TWO CENTURIES OF WARFARE

OF

WARFARE

CHRISTOPHER CHANT · RICHARD HOLMES · WILLIAM KOENIG

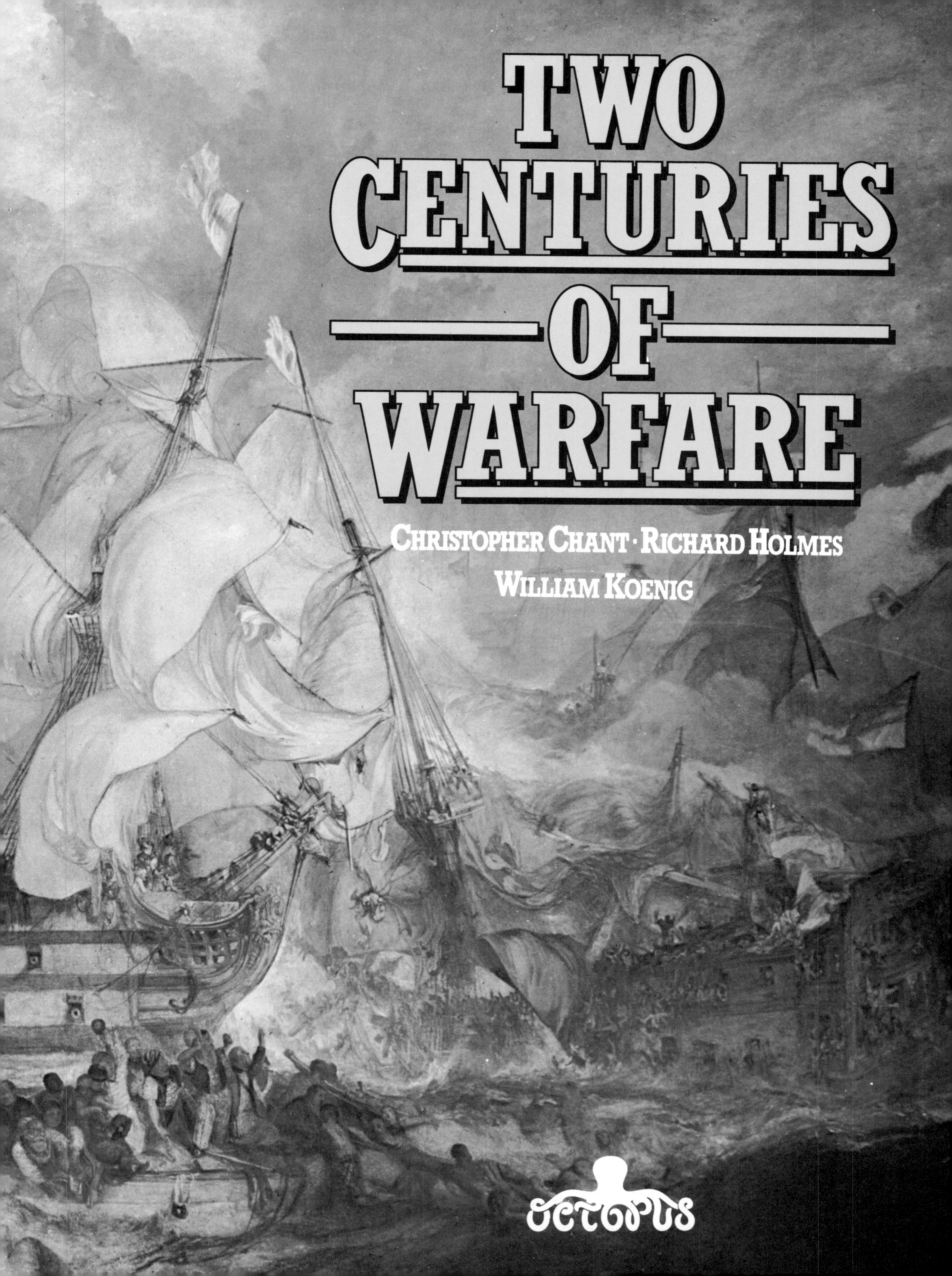

TWO CENTURIES OF WARFARE

Christopher Chant · Richard Holmes

William Koenig

OCTOPUS

First published 1978 by
Octopus Books Limited
59 Grosvenor Street
London W1

© 1978 Octopus Books Limited

ISBN 0 7064 0618 4

Produced by Mandarin Publishers Limited
22a Westlands Road
Quarry Bay
Hong Kong

Printed in Hong Kong

Contents

Introduction

It is a solecism common to a large proportion of those interested in military history to regard battles and even campaigns in isolation rather than as part of a larger canvas. The same may be said, moreover, of theatres of war—all too often, for example, grand strategy (the interrelationship of economics, internal politics, external statesmanship, and the course of the war in theatres geographically divorced from each other) is totally ignored, which leads the incautious writer or reader to ask futile questions or to come to erroneous answers because the whole problem has not been considered.

Tactically, of course, each battle has its own fascination, but how much more there is to be gained from consideration of battles both tactically and strategically, that is, how the battles of each war affected the course of the conflict as a whole. This is particularly the case when different services are involved: although there were only two such services at the end of the 18th century, World War I saw the introduction of air services on a wide scale, and World War II saw the conscious adoption of 'triphibious' operations as a standard method of waging war, although there were still campaigns which could be, and were, waged by single services as part of the grand strategic plan. This tendency to regard land, sea and air forces as elements closely related for the conduct of major war has increased since the end of World War II: in Canada, for example, the three are now merely branches of the Canadian Armed Forces, and the services of other major powers are presently controlled by a committee including the service heads of the three services.

This realization that the three services are all components of the same machine does not, and should not, detract from the fierce rivalry between the services, which unless carried to ludicrous extremes can have the very useful effect of building up morale and increasing combat efficiency. This was not always the case, though, for realization of the interdependence of the services was not widespread in the late 18th and early 19th centuries. Indeed, the regard of any country was usually fixed on the service which was reckoned to have performed most creditably in the last war: in the case of Great Britain, this was usually the Royal Navy; in the case of France her army. The result was that the less regarded service usually found itself in the position of a poor relation, with a consequent disadvantageous effect on its morale, training and equipment.

Yet the interdependence of the two services was there for all to see: Nelson's victory, in brilliant tactical circumstances, in the Battle of the Nile isolated Napoleon Bonaparte in Egypt and dictated the final outcome of the war in this theatre. And despite the quite brilliant tactical victory he won at Austerlitz, only his refusal to accept the real value of seapower prevented Napoleon from realizing the long-term effects of Nelson's magnificent victory in the Battle of Trafalgar two months earlier, denying France the strategic use of the sea for military and civil purposes for the rest of the Napoleonic Wars, brought to a final end by the great Allied victory at Waterloo in 1815.

The American Civil War (1861–1865) was also largely dictated by seapower, despite the fact that most of the famous battles took place on land. Yet the fact that the Unionists took quick command of the sea allowed an interesting coastal campaign, and effectively denied the Confederacy the arms and other support that might have been brought in by sea. The cataclysmic Battle of Gettysburg must be seen in this context, and there were interesting 'naval' aspects of the Battle of Vicksburg.

Seapower played no part in the Franco-Prussian War of 1870–1871, whose outcome was decided in the Battle of Sedan—the war was too short for seapower, which neither side had in abundance, to play a part. Far more important, however, was the revelation provided by this war of the introduction of a new type of warfare, fought with the advanced weapons provided by the new technology and mass production, and controlled for the first time by specially trained, permanent staffs. The Germans took full advantage of both novelties, and soon the rest of the world followed, amazed by the Germans' swift and conclusive victory

over what was reckoned to be the best army in the world.

The new century once again proved the interdependence of naval and military matters, when the Japanese victory in the Battle of Tsushima, in the straits separating Japan from Korea, put paid to Russia's attempts to bring succour to her forces all but cut off in Manchuria, and in effect won the Russo-Japanese War for the Nipponese Empire. On land, the war was very hard fought, and served notice on those who were prepared to accept it that the era of 'Napoleonic' warfare, with morale and manoeuvre the dominating factors, was at an end: from now on, the machine-gun, artillery and barbed wire were to be paramount factors.

This lesson had not been fully learned by the time of World War I, however. But the war of movement ceased shortly after the Battle of the Marne, which finally halted the German drive into France, and by the time of the Battle of the Somme, the horrors of trench warfare were fully understood. Seapower also played a major part in World War I: despite the setback of the Battle of Coronel, the British soon disposed of the Germans' ambitions of waging a surface *guerre de course*, forcing them to turn to the submarine as a means of trying to starve Britain to surrender. The British surface blockade in the long run proved more decisive, though, so that starvation was of epidemic proportions by the middle of 1918 in Germany. And although the war's only major battle between surface navies, the Battle of Jutland, proved a tactical success for the Germans, the British Grand Fleet kept the strategic initiative and the blockade of Germany remained, finally sealing her fate.

By the time of World War II, airpower had become of major importance, especially tactically as an adjunct of land power in the German *Blitzkrieg* operations. But the first attempt to use airpower as a strategic weapon resulted in a disastrous German reverse that left Great Britain in the war, a small but poisonous thorn in the Germans' side when they launched their invasion of Russia in June 1941. Seapower also played a decisive part in World War II, both on and under the surface. The Battle of Cape Matapan, for example, so shattered the

power and morale of the Italian Navy that the course of the war in North Africa henceforth went far more the British way in the long term, culminating in the decisive Battle of El Alamein.

The Allied sea blockade of Germany combined with the bomber offensive to sap the Third Reich's industrial strength, and via that her armed strength, so despite final efforts such as the 'Battle of the Bulge', the defeat that had started with the Battle of Kursk in July 1943 overwhelmed Germany in 1945. Not even the German submarine effort could halt this process, despite the grave problems it posed until May 1943.

In the Pacific theatre, the war was fought primarily between the United States and Japan, and the former's great tactical and strategic victory in the Battle of Midway did more than just halt Japan's expansion. Having lost her most important aircraft-carriers, Japan could no longer hope to defeat the growing American land, sea and air effort in this vast ocean campaign.

Airpower had played a vital tactical and strategic role in World War II, and did so once again in the Korean War, where the tactical excellence of the American pilots was sufficient to overcome the tactical superiority of the Russian-built MiG jet fighters. With total air superiority, the United Nations' ground forces were finally able to force the Communists into a ceasefire and peace settlement. Airpower played a decisive part in the Arab-Israeli Six-Day War of 1967, moreover: Israel's great pre-emptive air strike on the Arab airfields at one blow gave Israel the tactical and strategic initiative she needed to make quick and decisive land advances.

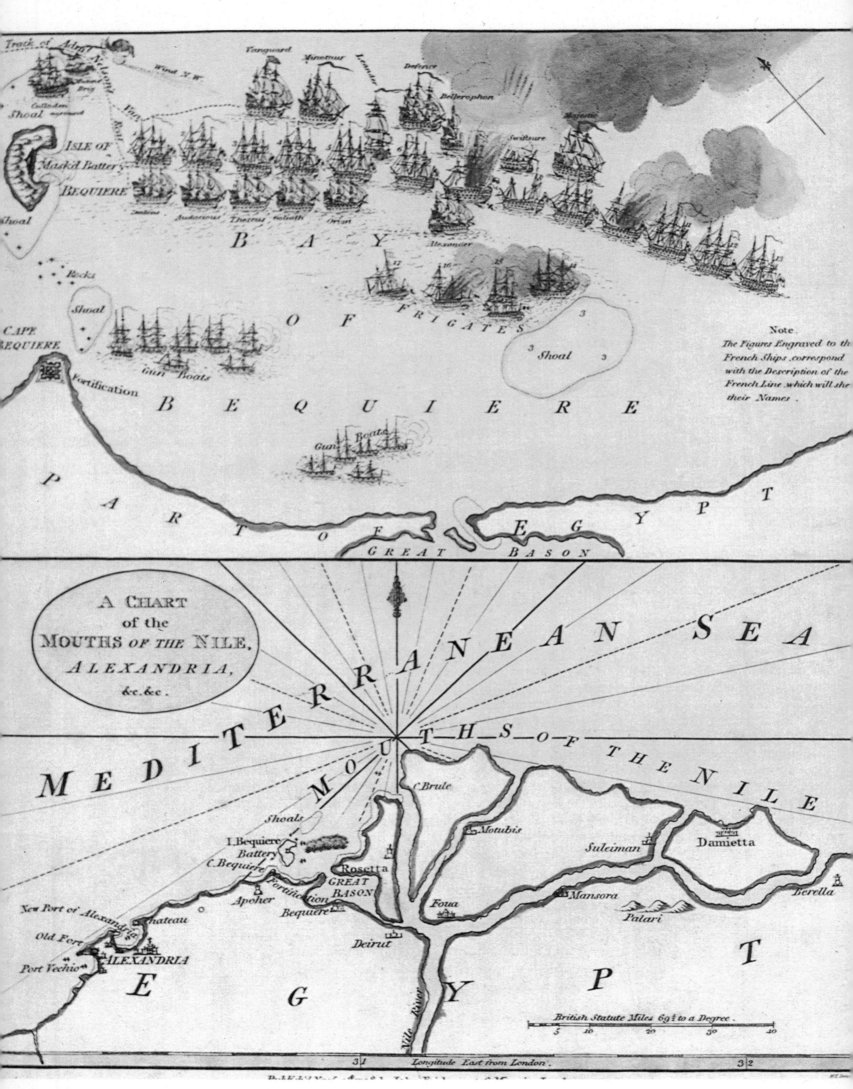

Track of Adm. Nelson's Route
Wind N.W.

Vanguard
Minotaur
Leander
Defence
Bellerophon
Majestic
Swiftsure

ISLE OF
Mask'd Batter
BEQUIERE
Shoal

Culloden aground

Rocks

Shoal

CAPE
BEQUIERE

Fortification

Gun Boats

Zealous   Audacious   Theseus   Goliath   Orion   Alexander

B   A   Y

O   F

F   R   I   G   A   T   E   S

Shoal
3
3   Shoal
3

B   E   Q   U   I   E   R   E

Gun   Boats

P   A   R   T   O   F   E   G   Y   P   T

GREAT   BASON

Note.
The Figures Engraved to th
French Ships correspond
with the Description of the
French Line which will she
their Names.

A CHART
of the
MOUTHS OF THE NILE,
ALEXANDRIA,
&c.&c.

M   E   D   I   T   E   R   R   A   N   E   A   N   S   E   A

M   O   U   T   H   S   o   f   T   H   E   N   I   L   E

C. Brule

Motubis

Shoals

I. Bequiere
Battery
C. Bequiere
Apoher
Fortification
Bequiere

Rosetta
GREAT
BASON

Suleiman

Damietta

New Port of Alexandria
Old Port
Port Vechio
ALEXANDRIA
Chateau

Deirut

Foua
Mansora
Palari
Berella

E   G   Y   P   T

British Statute Miles 69½ to a Degree.
5   10   20   30   40

34
Longitude East from London.
32

10

The Nile

Britain was almost continuously at war with revolutionary and Napoleonic France from 1793 to 1815. During this period there were a number of sea battles of significance, but two in particular stand out as landmarks in the development of tactics and the handling of fleets. The Battle of the Nile in 1798 was the first and most spectacular of the victories of Horatio Nelson, establishing him at that time as Britain's foremost fighting admiral and a brilliant if unorthodox tactician. Seven years later the Battle of Trafalgar became the most sophisticated expression of Nelson's style of tactics and immortalized him as one of the great naval strategists in western history. Nelson, however, appeared at a time when significant changes in tactics and technology were already having an impact on naval warfare. Thus it is useful to look backwards briefly before examining the Nile and Trafalgar.

In the two centuries preceding the encounter at the Nile, there had been few changes in naval tactics and gunnery. Prior to the reign of Henry VIII, ships had served as floating forts to be attacked and taken by storm by other floating forts. But when Henry VIII built battleships carrying heavy guns capable of firing broadsides, infighting came to be replaced by outfighting. During the Dutch wars of the mid-seventeenth century, an important advance in naval tactics took place: ships were formed into a line bow to stern so that the enemy was presented with the full fire power of the fleet. Fleets also began to be maneuvered skilfully and effectively. These changes were documented by a contemporary French observer of the Four Days Battle of 1665 in the Second Dutch War who noted, 'Nothing equals the beautiful order of the English at sea. Never was a line drawn straighter than that formed by their ships; thus they bring all their fire to bear on those who draw near them . . . They fight like a line of cavalry which is handled according to rule, and applies itself solely to force back those who oppose; whereas the Dutch advance like cavalry whose squadrons leave their ranks and come separately to the charge'. During the First Dutch War the British 'Generals at Sea', predecessors of the Admiralty, issued the first *Fighting Instructions* to the navy. In this document the formation of the 'line ahead' was made the obligatory and official tactic of both defense and attack and remained so until Nelson's time.

The first time the Royal Navy used heavy guns to any extent in a major action was against the Spanish Armada in 1588. This experience proved the guns to be ineffective at long range but good at short range for causing casualties and destroying the ability and will of the enemy to fight. Thus the gunnery doctrine of the British navy came to be to fight at close range, aiming at the enemy's hull with the object of causing maximum casualties, especially from splinters.

This gunnery doctrine was obviously in conflict with the officially prescribed tactic of the 'line ahead', adherence to which made it virtually impossible to close with an enemy ship. Each doctrine had its adherents within the Royal Navy. There were the 'mêléeists' who wanted tactics appropriate to forcing a fight at close range as required by the gunnery doctrine. They were opposed by a formalist school which maintained that in actions between fleets of comparable strength the British fleet was required to fight in a line stretching ship for ship parallel to that of the enemy. Breaking out of the line was forbidden unless the whole of the enemy line fell into disorder, in which case 'general chase' might be signaled. In spite of the contradiction between the gunnery doctrine and the tactic of the line, the formalist view was embodied in the *Permanent Fighting Instructions* issued by the Admiralty. These instructions robbed commanders of initiative and made it impossible to force a mêlée at close range. It was demonstrated over and over again that fleet actions characterized by rigid adherence to the 'line ahead' tended to be tactically indecisive. While this contradiction within British naval doctrine continued, the British fleet did not win a single tactical victory over a fleet of comparable strength. Rare victories occurred only when a British admiral decided that the enemy was flying in disorder, a situation in which the *Permanent Fighting Instructions* allowed him to order a general chase so that his ships could come up at close range.

While British naval tactics were frozen by the *Permanent Fighting Instructions*, the French navy encouraged the study of tactics and worked out an effective counter to the type of fighting imposed on the British. French tactics were based on a gunnery doctrine which had as its object not casualties at close range but material damage at long range. Rather than aiming low for the hull, French gunners fired high, often using chain shot to bring down masts and yards. And it must be remembered that during the eighteenth century the French were foremost among Europeans in gunnery and artillery expertise generally. Their tactics were thus well suited to countering

the rigid British line. In a battle situation a French fleet normally accepted the leeward position so that it could retire downwind refusing a close action but maintaining a duel at long range, a duel in which British gunnery caused few casualties, but French gunnery eventually crippled so many British ships that the fleet could no longer keep formation and had to retire for repairs. The strategic goal of the French was fitted to their tactical doctrine, which was not to destroy the enemy fleet but to gain command of the sea for a limited period to accomplish a specific objective. But the French never switched from defensive to offensive tactics to exploit their limited victories, so in the end their tactics were self-defeating, as they had always to fight the same British ships again once they had been repaired.

A classic example of the impotence of the British fixation on the 'line ahead' and the

French notion of a limited victory was the Battle of Chesapeake Bay on 5 September 1781. With nineteen ships of the line, Admiral Thomas Graves had been sent to relieve General Cornwallis, then besieged at Yorktown by the American General Washington and the French General de Rochambeau. The French Admiral de Grasse was caught in the bay with 24 ships, and on sighting the British fleet immediately tried to stand out against the wind. By the time Graves arrived, only the French van had managed to round Cape Henry and hence the fleet was at his mercy. Instead of reacting in terms of the situation, however, Graves noted that the number of enemy ships was comparable to his own and incredibly ordered 'line ahead' instead of 'general chase'. The French were given time to form their own line, and a typically indecisive 'line' style action followed, in which enough damage was inflicted on Graves' ships that he deemed it necessary to return to New York. Thus the fetish of the 'line' which for so long had exercised a paralyzing effect on British naval initiative lost a heaven-sent opportunity to raise the siege of Yorktown. Although tactically undistinguished, strategically Chesapeake Bay was the battle that helped decide the American Revolution.

Seven months later exactly the reverse situation occurred in the Battle of the Saintes, when a tactically revolutionary encounter turned out to have little strategic significance. The long paralysis imposed by the *Permanent Fighting Instructions* was decisively ended by Admiral George Rodney on 12 April, 1782. The French had been planning an attack on Jamaica and needed one of their temporary victories to clear Rodney's fleet from the path of their expedition. With the French for once holding the windward position, the two lines ran past each other on opposite tacks and another indecisive line action should have resulted. But the wind suddenly veered in Rodney's favor and, in flagrant disobedience of the sacred *Permanent Fighting Instructions*, he took his ship through the enemy line followed by the five ships astern of him. Two other British ships then broke through the French line in two other places. Cut at three points, the French line never reformed, with the result that a number of French ships were assailed by superior concentrations of British ships in a furious mêlée. In the most successful British fleet action for nearly eighty years, Rodney broke the long sequence of inconclusive line actions. Beyond averting the threat to Jamaica, however, the Saintes had no strategic significance, as the outcome of the American Revolution had already been decided.

The Glorious First of June

The next major departure from orthodox tactics occurred in the first great sea action of the French Revolutionary War and was known as the 'Glorious First of June' of 1794. A fleet under Admiral Howe had been waiting in the eastern Atlantic to attack a large grain fleet escorted by a squadron under Admiral Villaret-Joyeuse. Villaret-Joyeuse's sole order was to get the grain convoy through at all costs as it was desperately needed to stave off famine in central France. Indeed, Robespierre himself had told Villaret-Joyeuse that he was destined for the guillotine if he failed. After several days of maneuvering, on 1 June Howe stood down on the enemy in a classic line ahead. Unlike Rodney who had acted instinctively in response to a sudden opportunity, Howe

Opposite: Admiral George Rodney, victor of the Battle of the Saintes (**below**), the greatest tactical triumph of the Royal Navy in the American Revolutionary War, if not the most decisive in strategic terms. Rodney defeated de Grasse after the Americans had effectively won the war, but the Saintes confirmed British naval superiority before the French Revolution broke out.

deliberately threw away the *Permanent Fighting Instructions* and planned to have each of his ships cut through the French line under the stern of her opposite number and engage from leeward. Such a maneuver meant that a heavy raking fire could be poured into the hull of the enemy ship as the opposite British ship passed under her stern and also that the escape of disabled ships would be blocked as they could only retreat to leeward. In the event, the seamanship of most of Howe's fleet was not up to this maneuver and only seven of his 26 ships actually cut the French line. Even so, a desperate mêlée ensued in which a number of French ships were captured. But Villaret-Joyeuse had achieved his object of drawing Howe away from the grain fleet and as he later said, 'I saved my convoy and I saved my head'.

Howe's achievement that day was a significant step toward solving the two main problems faced by British commanders in actions against the French. The first problem was that the proficiency of both British and French in forming and maintaining the close hauled line of battle ahead almost invariably led to a stalemate. The unwillingness of the French to accept a decisive action posed the second problem, which was to 'fix' the enemy fleet. Both problems could be solved by breaking the enemy's line and getting to leeward of it. In fact breaking the line was a virtual necessity to obtain decisive action in the face of the elusive tactics developed by the French. Breaking the line at many points was a tactic first deliberately used at the Glorious First of June and thereafter came to be known as 'Lord Howe's Maneuver'.

It should also be noted that advances in tactics were closely related to advances in signaling. Only a primitive set of signals had been available for use with the few set maneuvers permitted by the *Permanent Fighting Instructions*, but by 1800 efficient signalling was possible and finally enabled admirals to have full tactical control over their fleets. Sir Hugh Popham's *Telegraphic Signals or Marine Vocabulary* was first published in 1800 and enabled commanders to say exactly what they pleased. Nelson's famous message at Trafalgar, 'England expects that every man will do his duty', was made with Popham's code. In fact, the Admiral's original message read 'England *confides* that every man will do his duty'. But to save time the signal lieutenant, John Pasco, recommended the substitution of the word 'expects' since that was in Popham's vocabulary, whereas 'confides' would have to have been spelled out.

In 1798 the ships of the Royal Navy were still classified as they had been during the Seven Years War of 1756–1763. There were lines of battleships whose emphasis was on fire power, cruisers whose emphasis was on speed and seaworthiness, and flotilla craft such as sloops and brigs for inshore work and subsidiary services. Battleships were further classified as first and second rates, which were three deckers of 90 guns or more and as third and fourth rates, which were two deckers usually mounting 74 and 64 guns. At the time of the Battle of the Nile the standard ship of the line in the Royal Navy was the 74.

Throughout the greater part of the eighteenth century British naval construction and design was generally inferior to that of the French and Spanish whose ships were larger in tonnage and correspondingly large in scantling with stout sides not easily pierced by shot. The *Tonnant, Canopus* and *Malta*, all ships of the line captured at the Battle of the Nile, were declared to be the 'finest on two decks ever seen in the British navy; . . . their qualities in sailing and carrying sail have rarely, if ever been surpassed'. The former French ship, *Le Franklin*, taken into British service as HMS *Canopus* after the Nile, was so admirably designed that British dockyards were ordered to build eight more like her. This design superiority, however, was more than balanced by the superior strategy, seamanship and discipline of the British navy, the greatest in the world at this time.

Improving British Gunnery

Toward the end of the eighteenth century, British gunnery was improving through more rapid rates of fire and the introduction of the carronade, so called because it was first cast at the Carron Foundry in Stirlingshire. The carronade was a short piece with a large bore, light and easy to handle in close fighting. Firing a heavy shot, it substantially increased the fire power of the battle fleet. First introduced in 1779, the carronade played a leading role at the Battle of the Saintes where more men were killed in the French flagship than in the entire British fleet. Ideally suited to traditional British gunnery doctrine, the carronade made British battleships even more formidable at a time when the contradiction between gunnery doctrine and tactical doctrine was being resolved by such commanders as Rodney, Howe

Above: The situation at the close of the action on the Glorious First of June. HMS *Defence*, lying completely dismasted.
Above center: HMS *Canopus* was the French *Franklin* before her capture at the Nile. This fine two-decker was taken into the British Fleet and served for nearly a century more.
Above right: Battle of St. Vincent, 1797, when the British Fleet under Jervis defeated the Spanish off the Portuguese coast.

and Nelson. The Saintes, the Glorious First of June, Camperdown, St. Vincent, the Nile, Copenhagen and Trafalgar were all carronade actions fought at close range. With these developments in technology and tactics the stage was set for what has been called the 'golden age of the sailing navy, the prolonged wars against revolutionary and Napoleonic France'.

The *Ancien Régime* in France came to a bloody end with the outbreak of the French Revolution in 1789. The Revolution had supposedly ended with the abolition of absolute monarchy through the Constitution of 1791, but the outbreak of foreign war and the destruction of the throne in 1792 were followed by the execution of Louis XVI early in 1793. The revolutionary ardor in France and the execution of its king, a relative of other crowned heads in Europe, raised the fears of the conservative monarchies, and the new republic quickly found itself assailed by a coalition of Britain, Austria, Prussia, Spain, Piedmont and Holland. Infused with a revolutionary nationalism, however, the raw armies of' the republic were able to turn a defensive into an offensive war and carry the revolution beyond the borders of France. By 1795 French arms had overrun the Low Countries and had extracted favorable treaties with Prussia and Spain, Austria was hesitating. In one of the classic instances of great generalship, a young republican officer named Napoleon Bonaparte then conducted a swift and decisive campaign in Italy which forced a peace settlement from Austria in 1797.

Supported by its small ally Portugal, Britain alone still stood against France and Britain had opened negotiations. As the Allies one after the other had deserted the 'First Coalition', the position of the British fleet in the Mediterranean had become increasingly untenable. With the fall of Leghorn in 1796, the Mediterranean squadron had no more bases and faced the real possibility of being overwhelmed by the combined French and Spanish fleets. The Cabinet therefore ordered the Mediterranean to be evacuated and concentrated on the defense of England and Ireland. The Directory, the five-man executive committee of the National Convention which had governed

Far right: A contemporary drawing showing the construction of a 24-pounder carronade.

France since 1795, saw Britain's willingness to negotiate as an indication of weakness and made impossible demands. Correctly perceiving that France had no genuine interest in peace, Britain broke off the negotiations and prepared to defend herself alone.

The Directory believed Britain to be on the verge of revolution and openly proclaimed its intentions. 'It remains, fellow citizens, to punish the perfidy of the Cabinet of England, that has corrupted the courts of Europe. It is in London that the misfortunes of Europe are planned; it is in London that we must end them', announced a French manifesto of 1797. The Directory wanted to accomplish this goal through an invasion of England, a project which had not been successfully attempted since 1066. In October of 1797 command of the 'Army of England' was given to a 29-year old Corsican officer who had already proved his brilliant grasp of military affairs in the Italian campaign, which had resulted in the withdrawal of Austria from the war and the British fleet from the Mediterranean. Napoleon Bonaparte was immensely popular as a result of these exploits and had a genuine flair for politics, which made the Directory anxious to remove him from the seat of power on Paris. On 23 February, 1798, however, a surprised Directory heard Bonaparte report that a landing on the English coast was not feasible: '. . . make what efforts we will, we shall not for many years acquire control of the seas. To make a descent on England, without being master of the sea, is the boldest and most difficult operation ever attempted'. As an alternative Bonaparte proposed an invasion of Egypt. By reviving old dreams of colonizing the Levant and capturing the rich eastern trade, such a project had a ready appeal in France. Talleyrand supported the project strongly for these reasons and also because he wished to avoid a further direct clash with Britain. The remainder of the Directory wanted to continue the war with Britain, but since the invasion was not possible the Egyptian project offered a means of continuing the hostilities and also of removing the over-popular young general even farther from Paris. As a Corsican, Bonaparte himself was more oriented toward the Mediterranean and the

Description of a 24 Pounder Carronade on a Carriage with an Inclined Plane, agreeable to a plan suggested by Captain Schank, by which it can be seen Guns of all kinds can be mounted either on board Ship, or on Shore, in Forts &c. &c. &c. ___ complete Experiments have been made on board the Wolverene Gun-Vessel, several Revenue Vessels, Merchant-Ships & Gun Boats, and reports of the experiments made, with the Utility of the Invention, is approved of and lodged in the Admiralty.

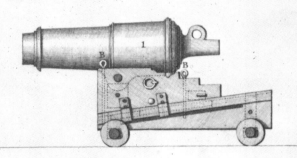

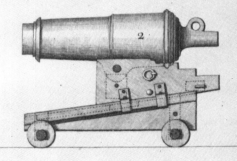

Plan of the lower Carriage.

Scale of Feet.

Section of the Carronade and Carriage.

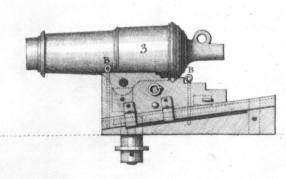

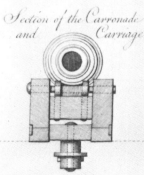

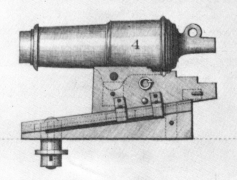

References.

1. & 2. The Carronade mounted on a Carriage with Trucks, describing as at 1, the lower and upper Carriages fixed with the bolts B.B. & at 2, the bolts taken out and the upper Carriage shewn recoiled.

3. & 4. The Carronade mounted on a Carriage fitted with a Spindle to be used on slides, describing the Carriage fixed as at 3, with the bolts B.B. and at 4, the bolts taken out and the upper Carriage shewn recoiled.

N.B. It is particularly recommended that a middle Breeching should be used, ___ and it is to be observed that the Inclined Plane is applicable to Gun Carriages of all descriptions, & is not meant to be confined to Carronades only. The Recoil of the Gun in Carriages on this principle is so gentle, that it may be fired athwart-ships in Boats, or in any other Situation without the least danger.

Above: Nelson receives the surrender of the Spanish captain of the *San Josef* after the Battle of St. Vincent.

Below: A 32-pounder carronade. Carronades had great penetrating power for their size, and lightness enabled them to be handled by small crews.

Levant and, tending to ignore Britain, Prussia and the other northern European states, simply was not interested in the invasion of England. As he told his secretary in 1798, 'This little Europe is too small a field. Great renown can only be won in the east'. Thus the Egyptian in expedition was an acceptable compromise, and so from command of the 'Army of England' in October 1797 Bonaparte passed to command the 'Army of the Orient' in March 1798.

The plan approved by the Directory had as its goal the weakening of British power by threatening India and disrupting the rich British trade with the east. Such a move would indeed have touched Britain in a vital spot, as its industry and commerce were now closely bound up with that of Asia. Deprived of India, Britain could not have carried on her extensive commerce with the East Indies and China, a commerce which was almost essential to her survival as a first class power. French contacts were already well developed with Tipoo Sahib, Sultan of Mysore, who was seeking French aid to expel the British from India. (The Sultan was defeated and killed by the future Duke of Wellington at Seringapatam in 1799.) Bonaparte was thus ordered to occupy Egypt and exclude the British 'from all their possessions in the east to which the General can come'. He was further ordered to cut through the Isthmus of Suez to assure French possession of the Red Sea, to better the condition of the people of Egypt and to improve relations with Turkey, one of the few states not at war with France.

Similar plans had appeared a number of times before in French history. Hence the proposal was neither original nor novel, yet was appealing to latent but longstanding French aspirations toward colonizing Egypt and Syria and challenging British power in India and Ceylon. Although advertised as a grandiose blow against British power in the east, the expedition was in fact organized as a practical colonizing venture, including in its complement a corps of engineers, mathematicians, geologists, chemists, artists and others to assist in the foundation of a permanent colony. The international situation was also propitious for such a venture, for Britain's energies were focused on defense of the Channel, Austria was already beaten and Turkey was likely to welcome the expulsion of the Mamelukes from Egypt.

A French Base in Egypt

The future Emperor of France, however, entertained larger aspirations. His idea was to establish a permanent French colony in Egypt as a base from which to menace British interests in India and Ceylon. After conquering the east and founding a great French empire upon the ruins of the British, he wanted to mobilize the Greeks and other Christians, seize Constantinople and smash Turkey, and then 'take Europe in the rear'. And while he could not dream of transporting the 'Army of England' across the Channel for fear of the British Navy, Bonaparte could be quite certain that the passage of the 'Army of the Orient' to Egypt would not be disputed, since British squadrons had been absent from the Mediterranean for over eighteen months.

Speed and secrecy in mounting the expedition were imperative, and both were achieved to a remarkable degree. Speed was needed not because of the British Navy but because in August the Nile River would be in flood, greatly hampering the advance on Cairo and increasing Egyptian opportunities for resistance. The expedition sailed with little more than two month's preparation. The secrecy was so thorough that Bonaparte had defeated the Mameluke armies at the Battle of the Pyramids and occupied Cairo before the British even discovered where the expedition had gone.

Preparations for the expedition were spread between Toulon, Marseilles, Genoa, Corsica and Cività Vecchia. Escorted by thirteen ships of the line, seven frigates and a few gunboats, 300 transports carried 30,000 infantry, 2800 cavalry, 60 field and 40 siege guns, two companies of sappers and miners and a bridging train. The naval forces were commanded by forty-five year old François Paul Brueys d'Aigalliers, who had been a mere lieutenant at the outbreak of the Revolution in 1789. As three-quarters of the officers of the French navy had either been guillotined or driven into exile during the Revolution, Brueys had rapidly been promoted to flag rank. Dismissed during the Reign of Terror in 1793, he had come to the notice of Bonaparte at Ragusa during the Italian campaign. On Bonaparte's strong recommendation, the Directory had appointed Brueys to command the Toulon fleet in 1797, although he was in no way qualified for such a position. Admiral Pierre de Villeneuve, destined for command of the Franco-Spanish forces at Trafalgar seven years later, served as second in naval command, Count Honoré Ganteaume as chief of naval staff, while Rear Admiral Decrès was in charge of the transports.

Brueys' squadron was made up of the remnants of the French Mediterranean fleet, ships that had managed to escape destruction by the British at the evacuation of Toulon in 1793 and which were 'old and rotting, not even able to support the firing of their guns if it became at all heavy'. Some of the guns even had to be unshipped as it was doubtful whether the decks would continue to bear their weight. The crews were in little better condition, for the seamen of the First Republic were badly fed, badly paid and without even a change of clothes. A report to the Directory made a few days before the battle said simply, 'On the whole our ships are very poorly manned, and in my opinion it needs much courage to command such an ill-prepared fleet'.

With Bonaparte and his staff billeted aboard Brueys' huge flagship *L'Orient*, the expedition sailed from Toulon in mid-May. Bonaparte was not a man of the sea and earlier had written to Brueys to request a comfortable berth, 'suitable for a commander-in-chief who expects to be seasick the entire voyage'. After capturing and looting Malta on the way, the expedition arrived at Marabut, a little fishing village four miles west of Alexandria. Here 5000 troops were landed to seize Alexandria so that the rest of the forces could disembark in leisurely safety and the transports shelter in the harbor. With a full month before the beginning of the flood season, Bonaparte marched on Cairo. He occupied that city two days after defeating the Egyptian forces on 21 July at the Battle of the Pyramids, and began to consider how to pacify and administer Egypt, penetrate to Suez and convoy regiments down the Red Sea toward India.

While Bonaparte was organizing his Egyptian expedition, his nemesis-to-be was enjoying a rest and considerable fame at his home in England. At thirty-nine years of age, Horatio Nelson was

Left: Admiral François Brueys, the ill-fated commander of the French Fleet at the Battle of the Nile.

already a rear-admiral of twelve month's seniority. He had gone to sea at twelve, become a lieutenant at nineteen and commanded a ship at twenty. His first action as a commander had been off Toulon in 1795 and although the action in general had been inconclusive, Nelson had distinguished himself and launched a glorious career which was to last just ten years. Already his characteristic qualities of instant decision and brilliant tactical insight, his penchant for swift and audacious action, and his supreme urge to victory were being noted by his colleagues and superiors.

Nelson's role in the Battle of St. Vincent on 14 February, 1797 presaged the brilliance and daring which was to be more fully revealed at the Battle of the Nile the following year. The squadron of Sir John Jervis had sighted a Spanish fleet off Cape St. Vincent, disordered and in two straggling groups. Although outnumbered by nearly two to one, Jervis tried to even the odds by leading his line between the two groups of Spanish ships to force them farther apart. Completing this maneuver successfully, Jervis then tacked to sail back between the enemy but missed his timing so that the Spaniards could reunite before the British fleet could pass through again. Serving as commodore in the third ship from the rear, Nelson saw the situation developing, took his ship out of the line and attacked the Spanish from windward in a desperate attempt to delay the junction of the enemy. Jervis then ordered the rear ships to Nelson's support and a furious mêlée took place with Nelson himself capturing two ships at the head of boarding parties. No officer would have dared attempt such a move twenty years before and even in 1797 it was very bold. Many of his fellow officers thought Nelson should be reprimanded for breaking the line and even he was uncertain if Jervis would approve.

Already minus an eye from shell splinters and having lost an arm leading an unsuccessful expedition against Tenerife in 1797, Nelson was knighted for his part in the Battle of St. Vincent. In the Spring of 1798, his arm now healed, he asked the Admiralty for employment and was sent in the fast 74-gun *Vanguard* to serve under Jervis at the blockade of Cadiz. The British were by this time aware that an expedition was being prepared at Toulon, but British agents had been unable to penetrate French security to discover its purpose and destination. Hence it was deemed necessary for a squadron to re-enter the Mediterranean and keep watch off Toulon. As the Admiralty wrote to Jervis, 'When you are apprized that the appearance of a British squadron in the Mediterranean is a condition on which the fate of Europe may at this moment be said to depend, you will not be surprised that we are disposed to strain every nerve, and incur considerable hazard in effecting it'.

Nelson Enters the Med.

Hence Nelson was ordered by Jervis into the stormy Gulf of Lyons on 2 May 'to endeavour to ascertain the real object of the preparations in the making by the French'. Arriving on 17 May Nelson had at his disposal two other 74's, three frigates and a sloop. Ten more ships of the line

were promised as soon as reinforcements arrived from England. Although both Jervis and the Admiralty were very impressed with Nelson's abilities, the only independent operation conducted by him up to that time had been the ill-fated assault on Tenerife. The Admiralty was gambling with Nelson and both knew it.

A spell of heavy weather on 20 May dismasted the *Vanguard* which was only saved from being wrecked by being taken in tow by one of her sister ships. Assuming that the *Vanguard* would have to put into Gibraltar for dockyard repairs, the frigates returned to base. Weather notwithstanding, Brueys sailed from Toulon that same day, setting a course between Corsica and the Italian mainland. The *Vanguard* was in fact repaired at sea from the resources of her companions. French security was so thorough that it was only on 28 May that Nelson finally learned of the departure of the French expedition from a passing merchantman.

On 7 June ten 74's and a frigate joined Nelson. These were Captains Troubridge in the *Culloden*, Darby in the *Bellerophon*, Louis in the *Minotaur*, Peyton in the *Defence* (the oldest ship in the fleet with thirty-five years of service), Hood in the *Zealous*, Gould in the *Audacious*, Westcott in the *Majestic*, Foley in the *Goliath*, Hallowell in the *Swiftsure*, and Miller in the *Theseus*. The *Leander* under Captain Thompson was a 50-gun frigate then eighteen years old. Already with Nelson were the *Orion* under Captain Saumarez, the *Alexander* under Captain Ball and the eighteen-gun sloop *Mutine*. Jervis had received only eight ships from England but still sent Nelson the ten originally promised. As befitted the importance of his mission, Nelson now had what was prob-

Above: Admiral Sir John Jervis, victor at St. Vincent, who sent Nelson to the Mediterranean prior to the Battle of the Nile.

Opposite: Admiral Horatio Nelson, with the Battle of the Nile in the background.

Above: The launching of HMS *Alexander*, which joined Nelson's squadron on the way to Egypt. It was typical of the British 74s of the period, which formed the backbone of the British Fleet. **Opposite above:** British Fleet about to engage the French at anchor at the start of the Battle of the Nile. The British are sailing in time-honored fashion, in the 'line ahead'. **Opposite below:** The moment when *l'Orient*, the French flagship, blew up. The entire crew was lost. **Below:** A 32-pounder gun, the heaviest weapon normally carried on board British ships. Its long barrel gave it range and and accuracy which the the carronade lacked, but it needed a much larger crew to man it.

ably the finest squadron of 74's ever assembled. And although his original orders had been to gain intelligence, Nelson was now instructed to use 'his utmost endeavours to take, sink, burn or destroy the armament preparing by the enemy at Toulon'.

Once his squadron was assembled, Nelson disappeared into the Mediterranean on his search for the French expedition and was not heard from for almost two months, causing great anxiety to Jervis and the Admiralty. Nelson first followed Brueys' own course down the coast of Italy searching for information. Sicily was considered the most likely goal of the French, but Nelson felt that if the French passed Sicily, the destination was definitely Alexandria. Writing to Lord Spencer, he commented, 'I shall believe they are going on with their scheme of possessing Alexandria and getting troops to India – a plan concerted with Tipoo Sahib, by no means so difficult as might at first view be imagined'. By 22 June he had learned of the fall of Malta and believed that if the French were at Sicily, information would by then be plentiful. With most of his captains concurring, Nelson concluded that Alexandria was the goal and made directly there, only to discover an empty harbor on 26 June.

The search was greatly hampered by the absence of the frigates to extend its range, but the squadron could not be broken up to compensate as its power lay in concentration. 'No frigates to which has been, and may be again, attributed the loss of the French fleet', Nelson wrote despairingly to his friend William Hamilton, British Ambassador at Naples. The search

was renewed and on 19 July Nelson touched in at Syracuse, 'as ignorant of the situation of the enemy as I was twenty-seven days ago'. Next arriving in the Gulf of Koroni in Greece, he learned that the French had been sighted a month before off Crete and sailing southeast. After six weeks of searching had come the first ray of hope and, making direct to Alexandria, morale was lifted still further when the harbor was found to be full of French transports protected by shore batteries. On the following day, 1 August, the frustrating quest came to an end when the *Zealous* reported the French warships peacefully anchored fifteen miles away in Aboukir Bay. Having eaten little for days due to tension, Nelson crowded on sail and ordered dinner.

The irony of the chase is that it was unnecessary. Nelson and his captains had originally guessed too well that Alexandria was the target. As a precaution Bonaparte had steered a course for southern Crete instead of directly for Alexandria. Nelson had actually overtaken the slow moving French convoy, beaten it to Alexandria and sailed off to the north as the French arrived from the northwest. On the night of 22 June the two fleets had even been within one hundred miles of each other but on diverging courses. Had Nelson had his frigates, however, even Bonaparte's precautions would not have saved the French force from detection.

The search was not a complete waste of time. During the weeks at sea, Nelson had carefully drilled his ships and planned tactics to meet any contingency. If the French were caught at sea, he planned to divide his ships into three squadrons, two to attack the escort and the third, the transports. Conversely, an anchored opponent must be allowed no further time in which to prepare. Hence the attack must begin on sighting the enemy. If the strength of the opposing fleet was comparable to his own, Nelson hoped to obtain at least a limited victory by concentrating a superior force on one part of the enemy while containing the rest. His tactic was to pit two of his ships against one of the enemy's and gradually move along the anchored line, blasting it ship by ship. Regular tactical sessions were held with his captains so that, whenever and in whatever

circumstances battle finally came, appropriate action would have been discussed in principle if not in detail. In terms of possible tactics, Nelson wanted his captains to know his mind beyond possibility of misunderstanding.

Bruey's Fleet at Aboukir

When British ships hove into sight off Aboukir Point about two o'clock in the afternoon, Brueys' fleet had been settled in the bay for weeks. After the debarkation of the expedition at Alexandria was complete, Brueys' orders from the Directory had been to go to Corfu both to protect the Ionian Islands and to safeguard his ships. Bonaparte had, however, countermanded these orders and required Brueys to remain at Alexandria, presumably in case the general wished to return to France without delay. The execution of this new order having been left entirely to him, Brueys had moved his ships from the security offered by Alexandria Harbor to Aboukir Bay where he lay awaiting further orders from Bonaparte. Brueys was apparently haunted by a fear of running aground and although his largest ship drew only 22 feet and Alexandria offered a minimum of 27 feet, he decided not to risk it.

Aboukir Bay extends in a semi-circle sixteen miles across from Aboukir Point to the Rosetta Mouth of the Nile River which gave its name to the coming battle. At the site of the ancient city of Canopus lay the then-village of Aboukir. The coast shelves gradually so that the ships had to be moored three miles from shore. The only natural protection was the small island of Aboukir and some rocks and sandbanks. Still, Aboukir could have been made an almost impregnable position had Brueys so chosen. It was already known that the British were again loose in the Mediterranean, for British frigates (actually searching for Nelson at Jervis' orders) had been seen off Crete. Even the knowledge that a British squadron was surely searching for him did not move Brueys to send out guard frigates. Although events were to prove Brueys a most courageous man, he had no orders to seek action and indeed no orders but to remain where he was. He had never commanded a squadron in battle and therefore thought the best course was to wait passively in the bay in a defensive position. Some of his more experienced captains such as Blanquet du Chayla, a veteran of thirteen battles, and Dupetit-Thouars argued that the best chance lay at sea where time and place could be selected with surprise and the wind in their favor. Supported by Ganteaume, the chief of naval staff, who pointed out the poor condition of the ships and how impossible it would be for them to fight on the open sea, Brueys elected to remain at Aboukir.

It was axiomatic in those days that ships could not stand up to shore batteries, a truth which had often been proven, so the proper defense for a fleet in Brueys' position was to anchor in a line which was incapable of being turned and in which the ships were closed up to prevent penetration by the enemy. In effect this arrangement converted the fleet into a long floating battery which should have been able to repulse even repeated assaults by a superior force. During the American Revolution this type of defense had been successfully used by the British admirals Barrington at St. Lucia in 1778 and Hood at St. Kitts in 1782 against heavy French attacks. Attacking a strong anchored position was a risky affair, and although in 1801 Nelson himself boldly attacked a powerful Danish fleet in defensive position in Copenhagen harbor, he would have been the first to admit how close he came to failure.

This pattern of defense was in fact adopted by Brueys, who anchored his battleships in a line extending from Aboukir Island. Five 74-gun ships – *Le Guerrier*, *Le Conquérant*, *Le Spartiate*, *L'Acquilon* and *Le Peuple Souverain* – made up the van. In the center was the 80-gun *Le Franklin*, the massive *L'Orient* which at 120 guns and 1000 men was larger than any ship in the British navy, *Le Tonnant* at 90 guns, and two 74's, *L'Heureuse* and *Le Timoléon*. The rear was composed of *Le Mercure* at 74 guns, the 80-gun *Le Guillaume Tell* which served as Admiral Villeneuve's flagship and the 74-gun *Le Généreux*. Brueys and his four frigates, the 40-gun *La Diane* and *La Justice* and the 36-gun *L'Artémise* and *La Sérieuse*, anchored inside his battle line. He expected any attack to come on the rear and center because of the shoals and had therefore positioned his more powerful units there. Every advantage thus lay with Brueys at Aboukir. He had a heavier weight of metal, an equal number of battleships, frigates, a relatively secure natural position, and above all time to prepare his defenses. In the aggregate, these factors meant that his fleet should have been able to withstand any attack mounted by Admiral Horatio Nelson.

His own mistakes and other circumstances, however, neutralized these advantages for Brueys. From Aboukir Point shoals covered by broken water stretched northeast toward the island and continued in the same direction beyond the island for another two miles. Another irregular shoal lay within the bay itself. To make his line incapable of being turned, Brueys had only to anchor his van as close as possible to the island and his rear close in upon the inner shoal. Then if his ships lay close enough together, his line could neither be turned nor penetrated. But dominated by his obsession of running aground and expecting the British to have as much respect for the shoals as himself, he left a generous margin of safety, anchoring the lead ship of his van too far off the island and his entire line a thousand yards farther out than necessary. With two ship lengths between them, his vessels were also anchored too far apart. Had he also made a strongpoint of Aboukir Island, he could have provided powerful support for his van but as it was, he established only a weak battery of half a dozen six-pounders and a few mortars on the island, not even enough to command the passage between the island and the lead ship of the van. A further problem was that his ships had been stripped of supplies for the troops marching on Cairo. Therefore each day almost half of his manpower was employed ashore either digging wells or searching for food. These work and forage parties were subject to attack by the local population, so Brueys found it necessary to requisition a further 50 men to protect them.

When *L'Heureuse* sighted the *Zealous* early in the afternoon of 1 August, Brueys received the news without alarm. He ordered signals to be made for the work parties ashore to return but more than 4000 men did not reach their ships in time and watched the battle from ashore. Only at this point did Brueys finally order hawsers to be strung between his ships to prevent the enemy breaking through. He believed he had ample time to further his defenses, since standard procedure for a French admiral in Nelson's situation would have been first to make a careful reconnaissance and then test the enemy's reaction to a distant cannonade. This belief was strengthened by the fact that the day was already advanced and that when sighted Nelson's ships were somewhat scattered and obviously not in battle formation.

The British squadron had, however, standing orders that an anchored enemy was to be given no more time to prepare; despite the time and disordered condition of the fleet, the attack began immediately. Although the *Alexander* and the *Swiftsure* were away scouting and the *Culloden* was towing a captured French brig, Nelson signaled an attack on the van and center because this was the weaker part of the French line and could not easily be reinforced due to the wind. A top-gallant breeze, just enough to ensure ease of maneuver, was blowing north-northwest. As Captain Berry of the *Vanguard* later wrote, 'His idea in this disposition of force was, first to secure the victory, and then to make the most of it according to future circumstances'. At 1500

hours the 'prepare for battle' signal appeared. By 1730 the British ships were in line and abreast of Aboukir Island, coming from the north west.

The lead ship in the British line was the *Zealous* under Captain Hood who proceeded slowly, sounding carefully to avoid the reef and shoal. The second ship was the *Goliath* under Captain Foley, one of the most experienced captains in the fleet. As the *Goliath* rounded the island, Foley saw that with luck he could cut between *Le Guerrier* and the island, thus attacking from the side on which the French were unprepared and might not even have their guns run out. They would thus be caught between two fires as other British ships attacked from the outside. Foley also saw that Brueys' position was defective in that he had allowed 500 feet between his ships, a space large enough for the attackers to sail through and take up positions from which the French ships could be raked from bow or stern but at which they could make no effective retaliation without cutting their cables. Foley was more confident about sailing near the island than was Hood because he possessed a French atlas only twenty years old showing the depths of water in the bay.

Foley's decision to cut inside the French line was exactly the kind of spontaneous initiative required by Nelson from his captains and decisively shaped the course of the battle. The *Goliath* was followed by the *Zealous*, *Audacious*, *Orion* and *Theseus* while the *Vanguard* and the rest of the line attacked from the seaward side, thus effectively doubling and overpowering the

Above: *Le Tonnant*, with its 90 guns, fights to the last, surrounded by British ships.

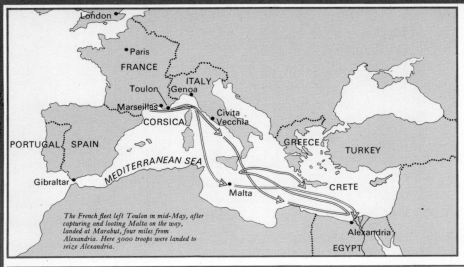

The French fleet left Toulon in mid-May, after capturing and looting Malta on the way, landed at Marabut, four miles from Alexandria. Here 5000 troops were landed to seize Alexandria.

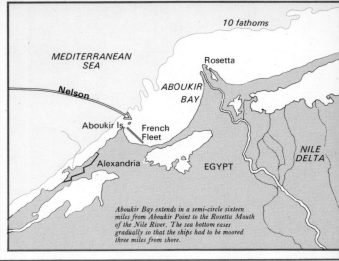

Aboukir Bay extends in a semi-circle sixteen miles from Aboukir Point to the Rosetta Mouth of the Nile River. The sea bottom eases gradually so that the ships had to be moored three miles from shore.

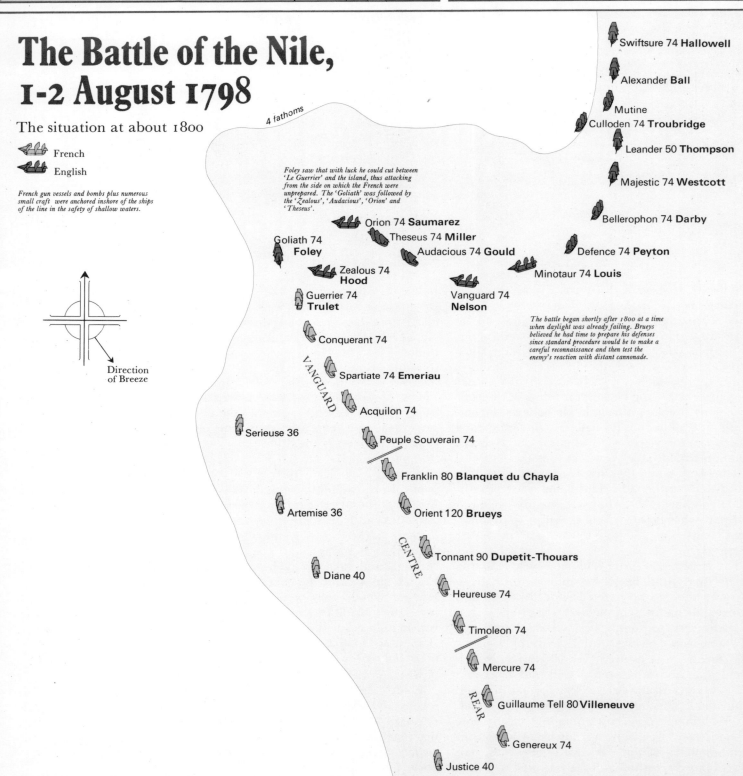

The Battle of the Nile, 1-2 August 1798

The situation at about 1800

French

English

French gun vessels and bombs plus numerous small craft were anchored inshore of the ships of the line in the safety of shallow waters.

4 fathoms

Foley saw that with luck he could cut between 'Le Guerrier' and the island, thus attacking from the side on which the French were unprepared. The 'Goliath' was followed by the 'Zealous', 'Audacious', 'Orion' and 'Theseus'.

Direction of Breeze

Swiftsure 74 **Hallowell**

Alexander **Ball**

Mutine

Culloden 74 **Troubridge**

Leander 50 **Thompson**

Majestic 74 **Westcott**

Bellerophon 74 **Darby**

Orion 74 **Saumarez**

Theseus 74 **Miller**

Goliath 74 **Foley**

Audacious 74 **Gould**

Defence 74 **Peyton**

Zealous 74 **Hood**

Minotaur 74 **Louis**

Guerrier 74 **Trulet**

Vanguard 74 **Nelson**

Conquerant 74

The battle began shortly after 1800 at a time when daylight was already failing. Brueys believed he had time to prepare his defenses since standard procedure would be to make a careful reconnaissance and then test the enemy's reaction with distant cannonade.

VANGUARD

Spartiate 74 **Emeriau**

Acquilon 74

Serieuse 36

Peuple Souverain 74

Franklin 80 **Blanquet du Chayla**

Artemise 36

Orient 120 **Brueys**

CENTRE

Tonnant 90 **Dupetit-Thouars**

Diane 40

Heureuse 74

Timoleon 74

Mercure 74

REAR

Guillaume Tell 80 **Villeneuve**

Genereux 74

Justice 40

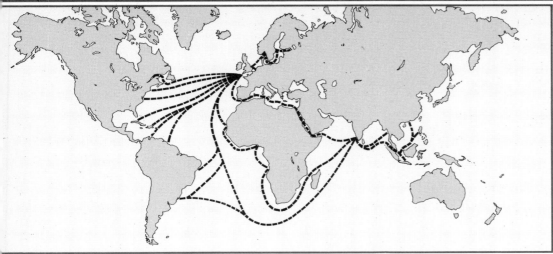

Trade and Shipping Routes of the World

The pattern of 19th and 20th century shipping was already emerging at the end of the 18th century. Although most of 'world' trade was intra-European, though the Mediterranean, North Sea, and Baltic, the amount of trade between Europe and North America was growing fast. Trade with the West Indies was declining, but trade to the Far East around the Cape of Good Hope to India and the 'country trade' between India and China was increasing. The extensive Pacific trade which exists today was virtually non-existent 200 years ago.

The situation at about 2200

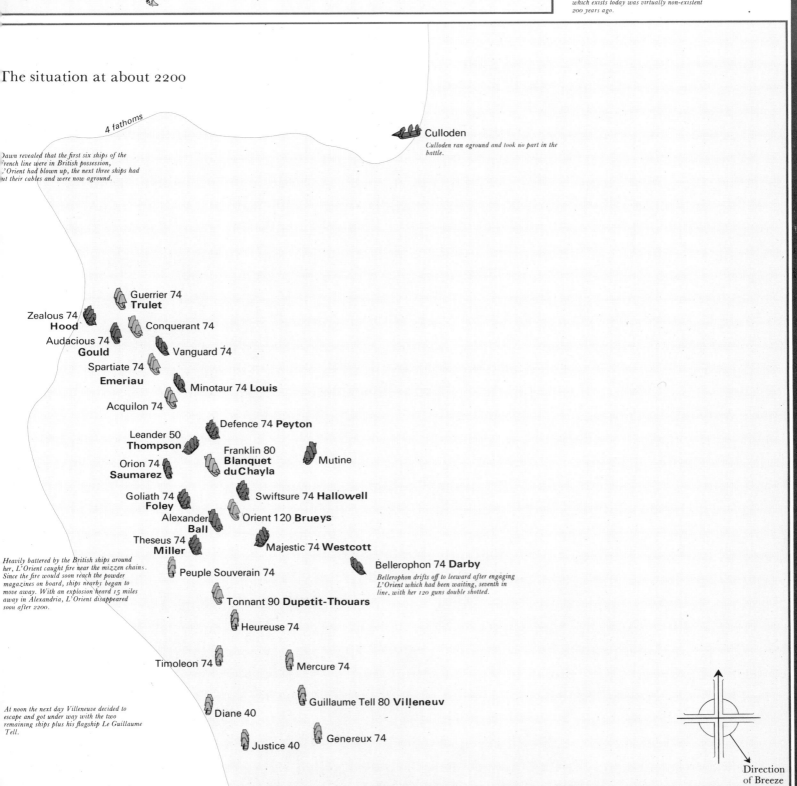

4 fathoms

Culloden

Culloden ran aground and took no part in the battle.

Dawn revealed that the first six ships of the French line were in British possession, L'Orient had blown up, the next three ships had cut their cables and were now aground.

Guerrier 74 **Trulet**

Zealous 74 **Hood**

Conquerant 74

Audacious 74 **Gould**

Vanguard 74

Spartiate 74 **Emeriau**

Minotaur 74 **Louis**

Acquilon 74

Defence 74 **Peyton**

Leander 50 **Thompson**

Franklin 80 **Blanquet du Chayla**

Mutine

Orion 74 **Saumarez**

Goliath 74 **Foley**

Swiftsure 74 **Hallowell**

Alexander **Ball**

Orient 120 **Brueys**

Theseus 74 **Miller**

Majestic 74 **Westcott**

Bellerophon 74 **Darby**

Heavily battered by the British ships around her, L'Orient caught fire near the mizzen chains. Since the fire would soon reach the powder magazines on board, ships nearby began to move away. With an explosion heard 15 miles away in Alexandria, L'Orient disappeared soon after 2200.

Peuple Souverain 74

Bellerophon drifts off to leeward after engaging L'Orient which had been waiting, seventh in line, with her 120 guns double shotted.

Tonnant 90 **Dupetit-Thouars**

Heureuse 74

Timoleon 74

Mercure 74

At noon the next day Villeneuve decided to escape and got under way with the two remaining ships plus his flagship Le Guillaume Tell.

Diane 40

Guillaume Tell 80 **Villeneuv**

Justice 40

Genereux 74

Direction of Breeze

27

enemy van. As Nelson later explained his tactic to Lord Howe, 'By attacking the enemy's van and centre, the wind blowing directly along their line, I was enabled to throw what force I pleased on a few ships'. And thanks to Foley, Nelson's tactic was working even better than he could ever have hoped.

The battle began shortly after 1800 at a time when daylight was already failing. The French van fought stubbornly but was doomed by the overwhelming concentration of power focused on it. The lead ship, *Le Guerrier*, was engaged by the *Goliath* and dismasted within ten minutes. Her commander, Captain Trulet, refused to strike his colors for over three hours even after being reduced to sporadic fire from one stern gun and the ship finally had to be boarded. The second in the line, *Le Conquérant*, faced both the *Audacious* and the *Zealous*. As British ships began to pass down the outside of the French line, *Le Guerrier* and *Le Conquérant* were attacked from both sides but had barely enough men aboard to serve their guns on one side. Fully engaged by the *Goliath*, raked by the *Audacious* and subject to the passing fire of the *Orion* and *Theseus*, *Le Con-*

quérant had to strike after about twenty minutes. Captain Gould of the *Audacious* later wrote of *Le Conquérant* that 'the slaughter became so dreadful in the ship that the French officers declared it was impossible to make their men stand to their guns'. The *Audacious* should actually have moved farther down the French line as the *Goliath* and the *Zealous* alone could have beaten the lead ships. The *Theseus* and the *Orion* soon arrived and moved farther down the line, the *Orion* attacking the fifth French ship which was *Le Peuple Souverain*.

Moving down the outside of the French line, the *Vanguard* became locked in a heavy duel with the third French ship, *Le Spartiate*. At first the *Vanguard* suffered heavy damage and casualties from the fire of her adversary and *L'Acquilon* next in line. The *Vanguard* was in fact almost forced to break off the attack but the timely arrival of the *Minotaur* gave the battered ship some relief by diverting the fire of *L'Acquilon*. During the action with *Le Spartiate* Nelson received a nasty wound above his blind eye, rectangular and three inches long, which covered his good eye with blood and skin and gave him a concussion. But for this wound, he later said, he would have

annihilated the French fleet. As it was, the wound was messy and painful and left him 'stone blind' for a time. *Le Spartiate* put up a terrific resistance but with 49 shot holes below water line on the port side and 27 on the starboard, her magazines flooded and her guns out of action, her colors were finally hauled down. At the end Nelson refused to take Captain Emeriau's sword, saying to the officer who brought it, 'Return it to him. He has used it so well'.

While this clash was occurring, the *Defence* passed the *Minotaur* and engaged *Le Peuple Souverain* from the outside. Soon after, the *Orion* shifted from *Le Peuple Souverain* to the sixth ship in the line, *Le Franklin*, which had thus far escaped attention. The *Bellerophon* should have engaged *Le Peuple Souverain* from the outside but instead was the first ship to tackle the huge *L'Orient* which had been waiting, seventh in the line, with her 120 guns double shotted. For an hour the *Bellerophon* was blasted by a ship almost twice her size until finally, dismasted and a virtual wreck, with the captain wounded and 200 casualties, she had to cut her cable and drift off into the smoke to leeward. The *Majestic*

Below: The scene of carnage on the decks of *Le Tonnant*. Captain Dupetit-Thouars can be seen resting on his shattered stumps in a tub of bran (center) continuing to direct the hopeless fight against the British.
Overleaf: Another view of *Le Tonnant*. After her captain was killed, her crew committed his body to the waters of Aboukir Bay before surrendering.

groped its way down the blazing line and eventually engaged *L'Heureuse* but at a disadvantage. Her captain was killed, and under the command of a lieutenant the *Majestic* finally swung clear and began to fire on the bow of *Le Timoléon*, the last ship of the center division.

The first phase of the battle ended just after 2000 hours, during which time most of the ships retained their original positions and the battle moved farther down the line as more British ships came up. The arrival of the *Alexander* and the *Swiftsure* marked the next phase which revolved around the French center. The distance of these two ships from the remainder of the British squadron enabled them to function as a mobile reserve and attack the French line where it would be most effective. The last British ship, the *Culloden*, had grounded on a shoal near Aboukir Island. The frigate *Leander* and the sloop *Mutine* had been trying to help her get off but they now joined the fight with the *Alexander* and *Swiftsure*. The arrival of these fresh ships turned success into total victory.

Now that the van had been destroyed, the British ships began to move down the line to attack the center and especially to cluster around *L'Orient*. This massive ship was the keystone of the French defense and on her fate hung the victory. The *Swiftsure* anchored outside the line and the *Alexander* on the inside. Her cable cut by a shot, *Le Peuple Souverain* then drifted out of line, leaving a gap through which the *Leander* sailed to rake both *Le Franklin* and *L'Orient*. Heavily battered by the British ships around her, *L'Orient* caught fire near the mizzen chains, causing the *Swiftsure* to bring every gun to bear on that point. Early in the battle Brueys had lost both legs and was wounded in the head but he refused to be taken below, saying 'A French admiral dies giving orders'. He was seated in an armchair, tourniquets on both legs and giving orders, when a shot from the *Swiftsure* cut him in half.

The fire in the flagship spread and grew with heat so intense that sailors began to jump overboard and pitch melted in the seams of the neighboring *Swiftsure*. Since the fire would soon reach the large powder magazines on board, nearby ships began to move away and rescue *L'Orient*'s sailors from the water. Still on board were Commodore Casabianca and his son, the subject of Felicia Hemans' popular poem, *The Boy Stood on the Burning Deck*. Most reliable reports state that Casabianca preferred to stay on board *L'Orient* and be blown up rather than leave the ship and abandon his wounded son, though others claim that both father and son jumped at the last minute but were drowned before they could be picked up. With a noise heard fifteen miles away in Alexandria, *L'Orient* simply disappeared in a mighty flash soon after ten. With her went half a million pounds in bullion, three tons of silver plate and the principal treasures of the Knights of Malta. At the Battle of the Nile Bonaparte lost much of his loot and financial base.

After the explosion firing ceased for almost ten minutes but was resumed by *Le Franklin*, flagship of Admiral Blanquet du Chayla. Blanquet had been severely wounded in the head

Above: Captain Dupetit-Thouars gave his final orders before he died: to nail the tricolor to the mast and to scuttle *Le Tonnant* before surrendering.

but continued to fight stubbornly. *Le Franklin* had been heavily battered in the attack on the center and at the time of the explosion the main and mizzen masts were down and all guns on the main deck dismounted. Only 80 fathoms to windward, the explosion of *L'Orient* had caused fires on *Le Franklin*, but these were extinguished and the action renewed. Nelson had now given the order for all ships to join the fighting at the center. *Le Franklin* was surrounded by enemy ships. With two-thirds of her company killed or wounded, Blanquet himself unconscious and only three lower deck guns still operational, the ship struck after an hour's fighting. Afterward Blanquet revived and inquired why the guns were silent. Informed that only three guns were still serviceable, he responded, 'Never mind, go on firing. The last shot may bring victory'.

Le Tonnant had also taken a severe pounding. At the time *L'Orient* blew up, she was razed to the deck and low in the water but still firing. Hit in both arms and with a leg shot off, Captain Dupetit-Thouars had himself placed in a tub of bran and continued shouting orders, the last of which, given just before he died, was to nail the colors to the mast and scuttle the ship before surrendering. *Le Tonnant* slipped her cable to avoid the explosion of *L'Orient* and at dawn was grounded a mile from her original position. As a gesture to his last order, the crew committed their captain's body to the deep before surrendering.

Until the explosion of *L'Orient* the last three ships in the French line – *Le Guillaume Tell*, *Le Généreux* and *Le Timoléon* – had scarcely fired a shot. Because of the thick smoke obscuring the line and his own wounds, Brueys was unable to give orders for the rear to assist the van and center. Admiral Decrès wrote in his diary, 'For four fatal hours the rear had seen nothing but the fire and smoke of the battle. It had remained at its moorings without firing a shot, waiting for signals that were not to be made, for the Commander-in-Chief had long lost the power to make his wishes known'. Villeneuve was later accused of standing by while the remainder of the fleet was destroyed, but since he was to leeward of the battle, how could his ships 'have weighed and tacked to get within range of the fighting before

the ships engaged had been disabled ten times over?' as he later wrote to Blanquet du Chayla. Had he weighed anchor, wind and current might well have carried him farther from the battle, in which case he would have been accused of flight. The only way one part of the line could have aided the others would have been for the engaged ships of the van and center to cut their cables and drift toward the rear. But when *Le Peuple Souverain* involuntarily took such an action because her cable had been shot away, it left a gap in the line through which the *Leander* then came. After the explosion of *L'Orient* Villeneuve shifted the anchorage of the rear farther to the east to wait for daylight to reveal the situation to him.

Dawn revealed that the first six ships of the line were in British possession, the seventh had blown up and there were six survivors. *Le Tonnant*, *Le Mercure* and *L'Heureuse* had all cut their cables to avoid the explosion and were aground. Of the smaller French frigates, *La Sérieuse* had run aground early in the battle, her rudder wedged by a piece of shot fired from a mortar on the poop of the *Goliath*. Although she should have kept well clear of the ships of the line, *La Sérieuse* had attacked the *Goliath*, causing Captain Foley to exclaim, 'Sink that brute, what does he here!' *L'Artémise* was sunk after the main battle. At noon Villeneuve opted for escape and got under way with the two remaining frigates, his flagship *Le Guillaume Tell*, *Le Généreux* and *Le Timoléon*. In an ineffectual attempt to turn, however, *Le Timoléon* ran aground and lost her foremast, after which her crew fired her and escaped ashore. The other four ships made good their escape.

Truly the most spectacular of Nelson's victories, the Nile virtually annihilated an entire fleet. A British sailor wrote that in the morning he '. . . went on deck to view the state of the fleets, and an awful sight it was. The whole bay was covered with dead bodies, mangled, wounded and scorched, not a bit of clothes on them except their trousers'. 'Victory is a name not strong enough for such a scene' was Nelson's comment. Of Brueys' thirteen ships of the line and four frigates, eleven of the line and two frigates were lost. Seven French captains and an admiral were killed and three captains wounded. Over 5000 French sailors were killed or missing, 3100 prisoners were put on shore and 400 others – officers, carpenters and caulkers – were carried off. Six French ships of the line were taken into British service and the rest stripped and destroyed as not worth repair. Bonaparte formed the survivors of the battle into a 'Nautic Legion' which served with his Army of the Orient but did not distinguish itself in any sense.

In the British squadron there were no ships beyond repair, but most had sustained heavy damage. Among nine of Nelson's battleships there was a total of two masts still standing but much of the loss in masts, spares and equipment was made good from the wreckage and prizes. Total British casualties were 218 killed and 677 wounded, a ratio of 1–10 in favor of the British. In addition to Nelson, three captains had been wounded and one killed.

The immediate result of the battle was to

Above: *L'Orient* in flames during the final stages of the Battle of the Nile.
Below: A contemporary broadsheet celebrating the British victory at the Nile.

ADMIRAL NELSON'S GLORIOUS VICTORY over the FRENCH FLEET off the MOUTH of the NILE on the 1st AUG! 1798.

(a) Mons.r Poussaculque, the French Commissary viewing the Engagement from the Castle of Bequires. b.b. The French Line. c. The English Line.

ADM.L LORD NELSON.

CAPT.N BERRY.

The Leander, capt. T.B.Thompson, which broke the French Line.

News my Boys from the Nile.

— *Christmas.* —

'Tis come, the day of health, the saving morn,
The Son of God, the babe of love is born.
Behold! all Heaven descends upon the wing,
And choiring Angels, Glory, Glory, sing;
Glory to God, from whom such bounties flow,
And peace on Earth, good will to Men below.

An honest man is the
noblest work of God.

Should some slight faults escape my pen,
With candor yet approve;
The boys can't reach the feats of men,
I'm sure at least I strove. —

Henry Vinicombe, Christmas, 1798.

Published 9.th Nov.r 1798 by LAURIE & WHITTLE, 53 Fleet Street, London.

CAPT.N DARBY.

CAPT.N WESTCOTT
killed on board the Majestic.

The L'Orient blown up.

Success to the Jolly Tars of Old England.

maroon the Army of the Orient in Egypt and cut it off from supplies and reinforcements. Despite Bonaparte's reassurance, 'Come, come, gentlemen, our fate is in our own hands', the news from Aboukir Bay greatly depressed the French expeditionary force which found itself in a difficult defensive war as the people of Egypt became openly hostile. After a disastrous campaign in Syria, Bonaparte slipped back to France aboard a frigate, arriving on 9 October, 1799. The Army of the Orient finally surrendered to Britain in 1801. The Battle of the Nile thus directly rendered the Egyptian project abortive and prevented any attempts to launch attacks on India or British trade with the east.

British Supremacy in the Med.

Once again supreme in the Mediterranean, Britain's influence quickly revived and the strategic islands and bases again began to pass under her control. More important, the enemies of France were given new heart and a second coalition of Britain, Austria, Russia, Naples, Portugal and Turkey renewed the war against France. A Russo-Turkish fleet entered the Mediterranean to aid the British and while Bonaparte struggled in Syria, his country was hard-pressed with a series of military reverses. Dependent on army support and funds from conquered terri-

tories, the Directory in 1797 had hesitated to end both the war and its expansionist foreign policy, a policy to which Bonaparte was closely allied. In 1798 its policy of aggression was resumed at a moment when France had come to favorable terms with all its adversaries except Britain. The Egyptian expedition had revived the fears of the conservative monarchies about France, resulting in the 'Second Coalition' whose initial successes in turn completed the ruin of the already unpopular Directory. Although the débâcle of the Egyptian plan was the first serious reverse in his meteoric career, Bonaparte opportunely returned at a time when his beleaguered countrymen were ready to hail him as their savior and install him as First Consul of the Republic.

News of the victory was received with wild rejoicing in England. Nelson was created Baron of the Nile and Burnham Thorpe (his birthplace); he received a pension from Parliament and many other honors. By demonstrating through his own tactical genius that Bonaparte was not superhuman, Nelson had inspired the rest of Europe to continue to resist French expansion. He was now acknowledged as the greatest fighting admiral of the age, known for his swift and audacious attack and for exploiting to the fullest any success over the enemy. By his insistence on not just the defeat but the complete destruction of the enemy,

he had revolutionized the whole concept of fleet action. The Nile also established a new tradition of leadership, for Nelson had proved another revolutionary proposition; that a resounding victory under sail could be won not through centralized command by written instructions, nor centralized command through signals, but by broad directives giving scope for independent action by subordinates. It is true that Nelson had excellent captains under his command, drawn from Jervis' Mediterranean fleet which was famed for its discipline and standards of seamanship. He was close to these men and remarked proudly after the battle, 'They are my children, they serve in my school and I glory in them'. Seven years later this same element of leadership was to be a vital factor at Trafalgar.

It would be incorrect to say that the Nile was a battle between comparable fleets. The French ships and crews were in poor condition, led by an admiral who had yet to command in battle. Pitted against him was the most brilliant and formidable sea fighter of the time in command of as fine a squadron of ships and crews as could then be had. Brueys has often been criticized for not meeting Nelson at sea and thus preventing the fatal concentration on one part of his line. Given the state of his ships and crews, however, it seems conjectural whether the French fleet would have fared any better under sail than at anchor. Where Brueys can be faulted is in not having guard frigates out and not preparing his defensive position properly. Criticism has also been leveled at Villeneuve, for had he sailed as soon as he saw Nelson's design, he could have captured the *Culloden* and prevented the *Alexander* and *Swiftsure* from entering the bay. Yet surely this was too much to expect of a thirty-five year old admiral who had been given no contingency orders. At best he could have been expected to order *L'Heureuse* and the remainder of the line to weigh at dawn, in which case five of the line might have escaped instead of two.

The Nile was the first encounter between the grandiose plans of Napoleon Bonaparte and the tactical genius of Horatio Nelson, an encounter from which the French Revolutionary Navy never really recovered. From 1798 the maritime ascendancy of Britain was definitely established and was to be one deciding factor in the struggle between France and Britain which lasted until 1815. The second encounter between the strategy of Bonaparte and the tactics of Nelson was to occur at Trafalgar in 1805, but this battle had not nearly the strategic significance of the Nile. As Bonaparte noted during his exile on St. Helena, 'I made one great mistake, my decision to invade Egypt'.

35

Trafalgar 1805

Early in the morning lookouts reported the masts of the enemy fleet some ten miles to leeward. Bringing with it the promise of fairer weather, daylight then revealed the enemy, now only nine miles distant. At 0540 the signal to form the order of sailing was made, followed at 0600 by 'prepare for battle'. Although he had carefully held the windward position during the night, the admiral was fearful lest the enemy decline battle as it had so often in the past and he ordered frequent signals to 'make more sail'. Having pursued this enemy fleet for almost six months, the admiral was in no mood to let it run back into

Cadiz and so elude him again. His burning ambition was the complete destruction of his enemy and today, the 21st of October 1805, was the day that history had allotted. Horatio Nelson was to smash the combined Franco-Spanish fleet off Cape Trafalgar and put a final end to any notions that the usurper Napoleon Bonaparte entertained of challenging British mastery of the seas.

The encounter off Trafalgar that day was the final dénouement of a train of events set in motion seven years earlier. Finding the reputation of their brilliant young general, Bonaparte, to be 'excessive and opportune', the French Directory had tried to get him away from Paris by giving him orders to end 'the perfidy of the Cabinet of England' through invasion by the Army of England, poised on the shores of the Channel. Seven years later in 1805, this army was still waiting to cross the Channel. In the meantime, Bonaparte had abandoned the original plan to invade England as not feasible and embarked on his ill-fated Egyptian adventure. Returning to a France hard pressed by the armies of the Second Coalition in 1799, he had been welcomed as a savior by his countrymen who made him First Consul of the Republic on the fall of the unpopular Directory. An abortive royalist plot to kidnap him in 1804 had led Bonaparte to consolidate his power by establishing himself as Emperor Napoleon I.

The war between Britain and revolutionary France had been ended in 1802 by the uneasy Peace of Amiens but after a brief respite had broken out again in May 1803. By now accepting that decisive victory would not be possible until French troops were on British soil, Napoleon's immediate objective in 1803 was the invasion of England. He thus began to assemble four of his best veteran divisions, along with transports and supplies, at Boulogne. But in 1803 the plans for invasion were beset with the same problem which had caused Napoleon to declare invasion not feasible in 1797 – how to obtain control of the Channel for passage of the invasion army. It was not that France did not have adequate naval

Below: Salute to the *Victory* returning to Portsmouth under jury-rig from the Battle of Trafalgar.

forces. Ganteaume lay at Brest with 21 of the line while Latouche-Tréville, France's ablest admiral, had a further twelve of the line at Toulon. Smaller squadrons under Missiessy and Gourdon lay at Rochefort and Ferrol respectively. Already a sympathizer in 1803, Spain became a formal ally of France the following year, adding 32 of the line to Napoleon's forces. Since the Dutch fleet was also arrayed against Britain, the Royal Navy's margin of superiority was indeed slender.

At the outbreak of war Britain had adopted her traditional defense strategy which was to prevent a direct threat to the home islands, to maintain control of the Mediterranean, and to assist such allies as she may have had with her naval forces. A strong force under Admiral Cornwallis blockaded Brest and guarded the approaches to the Channel. Smaller squadrons blockaded Rochefort and Ferrol while the blockade of Toulon and other operations in the Mediterranean were directed by Nelson. The lesson of the French expedition against Egypt in 1798 which had followed the withdrawal of the British fleet from the Mediterranean had been well learned in London. As a result British naval strategy in the Mediterranean was to prevent the Toulon squadron escaping to succor the French colonies, launch a new threat against Egypt or join the Brest fleet in the Channel. Nelson's task was to check the French at sea, while Hugh Elliott,

Below: Admiral Pierre de Villeneuve, Nelson's adversary at Trafalgar.

British Minister to the Court of Naples, tried to stem their advance on land through diplomacy.

In the face of the British naval blockades, Napoleon's preparations at Boulogne stood so little chance of success that some of his contemporaries such as the Austrian Chancellor believed the whole project to be a camouflage for a contemplated struggle with Austria. In actual fact, however, the chief aim of Napoleon's naval strategy for over two years was to divert by a series of eccentric maneuvers enough British ships from the blockades to enable his naval forces to combine and concentrate in superior numbers in the Channel before sufficient British ships could re-assemble to pose a threat to the invasion flotilla. Trafalgar came at the end of the last of these maneuvers.

The core of all of Napoleon's naval plans was to have the Toulon fleet break out and combine with the Brest fleet in the Channel, along with such other ships as were able to escape the blockades. Knowing the British feared that, thwarted by the blockades in his plan to invade England, he would reopen his ambitions in the east. Napoleon encouraged their concern assiduously. Indeed, the threat was all the more effective because it was genuine; Napoleon was already looking beyond the defeat of Britain to the realization of his dreams of an eastern empire. As a first step in this deception French forces occupied Taranto, from which they could threaten Greece, Egypt and, above all, Sicily. Greece was the key to the maintenance of the Ottoman Empire, which all powers except France had a vested interest in preserving. French control of Egypt renewed the threat to India and the eastern trade routes while Sicily was essential to the maintenance of British maritime power in the Mediterranean. A series of clever intelligence plants by the French was contrived to further confirm the British in their fears for the east.

The first French maneuver to gain the Channel had been scheduled for February of 1804 but was aborted due to the royalist plot against Napoleon. A second plan had to be cancelled in the summer of that year because of the death of Latouche-Tréville, commander of the Toulon fleet, who was succeeded by Admiral Pierre de Villeneuve. A forty-two year old Provençal of aristocratic background, Villeneuve had been a pupil of Suffren, the greatest naval tactician ever produced by France. Surviving the revolutionary purges of the naval officer corps, Villeneuve had been promoted to the rank of rear-admiral at the age of 33 and had commanded the French rear at the Battle of the Nile in 1798. Initially criticized for his failure to support the center and van in that battle, his reputation had quickly shifted from goat to hero as it was realized that he was the one French admiral clever enough to have escaped the clutches of Nelson. After his brave and resolute defense of Malta against the British in 1800, his reputation was completely cleared of any stigma resulting from the Nile.

A third plan failed early in 1805 when heavy weather dismasted several of Villeneuve's ships and forced him back into Toulon only two days after his departure. Playing on the obsessive fear for the eastern Mediterranean which he

had held since 1798, strong efforts were made to convince Nelson that this expedition was headed eastward, efforts which did succeed in drawing him to Greece and Alexandria. 'I have not the slightest doubt but that the destination of the French Armament was Alexandria', Nelson wrote at this time. Although his tactics of deception had drawn Nelson to the east as planned and his fleet had been able to escape, Napoleon was becoming increasingly frustrated with his admirals. 'What is to be done with admirals who . . . hasten home at the first damage they receive?' and again, 'The great evil of our navy is that the men who command it are unused to the risks of command', he complained.

Thwarted so far in his plans to uncover Brest and launch the invasion, Napoleon conceived a last plan which is known as his 'grand design' for the campaign. Missiessy, who had already escaped to the West Indies as part of the previous plan, was ordered to remain there and in due course join other French forces off Martinique. Ganteaume was to take his fleet immediately from Brest to Ferrol where he was to drive off the blockade squadron, collect Gourdon's ships, and sail for Martinique to combine with Missiessy and Villeneuve. Returning to drive the British forces out of the Channel, he was to proceed to Boulogne where he was expected by mid-July with his combined fleet of over 40 sail. If Villeneuve failed to make the *rendezvous*, Ganteaume was to wait 30 days and then try to fight his way through to Boulogne with 25 instead of 40 sail. After breaking out of the Mediterranean, Villeneuve was to relieve the blockade of Cadiz and, having released the Spanish ships there, proceed to Martinique and wait 40 days for Ganteaume.

If Ganteaume did not appear, he was to land his 3500 troops, harass the British in the West Indies as best he could and then sail east, taking a station off the Canary Islands on the route to the East Indies. If Ganteaume had not appeared there after twenty days, Villeneuve was to return to Cadiz for further orders.

Napoleon felt that such maneuvers would draw not only Nelson's squadron but at least twenty other battleships in pursuit, if for no other reason than to save the rich West Indian sugar harvest. Thus the main point of the grand design was to create a diversion on the other side of the Atlantic to draw off enough British ships for the French fleet to gain temporary supremacy in the Channel. The grand design was a masterful plan on paper conceived by a brilliant military mind – but a mind which never understood that a

Above: Procession of the British Fleet past the Castle of Elsinore on its way to Copenhagen, 30 March, 1801. Nelson's bold stroke which destroyed the Danish Fleet frustrated Napoleon's plans to break British mastery of the seas.

Left: Admiral Sir Robert Calder, one of Nelson's few professional enemies, was nevertheless allowed to proceed home in his flagship to face court-martial on the eve of Trafalgar. Although this weakened Nelson's fleet, it was a characteristically generous gesture on the part of this great man.

Right: Rear-Admiral Cuthbert Collingwood, who led the second line in his flagship *Royal Sovereign* at Trafalgar. He was an able subordinate, much respected by Nelson.

Below: The Battle of Copenhagen, 1801. The Danish Fleet was a sitting duck which Nelson proceeded to capture and destroy. Rather than risk the destruction of their city by bombardment, the Danes capitulated immediately.

squadron of ships could not be moved about like regiments of soldiers. Ignoring the winds and obvious countermoves of the enemy, indeed the essential differences between land and sea strategy, Napoleon dismissed the possibility of serious opposition until the final combination of his forces gave him overwhelming superiority. What Napoleon's admirals thought of the grand design is not on record except for Admiral Decrès, then Minister of Marine, who wrote to the Emperor, 'It is grievous to me to know the naval profession, since this knowledge wins no confidence nor produces any result in Your Majesty's combinations'.

The scope of the grand design was not suspected by the British but the renewed activity in the blockaded French ports made them aware that some plan was afoot and hence increased their vigilance. Nevertheless, on 30 March Villeneuve again made his escape from Toulon in circumstances remarkably similar to those which had enabled Brueys to come out in 1798. A storm blew Nelson's watching frigates away from their station off Toulon just before Villeneuve came out, then by sheer luck the French admiral learned the position of Nelson's fleet from a

neutral merchantman. With eleven of the line, eight frigates and 3000 troops, Villeneuve altered his course away from Nelson and ran down the coast of Spain. At Cartagena Villeneuve found no Spanish ships ready to sail and passed Gibraltar on 8 April. Since the squadron of Sir John Orde blockading Cadiz had been shifted to the north to reinforce Cornwallis guarding the Channel, Villeneuve was able to add one French and six Spanish ships to his forces without hindrance at Cadiz. Arriving at Fort Royal, Martinique on 14 May, Villeneuve received new orders which instructed him to seize some of the British possessions in the West Indies and then return in 35 days to join Ganteaume off Ferrol. The latter had been as yet unable to leave Brest without a fight which would have contravened Napoleon's orders to avoid contact with the enemy. Shortly thereafter, Villeneuve learned of Nelson's arrival in the Caribbean and, having achieved the main objective of drawing a substantial enemy force away from Europe, decided to return at once with his eighteen sail.

Only on 4 April did Nelson learn of the French sortie, after which he lay off Sardinia waiting for more definite information. On the eighteenth he learned that the French had been seen off Cape de Gata ten days before and realized that Villeneuve was headed not east, but for the Atlantic with ten days start. On 5 May, at Gibraltar, Nelson confirmed that Villeneuve had set course for the Caribbean. Leaving a squadron of frigates and one of the line to guard the Mediterranean, he set sail for the West Indies with nine of the line, making the crossing in only ten days. Characteristically, Nelson planned to attack the French as soon as they could be located, overcoming the disparity in numbers with his tactic of overwhelming one part of the enemy line and then dealing with the disorganized and demoralized remainder. Due to misleading intelligence, the British squadron did not catch the French fleet before the latter had shaped a northerly course for Ferrol. Nelson, however, soon came to believe that Villeneuve had indeed returned to Europe but had not the slightest clue as to whether Ireland, the Channel, Ferrol or Cadiz was his adversary's destination. Since the first three possibilities lay within Cornwallis' sphere of operations, Nelson's obvious duty was to cover Cadiz and the possibility that Villeneuve might be returning to Toulon.

Sending the brig *Curieux* to England to report the latest news to the Admiralty, Nelson sailed east to Cadiz where he met Rear Admiral-Collingwood patroling with six of the line but found no sign of the enemy. Leaving Collingwood on his station, Nelson made a sweep to the west and north in the Atlantic searching for the elusive French squadron. By luck he learned from an American ship that Villeneuve had steered a northerly course, information which caused him to join Cornwallis immediately off Ushant on 15 August in case Villeneuve was making for the Channel. When he heard the latest news from Cornwallis, however, Nelson decided to return to England for some long overdue shore leave. Despite the fact that he was a relatively healthy man, 'afflicted only with seasickness, to which he was so accustomed that he did not allow it to trouble him', he had been at sea continuously for two years and desperately needed a rest.

The news given Nelson by Cornwallis was that the *Curieux* had spotted the French fleet on a northerly course for the Bay of Biscay, raising the possibility that the French objective was the Channel. When Sir Charles Barham, First Lord of the Admiralty, received this intelligence, he had immediately disposed the fleet to meet the challenge. Cornwallis was ordered to raise the blockade of Brest, leaving only a few frigates on guard, and with twenty of the line to cruise thirty leagues out to the southwest for a week to intercept the French. Sir Robert Calder's blockading force off Ferrol and Corunna was reinforced to fifteen ships. Thus two strong forces were prepared to intercept Villeneuve in the north, but these moves left Brest and Rochefort uncovered. The grand design was working, though not in the way originally planned. Napoleon was in a state of frustrated excitement and, writing to Decrès, said 'I do not understand Ganteaume's inactivity'. Messengers were sent to order the reluctant admiral to sail immediately for Boulogne. 'Hold command of this passage for three days, and you will give us the means of putting an end to British pretensions . . .' he implored Ganteaume. Unfortunately for the grand design, Ganteaume could not be persuaded to put out until 21 August, by which time Cornwallis was back on station to send the cautious French admiral running for shelter after an exchange of sporadic gunfire.

On 22 July while steering for Ferrol, Villeneuve had the bad luck to cross courses with Calder's fifteen ships 100 miles west of Cape Finisterre. The outnumbered Calder attacked but the action was inconclusive due to a thick mist. After two days of contact Villeneuve was able to make off south southeast and run into Vigo, having lost only two crippled Spanish ships which were made prizes by the hungry Calder. With many sick and seriously short of food and water, the French forces next put into Ferrol on 28 July where they were joined by the five ships of Gourdon and eleven Spanish ships. With over thirty sail at his disposal, Villeneuve was urged by Napoleon 'Leave at once. You have only to sail up the Channel to ensure our becoming masters of England'. But Villeneuve's ships were in poor condition after their long voyage and the clash with Calder while at least a

dozen of his ships were no more than floating barracks for the troops he still had aboard. His lack of enthusiasm showed in a letter to Decrès: 'When I leave here with 29 ships, I'm supposed to be capable of fighting about the same number. I don't mind telling you I shouldn't like to meet twenty'. Again prevented from trying for the Channel by northeast winds, and certain that by now the opposing forces had concentrated to block him, Villeneuve convinced himself that the grand design was no longer feasible and sailed south for Cadiz on 19 August, hoping that from southern Spain he could engage the enemy on better terms.

What a Navy! What an Admiral!

Already disillusioned with Villeneuve for retreating in the face of Calder's inferior force, Napoleon was now furious, 'What a navy! What an admiral!' As soon as word of Villeneuve's move to Cadiz reached him on 23 August, Napoleon knew that the grand design was a total failure and that the opportunity to invade England had been irretrievably lost. Even before this turn of events, however, he was aware that forces elsewhere were again combining against him and would have to be dealt with soon. English diplomacy had finally persuaded Russia and Austria to join in the Third Coalition against Napoleon. Well aware of the progress of the Third Coalition, Napoleon's 'cold and marvellous brain saw every movement; and like some gross spider he lurked in wait to dash at the first victim who should be entangled in his web'. Already quiet arrangements were being made to counter a potential Austrian attack on northern Italy and even before the naval war reached its climax, Napoleon knew that he would have to strike southeast to crush Austria before the winter. On 8 August Prussia was offered the bribe of Hanover

Below: Admiral Gravina, who commanded the Spanish squadron of fifteen ships of the line at Trafalgar. Although part of Villeneuve's fleet, the Spanish had an independent command.

Above: The exposed Danish Fleet is destroyed by Nelson at Copenhagen in 1801.

in return for her neutrality and the order for the Imperial Guard to march from Paris to Boulogne was cancelled. News of Villeneuve's latest failure was just the last straw. The day following the receipt of this news the Grand Army began to move toward the Rhine in forced marches. 'I want to be in the heart of Germany with 300,000 men before anybody knows about it', wrote the Emperor. The War of the Third Coalition was to be decided not at sea or in England, but in Germany.

On 21 August the combined fleet of Villeneuve reached Cadiz. With only three of the line Collingwood did not dispute its entry, knowing that he would shortly be reinforced and that the combined fleet could not then escape without a battle. A hastily assembled British force established a full blockade close in. As an epidemic had ravaged the Cadiz area and food and naval supplies were known to be scarce, there was every hope that Villeneuve would come out before winter gales made maintenance of the blockade difficult. Villeneuve was in fact actually refused supplies by the local authorities until a direct order came from Madrid, and on 28 September Nelson himself arrived in the 100-gun *Victory*. Having been allowed but a short rest in England after his arduous two years at sea, Nelson had again been appointed to command in the Mediterranean since this was now the focal point of the naval war.

Since his victory at the Nile Nelson had fallen into some personal disfavor with the English establishment because of his highly visible affair with Emma, the young and beautiful wife of the elderly Sir William Hamilton, British Minister at Naples until 1800. But his rejection of his wife Fanny and Emma's unfortunate effect on his naval and diplomatic judgment in the aftermath

of the Nile tended to be forgotten even by the Establishment after his victory at Copenhagen in 1801. The battle in which he shattered a Danish fleet anchored in a well prepared defensive position and supported by strong shore batteries, Copenhagen finally established Nelson's reputation even among his enemies. From the outbreak of war in May 1803 until August 1805 Nelson was continuously at sea maintaining the blockade of Toulon and protecting the Mediterranean generally – no mean feat since the British had few bases east of Gibraltar. Hugh Elliott at Naples wrote of this period to Nelson '. . . to have kept your ships afloat, your rigging standing, and crews in health and spirits – is an effort such as was never realized in former times, nor I doubt, will ever again be repeated by any other admiral. You have protected us for two long years, and you have saved the West Indies.' Now the man of the hour in England, Nelson sailed for his post with the clamor of the populace ringing in his ears. 'I had their huzzas before – I have their hearts now!', he reportedly said to Captain Hardy of the *Victory* as they put out to sea. His reception by the bored and restive fleet off Cadiz was equally warm and sincere.

Preparations for the battle Nelson felt must soon come began on his arrival. His first act was to abandon Collingwood's close blockade and adopt his favorite tactic of the loose blockade. Regular meetings were held with the captains of the fleet, meetings at which Nelson expounded his tactics and discussed them thoroughly so that there could be no possibility of misunderstanding and a minimal need for signals. One element of Nelson's success as a commander was definitely his penchant for thorough preparation. The Admiral soon unveiled his plan for the battle which was accepted enthusiastically by his cap-

Left: HMS *Victory*, Nelson's flagship, as she appeared at Trafalgar. A first-rate, 100-gun ship of the line, she can be seen today at Portsmouth, England, restored to her 1805 condition. It is not generally known the *Victory* fought in the American Revolutionary War, but at that time there were many differences in her appearance. **Top left:** Contemporary broadsheet giving a graphic impression of how Collingwood and Nelson used their columns to shatter the Franco-Spanish line. **Top right:** *Bucentaure* fires the first shots of the Battle of Trafalgar at *Victory* and the frigate *Euryalus*.

tains and became known in the fleet as the 'Nelson touch'. In this plan Nelson argued that the old line ahead tactic was outdated for several reasons. No day was long enough to arrange two large fleets in line ahead and still fight a decisive action. Mutual support was the aim of the line ahead but, said Nelson, mutual support could best be given by getting alongside the enemy rather than in the formal line of battle. Thus the order of sailing was to be the order of battle and the aim of the 'Nelson touch' was to break up the enemy line and force a general mêlée.

Distilling the 'Nelson touch' into a secret memorandum for his captains, Nelson wrote that he wanted to attack from the windward on an enemy in the traditional close-hauled line ahead, the standard situation confronting British admirals in actions against the French. The fleet was to attack in two, or if there were enough ships, three lines. The lee division under Collingwood was to be the main striking force, cutting through the enemy line about twelve ships from the rear and forcing a close action by the use of Lord Howe's maneuver. The weather division under Nelson was to contain the rest of the enemy fleet and prevent it from assisting the outnumbered rear which was being overwhelmed by the lee division. This was to be accomplished by threatening the van and center and then, when the lee division was fully engaged, attacking the enemy flagship and neighboring ships to paralyze the enemy command. Like the lee division, the weather division would approach in line abreast and use Lord Howe's maneuver to get close action. The goal was the capture or destruction of the entire enemy fleet.

Here Nelson was again applying his favorite tactic, that of overwhelming an inferior part of the enemy line while containing the rest, through a battle plan which was the ultimate expression of his genius. The essence of Nelson's plan was to cut the enemy line into three parts to enable him to concentrate his whole strength on little more than half of that of the enemy in a general mêlée while the remainder of the enemy lay powerless to intervene due to the wind. Collingwood was to have complete control of the lee division in accord with Nelson's belief that subordinates should be given freedom to act within the confines of his broad plan. Nelson concluded his secret memorandum 'Something must be left to chance; nothing is sure in a sea fight beyond all others. Shot will carry away the masts and yards of Friends as well as Foes; but I look with confidence to a Victory before the Van of the Enemy can succour their Rear . . . In case Signals can neither be seen nor perfectly understood, no Captain can do very wrong if he places his ship alongside that of an Enemy.'

Crossing the 'T'.

At first glance the Nelson touch seems open to the criticism that in attacking the enemy line at right angles rather than parallel, the enemy was being given a highly desired opportunity to cross the 'T' of Nelson's two divisions. 'Crossing the T' is a naval maneuver in which a battle line sails at right angles across the head of the opposing line, thus blasting the enemy with its entire broadside from a postion at which the enemy can make little or no retaliation. In fact, however, Nelson's plan was to approach in line abreast rather than in line ahead, spreading his ships out as they approached the French line so that his 'T's' would not be crossed. As it was, however, he decided to attack with such speed that his ships never got into proper line abreast and appeared to be attacking in a disorganized line ahead. The ultimate weakness of the Nelson touch was that the first ships to attack would have some unpleasant minutes initially, taking the full brunt of enemy fire before the slower ships could come up to support them. At the time Nelson felt this was a risk worth taking to prevent the enemy from escaping, as French gunners still fired high to dismast rather than low to sink and the heavy swell that day was likely to make their aim erratic.

The British fleet consisted of three 100-gun ships including the venerable *Victory*, four 98's, one 80, sixteen 74's and three 64's. Four veterans of the Nile were among these vessels, the *Bellerophon*, the *Defence* and two captured French ships, the *Spartiate* and the *Tonnant*. Second in command was Cuthbert Collingwood, then 57, a senior and distinguished admiral who was a close friend of Nelson. He had made his reputation at the Glorious First and Cape St. Vincent. The other two flag officers in the fleet were Rear-Admirals Louis and the Earl of Northesk, Calder having been recalled to England. Shortly before the battle five of Nelson's ships under Louis had to be sent into the Mediterranean on convoy duty and to provision at Gibraltar. This left only 22 available on the day of the action, and the notion of a third group to act as a mobile reserve had to be dispensed with.

Having no further illusions about Villeneuve, Napoleon determined to replace him with Admiral Rosily. At the same time the Emperor decided he needed to take action against a joint Anglo-Russian force under General Sir James Craig which was threatening Italy from Malta. Rosily was dispatched to Cadiz bearing orders relieving Villeneuve but no advance notice of his dismissal was sent. His successor was apparently to be the bearer of the bad tidings. Instead,

Below: The day after Trafalgar remnants of the shattered French Fleet were able to make good their escape.

Villeneuve received orders to leave Cadiz immediately, pick up the Spanish squadron still at Cartagena, and then support General Saint-Cyr at Naples. Villeneuve was not to hesitate to attack any British force of equal or inferior strength. 'He reckons the loss of his ships as nothing, provided they go down in glory', wrote Decrès to which Villeneuve replied, 'As the Emperor thinks that only boldness and determination are necessary for success at sea, I shall satisfy him on that score'.

Why Napoleon did not notify Villeneuve of his dismissal is puzzling, but perhaps his contempt for the Admiral led the Emperor to believe that he would not leave port under any circumstances. Whatever the reason, it was to prove a costly error, for having heard rumors of his replacement and even talk of a court martial, Villeneuve put out to sea on 19 October after hearing that Nelson's fleet had been weakened by the detachment of Louis' squadron. In this final effort to redeem himself Villeneuve was to find that fortune dealt more harshly with him than the court martial and disgrace he feared to face. For while Napoleon was accepting the surrender of 30,000 Austrians at Ulm on 21 October, Villeneuve found Nelson waiting for him before the Straits of Gibraltar.

Villeneuve had 33 of the line, although fifteen of these were Spanish. and Napoleon allowed two of these as the equivalent of one French ship. There were command problems as well. Aside from the fact that the Spanish heartily detested the French, Admiral Gravina was not under Villeneuve's orders. He had an independent command with instructions to give the French assistance. In these circumstances it was difficult for Villeneuve to get agreement even on the order of battle. Agreement was finally reached, however, with the van to be commanded by Admiral Alava in the 112-gun *Santa Ana* and the rear by Admiral Dumanoir le Pelley in the 94-gun *Formidable*. The center was commanded by Villeneuve himself in the 80-gun *Bucentaure* with Admiral Cisneros second in command in the 130-gun *Santissima Trinidad*, the most heavily armed ship of its time. A twelve ship reserve was under Admiral Gravina in the 112-gun *Principe de Asturias*. The French forces consisted of four 80's and fourteen 74's while the Spanish had one 130, two 112's, one 100, two 80's, eight 74's and one 64; in all, a formidable fleet.

Having faced Nelson before at the Nile, Villeneuve knew what to expect of his opponent. 'The enemy will not trouble to form a line parallel to ours and fight it out with the gun', he wrote, no doubt remembering Nelson's hasty and unorthodox attack seven years earlier. 'He will try to double our rear, cut through the line, and bring against the ships thus isolated, groups of his own to surround and capture them.' As ever Villeneuve was pessimistic about his captains and the prospects: 'All we know how is to form a line, which is what the enemy wants us to do; I have neither the time nor the means to adopt other tactics, nor is it possible with the captains commanding the ships of the two navies . . .' And yet he was determined to fight, ending his written instructions to his captains with a quite Nelsonian turn of phrase, 'Captains must rely on their courage, and love of glory rather than upon the signals of the Admiral, who may be already engaged and wrapped in smoke . . . The captain who is not in action is not at his post'. On the basis of his experience at the fiasco of the Nile where he had received no orders from Brueys,

was Villeneuve in effect taking a leaf from Nelson's book and giving his captains some scope for independent action to forestall such a situation arising in his own command?

In accord with his ideas of the loose blockade, Nelson had been stationing his ships about fifty miles off Cadiz and relying on his frigates to warn him of any enemy sortie. About six in the morning of the 19th, he learned that the enemy was on the move and immediately set his own course to the southeast to get between them and the Straits of Gibraltar. Arriving off Gibraltar early in the morning of 20 October, he lay midway between Cape Trafalgar and Cape Spartel. Unfortunately for Villeneuve, the 19th had not been a very auspicious day for a sally, since light winds prevented all of his ships from clearing the harbor before dark, and the combined fleet was not really at sea before noon on the 20th. Four more hours were consumed by forming the battle order before the run toward the straits could begin.

'The Fleet is Doomed'.

After running in his regular line all night and sighting the British fleet between four and five in the morning of the 21st, Villeneuve suddenly decided about eight to reverse course to the north so that Cadiz would be under his lee if retreat became necessary. It was this maneuver which excited Nelson with the thought that the enemy might escape and caused him to sacrifice the finer points of his battle plan by rushing into action. The wind was light and the swell heavy, however, so that it was ten before the maneuver was completed. Gravina's reserve was now at the rear and Dumanoir's rear divisions had become the van. The Allied line was somewhat confused, being curved with many ships bunched two and three deep. With the enemy bearing down only five miles away, a Spanish captain was moved to remark to his first lieutenant, 'The fleet is doomed. The French admiral does not understand his business. He has compromised us all'.

The British ships in their two divisions were bearing down rapidly, as Nelson feared the enemy would deny him his battle by running for Cadiz. The growing swell suggested the approach of a storm which would be especially dangerous for damaged ships on a lee shore, so Nelson signaled to prepare to anchor at the close of the day, followed by the famous signal 'England expects that every man will do his duty'. Seeing the flags hoisted on the *Victory*, Collingwood growled impatiently, 'I wish Nelson would stop signaling, as we all know well enough what we have to do'.

His own column held back by the slower ships to the rear, Nelson was chagrined to see Collingwood in the 100-gun *Royal Sovereign* come under fire first, exclaiming 'See how that noble fellow, Collingwood, takes his ship into action. How I envy him!' And indeed, Collingwood was the picture of calm, walking the break of the poop 'with his little triangular gold-laced cocked hat, tights, silk stockings (easier to cut off in case of a leg wound) and buckles, musing over the progress of the fight, and munching an apple', as one of his lieutenants described the scene. Seeing

that the sixteenth ship from the end of the enemy line was the 112-gun *Santa Ana* of Admiral Alava, Collingwood made direct for her and gave her two broadsides at close range within five minutes which caused about one hundred casualties. The two ships were so close that they then locked yards while the French ship *Fougeux*, which had fired the opening broadside of the battle into the *Royal Sovereign*, continued a heavy assault on Collingwood's flagship which now lay between the two Allied ships. A furious muzzle to muzzle duel ensured between the three ships. Collingwood later said of the *Santa Ana* that she was a 'Spanish perfection . . . She towered over the *Royal Sovereign* like a castle. No one fired a shot at her but ourselves, and you have no conception how completely she was ruined'.

This proud assertion was not entirely accurate since the second British ship to come up, the 74-gun *Belleisle*, poured her first broadside into the *Santa Ana* and then locked yards with the *Fougeux* for an hour in another muzzle to muzzle contest. By that time the *Belleisle* was reduced to a wreck and was only saved from complete destruction by the intervention of fresh British ships. The *Fougeux* also badly blasted the 74-gun *Mars*, the next British ship to enter the battle, which was at the same time raked by the *Pluton*. Her masts and rigging destroyed, the *Mars* drifted away in an unmanageable state with heavy casualties and a dead captain. 'A cannon shot [from the *Fougeux*] killed [Captain] Duff, and two seamen who were immediately behind him. The ball struck the captain on the chest, and carried off his head. His body fell on the gangway, where it was covered with a spare colour until after the action', wrote one of the few survivors of the badly mauled vessel.

The remainder of the lee division continued to come up and one by one sail into the mass of the enemy rear. By one in the afternoon seventeen of the Allied ships had been separated from the center of their line and were assailed by the fifteen ships of the lee division in a confused mêlée. Having lost all of her masts and with Admiral Alava severely wounded, the *Santa Ana* struck at 1415. The *Royal Sovereign* was so badly damaged that she had to be taken in tow by the frigate *Euryalus* which also made the necessary signals since the flagship had not enough rigging left to hoist signal flags. The 80-gun *Tonnant* had fought a heavy action with the 74-gun *Algesiras* in which the French admiral Magon, second in command of the Allied rear, was killed and his ship captured by boarding. The flagship of Admiral Gravina, the 112-gun *Principe de Asturias*, was engaged first by the 74-gun *Revenge* and then other ships fought her assailants off. Mortally wounded, Gravina all too prophetically said 'I am a dying man, but I hope I am going to join Nelson'. The other ships fought at close range, often yard arm to yard arm, and with much boarding. At 1630 the lumbering 98-gun *Prince* finally came up to join the battle, though so late that she suffered no casualties at all. And at 1745 the French ship *Achille* blew up with most of her crew to end the battle of the rear, a battle which had gone exactly according to plan.

Fearful that the enemy would escape if he did

Above: Captain Harvey of the *Téméraire* led his seamen and marines in clearing the decks of enemy boarders.

rear, but instead of ordering Dumanoir to tack about he merely signaled that ships not engaged should get into action. Dumanoir therefore did nothing, as there were no British ships anywhere near him. Had he immediately come about, the *Victory* and the other lead ships might have been cut off and overwhelmed before the rest of the weather division could support them. As it was, the *Victory* drew heavy fire from a number of Allied ships, fire which riddled her sails and smashed her wheel so that she had to be steered by tiller from the gun room, an emergency measure requiring a number of hands urgently needed for other duties. 'This is too warm work, Hardy, to last long', remarked Nelson to his captain. Searching for Villeneuve's flagship, the *Victory* located her quarry about twenty minutes later. Passing under the *Bucentaure's* stern, the British flagship raked her with a treble-shotted broadside which sent shot crashing all the way to her bow, dismounting about twenty guns and causing nearly 400 casualties. Now being raked herself by other French ships, the *Victory* passed by the *Bucentaure*, leaving her disabled and easy prey for other British ships.

Immediately astern of the *Bucentaure* was the 74-gun *Redoutable* of Captain Jean Lucas, one of the finest fighting captains in the French navy. With a decided preference for obtaining his victories through boarding, Lucas had trained and equipped his crew well in the use of the grenade, cutlass, pistol and bayonetted carbine. At the opening of the action, Lucas had, as he wrote in his own account of the battle, 'laid the *Redoubtable's* bowsprit against the *Bucentaure's* stern, fully resolved to sacrifice my ship in defense of the

not attack immediately, Nelson ordered his faster ships to crowd on sail and engage the center. As Collingwood's division was already engaged, the columns were not even but the battle plan had always been intended to be flexible enough to meet whatever situation developed. At 1215, at the head of the weather division, the *Victory* came under fire from the *Heros*, whose gunners were aiming high in the French custom. At this moment Villeneuve in the 80-gun *Bucentaure* realized the need for his van to aid the center and

admiral's flag'. Although unable to prevent the *Victory* from raking the *Bucentaure* to such terrible effect, Lucas quickly closed with Nelson's now battered ship, laying his poop abeam his opponent's quarterdeck, after which the two ships became locked together by their rigging. Then, wrote Lucas, 'In this position the grapnels were flung. Those aft were cut loose but those forward held. Our broadsides were fired muzzle to muzzle, and there resulted horrible carnage'. The deck guns of the *Victory* were now almost silent

from loss among their crews, but the lower deck guns were still active. Lucas ordered his lower gun ports shut and continued the battle with his deck guns. Both crews were anxious to board, but the English were prevented by French musketry and grenades which made the upper deck of the *Victory* all but untenable. The boarders of the *Redoubtable* were frustrated because both ships were rolling and by the height of the *Victory* which made it difficult to cross. They tried to lower the main yard of the *Redoutable* to serve

Far right: The diminutive Captain Lucas, known in the French Navy as le petit Lucas, fought with incredible bravery and doggedness even after his ship, *Redoutable*, was boarded. He survived to become an admiral. **Below:** The *Redoubtable* under heavy fire from two British ships. This French picture inexplicably shows the right-hand British ship to be the *Sandwich*, but there was no ship of that name at Trafalgar.

as a bridge but this attempt was foiled by the *Victory*'s marines who also wiped out a small party who got aboard by the anchors.

Having barely beaten off these boarding parties of her adversary, the *Victory* was finally saved when the *Téméraire* poured a devastating broadside into the *Redoubtable* which ended her capacity to fight. 'It would be difficult to describe the horrible carnage caused by that broadside', wrote Lucas. 'More than 200 of our brave lads were killed or wounded. I was wounded at the same instant'. A third British ship then came up and opened fire at pistol range. Locked together with the *Victory* and the *Téméraire*, whose two topmasts had fallen on the *Redoutable* in exchange for the latter's mainmast which lay on the *Téméraire*, Lucas' ship was a riddled wreck in less than half an hour. Out of control, the *Fougeux* had drifted up from the rear and also became entangled with the other ships. Having tried to prevent Nelson from passing through the Allied line and thus cutting it off from Cadiz, Lucas had precipitated the fiercest scene of the battle, but now, with all his guns dismounted or shattered and 522 of his complement of 643 killed or wounded, he struck his colors at 1420, secure in the knowledge that his ship would soon founder.

Before the battle began, Nelson had been advised to cover his uniform coat with its easily recognizable admiral's stars so that he would be less easy prey for sharpshooters but he had refused as, he said, he wanted to inspire the crew. While pacing the quarterdeck with Hardy about 1315, Nelson fell to the deck, hit by a marksman about fifteen yards away in the mizzentop of the *Redoutable* which had a contingent of Tyrolean sharpshooters aboard. The ball struck him in the chest and lodged in his spine. Groaning 'They have done for me at last. My backbone is shot through', he was carried below and died three hours later. His last words were 'Thank God I have done my duty'.

The 98-gun *Téméraire* had been the second ship of the weather division to come up and, after engaging the *Neptune* in a hot action, had drifted across the bows of the *Redoutable* and brought her port battery to the support of the hard pressed *Victory*. The *Fougeux* had drifted up from the rear but was broadsided to such effect by the *Téméraire* that she ran foul of her attacker. Unable to resist further, she was then boarded from the *Téméraire* while the four ships lay locked together. About 1415 Hardy managed to cut the *Victory* loose of the tangle and tried to head north,

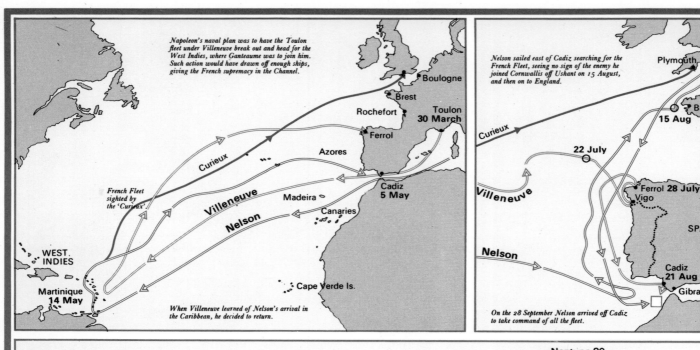

Napoleon's naval plan was to have the Toulon fleet under Villeneuve break out and head for the West Indies, where Ganteaume was to join him. Such action would have drawn off enough ships, giving the French supremacy in the Channel.

French Fleet sighted by the 'Curieux'.

WEST INDIES
Martinique 14 May

Cape Verde Is.

When Villeneuve learned of Nelson's arrival in the Caribbean, he decided to return.

Nelson sailed east of Cadiz searching for the French Fleet, seeing no sign of the enemy he joined Cornwallis off Ushant on 15 August, and then on to England.

On the 28 September Nelson arrived off Cadiz to take command of all the fleet.

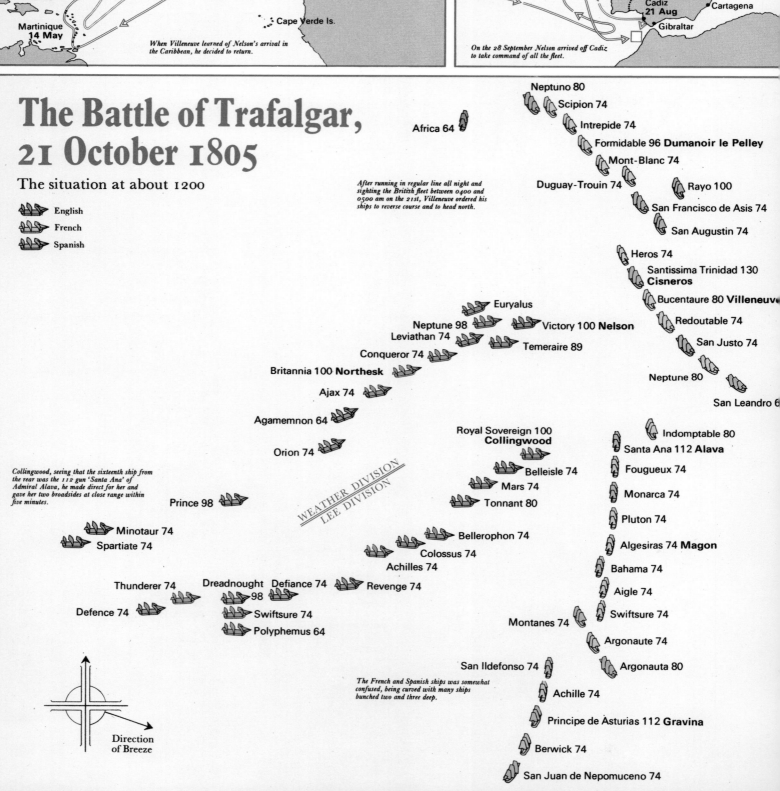

The Battle of Trafalgar, 21 October 1805

The situation at about 1200

- English
- French
- Spanish

After running in regular line all night and sighting the British fleet between 0400 and 0500 am on the 21st, Villeneuve ordered his ships to reverse course and to head north.

Collingwood, seeing that the sixteenth ship from the rear was the 112 gun 'Santa Ana' of Admiral Alava, he made direct for her and gave her two broadsides at close range within five minutes.

The French and Spanish ships was somewhat confused, being curved with many ships bunched two and three deep.

Direction of Breeze

Neptuno 80
Scipion 74
Intrepide 74
Formidable 96 **Dumanoir le Pelley**
Mont-Blanc 74
Duguay-Trouin 74
Rayo 100
San Francisco de Asis 74
San Augustin 74
Heros 74
Santissima Trinidad 130 **Cisneros**
Bucentaure 80 **Villeneuve**
Redoutable 74
San Justo 74
Neptune 80
San Leandro 6

Africa 64

Euryalus
Neptune 98
Leviathan 74
Conqueror 74
Britannia 100 **Northesk**
Ajax 74
Agamemnon 64
Orion 74

Victory 100 **Nelson**
Temeraire 89

Royal Sovereign 100 **Collingwood**
Belleisle 74
Mars 74
Tonnant 80

Prince 98

Minotaur 74
Spartiate 74

Thunderer 74
Defence 74
Dreadnought 98
Defiance 74
Swiftsure 74
Polyphemus 64

Revenge 74

Bellerophon 74
Colossus 74
Achilles 74

Indomptable 80
Santa Ana 112 **Alava**
Fougueux 74
Monarca 74
Pluton 74
Algesiras 74 **Magon**
Bahama 74
Aigle 74
Swiftsure 74
Montanes 74
Argonaute 74
Argonauta 80
San Ildefonso 74
Achille 74
Principe de Asturias 112 **Gravina**
Berwick 74
San Juan de Nepomuceno 74

WEATHER DIVISION
LEE DIVISION

54

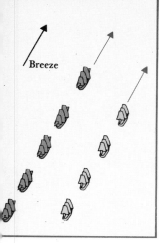

Breeze

The diagram illustrates the line ahead tactic of both defense and attack. Where ships would follow each other on a parallel course this tactic proved to result in an indecisive victory.

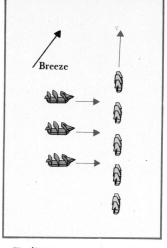

Breeze

The meleeists however, wanted tactics which forced fighting at close range. Nelson's tactic at Trafalgar indicated hoe effective this method was against a confused enemy.

The situation at about 1400

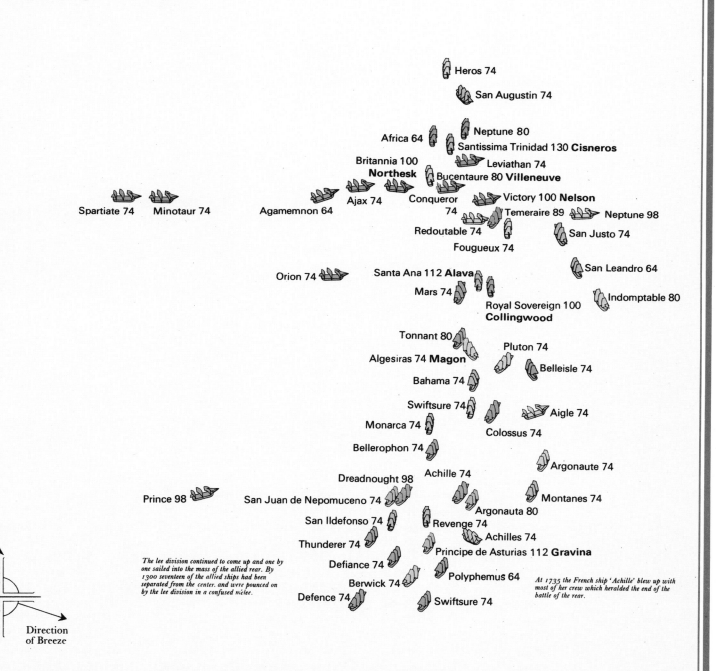

At 1400 Villeneuve finally ordered the van, under Dumanoir, to tack around and support the centre. The wind was so light that it required two hours for the van to accomplish the manoeuver.

Neptuno 80

Scipion 74

Duguay-Trouin 74

San Francisco de Asis 74

Mont-Blanc 74

Intrepide 74   Rayo 100

Formidable 96
Dumanoir le Pelley

As Dumanoir approached the rear with five ships. Collingwood ordered six ships to form a line. Since Gravina was breaking off action and making his escape, Dumanoir decided to sail south about 1630.

Heros 74

San Augustin 74

Neptune 80

Africa 64   Santissima Trinidad 130 **Cisneros**

Britannia 100   Leviathan 74

Northesk   Bucentaure 80 **Villeneuve**

Agamemnon 64   Ajax 74   Conqueror   Victory 100 **Nelson**

Spartiate 74   Minotaur 74   74   Temeraire 89   Neptune 98

Redoutable 74   San Justo 74

Fougueux 74

San Leandro 64

Orion 74   Santa Ana 112 **Alava**

Mars 74   Indomptable 80

Royal Sovereign 100
Collingwood

Tonnant 80

Pluton 74

Algesiras 74 **Magon**

Belleisle 74

Bahama 74

Swiftsure 74   Aigle 74

Monarca 74   Colossus 74

Bellerophon 74

Argonaute 74

Achille 74

Dreadnought 98   Montanes 74

Prince 98   San Juan de Nepomuceno 74   Argonauta 80

San Ildefonso 74   Revenge 74

Thunderer 74   Achilles 74

Defiance 74   Principe de Asturias 112 **Gravina**

Berwick 74   Polyphemus 64

Defence 74   Swiftsure 74

The lee division continued to come up and one by one sailed into the mass of the allied rear. By 1300 seventeen of the allied ships had been separated from the center. and were pounced on by the lee division in a confused melee.

At 1735 the French ship 'Achille' blew up with most of her crew which heralded the end of the battle of the rear.

Direction
of Breeze

but with her masts badly damaged, her rigging in shreds and badly holed in the hull, the *Victory* could take no more part in the battle and had to anchor. Later Hardy bore the news of Nelson's death to Collingwood who took command, transferring his flag to the *Euryalus*.

By 1400 other British ships were coming up and surrounding the crippled *Bucentaure*. At this point Villeneuve belatedly realized Dumanoir's failure to support him and finally made the signal which he should have made several hours earlier. The wind, however, was so light that it required more than two hours for the van to tack around and some ships accomplished this maneuver only by using boats. Ten ships finally came around and bore down on the battle. By this time, however, the *Bucentaure* had been so badly mangled that 'her upper decks and gangways heaped with dead and wreckage . . . presented an appalling spectacle'. Displaying throughout the calmest courage, Villeneuve finally exclaimed 'The *Bucentaure* has played her part, mine is not yet over'. But unable to transfer his command to a fresh ship from the van because all of the *Bucentaure*'s boats had been destroyed, Villeneuve realized that he was trapped aboard a ship unable to defend itself while the rest of his fleet continued the fight. Accepting the inevitable, he allowed the colors to be struck rather than see his crew uselessly slaughtered.

As Dumanoir's ships approached the battle the resistance of the Allied center had already been broken, but ten fresh ships could have saved the day since many British ships were now too badly mauled to fight. The action at the rear was still hot as Gravina held his own despite the fact that he was badly wounded and the concentration of enemy ships around him increasing. Taking as his first target the last ships of the weather division to come up, the *Spartiate* and the *Minotaur*, which were heading to protect the helpless *Victory* and *Téméraire*, Dumanoir quickly found that these ships were supported by the *Ajax*, *Orion* and *Africa*. In the face of this firepower and the fact that his commander-in-chief was now a prisoner, Dumanoir moved toward the rear with five ships. The other ships of the van moved to leeward. Seeing this new threat developing, Collingwood ordered six of his freshest ships to haul out and form a line to windward. Since Gravina was now breaking off the action and making his own escape, Dumanoir found it prudent to sail south about 1630.

The End of the Battle

With the departure of the French van, the battle was now over. The remainder of the day was given to the taking and manning of prizes and assisting the more badly damaged British ships. Of the seventeen ships engaged by Collingwood, eleven were prizes and one had blown up. Nelson's column had taken six. Dumanoir had escaped with four ships to the south while four from the van and four from the center had joined three survivors of Gravina's division and made off to the northwest. The combined Allied fleet had lost eighteen of its 33 ships and suffered 5860 dead and 20,000 prisoners. All of the prizes were totally or partially dismasted and in general

heavily damaged. By his failure to observe Nelson's earlier order to anchor at the end of the day, Collingwood saw all but four of his prizes sunk, wrecked or retaken by their own crews in the storm which blew up after the battle. No British ship was taken by the enemy but there had been heavy losses in masts and rigging, not to mention 1690 casualties. The escaping Allied ships made their way into the safety of Cadiz except for Dumanoir's four ships, which were all taken in a heavy fight with five of the line under Sir Richard Strachan off Ferrol on 2 November.

Thus ended not only the last fleet action of the Napoleonic Wars but the last major engagement between sailing fleets at sea. The radical tactics of Nelson had made Trafalgar the most decisive tactical victory ever achieved in an action in which both fleets had freedom to maneuver. But it would seem that few of Nelson's contemporaries appreciated the brilliance of the 'Nelson touch'. Although grasping that it had forced the enemy to stand and fight at a disadvantage, they tended to see it merely as a triumph for the principles of close action and support. Perhaps bemused by Nelson's last minute decision to rush into action

without forming his two divisions into proper line abreast, their lack of understanding of the 'Nelson touch' led them to carry the principle of close action to extremes in the years following Trafalgar. Not realizing how carefully tactics and gunner methods had been matched in that epic encounter, they proceeded to sacrifice the long range hitting power of their ships to make them more formidable at short range by increasingly arming them with carronades rather than cannon. Thus British ships could only develop their full fighting power in close, a fact which cost the British navy unnecessary losses in the American War of 1812. In the era of the *Permanent Fighting Instructions* tactics had been devised without regard to gunnery doctrine, but after Trafalgar new gun armaments were to be developed to a state which demanded battle conditions not always able to be provided by tactics.

Trafalgar was an excellent example of the superiority of British seamanship and gunnery in that period. In the light wind of that day, the British ships were better sailed and maneuvered and their gun crews better trained. Nevertheless the French defeat at Trafalgar can be said to have been due as much to their own errors as to the skill of their opponents, a statement also true of the Nile. Villeneuve had failed to signal his van in time, a failure difficult to understand since he was well aware of the style of Nelson's tactics. Dumanoir exercised no initiative about getting into action and had to be ordered to fight despite Villeneuve's pre-battle admonition that captains not in action were not at their posts. Even then Dumanoir allowed his force to split into two parts, when as a compact unit it could have made a significant impression on the battle at that time. Holding the windward position, Gravina on seeing the attack developing should have brought his twelve ships up to support the center, which was Villeneuve's original concept of the reserve division, but instead he remained at the rear. The French cause was also weakened by the lack of enthusiasm of their Spanish allies about the war in general and the French in particular. Indeed, several Spanish ships had to be fired on by the French to keep them in the line and when captured, the Spanish crews offered to help their captors man their guns!

Above: The scene on board the *Victory* just after Nelson was wounded. In the foreground a marine and a midshipman take aim to kill the French sharpshooter, but all around the gun crews continue at their stations.

Left: The end of the battle. Remnants of the Franco-Spanish fleet make their escape with the British in pursuit. **Right:** Nelson was removed to the cockpit to join the scores of casualties already there Nelson already knew that he was mortally wounded. He tried to cover his decorations so that the sailors would not recognize him as he was carried below. **Below:** By the closing stages of the battle, *Victory* was heavily damaged, particularly in her rigging.

Without Nelson, however, there would have been no such victory. It was Nelson's strategy of the loose blockade which brought Villeneuve out of both Toulon and Cadiz, not the close blockade of Collingwood. With the same style of leadership he had displayed at the Nile, Nelson again inspired the best from his captains and crews. Disregarding dogma, his tactics enabled his force to engage and vanquish a numerically superior enemy. Obsessed with annihilating his enemy, he was contemptuous of what he called a 'Lord Howe victory'. He believed that the Glorious First of June had been a strategic failure and only a half-developed tactical success. His goal at Trafalgar had been the capture or destruction of twenty enemy ships, and with eighteen actually taken the goal was very nearly achieved.

In addition to a posthumous earldom, a grateful nation gave Nelson a state funeral at St. Paul's Cathedral in London and transmuted his fame into a schoolboy legend of impetuous daring. In the words of a modern historian of this period, 'The breadth and vigor of his strategic conceptions, which constituted the real proof of his genius, formed only a small part of the legend, his flashes of un-British emotionalism and theatricality were carefully edited, and the ill-savor of his affair with Lady Hamilton was passed over in embarrassed silence.' Collingwood took over Nelson's burdens as commander-in-chief in the Mediterranean until his own death five years later. Fate continued to deal cruelly with Villeneuve, whose main failing had been to recognize that the French with their poorly fitted vessels and sickly and ill-trained crews could not defeat the British even when numerically superior. After four months in England Villeneuve was repatriated to France in 1806, and Napoleon ordered him not to come to Paris. Having survived the battle he could not survive disgrace and committed suicide the next day. 'He was a gallant man, although he had no talent', remarked Napoleon and ordered him buried without honors.

Trafalgar did not save England, as the instigator of the train of events leading to the battle had broken his camp at Boulogne two months earlier and rushed across Europe in forced marches to meet the threat on land of the Third Coalition. First defeating the Austrians at Ulm on 17–21 October, Napoleon decisively wrecked the coalition on 2 December at Austerlitz where in a brilliant piece of generalship and deception

he defeated the Austrians and Russians. This victory forced Austria to withdraw from the coalition and convinced Prussia, then holding the balance of power in Europe, to remain neutral for the time being. Trafalgar thus occurred months after Napoleon had accepted the grand design as a failure.

Nor did Trafalgar destroy the naval power of Napoleon: the Brest fleet was still intact and a new force was soon created at Toulon. In fact, Napoleon had at his disposal a combined total of 62 French, Spanish and Dutch ships of the line. Depending on the success of his diplomacy, more could have been added from Russia, Sweden and Denmark, a possibility which led the British to destroy the Danish fleet at Copenhagen a second time in 1807 to prevent it from falling into French hands. Already disillusioned with his admirals and the failure of his naval strategy, Napoleon was convinced by Trafalgar to end his attempts to contest supremacy of the seas with the British. The remains of the navy and the large fleet of privateers were used only for commerce raiding, which was sufficiently destructive but could not be a decisive factor in the overall struggle. After Trafalgar French arms were confined to the continent, and it was on the continent that Napoleon would have to be defeated. Napoleon was not in fact defeated until 1814 when a Russian army marched into France, occupied Paris and captured him. Although in his last exile at St. Helena, Napoleon said 'In all my plans I have always been thwarted by the British Fleet', it was not in fact British supremacy at sea which ultimately undid him but Russian bayonets and the unpopularity of his administration in France.

Although when he read the dispatch of the victory, George III was speechless for a full five minutes, no doubt causing some consternation among his entourage. Trafalgar was probably not even fully appreciated in England at that time. The news of the victory was overshadowed by the news of the death of Nelson, who was truly a national hero. The momentous events on the continent such as Ulm and Austerlitz, the end of the Holy Roman Empire, the eclipse of Austria as a military power, and the short-lived Prussian alliance with France must have seemed far more important to the people of England. The strategic results of Trafalgar were perhaps minor compared to those of the Nile, but its effect on naval tactics and leadership made it later recognized as one of the epic events in naval history.

Below: England was plunged into grief by the death of Nelson, despite the rejoicing over the good news of his victory. His body was brought up the Thames to lie in state at the Royal Naval Hospital, Greenwich, before being taken to its final resting place in St. Paul's Cathedral.

Austerlitz

1805

Opposite right: Napoleon surrounded by battle honors in a contemporary broadsheet celebrating the victory of Austerlitz. **Below:** The battlefield of Austerlitz at 1000 hours on 2 December, 1805.

On 2 December, 1805 the French *Grande Armée* met the combined armies of Russia and Austria near the Moravian village of Austerlitz. The French were ostensibly at a disadvantage. They were deep inside hostile territory, heavily outnumbered and faced by an aggressive and confident enemy. Yet within the space of a few hours the *Grande Armée* had won its most spectacular victory, routing the Allied armies, forcing Austria out of the war and sending a thrill of horror throughout Europe.

The dramatic and far-reaching consequences of Austerlitz should not be permitted to obscure its equally significant background. Few battles can usefully be studied outside their diplomatic and military context, and Austerlitz, the culmination of a campaign of movement and a war of alliances, is certainly not one of them. The diverse elements which brought about Austerlitz account, in themselves, for much of the battle's course and character. The midwinter clash in Moravia was not simply one of a series of battles; it was the focal point of a campaign and was to leave its stamp on Europe for the next decade.

From 1792 to 1797 Revolutionary France had been at war with the 'First Coalition', a tenuous alliance between England, Prussia, Russia, Austria and Spain. By 1797 only England continued the struggle. A French expedition to Egypt in 1798 met with success on land, though the destruction of the French fleet in Aboukir Bay (Battle of the Nile) ensured the expedition's ultimate failure. The leader of the abortive descent on Egypt was the young General Napoleon Bonaparte.

Born at Ajaccio in Corsica in 1769, Bonaparte had been commissioned into the French artillery in 1785. The upheavals following the Revolution of 1789 facilitated his rapid promotion; in 1793 he distinguished himself at the siege of Toulon and, three years later, commanded the French army in Italy. Bonaparte's Italian campaign of 1796 established him as a commander of the first order, raised him to eminence within France and brought him to the notice of Europe at large. Undaunted by his failure in Egypt Bonaparte, on his return to France, was instrumental in removing the Directory and replacing it by the

Consulate, with himself as First Consul. After some six months of frenzied political and administrative work, Bonaparte took the field once more.

His adversaries were now the members of the 'Second Coalition', formed in 1798, which was to meet with as little success as the first. A Russian army under Marshal Suvorov reached Zurich, only to be defeated by General André Massena in September 1799. Austrian successes in northern Italy, however, compelled Bonaparte's personal intervention, and on 14 June 1800 he defeated General Melas at Marengo. In February 1801 France and Austria made peace at Lunéville and, the following month, Spain, who had already been giving France naval support, made a formal alliance with her. A series of fruitless military and diplomatic maneuvers failed to produce any result in the Anglo-French struggle, and March 1802 saw peace concluded at Amiens.

Much as it was welcomed on both sides of the Channel, peace did not survive for long. French moves in Europe and the West Indies, matched by a marked reluctance on the part of Britain to relinquish Malta, brought about a renewal of war in May 1803. The British at once blockaded France and began to seize French overseas colonies. Bonaparte responded by closing European ports to English trade and concentrating an army of invasion on the channel coast. Britain set about the formation of a 'Third Coalition'; Russia joined eagerly enough, followed in August 1805 by Austria and subsequently by Sweden and Naples. Prussia, deluded by French diplomacy, decided, for a while at least, to remain neutral, but Spain, Bavaria and Württemberg adhered to France.

The Coalition's plan involved five major armies. An Austro-Russian force of some 94,000 men was forming under the Archduke Charles in

northern Italy. These forces were to be linked by a smaller Austrian army, commanded by the Archduke John, in the Tyrol. To the south a small Anglo-Russian force was to sail from Corfu to Naples, and, aided by the Neapolitans, was to march into northern Italy. In the Baltic a tripartite English, Russian and Swedish force was to move from Stralsund to Hanover, threatening Holland and putting pressure on the Prussians. The main blow was to be delivered by the Austro-Russian army in the center which, when fully concentrated, was to invade France by way of Strasbourg. The Archdukes would accompany this move by advancing through Switzerland into France. If the main force incurred a reverse, the Archduke Charles was to defend the line of the River Mincio and send reinforcements to the north. The plan relied heavily on British gold financing continental manpower, backed by the British fleet; it was, inevitably, fraught with the problems which so often attend alliances.

One of the most serious difficulties was that of command. The Austrian Aulic Council remained preoccupied with northern Italy, home of the Archduke Charles' disproportionately powerful army. The Austrian element of the central army was commanded by the Archduke Ferdinand, but the Emperor Francis had instructed him to obey the orders of the Chief-of-Staff, General Mack. Francis himself proposed to take personal command of the central army once the Russians had armed. The leading Russian force, under the eccentric veteran Marshal Kutusov was due to arrive in Bavaria toward the end of October, closely followed by another army under General Buxhowden, with a third army under Marshal Bennigsen operating to its north. Kutusov had been instructed by the

Tsar to obey the orders of the Emperor Francis or one of the Archdukes, but not those of any other Austrian general. These arrangements made chaos an integral part of the Allied command, chaos which was to worsen with a series of violent personal disagreements between commanders. The tottering edifice was crowned with supremely bad staff-work which failed to take into account the fact that the Austrian and Russian calendars differed by ten days. This oversight was to result in the Austrian force under the divided command of Ferdinand and Mack remaining dangerously isolated in the Ulm-Augsburg area.

Napoleon Crowns Himself Emperor

While Allied machinations went on, Bonaparte, elevated in December 1804 to the dignity of Napoleon I, Emperor of the French, concentrated his army on the Channel coast with the apparent intention of invading England. A descent on England was certainly not a viable proposition unless the combined French and Spanish fleets could destroy the British fleet and thus guarantee free passage for the invasion force. It is, indeed, open to discussion as to how seriously Napoleon took the planned invasion. Nevertheless, if the Emperor had any doubts he kept them to himself, and the summer of 1805 saw the *Grande Armée* massed in the area of Boulogne, with detachments in Holland, Hanover and Brittany.

After assessing the various Allied threats, Napoleon adopted a strategic plan which, in contrast to that of the Allies, was as brilliant and incisive as it was hazardous. The invasion of England was postponed—a postponement which was to be turned into cancellation with the defeat of the French fleet at Trafalgar on 21 October, 1805. The *Grande Armée* was to march to

the Danube with all possible speed, collecting the Bavarians *en route* with the intention of encircling Ferdinand and Mack, before moving eastwards to deal with the advancing Russians. The envelopment of Mack depended upon the French advance being carried out in secrecy and with great rapidity. The accomplishment of a swift and secure maneuver over such distances, with an army of over 200,000 men was in itself a strategic novelty. Marlborough had accomplished it for the Blenheim campaign of 1704, but the problems facing Napoleon, in terms of supply and transport, were infinitely greater.

Napoleon's task was facilitated by the composition and organization of the *Grande Armée*. The French army of 1805 was the result of the fusion of many disparate elements into a cohesive and vibrant whole. The wars of the Revolution had not only put an unprecedentedly large number of Frenchmen into uniform but they had also allowed the creation of an army in which rank was no longer the prerogative of an aristocratic minority. Most of Napoleon's senior commanders in 1805 had risen from the ranks by merit; only two of them, Marshals Augereau and Bernadotte, were over forty years of age. The organizational basis of the *Grande Armée* was the corps, a large all-arms group formed of several divisions. The corps of the *Grande Armée* differed in size according to their role; they were, however, flexible formations, well-suited to overcoming the logistic problems posed by Napoleon's strategic plan.

Napoleon dictated his orders to Count Daru, Intendant General of the *Grande Armée*, on 13 August. He decreed the simultaneous advance of what he termed 'my seven streams'. Bernadotte, with 17,000 men of 1st Corps, was to march from

Hanover to Bavaria by way of Würzburg—
13,000 men were to remain in Hanover in case
of an Allied landing in north Germany. Marshal
Marmont's 2nd Corps, 20,000 strong, was to
join Bernadotte at Würzburg, having marched
by way of Mainz and Frankfurt. The most
able of Napoleon's marshals, the level-headed
Davout, was to lead the 26,000 men of his 3rd
Corps from its camp at Ambleteuse, on the
Channel coast, to Mannheim. Marshal Soult was
to take the 4th Corps, 40,000 men, from Boulogne
to Spires, where a division would be detached to
strengthen 5th Corps under Marshal Lannes.
The red-headed Marshal Ney—'bravest of the
brave'—would link up with Lannes at Strasbourg
with the 24,000 men of 6th Corps, having
marched from Montreur on the Channel coast.
Marshal Augereau's 7th Corps was to march from
Brittany to the Rhine, bringing up the rear.

The advancing infantry were preceded by the
cavalry of the *Grande Armée*, 22,000 horsemen
under the flamboyant Marshal Joachim Murat.
Part of Murat's force was employed with 5th
Corps in the Black Forest, drawing Mack
westward and distracting him from the danger
looming to the northwest. Napoleon himself
was accompanied by the Imperial Guard under
Marshal Bessières, 7000 strong.

Its itineraries laid down by meticulous staff-
work, the *Grande Armée* surged eastward in
September and early October, and the jaws of
the trap closed about the unwary Mack. The
latter, hindered by bad relations with Ferdinand
and his divisional commanders, concentrated on

Ulm. On 13 October Lannes took Elchingen and
its half-demolished bridge after a brisk engagement. Ferdinand, following yet another dispute
with Mack, broke out of the Ulm position on the
night of 14/15 October, but, pursued hard by
Murat, only a very small proportion of his force
actually managed to escape. On the 17th Mack
agreed to surrender if Russian help had not
materialized by the 26th. However, for reasons
which remain unclear, he capitulated early, on
20 October, with nearly 30,000 men.

Kutusov had indeed been making for Ulm, but
was too far away to be of any assistance to Mack.
He reached Braunau on the River Inn on the 20th,
but even though he had assimilated a stray
Austrian division, he had only 40,000 men
immediately available. He heard of the Ulm
capitulation on 23 October, and at once fell back
over the Inn, burning its bridges behind him.

The second phase of the campaign began on
26 October, when the *Grande Armée* set along the
Danube. The French crossed the Inn on 29/30
October, but the pace of the advance was slowed
down by bad weather. Ney had been sent to
contain the Austrians in the Tyrol, while Marmont, in the Salzburg area, checked any threat
from the Archdukes Charles and John.

The bulk of the *Grande Armée*—Soult, Lannes,
Bernadotte and Murat—moved along the right
bank of the Danube. Davout's troops linked the
main body with Marmont, while Marshall
Mortier, with Gazan's and Dupont's divisions,
followed the left bank of the Danube.

Kutusov fell back with the stubbornness and

Opposite: Napoleon enters Vienna after his victory at Ulm. The composer Beethoven, who had written his Eroica Symphony in honor of the 'liberator' of the Habsburg Empire, changed his dedication of the 3rd symphony after the French troops arrived. **Left:** Marshal Bernadotte, whose army occupied the Pratzen Plateau after the battle. He was later forced upon the Swedes as their King by Napoleon, and he betrayed his former chief as the tide of battle flowed against him after the disastrous Russian campaign.

The Battle of Austerlitz, 1805

At the onset of war, Britain immediately set about the formation of a 'Third Coalition'; Russia joined eagerly followed in 1805 by Austria, Sweden and Naples. Prussia remained neutral, but Spain, Bavaria and Wurttemberg adhered to France.

The Coalition's plan involved five major armies, the main blow was to be delivered by the Austro-Russian army which, when fully concentrated, was to invade France by way of Strasbourg, accompanied by the Archdukes advancing through Switzerland into France.

After assessing the various Allied threats, Napoleon issued his orders. The 'Grande Armée' was to march to the Danube with all possible speed, encircle Ferdinand and Mack, before moving eastwards to deal with the advancing Russians. The plan depended upon secrecy and great rapidity.

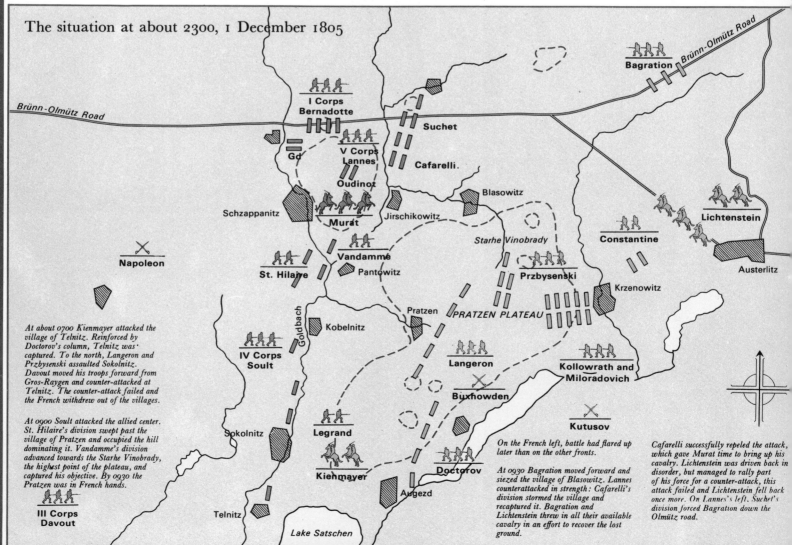

The situation at about 2300, 1 December 1805

At about 0700 Kienmayer attacked the village of Telnitz. Reinforced by Doctorov's column, Telnitz was captured. To the north, Langeron and Przbysenski assaulted Sokolnitz. Davout moved his troops forward from Gros-Raygen and counter-attacked at Telnitz. The counter-attack failed and the French withdrew out of the villages.

At 0900 Soult attacked the allied center. St. Hilaire's division swept past the village of Pratzen and occupied the hill dominating it. Vandamme's division advanced towards the Starhe Vinobrady, the highest point of the plateau, and captured its objective. By 0930 the Pratzen was in French hands.

On the French left, battle had flared up later than on the other fronts.

At 0930 Bagration moved forward and siezed the village of Blasowitz. Lannes counterattacked in strength: Cafarelli's division stormed the village and recaptured it. Bagration and Lichtenstein threw in all their available cavalry in an effort to recover the lost ground.

Cafarelli successfully repeled the attack, which gave Murat time to bring up his cavalry. Lichtenstein was driven back in disorder, but managed to rally part of his force for a counter-attack, this attack failed and Lichtenstein fell back once more. On Lannes's left, Suchet's division forced Bagration down the Olmütz road.

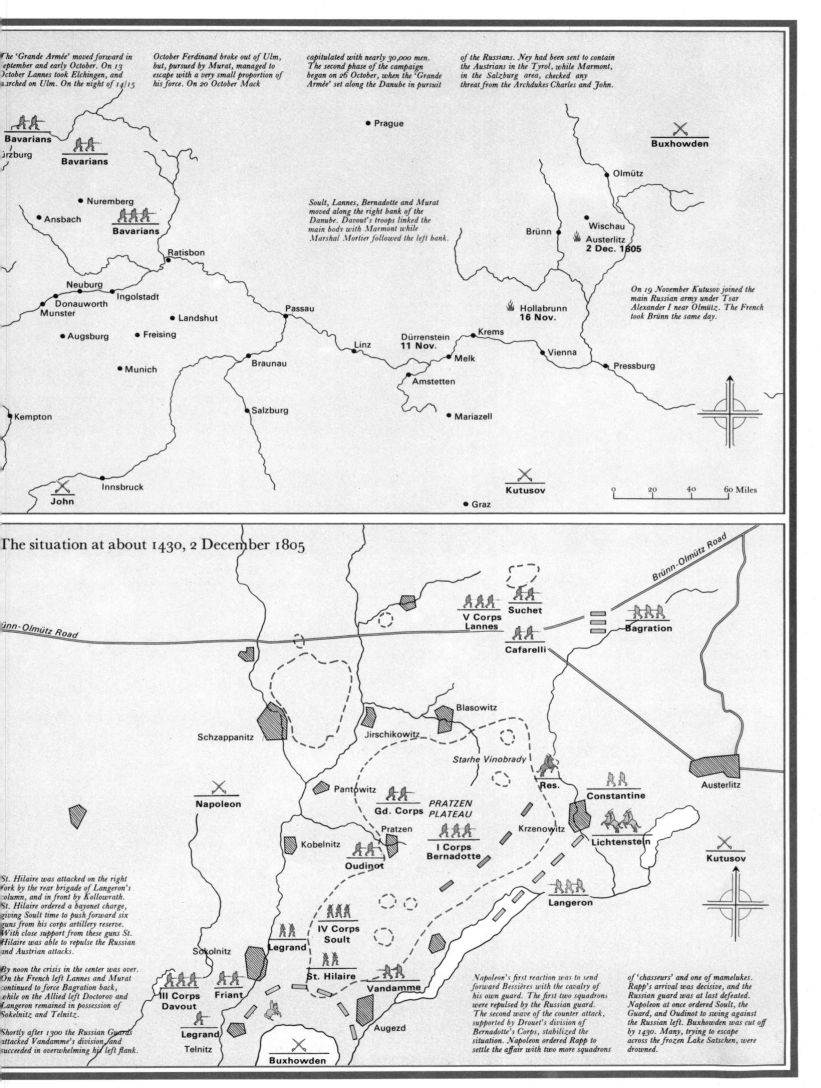

The 'Grande Armée' moved forward in September and early October. On 13 October Lannes took Elchingen, and marched on Ulm. On the night of 14/15 October Ferdinand broke out of Ulm, but, pursued by Murat, managed to escape with a very small proportion of his force. On 20 October Mack capitulated with nearly 30,000 men. The second phase of the campaign began on 26 October, when the 'Grande Armée' set along the Danube in pursuit of the Russians. Ney had been sent to contain the Austrians in the Tyrol, while Marmont, in the Salzburg area, checked any threat from the Archdukes Charles and John.

Soult, Lannes, Bernadotte and Murat moved along the right bank of the Danube. Davout's troops linked the main body with Marmont while Marshal Mortier followed the left bank.

On 19 November Kutusov joined the main Russian army under Tsar Alexander I near Olmütz. The French took Brünn the same day.

Bavarians
Würzburg
Bavarians
• Nuremberg
• Ansbach
Bavarians
Ratisbon
Neuburg
Ingolstadt
• Donauworth
Munster
• Landshut
Passau
• Augsburg
• Freising
Linz
• Munich
Braunau
• Salzburg
Innsbruck
John
• Kempton

• Prague
Buxhowden
• Olmütz
Brünn
• Wischau
Austerlitz
2 Dec. 1805
Hollabrunn
16 Nov.
Dürrenstein
11 Nov.
Krems
Melk
Vienna
Pressburg
Amstetten
• Mariazell
Kutusov
• Graz

0   20   40   60 Miles

The situation at about 1430, 2 December 1805

Brünn-Olmütz Road

V Corps Lannes   **Suchet**
Cafarelli   **Bagration**

• Blasowitz
Jirschikowitz
Schzappanitz
Starhe Vinobrady
Napoleon
Res.
• Pantowitz   **Constantine**
Gd. Corps   *PRATZEN PLATEAU*   Krzenowitz
Pratzen   **Lichtenstein**
• Kobelnitz   **I Corps Bernadotte**   Austerlitz
Oudinot   **Kutusov**

St. Hilaire was attacked on the right flank by the rear brigade of Langeron's column, and in front by Kollowrath. St. Hilaire ordered a bayonet charge, giving Soult time to push forward six guns from his corps artillery reserve. With close support from these guns St. Hilaire was able to repulse the Russian and Austrian attacks.

IV Corps Soult
Sokolnitz   **Langeron**
Legrand
St. Hilaire
Vandamme
III Corps Davout   **Friant**
Legrand
Telnitz   Augezd
Buxhowden

By noon the crisis in the center was over. On the French left Lannes and Murat continued to force Bagration back, while on the Allied left Doctorov and Langeron remained in possession of Sokolnitz Land Telnitz.

Shortly after 1300 the Russian Guards attacked Vandamme's division, and succeeded in overwhelming his left flank.

Napoleon's first reaction was to send forward Bessières with the cavalry of his own guard. The first two squadrons were repulsed by the Russian guard. The second wave of the counter attack, supported by Drouet's division of Bernadotte's Corps, stabilized the situation. Napoleon ordered Rapp to settle the affair with two more squadrons of 'chasseurs' and one of mamelukes. Rapp's arrival was decisive, and the Russian guard was at last defeated. Napoleon at once ordered Soult, the Guard, and Oudinot to swing against the Russian left. Buxhowden was cut off by 1430. Many, trying to escape across the frozen Lake Satschen, were drowned.

Above: Marshal Joachim Murat, who commanded the advance guard, failed to follow the Russians and made straight for Vienna. Kutusov's forces made good their escape, forcing Napoleon to follow him northward to Austerlitz.

determination he was famed for. The French, impeded by atrocious roads, were unable to encircle him as Napoleon had hoped. On 8 November Kutusov slipped across the Danube at Krens. Murat, commanding the French advance guard, failed to pursue the Russians, but made instead for the Austrian capital of Vienna, now lying open before him. He was within a few miles of the city when, on 11 November, he received a stern rebuke from Napoleon, informing him that 'there is no glory except where there is danger. There is none in entering a defenseless capital'. On the same day Mortier, on the left bank of the Danube, collided with the Russians at Dürrenstein. He had with him only Gazon's division, and lost heavily in a desperate action, being saved only by the timely arrival of Dupont.

The Austrians had declared Vienna an open city, but held the nearby Danube bridges in strength. On 12 November Murat and Lannes seized the bridges by a brilliant ruse, and at once moved in pursuit of Kutusov. Napoleon entered the capital the same day, well pleased with Murat's stratagem. The dashing Murat was not, however, destined to remain in favor for long, for on 13 November he was duped into accepting a brief armistice which enabled Kutusov's main body to make good the escape. Napoleon furiously repudiated the armistice as soon as he heard of it, and on 16 November Lannes threw General Oudinot's grenadiers at the Russian rear-guard, commanded by the staunch Prince Peter Bagration.

The Russians suffered severely in the confused and bloody action at Hollabrunn, but managed to slip away under cover of darkness. Bagration's steadfastness enabled Kutusov to continue his retreat unmolested, and on 19 November he joined the main Russian army, under Tsar Alexander I, near Olmütz. The French took Brünn the same day, but the *Grande Armée* had reached such a peak of exhaustion that, on 23 November, Napoleon was forced to suspend operations for the time being.

The overall strategic picture was now one of some peril for the French. The Archduke Charles, in a campaign which reflects unfavorably upon this otherwise capable general, had withdrawn from Italy under pressure from Massena, but was joined in Carinthia by John, who had marched via the Brenner Pass. The end of November saw the Archdukes in the Marburg area, watched by a part of Marmont's corps around Graz to the north. The main Austro-Russian army was strongly posted in the area of Olmütz, with secure lines of communication with Russia and Silesia. There was a very real danger that the *Grande Armée* would find itself cracked like a nut between the Archdukes from the south and the Austro-Russians from the northeast. Napoleon's danger was magnified by his logistic problems, which were largely responsible for keeping his army sprawled over a wide area from Brünn to Vienna, and then westwards along the Danube. There were few ways out of the situation. A retreat toward Ulm was, perhaps, the safest, but such a maneuver was an open admission of defeat.

Napoleon's solution to the problem was as dramatic as had been his original strategic plan. He decided to snap the mainspring of the Allied threat by persuading the Austro-Russian army around Olmütz to attack his concentrated forces between Brünn and Vienna. His first priority was to secure his southern flank. Marmont was ordered to remain on the defensive, and to avoid, at all costs, a pitched battle with the Archdukes. If necessary, he could be supported by Davout and Mortier, who were around Vienna. The second part of the plan was more hazardous. Soult and Lannes, with the guard and three cavalry divisions, were concentrated around Brünn, while a hussar brigade was sent forward to Wischau on the Olmütz road. As soon as the Allies had taken the bait and moved forward, Napoleon would summon Davout from Vienna and Bernadotte from Iglau. This assembled army would then be only slightly weaker than that of the Allies—75,000 against 88,000. Finally, the Allies would be induced to attack the deceptively weak French right; while this attack was in progress Napoleon would turn the Allied right, severing its lines of communication and inflicting a defeat on the Austro-Russian armies which would change the complexion of the war.

The plan depended very heavily upon the deception. If the Allied commanders realized what was afoot and declined to attack, Napoleon's position would worsen by the day, and he would probably be forced to retreat via Brünn, to the northwest, into Bohemia and thence to Württemberg. The French were aided, as they had been at earlier stages of the campaign, by the confusion and the bad feeling so prevalent in the Allied command. The reputation of the Austrian armies was low, in Russian eyes, following Ulm, and relations between the armies were not aided by the looting carried out by the Russians around Olmütz in what was, after all, Austrian territory. Efforts to persuade Prussia to join the Coalition had met with some success, but, although Prussian troops were on the move, the Prussian Foreign Minister, Count Haugwitz was—unbeknown to the Allies—negotiating with Napoleon.

The mood in the Allied camp was particularly bellicose. The Emperor Francis and his Chief-of-Staff, the pedantic General Weirother, favored a counteroffensive with the aim of recovering Vienna. The gay Russian firebrands surrounding Alexander were also loud in their demands for immediate attack upon the insolent French. There were, it is true, leveller heads in both armies; the Austrian Prince Karl Schwarzenburg joined Kutusov in demanding caution.

Napoleon's stratagems, however, poured fuel on the fires of Russian temerity. On 28 November he sent General Savary to negotiate with the Tsar, a mission the Allies instantly interpreted as a sign of weakness. Why would he negotiate if he were not in difficulties? Further credence was given to this viewpoint by a meeting between Napoleon and Count Dolgoruki, at which Napoleon appeared to ask for terms. Dolgoruki returned to the Allied camp convinced that the French were trying to buy time; his evidence simply confirmed the Allied leaders in their belief that they were dealing with a beaten man.

Napoleon had chosen his battlefield as early as 21 November, long before the Allies had taken the bait. He had ridden over Moravia for several days, and on the 21st he pointed to a stubby hill, the Santon, north of the Brünn-Olmütz road near the village of Austerlitz, and remarked to his staff, 'Gentlemen, examine this ground carefully, it is going to be a battlefield; you will have a part to play upon it'. The main road from Vienna to Olmütz ran north to Brünn, where it turned sharp right and ran northeast toward Olmütz. It was a straight, tree-lined highway, and was to mark the northern limit of the battlefield. To its north lay the wooded foothills of the mountains of Moravia.

The village of Austerlitz—a group of houses clustered around the residence of Count Kaunitz—lay just south of the road, about fifteen miles from Brünn. Two miles west of Austerlitz the ground rose rapidly into the Pratzen Plateau, just under 1000 feet high at the Starhe Vinobrady, its highest point. The village of Pratzen lay in the neck of a small valley on the western edge of the plateau, with the Goldbach stream running north-south about a mile west of the village. Parallel with the northern edge of the Pratzen, the Goldbach forked around another piece of high ground, just south of the Brünn-Olmütz road. The village of Puntowitz lay near the fork, with Kobelnitz, Sokolnitz and Telnitz further downstream. The Goldbach itself was a shallow marshy stream, easily fordable. South of Telnitz it was fed by two lakes which, naturally enough in December, were ice-covered.

The French Move Into Position

The French army began to slide into position west of the Goldbach on 29 November. Lannes held the northern sector, around the Santon, with the divisions of General Suchet and Cafarelli; the field defenses were placed on the Santon itself, the cornerstone of the French left. On Lannes' right, Murat's cavalry and horse artillery bivouacked around Schzappanitz, with Oudinot's grenadiers to their north. Bernadotte's corps, still on the march, were to take position behind Oudinot on arrival. Soult's 4th Corps was more widely extended. Generals Vandamme and St Hiliare were along the line of the Goldbach north of Puntowitz—south of this village General Legrand's division held Kobelnitz, Sokolnitz and Telnitz with small detachments. Davout's corps, when it arrived, would strengthen the dangerously over-extended Legrand.

Across the Goldbach the ponderous Allied army moved into position on 1 December. Alexander and Francis set up their headquarters in the village of Krzenowitz where, in the fatal tradition of the Allied command, the inevitable Council of War took place on the afternoon of 1 December. Kutusov was nominally Commander-in-Chief, but naturally his authority did not extend to the monarchs, whose adherents at once resumed their squabbles. Kutusov himself, seated in his traveling armchair, dozed intermittently throughout the Council, well fortified by several bottles of his favorite wine. Francis was by now less enthusiastic about an immediate advance on Vienna, but the young Alexander was carried away by the advice of hotheads surrounding him.

The Allied plan was the work of Weirother, who arrived at Kutusov's quarters just after midnight, bringing with him a vast map of the area. He then proceeded to read out the dispersions in what General Langeron, an *emigré* Frenchman in Russian service, called 'an elevated tone and with an air of boastfulness that proclaimed his ultimate conviction of his merit and our incapacity'. Kutusov was by now asleep, and

Left: Marshal Bessières, commander of the 7000 men of the Imperial Guard, which remained under the personal control of Napoleon.

Leuthen: Oblique Order

On 5 December, 1757 Frederick the Great of Prussia attacked an Austrian army under Field-Marshal Daun and Charles of Lorraine at Leuthen in Silesia. The odds were heavily against the Prussians, who were outnumbered by nearly three to one. The Austrian position was, furthermore, a strong one, running from Sagschütz in the south to Nippern in the North, squarely blocking the Breslau road, Frederick's main line of advance. The Prussian plan was simple enough. Frederick intended to make a feint against the Austrian right while the main weight of his army, swinging south of the Breslau road, struck the Austrian left around Sagschütz. The Prussian advance guard ejected an Austrian detachment from the village of Borne at first light, and Frederick sent a small force to threaten the Austrian right while the remainder of his army, in two huge columns, marched southeast, hidden from the Austrians by rising ground west of Leuthen.

The blow fell on Sagschütz at about midday. The Austrian commander in this sector, General Nadasti, was overwhelmed, and the battle swept on to Leuthen itself which, stoutly held by infantry sent forward by Charles of Lorraine, was finally carried by a brilliant charge by the Prussian Guard. Frederick's progress now became more difficult, for the Austrian troops around Frobelwitz had time to change front to meet the threat. Nevertheless, by late afternoon General Lucchessi's last cavalry counterattack was repulsed, and the position had collapsed completely by nightfall. The Austrian army was routed, with heavy losses in men and equipment, and Breslau fell two weeks later.

Napoleon called Leuthen 'a masterpiece of movements, maneuvers and resolution'. The tactics which Frederick employed were, however, far from new. The Theban general Epaminondas pioneered oblique order at Leuctra in 371 BC, when his force of 6000 defeated 10,000 Spartans. As Sir Basil Liddell Hart puts it, 'the oblique order which Frederick made famous was only a slight elaboration of the method of Epaminondas'. Furthermore, Frederick's oblique order was not universally successful. At Prague in 1757 the Austrians had time to change front to meet the attack, and at Kolin in the same year the Prussian attack was fatally disorganized by the fire of Austrian light troops.

Frederick pointed out that oblique order had three major advantages. It permitted a small force to defeat a larger, it attacked the enemy at a decisive point, and, if the attacker suffered a reverse, it enabled him to retain unengaged troops to cover his withdrawal. The benefits of oblique order have not escaped more recent military commanders. The Austro-Russian plan for Austerlitz was a variation on oblique order, as was Napoleon's own counter-plan. Subsequent use of oblique order has often been directed towards 'single envelopment', outflanking the enemy rather than 'rolling up' his exposed flank. The special conditions of desert warfare are ideally suited for such maneuvers; Allenby forced the Turks from the Gaza line by thrusting to Beersheba in 1917, and Rommel employed similar tactics with great success in the Western Desert in 1941–42. Although oblique order and outflanking attacks have produced an impressive list of victories—Leuctra, Leuthen, Chancellorsville and Gazala, to name but a few—they have similarly resulted in disastrous failures. Napoleon's outflanking attack at Leipzig, the Battle of the Nations, in 1813 proved abortive, as did a similar Union attempt at the First Battle of Bull Run in 1861. The success of oblique order depends, as Frederick himself realized, upon mobility and deception; the enemy must remain fixed in his defensive position while the attacking force carries out its outflanking move. To employ such tactics against an enemy who retains the liberty to maneuver as he pleases is, as generations of soldiers have discovered to their peril, disastrous.

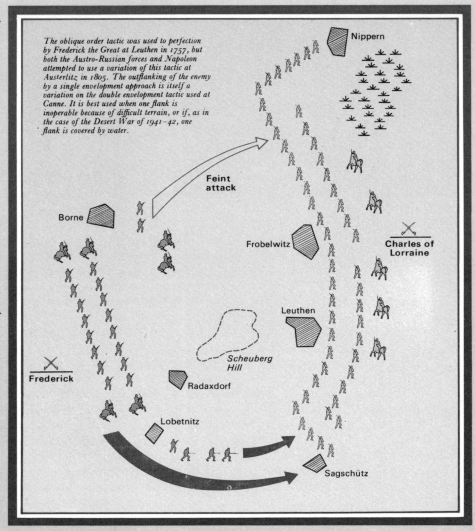

The oblique order tactic was used to perfection by Frederick the Great at Leuthen in 1757, but both the Austro-Russian forces and Napoleon attempted to use a variation of this tactic at Austerlitz in 1805. The outflanking of the enemy by a single envelopment approach is itself a variation on the double envelopment tactic used at Canne. It is best used when one flank is inoperable because of difficult terrain, or if, as in the case of the Desert War of 1941–42, one flank is covered by water.

Left: Frederick the Great.

of the assembled Allied commanders, Langeron noted that only the conscientious little General Doctorov actually appeared to pay attention.

Weirother's plan was to turn the French right by crossing the Goldbach between Telnitz and Sokolnitz, exploiting the crossing by swinging north and cutting the French to pieces as they fell back on Brünn. General Kienmayer, with the Austrian cavalry on the Allied left, was to swing left once across the Goldbach, and sever the Brünn-Vienna road. On the Allied right, Bagration was to launch an attack along the Brünn-Olmütz road, taking the Santon and unhinging the French left.

The crossing of the Goldbach was to be accomplished by General Buxhowden's corps. Doctorov would storm Telnitz with his 13,500 men, while Langeron, with just under 1200 men, would take Sokolnitz. General Przbysenski, on Langeron's right, would offer assistance as necessary. Once his initial objectives were taken, Buxhowden was to move against the French center around Kobelnitz. Simultaneously, a powerful corps of Austrians and Russians under Generals Kollowrath and Miloradovich, would move over the Pratzen Plateau and complete the French defeat. The Russian Imperial Guard, under the Grand Duke Constantine, was to remain in reserve, and the 4500 cavalry of Prince John of Lichtenstein were to link Bagration and Kollowrath.

Such, then, was Weirother's scheme. It looked attractive enough on the map, but was subject to severe practical limitations. Firstly, the Russian center would be uncovered at the crucial moment of the battle. Langeron pithily inquired what would happen if the French attacked the Pratzen, but the assembled commanders envisaged little possibility of such a move. Secondly,

Weirother's plan was not produced until the early morning of 2 December, and the first attacks were to go in at dawn. The remainder of the night would thus have to be spent moving into assault positions; it would be difficult to maintain secrecy, the troops would be unable to get any rest, and there was every chance that bad map-reading coupled with poor staff-work would produce serious delays. Finally, the task of unified central control was matched by divided command at lower levels.

Napoleon spent 1 December in inspections, waiting anxiously for news of the approach of the 3rd Corps. Without Davout the French right would be desperately weak, and there was some chance of Weirother's bookish plan succeeding. As news of the Allied movements reached Napoleon during the day, so his confidence grew. At last, at about 1600 hours, a staff officer arrived from 3rd Corps announcing that Davout was

Above: Napoleon dining on his favorite pre-battle supper of potatoes and onions fried in olive oil on the eve of the Battle of Austerlitz.

Below: Napoleon gives the order to advance as the battle begins.

Above: Napoleon inspects his Imperial Guard by torchlight on the eve of the battle.

close, and his leading division was at Gros Raygern, southwest of Telnitz. Napoleon issued his orders at about 2030. Lannes was to hold the Santon, backed by Murat's cavalry. Bernadotte was to deploy between Puntowitz and Jirschikowitz in preparation for an attack on Blasowitz. On the right, Legrand was to contain the attack across the Goldbach until Davout came up in support. In the center, meanwhile, Soult was to assault the Pratzen with the divisions of Vandamme and St Hiliare. Oudinot's grenadiers and the Imperial Guard were held in reserve; they could be used to bolster the southern flank or to reinforce a successful attack in the center.

Napoleon's customary pre-battle proclamation was distributed to his army. 'Soldiers!' it thundered, 'The Russian army is presenting itself before you in order to avenge the Austrian army of Ulm. These are the same battalions which you defeated at Hollabrunn, and which since then you have pursued steadily to this point ... This victory will end the campaign, and we shall be able to resume our winter quarters, where we shall be joined by the new armies that are forming in France, and then the peace I shall make will be worthy of my people, of you and of me.' This proclamation sent a shiver of excitement through the *Grande Armée*; morale rose with a bound. After dining gaily with his staff, on his favorite dish of potatoes and onions fried in oil, Napoleon visited his lines on a last inspection. He returned to his tent, and slept for less than an hour before being awakened with news of skirmishing in the area of Telnitz. Savary was sent off to investigate, and returned with the information that Legand had brushed with a detachment of Austrian Hussars, and that there were unmistakable signs of enemy movement in the Augezd area. Napoleon rose again, and set off on reconnaissance, accompanied by Soult and a small group of staff officers. He satisfied himself that the Allies were in fact making against his right, clashed with a Cossack picket, narrowly avoiding capture, and returned to his own lines. He dismounted in the safety of the French camp, and was greeted by a tremendous display of

confidence and enthusiasm; soldiers leapt to their feet to light his way with blazing wisps of straw, and frenzied shouts of 'Vive L'Empereur!' split the frosty night.

The Allied commanders were unaware of the cause of the blaze of light across the Goldbach. They failed to profit by the fleeting target it offered to their guns, and the massive troop movement went on. Napoleon, meanwhile, returned to his headquarters and dictated orders slightly modifying his dispositions. St Hiliare was to attack through Puntowitz rather than to follow Vandamme further north, and 3000 men of the 4th Corps were detailed to support the weak right wing until Davout reached the field in strength. His orders issued, Napoleon snatched some more sleep as his army moved forward into its final positions.

The adversaries completed their deployment in thick mist between 0400 and 0700 on 2 December. Despite the presence of a large part of the 3rd Corps at Gros-Raygen, the French were outnumbered by about three to one. Of the 73,000 French in the area, about 12,000 were too exhausted or too ill-equipped to fight. The Allies, on the other hand, expected reinforcements from Olmütz to raise their strength to 90,000 during the course of the day. They also had a comfortable artillery superiority, 178 guns as opposed to 139. The Allied deployment was predictably confused. Lichtenstein's cavalry was badly placed, three miles too far south near the foot of the Pratzen. The Allied left was in some disorder, as was the central force of Kollowrath and Miloradovich.

At about 0700 Doctorov's advance guard under Kienmayer clashed with the French 3rd of the Line in the village of Telnitz. After a short period of bitter hand-to-hand fighting, Kienmayer was reinforced by the bulk of Doctorov's column, and Telnitz was stormed. To the north, Langeron and Przbysenski assaulted Sokolnitz, falling on the French 26th Light Infantry, and carrying the village after a sharp fight. The 3rd fell back from Telnitz, screened by some of Davout's light cavalry, and rallied behind the Goldbach. Davout, moving with his customary energy, brought his tired troops forward from Gros-Raygen and counterattacked Telnitz with General Heudelet's brigade. Unfortunately one of Heudelet's regiments, the 108th of the Line, became disordered crossing a ditch and was cut up by some Austrian Hussars. The counterattack failed, and the subsequent French withdrawal was marred by an accidental engagement between the 108th and the 26th Light, retreating from Sokolnitz.

While the French right fought desperately against the advancing Allied columns, the French center prepared to assault. Napoleon, clad in his grey greatcoat sat his little Arab horse west of Puntowitz, surrounded by his marshals. The fog and the dense smoke of the campfires obscured the divisions of Vandamme and St Hiliare, but the Russian columns could be seen on the higher ground, moving continually southward. Soult was eager to unleash his attack.

'I beg Your Majesty to hold me back no longer,' he urged, 'I have 20,000 men to set in motion.'

'How long will it take you to climb the Pratzen?' inquired the Emperor.

Left: Napoleon orders his troops forward into the Austro-Russian lines at the start of battle.

'Less than twenty minutes, Sire,' replied Soult.

'In that case,' concluded Napoleon, 'we will wait for another quarter of an hour.'

Soult's attack went in at 0900. His men, fortified by a triple ration of brandy, advanced with determination, urged on by the shouts of their officers and the hammering of the *pas de charge*. Vandamme and St Hiliare both advanced in the same formation, battalion columns preceded by lines of skirmishes. St Hiliare swept easily past the village of Pratzen and occupied the hill dominating it. Vandamme, advancing towards the Starhe Vinobrady, the highest point of the plateau, was held up briefly, but went on to capture his objective.

Soult's advance had been partially shielded by the mist, and his attack was well under way before the Allied commanders could take counter-measures. Kutusov, accompanying Milorado-vich's force, realized the danger as soon as the French appeared on the plateau, but the two battalions he sent forward were quickly brushed aside. By 0930 the Pratzen was in French hands. At the same time, there was a brief lull in the south as the Allies reorganized in the captured villages of Sokolnitz and Telnitz. A French cavalry charge had delayed the Allied advance, and at about 1000 General Friant's division of the 3rd Corps counterattacked. General Lochet's brigade went boiling through Sokolnitz, only to be attacked in its turn by Langeron and the Kursk Regiment. The fighting eventually stabilized with the French in possession of the southern end of the village, which was by now crammed with the casualties of both sides. Doctorov remained secure in Telnitz, with fresh reserves at hand. Once

Left: Napoleon, on a bluff above the battle, directs operations as the French make for the Pratzen Plateau.

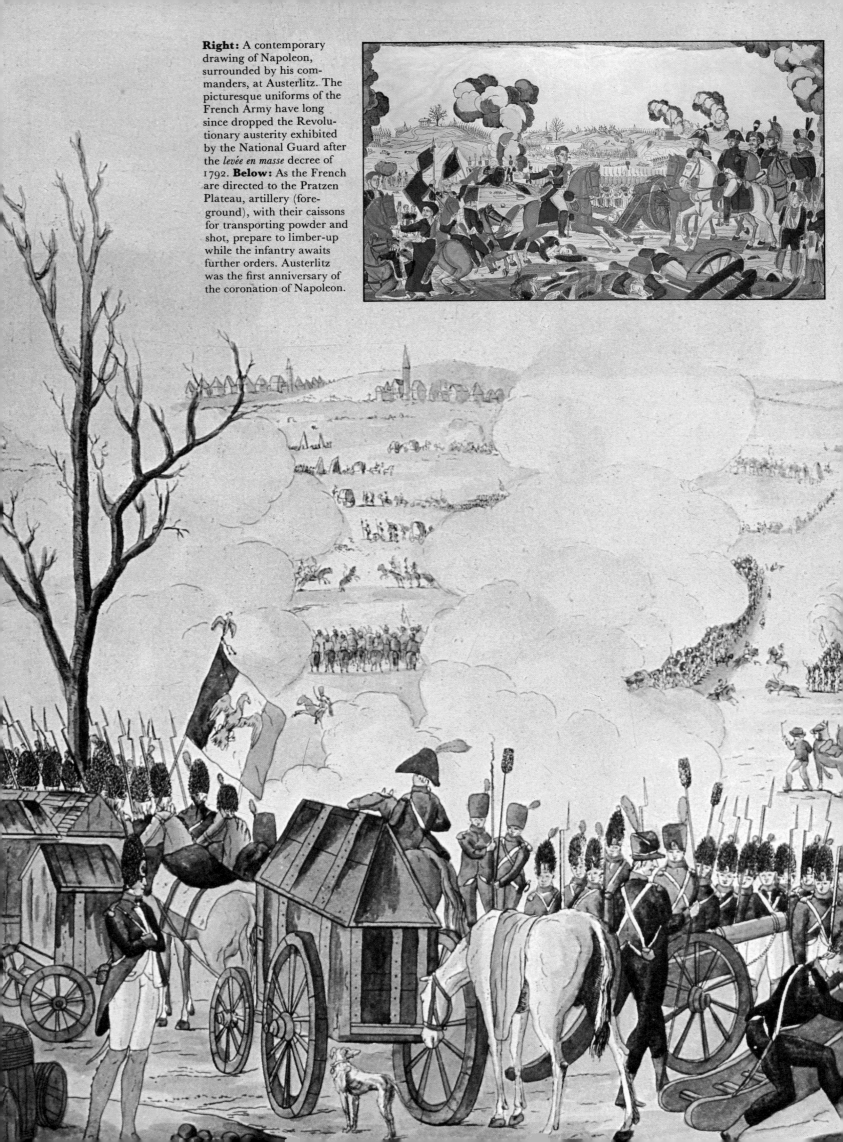

Right: A contemporary drawing of Napoleon, surrounded by his commanders, at Austerlitz. The picturesque uniforms of the French Army have long since dropped the Revolutionary austerity exhibited by the National Guard after the *levée en masse* decree of 1792. **Below:** As the French are directed to the Pratzen Plateau, artillery (foreground), with their caissons for transporting powder and shot, prepare to limber-up while the infantry awaits further orders. Austerlitz was the first anniversary of the coronation of Napoleon.

again, however, the defective Allied command took its toll. There was no attempt to launch a cohesive attack through Sokolnitz and Telnitz since the man who should have organized it, General Buxhowden, the overall commander in this sector, was incapably drunk.

By mid-morning, then, the picture was one of French success in the center, but a more desperate contest in the south. Away on the French left, battle had flared up later than on the other fronts. Lannes' task was to hold the Santon, and to prevent Bagration from swinging south against the Pratzen. To his right was Murat, whose cavalry were to be used to exploit the eventual French breakthrough. This plan was dislocated when, at about 0930, Bagration moved forward, seizing Blasowitz with two battalions of the

Russian Imperial Guard. Lannes, aware of the significance of the sound of gunfire from the Pratzen, counterattacked in strength. Cafarelli's advancing division, supported by General Kellerman's light cavalry, was charged by a mass of Russian horse. Kellerman waited until the Russian attack had spent its energy against the volleys of Cafarelli's infantry, and then swept forward and drove the Russians off. Lannes continued his advance, but was now heavily engaged by Bagration's 40 guns, and, though Lannes replied

with his own artillery, his corps ground to a halt. After an unproductive exchange of fire, both commanders lunged forward on their right. Bagration's attack on the Santon was thwarted by the tenacity of the 17th of the Line, but Lannes' assault on Blasowitz was successful, though at a very heavy cost.

Murat Cuts Off Buxhowden

The fall of Blasowitz gave Murat the opportunity of cutting Bagration off from the Allied center. Before Murat's attack got under way, Bagration and Lichtenstein—who had at last arrived in the right place—threw in all their available cavalry in an effort to recover the lost ground. Cafarelli, emerging from Blasowitz, was assailed by 40 squadrons of cavalry, but drove them off by sustained fire. Cafarelli's steadfastness gave Murat time to bring up the cavalry of Generals Nansouty and D'Hautpoul, huge *cuirassiers* with steel breastplates and sweeping horse-

hair plumes. They trotted forward in immaculate order and collided with Lichtenstein's horsemen with a crash which could be heard all over the battlefield. Lichtenstein was driven back in disorder, but managed to rally part of his force for a counterstroke against the over-extended French. This move was itself counterattacked by the 2nd *Cuirrassiers*, and Lichtenstein fell back once more. On Lannes' left, Suchet's division made progress in the face of heavy fire, slowly forcing Bagration down the Olmütz road. The engagement in the north prevented Bagration from intervening in the center, where the battle was nearing its climax.

The Allied center was by no means as denuded of troops as Napoleon had believed. Many Allied infantry had been detained behind the center as a result of the traffic jam caused by Lichtenstein's erroneous early morning deployment, and were thus in a position to engage Soult. Vandamme's division, on the high ground at the northern end of the Pratzen, was better placed to resist a

VENI
VIDI
VICI

ERGER ET. INV.F. 1806.

Left: Napoleon, who viewed himself as a reincarnation of Julius Caesar and the French Empire as a revival of the Roman, is portrayed in classical Empire style leading a Roman triumphal march. *Imperator* was the Roman title given to Caesar as the conquering hero of Gaul. The Emperor Napoleon, leading the latter-day Gauls to victory, came to Austerlitz, saw the Austrians and Russians, and conquered them.

counterattack than was St Hiliare, around the village of Pratzen. St Hiliare was attacked on the right flank by General Kamenski commanding the rear brigade of Langeron's column, and in front by Kollowrath's Austrians. Even the dogged St Hiliare was briefly nonplussed, but he recovered in time to order a desperate bayonet charge, giving Soult time to push forward six guns from his corps artillery reserve. With close support from these cannon St Hiliare was able to repulse the Russian and Austrian attacks. Vandamme consolidated his position on the northern end of the Pratzen with little difficulty for Miloradovich, although personally able, spent the morning making theatrical gestures and, like his tippling colleague Buxhowden, failed to organize a general counterattack.

By noon the crisis in the center was over. On the French left Lannes and Murat continued to force Bagration back, while on the Allied left Doctorov and Langeron remained in possession

of Sokolnitz and Telnitz, but were unable to advance further due to pressure from Davout, now supported by Oudinot's grenadiers, dispatched by Napoleon from his left. The Russian commanders in this sector were by now seriously preoccupied with events on their right, and perturbed by the absence of orders from Buxhowden.

Bagration was more fortunate in the latter respect for, in the early afternoon, he received intelligence of the collapse of the Allied center, and was ordered to hold open the Olmütz road as a line of retreat for the army. He responded by attacking Lannes' left to keep him engaged. Lannes at once swung his right wing forward, threatening to swing Bagration back against the mountains of Moravia. Bagration quickly realized what was afoot and straightened his line at right angles to the road. Under heavy pressure from Cafarelli, Suchet and Murat, the Russians were driven back, with heavy losses, beyond the point where the Austerlitz fork joins the Olmütz road.

Murat, possibly smarting under the reprimands which he received earlier in the campaign, decided not to launch his forces in an all out attack on the retreating Bagration. The Allied right thus managed to limp off the field, and the vital road remained open.

Napoleon and his entourage had ridden to the Starhe Vinobrady soon after midday. The Emperor had ordered the guard to cross the Goldbach, and had ensured that Bernadotte did not become seriously engaged against Bagration. At about this time he made the decision which was to result in the destruction of the Allied left. The French army was to swing to the right, and encircle Buxhowden in the Telnitz-Augezd area. Before this maneuver could be executed, the French center had to sustain the last major Allied effort; the charge of the Russian Imperial Guard.

Four battalions of the Semionovski and Preobrajenski regiments attacked Vandamme's division, but were forced back after causing heavy casualties. This determined attack was followed by a charge by the cavalry of the Russian guard, led by the swarthy Grand-Duke Constantine in person. The horsemen, fifteen squadrons of the finest youth in Russia, swirled over the 4th of the Line, took its eagle, and went on to maul the 24th Light. Vandamme had swung these two regiments around to cover his threatened flank and now, with the footguard renewing its attack on his front, he was in a desperate situation.

Napoleon ordered Bessières to support Vandamme with the cavalry of his own guard. Bessières sent forward two squadrons of *chasseurs*, only to see them driven back. He then pushed three squadrons of horse grenadiers and two more of *chasseurs* together with the horse artillery of the guard, into the fray. Bernadotte, to the northwest, had seen the dangerous plight of Vandamme, and, on his own initiative, ordered General Drouet D'Erlon's infantry division to intervene. A frightful *mêlée* was already in progress when Napoleon ordered one of his *aides de camp*, General Rapp, to settle the affair with two more squadrons of *chasseurs* and one of Mamelukes. Rapp's arrival was decisive, and the Russian guard was at last defeated. Prince Repnine, commander of the Tsar's chevalier guard, was captured with 200 of his men. All the artillery of the Russian guard fell into French hands. Napoleon looked on the scene with satisfaction, remarking that many fine ladies would weep in St Petersburg the next day.

The defeat of the Russian guard at last permitted Napoleon to carry out the great right-wheel which was to destroy Buxhowden. Bernadotte was directed to occupy the Pratzen, while Soult, the Guard, and Oudinot, swung against the Russian left. Buxhowden was cut off by 1430; an order sent by Kutusov some three hours earlier, telling him to retreat, did not arrive until the time for safe withdrawal was long past. As the French closed in, the Allied troops in the southern pocket fought desperately. Some managed to break out to the east before the ring was closed; many, trying to escape across the frozen Lake Satschen, were drowned. Przbysenski was captured and his column destroyed. Both Langeron and Doctorov got away, though the majority of their men were killed or captured.

The battle was over by 1700. To the north, Bagration was in full retreat, though Lannes and Murat failed to press him closely. In the center and south the French collected a rich body of prisoners and trophies. About 12,000 Allied troops were captured, with 180 guns and 50 colors. The Russians had lost some 11,000 men killed and the Austrians perhaps 4000. French casualties were altogether less heavy, and in killed, wounded and captured did not much exceed 10,000, most of whom were wounded.

Austerlitz was certainly no ordinary victory; it was the decisive battle upon which Napoleon had counted. Francis asked for an armistice the following day, and brought Austria out of the war; Alexander took his troops back to their Russian homeland. The news of Austerlitz broke William Pitt's heart; he died soon afterwards. Prussia, who had vacillated for rather too long, was forced to make a humiliating treaty. Finally, in the summer of 1806, goaded beyond endurance, she broke with France, only to suffer total defeat at Jena.

The campaign and battle of Austerlitz were triumphs of the Napoleonic system of central command. This was, in fact, the first occasion on which Napoleon had enjoyed undisputed command of the French army, unmolested by restive political masters or the bickering of other army commanders. The campaign represents the triumph of an overall strategic plan, differing radically from the piecemeal strategy employed by the Allies. Napoleon later wrote that 'the victory of Austerlitz was only the natural outcome of the Moravian plan of campaign. In an art as difficult as that of war, the system campaign often reveals the plan of battle.'

Napoleon's conduct of the battle shows the same qualities as his plan of campaign. The Allies were already off-balance before the first shot was fired; they were lured into launching an attack on an enemy they believed to be on the verge of collapse. To this masterly scheme of deception Napoleon added a sound tactical plan, based on concentration of force at the decisive point, which speedily threw the Allied machine into disorder. The Weirother plan was an altogether more risky venture. Its essential premise was that the French were already half-defeated. It contained no safeguard against a French attack across the Pratzen, and the southern striking force compromised more men than could effectively be employed in the marshy and broken ground around Sokolnitz and Telnitz. Perhaps the most dramatic point of comparison between the adversaries is that of command. Strong central control, with energetic subordinates characterized the *Grande Armée*; a disordered high command, with corps commanders of uncertain quality, was the hallmark of the Allied army.

Austerlitz was fought on the anniversary of Napoleon's coronation. His Moravian victory ensured the survival of the French Empire and earned the *Grande Armée* a role it was to retain for the next decade, that of the predominant weight in the balance of power. The Parvenu Empire came of age on the Pratzen Plateau on the morning of 2 December, 1805; as the sun of Austerlitz broke through the mist it heralded the birth of a new force in European politics.

Opposite: The meeting of Napoleon and the Habsburg Emperor Francis II after the battle.

Waterloo
1815

The invasion of Russia in 1812 proved a disaster for Napoleon. In an attempt to dominate all of Europe rather than merely most of it, the French Empire came crashing down around his ears after the Battle of Leipzig in 1813. By 1814 Russian troops were in Paris and Napoleon was forced into exile on the island of Elba just off the Italian coast.

The Congress of Vienna met to reconstruct the map of Europe, while Napoleon, unhappy and restless, plotted to regain France. His lightning return and reconquest of France sent the Bourbon King Louis XVIII scurrying back to England. Men sent to capture the Emperor fell in line behind him. Napoleon was master of France within

days. But could he once more become master of Europe? The Battle of Waterloo put paid to Napoleon's ambitions forever and saved Europe from another series of debilitating wars to prevent French hegemony on the Continent.

Napoleon's escape from the island of Elba brought unanimity and speedy decision to the hitherto dilatory and bickering Congress of Vienna. Within hours of receiving the news the Powers had reformed their Alliance and decided on war against their old enemy. The dispersal of their armies was halted and for the second time in just over a year France was threatened with invasion. Napoleon had landed in France with scarcely more than a battalion of troops, but the magic of his name was enough to destroy the stronger forces sent against him. The attitude of the French nation was well summarized by a Paris journalist:

'The Tiger has broken out of his den
The Ogre has been three days at sea
The Wretch has landed at Fréjus

The Buzzard has reached Antibes
The Invader has arrived in Grenoble
The General has entered Lyons
Napoleon slept at Fontainebleau last night
The Emperor will proceed to the Tuileries today
His Imperial Majesty will address his loyal subjects tomorrow.'

The author of this lampoon went to the heart of Napoleon s renewed popularity, which was based on his success and not on any deep loyalty to his person. Apart from the hard core of Bonapartists, most Frenchmen hated the thought of more years of war. In particular they dreaded the return of conscription. Napoleon may have claimed that he wanted peace, but the Congress Powers were soon massing a million men against him. Five armies were preparing to invade France. The Duke of Wellington had an army of British, German, Dutch and Belgian troops in the Low Countries, with Marshal Blücher's Prussians on his left flank. An Austrian Army was forming in the Black Forest, with more Austrians and Italians threatening

Below: Entry of the Allied sovereigns into Paris, 1814. Alexander I of Russia had Europe at his feet when Napoleon abdicated and left France for the Isle of Elba.

Above: Marshal Soult, Napoleon's Chief-of-Staff in his final campaign. Napoleon mocked him for his caution, but he had at least fought against Wellington in the Peninsular War.

to the borders of France and there were also strong Bonapartist factions in Belgium and Holland. The Emperor's decision was made in early May and in the first days of June his army began a carefully screened concentration on the Belgian frontier.

The Grande Armée Reassembled

From all over France 132,000 men were assembled, leaving the fortresses in the hands of the National Guard. Napoleon naturally assumed the supreme command, but he could no longer count on his old team of subordinates. Marshal Berthier, his matchless chief of staff, was dead, Marshal Murat he considered a traitor, and several other Marshals refused to serve because of age or their oaths of allegiance to Louis XVIII. Napoleon's appointments in 1815 have often been criticized by historians, and many of them were far from suitable. Marshal Soult, an able independent commander, became Chief-of-Staff although he had no training in staff work. Marshal Grouchy was originally selected to command the cavalry, for which he was well qualified, but was later given command of the right wing of the army despite the fact he had never commanded even a corps. The left wing was entrusted to Marshal Ney, whose defection to Napoleon's cause had been a vital factor in the triumphal progress to Paris; he was known to be a fighting, not a thinking, machine. Marshal Davout, the ablest of the Marshals, was left to hold Paris for the Emperor.

But if Napoleon's subordinates were unsuitable the plan he laid before them was worthy of the Emperor at his best. From French sympathizers in the Netherlands he had a very clear picture of his enemies' dispositions. The two armies were dispersed in loose corps groupings. The Prussians (105,000 infantry, 12,000 horse and 296 guns) lay within the area Liège-Dinant-Charleroi-Tirlemont, and Wellington's army (79,000 infantry, 14,000 cavalry and 196 guns) covered the area Brussels-Ghent-Leuze-Mons-Nivelles. It would take some days to concentrate the Allied forces and if he struck quickly Napoleon might prevent this movement altogether. The lines of communication of the two armies diverged; Wellington's running north from Brussels to Ostend and the Channel and Blücher's westwards into Germany from Liège. If surprised and forced to retreat the Allies would tend to fall back along these lines, wanting to get nearer the security of home, and making it easier for Napoleon to concentrate undisturbed on one army or the other. Napoleon's own deployment was ideally framed to assist such a move. Two wings under Ney and Grouchy were to lead the army and Napoleon and the main body would follow in a central position ready to throw their weight on one flank or the other. Moreover, the axis of advance was to be along the boundary between the two armies, a proverbially weak spot with all composite forces.

In Belgium the Allied commanders had little idea of Napoleon's preparations. Wellington had always laid great stress on intelligence, on knowing what was happening on 'the other side of the hill', but he was not allowed to send his scouts beyond the frontier and was misled by reports from the Prussians. He relaxed his guard, making only

the Riviera; behind them a Russian Army was marching to the Central Rhine.

Faced with these forces, Napoleon abandoned the pretence that war could be avoided. To the Bourbon army of 200,000 he added 80,000 volunteers, most of them veterans, and he hoped to raise a further 150,000 by re-conscripting the Class of 1815, the so-called Marie-Louises who had been pressed into service to defend '*la patrie en danger*' once before. Every available weapon was refurbished and the factories poured out new uniforms to clothe them. But time was not on Napoleon's side; he could only mobilize a proportion of the Allies' manpower and the French people would not tolerate the return of wartime conditions without the stimulus of victory. He could not afford to repeat the defensive strategy he had employed so skillfully in 1814 Napoleon must attack, and the obvious target was the Low Countries, where Wellington and Blücher were gathered. They presented the most immediate threat leisurely preparations to concentrate his army, and even advised the Duchess of Richmond that she might hold her famous ball on 15 June. But during the 15th the French army crossed the border and by nightfall Napoleon's headquarters were at Charleroi, his army concentrated and already between the Allies.

It was at the ball that Wellington first appreciated the danger in which the Allies stood. First came the news that the Prussian advance guard had met the French at Fleurus and been repulsed; this was serious enough because Blücher was committed to a forward concentration at Sombreffe, less than five miles away. Then during supper Wellington learned from the Prince of Orange that French scouts had reached Quatre Bras, a vital crossroads on the army's route to join Blücher. The Duke had been caught completely wrong-footed for, fearing a flanking move around his right he had begun to assemble his army at Nivelles, away from Quatre Bras and Sombreffe. Fortunately the Dutch commander at Quatre Bras realized the significance of the crossroads and disobeyed his orders to concentrate at Nivelles; two brigades held this crucial point, nearly 30 miles from Brussels. Wellington might well tell the Duke of Richmond that:

'Napoleon has *humbugged* me, by God! he has gained twenty-four hours march on me!'

'What do you intend doing?'

'I have ordered the army to concentrate at Quatre Bras; but we shall not stop him there, and if so I must fight him *here*,' he said, indicating one of the long ridges across the Brussels—Quatre Bras road, south of the village of Waterloo.

Wellington's prophecies were soon justified. He was able to hold Quatre Bras for the whole of the 16th, largely by bluff. Ney, facing a slight slope up to the crossroads, assumed that although it seemed very thinly held, it in fact concealed the full strength of the Allied army. His Peninsular experiences made Ney unusually nervous of attacking Wellington in a prepared position. But on the same day, the Prussians, caught too far forward by Napoleon's speed, were being mauled at Ligny, although decisive victory avoided Napoleon because his *corps de reserve* was not committed on either flank but spent the day marching and counter-marching between the two wings. Nevertheless the Prussians were forced to withdraw, and the only question was which way they should move. The best roads led eastward, toward the Prussian base and General Gneisenau, Blücher's Chief-of-Staff, who considered that Wellington had failed in his promise to support his Allies, favored this route. Blücher had been rolled on by his wounded horse while leading a cavalry charge during the battle, but he was still full of fight. Trusting to doses of gin, rhubarb and garlic to cure his injuries, and possibly remembering that Wellington's promise had been conditional on his not being attacked himself, Blücher insisted on a more northerly withdrawal, to the town of Wavre, from where he could either support Wellington or still withdraw to the west if necessary.

Wellington did not know of Blücher's decision until nearly 0800 the following morning. It was clearly impossible to hold Quatre Bras any longer and Wellington immediately began moving off

his troops. Had Ney obeyed the Emperor's orders to resume his attack Wellington might have been too late, but the French troops were still foraging for their breakfast. Even Napoleon did not really grasp the urgency of the situation until the middle of the morning, when he moved to reinforce and hasten the dull-witted Ney. By 1400 Wellington had withdrawn all his infantry and only a screen of cavalry and light artillery remained to face the mass of French lancers, led by Napoleon himself, which was appearing over the southern slopes. The British horse batteries fired one round in greeting, then limbered up and galloped for the bottleneck of the one road through Genappe. Their shots were echoed by thunderclaps as a tremendous storm swept southward, drenching the fields and confining movement to the one major road. Dispiriting though the rain was, it saved the Allied army from serious loss. Confined to the roads Napoleon's cavalry could not come to grips with their enemies' rearguard and the pur-

Above: Marshal Ney, 'bravest of the brave', whose reckless daring was not enough to turn the tide of battle in favor of the French. He was executed for treason after Napoleon's exile to St Helena.

Right: William, Prince of Orange, at Waterloo, who had recently become William I, first King of the Netherlands, after the liberation which followed the Battle of Leipzig in 1813. His family had traditionally held the position of *stadhouder* of the Netherlands in the years of the Dutch Republic, which collapsed in 1795. **Center above:** Charge of the 1st Life Guards at Genappe on 17 June, the day before Waterloo. **Center below:** Wellington orders his men to charge during the last phase of the battle.

suit died out. Napoleon's great fear was that, having concentrated his main effort against Wellington, he would not be able to catch the Duke, and would thus lose the benefits of his initial move. It was therefore with great relief that Napoleon rode along his outpost line in the early hours of the 18th and saw a long line of bivouac fires, marking the position of the Allies along the ridge to the north. '*Je les tiens donc, ces Anglais*' ('I have those English now!'), he remarked.

Wellington had taken up a position along a low ridge just south of the hamlet of Mont-St Jean. Most of his army was posted on the reverse slope and could therefore, by lying down, protect themselves against the worst effects of the French artillery fire. On the forward slope was a strong skirmishing line, strengthened by the garrisons of a number of farms which Wellington had occupied to break the first force of the French attacks. The greatest weight was placed to the right of the Brussels road, which bisected the position. Wellington expected Napoleon to maneuver around

Left: Prince Blücher under his horse when the French cavalry pushed both aside. Blücher may have been down but was by no means out of the battle. **Below:** The Death of Frederick William of Brunswick at Quatre Bras on 16 June, 1815.

Above: Napoleon, sketched from life. Once trim and lithe, Napoleon developed a degree of corpulence in his later years that he would once have deplored in others.

Opposite top: The exterior of Hougoumont at the start of the battle. One of the strongly built farmhouses, fortified by Wellington as field defenses, Hougoumont had walls several feet thick which could stand bombardment.
Opposite bottom: The interior of Hougoumont during a later stage of the battle.

this flank rather than mount a frontal attack and in case the French should make a really broad sweep to the west, 17,000 men were placed at Hal, nearly ten miles away, thereby condemned to play no part in the coming battle. Wellington was content to accept weakness on his left flank because he expected to be supported there by the Prussians. He had told Blücher that he would march at dawn, supported by two more divisions. Wellington expected that they would make their presence felt by midday. Until then his own army had to hold off the French assaults unaided. Wellington had 67,661 men drawn from several nations under his command, composed of 49,608 infantry, 12,408 cavalry and 5645 artillerymen, with 156 guns. The backbone of the army were the British regiments, especially those which had served in Spain, and some experienced Hanoverian and King's German Legion units. However, most of his troops were untried in war and some of the Allied forces were decidedly unreliable. The first shots fired at the Duke of Wellington on the battlefield of Waterloo came from a battalion of Nassauers who panicked at the sight of the French troops deploying in front of them. To hold this heterogenous force together required leadership of the highest quality and the ability to juggle reserves into danger spots with absolute precision.

On the other side of a slight valley Napoleon had 71,947 men: 48,950 infantry, 15,765 cavalry and 7232 artillerymen with 246 guns. They were generally much more experienced troops and Napoleon had no problems of international cooperation. In fighting the battle Napoleon intended to exploit his superiority in artillery and cavalry, and told brother Jerome:

'I shall have my artillery fire and my cavalry charge, so as to force the enemy to disclose his positions, and, when I am quite certain which positions the English troops have taken up, I shall march straight at them with my Old Guard.'

He was scathingly contemptuous of those on his staff who spoke well of the English Army and its commander: 'Just because you have been beaten by Wellington, you think he's a good general. I tell you, Wellington is a bad general, the English are bad troops, and this affair is nothing more than eating breakfast.'

The Emperor was also confident that he could deal with Wellington without any interference by the Prussians:

'The Prussians and English cannot possibly link up for another two days after such a battle.'

Two Crucial Decisions

In his sublime and unshakable assurance, Napoleon made two crucial decisions. He postponed the main attack from 0900 to 1300, to allow time for the ground to dry, which would permit the artillery to move more easily and improve the ricochet effect of their shots. Secondly, he neglected to send clear and early orders to Grouchy to advance to Wavre as quickly as possible, and to keep in touch with his own operations. It is clear from the wording of his despatch that Napoleon believed that only a fragment of the Prussian army was at Wavre, rather than its full strength. Grouchy followed orders only too closely and by refusing to use his initiative and move closer to Water-

loo, he ensured that nothing interfered with the Prussian corps which were marching to join Wellington.

Time is usually of vital importance in warfare and clearly the decisive moment in the battle of Waterloo would be the arrival of Blücher's Prussians. If Napoleon had not driven Wellington from the battlefield by then, he would inevitably face defeat and the loss, for the second time, of his Empire. Neither side knew exactly when the Prussians would appear and the suspense was increased when Bülow's corps, which had not been engaged on the 16th, was ordered to lead the advance. Its line of march lay across that of two other corps which were recovering from Ligny. By the time Bülow had emerged from the resulting confusion there was no possibility of his corps intervening before four in the afternoon.

While he waited for the ground to dry Napoleon deployed his army in parade array. Along the front of his position were the corps of General Reille, on the left, and of Count d'Erlon on the right. This thick line of infantry was supported by a great battery of 84 guns to its front, west of the Waterloo road. Behind it, along the same road, were General Lobau's corps and the Imperial Guard itself, and on either side of them were the cavalry under Kellermann and Milhaud.

As the two armies surveyed each other across the scant half mile of wheat which separated them Napoleon made his first move. Perhaps appreciating Wellington's concern about his right flank, he ordered a diversionary attack on the Château d'Hougoumont. Hougoumont was an ancient, partly fortified manor house, surrounded by a high wall and an orchard and wood. It was held by four light companies of the Guards, reinforced by 300 Hanoverian Jaegers and the same battalion of Nassauers who had so nearly shot the Duke. At 1150 the Château came under fire from the artillery of the French left wing and four regiments of Jerome Bonaparte's division advanced to the attack, preceded by a dense crowd of *tirailleurs*. Once the latter reached the southern edge of the woods, the Allied light infantry fell back to their prepared positions in the Château, its walled garden, and the orchard. The French could make no impression on these defenses and most of Jerome's division was soon milling about in the woods, under heavy shrapnel fire from Bull's howitzer battery, which Wellington brought to a position behind the Château over which the high-trajectory howitzers could safely fire. The French attack was checked by this fire and a sudden counterattack drove them from the woods altogether. This was no great matter, for the attack was only intended as a feint. However Jerome was so incensed that, instead of holding back and relying on his artillery to batter Hougoumont, he sent in his own infantry and troops from Foy's division. This attack was more successful, re-occupying the woods, entering the orchard, and then reaching the walls of the Château itself on the western side. However, Wellington was watching the struggle from the hill to the northeast and he sent forward a battalion of Coldstream Guards, in two bodies. Four companies retook the orchard and another four swept into the rear of the French troops who

Right: Napoleon was obliged to flee from the battlefield of Waterloo when the defenses of the Old Guard collapsed around him in the afternoon of 18 June. **Far right:** The Scots Greys stormed into the center of the French forces when Lord Uxbridge's heavy cavalry brigades attacked the exposed flank of d'Erlon's columns. **Below:** The *mêlée* at the center of the British position on the afternoon of the battle.

had just forced the northern door of the Château for the second time. Soon after this Wellington sent the 3rd Guards into the orchard, which meant that almost all of General Byng's Guards Brigade had been drawn down into the area of the Château. To support them Wellington brought up two brigades, du Plat's of the King's German Legion and then Halkett's Hanoverians, from the rear of his right flank. Although these troops were tied down for the rest of the day in the continuing fight for Hougoumont Wellington used only 3500 troops in all, as opposed to the 14,000 Frenchmen engaged in the struggle. Nearly all of Reille's corps was involved, but to no avail; as a diversion the attack on Hougoumont was a failure, for Wellington moved no troops from his center. Furthermore, by holding the Château, Wellington

confined the French attacks east of the Brussels road, which often came under enfilade fire. As many as 10,000 men were killed and wounded around Hougoumont, three-quarters of them French, and although the Château buildings caught fire at one stage the Guardsmen were not driven out. The only Frenchmen who entered the courtyard of Hougoumont were prisoners.

Although the fighting there continued throughout the day, it was soon obscured in the greater struggle about to commence. Just before Napoleon began the great bombardment which was to signal his attack on the center, movement was seen on his far right flank beyond the Bois de Paris. At first it was thought to be Grouchy, but a hussar soon brought the news that these were Prussian troops, in fact the leading elements of

Right: 'Scotland Forever', the charge of the Scots Greys. **Below:** The charge of the Life Guards at Waterloo.

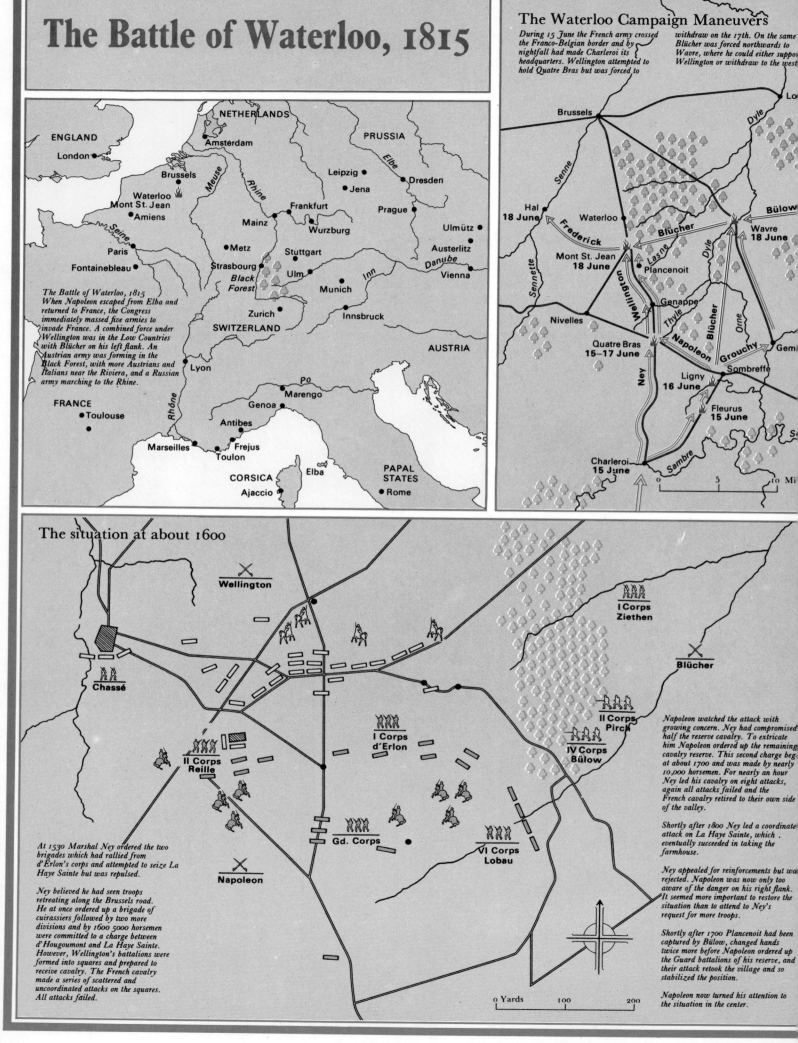

The Battle of Waterloo, 1815

The Waterloo Campaign Maneuvers

During 15 June the French army crossed the Franco-Belgian border and by nightfall had made Charleroi its headquarters. Wellington attempted to hold Quatre Bras but was forced to withdraw on the 17th. On the same Blücher was forced northwards to Wavre, where he could either suppo Wellington or withdraw to the west

The Battle of Waterloo, 1815
When Napoleon escaped from Elba and returned to France, the Congress immediately massed five armies to invade France. A combined force under Wellington was in the Low Countries with Blücher on his left flank. An Austrian army was forming in the Black Forest, with more Austrians and Italians near the Riviera, and a Russian army marching to the Rhine.

The situation at about 1600

At 1530 Marshal Ney ordered the two brigades which had rallied from d'Erlon's corps and attempted to seize La Haye Sainte but was repulsed.

Ney believed he had seen troops retreating along the Brussels road. He at once ordered up a brigade of cuirassiers followed by two more divisions and by 1600 5000 horsemen were committed to a charge between d'Hougoumont and La Haye Sainte. However, Wellington's battalions were formed into squares and prepared to receive cavalry. The French cavalry made a series of scattered and uncoordinated attacks on the squares. All attacks failed.

Napoleon watched the attack with growing concern. Ney had compromised half the reserve cavalry. To extricate him Napoleon ordered up the remaining cavalry reserve. This second charge beg at about 1700 and was made by nearly 10,000 horsemen. For nearly an hour Ney led his cavalry on eight attacks, again all attacks failed and the French cavalry retired to their own side of the valley.

Shortly after 1800 Ney led a coordinate attack on La Haye Sainte, which eventually succeeded in taking the farmhouse.

Ney appealed for reinforcements but wa rejected. Napoleon was now only too aware of the danger on his right flank. It seemed more important to restore the situation than to attend to Ney's request for more troops.

Shortly after 1700 Plancenoit had been captured by Bülow, changed hands twice more before Napoleon ordered up the Guard battalions of his reserve, and their attack retook the village and so stabilized the position.

Napoleon now turned his attention to the situation in the center.

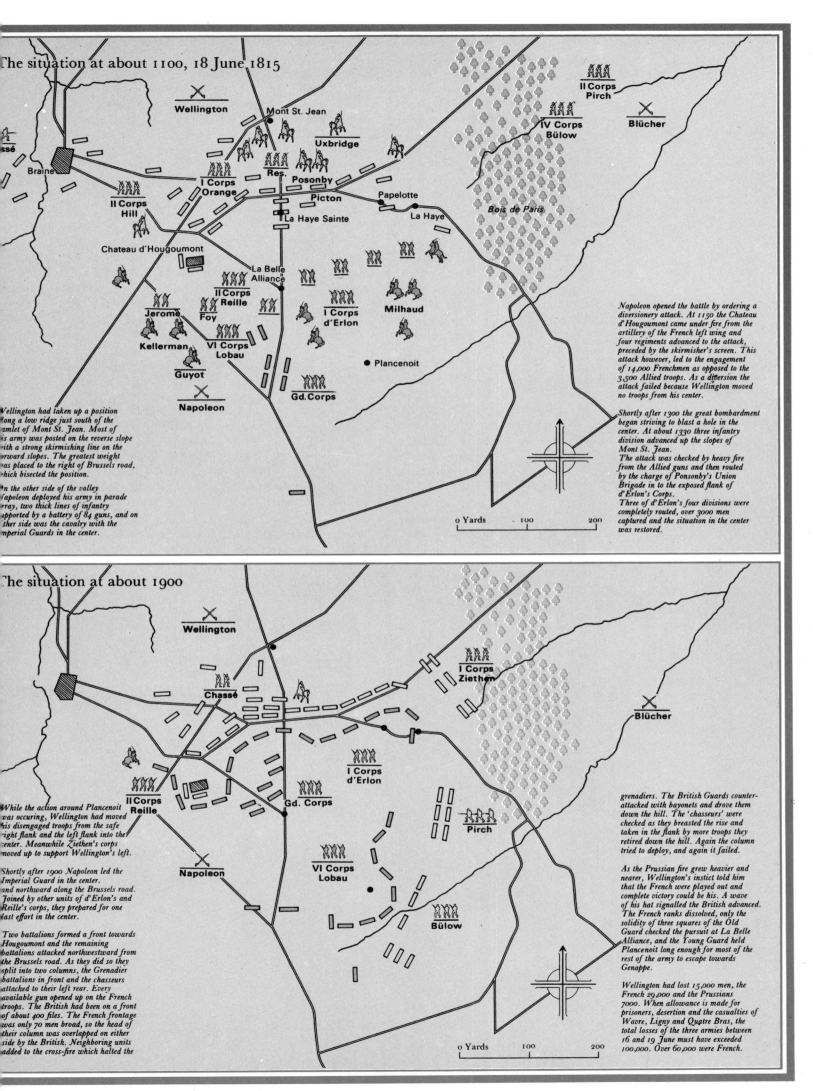

The situation at about 1100, 18 June 1815

Wellington

Mont St. Jean

Uxbridge

Braine

I Corps
Orange

Res.

Posonby

Picton

Papelotte

II Corps
Hill

La Haye Sainte

La Haye

Bois de Paris

II Corps
Pirch

IV Corps
Bülow

Blücher

Chateau d'Hougoumont

La Belle
Alliance

II Corps
Reille

Jerome

Foy

I Corps
d'Erlon

Milhaud

Kellerman

VI Corps
Lobau

Guyot

Plancenoit

Napoleon

Gd. Corps

Wellington had taken up a position along a low ridge just south of the hamlet of Mont St. Jean. Most of his army was posted on the reverse slope with a strong skirmishing line on the forward slopes. The greatest weight was placed to the right of Brussels road, which bisected the position.

On the other side of the valley Napoleon deployed his army in parade array, two thick lines of infantry supported by a battery of 84 guns, and on either side was the cavalry with the Imperial Guards in the center.

Napoleon opened the battle by ordering a diversionery attack. At 1150 the Chateau d'Hougoumont came under fire from the artillery of the French left wing and four regiments advanced to the attack, preceded by the skirmisher's screen. This attack however, led to the engagement of 14,000 Frenchmen as opposed to the 3,500 Allied troops. As a diversion the attack failed because Wellington moved no troops from his center.

Shortly after 1300 the great bombardment began striving to blast a hole in the center. At about 1330 three infantry division advanced up the slopes of Mont St. Jean.
The attack was checked by heavy fire from the Allied guns and then routed by the charge of Ponsonby's Union Brigade in to the exposed flank of d'Erlon's Corps.
Three of d'Erlon's four divisions were completely routed, over 3000 men captured and the situation in the center was restored.

0 Yards   100   200

The situation at about 1900

Wellington

I Corps
Ziethen

Chassé

Blücher

II Corps
Reille

I Corps
d'Erlon

Gd. Corps

Pirch

Napoleon

VI Corps
Lobau

Bülow

While the action around Plancenoit was occuring, Wellington had moved his disengaged troops from the safe right flank and the left flank into the center. Meanwhile Ziethen's corps moved up to support Wellington's left.

Shortly after 1900 Napoleon led the Imperial Guard in the center and northward along the Brussels road. Joined by other units of d'Erlon's and Reille's corps, they prepared for one last effort in the center.

Two battalions formed a front towards Hougoumont and the remaining battalions attacked northwestward from the Brussels road. As they did so they split into two columns, the Grenadier battalions in front and the chasseurs attached to their left rear. Every available gun opened up on the French troops. The British had been on a front of about 400 files. The French frontage was only 70 men broad, so the head of their column was overlapped on either side by the British. Neighboring units added to the cross-fire which halted the

grenadiers. The British Guards counter-attacked with bayonets and drove them down the hill. The 'chasseurs' were checked as they breasted the rise and taken in the flank by more troops they retired down the hill. Again the column tried to deploy, and again it failed.

As the Prussian fire grew heavier and nearer, Wellington's instict told him that the French were played out and complete victory could be his. A wave of his hat signalled the British advanced. The French ranks dissolved, only the solidity of three squares of the Old Guard checked the pursuit at La Belle Alliance, and the Young Guard held Plancenoit long enough for most of the rest of the army to escape towards Genappe.

Wellington had lost 15,000 men, the French 29,000 and the Prussians 7000. When allowance is made for prisoners, desertion and the casualties of Wavre, Ligny and Quatre Bras, the total losses of the three armies between 16 and 19 June must have exceeded 100,000. Over 60,000 were French.

0 Yards   100   200

Bülow's corps. Napoleon was not yet committed to the main assault on Wellington's position and he could have waited for Grouchy before beginning the attack, but once again his overwhelming confidence drove him on. 'This morning we had ninety chances in our favor. Even now we have sixty chances, and only forty against', he assured Soult. He did send a new order to Grouchy, instructing him to march directly towards the main body, but by the time that he received this order it was too late for Grouchy to affect the issue. Napoleon also moved the cavalry of his central reserve to meet the Prussians and sent Lobau's 6th Corps after them. Lobau took up a position in advance of the village of Plancenoit, at right angles to the main line, and waited for Bülow to emerge from the Bois de Paris.

Having taken these precautions, Napoleon finally cast the die. Shortly after 1300 the great bombardment opened, striving to blast a hole in the center of the Allied position through which d'Erlon's infantry could advance and ensure a quick victory. However, the only target facing the French artillery was General Bylandt's brigade, standing rather in advance of the rest of the line, and a few scattered guns. Bylandt's brigade was shaken and withdrew to the line of the other Allied brigades, but otherwise the French gunners did almost nothing to prepare for the advance of the d'Erlon's men, which began at about 1330. Three of d'Erlon's divisions adopted an unusual formation for their attack. Each battalion was deployed in a three-deep line, and the battalions formed one behind another in a vast column up to 200 files broad and 24 or 27 ranks deep. His-

torians have criticized the choice of this formation, rather than one of the more usual combinations of battalion columns or lines, for although it had depth, it lacked flexibility and the rear units had little chance to maneuver. However, French units often adopted this formation when massing in reserve or moving up in support and it may be that d'Erlon, overestimating the effect of the preliminary barrage and underestimating the steadiness of the troops before him, imagined that he had only to walk through an already shattered enemy.

If this was the case, d'Erlon was soon to be disillusioned. As the blocks of blue-coated figures began to ascend the slopes of Mont-St Jean, the Allied guns tore long and bloody lanes through them. Only Bylandt's brigade did not wait for their approach, falling back in a more or less orderly fashion to the woods in the rear, where they sat out the battle, smoking and drinking coffee. But the rest of Picton's division lay in wait as the French mass lapped around the farm of La Haye Sainte and into the farms of Papelotte and La Haye. As the French lines reached the forward edge of the crest, the gunners at last abandoned their pieces, but instead of retiring to the shelter of the infantry battalions many streamed to the rear. It seemed that the French battalions had only to rally their lines, disordered in crossing the fields and by the artillery fire, to complete the rout of the center. However, the Allied line at this point was under the command of Lieutenant-General Sir Thomas Picton, a Peninsular veteran who thoroughly understood the business in hand. His division rose from the ground and poured a

Below: Highland troops between La Haye and La Belle Alliance close in for the kill on the afternoon of Waterloo.

tremendous volley into the startled French. Pack's brigade of Highlanders flung themselves on the staggering column, followed by Kempt's brigade led by Picton himself. As Picton urged his troops on, one French bullet found its mark in his temple, killing him instantly, and although his valiant troops mangled the first lines of French infantry, they could not cut their way through all the twenty-odd ranks which faced them. They might yet have been overborne by sheer weight of numbers. Moreover, the center of the whole Allied line was threatened by a charge by French *cuirassiers* on d'Erlon's left flank. However Wellington, having overseen Picton's attack, had moved back to the center and was ready with the right riposte. The German infantry battalions west of the Brussels road moved into square and through the intervals thus formed Lieutenant-General Lord Uxbridge, commander of the cavalry, led Somerset's Household Brigade and Ponsonby's Union Brigade. These were both composed of heavy cavalry, and men and horses were perfectly fresh. The *cuirassiers* had not rested properly during the previous night and were now blown by the uphill charge. They were swept contemptuously aside and the British heavies crashed into the exposed flank of d'Erlon's corps. Almost simultaneously the Household Brigade struck the westernmost division and the Union Brigade carved into the two center divisions. As the Scots Greys passed through the ranks of the Gordons, many Highlanders hung on to their stirrups, and shrieking 'Scotland for ever' cavalry and infantry hurtled forward together. Even if there had been time, the clumsy French columns could not have deployed into squares, but as it was they were taken completely by surprise. Instead of presenting a solid front to their enemies the infantry had to rely on their individual efforts; a survivor described the result thus:

'In vain our poor fellows stood up and stretched out their arms; they could not reach far enough to bayonet those cavalrymen mounted on powerful horses, and the few shots fired into this chaotic *mêlée* were just as fatal to our own men as to the English. And so we found ourselves defenseless against a relentless enemy who, in the intoxication of battle, sabred even our drummers and fifers without mercy. That is where our eagle was captured; and that is where I saw death close at hand, for my best friends fell around me and I was expecting the same fate, all the while wielding my sword mechanically.'

Three of d'Erlon's four divisions were completely routed; over 3000 men were captured and the situation in the center was completely restored. But the British cavalry were drunk with their success. In the exhilaration of the charge they believed themselves invincible. 'At this moment,' wrote one Scots Grey, 'Colonel Hamilton rode up to us crying, "Charge! Charge the guns!" and went off like the wind up the hill towards the terrible battery that had made such deadly work among the Highlanders. It was the last we saw of our colonel, poor fellow! His body was found with both arms cut off... Then we got amongst the guns, and we had our revenge. Such slaughtering! We sabred the gunners, lamed the horses, and cut their traces and harness. I can hear the Frenchmen yet crying "*Diable!*" when I struck

at them, and the long-drawn hiss through their teeth as my sword went home... The artillery drivers sat on their horses weeping aloud as we went among them; they were mere boys, we thought.'

By now the British cavalrymen were exhausted and surrounded on all sides by the French army. As they struggled to recross the valley they were particularly harassed by the lancers of General Jacquinot's brigade which attacked from the east, and scarcely half the troopers returned unharmed. The British cavalry had always been difficult to control, but never was its dash and strength more tragically wasted. An important part of Wellington's reserve had been dispersed and his ability to counterattack future French assaults had been drastically reduced.

However, this rash charge consumed more time, and it was 1530 before Marshal Ney led the next attack forward. With the only two brigades which had rallied from d'Erlon's corps he attempted to seize La Haye Sainte and was repulsed after some stiff fighting around the farmhouse. But Ney believed that he had seen troops retreating along the Brussels road. In fact these were only columns of wounded and transport but Ney was sufficiently deceived to order up a brigade of *cuirassiers* to hurry the apparent retreat. Two more divisions of cavalry followed, more or less on their own initiative and by 1600 hours 5000 horsemen were committed to a charge between Hougoumont and La Haye Sainte. Cramped into a front considerably less than a thousand yards wide the French cavalry were an ideal target for Wellington's artillery, which once again he had ordered to keep firing as long as possible, leaving their guns only at the last moment for the protection of the infantry squares behind them. Captain Mercer's 'G' Troop, Royal Horse Artillery, scorned even this precaution, distrusting the steadiness of the Brunswickers in their rear, and by the tempest of their fire they kept their front clear. Everywhere the infantry held firm, despite 'the awful grandeur of that charge. You perceived at a distance what appeared to be an overwhelming, long moving line, which, ever advancing, glittered like a stormy wave of the sea when it catches the sunlight. On came the mounted host until they got near enough, while the very earth seemed to vibrate beneath their thundering tramp'. However, the *cuirassiers* had no support except from a long range artillery bombardment, which had to cease as they approached the Allied line. D'Erlon's troops had been surprised by cavalry in an unsuitable formation and cut to pieces, but Wellington's battalions were formed in squares and 'prepared to receive cavalry'. As soon as the first impact of their charge was broken by the rolling volleys of musketry the French were split into small groups of squadrons which attempted scattered and uncoordinated attacks on the squares until at last the mass of them were forced into the bottom of the valley. Here they reformed and returned to the charge. However, their horses were so tired that they could only walk forward, and this attack was broken up by artillery fire before it reached the top of the hill.

Napoleon watched the attack with growing

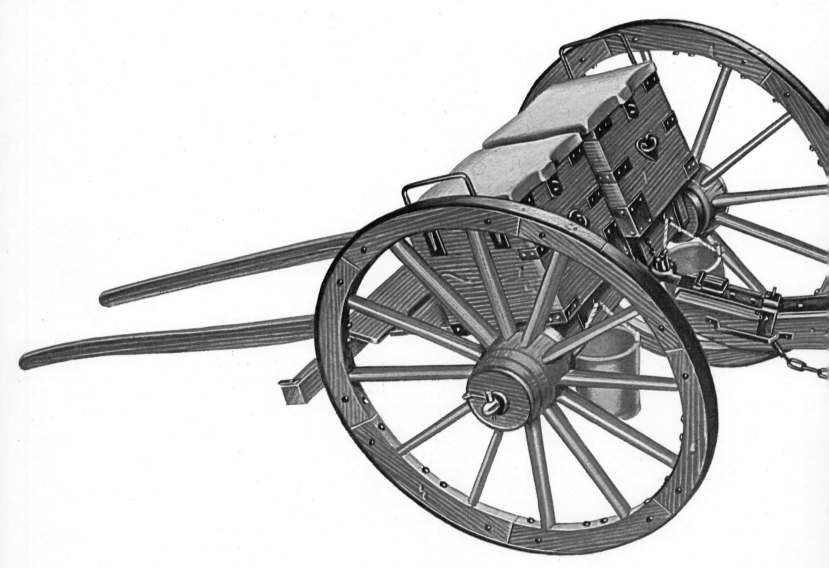

concern. Bülow was clear of the Bois de Paris and, forcing Napoleon's right flank back toward Plancenoit, threatened the rear of the whole French line. Yet there was no sign that Wellington was on the verge of defeat and Ney had compromised half the reserve cavalry. To extricate him Napoleon ordered forward General Kellermann's wing of the cavalry which had been waiting west of the Brussels road. Kellermann would have queried the wisdom of this order, but his divisional generals would not wait for an answer. As they advanced General Guyot followed with the Empress's Dragoons and the Horse Grenadiers, Napoleon's last reserve of cavalry. This second great charge began at about 1700 and was made by nearly 10,000 horsemen, on a front of 500 yards. Again the first charge failed, but for nearly an hour Ney led the French cavalry in charge after charge. At least seven or eight attacks were made and Ney had his fourth horse killed under him. At one stage he was seen hacking at a British gun with his sword as rage and frustration overpowered him.

The scene inside the squares was almost indescribable. Around them, at twenty or thirty yards distance, was a rampart of dead or wounded men

and horses, which increasingly impeded French efforts to charge home. 'Inside them we were nearly suffocated by the smoke and smell from burnt cartridges' wrote Ensign Gronow of the 1st Foot Guards. 'It was impossible to move a yard without treading upon wounded comrades, or upon the bodies of the dead; and the loud groans of the wounded and dying was most appalling.' Above the groans came the volleys of musketry and the sounds of bullets striking steel *cuirassiers*, like 'the noise of a violent hailstorm beating upon panes of glass'. The 40th Regiment was greatly amused by the gesticulations and grimaces with which the *cuirassiers* faced the barrier of casualties

Opposite: La Belle Alliance, the farmhouse used by Napoleon as his headquarters during the battle. Waterloo is often called the battle of La Belle Alliance by the French for this reason. **Left:** The 3rd Regiment of Foot Guards repulses the final charge of Napoleon's Old Guard during the closing stages of battle.

Below: A British 9-pounder gun and limber first introduced during the Peninsular Campaign and used by Wellington at Waterloo. Although its range at ground level was only 400 yards, the range could be increased to 2,400 yards if the gun was elevated to ten degrees. It required a crew of seven.

and the storm of fire. Ordering their men to 'Prepare to receive cavalry' the officers added 'Now, men, make faces!' As the baffled *cuirassiers* fell back to prepare for yet another charge the Allied infantry came under fire from a battery of horse artillery at point blank range, which swept away whole files. To the diminishing squares, the cavalry charges were a welcome relief, giving them a chance to hand out punishment as well as take it. But despite the casualties the squares stood firm, apparently rooted to the spot. Among them rode Wellington, strengthening the infantry's resolve by a word, or ordering a counter-charge by his own weakened cavalry. 'We had a notion that while he was there nothing could go wrong', wrote one of his staff afterwards. In the end it was the French whose willpower gave way and the exhausted cavalry retired to their own side of the valley.

Ney's thoughts again turned to the infantry. A division and a half of Reille's corps had not been embroiled in the Hougoumont, and by 1800 Ney was leading them up slopes strewn with the bloody evidence of his previous failures. This attack, although supported by horse and guns, was no more successful. The area was now thickly held by Wellington's artillery and infantry and he was there himself to see the advance checked in front by Maitland's Guards Brigade and to order Adam's to a position on the flank of the French columns. For ten minutes the French stood in this killing ground, losing 1500 men out of 6000. Then they too turned their backs on the Allied line.

Napoleon saw this, but still he did not despair. He recognized the importance of La Haye Sainte, standing in easy range of the Allied center, and sent Ney categorical orders to capture it. Ney managed to scrape together a force of all arms,

chiefly from the remnants of d'Erlon's divisions, and soon had the farmhouse surrounded. The 2nd Light Battalion of the King's German Legion under Major Baring had held the farm against all comers throughout the day, but ammunition for their rifles was becoming scarce. A rash attempt to assist the garrison met with disaster when French cavalry emerged from the dead ground and caught half a brigade in line. Shortly after 1800 the defenders' ammunition gave out, and after holding their position with the bayonet for some minutes, Baring and 42 other survivors out of a garrison of 376 broke out of the doomed farm. At last Ney could report success to his Emperor. Artillery and *tirailleurs* pressed forward and the whole center of Wellington's line came under their fire. The rallied elements of d'Erlon's corps were pressing forward again, but to be sure of victory Ney needed fresh troops. Now was the time for Napoleon to throw in his last reserve, the Imperial Guard itself.

Ney's Appeals Rejected

But the Emperor rejected Ney's appeals: '*Des troupes! Où voulez-vous que j'en prenne? Voulez-vous que j'en fasse?*' ('Troops! Where do you expect me to get them from? Do you want me to make some?'). Having ignored or underestimated the Prussian threat all day, Napoleon was now only too aware of the danger. Plancenoit had been captured by Bülow shortly after 1700. Napoleon had ordered up the Young Guard Division of his reserve and their attack drove the Prussians back beyond the village, but Bülow was soon reinforced by Pirch's corps and the Young Guard was overborne and forced out of Plancenoit again. Prussian artillery brought the Brussels road under fire. It seemed more important to Napoleon to restore the

situation on his right flank than to attend to Ney's request for troops. Of the fourteen Guard battalions available to him, Napoleon put eleven in a line of squares east of the Brussels road. One battalion remained to guard the Emperor's person, and the remaining two stormed into Plancenoit and retook the village with the bayonet. Although they were unable to drive the Prussians further back the position had been stabilized and Napoleon could turn his attention to Mont-St Jean and the center of Wellington's army.

But he had once again underestimated his opponent. No one who knew Wellington's capabilities as a general would have allowed him even a moment to recover his balance. As soon as he heard the news of the fall of La Haye Sainte, Wellington moved to the point of greatest danger. At 1600 he decided that his extreme right flank was safe and had moved Chassé's Dutch-Belgian Division from there to a more central position on the Nivelles road behind the main line. His foresight was now justified, as he could bring them into the front line at the critical point. There were then twice as many brigades in the area immediately west of the Brussels road as there had been at the beginning of the battle, but the reliability of some of these units was doubtful. To strengthen them Wellington sent for every available gun and formed Vivian's and Vandeleur's brigades of light cavalry in a continuous line behind the infantry. They were there not just to support the front line but also to block any possible retreat to Brussels. To the west of this section of the line were Maitland's Guards brigades and Adam's brigade of light infantry, almost all Peninsular veterans. Beyond them was the still defiant bastion of Hougoumont. But undoubtedly the greatest strength in this grouping was the presence of Wellington

himself, restraining troops who jibbed at standing under fire without being able to reply and encouraging all to 'Standfast! .... we must not be beat —what will they say in England?'

Meanwhile Prussian assistance was approaching rapidly, as the first troops of General Graf von Ziethen's corps, led by General Müffling, moved up to reinforce Wellington's left. Ziethen had left Wavre for Mont-St Jean about 1400, but at 1800, as he approached Ohain, a junior officer told him that Wellington was in retreat. (He had, like Ney, been deceived by the sight of transports moving the wounded to the rear.) Ziethen decided to turn south to aid Bülow at Plancenoit, but Müffling had appeared in the nick of time and persuaded him to carry out his original orders.

It was shortly after 1900 when Napoleon led the Imperial Guard past his command post at La Belle Alliance and northward along the Brussels road. Authorities disagree about the number and composition of this column but it was probably made up of nine battalions of the Old and Middle Guards. About 600 yards short of the Allied line Napoleon handed over command to Ney; as he watched the Guard march past him he was saluted with cheers and cries of '*Vive l' Empereur!*' In the wake of the 'Immortals' other units of d' Erlon's and Reille's corps prepared for one last effort, encouraged by the Emperor's assurance that the ominous masses appearing in the northeast were not Prussians but Grouchy's long-awaited corps. But this elation did not last very long; a cannonade from the right flank and the rear of the advance announced that the approaching troops were in fact Prussian, whatever the Emperor might say. In the general hesitation only the Guard continued to move forward; the rest of the army waited to see whether they could ensure victory in the same way that they had completed many of Napoleon's greatest triumphs.

The details of the actual assault are far from certain. Two battalions formed a front toward Hougoumont and the remaining battalions attacked north-westward from the Brussels road. As they did so they split into two columns, the grenadier battalions in front and the *chasseurs* echeloned to their left rear. This move may have been intentional, or it may have been caused by the uneven ground and the tendency of the leading battalions to step faster than those behind when they came under fire. Wellington was with Maitland's Guards Brigade as they waited, lying down, for the leading column. Every available gun, double-shotted or with canister, opened up on the French troops, but ignoring this curtain of fire they pressed on at the *pas de charge*. There was no move from the British line as the French came to within forty yards of them. Then, above the drums, came the Duke's order 'Now, Maitland! Now is your time!—Stand up Guards! Make ready! Fire!' The Guards had been on a front of about 400 files. The French frontage was only 70

Right: The blazing remains of La Haye Sainte (center) as night descends over the carnage after the battle. **Far right:** Napoleon on the *Bellerophon*. **Below:** Blücher and Wellington meet after the battle at La Belle Alliance. Blücher, after having been ridden over by his own cavalry, had been forced to swallow a mixture of garlic and rhubarb, a point which Wellington noticed when they embraced to celebrate their victory.

the Allied army turned on him, he saw that the French right wing was crumbling, but that the main body of the enemy had not yet broken. However, instinct told him that the French were played out and complete victory could be his. A wave of his hat signaled his decision to the army; cheering, the long-tried regiments swept forward.

The Imperial Army fell apart; 'Sauve qui peut' was now the cry and as the French ranks dissolved the British and Prussian light cavalry rushed upon them. Only the solidity of three squares of the Old Guard checked the pursuit at La Belle Alliance and the Young Guard held Plancenoit long enough for most of the rest of the army to escape towards Genappe. But Napoleon's attempt to rally the survivors there or at Quatre Bras failed, and it was only at Phillipeville, across the French border, that the rabble began to coalesce into an army again.

The Price of Victory

On the battlefield itself over 40,000 men lay dead or wounded, beside an untold number of horses. Wellington had lost 15,000 men, the French 29,000 and the Prussians 7000. When allowance is made for prisoners, desertion and the casualties of Wavre, Ligny and Quatre Bras, the total losses of the three armies between 16 and 19 June must have exceeded 100,000. Over 60,000 of these casualties were French, yet in numerical terms their army had not been destroyed. There were 117,000 troops available between Belgium and Paris, excluding fortress troops and conscripts; the Allied armies were scarcely more numerous than this field force. Politically, however, Waterloo had sealed the Emperor's fate. On returning to Paris he found little support in the Chamber of Deputies and on 22 June he abdicated in favor of his son. In exile he blamed subordinates such as Soult, Grouchy and Ney for his defeat, but he had chosen these men himself, after having known them for many years. What Napoleon could not bring himself to admit was that, after his initial success, he had been mastered by overwhelming self-confidence, so that he was no longer capable of seeing any flaws in his own appreciation of the situation and his own plans. The rest of his army were seized by the same failing; so great was their confidence in the Emperor that they attempted the impossible, and continued the struggle to the limit of human endurance. In the words of one English officer 'By God! Those fellows deserve Bonaparte, they fight so nobly for him'. The most serious error Napoleon made was to despise Wellington. The 'Iron Duke's' army had little chance of achieving total victory on its own, and the appearance of a growing mass of Prussian troops in the northeast certainly tipped the balance in the Allies' favor, but there would have been no victory waiting when they finally reached the battlefield had it not been for Wellington. As Harry Smith of the 95th said of Waterloo, every moment was a crisis, and without Wellington's knack of being ready with the right answer at every critical point, the result might have been completely different. Wellington's judgement was always reliable and as he immodestly put it: 'By God! I don't think it would have done if I had not been there'.

men broad and so the head of their column was overlapped on either side by the British. Neighboring units added to the crossfire which halted the Grenadiers; then the cheering British Guards were on them with the bayonet, driving them down the hill. As the western column breasted the rise they were met and checked by Adam's Brigade. Colonel Sir John Colborne wheeled the 1st/52nd until they stood parallel to the *chasseurs'* left flank. Again the column tried to deploy under a withering cross-fire and again it failed. The advance of the 52nd completed the defeat of the Imperial Guard.

The impossible had happened, and as the Prussian fire grew heavier and nearer the spirit of the French army began to waver. Wellington sensed this and moved to a mound beside the Brussels road, from which he could survey the battlefield and could be seen by his own army. As all eyes in

Hampton Roads

1862

In the several centuries preceding Trafalgar there had been virtually no change in naval tactics or technology, but by the time of Navarino the outlines of a coming revolution in technology were clear. The adaptation of the steamship and the iron ship, both known before the end of the eighteenth century, heralded the advent of the most important innovation of the nineteenth century, the armored warship. The death knell of the old wooden warships of Nelson and Codrington had been sounded in 1853 when a Russian squadron equipped with shell firing guns had blasted a Turkish squadron to bits at the Battle of Sinope. But it was only in the American Civil War of 1861–1865 that armored vessels were first used extensively and faced each other in action. An armored warship made the first naval challenge of the South against the North at the Battle of Hampton Roads in March 1862, a challenge which, if successful, might have changed the course of the war.

In the years before the Civil War, the American navy was undergoing a transition from sail to steam in common with the European navies. At that time, steam was still generally supplementary to sail in sea-going ships since engines were very inefficient and consumed huge quantities of coal. In 1842 the American navy had acquired its first steam screw propeller warship, the *Princeton*, whose engine, propeller and main armament were designed by the Swedish engineer John Ericsson. In that same year, a commission for an armored harbor defense craft was obtained by Robert L. Stephens, but the vessel was never completed. Despite this failure, the navy was definitely aware of the growing trend toward armored ships or 'ironclads', as they were called. In the Crimean War of 1853–1856, France had used armored floating batteries with so much success that Napoleon III ordered four ironclad warships to be built. First to be completed in this group was the *Gloire*, the most powerful warship of her time. To counter this threat to her naval supremacy, Britain completed her own ironclad, the *Warrior*, a year later. With only Stephens' ship, perpetually under construction, the American navy had no ironclads at the outbreak of war. It did have, however, six new first class steam frigates, the best known of which was to be the *Merrimack*, and twelve steam sloops. All told, 42 ships were in commission.

Along with the shift to steam, new ordnance was being introduced. After some experimentation with gun barrel pressures, a young lieutenant named John Dahlgren successfully began to design guns of larger caliber after 1847. The 'Dahlgrens' were smooth bores and fired both shot and shell. Guns under eight-inch bore often had rifled barrels, making them more accurate than the smooth bores. Although Dahlgren could produce a thirteen-inch gun, the new steam frigates of the American navy were armed with nine, ten and eleven-inch guns. On the eve of the war, therefore, the navy was a small but relatively modern force, augmented by a large merchant marine and abundant shipbuilding resources.

The long-standing and deeply divisive issue of the extension of slavery to the new states being formed in the American West came to a final crisis in December 1860 when South Carolina seceded from the Union, followed by six other states. With Jefferson Davis as their president and

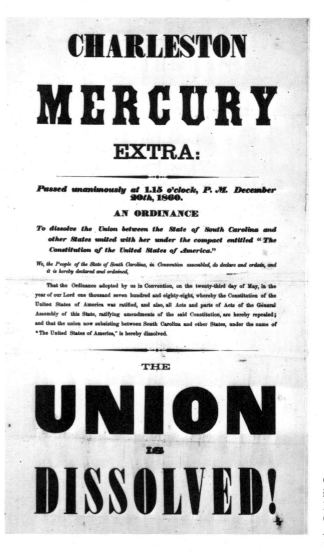

Opposite: The inauguration of Jefferson Davis as President of the Confederate States of America.

Far left: The unfinished dome of the Capitol as seen from Pennsylvania Avenue, as Lincoln's carriage proceeds to the inauguration, 4 March, 1861. **Below:** Abraham Lincoln, 16th President of the United States.

Montgomery, Alabama as their first capital, these seven formed the original Confederate States of America. By following a policy of inaction, President James Buchanan tried not to aggravate the situation but his successor Abraham Lincoln, taking office early in 1861, quickly realized force was the only means of preserving the Union. Opinion in the North was deeply divided, however, and the new president knew the first act of overt war would have to come from the South. The Confederates obligingly fired on Fort Sumter in Charleston harbor on 12 April, an act which solidly united the North, not for long, but long enough for Lincoln to act. He issued a proclamation declaring a state of insurrection and called for a volunteer army to re-establish order. Four additional Southern States then parted company with the Union.

Correctly interpreting Lincoln's insurrection proclamation to mean that the South was to be invaded, President Davis called for volunteers to defend the Confederacy. At the same time he called for privateers to sail under Confederate letters of marque with two objectives in mind. First, it was hoped that these raiders would so disrupt the commerce of the North that the European powers would intervene on the side of the South. Second, since almost all of the exports of the South went through the six ports of Norfolk, Virginia; Wilmington, North Carolina; Charleston, South Carolina; Savannah, Georgia; Pensacola, Florida; Mobile, Alabama, and New Orleans, Louisiana, the North would certainly establish a blockade, and it was also hoped that the privateers would distract the Northern Navy from the blockade.

The advantage in the war initially lay with the South as North had to be the aggressor, literally conquering and occupying the eleven states of the Confederacy one by one. Such an advantage, however, was ultimately offset by the fact that the North possessed two thirds of the nation's

population and virtually all of its industry. The economy of the South was basically agricultural and badly balanced in its heavy dependence on the export of cotton. The South had therefore to import nearly all of its iron, arms, equipment, clothing and even some food. Fully aware of their inferior economic, industrial and demographic position, Southern leaders firmly believed that the European powers and especially Britain would intervene in their favor because of Europe's need for Southern agricultural products, especially cotton. With five million people in Britain dependent on the textile industry for their livelihood and 80 per cent of Britain's cotton supplied by the South, so this view ran, the North would not dare interfere with the movement of

Above: President Lincoln, flanked by Allan Pinkerton and General McClernand, on the battlefield of Antietam, 3 October, 1862. The fight for control of northern Virginia and Maryland continued throughout the war.

Left: Lincoln's inauguration at the Capitol.

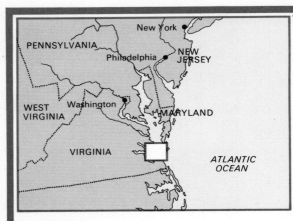

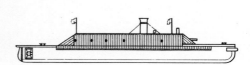

The 'Merrimack' was a 'casemate' ironclad because she had a sloping iron box superimposed on the wooden hull of a former frigate. The large single screw and rudder were under water, making her invulnerable to shell fire. Apart from her powerful guns, she had another offensive weapon—a heavy projecting ram at the bow.

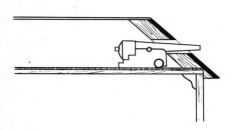

The guns of the 'Merrimack' inside the iron 'casemate' in a battery reminiscent of the ships of the line of sailing days. The sloped armor plating offered further protection, because solid shot and spherical shells tended to be deflected.

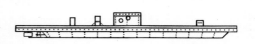

The 'Monitor' was much smaller than the 'Merrimack' and had an iron hull with an armored raft superimposed. On this raft was a cylindrical turret containing only two guns, but as the turret revolved, the same degree of firepower could be brought to bear.

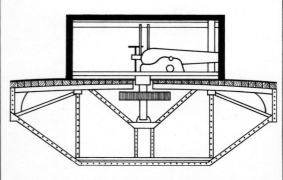

The 'Monitor's turret as designed by John Ericsson contained two 11-inch smooth-bore guns. Its armored roof and sides gave complete protection to the crew, and steam training machinery gave a 360 degree field of fire.

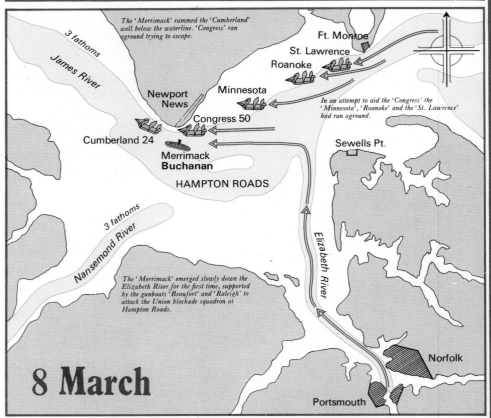

The 'Merrimack' rammed the 'Cumberland' well below the waterline. 'Congress' ran aground trying to escape.

In an attempt to aid the 'Congress' the 'Minnesota', 'Roanoke' and the 'St. Lawrence' had run aground.

The 'Merrimack' emerged slowly down the Elizabeth River for the first time, supported by the gunboats 'Beaufort' and 'Raleigh' to attack the Union blockade squadron at Hampton Roads.

3 fathoms

James River

Ft. Monroe
St. Lawrence
Roanoke
Minnesota
Newport News
Congress 50
Cumberland 24
Merrimack **Buchanan**
HAMPTON ROADS
Sewells Pt.

3 fathoms

Nansemond River

Elizabeth River

Norfolk

Portsmouth

8 March

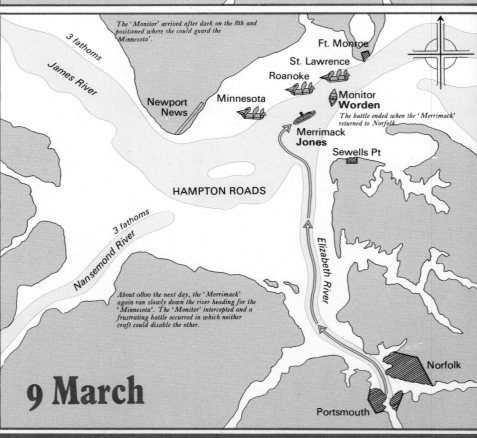

The 'Monitor' arrived after dark on the 8th and positioned where she could guard the 'Minnesota'.

The battle ended when the 'Merrimack' returned to Norfolk.

About 0800 the next day, the 'Merrimack' again ran slowly down the river heading for the 'Minnesota'. The 'Monitor' intercepted and a frustrating battle occurred in which neither craft could disable the other.

3 fathoms

James River

Ft. Monroe
St. Lawrence
Roanoke
Minnesota
Newport News
Monitor **Worden**
Merrimack **Jones**
Sewells Pt
HAMPTON ROADS

3 fathoms

Nansemond River

Elizabeth River

Norfolk

Portsmouth

9 March

cotton for fear of provoking Britain to intervention on the side of the South. As Senator Hammond of South Carolina succinctly put this disastrous view in 1858, 'No power on earth dares make war on it. Cotton is King'.

But to the bitter disillusionment of Southerners everywhere, Lincoln did make war on King Cotton and Britain did not intervene. Provoked by Davis' call for privateers, the blockade was imposed immediately and within a year had become reasonably effective. King Cotton diplomacy came undone for two reasons. At the outbreak of the war in 1861, Britain already had a large oversupply of cotton on hand while during the war new sources of supply were developed in Egypt and India. A certain amount of Southern cotton also got through the blockade. At the same time, crop failures in Britain during the war years made necessary the import of Northern wheat for which Britain gladly exchanged munitions. Generally speaking, the war worked to the advantage of Britain which supplied both sides with munitions, captured most of the North Atlantic carrying trade, and imported Northern grains.

The privileged classes in Britain were basically sympathetic with the South, viewing the war as an attempt by the North to dominate the South and gladly watching the weakening of the growing power of the United States. The failure of the 'detestable' democratic experiment in America would slow down the demand for reform in Britain just as the ultimate victory of the North contributed to the ferment leading to the English Reform Bill of 1867. Seeing the North as fighting for free labor and democracy, the British working classes would never have willingly consented to intervention on behalf of slavery. Thus while the British Prime Minister Lord Palmerston was quick to assert and defend what he considered to be British rights, he proclaimed British neutrality at the outset. The formal neutrality of Britain actually worked to the advantage of the North as it forced all British trade with the blockaded states into clandestine channels and deprived such trade of official British protection. The Southern military successes early in the war led to doubts in Europe about the ability of the North to subdue the rebellious states. Britain and France made unsuccessful offers of mediation and considered intervention. The Union victory at Antietam in September 1862, however, caused Britain to be more judicious in this policy, and it was dropped completely after the Union suc-

Left: The bombardment of Fort Sumter by the South Carolina batteries, 13 April, 1861. These guns heralded the start of the Civil War which was to last four years.
Above: The interior of Fort Sumter during the bombardment. **Right:** The floating battery in Charleston Harbor during the attack on Fort Sumter.
Below: The battered and conquered fort, with the Confederate flag waving over it.

cesses at Gettysburg and Vicksburg in 1863. This fact became apparent even to the Confederate government, which recalled its agents from London in late 1863.

The first miscalculation of Confederate naval policy was to provoke the blockade at the outset, but having done so the primary task of the Southern navy was to break or circumvent the blockade as the Confederate Secretary of the Navy, Stephen R. Mallory, clearly recognized. Since the South had no ships of its own, Mallory decided the real answer to breaking the blockade was ironclads. In May 1861 he sent Commander James Bulloch to England to procure warships and especially ironclads. Somewhat optimistically, Mallory even hoped to buy one of the *Gloire* class from France. At the same time, a program to produce two powerful ironclads at Memphis, Tennesee and two more at New Orleans was launched despite the South's manifest inadequacies in materials and skilled work-

men. When Virginia had seceded from the Union on 17 April, the Confederates happily came into possession of the Norfolk Navy Yard and with it many naval guns, a large quantity of urgently needed powder and the almost new steam frigate *Merrimack*. Fired and scuttled by the Union personnel of the yard before they escaped, this ship had only burned to the water line and was easily salvageable. Mallory authorized her conversion to an ironclad on 11 May, thus launching the first Confederate challenge to the partly effective Union blockade.

A large wooden frigate, the *Merrimack*'s hull had only been slightly damaged. Her upper works were removed and a casement with sloping sides and curved ends was constructed. The casement was protected by two layers of iron plate, each of which was two inches thick and rolled from railroad rails. Mastless, the one-funnel vessel had an engine which could barely move her when the tide ran against her. Mount-

Left; below left: Destruction of the US Navy Yard at Norfolk, Virginia involved the burning of several American ships.
Below: A French impression of the fight between the *Monitor* (center) and *Merrimack* (left). The *Minnesota* is firing on the right. **Bottom:** The *Monitor* engaged the *Merrimack* at close range, and the clouds of powder-smoke soon obscured everything.

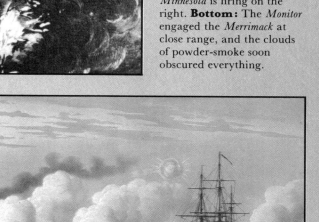

ing a total of ten guns, the *Merrimack* had seven-inch rifled guns fore and aft, each of which could be trained on the keel line or on either beam. Her broadside consisted of one six-inch rifled gun and three nine-inch smooth bores. With a complement of 320 men, mostly from the army, she was under the command of Captain Franklin Buchanan. On completion in March 1862 she was renamed the *Virginia*, but this name has fallen into disuse she remains known as the *Merrimack*.

The conversion of the *Merrimack* was no secret and had brought counter measures in the North. To the pleasant surprise of Secretary of the Navy Gideon Welles, who was very conscious of the $500,000 which had been spent on Stephens' ironclad since 1842, Congress voted funds for one or more ironclads in 1861. Three contracts were let but the first ship actually to be launched was a radically designed craft by John Ericsson who had earlier designed the *Princeton*. Using a design which had been rejected by the French during the Crimean War, Ericsson laid his ship down on 25 October, 1861 and delivered her on 19 February, 1862. The essence of Ericsson's idea was to place one or two heavy guns in a revolving turret protected by strong armor. A similar idea for a turreted ship had been unsuccessfully proposed to the Royal Navy in 1860 by Captain C. P. Coles who designed such a ship for Denmark the following year.

Displacing 1225 tons, Ericsson's ship was a shallow hull with one turret almost in the center. Fixed on a pivot rotated by a steam engine, the turret was twenty feet in diameter, nine feet high and protected by eight layers of one-inch iron. The deck was armored with two layers of half-inch iron plate. Above and near the waterline, the hull was secured with a belt of five one-inch layers of iron bent outwards to prevent ramming. A four foot high conning tower made of nine-inch iron logs with half-inch sight holes was placed forward and obstructed the front field of fire. The armament was two eleven-inch smooth bores which fired 166 pound shot at a very slow rate. With a length of 172 feet and a beam of 41 feet, the ship was made barely seaworthy by concentrating the heaviest armor in the turret. The crew of 65 under Lieutenant J. L. Worden were all volunteers as the ship was considered a dubious if not dangerous experiment in naval architecture. Named the *Monitor*, the strange appearance of the ship earned her the unflattering sobriquet 'cheesebox on a raft'. Like the *Merrimack*, the *Monitor* presented no unarmored target to the enemy but had two distinct advantages over her Confederate rival. She was much handier and had a draught of 10½ feet compared to the 24 feet of the *Merrimack*, an important factor for operations in shallow coastal waters.

Merrimack Rushed into Action

Well aware of the construction of the Union ironclads, Secretary Mallory wanted the *Merrimack* in action before any Union ironclad could appear to oppose her. Hence the *Merrimack* was rushed into action with such despatch that when she got under way for the first time on the morning of 8 March, 1862, her crew thought she was going for a trial run. That bright and calm morning proved to be more than a trial run, however, as the *Merrimack* came slowly down the Elizabeth River supported by the gunboats *Beaufort* and *Raleigh* to attack the Union blockade squadron in Hampton Roads. The two wooden Union ships anchored off Newport News. The 24-gun sloop *Cumberland* and the 50-gun frigate *Congress* were the immediate targets. Intent on achieving decisive results that day, Buchanan planned to use his ram, possibly because powder and shot were scarce in the Confederacy.

As the *Merrimack* approached the *Cumberland*, both Union ships and shore batteries poured a violent fire at her. To the amazement of onlookers, projectiles bounced off her armor 'like India-rubber balls' while her own shells were smashing the two wooden ships. Undeterred by the Union fire, the *Merrimack* rammed the *Cumberland* forward well below the waterline, ripping open a gaping hole. With her crew still manning their guns, the *Cumberland* rapidly began to sink. The ram, however, wedged into her hull, trapping the *Merrimack* and taking her down with the *Cumberland*. Had the officer on the forward deck of the *Cumberland* had the presence of mind to let go her starboard anchor, it would have fallen on the deck of the *Merrimack* and ensured that she met the same fate as her victim. With water already over her forward deck, the ram suddenly broke off, freeing the attacker and

allowing the attacked to sink even more rapidly. As it was, the Confederate craft did ship some water as a result of the ramming.

While the *Cumberland* was being destroyed, the *Congress* had run aground in shoal water in a futile effort to escape. Taking up a position where she could rake the *Congress*, the *Merrimack* blasted the helpless ship for an hour until she was afire, her captain dead and had no guns operating, at which time the executive officer hoisted a white flag. By now both the day and the tide were ebbing, and Buchanan withdrew his ship, well satisfied with his day's work. While his own ship had lost her ram, had two guns disabled and suffered two killed and eight wounded, she had destroyed two enemy ships and killed 257 Union officers and ratings. Three more large wooden ships – the *Minnesota*, *Roanoke* and *St. Lawrence* – had run aground trying to aid the *Congress* and remained easy prey for the next day's operations. Unfortunately Buchanan himself had been wounded seriously enough for command of the *Merrimack* to pass to Lieutenant Catesby Jones.

When news of the *Merrimack*'s first raid was telegraphed to both sides there was deep rejoicing in the South but genuine panic in the North. It was feared the invincible Southern warship would raid Northern ports and even appear in the Potomac River to bombard Washington. Such fears were unfounded because of the deep draught and unseaworthiness of the *Merrimack* which had trouble just navigating Chesapeake Bay, but the results of her first day's operations seemed to more than justify this consternation to Northern observers. Even before her appearance, the news about the *Merrimack* had been so alarming that the *Monitor* had been rushed to completion and had left New York on 6 March, towed by a seagoing tug. She had had only a few days of tests and her trip south was so difficult that a less resolute person than Worden might well have turned back as the ventilation system broke down and water poured into the low beam craft. By dint of strenuous effort, however, the *Monitor* arrived at the mouth of Chesapeake Bay on the afternoon of the eighth. Hearing the sound of gunfire, Worden proceeded directly to Hampton Roads, arriving after dark, and was immediately ordered to a position where he could guard the stranded *Minnesota* against the depredations of the *Merrimack*, expected to be renewed the next day. In the light of the burning *Congress*, the Confederates also saw the *Monitor* take up her position and knew that the next day promised not easy pickings but a serious fight.

About eight the next morning, the *Merrimack* again ran slowly down the river headed for the *Minnesota*. With the guns of the Southern vessel pounding away at her, the *Monitor* crept forward to intercept and finally fired her own two guns at virtually point blank range. A frustrating encounter followed in which neither vessel could cripple the other even at close range. The *Merrimack* had been provided only with shells whereas solid shot was needed to penetrate the turret of the *Monitor* whose smooth bores were equally ineffective against the iron mail of the *Merrimack*. Worden soon grasped this fact and tried to ram his opponent but missed her propeller, the only vulnerable point at which the *Monitor* could strike, and did no damage to either ship. The sluggish duel continued, the *Merrimack* letting loose a broadside every fifteen minutes and the *Monitor* firing her guns about every seven minutes. Seeing that he was apparently doing no damage to his adversary, Jones then decided that his best course was to attack the grounded *Minnesota* rather than continuing to pound at the seemingly indestructable *Monitor*. In turning toward the *Minnesota*, however, the heavy draught of the *Merrimack* caused her to run aground for fifteen minutes. Then, abandoning any assault on the wooden ship, Jones turned again on the squat *Monitor* and determined to run her down, but his ship was unwieldy and difficult to handle in the narrow shoal channel. His nimbler opponent was able to avoid the main impact and the only result was a bad leak in the bow of the *Merrimack* caused by the sharp edge of the *Monitor*'s armored belt.

After two hours of combat, neither ship had succeeded in disabling the other, but now the *Monitor* hauled off to shallow water to replenish her empty powder and shot lockers in safety, away from the heavy draught *Merrimack*. Although thus far the *Monitor* had seemed to have the upper hand, the astonished Southerners saw this move as a retreat. When the *Monitor* renewed the action at 1130, the *Merrimack* was able to end the battle by changing her tactics. All her fire was concentrated on the conning tower of her enemy. While peering through a sight hole, Worden was stunned and temporarily blinded by a shell burst on the conning tower. Even so, he was still able to order the *Monitor* to sheer off and return to shallow water where she remained for twenty minutes. Unable to pursue the *Monitor* into her sanctuary, the Confederate ironclad assumed her adversary was finally out of action and returned to Norfolk. The *Monitor* shortly came out again to guard the *Minnesota* until the latter was afloat. The Battle of Hampton Roads was over.

Both ships had lacked the offensive power to destroy each other; hence neither suffered much damage in what was the first action between ironclad warships. The *Monitor* received 22 hits and had six wounded including Worden, while the *Merrimack* took twenty hits with two killed and nineteen wounded. Her armor was never penetrated but was broken in a few easily reparable places. Every solid hit by the heavy shot of the *Monitor* did, however, cause considerable concussion in the casement of the *Merrimack*. In retrospect, the *Monitor* should have concentrated her fire on one point to break the armor of her opponent just as the *Merrimack* finally focused her fire on the conning tower of the *Monitor* to put her out of action. But it must also be remembered that the *Monitor* had been in commission less than two weeks and with her crew not yet shaken down, she had barely enough training to operate as a ship when the battle occurred. In tactical terms, the battle was a stalemate with perhaps a slight edge to the *Merrimack* which was basically a more powerful ship than the *Monitor*. Perhaps the *Merrimack* did in fact win, since the *Monitor* declined to prevent her from resuming her raids

a month later. Thoroughly refitted and equipped now with solid shot for her guns, the *Merrimack* sallied forth again on 11 April, but the *Monitor* refused battle as Union officials were well aware that her turret could be pierced by solid shot. Had the *Merrimack* been firing solid shot on 9 March as well, the story of the battle would likely have been different.

Although a tactical stand-off, the battle at Hampton Roads on 9 March had far reaching strategic consequences. In local terms, the *Merrimack* seriously impeded the communications of General George B. McClellan's controversial Peninsula Campaign. With the object of capturing Richmond, Virginia, now the capital of the Confederacy, McClellan had planned to use the channels of the James, York, and Rappahannock Rivers for water transport of supplies and equipment while moving his troops up the peninsulas formed by the three rivers. His movements could then also be supported by Union gunboats on the rivers. While the *Merrimack* was in action, however, she controlled the James

Below: Lieutenant Catesby Jones, CSN, Commander of the *Merrimack*.

Below: The Battle of Hampton Roads took place under the eyes of the Federal Army. **Right:** The *Monitor*'s low profile made her difficult to hit, and shells tended to glance off the flat deck.

Left: General Robert E. Lee, commander of Confederate forces in Virginia and the South's greatest hero. **Bottom right:** A modern Monitor used on the Mekong River by American forces in Vietnam in 1971.

River and McClellan's main effort had to be shifted to the York River. The flow of supplies was also hindered. McClellan's forces did suc- seed in forcing the Confederates to evacuate Norfolk on 1 May. Because of her deep draught, always her main weakness, the *Merrimack* could escape no more than a few miles up river and had to be blown up, thus changing the local strategic situation radically. Even with control of the rivers and support of Union gunboats, including the *Monitor*, McClellan was still defeated by the Confederate General Robert E. Lee in the Seven Day Battle in June. Thwarted in his drive on Richmond, McClellan was forced to withdraw under cover of the guns of the Union ships and the Peninsula Campaign ended in failure. In the end the deep draught of the *Merrimack* proved her undoing. Unsuited for the shallow coastal waters in which she was built to operate, she was also prevented from escaping by the same weakness.

In broader terms, the North believed the *Monitor* to be the only defense it had against the awesome power of the *Merrimack*. In an effort to preserve her for a real emergency, the *Monitor* was ordered not to accept battle unless the *Merri- mack* again attacked the wooden ships on blockade duty, now anchored farther out. Since the *Merrimack* contented herself with bombarding coastal installations and capturing some small craft, the *Monitor* remained watchful but did not offer a second battle. The Union Navy was most impressed with the design of the *Monitor* and ordered 21 similar ships, thus inaugurating a distinct class of ironclads known as 'monitors'. The impact of the *Monitor* itself was so great that the design was adopted by some European navies and monitors played a disproportionate role in the reconstruction of the American navy in the 1880's. Such ships were still in use in both the British and American navies until after the First World War. The last monitor was not removed from the American Navy List until 1937 while 'monitor type' ships were in use in 1974 as convoy escorts on the run up the Mekong River to the besieged Cambodian capital of Phnom Penh. Always barely seaworthy, the original *Monitor* foundered at sea on 29 December, 1862, taking sixteen of her 65-man crew down with her.

Southern naval policy as a whole was a failure. The privateers were driven off the seas within a year due to the blockade and the closure of neutral ports to them, leaving them with no place to dispose of their prizes. Bulloch found the

neutrality of England enforced enough that he had to procure ships and supplies clandestinely. He nevertheless arranged for the purchase or building of eighteen commerce raiders, the best known and most successful of which were the *Alabama*, *Florida* and *Shenandoah* which accounted for more than sixty Union ships between them. All, told, the commerce raiders took around 250 Northern ships but though highly successful, this activity did not have the desired effect of provoking European intervention though it did force the commerce of the North largely out of Northern into foreign and particularly British bottoms. Throughout the war the commerce of the North with Europe continued to increase.

The best hope of the South had rested on the ironclads breaking the blockade and here also Southern plans came to nought. The Confederacy built about 25 ironclads and bought one from France, but only half of these ever saw action. The *Merrimack* was the first and most successful of these ships, having sunk two Union ships. Other Southern ironclads were able to sink only one more ship and damage a few others. Mostly for technical reasons, the Southern ironclads never seriously impaired Union naval activity. Facing a well-equipped, efficient and numerically superior enemy, perhaps the Confederate sailors in their improvised ships experienced some feeling of awe and hopelessness as well. On the eve of the battle of Albemarle Sound in 1862, the Southern commander sighed 'Ah! If we could only hope for success . . .' as he faced sixteen Union ships mounting 54 guns with his eight ships and nine guns. The Union, for its part, ultimately had about 65 assorted ironclads.

The *Merrimack* was the first ironclad challenge made by the South to the blockade, but a second and far more serious threat appeared on the other side of the Atlantic in 1863. From the British builders of the Confederate commerce raider *Alabama*, Southern agents contracted for two powerful steam ironclad warships. These ships were fitted with iron rams to destroy the Union blockade ships while their nine-inch rifled guns could have held Northern seaports hostage to bombardment. Known as the 'Laird Rams' after their builders, the Laird Brothers of Liverpool, the ships were widely known to be destined for the use of the Confederacy. The North watched their progress with growing alarm and applied increasing diplomatic pressure on the British government to seize them. Finally the American Ambassador to Britain, Charles Francis Adams, threatened war to Earl Russell, the British Foreign Secretary, by writing 'It would be superfluous for me to point out to your Lordship that this is war . . .' Had the rams reached America, the South would probably have achieved its independence and the North would certainly have gone to war with Britain, but in the end the British government ordered the rams held and then purchased them for the Royal Navy. This ended the last chance of the South to challenge the blockade.

Despite the short lived threat of the *Merrimack*, the Southern ironclad program never really menaced the blockade. And the blockade was the main instrument of the North for causing the economic chaos which so weakened the South internally that the Union armies were able to gain ascendancy. It is significant that the major victories of the North did not occur until the South was suffering from shortages caused by the blockade. Thus the Southern failure to break or circumvent the blockade was one of the major factors leading to its ultimate defeat.

The Battle of Hampton Roads on 8–9 March, 1862 did not revolutionize naval warfare as is often asserted. That revolution had already occurred when France launched the *Gloire* in 1860. The unique feature of Hampton Roads was that on the 8th wooden ships had to oppose an ironclad for the first time while, far more significantly, the first clash of ironclads came the following day. The day of the armored ship had dawned and while it did not really come into its own until the First World War, its progressive development was to dominate the direction of naval technology for the next half century.

Left: General George McClellan, Lee's opponent in Virginia and Lincoln's challenger for the Presidency in 1864.

Vicksburg

1863

Below: Confederate
pickets near Charleston
harbor in 1861. **Right:**
The bombardment of Fort
Sumter in April 1861,
which began hostilities in
the Civil War.

The American Civil War was the greatest blood-letting between Waterloo and the outbreak of the First World War. More Americans died in the War Between the States than in either of the two world wars. But the eventual outcome was in considerable doubt during the first two years of the war. The British gave overt and covert assistance to the Confederacy in various forms; the Union blockade was run by British ships which brought military supplies to the South; ships built in England flew the Confederate flag and harassed American commerce. But British support for the Confederacy melted away during the first week of July 1863. In that week the South suffered two cruel blows from which it never recovered. The Battle of Vicksburg split the South; the Battle of Gettysburg forced the South into a permanent defensive posture. The loss of these two epic battles convinced Britain and any other potential ally of the South that the war could only be won by the Union.

In November 1860 the Republican candidate, Abraham Lincoln, was elected President of the United States of America. His election came at

Above: The New Jersey Brigade parades before President Lincoln; from a sketch made by Artemus Ward.

a crucial time. For years public opinion in the Northern States had been offended by the survival of slavery in any part of their country. Conversely, the Southern States had resented attacks on a system held to be essential to their prosperity, and integral to their whole culture. Far from appreciating that their slave-holding civilization was fast failing in economic terms, and that its effects were almost as degrading to the whites as to their black slaves, the protagonists of the South built up an ideal picture of its way of life. In this idyll, every Southerner was an honorable, chivalrous, Christian gentleman. Those who owned slaves were careful of their property, kind and humane if only from motives of self-interest. Those who did not were freed from the depressing tasks of society, from the hewing of wood, and the drawing of water. The Northerners, or 'Yankees', were regarded as mere mechanicals, social inferiors, lacking the civilized graces of the South, and concerned only with vulgar practices such as trading or making money. These 'barbarians', seeking to exclude the extension of slavery to the newly occupied Federal Territories, and advocating its abolition throughout the Union, were at best dangerous radicals, at worst apostles of a black insurrection that would spread murder, arson, rape and pillage throughout the South.

On the Northern side an equally powerful stereotype was created. The practice of duelling, still existing in parts of Southern society, was no better than murder, and its hot-tempered practitioners tainted the whole South as a community of partly-civilized bullies. The popularity of Harriet Beecher Stowe's novel '*Uncle Tom's Cabin*' created a belief that all Southern plantation owners were cruel and brutal slave-drivers. Few Northerners had any high regard for the characters of the Negro slaves themselves, but most shared a feeling of loathing for the slave system

and detestation of slave owners. A series of 'Personal Liberty Laws' in the Northern States, passed by legislatures where the Republicans had a majority, did everything possible to hinder the return of fugitives, and were themselves contrary at least to the spirit of the US Constitution, which protected the property, including slaves, of every citizen. The Republican Party itself was formed after Southern pressure had forced the acceptance of slavery in some of the new Western states. When, in 1860, the coalition of Northern conservatives and Southern moderates forming the Democratic Party was defeated, most Southern leaders determined that, if slavery were to continue, the Union must come to an end.

Seven of the slave states withdrew from the Union between December 1860 and February 1861, claiming that as sovereign states they had the right to secede from an association they had once freely joined. Together they formed a new Confederacy, which proceded to take possession of all government property and public buildings under its control. Lincoln, in his inaugural address, declared that all the ordinances of secession passed by the Southern state legislatures were invalid, and announced his intention of occupying and holding all places and property belonging to the Government of the United States. The Confederate Congress called for 100,000 volunteers to resist any invasion, and on 12 April their batteries opened fire on Fort Sumter, at the entrance to Charleston Harbor, South Carolina. On the 14th the small garrison of US troops there laid down its arms, but the following day Lincoln asked the States of the Union to call out their militia to provide him with 75,000 men, for the purpose of quelling insurrection.

Lincoln had said in 1858 that a house divided against itself could not stand; it must either be all slave or all free; the proponents of slavery must

extend the legality of that institution throughout the Union, or its opponents must ensure its total abolition. Now four of the remaining eight slave states left the Union, rather than send their militias to fight against their Southern neighbors. Taking their stand on the principle that the Union was made up of sovereign states, who having freely entered it could freely leave, they turned their back on Washington, and joined the Confederacy, with its new capital at Richmond, Virginia. Lincoln met this threat by doubling the size of the US Regular Army, and adding to the militia a force of 200,000 volunteers, newly formed and enlisted for three years full-time service.

Union troops then marched against Richmond,

but were thrown back at the First Battle of Bull Run (July 1861), and for a time Washington itself was threatened. For four more years two great armies operated in this eastern theater, with the rival capitals within 100 miles of each other. The South, hopelessly outmatched in industrial and financial resources, and with half the population of the Union, had either to defeat the Northern troops in battle and impose its peace terms on a defeated Union, or to prolong hostilities until the North grew tired of the profitless struggle. Nevertheless, if the Union could bring to bear its vastly superior economic strength, and if her diplomats kept European powers from intervening against her, then the Confederate cause was doomed, and could not be saved by the most desperate valor or the most noble sacrifice.

Yet in the early months of 1863 the Confederate Army was still in the field, still with a chance of securing victory in battle, and still buying time, with its soldiers' blood, for the life of the Confederacy. In the east General Robert E. Lee's Army of Northern Virginia was well led, adequately armed, and consisted of veterans of more than a year's hard fighting. The Yankees were still prevented from marching on Richmond, and Washington still had cause to fear the dreaded 'rebel yell'. On the western front the outlook was grimmer. At the mouth of the Mississippi, New Orleans, the South's strategic seaport and commercial capital, had been captured by the US Navy in April 1862, and Admiral David G. Farragut and his deep-sea squadron could ply the lower stretches of the river with impunity. The headwaters of this mighty river and its great tributaries, the Ohio and Missouri Rivers, were in the North, so that another armada was gradually fighting its way downstream. But the river was still not open to Northern commerce. The great citadel of Vicksburg, frowning above the river on

Above: A sketch made during the First Battle of Bull Run, where the South proved that the Union would have no easy victory.

Left: Admiral David Farragut, whose Union Navy blockaded Southern ports and whose river fleet attempted to cut the Confederacy in two by driving up the Mississippi.

Above: The Federal gunboat *Cairo*, which drove up the Mississippi to Vicksburg. This ship was later sunk and her wreck was recently salvaged. **Above center:** A river steamer, the stern-wheeler *Conestoga*, converted into a gunboat for use on the Mississippi.

Below: The USS *Rattler*, another Mississippi stern-wheeler, typical of many river craft converted to gunboats for the river campaign.

its high bluffs, blocked the passage 400 miles from the sea. As long as it held out the Confederacy could still draw supplies, men and money from across the river.

At the same time the corn and wheat growers and meat producers of the Middle West were denied their traditional outlet to the sea. Their produce had now to go east by rail, or by steamboats and schooners on the Great Lakes. As the monopoly financiers who controlled these routes increased their freight rates, so the farmers and cattlemen of Illinois, Indiana and Ohio cooled in their ardor for the war. Peace party men began to win elections. There was talk of secession in the western states, of recognizing the Southerners' independence in return for their opening the river. The longer Vicksburg remained in Confederate hands, the greater the chance that the United States would be forced to give up the war. But if Vicksburg fell to the Union the Confederacy would be cut in two, the Mississippi would become a highway for the US Navy, and from it troops could push eastward to Alabama, Georgia, and the sea.

So far in the war, the descent of the Mississippi and Ohio Rivers had been achieved by gunboats and troop transports operating on the river itself, while a powerful army marched parallel to it, but up to fifty or sixty miles inland. The same technique was used for the ascent of the Ohio's major tributaries, the Cumberland and the Tennessee, which flowed through rebel territory.

It was difficult for the Confederates to counter this strategy. On the one hand, they could concentrate their forces and march inland against the invader. But to do this meant leaving the river virtually defenseless against the Union flotillas, and risking the loss of those very towns and cities they were meant to be saving. On the other hand, they could throw strong garrisons into all the river towns, and man their defenses in strength. This, however, merely invited the Union forces on land to close up behind them, cut off their supplies and starve them into surrender. Thus the Confederates had been obliged to abandon a number of important centers on the river because they were outflanked by powerful armies operating in their hinterland.

At the end of November 1862 the Union troops moved to repeat the same technique against Vicksburg. Major-General Ulysses S. Grant, commanding the Union armies of the Tennessee and Mississippi, marched south, following the Mississippi Central Railroad from Grand Junction, where it joined the Memphis to Corinth line which ran along the Union front. His subordinate, Major-General William T. Sherman, steamed down the river from Memphis, to threaten Vicksburg's frontal defenses. As an added threat to the Confederates, Major-General Nathaniel P. Banks was to move upstream from New Orleans, supported by Admiral Farragut's warships, to threaten Port Hudson, most southerly of the Confederate river citadels, 250 miles (by river) below Vicksburg.

This time the plan failed. Two large-scale raids by the Confederate cavalry succeeded in cutting Grant's supply lines and even severing his communications with the outside world, so that he was forced to retrace his steps to Grand Junction. January 1863 found Grant back where

Above: The Confederate ram *Arkansas* runs through the Union fleet off Vicksburg. Fired by the example of the *Merrimack*, the Confederates built a number of ironclad rams in an attempt to counter Federal naval supremacy. **Left:** General Ulysses Simpson Grant in a sober moment.

The Battle of Vicksburg, 1863

The Battle of Vicksburg, 1863.
For years public opinion in the
Northern States had been offended by the
survival of slavery in any part of their
country. Conversely, the Southern States
had resented attacks on a system held to
be essential to their prosperity and
integral to their whole culture. When in
1860, the Democratic Party was
defeated, most Southern leaders
determined that, if slavery were to
continue, the Union must come to an end.
Seven of the Slave States withdrew from
the Union between December 1860 and
February 1861.

The maneuvers leading to the siege of Vicksburg

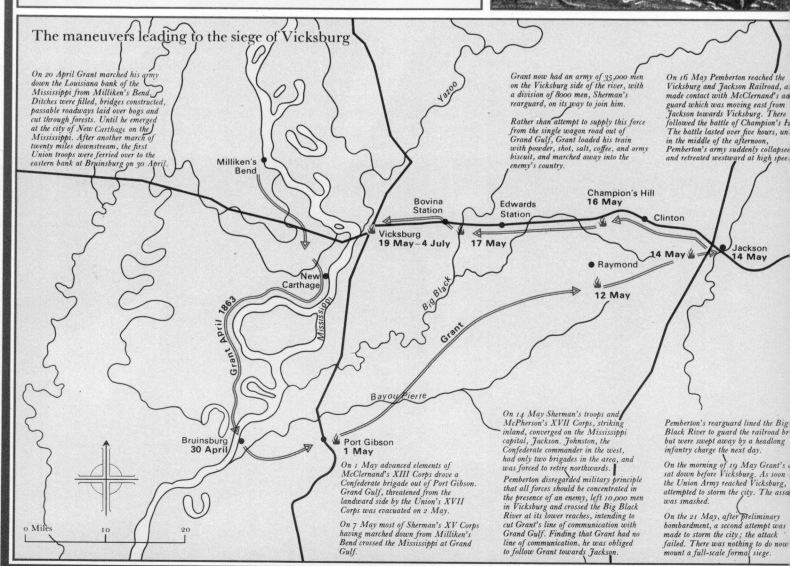

On 20 April Grant marched his army
down the Louisiana bank of the
Mississippi from Milliken's Bend.
Ditches were filled, bridges constructed,
passable roadways laid over bogs and
cut through forests. Until he emerged
at the city of New Carthage on the
Mississippi. After another march of
twenty miles downstream, the first
Union troops were ferried over to the
eastern bank at Bruinsburg on 30 April.

Grant now had an army of 35,000 men
on the Vicksburg side of the river, with
a division of 8000 men, Sherman's
rearguard, on its way to join him.

Rather than attempt to supply this force
from the single wagon road out of
Grand Gulf, Grant loaded his train
with powder, shot, salt, coffee, and army
biscuit, and marched away into the
enemy's country.

On 16 May Pemberton reached the
Vicksburg and Jackson Railroad, and
made contact with McClernand's aa
guard which was moving east from
Jackson towards Vicksburg. There
followed the battle of Champion's h
The battle lasted over five hours, un
in the middle of the afternoon,
Pemberton's army suddenly collapsed
and retreated westward at high speed

On 1 May advanced elements of
McClernand's XIII Corps drove a
Confederate brigade out of Port Gibson.
Grand Gulf, threatened from the
landward side by the Union's XVII
Corps was evacuated on 2 May.

On 7 May most of Sherman's XV Corps
having marched down from Milliken's
Bend crossed the Mississippi at Grand
Gulf.

On 14 May Sherman's troops and
McPherson's XVII Corps, striking
inland, converged on the Mississippi
capital, Jackson. Johnston, the
Confederate commander in the west,
had only two brigades in the area, and
was forced to retire northwards.

Pemberton disregarded military principle
that all forces should be concentrated in
the presence of an enemy, left 10,000 men
in Vicksburg and crossed the Big Black
River at its lower reaches, intending to
cut Grant's line of communication with
Grand Gulf. Finding that Grant had no
line of communication, he was obliged
to follow Grant towards Jackson.

Pemberton's rearguard lined the Big
Black River to guard the railroad br
but were swept away by a headlong
infantry charge the next day.

On the morning of 19 May Grant's
sat down before Vicksburg. As soon
the Union Army reached Vicksburg,
attempted to storm the city. The ass
was smashed.

On the 21 May, after preliminary
bombardment, a second attempt was
made to storm the city; the attack
failed. There was nothing to do now
mount a full-scale formal siege.

Milliken's Bend

Bovina Station

Vicksburg 19 May–4 July

17 May

Edwards Station

Champion's Hill 16 May

Clinton

14 May

Jackson 14 May

Raymond

New Carthage

12 May

Grant April 1863

Grant

Bayou Pierre

Bruinsburg 30 April

Port Gibson 1 May

0 Miles   10   20

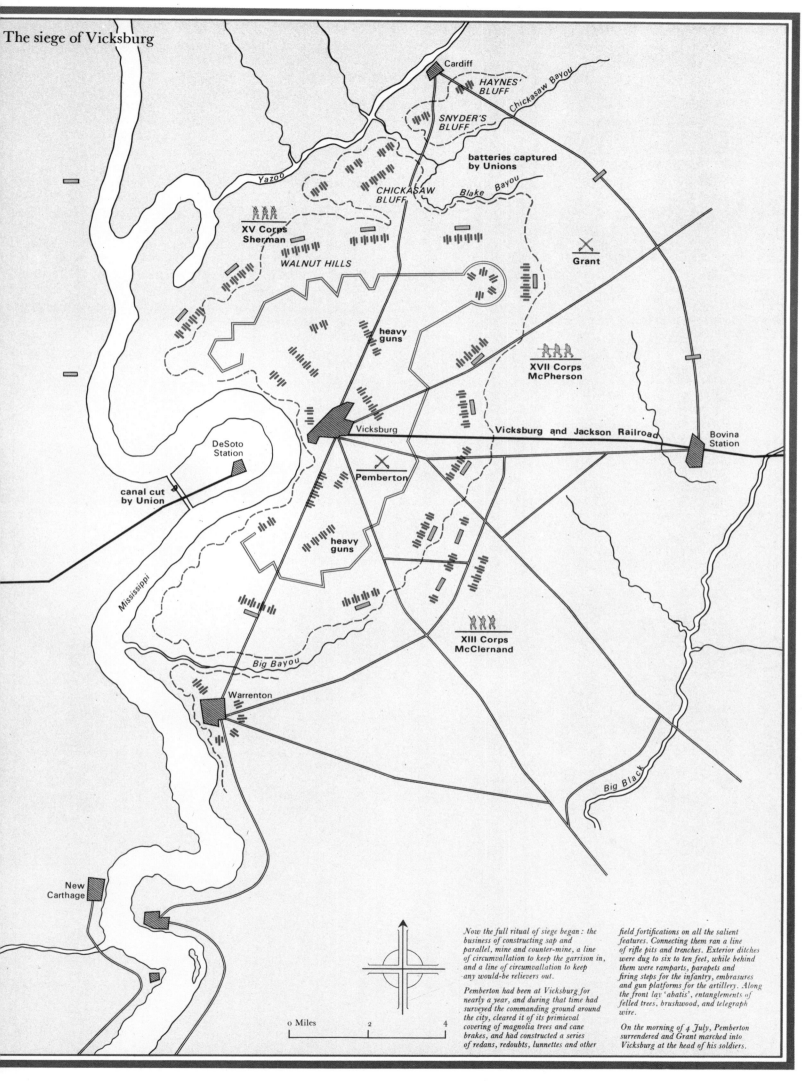

The siege of Vicksburg

Cardiff

HAYNES'
BLUFF

SNYDER'S
BLUFF

Chickasaw Bayou

batteries captured
by Unions

Yazoo

CHICKASAW
BLUFF

Blake Bayou

XV Corps
Sherman

WALNUT HILLS

Grant

heavy
guns

XVII Corps
McPherson

Vicksburg

Vicksburg and Jackson Railroad

Bovina
Station

DeSoto
Station

Pemberton

canal cut
by Union

heavy
guns

Mississippi

Big Bayou

XIII Corps
McClernand

Warrenton

Big Black

New
Carthage

0 Miles   2   4

*Now the full ritual of siege began: the
business of constructing sap and
parallel, mine and counter-mine, a line
of circumvallation to keep the garrison in,
and a line of circumvallation to keep
any would-be relievers out.*

*Pemberton had been at Vicksburg for
nearly a year, and during that time had
surveyed the commanding ground around
the city, cleared it of its primieval
covering of magnolia trees and cane
brakes, and had constructed a series
of redans, redoubts, lunnettes and other*

*field fortifications on all the salient
features. Connecting them ran a line
of rifle pits and trenches. Exterior ditches
were dug to six to ten feet, while behind
them were ramparts, parapets and
firing steps for the infantry, embrasures
and gun platforms for the artillery. Along
the front lay 'abatis', entanglements of
felled trees, brushwood, and telegraph
wire.*

*On the morning of 4 July, Pemberton
surrendered and Grant marched into
Vicksburg at the head of his soldiers.*

he had begun. The New Orleans troops had not even started, and Sherman's river expedition had failed to make any impression on either the defenders or the defenses of Vicksburg.

The natural defenses of this city were of a completely different order from anything the Union forces in the west had previously met. The Mississippi River, here well into its mature stage, swings to and fro across its flood plain for hundreds of miles above and below the city. Both banks along virtually the whole stretch are lined with mudbanks, swamps, marshes and tangled under-brush, pierced by tributaries, channels, and innumerable watercourses, large and small. There was almost no place for an army to land, nor, having landed, any clear way for it to move. At Vicksburg there were a series of high bluffs, rising some 200 feet from the waterside. These allowed firm standing at the river's edge, which was why the first settlement had been made there and why it had developed into a thriving river port with docks, wharves, and railway yards. But to attempt to land troops in the teeth of the batteries and earthworks was impossible. The river, about a half-mile wide, curved sharply and

did not allow the gunboats either to outrange the shore batteries or to outmatch them in weight of metal. The slow, unarmored transports would be sitting targets as they ran in to put the troops ashore. Any that did land would be too few to resist the inevitable counterattack.

If Vicksburg were to fall, the assault had to be made from the landward side. Sherman tried to steam along the slow, muddy Yazoo River, a tributary entering the Mississippi five miles above Vicksburg itself. At Chickasaw Bayou, a few miles upstream, he landed and tried to climb out to the Walnut Hills, a ridge of high ground connected to the Vicksburg Bluffs. On 29 December he made his move. The Confederates manned the high ground with artillery and infantry. At the base of the hills, and on their slopes, more infantry con-cealed in rifle pits poured a deadly fire on the blue-clad attackers. Trapped in a tangle of swamps and thickets, the Union soldiers floundered helplessly toward their objective, then stopped. Sherman pulled them out, with the loss of more than 1700 men. The Confederates had lost 200 at the most, and were as secure as when they had started. They watched Sherman re-embark his

troops and steam away upstream, back to his moorings at Milliken's Bend twenty miles away, where he was joined by General Grant in his headquarters steamer, the *Magnolia*.

In theory, an army on one side of a river desiring to attack an enemy on the other has only to walk along the bank until the enemy's defenses have been passed, and then cross over. In fact this was just what Grant's men could not do in the winter of 1862–63. There was no point in crossing upstream of Vicksburg, since the Yazoo still lay between them and their prize. And if they crossed the higher reaches of the Yazoo, how were they to be supplied with that river blocked by Confederate batteries at Snyder's Bluff, at the Vicksburg end? Nor could they go downstream on the Louisiana bank, because the country was so low-lying that progress was impossible until the spring.

Yet if the river was high, then its waters might be put to use, and no less than four different schemes were evolved to this end. At the most, they would result in the army getting below Vicksburg in comfort and safety. At the least, they would keep the soldiers and sailors busy, and

Right: Blacks were used to dig a canal for Federal ships, which hoped to bypass Vicksburg.

Below: The fight in the crater of Fort Hill after the explosion of the mine, 25 June, 1863.

prevent them becoming demoralized while sickness increased and repeated stories magnified the impregnable nature of Vicksburg's defenses and the disastrous repulse of Sherman's expedition.

The first plan was the simplest. Vicksburg lay in the state of Mississippi, on the outside of a hairpin bend in the river. The Union army held the narrow promontory of Louisiana soil forming the inside of the hairpin. If a canal were cut across this, then riverboats could bypass the city and the mighty Mississippi might even change its course altogether, scouring out a new channel through the canal, and reducing Vicksburg to an inland town. Several weeks hard digging ensued, encouraged by the personal interest of President Lincoln himself. The design, however, was faulty. The defenses of Vicksburg would have been quite as strong behind a muddy slough as behind a river, perhaps stronger. Furthermore the Confederates, when they saw what was intended, simply built shore batteries at Warrenton, below

the canal's planned exit, blocking the river as effectively as before. The canal entrance joined the river in a backwater, so that there was no stream to deepen the canal. Eventually, in early March, the river rose, broke through the upper dam, and covered the whole peninsula, to the discomfort of Sherman and his XV Corps, who had been engaged on the work. Stores were lost, cattle drowned, camps flooded out, and men obliged to run for their lives or take to the trees for safety.

The next plan was more ambitious. The Louisiana side of the river was low-lying and contained numerous watercourses. Fifty miles above Vicksburg lay Lake Providence, separated from the Mississippi by a levee or embankment to prevent flooding. If this were cut, boats could float for 200 miles along tributaries of the Red River, which had its origins far to the west, but joined the Mississippi above Port Hudson. A steamboat was hauled overland into the lake, but after several days exploring reported that the waterways were impassable. The abnormally high rainfall had caused more problems than it solved for the sailors, since the main channels were lost in overflow swamps, with submerged tree stumps sticking up to hole the unwary. This project too was abandoned when it became clear there was no navigation for large steamers, since there were not enough shallow draft vessels to lift the army over such a distance.

Meanwhile there were plans to find a way on the eastern bank, into the Yazoo, and behind the Confederate forts which blocked the river at Snyder's Bluff. The Yazoo and its upper tributaries, the Tallahatchie and Coldwater, formed one long stream running roughly parallel to the Mississippi, and at one time linked to it, some 200 miles above Vicksburg, by a bayou known as

Yazoo Pass. This had been closed some years before the war by a levee. The plan now suggested by Rear-Admiral David D. Porter, commanding the Mississippi Flotilla, was to cut the levee and allow the mighty Mississippi to raise the level of the Yazoo and its headwaters. Then his ships could steam down through enemy country, take all the river defenses in the rear, capture the Confederate boatyards at Yazoo City, where several large vessels were under construction, and move down to land an army on the high ground upstream of Snyder's Bluff, thus bringing it at last within reach of Vicksburg.

On 3 February, 1863 the levee was blown up and the river poured in, down a drop of eight feet or so, cutting a passage 40 yards wide. Some days elapsed before the levels were matched and the torrent slackened enough for steamboats to navigate without the risk of damage. Scarcely had the little fleet begun its passage when it was

stopped by the discovery that Confederate working parties had been that way before them. The Yazoo Pass was deep enough indeed, but it was narrow, and great trees had been felled across the waterway. It took another two weeks to clear it as far as the Coldwater River, at a time when speed was vital to the success of Union plans.

The gunboat fleet consisted of two ironclads, six shallow-draft, lightly armored 'tinclads', and two rams, with 4000 soldiers in transport steamers following close behind. The commodore, Lieutenant-Commander Watson Smith, although a brave and gallant officer, was ill-suited to this command. A professional deep-sea sailor, he hated operations where there was no room to swing, no water below his keel—indeed no keel, since he was now in flat-bottomed river boats. Moreover, he was becoming ill, and lacked both the spirit and the strength to urge on the expedition at the greatest pace. When they finally reached the junction of the Tallahatchie and the Yazoo on 10 March, it was found that the Confederates had made good use of the time. A fort of cotton bales and earth banks had been thrown up at one of the numberless hairpin bends through which the river meandered. Named Fort Pemberton in honor of the Confederate general, it was armed with field guns and three rifled cannon.

The same insoluble problem now faced Smith as faced Porter on the big river. The gunboats could not silence the batteries, and the troops could not get ashore into the flooded country above them. The two ironclads, attacking head-on, side by side down the narrow river, were riddled by the rifled guns of the fort. Smith, a dying man, handed over command to Lieutenant-Commander J. P. Foster, and went back upstream.

Foster, reinforced by another brigade of infantry, held on until 5 April, but finally had to steam back 200 miles the way he had come. He was only just in time, for the Confederates were moving troops to this river system in large numbers to cut off the entire expedition.

While these events were taking place, Admiral Porter conceived another plan. It was clear that even if Fort Pemberton fell, the Confederates were now fully aware of what was going on, and would be able to delay the advance on Yazoo City for months. Therefore he himself would take five stern-wheel ironclads, which had not gone with Smith, and try another route. This involved going up the Yazoo from the Mississippi, but, before reaching Snyder's Bluff, turning up a sluggish backwater called Steele's Bayou. An even narrower channel, Black Bayou, ran across from its higher reaches to join Deer Creek. This was a shallow and winding river, but if the fleet ascended this it could go through another bayou, Rolling Fork, and get into the Sunflower River. This flowed into the Yazoo above Snyder's Bluff, twenty miles as the crow flies from their starting point at Milliken's Bend, but two hundred miles by this river route. An infantry column led by General Sherman was ordered to march through the swamps along the banks, and the fleet started out on 14 March.

The difficulties of this route proved insurmountable even to Porter, despite his irrepressible sea-dog (or rather, river-dog) spirit. The watercourse wound in and out in tortuous serpentine bends, so that the five steamers, in line astern, at times found themselves apparently in line abreast, three going forward and two back, with narrow necks of land between them. The slightest error by the pilots, or delays by helmsmen, put them into the bank. There great trees overhung them, with branches to damage the smoke stacks, snag their guys and stays, or smash their wooden superstructures into splinters. When anxious officers reported increasing damage to their vessels' upper works, Porter told them all he required was an engine, guns, and a hull to float them. Birds' nests, fledglings, twigs and tree-rats fell from overhanging boughs in a ceaseless shower, and any sailor incautious enough to appear on deck risked being sniped at by Con-

federate marksmen or swept off by low branches. At one point, Porter's flagship with a 42-foot beam was going along a 46-foot wide waterway. Wooden bridges had to be rammed and carried away. Time after time, a gunboat would come to a halt, while her crew swarmed over the side with axes or ropes to free her. As the Union flotilla inched its way along, Confederate troops moved up to meet it, sending their pioneers ahead to fell more trees and prevent Porter from retracing his course. The forest seemed to be closing in on him, like the flesh around a healing wound.

Sherman and his men, still floundering through the swamps along Deer Creek could not come up in time to help, so Porter had to give up. He dropped back down river to the soldiers, un-shipped his rudders, and let them haul him out stern first. Cutting through the new-felled trees, and overcoming numerous obstacles, the flotilla emerged safely into the broad waters of the Mississippi on 24 March. So far, the Confederates were still winning.

It must be remembered that the vessels forming Porter's Mississippi Flotilla were quite different from those of the West Gulf Squadron operating in the lower river under Farragut. The latter were seagoing warships, steam-engined, paddle-driven, but with a high freeboard, and fitted with masts and yards to carry sails. Although restricted to the deepest part of the navigable channel, they could make reasonable headway against the strong river current, and indeed in 1862 Farragut had steamed all the way up to Vicksburg with a brigade of troops before Confederate movements lower down forced him to go back. Porter's vessels were true river boats. With fore and aft decks just above the water line, and their vulnerable boilers, steam tubes, paddle wheels and gun batteries under a high, armored, central section, they well deserved their nickname 'Turtles'. But, driven only by the type of engine designed for peaceful river traffic, they lacked the power to move upstream at anything more than snail's pace. Thus any gunboat or transport going below Vicksburg would never get back up again as long as Confederate batteries remained in place.

Below: A rare photograph of Vicksburg under Union fire during an early stage of the siege.

Grant's decision to send seven gunboats, a ram, and three cargo steamers past Vicksburg on the night of 16 April, 1863 signaled that he was fully committed to an irrevocable plan. On the 20th his army began to march down the Louisiana bank from Milliken's Bend. The river had begun to fall, and the land, although still half-drowned, allowed his scouts to find a way along which to march. Ditches were filled, bridges constructed, passable roadways laid over bogs and cut through forests. For a week they struggled on, hauling guns, wagons, and horses through the mud, and at last emerged, triumphant, at the city of New Carthage on the Mississippi. More transports had run past Vicksburg to meet them and after another march of twenty miles downstream, the first Union troops were ferried over to the eastern bank at Bruinsburg on 30 April.

This landing took the Confederates by surprise. They were still expecting the main attack to come from the north, and had been confirmed in this view by a feint attack by Sherman against Snyder's Bluff on the 28th. Meanwhile, Farragut had run his flagship and another man-of-war up past the Confederate batteries at Port Hudson, and on the 29th joined with Porter in a bombardment of Grand Gulf, a well-fortified city some fifty miles below Vicksburg, but well upstream of Bruinsburg. At the same time, 100 miles inland, in one of the most successful cavalry

raids of the war, Colonel Benjamin Grierson rode south from La Grange, Tennessee, for 400 miles through Confederate territory until he came out before the Union lines at Baton Rouge. Brushing aside attempts by scratch Confederate forces to stop him, he spread alarm and confusion all the way, burning stores and contraband, and wrecking the Mobile and Ohio Railroad as he went.

The hope that Grant could be resupplied by vessels coming upstream from Baton Rouge came to nothing. Banks, fearing that Confederate forces from northwestern Louisiana might attempt to recapture New Orleans, had moved up the Red River to meet them. He could not return to march on Port Hudson, the lowest Confederate stronghold on the Mississippi, until the middle of May. And Port Hudson was strong enough to stop any cargo-boat, for it had stopped most of Farragut's deep-water warships, sinking one, and turning back all except his flagship and one other. No more supplies were coming down from Milliken's Bend, for the Vicksburg gunners had improved with practice, and several Union supply steamers and coal barges had by now been sunk or driven ashore.

But Grant was not to be stopped. The previous year his army had lived very well from commandeered supplies, as it retreated after the Confederate cavalry had cut its supply lines. Now, marching through the same type of well-stocked

countryside, it would do so as a deliberate act of policy. Moreover, the citizens of Mississippi would supply not only meat, poultry, vegetables and forage, but also vehicles and cattle for the army's train. An army living off the country needed few wagons to carry its food, but an army meaning to fight needed a great many to carry its munitions, and most of Grant's military train was still plowing its way along the Louisiana road to New Carthage, as working parties strove desperately to repair and improve the highway. To take its place, the bluecoat soldiers rounded up everything on wheels within their reach, from tumbrils and hay-carts to the finely-made sprung coaches of plantation owners. Teams of mules, oxen, draft and carriage horses were harnessed up with ropes or whatever tackle could be found, providing the army with the mobility it needed if it was to exploit the enemy's surprise.

On 1 May advanced elements of Major-General John A. McClernand's XIII Corps drove a Confederate brigade out of Port Gibson. Grand Gulf, threatened from the landward side by the Union's XVII Corps was evacuated on 2 May, and its defenders joined the Confederate forces sent from Vicksburg to hold the line of the Big Black River. On 7 May most of Sherman's XV Corps, having marched down from Milliken's Bend, crossed the river at Grand Gulf. Grant now had an army of 35,000 men on the Vicksburg side of the river, with a division of 8000 men, Sherman's rearguard, on its way to join him.

Rather than attempt to supply this force from the single wagon road out of Grand Gulf, Grant loaded his motley train with powder, shot, salt, coffee, and army biscuit, and marched away into the enemy's country. On 14 May Sherman's troops and Major-General James B. McPherson's XVII Corps, striking inland, converged on the Mississippi state capital, Jackson. General Joseph E. Johnston, the Confederate commander in the west, had only two brigades in the area, and was forced to retire northward. Nevertheless, Confederate reinforcements were on the way from the

east. Joe Johnston would have 15,000 men available in a few days, and another 9000 in a week. He sent word to Lieutenant-General John C. Pemberton, commanding the Confederate Military Department of Mississippi, to add the garrisons of Vicksburg and Port Hudson to his field army and march to form, with Johnston, a combined Confederate force of about 50,000 men. But Pemberton, although under Johnston's command, had orders from President Jefferson Davis that Vicksburg and Port Hudson were to be garrisoned at all times. Therefore, in disregard of the military principle that forces should be concentrated in the presence of an enemy, he left 10,000 men in Vicksburg, and crossed the Big Black River at its lower reaches, intending to cut Grant's lines of communication with Grand Gulf. Finding that Grant too had ignored military convention by having no lines of communication, he was obliged to follow Grant toward Jackson. On 16 May he reached the line of the Vicksburg and Jackson Railroad, and made contact with McClernand's advance

guard which was moving east from Jackson toward Vicksburg. There followed the battle of Champion's Hill, one of the most hard-fought conflicts of this campaign. The tide of battle swayed to and fro for more than five hours, until suddenly, in the middle of the afternoon, Pemberton's army collapsed and retreated westward at high speed. The Confederates lost 6000 men, killed, wounded or captured, out of 23,000, and 27 guns out of 60. Grant had suffered severe losses too, amounting to more than 400 killed, and nearly 2000 wounded.

Grant Held the Field

But Grant held the battlefield. Pemberton succumbed to the temptation to retire behind his defenses, rather than escape northward and join Joe Johnston. His rearguard lined the Big Black River to guard the railroad bridge, but were swept away by a headlong infantry charge the next day, losing another 1700 men and eighteen guns captured. On the morning of 19 May Grant's Army

Left: The USS *Indianola* runs the gauntlet of Confederate batteries at Vicksburg in February 1863 to join the *Queen of the West.*

sat down before Vicksburg. Sherman led his men up the abandoned landward slopes of the hills he had attempted to take from Chickasaw Bayou the previous December. Snyder's Bluff and the adjacent strong-point, Haynes' Bluff, fell after a short engagement. Porter's supply vessels steamed up the Yazoo to reconnect the army with its base. Grant's risky but calculated gamble had paid off handsomely.

Indeed, as Sherman told him, Grant would have scored a major victory even if Vicksburg held out. Within twenty days of crossing at Bruinsburg his army had captured the state capital, destroyed vast quantities of strategic supplies, and had marched about for 180 miles in enemy territory, in a countryside so cut up by ravines, thickets, and canebrakes as to make it perfect for defense. It had fought five major engagements, had captured 61 fieldpieces and 27 heavier guns, and taken prisoner more than 6000 enemy soldiers. It had done all this on five days' official rations, and at a loss of only 2000 killed or missing and 7400 wounded, out of the 43,000 men who crossed the river. And now this army was in reach of Vicksburg.

It was in no mood to hesitate. The Union army had seen its opponents fleeing in panic before it and as soon as it reached Vicksburg, attempted to follow them into the defenses and take the place by storm. Grant soon realized he had misjudged the defenders' morale. Ten thousand of them had not been involved in the recent fighting, and were determined to show that they would not be panicked. The Federal assault was smashed. Grant paused to reconsider. Two days later, after a preliminary bombardment, he tried again, only to be driven back with heavier casualties. Pemberton's men had obviously regained their nerve. Grant had suffered 1000 casualties in the first assault, and 3000 in the second.

There was nothing to do now but mount a full-scale formal siege. Grant's soldiers did not welcome the prospect; they had spent a winter digging canals, and with the joyous dash across the river had felt they had at last exchanged the pick and shovel for the rifle. Now the realization came that all three implements had their proper place in the soldier's armory. The failure of the two assaults proved to the men that they were, despite their recent success, not invincible, and that a determined, well-defended enemy had to be treated with proper caution.

Now the full ritual of a siege began, as elaborate, predictable and formal in its procedures as the steps of a courtly dance: the business of constructing sap and parallel, mine and counter-mine, a line of circumvallation to keep the garrison in, and a line of countervallation to keep any would-be relievers out. As the pioneers and sappers sweated and dug, the infantry exchanged shots from rifle pits and trenches, or over parapets. Sometimes the two sides were near enough to throw hand grenades at each other. Sometimes, by a strange camaraderie in this sad war between brothers, men exchanged not bombs, but conversation, gibes, news, or even Confederate tobacco for Yankee 'hard-tack' biscuits.

The siege resolved itself into a duel between the skill and cunning of the opposing chief engineers, Captain F.E. Prime, succeeded by Captain Cyrus B. Comstock, United States Corps of Engineers, and Colonel H.S. Lockett, Confederate States Engineers. The Union forces, in fact, were short of trained military engineers. Some of Grant's troops came from the urban eastern seaboard. A few others came from the far western frontier, but the vast majority came from the Midwest agricultural area, the very region whose prosperity depended on the opening of the Mississippi and the fall of Vicksburg. Nearly all were wartime volunteer units, for the small US Regular Army

was either with the Army of the Potomac, or still in its peacetime location, deployed against the bands of Indians who threatened the outlying settlements. These volunteer soldiers brought with them ample skills from their peacetime occupations to meet all the needs Grant had for pioneers and field engineers, as their recent feats as road builders and canal cutters had proved. But what they lacked were the esoteric skills of the siege engineer. Grant, remembering his days as a cadet on the banks of the Hudson, recalled that West Point had taught future regular officers the rudiments of siege engineering, and therefore ordered every West Point graduate in his army to report to the four regular Engineer Corps officers, to act as assistant engineers.

During a truce called to bury the Union dead of 19 and 22 May, both chief engineers took the chance to view their enemy's works. Lockett was greeted by Sherman himself, who handed over some private letters to be delivered to Vicksburg addresses. After some courteous exchanges, Lockett found that Sherman detained him in conversation, each politely complimenting the other on their engineers' prowess. Sherman's unwonted civility served a useful military end, for the Confederate engineer complained in his memoirs that he was thus prevented from viewing a number of points he wished to see.

For all his Southern politeness, Lockett had prepared a vigorous reception for his Yankee visitors. He had been at Vicksburg for nearly a year, and during that time had surveyed the commanding ground around the city, cleared it of its primeval covering of magnolia trees and canebrakes and, using slaves to shift great quantities of earth, had constructed a series of redans, redoubts, lunnettes, and other field fortifications on all the salient features. A line of rifle pits and trenches connected them. When Pemberton and his field army were

driven in by Grant, fatigue parties were at once sent off to repair and strengthen the works. Exterior ditches were deepened to six or ten feet, while behind them were ramparts, parapets and firing steps for the infantry, embrasures and gun-platforms for the artillery. Along the front lay *abatis*, entanglements of felled trees, brushwood, and telegraph wire.

During the siege work went on behind the lines. Covered ways were built to foil the Union sharpshooters. New traverses were constructed, damage repaired, guns shifted to fresh positions, retrenchments, or inner lines, thrown up, and every effort was made to foil the slow but steady approach of the besiegers' lines.

On the Union side, the conventional techniques of siege warfare were carefully employed. At dusk, sappers went out in a line pointing like a finger toward the heart of the enemy position. Each man, with pick, shovel, and wickerwork *gabion* for protection against snipers, stopped five feet from his neighbor, and then began to dig. Before daylight each had covered his own foxhole with the *gabion*, and burrowed through to link up with his neighbor. During the day other working parties, usually provided by the infantry, widened and deepened the new portion of the sap, and further improved the rear sections—some of which could accommodate men marching in columns of fours. The next night the whole process was repeated. To prevent the defenders shooting down the sap in enfilade, sap-rollers filled with cotton were pushed ahead. After Confederate exploding bullets had set fire to the cotton, care was taken to see it remained damp.

So the siege went on, lengthening from days to weeks. In the middle of June, the call went out in the Union lines for any men who had worked in coal mines. From the most experienced of these a detachment of 36 miners was formed, under Lieu-

Below: The Federal monitor *Ozark* on the Mississippi in 1864. The bare outline of the original *Monitor* has been cluttered with the superstructure and deck fittings of a conventional warship. By this time the Mississippi had been entirely cleared from source to mouth.

tenant Russell of the 7th Missouri Infantry and Sergeant Morris of the 32nd Ohio. On the night of 22 June, the head of the flying-sap (the rapidly-dug night work) reached the wall of a redan held by the 3rd Louisiana Infantry. Confederate counter-mines were started to try and get under the sap, but the Union miners dug into the wall and sank a series of galleries into the earth below the fort. By the 25th the mine was fully dug. More than a ton of gunpowder was carried on the miners' backs, in 25-pound grain sacks, run across the open space between the sap head and the mine entrance, and then packed away below, tamped down with earth from the diggings.

The mine was exploded, blowing up the redan and leaving a breach into which poured men of the 31st and 45th Illinois Infantry. The 3rd Louisiana rushed to plug the gap, and 30 men in the storming parties went down before a hail of musketry. Nevertheless enough ground was held for another mine to be dug, and a further explosion of equal power, on 1 July, demolished the rest of the redan. This time the Union troops did not attack, but poured in such a storm of missiles that the Confederate pioneers found that as fast as they shovelled in earth from either side, it was blasted out again by Yankee fire power. Lockett himself was on hand to supervise their work, having narrowly escaped death in the explosion, as he had just been inspecting the Confederate mines.

These countermines, so close to the Union galleries that men could hear the orders and conversation of their foes through the earth, were collapsed by the concussion, or blown into the air. One black man was carried upwards by the blast and, incredibly, survived, coming down unhurt inside the Union lines. At length Lockett sent for tents and canvas wagon covers, had them filled with earth under cover, and gradually pushed the giant 'sausages' across to seal the gap. But nearly 100 Confederates had been killed or wounded by the explosion or the subsequent firing, and the Federal hold drew tighter around Vicksburg.

That other branch of siege warfare, the artillery, required as much improvization as the engineers. Grant's siege train consisted of six 32-pounders, and there was not another siege gun to

be had in the whole of the West. However, the Navy supplied a heavy battery manned by sailors, and the army's field guns were pressed into service, despite their lack of range and accuracy, so that by 30 June there were 220 guns in position against the city. The flat trajectory of the field pieces prevented full use being made of their power. Shells either flew over the parapets to burst inside the defenses, which were built of the thick red clay of which the Vicksburg Bluffs consisted, or else dropped short, to the annoyance of the Union infantry in their trenches. To drop bombs just inside the ramparts, mortars were made, by selecting logs of suitable length and diameter, boring out a tube, binding them with iron hoops, and then using a reduced charge to lob six- or twelve-pound shells into the enemy's positions.

The Confederate artillery had its own problems. Field and garrison guns together numbered 102, but, like most armies under siege, ammunition was limited and could not be replenished. Either in order to conserve ammunition against an assault, or because they had been dismounted by Union bombardment, the Confederate guns fell silent for long periods, allowing the besiegers to dominate the ground before them.

The river batteries, stripped of their land-service guns, but still well armed with coastal artillery pieces, continued a stout resistance. Union bomb schooners, each mounting a thirteen-inch mortar throwing a 200-pound projectile, kept up an incessant fire, day and night, joined from time to time by gun-boats from the flotilla. Good shooting by the Confederates sank the ironclad *Cincinnati*, but heavy naval guns mounted in scows established themselves opposite Vicksburg, enfilading part of the defense line and causing it to be abandoned.

Other gun-boats, accompanied by an infantry division, went up the Yazoo, past the abandoned defenses where the ironclad *Cairo* had gone down the previous November, and so on up to Yazoo City. There, Union soldiers burned anything left unscorched by its retreating garrison, while the gun-boats chased Confederate vessels up the narrow channels and backwaters where the expeditions had failed during the winter.

Within the walls of Vicksburg, men began to realize that there was no prospect of relief. Johnston had been able to scrape together a bare 30,000 men. Southern railroads had been somewhat inadequate even before the war. Now, with spares and raw materials cut off by the Union blockade, they could not cope with the wear and tear of ordinary traffic, increased as it was by military requirements. Far less could they repair the damage caused by Union raiders. Sherman's men, before evacuating Jackson, had devastated tracks, rolling stock, and railroad installations of every kind, rendering it useless to the Confederates as a communications center. Lee had refused to march west to help, and had told Davis frankly that he must risk losing either Mississippi or Virginia. Early in June, therefore, Confederate soldiers were marching not west, but north, where they would find their enemy at Gettysburg. Grant, on the other hand, was receiving massive reinforcements. From 43,000 at the end of May, his army grew to 72,000 by the middle of June. He even spoke of letting Johnston through into Vicksburg and increasing the number of future prisoners by 30,000. The only attempt by the Confederates to interfere on the Louisiana side was made on 7 June, when 3000 of them attacked the small garrison left at Milliken's Bend, but they were soon driven off.

Trench Warfare

Outside Vicksburg, Grant's men suffered the discomforts and boredom of trench warfare. All winter they had been frozen or wet through, up the river. Now they were baked in the 20,000 yards of dusty trenches, parched with thirst, unable to wash, and enduring the lot of anyone rash enough to fight in the Southern summer.

Inside, the situation was far worse. The besiegers, amply supplied, poured in musketry and artillery fire without a break. The defenders, husbanding their ammunition, made little reply. Food ran short. Mule stew, roast rat and cane shoots became desirable delicacies. Coffee gave out and was replaced by an ersatz brew of yams and blackberry leaves. As a substitute for flour, ground peas and cornmeal were issued. Soldiers became too weak to do more than man their positions. Union saps had reached the walls in a dozen places, and soon the numerical superiority of the attackers would enable them to swarm over in irresistible strength. Expedients such as the preparation of fougasses or the rolling down of fused artillery shells could only delay the inevitable.

On the night of 2 July Pemberton called a council of war. He told the officers present that there was no hope of relief, nor any hope that the garrison could cut its way out. The question was—surrender or not. Beginning with the junior officer present, according to military custom, the vote was taken. All except two voted to surrender while there was still a chance of making terms. Pemberton accepted the verdict. At 1000 on 3 July white flags were run up in the Confederate lines and a party went out under a flag of truce to parley.

At first Grant would offer nothing but his famous formula 'unconditional surrender', promising only that the garrison would receive the conventional respect due to prisoners of war who had fought bravely and endured much. At 1500 Pemberton came out, and the opposing commanders met face to face. They had little to say to each other, but their staff kept the talks going, and it was eventually agreed that Grant would send in his final terms in a letter at 2200. Meanwhile the ceasefire extended all along the front, and men on both sides had left their lines to gossip with their opponents. Both armies had recruited units from Missouri, a state claimed by North and South alike. Here was literally a case where families had been divided by the Civil War, but for a time several brothers and numerous cousins, Blue and Grey, met each other without rancor.

Grant eventually offered a concession. If Vicksburg surrendered, the garrison would be disarmed and released on parole, not to fight again in the war unless duly exchanged for a Union prisoner of war. Officers would be allowed to keep their sidearms, and mounted officers their horses. Personal baggage, rations, and clothing could be retained, but nothing else. Civilians would be protected, but no guarantee could be given about their property, including slaves. Thus he set the pattern for another surrender that he would take at Appomattox Court House. Years afterwards he wrote of Vicksburg, 'The men had fought so well that I did not want to humiliate them. I believed that consideration for their feelings would make them less dangerous foes during the continuance of hostilities, and better citizens after the war was over'.

So, on the morning of 4 July, Pemberton surrendered and Grant marched into Vicksburg at the head of his victorious soldiers. There was no cheering, no victory parade, merely the businesslike work of taking over strongpoints, stores, and munitions. The defenders gave up 172 pieces of artillery and 60,000 small-arms, most of the latter being new Enfield muzzle-loading rifles, brought in by blockade-runners. These were better arms than many of Grant's regiments carried, and he authorized all colonels of units equipped with old US or Belgian muskets, or more modern, but nonstandard calibre pieces, to exchange them for the captured weapons.

Southern apologists have tried to minimize the extent of the disaster. The Mississippi could still be crossed, for there was only one Union steamboat to patrol every ten miles of river, and only fifty places for them to be based. Confederate guerrillas, equipped with light artillery, could still harry passing traffic. The trans-Mississippi states had provided few supplies to the eastern states and were more of a liability than an asset.

Yet Jefferson Davis had tied his own prestige to the proposition that Vicksburg was impregnable. The propaganda effect of its fall was considerable. The South lost 30,000 men and arms it could ill afford. Port Hudson, which had been besieged by the Union troops from New Orleans since 26 May, surrendered on 9 July, on hearing the news of Vicksburg's fall. A week later the riverboat *Imperial* arrived at New Orleans, having steamed for a thousand miles from St Louis without hindrance. The Confederate stranglehold on the trade and traffic of the Mississippi had been broken. Lincoln, translating the river's Indian name, pronounced the epilogue: 'The Father of Waters again goes unvexed to the sea.'

Gettysburg

1863

Gettysburg, rightly termed 'the greatest battle ever fought on the American continent', was the climax of General Robert E. Lee's invasions of the North in the summer of 1863. It was also, in a sense, the climax of the American Civil War as a whole. In May the Confederate Army of Northern Virginia had defeated 'Fighting Joe' Hooker at Chancellorsville, a victory marred by the accidental death of Lee's ablest lieutenant, General 'Stonewall' Jackson. Within the next two months, however, the balance of the war was to swing against the Confederacy. In the west Major-General Ulysses S. Grant's successful attack on Vicksburg gave Union forces control of the Mississippi Valley. There were other Union successes further west, at Alexandria and Port Jackson, while in Tennessee the Confederates were forced back to Chattanooga. It was at Gettysburg,

though, that the major clash occurred, between Lee's Army of Northern Virginia and the main Union force, the Army of the Potomac.

Lee's army was reorganized into three corps following Chancellorsville. The methodical Lieutenant-General James Longstreet—Lee called him 'my old warhorse'—commanded I Corps, while the newly-promoted Lieutenant-Generals Richard Ewell and A.P. Hill led II and III Corps respectively. Ewell had lost a leg at Groveton nine months previously; suitably equipped with a wooden one, he remained cheery and popular. The red-bearded Hill was one of Lee's most pugnacious generals, with a good record as a divisional commander. Lee himself was a general of remarkable ability. A regular colonel on the outbreak of war, Lee had reluctantly accepted command of the forces of his native state, Virginia.

Far left: General Robert E. Lee, commander of Confederate forces at Gettysburg, who held off the Army of the Potomac for four years in Virginia and Maryland. **Left:** An early portrayal of Ulysses S. Grant, Lee's protagonist in the last stages of the war in Virginia, who was besieging Vicksburg at the time of the Gettysburg campaign.

Below: The slaughter at the Battle of Gettysburg, the most decisive conflict of the Civil War.

Above: Confederate winter quarters at Manassas, Virginia in March 1862. Manassas was the site of the First Battle of Bull Run, which gave the Union a healthy respect for Southern fighting skill and strength.

General Winfield Scott, who at the time commanded the Union armies, thought that the loss of Lee was equal to that of 50,000 veterans. In June 1861 Lee was appointed chief military adviser to the Confederate President Jefferson Davis, and a year later he took over command of the Army of Northern Virginia. The gentlemanly, courteous Lee had a record of almost uninterrupted success behind him when he moved north in June 1863. His 70,000 men, although fewer in number than their opponents, and in most respects miserably ill-equipped, were in excellent spirits, with no doubt of their ability to inflict yet another defeat upon the Army of the Potomac.

Lee's strategic aim was threefold. He sought to engage Hooker in a major battle, hoping that another defeat would weaken Union resolve to continue the war, and would increase the Confederacy's chance of recognition by foreign powers. Secondary motives for the invasion were the hopes of reducing Grant's pressure on Vicksburg, and of acquiring much-needed equipment and supplies in the North.

On 3 June Lee left his position on the south bank of the Rappahannock and set out for Culpepper. Once there he swung north, with Ewell's corps leading, followed by Longstreet and Hill. Ewell took Winchester on 15 June, after roughly handling a Union defending force. Hooker, meanwhile, was marching parallel to Lee, keeping his army between Lee and Washington.

Lee naturally intended to use his cavalry under the dashing Major-General J.E.B. Stuart to screen his advance, and ordered Stuart to cross the Potomac and station himself to Ewell's north and west. Stuart left two of his brigades to cover the passes through the Blue Ridge mountains to Lee's right rear, and set off with the remaining three, intending to ride right around Hooker's army, and then to move north to join Ewell. But Stuart found the going much harder than he had anticipated, and he was out of contact with Lee for eight days from 25 June onwards, thus depriving Lee of 'the eyes of his army'.

Ewell's corps was by now dispersed on a thirty-mile front, between Carlisle and York, gathering supplies. Hill was moving through the mountains in the Cashtown area, with Longstreet to his rear at Chambersburg. Lee had already ordered Ewell to cross the Susquehanna and take Harrisburg, when, on the evening of 25 June, he received some alarming news. One of Longstreet's scouts reported that the Union Army, after concentrating at Frederick, had moved rapidly northward on the front Emmitsburg-Westminster. Nor was this new energy accidental; Hooker, after yet another disagreement with President Lincoln, had been replaced by Major-General George Meade.

Lee at once set about driving his army west of Gettysburg. Unfortunately, with Stuart miles away to the east, he had no accurate intelligence of Meade's movements. On the evening of 30 July Hill's leading divisional commander, Heth, asked Hill for permission to march to Gettysburg next morning to obtain some shoes which he had heard were stored there. Hill cheerfully gave permission; there were some Union cavalry in the town, but he attached no particular significance to their

presence; Heth's infantry, he thought, should be able to dislodge them quickly enough.

The cavalry in question were, in fact, two brigades of Major-General John Buford's 1st Cavalry Division. Buford, a capable and experienced officer, realized that there were sizable Confederate forces in the area. On the night of 30 June/1 July he sent this intelligence back to Major-General John Reynolds, whose I Corps was encamped to the south. Reynolds relayed the information back to Meade, who responded by ordering Reynolds to move to Gettysburg at dawn to support Buford's cavalry.

At 0800 on 1 July Buford's scouts made contact with Heth's, in skirmishes on the Cashtown Road. Heth rapidly deployed two of his four brigades, sent forward some artillery, and attacked. Buford's cavalrymen, fighting dismounted, gave a good account of themselves, supported by one battery of guns. It was clear, however, that the cavalry could not hold on indefinitely in the face of growing Confederate pressure.

To Buford's rear was the small town of Gettysburg, from which roads radiated like the spokes of a wheel. On his immediate left was the Hagerstown Road, with the Emmitsburg Road to its south. Running into Gettysburg from due south was the Taneytown Road, with the Baltimore Pike on its right. The Carlisle and Harrisburg Roads ran north and northeast respectively, with the York and Hanover Roads running east. The main features of the terrain were two ridges, running more or less parallel, north to south. Seminary Ridge, so called from a Lutheran

Above: J.E.B. Stuart, the most daring cavalry commander of the Civil War, leads his men on a reconnaissance mission. **Left:** General James Longstreet, whom Lee called 'my old warhorse', commanded I Corps at Gettysburg.

149

seminary near the town, stood west of Gettysburg, immediately behind Buford's position. Due south of the town ran Cemetery Ridge, with Cemetery Hill at its northern end, and Culp's Hill to its northeast. At the southern end of Cemetery Ridge were two distinctive hills, Big and Little Round Tops. Just west of Little Round Top, in the valley of a small stream, Plum Run, was a rough, boulder-strewn area known as Devil's Den.

Gettysburg was thus amply provided with roads, and, on the morning of 1 July, the rival armies percolated down them into the fighting. Although both Lee and Meade were quite pre-

pared to fight, Gettysburg was in no sense a planned battle; once initial contact had been made both sides simply concentrated on Gettysburg as quickly as possible.

Reynolds was nearing Gettysburg at the head of his leading formation, Wadsworth's division, when he heard the sound of gunfire. Ordering Wadsworth to press on cross-country, he galloped forward, and conferred briefly with Buford at the seminary. Wadsworth's men checked the Confederate advance, and then briskly counterattacked, badly cutting up one of Heth's brigades. Reynolds himself was killed soon after this counterattack started, and fresh Confederate troops, Pender's division of Hill's corps, arrived, forcing Wadsworth onto the defensive. Doubleday's division of I Corps in turn came into action, soon followed by Major-General Oliver Howard's XI Corps. The Confederates were also being reinforced rapidly, with Rodes' division of Ewell's Corps advancing against Gettysburg from the northeast.

The battle was well under way before either Lee or Meade was fully aware of its significance. Lee arrived on the field while Heth's initial attack was in progress, but it took him some time to sanction the commitment of Pender's division. Meade was at Taneytown, a few miles south of Gettysburg. Deciding that he must remain there to concentrate his army, he sent Major-General Winfield Scott Hancock of II Corps forward, ordering him to take command of all Union troops engaged, and authorizing him to fight or withdraw as he thought fit. Hancock was well suited to this difficult task; he was tough, level-headed, and popular with the troops.

Lee sent Pender's division forward when he saw Rodes attack from the northeast. Howard's XI Corps managed to get into line at Doubleday's left, on the axis of the Carlisle road, in time to meet Rodes' attack, but at this point another of Ewell's divisions, under the vinegary Jubal Early, deployed down the Harrisburg road. Despite the hammering it had received at Chancellorsville, and its low reputation in the Army of the Potomac, XI Corps fought well, but it suffered heavily and was forced back through Gettysburg. The collapse of XI Corps necessitated the withdrawal of I Corps, and, accompanied by some very vicious fighting along the western slopes of Seminary Ridge, Doubleday fell back onto Cemetery Hill. As daylight faded the two battered Union corps reorganized on Cemetery Hill. Hancock decided to stay and fight, believing that a withdrawal would imply a Confederate victory, and knowing that reinforcements, in the shape of Major-General Henry Slocum's XII Corps and Major-General Daniel Sickles' III Corps, were close at hand.

On the Confederate side, Lee authorized Early to attack Cemetery Hill if he considered it practicable. Early eventually decided against an attack, and was supported in this view by Ewell, who arrived on the scene with his third division, Johnson's, shortly before nightfall. Early's failure to attack Cemetery Hill has been severely criticized. It is likely that an attack, launched at about 1600, could have succeeded; the loss of Cemetery Hill would have compromised I and

Sedan 1940: Breakthrough

The concept of breaking an enemy's front by direct assault has little to recommend it in terms of subtlety. It has, however, proved a useful means of attaining victory, though its successful employment has tended to depend upon the technical superiority of the attacker. In May 1940 the Germans used the tactics of blitzkrieg against the Allies who, beset by an essentially defensive strategy, spread their strength too widely. The main weight of the German blow was delivered by Rundstedt's Army Group A which, spearheaded by seven panzer divisions, crashed through the Ardennes and broke the Allied line at Sedan on the Meuse. A rapid Allied collapse followed as the panzers pressed on into France; reaching the Channel near Boulogne, they cut the Allied armies in half. The British, together with numerous French, were evacuated from Dunkirk, but France, paralyzed by the defeat, capitulated in mid-June. Blitzkrieg depended for its success upon the mobility and striking power of the panzers and *Luftwaffe*; it also relied upon the moral collapse of the defenders. It was used, again with considerable success, against Russia in the summer of 1941, but thereafter its results became less assured, and a German attempt to achieve an armored breakthrough at Kursk in July 1943 proved an expensive failure.

The tactics which won the 1940 campaign were revolutionary only in their technical ingredients, armor and air power. The concept of smashing the enemy's front is as old as warfare itself; indeed, the prime tactic of the armored horseman of medieval times was the charge *en masse*, usually directed at a weak point in the enemy's battle-line. Such a charge usually proved successful if the cavalry came to handstrokes with the opposing infantry, but the supremacy of the armored horseman was eroded by English longbowmen, Turkish horse-archers, Swiss pikemen and ultimately by the rise of firearms.

Many of the battles fought in the 17th and 18th centuries developed into mere slogging-matches in which lines of infantry exchanged murderous volleys while cavalry sought to find an opening for decisive action. Even the Duke of Marlborough's great victory at Blenheim (1704) exhibited little tactical sophistication. It was Napoleon who reintroduced conclusive means of breaking his enemy's front. He did so by concentrating his artillery against a selected point and smashing a breach through which his *masse de décision* would surge. Austerlitz was not the typical Napoleonic battle; Eylau, Wagram, Borodino and Waterloo, where the French artillery was massed in great batteries, and a tactical decision was sought by combined-arms assaults following preparation by the guns, are more indicative of the techniques which characterized the Emperor's battles. Such techniques were not always fruitful; at Borodino the bombardment proved less effective than had been expected, and the assault stuck fast in the face of staunch Russian resistance, while at Waterloo Wellington's skillfully-deployed forces offered a poor target for the French cannon, many of whose rounds were harmlessly absorbed by the damp ground.

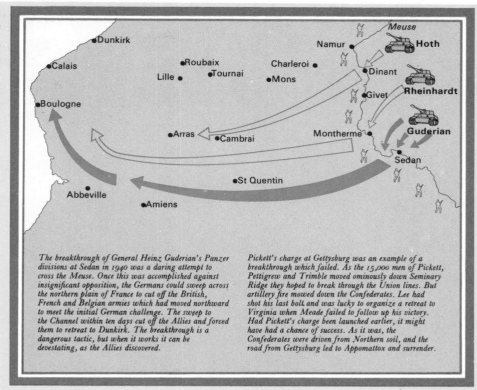

The breakthrough of General Heinz Guderian's Panzer divisions at Sedan in 1940 was a daring attempt to cross the Meuse. Once this was accomplished against insignificant opposition, the Germans could sweep across the northern plain of France to cut off the British, French and Belgian armies which had moved northward to meet the initial German challenge. The sweep to the Channel within ten days cut off the Allies and forced them to retreat to Dunkirk. The breakthrough is a dangerous tactic, but when it works it can be devastating, as the Allies discovered.

Pickett's charge at Gettysburg was an example of a breakthrough which failed. As the 15,000 men of Pickett, Pettigrew and Trimble moved down Seminary Ridge they hoped to break through the Union lines. But artillery fire mowed down the Confederates. Lee had shot his last bolt and was lucky to organize a retreat to Virginia when Meade failed to follow up his victory. Had Pickett's charge been launched earlier, it might have had a chance of success. As it was, the Confederates were driven from Northern soil, and the road from Gettysburg led to Appomattox and surrender.

As the 19th century went on, so the increased power of artillery gave new hope to generals who sought to achieve breakthrough on the Napoleonic pattern, but, as the Confederates discovered at Gettysburg and the Prussians at Saint-Privat, infantry armed with rifled weapons could inflict frightful casualties upon an attacker unless the assault had been meticulously prepared by shell-fire. Once infantry had realized that the spade was more important than the bayonet it became almost impossible for attackers to achieve a clean breakthrough, however powerful their artillery; the Battle of the Somme illustrated the strength of defense in depth against heavy bombardment and determined infantry assault. The German March Offensive of 1918 employed infiltration and a hurricane bombardment with considerable success, but it was the tank which provided the real answer to linear defense based upon barbed wire and trench-systems.

In the interwar years the Germans correctly assessed the importance of the tank supported by the dive bomber, and the breakthrough at Sedan in May 1940 was the price which the Allies paid for tactical obsolescence. There have, however, been suggestions that the postwar development of anti-tank weapons has rendered the tank itself obsolete. The major powers continue, nevertheless, to place great reliance upon armor; NATO forces in Germany face the specter of a Warsaw Pact blitzkrieg, supported by chemical and nuclear weapons, which could, so its authors believe, bring Soviet tanks to the channel coast within a week of its commencement. The concept of breakthrough, old though it may be, remains, in the opinion of many military authorities, viable. It remains to be seen, however, whether the tactical wheel has not once more come full circle and provided the defender with weapons which would enable him to halt an armored onslaught as firmly as the German machine guns checked British infantry on the Somme.

XI Corps, and made the eventual Union position untenable.

Lee conferred with Longstreet on Seminary Ridge after dark. The latter's troops were still on the march, but Longstreet himself was certain enough what they should do when they arrived. Lee announced his intention of attacking next morning, and proposed to move Ewell to the right to do so. Longstreet strongly disagreed, advocating instead a broad swing to the south, round the Union left flank and into the Union rear. Lee, however, had no idea of the whereabouts of the bulk of Meade's army, and such a move could end in disaster if it was itself outflanked by fresh troops. Once again, the absence of Stuart had a fatal influence on Confederate decision-making; supplied with accurate intelligence of Meade's movements, Lee would probably have carried out the plan suggested by Longstreet. The discussion ended with Lee gesturing towards Cemetery Ridge, stating forcefully that 'The enemy is there and I am going to attack him'. Longstreet rode back to his corps, dispirited; his dejection and irritation at Lee's decision were to have an important influence on the battle.

Ewell rode to Lee's headquarters later that night, with the news that Johnson's patrols had found Culp's Hill unoccupied. Ewell had been strangely indecisive during the latter part of 1 July, but by now he had recovered his composure. He suggested an attack on Culp's Hill, with the intention of placing artillery there to dominate Cemetery Hill and dislodge Union forces from it. Lee at once agreed. Such an attack, launched simultaneously with an assault against Cemetery Ridge from the west, seemed to offer a good chance of inflicting a decisive defeat on Meade. Unfortunately for Lee, Johnson's patrols were wrong. Culp's Hill was occupied in strength by XII Corps; its capture lay beyond Ewell's power.

Meade Arrives
Meade himself arrived on the field shortly after midnight. He confirmed Hancock's decision to stand and fight, aided by the knowledge that, with the exception of Major-General John Sedgewick's VI Corps, all his troops would be on the field by mid-morning. Sedgewick's men were on the march from Westminster, Maryland, some 37 miles away, and would not be up till well on into the afternoon. Meade spent the night putting his men into position. Slocum's XII Corps held Culp's Hill, with I Corps on its left, holding the ground west to Cemetery Hill, which was defended by the remnants of XI Corps. The Union line then ran south along Cemetery Ridge, held by Hancock's superb II Corps and Sickles' III Corps. Sykes' V Corps, an experienced formation, was in reserve on the reverse slope of the ridge. Meade himself set up his headquarters in a farmhouse behind II Corps.

The expected early-morning Confederate attack failed to materialize, and Meade ordered Slocum to prepare to attack Ewell. The former, though, advised that the terrain was unfavorable and that such an attack had little chance of success, and Meade concurred. Lee was also forced to modify his plans, in this case for an attack on

Culp's Hill. It had become apparent that Ewell's information was inaccurate, and the hill was strongly held. By now, however, it was too late to carry out Lee's original plan and move Ewell round to the right. Lee eventually ordered Ewell to attack if he saw a favorable opportunity, while Longstreet assaulted the southern end of Cemetery Ridge. Hill, in the center, was to assist Longstreet, and to attack if a suitable occasion arose.

Longstreet's attack could not be carried out until his corps was in position, and one of his divisions, Pickett's, was still well to the rear at Chambersburg. The remaining two were closer, but they still had some distance to cover. Longstreet was also preoccupied with the problem of getting his men to their concentration area unobserved, and he moved particularly slowly. There have been suggestions that he was sulking as a result of his disagreement with Lee the previous night, but the question remains unresolved. Whatever the reason, Longstreet's two leading divisions, commanded by Lafayette McLaws and John B. Hood, were not in position till mid-afternoon; by this time there had been a significant change in the Union dispositions.

Dan Sickles' III Corps had been posted on the southern end of the Union line, on Hancock's left. The corps was weak, containing only two divisions, and Sickles feared that he might be dislodged from his position. He had to hold the end of Cemetery Ridge, as well as the Round Tops on the extreme Union left. Furthermore, the ridge was nearly flat at its southern end, and Sickles considered that Confederate guns could engage it with success from the area of the Peach Orchard, on the Emmitsburg Road, half a mile to the west. Sickles informed Meade that he considered the Peach Orchard a better position for III Corps than the southern end of the ridge. Finally, when

his outposts reported Longstreet's advance, Sickles decided, on his own initiative, to move his corps forward into the Peach Orchard. This decision was to cost III Corps a severe mauling when Longstreet at last attacked.

While McLaws and Hood were forming up for their assault the latter noticed that the Round Tops were unoccupied, and requested permission to attack from the south and outflank the Union line. Longstreet, for reasons which remain unclear, refused, thereby missing an opportunity to turn Sickles incautious advance into a disaster.

By the time Meade learned of III Corps' move it was too late to countermand it, for Longstreet's attack, so long awaited, was at last ready. At about 1600 Hood and McLaws advanced against Sickles. Hood was wounded early in the action, but his men went on with the *élan* that could make charging Confederate infantry almost irresistible.

Above: Headquarters of General George Meade on Cemetery Ridge.

Below: Longstreet's attack on the center of the Union lines, in a sketch made at the time by A.R. Ward. **Overleaf:** Union forces fall on the Confederates who plunged into their lines during the afternoon of the second day of the Battle of Gettysburg.

McLaws crashed in against Sickles' right, and by about 1800 the Peach Orchard was lost and III Corps in retreat; Sickles himself was severely wounded, losing a leg. III Corps may have been roughly handled, but it was not routed, and its remnants were supported by V Corps and one of Hancock's divisions, leading to a hideous *mêlée* in the area around the Wheatfield and the Devil's Den. Hood's men eventually fought their way through the Devil's Den, and emerged facing the undefended Little Round Top.

The situation was now critical, for the loss of this salient feature would have imperiled the entire Union position. Fortunately for Meade, his chief engineer, Major-General Gouverneur

The Battle of Gettysburg, 1863

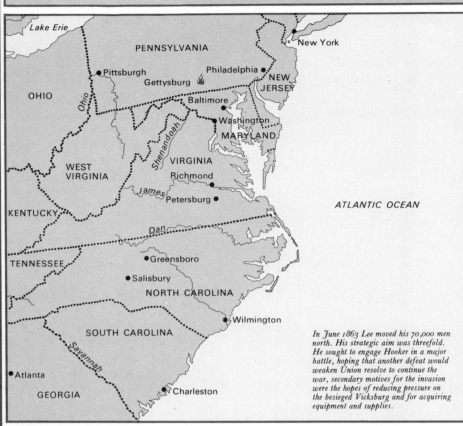

The maneuvers to Gettysburg

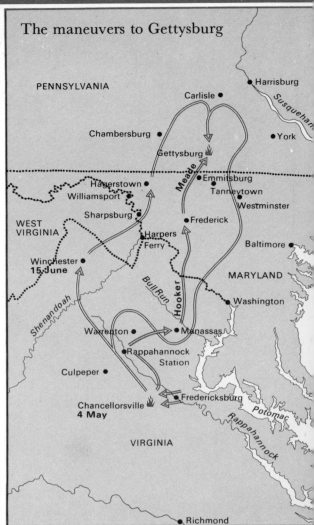

In June 1863 Lee moved his 70,000 men north. His strategic aim was threefold. He sought to engage Hooker in a major battle, hoping that another defeat would weaken Union resolve to continue the war, secondary motives for the invasion were the hopes of reducing pressure on the besieged Vicksburg and for acquiring equipment and supplies.

The situation on 2 July

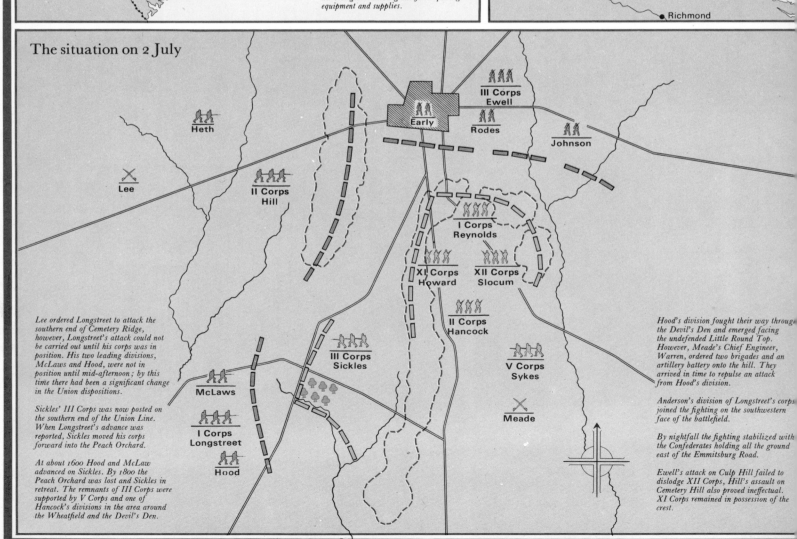

Lee ordered Longstreet to attack the southern end of Cemetery Ridge, however, Longstreet's attack could not be carried out until his corps was in position. His two leading divisions, McLaws and Hood, were not in position until mid-afternoon; by this time there had been a significant change in the Union dispositions.

Sickles' III Corps was now posted on the southern end of the Union Line. When Longstreet's advance was reported, Sickles moved his corps forward into the Peach Orchard.

At about 1600 Hood and McLaw advanced on Sickles. By 1800 the Peach Orchard was lost and Sickles in retreat. The remnants of III Corps were supported by V Corps and one of Hancock's divisions in the area around the Wheatfield and the Devil's Den.

Hood's division fought their way through the Devil's Den and emerged facing the undefended Little Round Top. However, Meade's Chief Engineer, Warren, ordered two brigades and an artillery battery onto the hill. They arrived in time to repulse an attack from Hood's division.

Anderson's division of Longstreet's corps joined the fighting on the southwestern face of the battlefield.

By nightfall the fighting stabilized with the Confederates holding all the ground east of the Emmitsburg Road.

Ewell's attack on Culp Hill failed to dislodge XII Corps, Hill's assault on Cemetery Hill also proved ineffectual. XI Corps remained in possession of the crest.

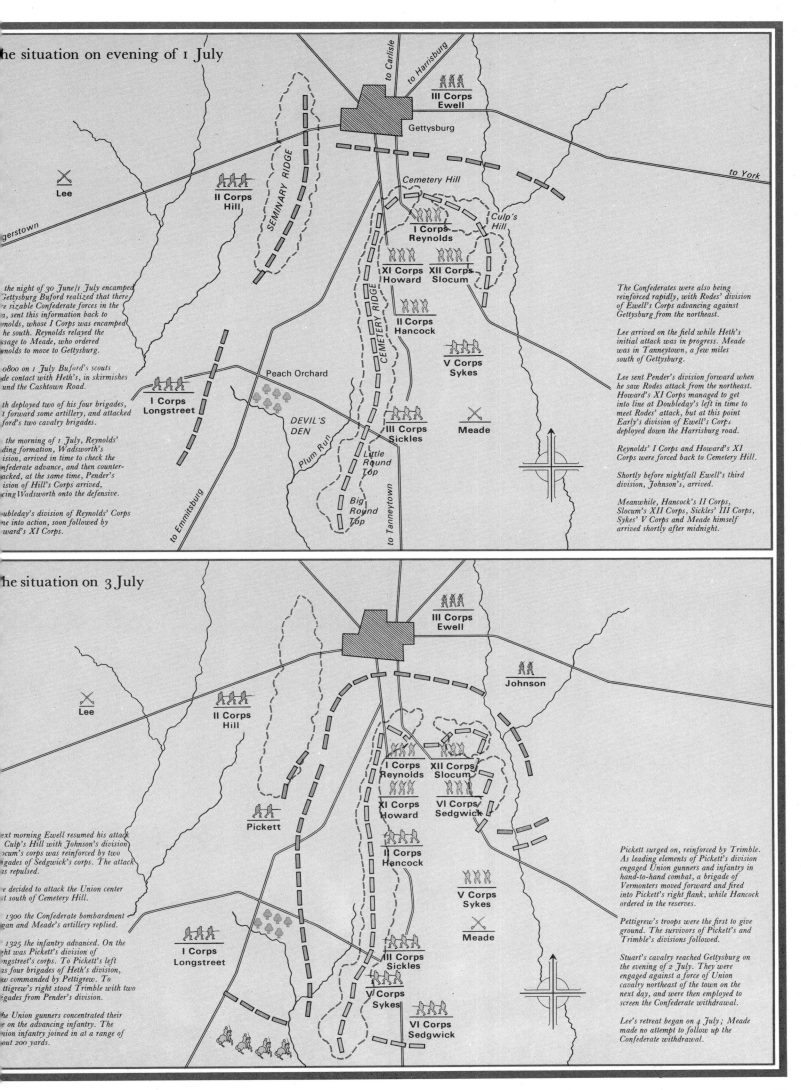

the situation on evening of 1 July

to Carlisle
to Harrisburg

**III Corps
Ewell**

Gettysburg

to York

SEMINARY RIDGE

to Hagerstown

Lee ✕

**II Corps
Hill**

Cemetery Hill

Culp's
Hill

**I Corps
Reynolds**

**XI Corps
Howard**

**XII Corps
Slocum**

CEMETERY RIDGE

**II Corps
Hancock**

**V Corps
Sykes**

Peach Orchard

**I Corps
Longstreet**

DEVIL'S
DEN

Plum Run

**III Corps
Sickles**

Meade ✕

Little
Round
Top

Big
Round
Top

to Emmitsburg

to Tanneytown

the night of 30 June/1 July encamped
Gettysburg Buford realized that there
re sizable Confederate forces in the
a, sent this information back to
ynolds, whose I Corps was encamped
he south. Reynolds relayed the
ssage to Meade, who ordered
ynolds to move to Gettysburg.

0800 on 1 July Buford's scouts
de contact with Heth's, in skirmishes
und the Cashtown Road.

th deployed two of his four brigades,
t forward some artillery, and attacked
ford's two cavalry brigades.

the morning of 1 July, Reynolds'
ding formation, Wadsworth's
vision, arrived in time to check the
nfederate advance, and then counter-
acked, at the same time, Pender's
vision of Hill's Corps arrived,
cing Wadsworth onto the defensive.

oubleday's division of Reynolds' Corps
ne into action, soon followed by
ward's XI Corps.

The Confederates were also being
reinforced rapidly, with Rodes' division
of Ewell's Corps advancing against
Gettysburg from the northeast.

Lee arrived on the field while Heth's
initial attack was in progress. Meade
was in Tanneytown, a few miles
south of Gettysburg.

Lee sent Pender's division forward when
he saw Rodes attack from the northeast.
Howard's XI Corps managed to get
into line at Doubleday's left in time to
meet Rodes' attack, but at this point
Early's division of Ewell's Corps
deployed down the Harrisburg road.

Reynolds' I Corps and Howard's XI
Corps were forced back to Cemetery Hill.

Shortly before nightfall Ewell's third
division, Johnson's, arrived.

Meanwhile, Hancock's II Corps,
Slocum's XII Corps, Sickles' III Corps,
Sykes' V Corps and Meade himself
arrived shortly after midnight.

the situation on 3 July

**III Corps
Ewell**

Johnson

Lee ✕

**II Corps
Hill**

**I Corps
Reynolds**

**XII Corps
Slocum**

**XI Corps
Howard**

**VI Corps
Sedgwick**

Pickett

**II Corps
Hancock**

**V Corps
Sykes**

Meade ✕

**I Corps
Longstreet**

**III Corps
Sickles**

**VI Corps
Sykes**

**VI Corps
Sedgwick**

ext morning Ewell resumed his attack
Culp's Hill with Johnson's division
ocum's corps was reinforced by two
gades of Sedgwick's corps. The attack
as repulsed.

e decided to attack the Union center
st south of Cemetery Hill.

1300 the Confederate bombardment
gan and Meade's artillery replied.

1325 the infantry advanced. On the
ght was Pickett's division of
ngstreet's corps. To Pickett's left
as four brigades of Heth's division,
w commanded by Pettigrew. To
ttigrew's right stood Trimble with two
gades from Pender's division.

e Union gunners concentrated their
e on the advancing infantry. The
ion infantry joined in at a range of
out 200 yards.

Pickett surged on, reinforced by Trimble.
As leading elements of Pickett's division
engaged Union gunners and infantry in
hand-to-hand combat, a brigade of
Vermonters moved forward and fired
into Pickett's right flank, while Hancock
ordered in the reserves.

Pettigrew's troops were the first to give
ground. The survivors of Pickett's and
Trimble's divisions followed.

Stuart's cavalry reached Gettysburg on
the evening of 2 July. They were
engaged against a force of Union
cavalry northeast of the town on the
next day, and were then employed to
screen the Confederate withdrawal.

Lee's retreat began on 4 July; Meade
made no attempt to follow up the
Confederate withdrawal.

K. Warren, was on the spot, and he at once appreciated the significance of Little Round Top. Galloping over to Sykes' corps, he ordered two brigades and a battery of artillery onto the hill. They arrived just in time, and were greeted by a vigorous attack from Hood's division, which was just—but only just—repulsed. Meanwhile, across the whole southwestern face of the battlefield, bitter fighting went on, with Anderson's division of Longstreet's corps joining in.

The Union artillery, under the capable Major-General Henry J. Hunt, had provided the infantry with superb close support throughout the attack in the area of the Peach Orchard, though it had lost some guns. Hunt also used his artillery in an effective if somewhat unconventional manner along the 'Plum Run Line' where there was a gap unheld by Union infantry. Hunt pushed a solid mass of 25 guns into the gap, and held the line unsupported. One Confederate regiment, the 21st Mississippi, actually got in among the guns as they were withdrawing, receiving and inflicting heavy casualties. By nightfall the fighting stabilized with the Union forces holding the Round Tops, the Plum Run Line, and Cemetery Ridge; the Devil's Den and much of the ground east of the Emmitsburg Road were in Confederate hands.

To the north, things went less well for Lee's army. Ewell had begun to bombard the area of Cemetery Hill and Culp's Hill when he heard Longstreet's guns announce that Hood and McLaws were going in. On Culp's Hill, XII Corps had been weakened by sending reinforcements to the southern end of the line, and when Ewell sent in Johnson's division it found only one brigade in position. Nevertheless, this formation put up a stiff resistance, aided by some troops sent over from I Corps. Johnson's men eventually managed to seize the lower part of the hill and some entrenchments, but XII Corps remained in possession of the crest.

Cemetery Hill was assaulted by Jubal Early, whose charge was warmly received by a particularly well-posted battery of I Corps artillery and by the massed guns of XI Corps. Despite some hand-to-hand fighting in the Union gun-line, Early's attack proved fruitless. Rodes, on Early's left, had been ordered to attack if he considered it feasible, but he decided against it; it was subsequently argued that had he supported Early, Cemetery Hill—as vital to the right of the Union line as was Little Round Top to its left—might have fallen. This must remain another of the unresolved problems of Gettysburg.

Both armies had suffered severely on 2 July. The dead and wounded lay in a broad swathe along the whole of the hook-shaped front, lying thickest in the Devil's Den—Wheatfield area, and in front of Cemetery Hill. The field hospitals on both sides were soon overloaded, and many of the wounded spent an agonizing night in the open. Meade held a conference of corps commanders at his headquarters. All agreed that retreat was out of the question, and that the army should stand and fight for at least another day before moving, if possible, onto the offensive.

Below left: A contemporary sketch by A. R. Ward of Cemetery Hill prior to Pickett's charge.
Bottom left: Pencil drawing of the battlefield taken from the junction of Gettysburg Pike and Taneytown Road on 3 July.
Below right: Major-General C.K. Warren, who attacked Little Round Top.
Bottom right: A.R. Ward sketching the Battle of Gettysburg, in a photograph taken by Matthew Brady, the greatest war photographer of the Civil War.

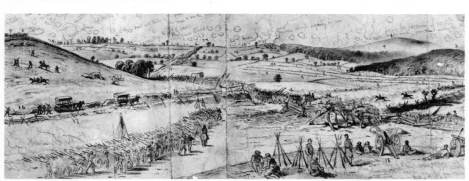

Meade announced that he suspected that Lee would attack the center of the Union position, in the area held by II Corps. He felt confident enough to repulse it; Sedgewick's VI Corps had arrived during the afternoon, and the Union artillery had adequate ammunition available—though Hunt had warned that there was none for 'idle cannonades, the besetting sin of some of our Commanders'.

Lee had less reason than Meade to feel satisfied with the result of 2 July. The opportunity opened by the ungarrisoned Little Round Top had been lost, and there had been little coordination behind the Confederate attacks. Had Longstreet and Ewell attacked simultaneously, and more promptly, things might well have gone differently.

Fighting flared up in the north early next morning. Johnson resumed his attack on Culp's Hill, to be met by the determined resistance of Slocum's corps, reinforced by two brigades of Sedgewick's. Despite a number of spirited attacks, Johnson's infantry could make no impression on the defenders, and were eventually forced to fall back. Over the remainder of the front things were relatively quiet. There were several minor exchanges of small arms and artillery fire, in one of which Pender was mortally wounded, but in the center and southern portions of the battlefield the Confederates were occupied in preparing for the assault which was to be the culminating point of the battle.

Pickett's Gallant Charge

Meade's prediction that Lee would attack the Union center proved correct. It was not, however, Lee's original intention. He hoped to use Longstreet's fresh division, under General George Pickett, to smash Meade's left in the Round Top area, but Longstreet pointed out that the confusion and close engagement in that vicinity made a set-piece attack difficult. Lee agreed, and decided instead to attack Meade's center just south of Cemetery Hill. The attack's objective was marked by a small clump of trees. One of Hill's brigades had reached the ridge top there on 2 July, but had been thrown back. Lee thought that Pickett's splendid division of fifteen Virginia regiments could punch through the Union line where a brigade had so nearly succeeded.

It was of paramount importance that the Union artillery should be as heavily engaged as possible before Pickett's attack went in. Hunt's gunners had been instrumental in repulsing Early's attack on Cemetery Hill on the previous day, and, given a chance, would inflict serious damage on Pickett as he crossed the open ground between the ridges. Early in the morning Lee told Longstreet's artillery commander, Colonel E.P. Alexander, of his plan, and Alexander set about concentrating his guns so as to be able to engage Cemetery Hill and the ground to its south. Alexander had 75 guns in line by 1000, while to his left Hill's corps had 63 more.

By 1300 an ominous silence reigned over the field. Alexander had moved into a suitable observation post at about midday. Once there, he received a note from Longstreet ordering him to advise Pickett not to attack if, in Alexander's opinion, the Confederate bombardment had not proved effective. Alexander, unwilling to take responsibility for such a decision, replied, warning Longstreet that ammunition was short, and that only one attack could be supported adequately. Even if this attack was successful it would, he predicted, be 'at a very bloody cost'. This opinion was shared by Brigadier-General A.R. Wright, whose Georgia Brigade had reached the ridge the previous day. 'It is not so hard to go there as it looks', he remarked to Alexander. 'The trouble is to stay there. The whole Yankee Army is there in a bunch.'

In fact, the Confederate attacking force was comfortably superior in numbers to the Union troops opposing it—perhaps 15,000 to 8000. Nevertheless, this superiority would be reduced as the advance progressed, first by the Union artillery and then by massed volleys of rifle fire. Meade also had reserves at his immediate disposal, to commit to the *mêlée* if Pickett actually reached the crest and, good though Pickett's Virginians were, Hancock's II Corps was in no way inferior. In the early part of the war Union infantry had shown a depressing tendency to break before a Confederate assault. By Gettysburg the overall quality of Union infantry was considerably high, and Hancock's men were among the best.

The assaulting units shook out into order west of Seminary Ridge. On the right was Pickett's division, with two brigades up and one in support. To Pickett's left stood four brigades of Heth's division, now commanded by Major-General J.J. Pettigrew who had taken over from the

Left: General George Pickett, whose heroic charge failed to break the Union forces. It was the most daring action of the battle and one of the most impressive infantry attacks in military history.

wounded Heth. Major-General Isaac Trimble, with two brigades from Pender's division, was to Pettigrew's right rear. Although the attack is usually known as Pickett's charge, Pickett himself had no authority over Pettigrew and Trimble.

At exactly 1300 two guns were fired by the Confederate Washington Artillery, signaling the beginning of the bombardment. The Confederate guns opened fire immediately, and Meade's artillery replied. For about half an hour the battle continued unabated, with clouds of dense smoke filling the depression between the ridges, and, in Alexander's words, 'missiles from every direction'. At 1325 Alexander was forced to advise Pickett to advance at once or not at all, otherwise ammunition would not permit him to give adequate support. No sooner had Alexander sent this note than the Union fire slackened as Hunt's guns withdrew from the Cemetery. Alexander sent a note to Pickett saying 'for God's sake, come quick'.

Pickett had, in fact, asked Longstreet whether he should advance when he received Alexander's

Above: Union and Confederate troops fire at each other at point-blank range during the closing stages of the action on 3 July.

reopened by Confederate guns. Those batteries with shells at hand fired with good effect as the infantry began to breast the rise, and were joined by the remaining batteries as the Confederates came within canister range. The Union infantry joined in at a range of about 200 yards. The effect on the advancing infantry was terrible. The Confederate ranks writhed like some hideous monster in agony, but continued to advance. Pettigrew's men were particularly hard hit, but Pickett surged on, reinforced by Trimble. With a low roar the leading elements of Pickett's division crashed into the Union lines, crossing a stone wall and engaging Union gunners and infantry in hand-to-hand combat. The fate of the battle, and, indeed of the war, hung in the balance. Hancock, however, had reserves at hand, and threw them in, while to his left a brigade of Vermonters moved forward and opened a brisk fire into Pickett's right flank, in an action similar to the British 52nd Regiment at Waterloo.

The gallant Confederate infantry could stand it no longer. Pettigrew's men, who had suffered heavily on 1 July, were the first to give ground. The survivors of Pickett's and Trimble's divisions followed. There were few enough of them; about half the attackers had been killed, wounded or captured. Pickett's division alone lost nearly 2900 men out of the 5000 who had initially moved over the crest of Seminary Ridge. Union losses, it is true, were not light. Hancock himself had been seriously wounded, his infantry were exhausted, and several of his batteries were crippled. Nevertheless, the Union line had held; Pickett's men had, despite their bravery and sacrifice, in the words of one Rebel, 'gained nothing but glory'.

Lee rode about the eastern slopes of Cemetery Hill alone, rallying the survivors of the charge. An English eyewitness described his conduct as 'perfectly sublime'. He rode slowly amongst the scattered groups of men, many of them wounded, and encouraged them to 'bind up their hurts and take up a musket'. The repulse, he told them, was his fault, not theirs, but they must rally now in case Meade counterattacked.

Meade considered his command in no condition to take the offensive. He had fresh troops available—part of VI Corps—but believed that a counterstroke was far too hazardous. His failure to turn the Confederate repulse into a rout was to cause Lincoln considerable dissatisfaction, but, under the circumstances, there was much logic behind Meade's refusal to compromise his victory.

There were many Confederates who hoped for a renewal of the action on 4 July, but Lee realized that he must withdraw to Virginia to reorganize. He ordered Ewell to fall back during the night to a position in line with Hill and Longstreet, in case of a Union counterattack. He then set about making arrangements for the transport of his wounded. Many of these could not be collected, and had to be left as a further burden on the already overworked Union medical services. Brigadier-General John Imboden, whose cavalry brigade had reached Gettysburg at noon on 3 July, was ordered to escort the column of wounded. Imboden moved out along the Chambersburg Pike, and then swung south to Williamsport, Maryland, where he crossed the Potomac.

first note. Longstreet, in an agony of indecision, could not bring himself to reply. Pickett saluted, galloped forward to his division, and began his advance. Longstreet rode over for an inconclusive conference with Alexander; while the two men were talking, Pickett's division emerged from cover. The Confederate guns ceased fire as the advancing troops passed through them and for some minutes a relative calm descended on the battlefield. There can have been few more impressive sights in the whole of military history than when the 15,000 men of Pickett, Pettigrew and Trimble marched down the slope of Seminary Ridge and into the valley beyond. They were in excellent order, with officers dressing the ranks as if on parade, colors fluttering overhead, and the July sun glinting off fixed bayonets.

The Union artillery opened up in earnest as the infantry reached the valley. Hunt's guns had, in fact, suffered surprisingly little. He had not intended to let them reply to the Confederate bombardment, but had been overruled by Hancock. The latter's batteries had expended most of their shells and roundshot but had canister available, a round with a devastating anti-personnel effect up to about 250 yards. The Union infantry, too, had suffered relatively few casualties from shellfire. Many of them were under cover and, on a ridgetop, they offered a difficult target; a good number of Confederate shells passed over the ridge to burst in the hollow to the east.

The Union gunners concentrated their fire on the advancing infantry, oblivious to the fire now

The plight of the wounded, riding, with the most rudimentary of medical attention, in unsprung wagons, was worsened by a blinding rainstorm which swept the field on the afternoon of 4 July. Imboden wrote that he learned more of the horrors of war in one night than he had in all the preceding two years.

Stuart's cavalry had at last reached Gettysburg on the evening of 2 July. They were engaged against a force of Union cavalry in an inconclusive action northeast of the town on the next day, and were then employed to screen the Confederate withdrawal. A Union cavalry brigade under Brigadier-General E.J. Farnsworth launched a fruitless attack on Longstreet's right rear late on 3 July; Farnsworth was killed and the attack speedily repulsed.

Lee's Retreat

Lee's retreat began on 4 July, the day that, away to the southwest, Vicksburg fell. Meade made no attempt to follow up the Confederate withdrawal. He moved off on 5 July, and marched to Emmitsburg before swinging down to the Potomac. The Confederates reached Williamsport only to discover that the river was unusually high, so the ford could not be used; moreover, Union cavalry had previously destroyed a pontoon bridge built by the Confederates in June. Lee deployed his army around Williamsport while his engineers worked desperately on a new bridge. Meade made contact with Lee's outposts on 11 July, but his corps commanders advised against an assault on the 13th. Meade proposed to attack the following day, but discovered that the main body of Lee's army had pulled back across the completed bridge during the night of 13–14 July.

The withdrawal of the Army of Northern Virginia across the Potomac effectively ended the Gettysburg campaign. It is a campaign which probably seems more decisive in retrospect than it did at the time. Satisfactory though the result was for the Union, Lincoln was disappointed in Meade's failure to pursue and make the victory conclusive. On the Confederate side, Gettysburg was seen as a defeat rather than a disaster. Lee made no attempt to avoid the blame, and wrote to Jefferson Davis offering to resign, an offer which Davis wisely declined. The battle had, however, been fought inside Northern territory, and Union as well as Confederate casualties had been heavy. Meade's army had lost 23,000 men, and the Confederates, according to their own figures, 27,500. This was a striking heavy overall percentage; about 30% of the participants in the battle had been killed, wounded or captured.

Gettysburg certainly did not make the defeat of the South inevitable. In outright strategic terms, it was probably less significant than the fall of Vicksburg, which cut the Confederacy in half. It was, for the Confederacy, the battle of lost opportunities. Lee, Longstreet, Stuart and Ewell have all been criticized for decisions at various stages of the action. Stuart's failure to maintain contact with the Army of Northern Virginia certainly placed Lee at an initial disadvantage. It is also difficult to view Longstreet's performance without questioning his judgement, particularly on the third day of the battle. Lack of coordination characterized the Confederate attacks; Pickett's charge, magnificent though it was, was launched too late, and with inadequate support.

The Union command, too, was by no means flawless. Sickle's advance to the Peach Orchard imperiled the entire Union right; the vital Round Tops were left ungarrisoned. Meade, although behaving with praiseworthy *sang-froid* during the battle, moved extremely slowly after it despite President Lincoln's impatience to follow Lee, and missed an opportunity of inflicting another, potentially more serious defeat on Lee at Williamsport. However, Meade should not be judged too harshly. He had taken over command of the Army of the Potomac only recently, and fought a difficult encounter battle against a determined enemy. He had, furthermore, held his army together in the face of pressure which, in previous actions, had invariably brought about its collapse.

It is profitless to speculate upon what might have happened at Gettysburg had events gone only slightly differently. What is certain is that the power of Lee's infantry had been sacrificed on the slopes of Cemetery Ridge, and that the Army of Northern Virginia, splendid fighting-machine though it remained, was never quite the same again. The war had come to Gettysburg because all the roads led there; after the battle, all the roads led to Appomattox.

Left: General Henry J. Hunt, who commanded the Union artillery superbly throughout the battle. His leadership kept the Round Tops and Cemetery Ridge in Union hands.

Sedan

If the dramatic Prussian victory at Königgrätz came as a shock to the Austrians, it was hardly less of a surprise for the French. The Second Empire of Napoleon III owed its prestige largely to its army, which had itself defeated the Austrians in 1859, and the implications of Königgrätz were, consequently, serious. Prussia had taken only six weeks to inflict a crushing defeat upon Austria, whereas in 1859 the French had taken considerably longer to win two infinitely less conclusive victories. The more perceptive French soldiers recognized the threat, and Königgrätz lent new urgency to their demands for military reform.

French diplomats and politicians, too, were nonplussed by Königgrätz and the subsequent creation of the North German Confederation. French demands for territorial cessions on the left bank of the Rhine were rejected by Bismarck, and France found herself without compensation for her non-intervention in the war. It was apparent to most Frenchmen that conflict with Prussia was, sooner or later, inevitable, but the growing liberalization of Napoleon's regime made harsh military service legislation impossible. The military reform of 1868 fell far short of the aims of its warmest advocate, the able Marshal Niel. More Frenchmen became liable for military service, but the reserve remained inadequately trained and the *Garde Mobile*, the French equivalent of the Prussian *Landwehr*, existed only on paper. The new law would not, moreover, take full effect for several years. Disaster might yet have been averted had French foreign policy reflected the temporary inferiority of French arms. Unfortunately the Imperialists, seeing their position at home weakened by the Liberal Empire, demanded, with increasing vigor, a hard line against Prussia. This policy led to a diplomatic clash over Luxembourg in 1867 and, in July 1870, to the confrontation which brought about the Franco-Prussian War.

One of the ironies of the situation was that, despite 1866, the French army appeared in many respects more than a match for the Prussians. It had considerable experience; French soldiers had fought in the Crimea, in Italy and in Mexico, but it was in Algeria that reputations had been made and new doctrines developed. The French invasion of Algeria in 1830 had been followed by years of intermittent fighting, and had witnessed the rise of a new style of commander and a new sort of tactics. Dash, drive and initiative were what mattered; the serried line of battle was replaced by the flying column, the European concept of major war by a series of ambushes and skirmishes. Algeria produced troops to match its tactics; *Spahis* and *Turcos*, *Chasseurs d'Afrique* and *Zouaves* gave fresh opportunities to the military tailor and dazzled an infatuated France with new tales of martial prowess.

Useful though the Algerian experience was, it was all 'in the small change of war', and was not strictly relevant to European conflict. There was, indeed, much in the Army of the Second Empire which made it ill-suited for a continental war. Its organization and training emphasized quality at the expense of quantity; the French were to find themselves at a constant numerical disadvantage in 1870. In 1866 a new infantry rifle, the *Chassepot*, had been adopted, but the tactics upon which its successful use depended had not been fully developed. French artillery had remained muzzle-loading, and France's possession of a machine-gun, the *Mitrailleuse*, was to do little to remedy the inadequacy of her field-guns. There were also serious deficiencies in the training of

Opposite: Napoleon III is consoled by Bismarck, whose Prussian armies gained a victory, two French provinces and an Empire at Sedan. Louis Napoleon was captured at Sedan, and finally retired to England where he died three years later.

Left: Napoleon III, Emperor of the French, who lost his crown as well as the battle and the war at Sedan.

staff officers and senior commanders, while the commissariat, the *Intendance*, was not equipped to deal with the problems posed by a major war.

Although the Prussian army had less experience than the French, its recent history made it much better suited to overcoming the organizational and administrative difficulties entailed in a struggle against another major European power. Its command and staff had learned invaluable lessons from 1866, its commissariat was well organized and its mobilization procedure skillfully prepared. The needle-gun might be inferior to the *Chassepot*, but Prussian artillery was notably more effective than that of the French. Furthermore, in 1870 Prussia would not fight alone. The forces of the North German Confederation backed her as a matter of course and, to the surprise and dismay of the French, the South German states decided, albeit reluctantly, to take the field alongside their fellow-Germans.

The Prussian General Staff finalized its plans for the invasion of France in the winter of 1868–69. An offensive by four armies was envisaged, although in fact only three were employed in 1870. With the cooperation of the South German states, Moltke and his collaborators could expect to field 484,000 men, while the anticipated French strength was something in excess of 250,000. The First Army was to concentrate around Wittlich, the Second around Homburg and the Third, which was to include the South German contingents, around Landau. The Fourth Army was to be in reserve, but in 1870 this formation was merged with the Second Army.

French plans were less concise. There were several schemes in existence for the invasion of Germany; the favorite one laid down a three-army organization, with a projected offensive from the area of Strasbourg to sever North and South Germany, frightening the South Germans into neutrality before swinging north to deal with the Prussians. On the eve of war this plan was modified to permit cooperation with the Austrians who, it was hoped, would mobilize in support of France. This the Austrians failed to do, and furthermore, for reasons which remain obscure,

the French Order of Battle was changed during mobilization to one of eight corps operating under the command of Imperial Headquarters.

War came in July 1870 as a result of the Hohenzollern candidacy. Prince Leopold of Hohenzollern-Sigmaringen had been offered the throne of Spain, vacant since the expulsion of Queen Isabella in 1868. His acceptance produced such a howl of protest from France that the scheme was dropped, but King Wilhelm refused to give the French Ambassador a formal assurance that it would never be renewed. Bismarck, who hoped that the incident would lead to war, was dismayed, but edited the celebrated Ems Telegram in such a way that the Ambassador's demand was made to appear insolent, and its rejection irrevocable. This inflamed public opinion on both sides of the Rhine, and on the afternoon of 14 July orders went out initiating the French mobilization. Prussia mobilized the following day; the recall of reserves, issue of equipment and transport of units to their concentration areas went on with a well-oiled slickness for which the German military machine became justly famous.

A Botched Mobilization

The French mobilization went less well, largely because the Minister of War, Marshal Le Boeuf, had decided to combine mobilizations and concentration in an effort to save time. Units left for the frontier before their reservists had rejoined, and the resultant chaos may be easily imagined. The lack of permanently-organized divisions and brigades meant that formations had to be patched together in haste. The brigade commander who sent an angry telegram to the Minister announcing that he could find neither his divisional commander nor his regiments was by no means an exception. There was a general lack of equipment of all sorts, and problems of food distribution led to some early lapses of discipline.

By 18 July three French corps—General Ladmirault's 4th Corps, General Frossard's 2nd Corps and Marshal Bazaine's 3rd Corps, were deployed between Metz and the frontier. To the south Marshal MacMahon's 1st Corps, composed large-

ly of troops from Algeria, was forming at Strasbourg. General Failly's 5th Corps, based at Sarreguemines and Bitche, connected the forces at Metz with MacMahon's corps at Strasbourg, while General Bourbaki and the Imperial Guard moved from Paris to Nancy. General Felix Douay's 7th Corps concentrated at Belfort. On 23 July Le Boeuf, before leaving for the frontier to take up his post as Major General (Chief-of-Staff) to the Emperor, ordered a tighter concentration in the north; Failly edged to his left, and Bourbaki took the Guard to Metz. Away in the rear, at Châlons, the 6th Corps assembled under Marshal Canrobert.

Napoleon arrived at Metz to take command on 28 July. He was physically ill and was, as the 1859 campaign had shown, no military genius; he failed to provide his army with the firm and incisive leadership which alone could save it. On 2 August Frossard took Saarbrucken, an easy if pointless success which no effort was made to exploit. Four days later the French were to be overtaken by a disaster of alarming proportions.

While the French corps shuffled into position along the frontier, in a fashion, as one historian cruelly remarked, reminiscent of customs men, the German concentration went on. Bavaria and Baden had begun their mobilization on 16 July, and Württemberg had followed two days later; over a million men reported for duty, and 462,000 of them moved to the frontier. Prince Frederick Charles, with the six corps of the Second Army advanced via Kaiserslauten towards Saarbrucken. The obstinate General von Steinmetz, commanding the First Army, moved from Trier to the Saar, coming up on the right of Frederick Charles. The Third Army, consisting of two Prussian corps, two Bavarian corps, and a division each from Baden and Württemberg, was under the command of the Crown Prince of Prussia; it concentrated in the area of Landau, taking rather longer to do so than Moltke would have wished. Moltke's plan, in fact, was for the Third Army to attack the right flank of the French corps around Metz while Frederick Charles attacked them from the front. This is reminiscent of the plan

which had won Königgrätz, and its appeal is obvious; it would have brought about a battle of encirclement east of Metz in which the full weight of the German armies could be deployed.

Steinmetz, 'the Lion of Nachod', had facilitated Prussian victory in 1866, but he was to imperil it in 1870. With scant regard for Moltke's strategy, he pushed ahead toward Saarlouis, risking entanglement with the Second Army, and becoming involved in a dispute with Moltke, appealing, over the latter's head, to the King. Even after direct orders to the contrary, he sent two of his corps, VII and VIII, toward Saarbrucken on 5 August, a move which was to bring them into contact with Frossard's 2nd Corps, holding the heights west of the town. The Battle of Spicheren flared up on the afternoon of 6 August. Frossard's men repulsed the first German attacks but as the afternoon went on, increasing pressure, particularly against his flanks, endangered Frossard's position. Although Bazaine's corps was within easy marching distance, no help came, and by the late evening Frossard was forced to retreat. His men had given a good account of themselves, but the battle augured badly for the French. Their artillery had been seriously outclassed, and Bazaine's failure to support his colleague revealed the reluctance of French commanders to march toward the sound of gunfire.

While the cannon roared at Spicheren, MacMahon was brought to battle in Alsace. The Third Army had crossed the frontier on 4 August, lacerating an outlying French division, that of General Abel Douay, at Wissembourg the same morning. MacMahon, an officer of vast experience if limited capacity, was undismayed by Douay's defeat. He asked the Emperor for more troops, and planned to make a stand on the ridge of Froeschwiller. Napoleon put Failly's corps at

Left: Marshal Bazaine, whose 3rd Corps was deployed between Metz and the frontier at the start of hostilities.

Above: Marshal Mac-Mahon, who was wounded at Sedan.

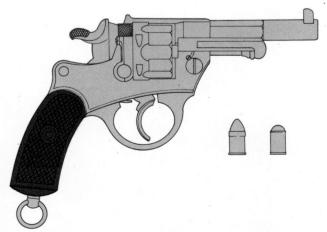

Right: A French revolver, 1869 model, used at Sedan. Caliber: 11 mm. Weight: 2.7 pounds. Capacity: six rounds. Length: 9½ inches.

Prince. The German artillery caused frightful casualties and, as more and more German troops came up to tip the scales against MacMahon, the situation worsened. The defense collapsed at about 1630, the division sent by Failly arriving only in time to cover the retreat. Failly heard of the disaster by telegraph, and fell back precipitately toward Phalsbourg, abandoning much of his equipment.

The battles of 6 August added a new air of gloom to the hesitation already prevailing at Imperial Headquarters. For the next few days the Emperor and his advisors struggled with the crucial problem of whether to concentrate on Metz or to fall back on Châlons. The catastrophic sequence of order, counterorder and disorder exercised its baleful influence on morale, which sank to a new ebb as the weather broke and turned the retreat into a nightmare.

On 9 August the French cabinet resigned, and a new one was formed by General Cousin de Montauban, Comte de Palikao, who was to act as both President of the Council and Minister of War. Energetic steps were taken to raise both troops and money; a state of siege was declared in Paris, and Marines, destined for northern Germany, were summoned to the capital.

The Retreat Goes On

In Alsace and in Lorraine the retreat went on. Bazaine suggested a concentration on Langres, but Napoleon at once vetoed the idea, since it presupposed the abandonment of the capital. What he failed to appreciate was that the defenses of Paris made it safe from a *coup de main*; his preoccupation with the city was undoubtedly more political than military. While the northern element of the French army lay at the mercy of its vacillating commanders, the southern portion— 1st and 7th Corps, and most of 5th Corps— struggled to Lunéville, and then moved by road and rail, on Châlons. The opportunity of joining the two wings of the French army on the Nancy-Metz axis was lost, and MacMahon's withdrawal left the northern corps dangerously exposed before Metz.

Moltke remained uncertain of MacMahon's line of retreat until 9 August, when he felt confident to issue a new directive, ordering the Third Army to move on Sarreunion, while the First and Second Armies marched on Boulay and St Avold respectively. Although the German forces were not victims of chaos on the French scale, there was considerable confusion to the rear of the marching armies, and friction between Moltke and Steinmetz imposed a further stress on operations. Furthermore, the German cavalry, although more enterprising than their adversaries, were far from perfect at their vital role of reconnaissance; the cavalry of the Third Army had contrived to lose contact altogether.

The Third Army, unopposed, reached Nancy on 14 August. On the same day the leading elements of the First Army engaged the French rearguard at Borny, just east of Metz. Napoleon, by now quite worn out, had handed over command of the Army to Bazaine, and the decision was at last taken to withdraw down the Verdun road to Châlons. The French lost valuable time on 14 and

his disposal, and MacMahon at once ordered him south. Failly's failure to support MacMahon was, like Bazaine's failure to aid Frossard, to be one of the *causes célèbres* of the war. Despite MacMahon's orders, he maintained that he could only produce one division immediately; the rest of the corps would move in its own good time.

On the morning of 6 August MacMahon, with just under 50,000 men, mostly of his own corps but including elements of the 7th Corps, was attacked by the Third Army. The Froeschwiller position, like that of Spicheren, was a strong one, and throughout a blazing August day Mac-Mahon's *turcos* and *zouaves* held off the Crown

15 August, much of it in forcing a way through the congested streets of Metz, and still more awaiting orders on the Gravelotte plateau. Bazaine, like Benedek, was personally brave, but totally unfitted by attitude, training or experience to command an army. He was mesmerized by the illusory security offered by Metz, and seemed reluctant to push on into open country.

On 16 August the Germans made Bazaine's decision for him. The Second Army had crossed the Moselle south of Metz on the 15th, and early the next day two German corps attacked the French advance guard at Mars-la-Tour. The Germans initially assumed that they had made contact with the French rearguard, but once the mistake was discovered they resolutely continued to attack, and as the remainder of the Second Army marched desperately to their assistance, Generals von Voigts Rhetz of X Corps and von Alvensleben of III Corps deceived Bazaine as to their real strength. A bitter day-long battle around Rezonville persuaded Bazaine that break-out to the west was impossible; he fell back onto the escarpment on the left bank of the Moselle, taking up a strong position running from St Privat in the north to Rozerieulles in the south. There, on 18 August, he was attacked in force. The Second Army bore the brunt of the battle, with the First intervening only against the extreme French left. The Prussian Guard, attacking the 6th Corps at St Privat, lost over 8000 men, but once again the German artillery proved decisive. Canrobert's men, after a brilliant defense, gave way at nightfall, laying bare Bazaine's right flank. The French fell back into Metz; they were never to leave it except as prisoners-of-war.

Napoleon had left Bazaine's army on the morning of 16 August, and had reached Châlons that evening. Châlons was, in peacetime, a huge military camp and Napoleon found it crammed with the troops making up his last army, the Army of Châlons. It included the three southern corps, 1st, 5th and 7th, parts of which were still arriving

by rail. All three were badly depleted. One eye-witness pointed out that 5th Corps was in a sorry state without actually having been engaged: 'It had left one of its brigades at Sarreguemines, a part of its baggage at Bitche, its morale bit by bit on the road, and, without having fought, it was more disorganized than those which had seen the enemy'. These three corps were strengthened, if the term can properly be used in this context, by the addition of recruits of the class of 1868 who were, naturally, totally untrained.

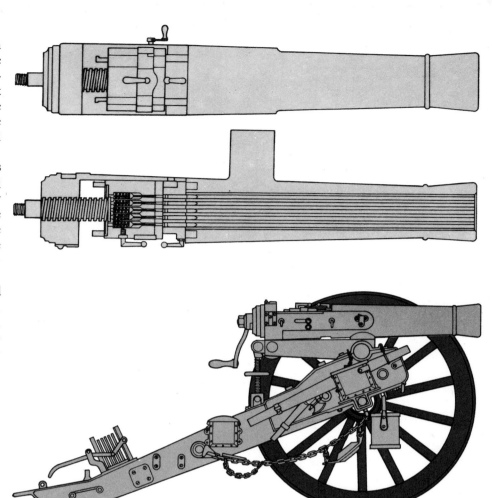

Above: The French *Mitrailleuse*, Model 1866, used at Sedan. This 13-mm artillery piece, invented by a French Captain of Artillery, consisted of 25 barrels fired in five tiers of five bullets enveloped by a bronze cover. Its rate of fire was 130 rounds per minute with a range of 1200 yards. It weighed approximately 800 kilograms (about 1760 pounds) and required six horses to transport it.

Far left: Frederick William, Prussian Crown Prince, commanded the Third Army at Sedan. **Left:** Prussian *Uhlans* enter a French town during the encirclement of Sedan.

Right: French and German cavalry engage at Mars-la-Tour, 16 August, 1870.
Below: Prussian Dragoons at Mars-la-Tour charge French infantry.

The newly-formed 12th Corps contained one division of such troops, one regular division, and a division of Marines who, although enthusiastic and bellicose, were unused to long marches.

The overall picture was uninspiring. One staff officer described the army as 'an inert crowd, vegetating rather than living'. Another witness likened Châlons to a beach with all manner of debris washed up on it. Discipline was poor; the breakdown of the *Intendance* during the retreat had made looting commonplace. Much vital equipment could not be provided; maps, guns and ambulances were all in short supply.

The army's fragile discipline was not reinforced by the presence at Châlons of eighteen battalions of Parisian *Garde Mobile*. These worthies had been close to mutiny ever since their arrival; they loudly demanded to be sent back home, and their employment in the field was certainly open to question.

The use of the *Garde Mobile* was one of the issues discussed at a Council of War held on 17 August. It was attended by the Emperor's cousin, Prince Napoleon, MacMahon, General Trochu of the 12th Corps, his Chief of Staff, General Schmitz and General Berthaut, commander of the Parisian *Garde Mobile*. All present realized that the fate of the regime as well as that of the army hung upon their decisions. Prince Napoleon counseled an immediate return to Paris by Emperor and army, and the appointment of Trochu, a well-known liberal, as Governor of the city. It was eventually decided that Trochu would hand his corps over to General Lebrun, and depart immediately for

The Battle of Sedan, 1870

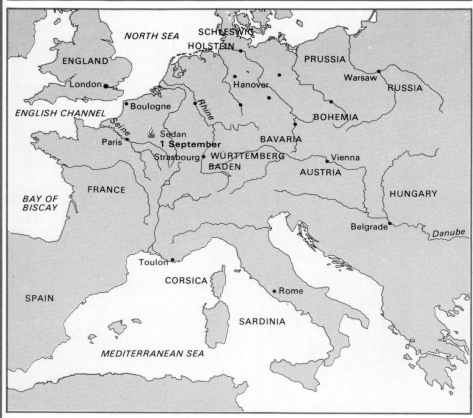

The situation on the 25 August

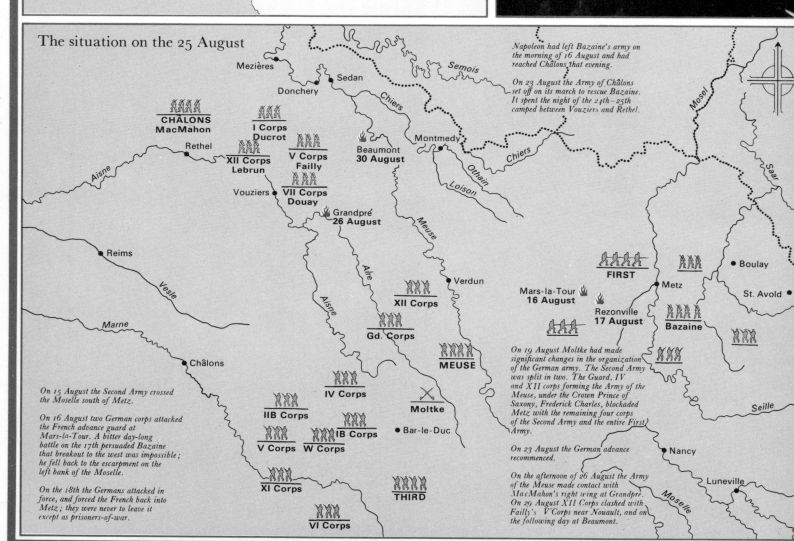

Napoleon had left Bazaine's army on the morning of 16 August and had reached Châlons that evening.

On 23 August the Army of Châlons set off on its march to rescue Bazaine. It spent the night of the 24th–25th camped between Vouziers and Rethel.

CHÂLONS
MacMahon

I Corps
Ducrot

XII Corps
Lebrun

V Corps
Failly

Beaumont
30 August

VII Corps
Douay

Grandpré
26 August

XII Corps

Gd. Corps

MEUSE

IIB Corps

IV Corps

Moltke

V Corps

IB Corps

W Corps

XI Corps

THIRD

VI Corps

FIRST

Mars-la-Tour
16 August

Rezonville
17 August

Bazaine

On 15 August the Second Army crossed the Moselle south of Metz.

On 16 August two German corps attacked the French advance guard at Mars-la-Tour. A bitter day-long battle on the 17th persuaded Bazaine that breakout to the west was impossible; he fell back to the escarpment on the left bank of the Moselle.

On the 18th the Germans attacked in force, and forced the French back into Metz; they were never to leave it except as prisoners-of-war.

On 19 August Moltke had made significant changes in the organization of the German army. The Second Army was split in two. The Guard, IV and XII corps forming the Army of the Meuse, under the Crown Prince of Saxony, Frederick Charles, blockaded Metz with the remaining four corps of the Second Army and the entire First Army.

On 23 August the German advance recommenced.

On the afternoon of 26 August the Army of the Meuse made contact with MacMahon's right wing at Grandpré. On 29 August XII Corps clashed with Failly's V Corps near Nouault, and on the following day at Beaumont.

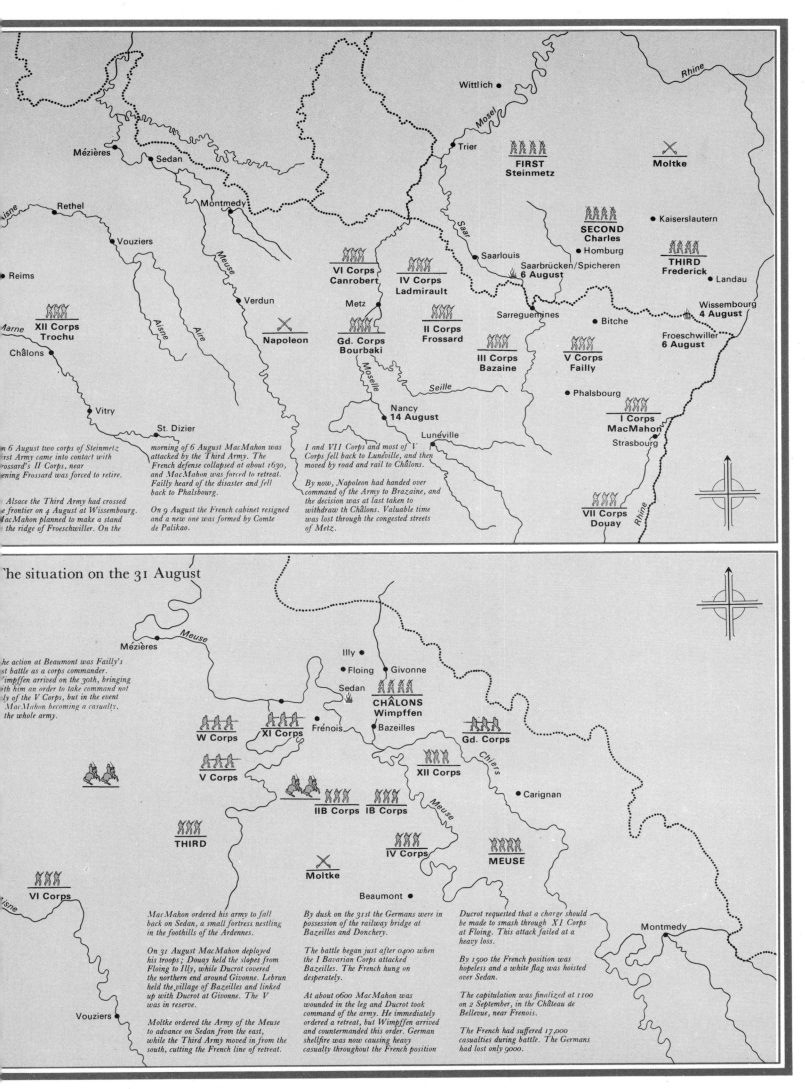

Wittlich •

Rhine

Mosel

• Trier

☖☖☖☖
FIRST
Steinmetz

✕
Moltke

Mézières •

• Sedan

Montmédy •

• Kaiserslautern

☖☖☖☖
SECOND
Charles

Saar

• Saarlouis

Saarbrücken/Spicheren
6 August

• Homburg

☖☖☖☖
THIRD
Frederick

Aisne

• Rethel

• Vouziers

☖☖☖
VI Corps
Canrobert

☖☖☖
IV Corps
Ladmirault

• Sarreguemines

• Bitche

• Landau

Wissembourg
4 August

• Reims

Meuse

• Verdun

Metz

• Sarreguemines

Aire

☖☖☖
XII Corps
Trochu

✕
Napoleon

☖☖☖
Gd. Corps
Bourbaki

☖☖☖
II Corps
Frossard

☖☖☖
III Corps
Bazaine

☖☖☖
V Corps
Failly

Froeschwiller
6 August

Marne

Châlons •

Moselle

Seille

• Phalsbourg

☖☖☖
I Corps
MacMahon

• Vitry

• St. Dizier

Nancy
14 August

Lunéville •

☖☖☖
VII Corps
Douay

Rhine

• Strasbourg

On 6 August two corps of Steinmetz
First Army came into contact with
Frossard's II Corps, near
ening Frossard was forced to retire.

Alsace the Third Army had crossed
e frontier on 4 August at Wissembourg.
acMahon planned to make a stand
the ridge of Froeschwiller. On the

morning of 6 August MacMahon was
attacked by the Third Army. The
French defense collapsed at about 1630,
and MacMahon was forced to retreat.
Failly heard of the disaster and fell
back to Phalsbourg.

On 9 August the French cabinet resigned
and a new one was formed by Comte
de Palikao.

I and VII Corps and most of V
Corps fell back to Lunéville, and then
moved by road and rail to Châlons.

By now, Napoleon had handed over
command of the Army to Brazaine, and
the decision was at last taken to
withdraw th Châlons. Valuable time
was lost through the congested streets
of Metz.

he situation on the 31 August

Meuse

Mézières •

• Illy

• Floing   • Givonne

• Sedan

☖☖☖☖
CHÂLONS
Wimpffen

he action at Beaumont was Failly's
st battle as a corps commander.
impffen arrived on the 30th, bringing
ith him an order to take command not
ly of the V Corps, but in the event
MacMahon becoming a casualty,
the whole army.

☖☖☖
W Corps

☖☖☖
XI Corps

Frénois •

• Bazeilles

☖☖☖
Gd. Corps

☖☖☖
V Corps

☖☖☖
XII Corps

Chiers

🐎🐎

🐎🐎
☖☖☖
IIB Corps

☖☖☖
IB Corps

Meuse

• Carignan

☖☖☖
THIRD

✕
Moltke

☖☖☖
IV Corps

☖☖☖☖
MEUSE

☖☖☖
VI Corps

Beaumont •

Montmédy •

sne

• Vouziers

MacMahon ordered his army to fall
back on Sedan, a small fortress nestling
in the foothills of the Ardennes.

On 31 August MacMahon deployed
his troops; Douay held the slopes from
Floing to Illy, while Ducrot covered
the northern end around Givonne.
Lebrun held the village of Bazeilles and linked
up with Ducrot at Givonne. The V
was in reserve.

Moltke ordered the Army of the Meuse
to advance on Sedan from the east,
while the Third Army moved in from the
south, cutting the French line of retreat.

By dusk on the 31st the Germans were in
possession of the railway bridge at
Bazeilles and Donchery.

The battle began just after 0400 when
the I Bavarian Corps attacked
Bazeilles. The French hung on
desperately.

At about 0600 MacMahon was
wounded in the leg and Ducrot took
command of the army. He immediately
ordered a retreat, but Wimpffen arrived
and countermanded this order. German
shellfire was now causing heavy
casualty throughout the French position

Ducrot requested that a charge should
be made to smash through XI Corps
at Floing. This attack failed at a
heavy loss.

By 1500 the French position was
hopeless and a white flag was hoisted
over Sedan.

The capitulation was finalized at 1100
on 2 September, in the Château de
Bellevue, near Frenois.

The French had suffered 17,000
casualties during battle. The Germans
had lost only 9000.

Above: French cavalry charge Prussian infantry at Gravelotte.

Below: Prussian cavalryman wounded at Gravelotte. Below right: Moltke meets King Wilhelm I at Gravelotte.

Paris. The *Garde Mobile* were to accompany him.

All might yet have been well for the luckless Army of Châlons had Bazaine and Palikao not intervened. The former sent a telegram, arriving on the afternoon of the 17th, announcing that he had won a victory at Rezonville, but would have to regroup before continuing his march on Châlons. One of his *aides de camp* arrived at Châlons the following day with a note confirming this, suggesting that Bazaine would swing north to elude the Germans. Palikao, dismayed by the reappearance of the suspect Trochu and the dangerous *Mobiles*, warned the Emperor by telegram that a return to Paris would be fatal; it was essential, as much for the safety of the regime as for the success of the campaign, to rescue Bazaine.

MacMahon can have had few illusions. His

army was not without value, but it was certainly incapable of a dash toward Metz in the teeth of the advancing Germans. His difficulties were increased by the presence of the Emperor, and by his nominal subordination to Bazaine who, on 18 August announced himself unable to give any instructions whatever, 'your operations lying at the moment entirely outside my zone of action'. Communications with Bazaine worsened after the telegraph line was cut, and dwindled to equivocal notes brought by couriers through German lines.

On 21 August Rouher, President of the Senate, met Napoleon, MacMahon and Courcelles, and stressed the importance of relieving Bazaine. Palikao re-emphasized the point by telegram the following day, warning that failure to aid Bazaine 'would have the most deplorable consequences in Paris'. Messages from Bazaine indicated that he

proposed to move via Montmédy, though Mac-Mahon was later to deny having received the most significant of these notes, dispatched on 20 August Pressure from the capital, added to indications that Bazaine was going to break out rather than wait lamely for aid, brought about a new and fatal change of plan, and on 23 August the Army of Châlons set off on its march to destruction.

The army moved slowly, its march made more difficult by heavy rain and muddy roads. It spent the night of the 24–25th camped between Vouziers and Rethel. Already MacMahon was deviating from his axis of advance toward Montmédy, since he was forced to remain close to the Reims-Mezières railway, to ensure supply. His two Reserve Cavalry Divisions, commanded by Generals Margueritte and de Bonnemains, had, by singular absence of logic, been ordered to screen the Rethel area, which was precisely that not threatened by the Germans.

Moltke had made significant alterations in the organization of the German armies. On 19 August he split the Second Army into two. The Crown Prince of Saxony was given three corps—the Guard, IV and XII Corps—forming the Army of the Meuse, with the task of pursuing Mac-Mahon. Frederick Charles, meanwhile, block-aded Metz with the remaining four corps of the Second Army and the entire First Army. The German advance recommenced on 23 August. The Third Army swung up toward Châlons, with the Army of the Meuse to its right. For several vital days, however, Moltke remained ignorant of MacMahon's intentions and, had the French fallen back on Paris, the elaborate German right-wheel would have come to naught. As it was, the

Above: French soldiers advance at Gravelotte. France's inability to take advantage of innumerable Prussian errors at Grave-lotte cost them the only opportunity they had in the war to stop the Prussian advance and stave off total defeat.

Below left: The Prussian breakthrough at Gravelotte set the stage for the encircle-ment of French forces at Sedan. **Below:** Gravelotte showed that properly handled, the *mitrailleuse* machine-gun and the *chassepot* rifle were deadly weapons against the Prussian infantry.

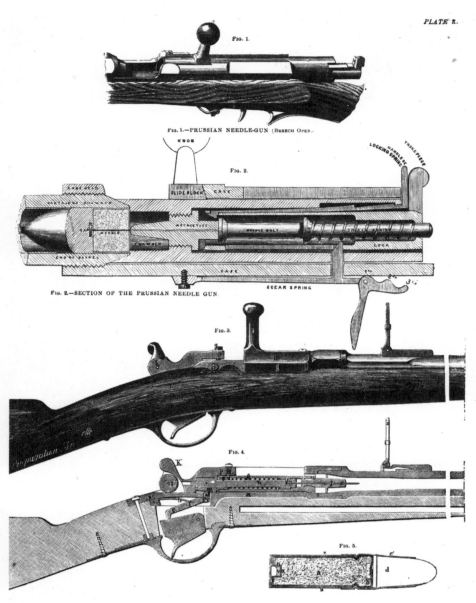

PLATE 2.

FIG. 1.—PRUSSIAN NEEDLE-GUN (BREECH OPEN).

FIG. 2.—SECTION OF THE PRUSSIAN NEEDLE GUN.

march on Montmédy played into Moltke's hands. He became increasingly certain that MacMahon was moving northeast, and on the afternoon of 26 August the cavalry of the Army of the Meuse made contact with MacMahon's right wing at Grandpré.

The Army of Châlons had struggled on, impeded by bad roads, appalling weather and dwindling supplies. On 26 August MacMahon realized that to continue was to risk encirclement, but his decision to fall back on Paris was greeted by a renewed protest from Palikao. The latter, never noted for his strategic prescience, maintained that MacMahon could easily brush aside the forces facing him, and that he was a clear 36 hours ahead of the Crown Prince. He ended by giving MacMahon an unequivocal order to press on. French movement, never particularly rapid, now became slower due to constant friction with hostile cavalry patrols. On 29 August there was a clash between 5th Corps and XII Corps near Noualt, and on the following day Failly was surprised at Beaumont.

The action at Beaumont cost the French well over 7000 men. It was Failly's last battle as a corps commander. It had already been decided to replace him, and his successor, General de Wimpffen, arrived on the evening of the 30th, bringing with him an order to take command not only of the 5th Corps, but, in the event of Mac-Mahon becoming a casualty, of the whole army.

MacMahon, dismayed by the misfortunes of his right wing, ordered his army to fall back on Sedan, a small fortress nestling in the foothills of the Ardennes. He probably intended to halt there to reorganize before moving off once more, though in quite what direction he was uncertain. Sedan, like Spicheren and Froeschwiller, was not without

its attractions as a defensive position. The River Meuse wound south of the town swinging north from Torcy to form the Iges Peninsula before running northwest towards Mezières. Its valley was wide and marshy and, if the bridges were blown, the river offered an excellent barrier against attack from the south. North of the river the ground rose sharply. Above Sedan itself lay the Bois de la Garenne, with the Calvaire d'Illy at its northern point. A narrow valley, the Fond de Givonne, cut away south towards Bazeilles, while a re-entrant ran from Illy itself to Floing in the valley of the Meuse. South of the river, at Frenois and Wadelincourt, rose another range of hills.

On 31 August MacMahon deployed his exhausted army to take best advantage of the position. Douay's 7th Corps held the slopes from Floing to Illy, while General Ducrot put his 1st Corps into line covering the northern end of the Fond de Givonne. Lebrun pushed one division of 12th Corps into Bazeilles, while the other two held the Fond de Givonne to link up with Ducrot on their left. The 5th Corps was placed in reserve.

Moltke viewed the situation with enthusiasm. Unless MacMahon moved rapidly eastward along the north bank of the Meuse, there was every chance that he could be trapped with the Belgian frontier at his back and German armies at both flanks. Moltke ordered the Army of the Meuse to advance on Sedan from the east. The Third Army was to move in from the south, sending its left wing across the Meuse to cut the French line of retreat.

By dusk on the 31st the Germans were in possession of the railway bridges at Donchery and Bazeilles—neither, by a combination of confusion and ill-luck, had been blown by MacMahon's engineers. As night fell the peril of the Army of

Châlons was clearly marked by the broad arc of German campfires. Ducrot appreciated the full seriousness of the army's plight. '*Nous sommes dans un pot de chambre*', he remarked, '*et nous y serons emmerdés*' (We are in a chamber pot, and we are about to be covered in shit).

The battle began just after 0400, when troops of I Bavarian Corps attacked Lebrun's Marines in Bazeilles. The Marines were regulars, and fought hard from houses and barricades, aided by some of the inhabitants. Before long the village was on fire, but the French hung on desperately. MacMahon rode forward at about 0600, but was wounded in the leg by a shell-splinter almost immediately. He thought Ducrot the most competent of the corps commanders, and sent him a note ordering him to take over. It took nearly two hours for the message to reach Ducrot, and by then the situation had worsened.

The leading formation of the Army of the Meuse, XII Corps, came into action on the Bavarian right, taking La Moncelle at 0630. Within half an hour the Saxons had 72 guns in line above the village, but it took them three hours to force General de Lartigue's division of 1st Corps out of Daigny, where Ducrot had posted it at first light. As soon as Ducrot learnt that he had succeeded to MacMahon's command, he ordered an immediate retreat. Lebrun objected that his men were doing well in Bazeilles, and it was not until after 0800 that Ducrot felt certain enough to order him to fall back.

At this delicate juncture Wimpffen arrived to turn chaos into catastrophe. MacMahon had been unaware that Wimpffen held a dormant commission; he had told him nothing of any overall plan, which is hardly surprising since such a plan probably did not exist even in MacMahon's

Top: French cannon protect the defenses around Sedan. **Above:** General Ducrot, whom MacMahon considered to be the best of his corps commanders.

Opposite top: The Prussian needle-gun (above) and the French *chassepot*, two key weapons in the Franco-Prussian War. The *chassepot*, a breech-loader, was potentially as dangerous to the Prussian as the breech-loading needle-gun was to both Austrians and French in the 1866 and 1870 wars. The difference was the men who fired them and the men who led them. **Opposite bottom:** French horse artillery, exhausted from the battle, bring up the guns for a final defense of the fortress of Sedan.

Right: A Krupp 1000-pounder gun. The breech mechanism was a horizontal sliding block.

Below: The last stand by the hapless and exhausted defenders of Sedan.

mind. Wimpffen was, however, convinced that withdrawal was out of the question. He ordered Lebrun to remain in Bazeilles, and told Ducrot that 'We need a victory, not a retreat'.

It was by now doubtful if the army could have retreated even if it were given the order to do so. The left wing of the Third Army, V and XI Corps, had begun to cross the Meuse at Donchery at 0400, and cut the Mezières road at 0730. The II Bavarian Corps deployed its guns around Wadelincourt, shelling the ramparts of Sedan and the all too visible French positions around them, while V and XI Corps moved on Fleigneux and

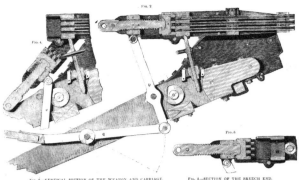

FIG. 2.—VERTICAL SECTION OF THE WEAPON AND CARRIAGE.
FIG. 3.—SECTION OF THE BREECH END.
FIG 4.—SECTION OF THE BREECH WITH THE BLOCK OR CLOSER DRAWN DOWN.

FIG. 1.—MITRAILLEUSE IN ACTION

Left: A French *mitrailleuse*, Napoleon III's secret weapon, which few French *poilus* knew how to operate. It was the forerunner of the modern machine-gun.

Above: The capture of Napoleon III at Sedan also cost the French Army 80,000 men, who went into Prussian captivity. It was the end of the French Empire and the Napoleonic dynasty. **Above right:** Prussian infantry charge the French defenses as their encirclement of Napoleon's forces became complete.

XI on St Menges. Guns of both corps came into action against the 7th Corps, and under cover of their fire, infantry pressed forward toward the Floing-Illy road. General Bernis' brigade of the 5th Corps Cavalry Division tried to check this advance, but was warmly received. The divisional commander, General Brahaut, was captured, with many of his troopers. Still more were killed or wounded, but some, more fortunate, found their way through the thin German cordon into Belgium and internment. There was an equally abortive charge by General de Gallifet's brigade of Margueritte's cavalry division.

German shellfire was now causing heavy casualties throughout the French position. The artillery of the Guard, under command of the brilliant Prince Kraft zu Hohenlohe-Ingelfingen,

was deployed above the Fond de Givonne, mercilessly raking 1st Corps, while the guns of V and XI poured shells into Douay's exposed lines. Despite this fire, Douay felt confident that he could hold out as long as the Calvaire d'Illy remained in French hands. At about 1100 Wimpffen promised Douay reinforcements to hold this vital point, but within an hour was forced to ask him to send a division to aid 7th Corps, which was to spearhead the planned breakout towards Carignan. Douay tried to hold the Calvaire with a scratch force, but his corps became increasingly shaky under the hail of shells, and the German infantry pressed closer.

Wimpffen's breakout never really got under way. The chaos within his defensive perimeter was so great as to make a cohesive move im-

possible. But while he remained preoccupied with the southeastern sector, matters continued to deteriorate in the north. German infantry had reached the Calvaire at about 1400, and both Douay's right and Ducrot's left had been forced back into the Bois de la Garenne. Douay's left, above Floing, was also in danger, as German infantry filtered down the edge of the Meuse valley. General Lièbert's division, holding this area, was forced to give ground, and eventually fell back off Sedan, suffering frightfully from shellfire in the process.

Ducrot's growing despair was reflected by his next decision. Although Wimpffen remained deluded by the prospect of a breakout to the east, Ducrot was horribly certain that the army's last chance of safety lay to the west. His own troops,

like those of the 7th Corps, were exhausted, and the remnants of 5th Corps could no longer be depended upon. He turned, therefore, to Margueritte, whose division of *Chasseurs d'Afrique* was largely intact. Ducrot requested Margueritte to smash through XI Corps near Floing, opening a gap through which the infantry could follow. Margueritte rode forward to reconnoitre while his division shook out into order. His jaw was smashed by a bullet, but he struggled back to his *Chasseurs* and pointed down the slope at the Germans before collapsing. He died some days later. The charge of Margueritte's division was as gallant as it was useless. Some skirmishers were cut down, but the main attack was stopped dead by the rapid fire of the German infantry. With supreme gallantry, the shattered squadrons re-

Above left and right: Two reconstructed episodes from the Battle of Sedan, photographed in 1890.

Below: In another reconstructed episode from the battle, French artillery is dragged into position near Sedan.

grouped and came on again and again. King Wilhelm, watching the battle from the heights above Frenois, could not resist exclaiming 'Ah! The brave fellows!'

The failure of the last charge, and of the forlorn infantry rush that accompanied it, was followed by the almost total collapse of 7th Corps, which streamed off to the questionable safety of the Bois de la Garenne or Sedan. Even the *Africains* of 1st Corps were demoralized by the crippling fire to which they had been subjected all day. By 1500 the guard had penetrated the splintered trees of the Bois de la Garenne, and 1st Corps' position, like that of 7th Corps, was hopeless.

Napoleon had spent the day riding about with fatalistic resignation, indifferent to the heavy fire. One of his staff was cut in half beside him, and others were wounded. But death eluded him, and when approached by Lebrun, Ducrot and Douay, he agreed that the situation was hopeless, sending Lebrun to find Wimpffen in order to negotiate terms. Wimpffen still hoped to salvage something from the wreckage. He ordered Lebrun to help him gather troops for a last attempt to break out and together, at the head of a few hundred men from a mixture of units, they surged into Balan, taking the Bavarians by surprise and seizing the village. The assault got no further, and Wimpffen had, at last, to admit defeat. The white flag was hoisted over Sedan even before he reached it, and General Reille was sent to Wilhelm with a note announcing that, having failed to die among his troops, Napoleon placed his sword in the King's hands.

There was more to the capitulation than the exchange of civilities between monarchs. Wilhelm, in his reply, appointed Moltke his plenipotentiary for the conclusion of terms. On the French side, it was less easy to find a negotiator. Wimpffen refused and offered his resignation, but Ducrot emphasized that, as Wimpffen had taken command when there was 'some honor and profit' in it, he could scarcely avoid this last cruel

responsibility. Wimpffen, accompanied by General de Castelnau, met Moltke and Bismarck at Donchery. The French generals were unable to wring any useful concessions out of Moltke. There was a moment when Bismarck implied that, if the Emperor were seeking an end to the war rather than the capitulation of the Army of Châlons, things might be different. But Castelnau killed this fleeting possibility by stressing that Napoleon's own surrender did not include that of France, and the meeting ended with Moltke pointing out the hopelessness of the French position, and warning that, if no satisfactory answer were received by 0900 the following day, his batteries would open fire once more.

The capitulation was finalized at 1100 on 2 September, in the Château de Bellevue, near Frenois. Napoleon had endeavored to see Wilhelm personally in the hope of producing improved terms, but he had been politely interrupted by Bismarck, and nothing had been achieved. The final terms were uncompromising. The entire army, with all its equipment, was to become prisoner-of-war. Officers were permitted to go free if they undertook not to take up arms against Germany during the course of the current war. Relatively few took advantage of this concession.

The French had suffered 17,000 casualties during the battle, and had lost a further 21,000 prisoners. The capitulation gave the Germans 83,000 more, with 449 field guns, 139 fortress guns, and a rich booty of horses, rifles and vehicles. The Germans had lost only 9000 killed and wounded. A comparison between the casualty figures reveals the predominant role played by the German artillery. The lesson of St Privat had not been wasted. German commanders were now content to let their artillery do their work for them, and the German gunners showed themselves worthy of this new confidence.

The consequences of Sedan cannot be measured in purely material terms. As Napoleon III was driven off to captivity, Bismarck sagely remarked

THE ILLUSTRATED LONDON NEWS

REGISTERED AT THE GENERAL POST-OFFICE FOR TRANSMISSION ABROAD

No. 1635.—VOL. LVIII.   SATURDAY, FEBRUARY 4, 1871.   PRICE FIVEPENCE

PROCLAIMING THE KING OF PRUSSIA AS GERMAN EMPEROR IN THE PALACE OF VERSAILLES.

Left: King Wilhelm I of Prussia is proclaimed German Kaiser in the Hall of Mirrors of the Palace of Versailles, 18 January, 1871. The German Empire, the Second Reich, was born out of the ashes of Sedan.

that a dynasty was on its way out. He was right; on 4 September the Regency in Paris fell, and was replaced by the Government of National Defense, an aggressively left-wing body pledged to continue the war. Its resistance was as remarkable as it was futile. Paris was beleaguered, and the provincial armies, one by one, were defeated. An armistice was concluded on 28 January, 1871, and in May the war was ended by the Treaty of Frankfurt. France lost Alsace and Lorraine, had to pay a substantial indemnity, and suffered three years of German occupation. The Treaty of Frankfurt, like that of Versailles nearly half a century later, brought peace but not forgiveness. The loss of Alsace-Lorraine was a source of continual bitterness to the French, while the new and aggressive German Empire, born as it was of military conquest, cast an alarming shadow over the future of Europe.

It is tempting to look upon French defeat in the Franco-Prussian War as inevitable. This is, however, to underestimate the fallibility of the German command, and the innate fighting qualities of the French soldier. What is certain, though, is that the defeat of the Army of Châlons was predictable and, at least until 23 August, avoidable. MacMahon's army was ruined as much by its own inadequacies as by the brilliance of its enemy. Impelled by political motives, and in defiance of military logic, it undertook a maneuver which would have taxed even a cohesive and well trained force. In the words of one French officer, MacMahon's success would have required a miracle; the age of miracles was over. As the German Empire was victoriously proclaimed in the Hall of Mirrors of the Palace of Versailles, Bismarck and Kaiser Wilhelm inaugurated a period of German hegemony in Continental Europe.

Opposite top: The Imperial Guard before their surrender at Sedan.
Opposite center: The French forces stampede as they enter Sedan in the closing phase of the action.
Opposite bottom: After the fall of Sedan, the Paris Commune took control of the capital, and Prussian forces surrounded Paris to begin their long siege of the city. Wounded were transported down the Seine to the Quai de là Megisserie.
Left: The capitulation of Bazaine and the Army of Metz, 27 October, 1870.

Tsushima

It was a perfect night. A full moon lit the smooth sea rendering excellent visibility. Within the harbor the fleet lay anchored in three lines with a row of five battleships on the outside. The ships and harbor installations were fully illuminated by electric lights since the Viceroy had thought it would be 'premature' to put them on a war footing. Twenty miles out, two guard destroyers had not interfered but had run into the harbor at full speed to raise the alarm which arrived simultaneously with the first torpedoes. Nine attacking destroyers ran along the line of battleships, each destroyer in succession firing its torpedoes and turning away at full speed. Searchlights vainly pierced the night while hastily manned guns banged away at an enemy no longer there. It was the night of 8 February, 1904, the night when Admiral Heihachiro Togo opened the Russo-Japanese War with a surprise attack on the Russian fleet at Port Arthur. As the war opened with this only moderately successful attack, so it was to end in a much different fashion a year and a half later at the Battle of Tsushima. The largest naval battle between Trafalgar and Jutland, Tsushima had a profound influence upon naval warfare and radically changed the structure of power in the Far East as a whole.

The war grew directly out of the competing imperialisms of Russia and Japan in Korea and Manchuria. In 1894–1895 Japan had fought China for primacy of influence in Korea and won Port Arthur and the Liaotung Peninsula by the Treaty of Shimonoseki. Russia had been pursuing a vigorous Far Eastern policy for decades and was now moving into Manchuria and Korea to compete with Japan. With the support of France and Germany, Russia had been able to force Japan to return her gains in the Sino-Japanese War to China, after which she then obtained a long lease on Port Arthur from China and began to develop it as the basis of her power in that area. During the Boxer Rebellion of 1900 in China, Russia took the opportunity to occupy much of Manchuria, from which she refused to withdraw. The Russian drive into Manchuria alarmed not only the Japanese, but also the British and Americans. The Russian threat brought Britain and Japan together in the Anglo-Japanese Alliance of 1902, the essence of which was that if Japan was at war in the Far East, Britain would intervene on the Japanese side if another power entered the war against her. The effect of the alliance was that Russia could not rely on French and German support against Japan as had been the case in 1895. Generally speaking, at this time Japan, Britain and the United States supported each other against Russia and France in the contest for power in the Far East.

It was not Manchuria, however, but Russian penetration into Korea that Japan found intolerable. Control of Korea was correctly seen as vital to the security of Japan or, as one Japanese statesman put it, Korea was 'an arrow pointed at the heart of Japan'. The Japanese had fought the Sino-Japanese War to remove the Chinese as rivals in Korea, only to see Chinese influence replaced by Russian. Russia in fact was virtually running the country. There had always been a strong 'war party' in Japan which advocated settling the Korean question by invasion and occupation, but as tension increased in 1903, the Japanese government first tried negotiations with

Opposite, above and below: Two Japanese portrayals of the attack at Port Arthur which inaugurated the Russo-Japanese War in 1904. The Japanese surprise attack which preceded a formal declaration of war effectively wiped out the entire Russian Far Eastern Fleet the first day. This forced Russia to send her Baltic Fleet to Asia if she were to combat Japanese naval power in the war.

Above: The capitulation of Port Arthur took place after several months of siege. The Russian garrison left the city as Japanese forces entered to occupy it.

Right: Court ladies at St. Petersburg make garments for the Russian soldiers at the front in the Far East. **Opposite top:** Officers of the Imperial Russian Guard leave St. Petersburg for the front. The journey on the recently-completed Trans-Siberian Railway sometimes took weeks. **Opposite bottom:** Admiral Heihachiro Togo, head of the Japanese Fleet and victor at Tsushima.

its rival. The Japanese suggested what amounted to a mutual recognition of their respective spheres of interest in Manchuria and Korea, but Russia dragged out the talks in the belief that she was strong enough not to have to accept any compromise. Also, Russia did not believe that Japan would dare to fight a European power. When asked if Russian policy might not provoke war with Japan, the Russian Foreign Minister replied 'One flag and one sentry; Russian prestige will do the rest'. Admiral Alexeiev, the Viceroy of the Far East and rumored illegitimate son of Czar Alexander II, was prominent among the 'hard

liners'. While negotiations limped along, Japan saw Russian influence in Korea increasing even more as Russians obtained land, timber and business concessions. Since it was obvious that no change in Russian policy was under consideration, Japan declared war on 10 February, 1904.

Japan was well aware of the role of naval power as her lines of communications depended on it. Possessed of a compact and modern fleet, it was only in 1892 that she decided to look outward by increasing her naval budget at the expense of the army. The one naval encounter of the Sino-Japanese War, the Battle of Yalu, had revealed Japanese sailors as disciplined and well trained while the victory had won the navy the enthusiasm of the nation. The officer who had fired the first shot in the Sino-Japanese War was Heihachiro Togo, now vice-admiral and head of the fleet. Of samurai origin, Togo was highly intelligent and experienced and as a young officer had trained in Britain with the Royal Navy. Japanese officers were often reported by their foreign contemporaries to be highly professional. This, coupled with the battle experience of the Sino-Japanese War, made the Japanese navy a modern and efficient fighting force.

Always attentive to British naval policy, Japan had decided to adopt its own 'two power standard' which meant that her navy should be stronger than the combined Pacific squadrons of any other two powers, excluding Britain. 'Any other two powers' meant Russia and France, and in 1896 a new naval program was launched. Armored cruisers and battleships were built in Britain but a fair number of light cruisers and torpedo craft were constructed at the Yokosuka and Kure dockyards. Japan was also largely dependent on Britain for guns, ammunition and coal. By 1904 the Japanese battle fleet was new

and homogenous due to Japan's late start in capital ship construction. All of Togo's battleships were less than ten years old and had similar speeds, turning circles and optimum gun ranges.

The two oldest battleships were the *Fuji* and *Yashima*, launched in Britain in 1896. Each was 12,500 tons, had a speed of eighteen knots and mounted four twelve-inch and ten six-inch guns. The *Hatsuse*, *Shikishima*, *Asahi* and *Mikasa* were new modern ships of 15,500 tons which could make eighteen knots and mounted four twelve-inch and fourteen six-inch guns. The *Mikasa* in particular had improved protection for her secondary armament and was one of the best of the world's pre-dreadnought battleships. To support her six battleships, Japan also had half a dozen armored cruisers – the *Asama*, *Tokigawa*, *Yakumo*, *Idzumo*, *Iwate* and *Adzuma*. These were 10,000 ton ships with twenty knot speed and mounted four eight-inch and fourteen six-inch guns. During the growing tension with Russia in 1903, Japan bought two new armored cruisers from Argentina with British aid. The *Kasuga* and *Nisshin* were both 7700-ton ships with twenty knot speed. The main armament of the *Kasuga* was one ten-inch gun forward and two eight-inch guns aft while the *Nisshin* mounted four eight-inch guns. The navy also had fourteen lighter cruisers and during the war armed 27 merchantmen as auxiliary cruisers.

Russia actually possessed three fleets – the Baltic, Black Sea and Pacific fleets. The Black Sea fleet was an instrument in Russia's age-old rivalry with Turkey and by the terms of the Treaty of London of 1870 was not permitted to pass through the Dardanelles, so it was not a factor in the Russo-Japanese War. Based at Port Arthur, the Pacific fleet contained seven battleships, six cruisers and several dozen destroyers

我驅逐艦隊於旅順港外近接
敵艦激戰大破敵隊

Opposite left: Transporting Russian soldiers across Lake Baikal on sledges. The problem of supplying an army thousands of miles away from the centers of population and industrial production proved insurmountable in the end.
Left: A Japanese version of the night attack at Port Arthur in 1904.

於黄海我軍大捷圖第一

定遠大火
發遠
靖遠沈没

Left: A Japanese artist's portrayal of the Battle of the Yalu River against China in 1894. The Sino-Japanese War of 1894–95 was the first time Japan put her fleet into action, surprising the world with the ability of an Asian nation to construct an effective, modern fleet. The world was shocked even more in 1904–05 when Japan was able to thoroughly defeat a major European state.

Top left: Japanese barbers and their clients aboard the *Mikasa*. **Top right:** The Japanese battleship *Hatsuse* in 1905. **Above center:** The Japanese battleship *Fuji* was built, like much of the Japanese Navy, in British shipyards. **Above:** The Japanese cruiser *Asama*, commanded by Admiral Uriu, which sank the *Variag*.

Left: The Japanese battle fleet, composed of *Mikasa* (foreground), and (left to right) *Shikishima, Fuji, Asahi, Kasuga* and *Nisshin* leave port to intercept the Russian squadron in the Strait of Tsushima.

and torpedo boats. By itself it was more than a match for Togo's fleet in terms of gun power and numbers of ships. In 1898 Russia had begun a capital ship program which made her the world's third power in battleships behind Britain and France by 1904, although the United States and Germany were rapidly catching up. Well aware of the progress of Russian naval expansion, the naval factor was a major reason why Japan elected to attack at the time and in the manner that she did. A Japanese naval delegation had visited Russian navy yards in the Baltic area in the autumn of 1903 and knew that an additional half-dozen battleships were destined for the Pacific within a year's time. Already outnumbered in terms of battleships in the Pacific, Japan had to act soon or war would not be possible in naval terms.

Japanese war strategy was to secure Korea and Port Arthur and then advance into Manchuria. To put troops into Korea, however, the Russian superiority in seapower had to be neutralized. Therefore Togo's plan was to destroy as many Russian ships as possible in three simultaneous actions at Port Arthur, the nearby Russian civil port at Dalny (Dairen), and Chemulpo (modern Inchon), the port of Seoul. Japanese intelligence had reported Russian ships at all three places but on the night of 8 February no ships were found at Dalny and only a cruiser and a gunboat were destroyed at Chemulpo where 2500 Japanese troops were also landed under naval cover. With the surprise attack on Port Arthur Togo had hoped to rob the Russians of their battleship supremacy, but the attack succeeded only in damaging two battleships and a cruiser. These were minor losses which were soon repaired, but Togo had seized command of the sea and forced the Russian fleet on the defensive, a position from which it never recovered. He had also insured that there would be a land battle for Korea and perhaps Manchuria

Below: The first shot fired by the main Japanese squadron.

浦潮港海軍之攻撃

八雲艦の砲撃ハ敵ニ尠小多大
の損害を加へ大勝利すて引揚
、露艦氷結困却の圖

as well. There was outrage in Russia at the immorality of the 'sneak' attack, but in Britain and the United States such a 'smart' move was generally admired.

Apart from three cruisers which raided from Vladivostok and were soon eliminated, the entire Russian Pacific Squadron was now bottled up in Port Arthur protected by formidable shore batteries. Togo made a number of efforts to destroy the fleet in the harbor but other than some skirmishing off Port Arthur, the Russian ships made no attempt to interfere with Japanese troop landings or communications. The Russian ships lay inert until the energetic Admiral Stephan Makarov arrived and rapidly began to whip them into fighting shape. Unfortunately in April Makarov's flagship, the *Petropavlovsk*, was sunk by a mine with no survivors. Without Makarov, the fleet took no further part in the war beyond several unsuccessful attempts to escape to Vladivostok. For their part, the Japanese lost the battleships *Hatsuse* and *Yashima* to mines in May but even so, the Russian squadron at Port Arthur showed no inclination to challenge Japanese control of the sea.

Japan prosecuted the war vigorously on land as well as sea. One Japanese army pushed south across the Liaotung Peninsula and soon had Port Arthur under siege while two other armies fought their way north into Manchuria. Although the Russians were pushed back to Mukden, the Russian Army remained intact and was receiving steadily increasing reinforcements. Then the

Japanese learned that their worst fears were about to be realized. The Russians had been giving some consideration to sending part of their Baltic fleet to reinforce the Pacific Squadron, but the news of the death of Admiral Makarov, the loss of the *Petropavlovsk* and the inactivity of the Port Arthur ships moved Czar Nicholas II and his advisors to make a final decision in this matter. The Russian plan was to relieve Port Arthur by sea, overwhelm the Japanese Navy with the now combined squadrons and thus delay the Japanese advance into Manchuria until enough reinforcements could arrive via the Trans-Siberian Railway for General Kuropatkin's army in Manchuria to turn the tide on land as well. In view of this turn of events, the main Japanese objective became to capture Port Arthur as soon as possible and destroy the Russian fleet there without risking their own fleet too much in the process.

The 'Second Pacific Squadron'

The man entrusted with command of what was called the 'Second Pacific Squadron' was the 56-year old son of an aristocratic and well to do family. Sinovie Rozhestvensky had joined the navy at 17, fought in the Turkish War of 1877–1878, served as Naval Attaché in London and after service in the Far East had become Naval Chief of Staff. He was a taciturn personality who rarely confided in his staff. In addition to his lack of command experience at sea, he combined a modest sense of tactics with a lack of imagination.

Opposite top: Russian staff officer patroling the Trans-Siberian Railway. Bicycles were often used by the gendarmerie of the railways in inspection tours.
Opposite below: How Russian soldiers traveled to the front lines on the Trans-Siberian Railway. Each railway car had 40 men; there was room for ten to sleep on the shelves. The rest slept on the floor.
Above: Japanese fleet in action off Vladivostok, Russia's principal port in East Asia.

It is not clear what Rozhestvensky's views on the mission of the Second Pacific Squadron were, but it is known that he rightly felt the venture was extremely dangerous and that it was his duty to lead it in person. Others had higher hopes. 'The Czar with his habitual optimism expected Rozhestvensky to reverse the war situation' wrote the Minister of Finance.

The five divisions of the Second Pacific Squadron did not weigh anchor until 15 October. The first division consisted of four new first class battleships – Rozhestvensky's flagship *Suvorov*, *Alexander III*, *Borodino* and *Orel*. These were 15,000-ton ships with eighteen-knot speed and mounting four twelve-inch guns. The six-inch armament was mounted in turrets which was an improvement over the sea drenched casemates still used by

other navies. Their speed and stability was reduced, however, by the extra ammunition, provisions and coal which they carried on the voyage east; they had to be handled carefully and it was dangerous for them to turn at more than twelve knots with their gun ports open. The second division was led by the *Oslyabya*, flagship of second in command Admiral von Felkerzam, a modern ship of the same class as the ships of the first division. Then there were two old battleships of 10,000 tons armed with four twelve-inch guns – the *Sisoi Veliky* and the *Navarin*. The division was completed by the *Nakhimov*, an old armored cruiser of 6000 tons built in 1882. With the exception of the *Oslyabya*, these ships were no longer suitable for front line service in 1904. With his flag in the *Oleg*, Admiral

Enkvist led the third division of eight cruisers. The remaining two divisions were made up of light cruisers and destroyers.

The heart of Rozhestvensky's squadron was obviously the five modern battleships which compared very favorably with the best Japanese ships. There were a few differences, however, which were to be significant. Aside from their slower speeds, the Russian ships had a slower rate of fire per minute on their big guns which were still fired by lanyard rather than electrically. Russian shells were also lighter than Japanese shells, a twelve-inch Russian shell weighing 732 pounds versus 850 pounds for a comparable Japanese shell. This gave the former a greater muzzle velocity and hence greater penetrating power and a flatter trajectory, which in turn

Opposite: Rozhestvensky's fleet in the Straits of Malacca. Apart from incidents with British in the Dogger Bank, along the African coast and near Malaya, the trip was 'uneventful'. **Left:** The Russian battleship *Orel* shortly after her capture by the Japanese in the Battle of Tsushima. **Above:** Admiral Rozhestvensky, commander of the ill-fated Baltic Fleet, which became the 'Second Pacific Squadron'.

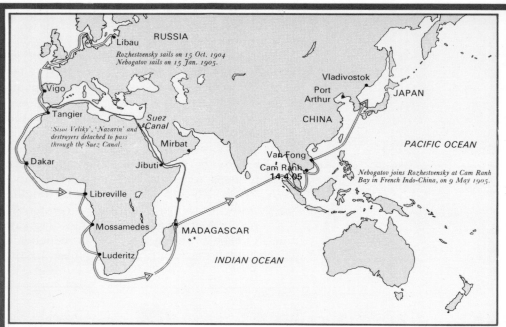

RUSSIA

Libau

Rozhestvensky sails on 15 Oct. 1904
Nebogatov sails on 15 Jan. 1905.

Vigo

Tangier

Suez Canal

'Sisoi Veliky', 'Navarin' and destroyers detached to pass through the Suez Canal.

Dakar

Mirbat

Jibuti

Libreville

Mossamedes

MADAGASCAR

Luderitz

INDIAN OCEAN

Vladivostok
Port Arthur

JAPAN

CHINA

PACIFIC OCEAN

Van Fong
Cam Ranh
14.4.05

Nebogatov joins Rozhestvensky at Cam Ranh Bay in French Indo-China, on 9 May 1905.

AUSTRALIA

The Battle of Tsushima, 27 May 1905

1. Iwate
2. Asama
3. Yakumo
4. Tokiwa
5. Adzuma
6. Idzum
7. Nisshin
8. Kasuga
9. Asahi
10. Fuji
11. Shikishima
12. Mikasa

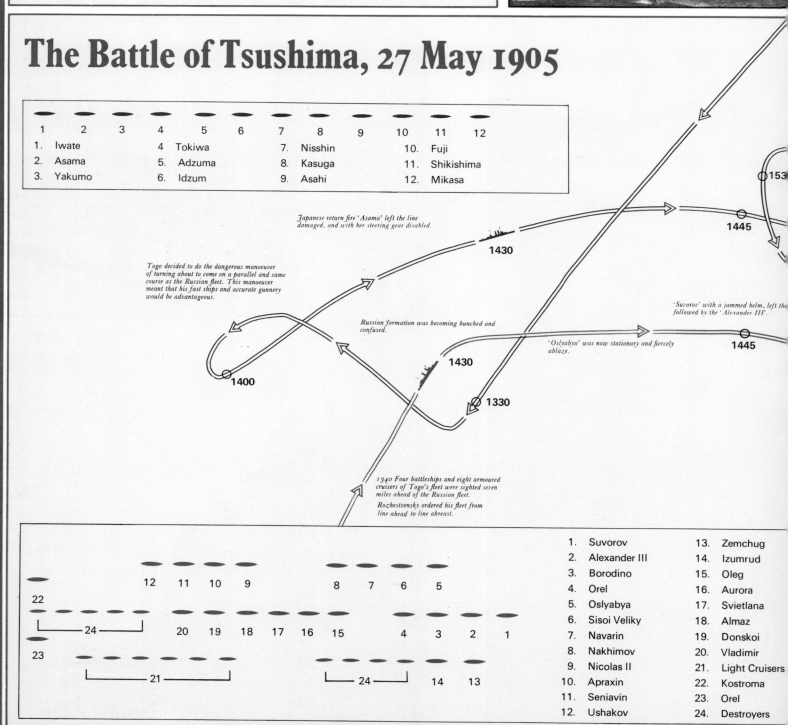

Japanese return fire 'Asama' left the line damaged, and with her steering gear disabled.

1430

Togo decided to do the dangerous manoeuver of turning about to come on a parallel and same course as the Russian fleet. This manoeuver meant that his fast ships and accurate gunnery would be advantageous.

Russian formation was becoming bunched and confused.

1400

1430

1330

1445

153

1445

'Suvorov' with a jammed helm, left the followed by the 'Alexander III'.

'Oslyabya' was now stationary and fiercely ablaze.

1340 Four battleships and eight armoured cruisers of Togo's fleet were sighted seven miles ahead of the Russian fleet.
Rozhestvensky ordered his fleet from line ahead to line abreast.

1. Suvorov
2. Alexander III
3. Borodino
4. Orel
5. Oslyabya
6. Sisoi Veliky
7. Navarin
8. Nakhimov
9. Nicolas II
10. Apraxin
11. Seniavin
12. Ushakov
13. Zemchug
14. Izumrud
15. Oleg
16. Aurora
17. Svietlana
18. Almaz
19. Donskoi
20. Vladimir
21. Light Cruisers
22. Kostroma
23. Orel
24. Destroyers

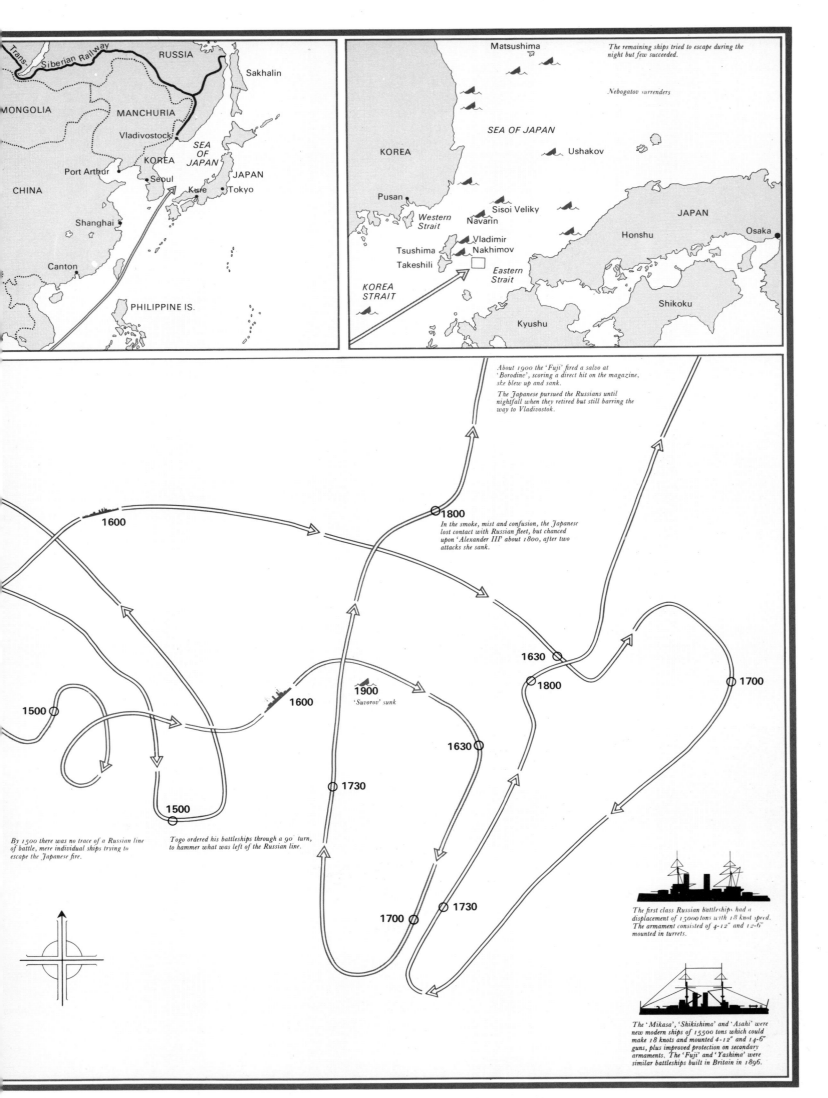

Trans- Siberian Railway RUSSIA
MONGOLIA
MANCHURIA
Sakhalin
Vladivostock
KOREA
SEA OF JAPAN
Port Arthur
Seoul
CHINA
Kure
JAPAN
Tokyo
Shanghai
Canton
PHILIPPINE IS.

Matsushima
The remaining ships tried to escape during the night but few succeeded.
Nebogatov surrenders
SEA OF JAPAN
Ushakov
KOREA
Pusan
Western Strait
Navarin
Sisoi Veliky
Tsushima
Vladimir Nakhimov
Takeshili
Eastern Strait
KOREA STRAIT
JAPAN
Honshu
Osaka
Shikoku
Kyushu

About 1900 the 'Fuji' fired a salvo at 'Borodino', scoring a direct hit on the magazine, she blew up and sank.

The Japanese pursued the Russians until nightfall when they retired but still barring the way to Vladivostok.

1600

1800
In the smoke, mist and confusion, the Japanese lost contact with Russian fleet, but chanced upon 'Alexander III' about 1800, after two attacks she sank.

1630
1800
1700

1500
1900 'Suvorov' sunk
1600

1500
1630

1730

By 1500 there was no trace of a Russian line of battle, mere individual ships trying to escape the Japanese fire.

Togo ordered his battleships through a 90° turn, to hammer what was left of the Russian line.

1700
1730

The first class Russian battleships had a displacement of 15000 tons with 18 knot speed. The armament consisted of 4-12" and 12-6" mounted in turrets.

The 'Mikasa', 'Shikishima' and 'Asahi' were new modern ships of 15500 tons which could make 18 knots and mounted 4-12" and 14-6" guns, plus improved protection on secondary armaments. The 'Fuji' and 'Yashima' were similar battleships built in Britain in 1896.

meant a greater margin of permissible error in estimating range. Since naval thought at that time assumed that battles would be fought between lines of battleships trying to force shells through the armor of their opponents, the duel between gun and armor was the dominant concept. The plain armor of the ironclads had first been superceded by compound armor, then Harvey (American) armor and finally Krupp (German) plate which was by far the hardest and was specified in all new Russian ships. At Tsushima the five modern Russian battleships all had Krupp armor, whereas only a few of the Japanese ships were so equipped.

All navies were at that time searching for an efficient armor-piercing shell and here the Russians were the most advanced with their AP shell which had a special cap to aid penetration. The shell had a relatively small bursting charge, however, which caused little damage and produced little smoke to help the gunlayers judge the fall of their shot. The British Navy was slow in this field and still used a 'common' shell with less penetrating power but a sizable bursting charge. Since the Japanese bought most of their ammunition from Britain, they also lacked a good AP shell but compensated by using a new explosive called *shimose* (after its Japanese inventor), which was more powerful than gun cotton with none of its disadvantages. *Shimose* had great explosive force which shattered the shell case into minute splinters (a single Russian sailor was wounded in 160 places by one shell burst) and also produced clouds of incapacitating smoke which caused headaches and giddiness and made it easier for Japanese gunners to gauge their accuracy.

The Dogger Bank Incident

Rozhestvensky's squadron faced severe problems from the outset. The crews had received no training and he was expected to remedy this lack en route. His new battleships had not completed their sea trials, while many of the remaining ships were simply too old for such a long trip.

Thus most of his ships suffered from engine trouble. Three ships were actually sent back as unfit once the voyage had begun. One Russian captain later wrote 'Our long voyage was a prolonged and despairing struggle with boilers that burst and engines that broke down. On one occasion, practically every ship's boilers had to be relit in the space of twenty-four hours'. And it was a long voyage, an impossible 18,000-mile route from the Baltic to Port Arthur along which there was not one Russian base. Coaling was to be done from 70 colliers chartered from the Hamburg-Amerika Line of Germany and the fleet included a number of stores and repair ships. After Rozhestvensky had talked the Navy Board out of giving him more antiquated ships, the fleet finally sailed in mid-October. Tension was high as rumors were rife of Japanese torpedo boats lying in wait along the route. After sailing all day on 24 October in mist and fog and keeping in bad contact, the ships of the first division saw small craft ahead and heard gunfire. Thinking their fears were realized, the ships opened fire and saw cruisers to the west also firing at them. After fifteen minutes of gunfire Rozhestvensky and Enkvist realized that they were firing on each other's ships. The small craft had been the Hull fishing fleet trawling the Dogger Bank, one of the busiest fishing grounds in the world. Felkerzam's ships had passed without incident, but Enkvist's ships had panicked and fired on the main fleet. One trawler was sunk and five more damaged while the Cruiser *Aurora* had taken five hits as well. Due to the rumors of the torpedo boats, Rozhestvensky had ordered his fleet to fire on any unidentified vessels which came too close.

What came to be known as the 'Dogger Bank Incident' caused an international uproar and raised the possibility of war between Britain and Russia. The British press called Rozhestvensky 'the mad dog' while Count Reventlow, naval correspondent of the *Berliner Tageblatt*, wrote trenchantly: 'The officers commanding the Russian ships must be all the time in an abnormal state of mind, and it is therefore not altogether

Below: Rozhestvensky's lost squadron. *Orel* (captured), in foreground, *Suvorov* in the center (sunk). Every ship in this illustration was either captured or sunk at Tsushima.

unjustifiable to ask . . . whether a squadron led as this squadron is led, ought to be allowed to sail the seas'. Britain put all its squadrons on a war footing and sent a strong force of heavy cruisers to shadow the Russian fleet all the way to North Africa. In his own report Rozhestvensky maintained that there had been at least two torpedo boats among the trawlers, although why these boats had fired shells rather than torpedoes and how they managed to find the Russian fleet which was thirty miles off its expected course in a fog remained unexplained. The Russian government had to accept this weak explanation and later adjudicated the matter with Britain at the International Court at The Hague.

After this less than auspicious start the fleet arrived at Tangier where Felkerzam with the *Sisoi Veliky*, *Navarin* and the destroyers were detached to transit through the Suez Canal while the remainder of the fleet went down the west coast of Africa and around the Cape of Good Hope to reunite off Madagascar. During the voyage Rozhestvensky attempted to drill his fleet in maneuvers and deployment, but the results revealed confusion and incompetence and brought the Admiral to a scarcely veiled contempt for some of his captains and officers. As the voyage progressed he became increasingly taciturn which made communication between him and his officers even more difficult than usual. Morale among the crews sank to very low levels from hard work and boredom, the breakdowns and defects in the ships, and the failures of seamanship but especially from the news the fleet received on arrival in Madagascar in early January.

At the siege of Port Arthur the Japanese had finally succeeded in capturing a key hill overlooking the city from which artillery fire could be directed into the harbor. With eleven-inch howitzer shells from enemy siege guns dropping on them, the ships of the First Pacific Squadron had come to an ignominious end within four days, never having properly engaged the slightly inferior enemy fleet. With the demise of the Port Arthur fleet, Russian naval strength in the Far East was reduced to one armored cruiser and some small craft at Vladivostok. Later in the month came the news that Port Arthur had capitulated after a five-month siege. The people of Russia were deeply shocked and believed that nothing was left. Whatever Kuropatkin's growing army in Manchuria or the vaunted Second Pacific Squadron could accomplish seemed almost irrelevant. Serious disturbances broke out in Russia which signaled the start of the Revolution of 1905, news of which further depressed Rozhestvensky's crews.

The loss of the Pacific fleet and the fall of Port Arthur changed the position of the Second Pacific Squadron. The relief of Port Arthur was no longer an objective nor could a junction be made with the Port Arthur ships to overwhelm the Japanese fleet. If the Japanese were to be confronted in battle, the Second Pacific Squadron would have to do so alone. The only reasonable course left was to proceed to Vladivostok and use that as a base from which to disrupt Japanese sea communications. The assumptions upon which the Baltic fleet had been dispatched to the Far East were now largely unfounded.

At Madagascar Rozhestvensky found that Felkerzam's ships needed at least two weeks for repairs, though Rozhestvensky wanted to push on and attack the Japanese fleet before it recovered from the long and wearing blockade of Port Arthur. The Japanese in fact were so worried about this very possibility that, fearful of a reverse

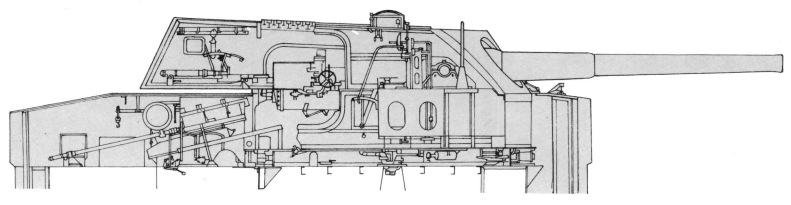

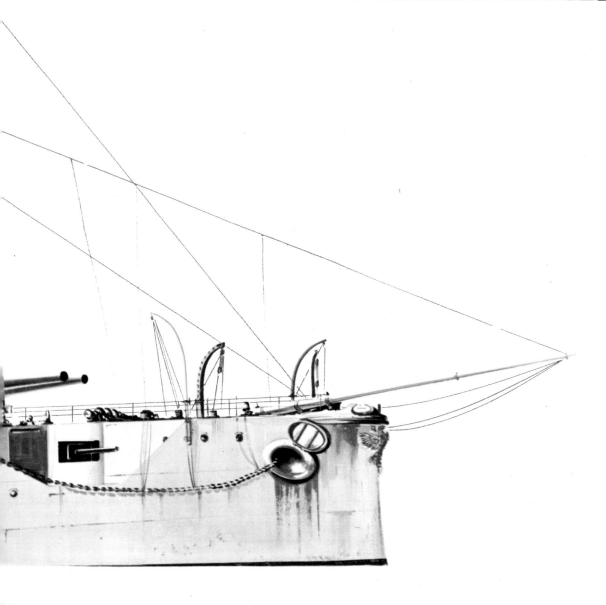

Above: The Battle of Tsushima was the total rout of the Russians. **Opposite:** Rozhestvensky's flagship *Suvorov* sinking in the Tsushima Strait.

at sea they began to stockpile matériel in Manchuria for a vigorous five-month campaign to prevent a disastrous peace settlement. In the event, however, Japanese fears were groundless as Rozhestvensky was also informed at Madagascar that another squadron had been despatched from the Baltic to reinforce him and that he was to await its arrival.

The reinforcement consisted of the same ancient ships which Rozhestvensky had persuaded the Navy Board not to send with him in the first place. Under the command of Admiral Nebogatov, the squadron consisted of the *Nicolas II*, an 1882 second-class battleship of 10,000 tons; the *Vladimir Monomakh*, a rigged cruiser of 6000 tons and equally ancient vintage; and three coastal defense ships, known derisively as 'flat-irons'. The *Apraxin*, *Seniavin* and *Ushakov* were small ships of 4500 tons, moderate armor and speed but large guns, the *Apraxin* having three ten-inch guns and the other ships four nine-inch guns. Among their crews these relics were termed the 'sink by themselves class'. After waiting until 16 March, Rozhestvensky sailed without Nebogatov, possibly hoping that the reinforcements would not catch up to him at all. Just before its departure, however, the Second Pacific Squadron suffered a further blow to its morale with the news of the Battle of Mukden. In the last great land battle of the war, 207,000 Japanese had attacked 276,000 Russians and forced them to retreat from Mukden at the end of February. The Japanese objective had not been the capture of territory but the destruction of the Russian Army in order to force Russia to the peace table. In this they had failed but the effect of the defeat, coming so soon after Port Arthur, was

shattering to Russian morale and brought the downfall of General Kuropatkin.

From Madagascar the fleet sailed across the Indian Ocean and on 14 April arrived at Cam Ranh Bay in French Indochina, having made a non-stop voyage of 4500 miles – the longest ever for a coal-fueled squadron without refueling. Probably with fresh orders about the reinforcements, Rozhestvensky tarried there long enough for Nebogatov to catch up and then the combined fleet of over forty ships sailed on into the South China Sea. Three possible routes to Vladivostok were now open to the Russian admiral. One route lay through the Korean Straits, passing the west coast of Japan into the Sea of Japan. The other two routes meant sailing around the east coast and using either the Tsugari or Soya Straits to the north of Japan. Had Rozhestvensky wished to attempt to avoid battle, he should have chosen one of the latter two straits, but instead he set his course for the Korean Straits, probably reasoning that avoiding battle served little purpose at this point.

Rozhestvensky apparently made few if any preparations for the battle he knew must lie ahead. He never consulted his three junior flag officers nor raised any discussion of contingencies. After the long voyage he apparently had a very low opinion of his subordinates and refused to consult them. In this event, however, they were even more in need of his detailed direction since they lacked initiative and skill. Also, signaling was chancey under the best of circumstances, so full orders were needed as Rozhestvensky would be unable to control his divisions in the heat of battle. But full orders were not given and a disorganized fleet approached the enemy. To

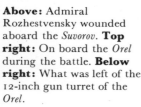

Above: Admiral Rozhestvensky wounded aboard the *Suvorov*. **Top right:** On board the *Orel* during the battle. **Below right:** What was left of the 12-inch gun turret of the *Orel*.

make matters worse, Felkerzam died on 23 May but the death of the second in command was kept from the rest of the fleet, which meant that it would have to turn to an already dead commander if Rozhestvensky had been put out of action.

Although he had mined and was patroling the Tsugari and Soya Straits, Togo was certain that his enemy would try the Korean Straits and had made his defensive dispositions accordingly. His heavy cruisers under Admiral Kamimura were based at Masampo, while his other ships were at Takeshii on the island of Tsushima. Tsushima lay in the middle of the Korean Straits and gave its name to the coming battle. Armed with squared maps of the area, four armed merchantmen and two old cruisers formed an outer guard line. Behind these were the four light cruisers of Admiral Dewa. The last concrete intelligence Togo had received was that the Russians had been sighted off the mouth of the Yangtse River on 25 May, but now he was worried as there had been no further news of them. As the Russian fleet approached the straits on the 26th, Rozhestvensky had ordered all wireless activity to cease and slowed his fleet so that their passage would be made in daylight as the night still held the terror of torpedo attacks. As daylight began to fade, Rozhestvensky gave the signal: 'Prepare for action.

Tomorrow at the hoisting of the colors, battle flags will be flown'.

Around 0300 on the 27th, the auxiliary cruiser *Sinano Maru* almost ran down a Russian hospital ship in the mist and soon sighted more ships. At 0500 she sent the urgent message 'Enemy fleet in sight in square 203. Is apparently making for the eastern channel' (between Tsushima and the Japanese mainland). At 0634 Rogo wired the Emperor 'I have just received news that the enemy fleet has been sighted. Our fleet will proceed forthwith to sea to attack the enemy and destroy him', after which the entire Japanese fleet put to sea. Around seven the first contact was made by the cruiser *Idzumi* which followed the Russians through the thinning mist for an hour until the *Suvorov* trained guns on her at 9000 yards. At nine the four cruisers of Admiral Kataoka's division appeared on the port side on a parallel course but later moved off. At eleven four light cruisers appeared again on the port side but quickly made off when the Russians sent a few rounds in that direction. The weather was now definitely poor with a heavy rolling sea and thickening mist.

By noon the Russian fleet was sailing at eight knots off the southern point of Tsushima. Hidden now from the watching enemy cruisers by the mist, Rozhestvensky made his only real tactical

Above: Looking forward from the hurricane deck of the shattered *Orel* after her capture.

canary yellow funnels which made them better targets than the slate grey Japanese ships on that dull day. Togo's line consisted of his battleships *Mikasa*, *Shikishima*, *Fuji* and *Asahi* supported by the armored cruisers *Kasuga* and *Nisshin*. Then followed Kamimura's armored cruisers *Idzuma*, *Adzuma*, *Tokigawa*, *Yakumo*, *Asama* and *Iwate*. As the Japanese line reversed its course, the *Suvorov* and *Oslyabya* opened fire, followed by the other ships in the still somewhat confused Russian formation. The Japanese line returned the fire more selectively, six ships concentrating on the *Oslyabya* and four on the *Suvorov* with telling effect. 'Shells seemed to be pouring upon us incessantly, one after the other' recalled one officer aboard the *Suvorov*. Serious fires broke out on the Russian flagship and the *Alexander III* but the *Oslyabya* was the hardest hit with fires, her fore turret out of action and a great hole in her bow at waterline where two twelve-inch shells struck simultaneously. In the opposing line, Togo's flagship *Mikasa* took a number of hits while the *Asama* left the line holed and with her steering gear entirely disabled.

The Japanese line was now curving around to starboard and ahead of the slow moving Russian formation. At about 1430 Rozhestvensky could have out maneuvered Togo by turning to port and passing astern of the Japanese, concentrating his fire on the ships of the enemy rear. But with three of his battleships already battered, Rozhestvensky instead allowed himself to be pushed around by the faster fleet and veered to starboard, throwing his gunners off-target in the process. With the enemy now almost in a semi-circle ahead of it, the Russian formation was becoming bunched and confused, the *Oslyabya* and *Suvorov* again the main targets of what was becoming a cross fire. The *Oslyabya* was now stationary and fiercely ablaze while the bridge of the *Suvorov* had been cleared by shell splinters. Rozhestvensky himself had been wounded in the head, back and legs. Moved to the conning tower, he was again wounded in the foot and lost consciousness. He was later evacuated aboard a destroyer. Now a burning ruin with an eight degree list to port and both funnels collapsed, the *Suvorov* had a jammed helm and turned a complete circle, followed by the *Alexander III*. The remainder of the formation was now in complete confusion with little semblance of a line. The ships behind the *Oslyabya* now pressed past that stricken vessel and watched in horror as she turned turtle and sank, a few frantic figures clinging to her keel. A destroyer was sent to inform Nebogatov that he was now in command.

Togo Finishes the Job

Taking his battleship division through two successive ninety-degree turns, Togo returned to hammer what was left of the Russian line. Kamimura's cruisers moved in to pound the hulks of the *Suvorov* and *Alexander III* at 3000 yards. By three o'clock there was no trace of a Russian line of battle, merely individual ships trying to escape the ring of Japanese fire. In the smoke, mist and confusion, the Japanese lost contact with the disintegrating Russian fleet but chanced upon the *Alexander III* about six

maneuver for the battle by ordering his fleet from line ahead to line abreast, possibly thinking that he could cross the Japanese T by turning to starboard or port as Togo arrived from the north in the traditional line ahead. The execution of the maneuver failed, however, and left the fleet in two parallel but unequal columns. At 1340 the four battleships and eight armored cruisers of the enemy were sighted seven miles ahead to starboard. Since noon the Japanese battle force had been cruising ten miles north of Okino-shima and with the enemy now in sight, Togo made the Nelsonian signal 'The Empire's fate depends on the result of this battle. Let every man do his utmost duty'. On its present bearing the Japanese fleet would have passed its enemy on an opposite and parallel tack, but Togo decided on the dangerous maneuver of turning about to come on a parallel and same course as the Russians. This maneuver meant that his ships would mask each others' guns temporarily. But afterwards his faster ships and more accurate gunnery would be in a position to inflict maximum damage for a longer period than if the fleets passed each other on opposite courses.

One line of four battleships was led by the *Suvorov*, while the remaining seven armored ships were led by the *Oslyabya* in a line to starboard. All the Russian ships were painted black with o'clock, low in the water but with her fires under control. After two attacks, she sank with but four survivors from her complement of 830. Subjected to repeated attacks by torpedo boats and destroyers, the *Suvorov* went down at seven with all hands. At the same time, the *Fuji* fired the last salvo of the main battle, scoring a direct hit on the magazines of the *Borodino*, which immediately blew up and sank leaving only one survivor.

By the end of the day the Russians had lost five battleships, three auxiliaries and suffered considerable damage to most of their other ships. Admiral Enkvist with the cruisers *Oleg*, *Aurora* and *Zemchug* had disappeared to the southwest and weeks later were interned in Manila. Nebogatov had collected the *Nicholas I*, *Orel*, *Apraxin*, *Seniavin* and cruiser *Izumrud* and remained undetected through the night by running without lights. At daybreak the Japanese battle line was north of the recent battle area, the fleet having withdrawn to allow attacks on the remaining Russian ships by torpedo boats and destroyers during the night but still barring the way to Vladivostok. As Nebogatov steamed toward the enemy in the morning he knew that a further clash was futile and hoisted the international signal of surrender. 'I'm an old man of sixty', he told his crew before going to surrender his sword to Togo. 'I shall be shot for this but what does that matter? You are young and it is you who will one day retrieve the honor and glory of the Russian navy. The lives of the 2400 men in these ships are more important than mine'.

The remaining ships tried to escape during the night but few succeeded. The *Ushakov*, *Navarin* and *Sisoi Veliky* were sunk while the *Nakhimov* and *Vladimir Monomakh* were scuttled off Tsushima. The destroyer to which Rozhestvensky had been evacuated was captured and the still unconscious admiral became a prisoner of Togo. Only one cruiser and two destroyers reached Vladivostok intact while a few other ships managed to make neutral ports where they were interned.

The battle was an utter disaster for Russia which lost 34 of 37 ships, 4830 dead, 5917 captured and 1862 interned in neutral ports. Japanese losses were one armored cruiser and two light cruisers badly damaged, three torpedo boats sunk, 110 killed and 590 wounded. When news of Tsushima reached Russia, it produced numbed despondency among the people and for the first time sentiment to end the war among the aristocracy. After Tsushima the war for all intents and purposes was over, although the Russian and Japanese armies continued to face each other in Manchuria. What the Japanese Army had failed to achieve had finally been accomplished by the navy at Tsushima: the annihilation of a major Russian force to bring Russia to the peace table. Tsushima made a profound impression in St. Petersburg precisely because it was so complete a disaster that Russia had no alternative but to pursue peace.

Immediately after the battle, the Japanese government asked President Theodore Roosevelt of the United States to use his good offices as mediator. After quietly sounding out the Russians, on 8 June Roosevelt formally wrote to each of the belligerents offering mediation. Russian and

Right: The doomed *Borodino*. There was only one survivor. **Below:** The body of the commander of the *Orel* is committed to the sea.

Japanese delegates met in August at Portsmouth, New Hampshire where the Treaty of Portsmouth was signed on 5 September. By this treaty, Japan received Russian railway rights in southern Manchuria and the ports of Dairen and Port Arthur in the Liaotung Peninsula. Russia recognized Japan's 'paramount political, military and economic interests' in Korea and also ceded the southern half of the island of Sakhalin to Japan, thus giving her complete control of the approaches to the Sea of Japan. With the loss of southern Manchuria, Russia was forced to give up her ambitious plans in the Yellow Sea area and concentrate on consolidating her remaining position. Japan became established as a continental Asiatic power and immediately proceeded to develop southern Manchuria. Japan also derived such prestige from being the only Asian nation to have defeated a western power that many Asians were ready to overlook her expansive ambitions and see her as the best available leader in the struggle against Western imperialism.

As Tsushima brought to an end a war which gave Japan increased territorial strength and prestige, so the battle also directly affected Japan's relationship with the United States. Up to 1904 American interests in the Far East had been largely assured by a system of competing powers in which no nation had military or naval preponderance. This system was further supported by the fact that the two leading naval powers in Asia – Britain and Japan – worked with the United States to counter the interests of Russia and her allies. The preservation of a balanced antagonism between Russia and Japan had become an essential ingredient of Roosevelt's Far Eastern diplomacy. The total destruction of Russian naval power in the Far East at Tsushima and the consequent diverting of her interests elsewhere destroyed this balanced antagonism. Roosevelt in fact had tried to get Russia and Japan into peace talks before Tsushima to preserve at least some of the naval balance which was changed still further as Britain increasingly withdrew her ships from the Far East to meet the rising challenge of German naval power in Europe. Of the half dozen major powers present in the Far East in 1904, only the United States and Japan remained to share or contend for mastery of the Pacific a few years after Tsushima.

This fact was quickly recognized by each government. In 1908 the Root-Takahira Agreement made an attempt to delineate the general position of the two powers in the Far East. Each government agreed to respect the 'existing status quo' in the Pacific, implying that America would give Japan a free hand in Korea while Japan would respect the American position in the Philippines. With the balanced antagonism between Russia and Japan destroyed at Tsushima, however, the United States had to redress the balance of naval power in the Far East shattered by Russia's defeats. Japan passed from being a 'sure' friend to a 'possible' enemy in American strategic planning, so a battle fleet had to be sent to the Pacific. Pearl Harbor in Hawaii was made the principal American base in the Pacific rather than Subic Bay in the Philippines, which was now exposed to a hostile Japan. The Philippines in fact had become a source of weakness rather than a strategic point from which American naval and diplomatic influence could be exerted in Asia. The powerful American fleet needed to defend the Philippines was as threatening to Japan as Japanese defenses were to the Philippines. After 1909, therefore, neither Japan nor the United States could assure protection for their territories by military or naval means without compromising the defenses of the other, a problem which defied solution by either side until 1941. Thus it could be argued that the consequences of Tsushima were hardly less important for the United States than those of Manila Bay.

The Lesson of Tsushima

The navies of the world drew an important lesson from the action at Tsushima. It was noted that the capital ships had been sunk by big guns while secondary armaments had been of little use due to the range and modest damage which they could inflict. Even before Tsushima, naval thinkers in Britain and the United States had been considering a new battleship design termed the 'all-big-gun' type. As a result of the experiments in America of Commander William S. Sims and his colleague Admiral Sir Percy Scott in Britain, the effectiveness of large guns at long range had been greatly increased. It was recognized that a main battery of large guns of the same caliber could concentrate a far heavier fire more accurately at greater distances than the mixed batteries of existing ships. The first all-big-gun ship to appear was the HMS *Dreadnought* in December 1906. Her 17,900 tons, 21 knots, heavier armor and above all her ten twelve-inch guns gave the *Dreadnought* twice the offensive power of any ship in existence and made every capital ship afloat obsolete. President Roosevelt saw the new design of battleship as necessary for the maintenance of American power in the Atlantic and Pacific, and in 1905 committed the United States to constructing dreadnoughts, the first of which was the 20,000-ton *Delaware*. With the HMS *Dreadnought* a new era in naval warfare was launched.

First Marne

1914

The First World War began with all participants believing it could never take place, and once it started in earnest, they believed it had to be short. All over by Christmas was the universal misconception. The weapons would be too terrible, the loss of men too great for any nation to withstand. It lasted over four years. The losses of men and materiel were greater than anyone envisioned. It is remembered by this generation as a war of attrition rather than of movement, with millions dying along the Western Front whose trenches could not be breached by any offensive, however great, until one side or the other was morally, spiritually and materially exhausted. These reminiscences are in the main correct, but it was not meant to be that way. Count von Schlieffen, whose master plan for winning the war for Germany against the Franco-Russian alliance was polished and perfected by 1905, intended Germany to knock France out of the war within a few weeks, enabling the huge German military machine to turn eastward and deal with Russia, whose mobilization plans took six weeks to bring their full strength into battle. The Schlieffen Plan called for Germany to mobilize 7/8 of her army along the Belgian and French borders, to sweep away Belgian opposition easily, and then to turn at the English Channel southward in order to complete a grand encirclement of Paris which would force a capitulation as humiliating as that suffered in 1870–71 by the French. 'Keep the right wing strong' were Schlieffen's dying words. When the war broke out in August 1914 the Schlieffen Plan had become an article of faith for every German staff officer. Had it been adhered to strictly, the war might have been short. Germany might have retained her mastery of Europe. But it was not to be. The Battle of the Marne saved the French, but it plunged the world into a conflict from which Western Civilization has yet to recover.

The last few days of August 1914 saw the French armies and the British Expeditionary Force in northern France in full retreat following the massive German thrust through Belgium. Twenty-eight days before seven German field armies had marched into Belgium, Luxembourg and eastern France. Slowly, inexorably, following the Schlieffen Plan which had been meticulously elaborated by the German General Staff they moved through Belgium in a gigantic sweep towards the west. The French battle plan, 'Plan 17', had envisioned the possibility of a German violation of Belgian neutrality, but expected it to be limited to a thrust through the region northeast of the Ardennes rather than a wide sweep which would carry the Germans north of the Meuse. Analyzing the situation based on German moves in the direction of Liège, General Joffre, the French Commander-in-Chief, came to a fatal decision. Believing that the German right would remain south of the Meuse, he prepared for what he believed would be the decisive counterstroke. The French 3rd Army (General Ruffey) and 4th Army (General de Langle de Cary) were ordered to advance northeast into the Ardennes to attack the supposed rear flank of the German forces. At the same time the 5th Army (General Lanrezac) was to push northwest into the region between Givet and Charleroi. With the aid of the British Expeditionary Force on his left, Lanrezac was to clear the region north of the Meuse and join the 3rd and 4th Armies in a converging attack on the overextended Germans. Unfortunately for the Allies, the Germans, by placing their reserve units into the front line were able to extend their march to the west before turning south without weakening their center. So, rather than striking a weak flank, the French attacked the German center.

By 20 August the French deployment had ended and Joffre was ready for a general advance. He believed that seven or eight German corps and four cavalry divisions were moving southwest into the gap between Givet and Brussels. Judging the strength of the German right correctly, Joffre deduced that the center was necessarily weak. The idea of the Germans putting their reserve units into the line had been suggested to him, but he rejected it as being most unlikely.

Opposite: *Cuirassiers* move up to the front after the start of World War One in 1914. Enthusiasm was high in every country, and flowers were strewn in the paths of troops marching toward the destruction of Western Civilization.

Below: French soldiers at the Gare du Nord, Paris, on their way up to the front.

During 19 and 20 August the Germans had checked their advance and fortified their center in the expectation of a French attack. On the foggy morning of the 21st the French marched into the trap. Instead of crashing through a weakened German center, 3rd Army was literally massacred in futile attacks on strong German positions. Throughout the 21st and 22nd, the armies of the two nations were locked in a continuous battle from Lorraine to a line south of Brussels. It was a murderous engagement with heavy French losses. By the evening of the 23rd the evidence before General Joffre was irrefutable: a continuation of the offensive against the German center was no longer possible.

The Critical Left Flank

But it was to the west, on the Allied left flank, that the situation was the most critical. The Allied forces totaled thirteen divisions of the French 5th Army and the five divisions of the BEF. Opposed to them were three German armies; the *First* (von Kluck) and *Second* (von Bülow) were moving from the north, while the *Third* (von Hausen) advanced from the east. The failure of the attacks of the 3rd and 4th Armies on 21 August and the crossing of the Meuse by elements of the *Third Army* exposed the French left flank. The 5th Army and BEF were in serious danger of being crushed by the superior numbers of the German right wing. During the 22nd and the morning of the 23rd the 5th Army and the British were desperately—and unsuccessfully—trying to check the German advance. In and around Charleroi the French were forced, by sheer weight of numbers, to give way. By the evening of the 23rd the line of the Sambre had been abandoned and the French 5th Army was in full retreat toward the south.

While the French left was fiercely engaged in the region Charleroi-Namur, the British deployed in the area Mauberge-Mons on the evening of 21 August. On the 22nd, the British moved into positions on the line Condé-Binche immediately to the left of the 5th Army. The British expected—or assumed—that the 5th Army was containing the German advance and that one or two corps faced their front. The actual situation, however, was quite different. In the face of German pressure the 5th Army was forced to give ground. The *First Army* was directly in front of the British while the *Second Army* was moving toward the British right. The BEF was in imminent danger of being outflanked on both right and left. Attacked by the Germans before Mons the British were saved from destruction only by an unparalleled standard of accurate and sustained musketry. But, devoid of the support of the 5th Army, and in fear of being overwhelmed, Sir John French, the Commander-in-Chief of the BEF, was forced to order a general retirement for the morning of the 24th. It was the start of the Great Retreat.

In the midst of the collapse of the French position, on the 25th General Joffre issued a General Order calling for the strategic withdrawal of his center and left, anchored on the fortress of Verdun. Meanwhile, he proposed to use elements of the 4th and 5th Armies, the BEF

and newly arrived colonial troops to form a 6th Army which would take its place on the French left and push back the German right. The new army was to be assembled between 27 August and 2 September and to advance from the base St Pol-Arras, or Arras-Bapaume. In order to make it easier to start a new offensive, all efforts were made to coordinate the retreat and so prevent the withdrawing forces from separating and losing their coherence.

Meanwhile the German right continued to push southwest in an effort to outflank the Allied left. From 25 August to the end of the month the Anglo-French left stubbornly resisted the German advance. But the weight of the German right wing was crushing and it constantly pushed back the BEF and adjacent 5th Army. Its left wing bent, its center hard pressed, the rest of the Allied line was forced to withdraw in a line with its threatened left to prevent the whole line from snapping like a bent twig. On 26 August the *First Army* severely mauled the British 2 Corps at Le Cateau. Arriving in the region Amiens-Péronne, von Kluck's troops made the placement of the newly formed 6th Army, which was still only partially ready to move into the line, impossible. Joffre had no recourse but to continue to withdraw towards Paris and the Marne.

As the German right wing wheeled south to pursue the retreating Allied left, the campaign approached a crisis. Whereas the original German plan had called for von Kluck to pass to the west of the French capital, the new line of march pulled the *First Army*—the right flank of the German forces—to the east of Paris. This drastically changed the Schlieffen Plan and exposed the Germans to a French counteroffensive. The newly formed 6th Army (General Manoury) and the troops under the command of the military governor of Paris (General Galliéni) which had previously been in some danger of being outflanked, were now offered the opportunity of attacking the German right flank as it swung east of the capital. Much has been made of the German decision to modify the original plan which called for a considerably wider enveloping movement that would have brought the *First Army* across the Seine between Paris and

Above: German soldiers pass a burning house in northern France as their advance continues. The Germans hoped to take France in six weeks in order to turn their attention on the Russians, who were still mobilizing while Belgium was being overrun.

Opposite top: French officers inspect artillery pieces during a lull in the fighting. **Opposite bottom:** The British Expeditionary Force arriving in Le Havre, 14 August, 1914. The British presence on the collapsing Western front saved Paris from encirclement and the French army from defeat.

The First Battle of the Marne, 1914

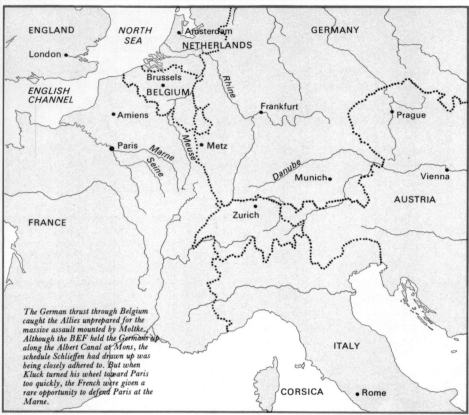

The German thrust through Belgium caught the Allies unprepared for the massive assault mounted by Moltke. Although the BEF held the Germans up along the Albert Canal at Mons, the schedule Schlieffen had drawn up was being closely adhered to. But when Kluck turned his wheel toward Paris too quickly, the French were given a rare opportunity to defend Paris at the Marne.

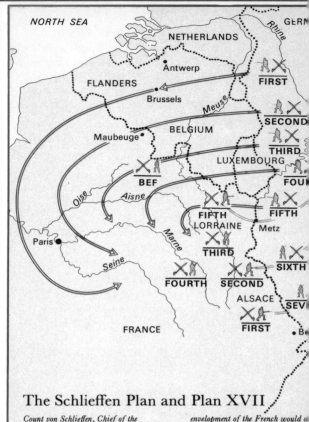

The Schlieffen Plan and Plan XVII

Count von Schlieffen, Chief of the German General Staff in 1905, perfected his plan to envelope the French by sweeping through Belgium and northern France, bringing his forces as far as the Channel to block the arrival of the BEF, and then encircling Paris, while the French sent the bulk of their forces to Alsace in Plan XVII. If the plan were carried out, a double

envelopment of the French would o bringing the desired victory within weeks. Then the Germans could se their main force against Russia, u took six weeks to mobilize. The p took courage and precision to carry In 1914 the Germans deviated from Schlieffen Plan, giving the Allies chance to turn the German flank at Marne.

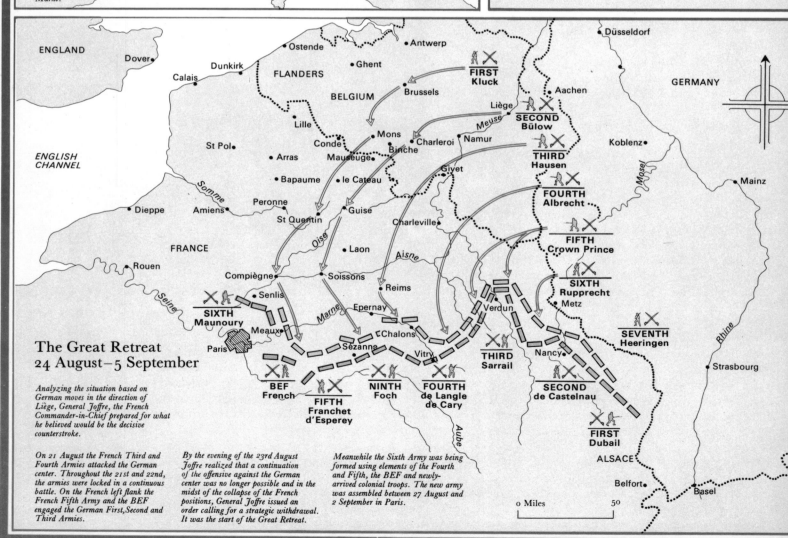

The Great Retreat
24 August – 5 September

Analyzing the situation based on German moves in the direction of Liège, General Joffre, the French Commander-in-Chief prepared for what he believed would be the decisive counterstroke.

On 21 August the French Third and Fourth Armies attacked the German center. Throughout the 21st and 22nd, the armies were locked in a continuous battle. On the French left flank the French Fifth Army and the BEF engaged the German First, Second and Third Armies.

By the evening of the 23rd August Joffre realized that a continuation of the offensive against the German center was no longer possible and in the midst of the collapse of the French positions, General Joffre issued an order calling for a strategic withdrawal. It was the start of the Great Retreat.

Meanwhile the Sixth Army was being formed using elements of the Fourth and Fifth, the BEF and newly-arrived colonial troops. The new army was assembled between 27 August and 2 September in Paris.

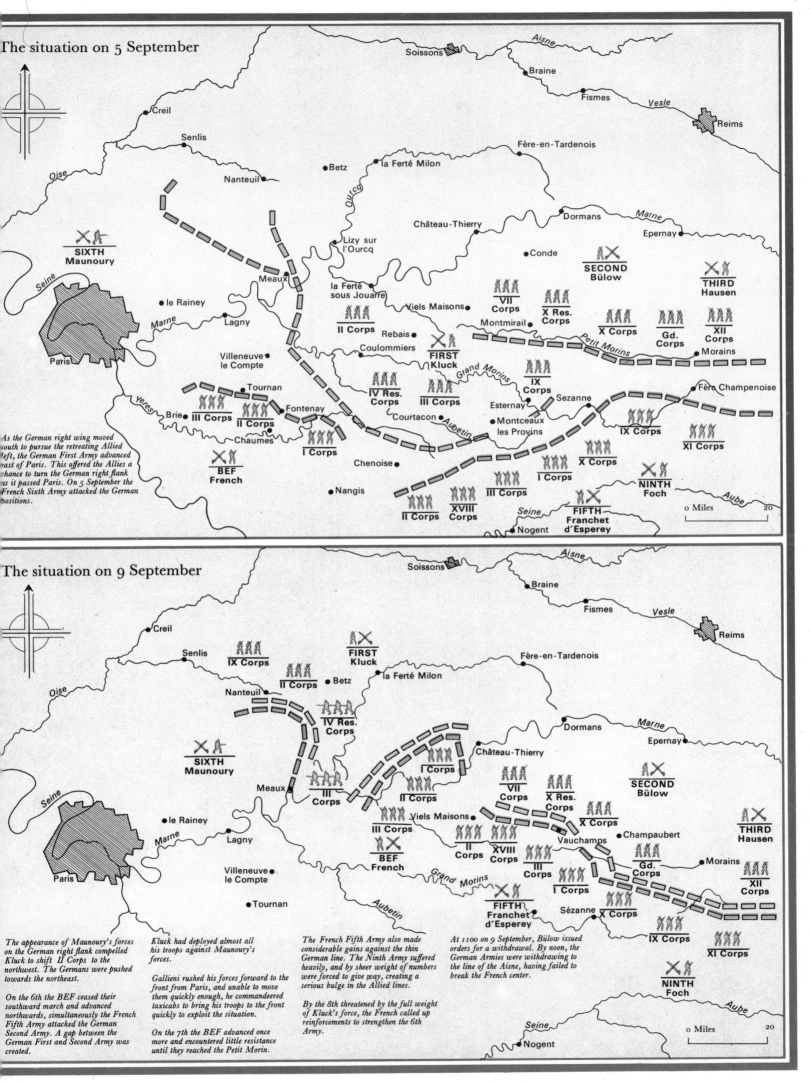

The situation on 5 September

SIXTH
Maunoury

VII Corps

SECOND
Bülow

THIRD
Hausen

X Res. Corps

II Corps

X Corps

Gd. Corps

XII Corps

FIRST
Kluck

IX Corps

IV Res. Corps

III Corps

II Corps

III Corps

IX Corps

I Corps

XI Corps

BEF
French

I Corps

X Corps

II Corps

XVIII Corps

III Corps

NINTH
Foch

FIFTH
Franchet
d'Esperey

0 Miles 20

As the German right wing moved south to pursue the retreating Allied left, the German First Army advanced east of Paris. This offered the Allies a chance to turn the German right flank as it passed Paris. On 5 September the French Sixth Army attacked the German positions.

The situation on 9 September

IX Corps

FIRST
Kluck

II Corps

IV Res. Corps

SIXTH
Maunoury

I Corps

VII Corps

X Res. Corps

SECOND
Bülow

III Corps

II Corps

X Corps

THIRD
Hausen

III Corps

II Corps

XVIII Corps

Gd. Corps

XII Corps

BEF
French

III Corps

I Corps

FIFTH
Franchet
d'Esperey

X Corps

IX Corps

XI Corps

NINTH
Foch

0 Miles 20

The appearance of Maunoury's forces on the German right flank compelled Kluck to shift II Corps to the northwest. The Germans were pushed towards the northeast.

On the 6th the BEF ceased their southward march and advanced northwards, simultaneously the French Fifth Army attacked the German Second Army. A gap between the German First and Second Army was created.

Kluck had deployed almost all his troops against Maunoury's forces.

Gallieni rushed his forces forward to the front from Paris, and unable to move them quickly enough, he commandeered taxicabs to bring his troops to the front quickly to exploit the situation.

On the 7th the BEF advanced once more and encountered little resistance until they reached the Petit Morin.

The French Fifth Army also made considerable gains against the thin German line. The Ninth Army suffered heavily, and by sheer weight of numbers were forced to give way, creating a serious bulge in the Allied lines.

By the 8th threatened by the full weight of Kluck's force, the French called up reinforcements to strengthen the 6th Army.

At 1100 on 9 September, Bülow issued orders for a withdrawal. By noon, the German Armies were withdrawing to the line of the Aisne, having failed to break the French center.

Above: French infantry dig in near the Marne. In the early days of the war trenches were not in evidence, as the war of movement was still employed by both sides. Only the French were moving backwards until they took a stand at the Marne. **Above right:** Headquarters of the British 2nd Cavalry Division on the Marne, September 1914.

Rouen. But the movement of von Kluck, while offering serious disadvantages to the right wing of the German armies did not in itself reverse the military situation. Coupled with the natural French desire to save Paris if they could, and the opportunity afforded by the river barrier of the Marne, von Kluck's march provided the opportunity for the Allies to strike at the German flank. It remained to be seen if the Allies could exploit a favorable situation on their left before

pressure on other sectors forced them to give way.

On 4 September the Allied front sprawled unevenly across northeastern France. On the far left, somewhat detached from the rest of the line, was the entrenched camp of Paris and the newly formed 6th Army. To the southwest stretched the five divisions of the British Army. Moving east, the 5th Army was on the line Dormans-Epernay, the 9th on the line Sézanne-Camp de Mailly-Sompius, and the 4th Army was astride the

Marne at Vitry-le-Francois. The line arched north to include the fortified region surrounding Verdun, held by the 3rd Army. Further to the east stood the 2nd Army, running across the Grand Couronne of Nancy and into Lorraine.

Except for the western edge of the battle line the German forces lay directly in front of the Allies. The *Sixth Army* was astride the Meurthe curving northwest to Pont-à-Mousson, opposite the 2nd Army. The *Seventh Army* covered the fortified region of Verdun on its left and faced the 3rd Army across the Argonne on its right. Dipping southwest from Rivigny to Vitry-le-Francois the *Fourth Army* faced the 4th Army. The German right wing, composed of the *First, Second* and *Third Armies* was across the Marne. The *Third Army* had bridged the river near Epernay and had reached the area just north of the line Sompius-Fère Champenoise which was held by the 9th Army. Directly to the west, the *Second Army* was

Above left: A Belgian friar offers drinking water to the German troops sweeping through Flanders in August 1914. **Above:** The Germans move field artillery forward to face the British and French on the Marne. The Eiffel Tower could be seen on the horizon as the Germans moved within twenty miles of Paris. **Below:** When the French inaugurated Plan XVII, they invaded Alsace and Lorraine as the Germans swept through Belgium and northern France. But these provinces were not un-protected. Here Germans counterattack in Lorraine, preventing this area from being overrun and thus covering their left flank.

Above: The 59th Field
Company of the BEF leaves
its bivouac near Mons, from
which the British were
forced to retreat after
having taken a stand on the
Albert Canal.

in the marshes of St Gond close to Ville-en-Tardenois, across the front of the 5th and 9th Armies. Between the *Second* and *First Armies* lay a gap of some twelve to fifteen kilometers, the *First Army* being somewhat northwest of its neighbor. Von Kluck's right stretched to Beauvais and Senlis, and his center continued to move south; on 3 September it was on the line Creil-Senlis-Nanteuil, and by the 4th it was astride the Marne just east of Meaux.

On 4 September, General von Moltke, Chief of the German General Staff, and nephew of the hero of Sedan and Königgrätz, issued the orders which sent the German right wing to the east rather than to the west of Paris. The *First* and *Second Armies* were to move southeast and roll up the 'defeated' Allied left while the German left effected a breakthrough west of Verdun. While the danger of a French sortie from Paris was not excluded, it was assumed that the pressure of the main German thrusts would be heavy enough to prevent an effective countermove.

The French, however, had the as yet unused 6th Army which was temporarily under the jurisdiction of the military governor of Paris, General Galliéni. On 3 September Galliéni had received reports that the Creil-Nanteuil line was no longer being pressed by German troops. On the 4th the southwest march of the *First Army* was confirmed along the line Nanteuil-Lizy-sur l'Ourcq. Galliéni quickly grasped the opportunity that was offered to him, and ordered Manoury to prepare to attack the flank of the *First Army* as it passed in front of Paris on 5 September. Later in

the evening of the 4th, Galliéni was able to convince Joffre to halt the general retreat. Joffre issued orders which called for a resumption of the offensive on the morning of 6 September. Galliéni's action had provided the French with the conditions necessary to halt their retreat and to strike at the flank of the German right wing.

The day of 5 September was one of intense expectation punctuated by sharp local clashes and severe fighting between the 6th Army and flank elements of the *First Army*. As the weight of Manoury's troops was felt on the *First Army's* flank, von Kluck was compelled to shift *II Corps* to the northwest. It was to prove a fatal mistake, and one which would have serious consequences for the cohesion of the German battle-line. Had von Kluck pulled his flank closer to his main body he would have been able to maintain his forces in a tighter formation. As it was, a full half of the *First Army* was dangerously separated from the rest of the German forces.

On the morning of 6 September Joffre issued his celebrated Order of the Day:

At the moment when a battle, on which the welfare of the nation depends, is about to begin, I have to remind all ranks that the time for looking back is past. Every effort must be made to attack the ememy and hurl him back. Troops which find advance impossible must stand their ground at all costs and die rather than give way. This is the moment when no faltering will be tolerated.

Responding to orders sent out on the evening of 4 September, the 6th Army attacked the

German positions on the Ourcq, to the east of Meaux, early on the 6th, pressing the flank and rear of the *First Army*. The German *IV Reserve Corps* was dealt a shattering blow by the 6th Army's left along the line Marcilly-Acy en Multien. The Germans were pushed back toward the northeast, threatening to expose the rear of the *First Army* to the 6th Army. But the arrival of units from *II Corps* on the 6th Army front enabled the Germans to check the advance.

On the same day, the BEF ceased their southward march and started north for the first time since 23 August. Advancing from the line Jouy le Chatel-Farmoutiers-Villeneuve le Comte, the British encountered quite heavy resistance at first, but this decreased throughout the afternoon. The advance elements of the *First Army* were withdrawing in accordance with von Kluck's transfer of *II Corps*. The *IV Corps*, the advance guard of the *First Army*, abandoned the Grand Morin at Coulommiers, and withdrew in the direction of Rebais. By nightfall the heights of the Grand Morin were entirely in British hands.

After shifting to the line Courtacon-Esternay-Sézanne on 5 September, the 5th Army was ordered to attack in the direction of Montmirail on the 6th. The assault was to be delivered in echelon, with the western flank of 5th Army somewhat north of the rest of the attacking force. The left wing of the 5th Army was to link up with the advance of the 6th Army along the Ourcq and encircle the isolated *First Army*. The 5th, however, ran headlong into the *Second Army* and a desperate fight ensued. On the left, the 18th Corps was able to wrest Courtacon from the Germans, while on the center the *Second Army* was forced to evacuate Montceaux les Provins and Courgivaux, and 1st Corps, on the right wing of the 5th Army gained Catillon sur Morin. It was, however, a somewhat disappointing day for the 5th Army. It had advanced only slightly on its left and had not been able to push the *Second Army* far enough to the northeast to effectively isolate the *First Army* from the rest of the German line.

The 9th Army, holding the French center, faced the left wing of von Bülow's *Second Army* and the right wing of von Hausen's *Third Army*. The

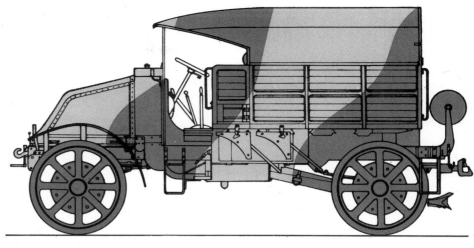

Above: French Renault artillery tractor. Towing capacity: 15 tons. Engine: six-cylinder, 60 bhp. Crew: four. Maximum speed: 42 mph.

9th Army commander, General Foch, was ordered to support the advance of Franchet d'Esperey's 5th Army on his left, and to stand on the defensive with his center and right. Attacked, and under the heaviest pressure, Foch's left lost Tarlus to the *Second Army's X Corps* and was in danger of losing Charleville as well. The 9th Army's center was pushed south of the St Gond marshes by the *X* and *Guard Corps* of the *Second Army*. On the 9th Army's right, the 2nd Corps and its supporting 9th Cavalry Division were both forced to give ground to elements of the *XII Saxon Corps* of the *Third Army*. By the end of 6 September Foch's army was very hard-pressed, having made no gains and been forced back on both flanks.

On the right of the Allied line, the French were mainly on the defensive trying to repel the attacks of the *Fourth, Fifth* and *Sixth Armies*. Here the situation was quite the reverse of that on the left: the Germans were resolutely carrying out their attacks trying to break the French line. The 3rd Army under General Sarrail was barely holding the line Vassincourt-Villotte-Ville-sur-Cousances.

A critical question had been posed by the result of the first day's battle: could the 6th Army batter the German right wing and separate the *First Army* from the rest of the German line before the pressure of the *Third, Fourth* and *Fifth Armies* crumpled the French center? Aware that the temporary advantage on the extreme west of the battle line could not last indefinitely, Manoury

Far left: General Galliéni, who commandeered the taxis of the Marne and moved his 6th Army forward in the 'Marne Maneuver' which turned the tide of battle in favor of France. **Left:** General Sir John French, Commander-in-Chief of the BEF.

pushed forward against the German right wing with every ounce of strength he possessed. Reinforced by 1st Cavalry Corps and the 61st Reserve Division on its left, 6th Army moved forward at dawn, only to grind to a halt. The German *IV Reserve Corps* had effected a tactical withdrawal late on the 6th and were now entrenched on the plateau of Trocy. The French line made little progress against the Germans, for von Kluck had placed the *II* and *IX Corps* in support of the *IV Reserve Corps*. Three of the four corps of the *First Army* had now shifted to face Manoury. Toward evening, *IX Corps* advanced against the 6th Army's left, threatening to outflank the French. The 6th Army had held its own against the Germans, but the original maneuver which had prompted the Battle of the Marne had been thwarted; von Kluck's change of front no longer offered the Allies the possibility of a flank attack. It remained to be seen if the Allies could hold in the center and right in these circumstances.

With only *III Corps* and cavalry of the *First Army* south of the Marne, British pressure was relatively minor on the second day of the battle, due to the skillful delaying action fought by the German cavalry under General von der Marwitz. Trying to maintain a bridgehead across the Marne at Coulommiers, von der Marwitz placed three cavalry divisions on the Grand Morin above the bridgehead, a position which was eventually taken by elements of the British 3rd Division. The three cavalry divisions (2nd, 9th and Guard) performed admirably, if not heroically, but were forced to withdraw by evening to the Petit Morin. By the end of the day's hostilities, the British were on the line La Haute Maison-Coulommiers-Jouy-sur-Morin.

To the right of the British, the 5th Army also benefited from German withdrawal north of the Marne. Moving into the vacuum, the 5th Army's left and center advanced with Montmirail as its goal, and achieved some ten kilometers in the face of relatively light resistance. The situation on 5th Army's right was considerably more difficult, as 1st and 10th Corps, on the right, were ordered to attack in a northeasterly direction to lessen pressure on the 9th Army. At the end of the day's fighting, 10th Corps had reached Charleville and was in effective contact with the left flank of the 9th Army.

The critical point in the Allied line was the frontage held by the 9th Army. Every effort was made by the Germans to break the French position and to relieve the pressure against their right. The 9th Army was heavily pressed throughout the day by the attacks of the *Second* and *Third Armies*. Foch ordered his left to maintain a defensive posture while his center and right held the line against the German assaults. Supported by an extremely heavy artillery preparation, *XII Corps* of *Third Army* repeatedly attacked the 2nd Corps on French right but made little progress. In the center the marshes of St Gond afforded a natural bastion for the 9th Corps and prevented

the Germans from seriously threatening the French position. The situation was altogether different on the French left. Although ordered by General Foch to attack in a northwesterly direction, two divisions on his left had to struggle hard to hold their ground against *X Corps* of the *Second Army*. Had it not been for the timely intervention of the 10th Corps (5th Army) operating on their left, the position might have collapsed.

Left: General von Moltke, nephew of the hero of Königgrätz and Sedan, who can be compared with his uncle in name only. He nearly suffered a nervous breakdown at the Marne and had to be relieved.
Below: French artillery returns German fire at the Marne, while a thinly protected observer directs the fire of his weapon.

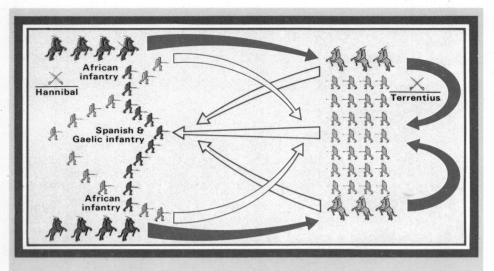

African infantry

Hannibal

Spanish & Gaelic infantry

African infantry

Terrentius

Cannae 216 BC: Double Envelopment

In August 216 BC a Carthaginian force under Hannibal defeated a Roman army well over twice its own size in what was to become known as the classic battle of envelopment. Hannibal drew up his army in a crescent, with Gauls and Spaniards in the center and the African veterans on both flanks 'refused'. His cavalry was stationed on the wings, and opened the battle by driving the Roman horse from the field. The Romans, ineptly led by the consul Terrentius Varro, attacked the Carthaginian center, which fell back steadily, permitting Hannibal's African troops to outflank them. Hannibal's victorious cavalry returned to complete the encirclement; the Roman army was 'swallowed up as if by an earthquake', and, according to one estimate, lost 70,000 of their 76,000 men.

The dream of Cannae has exercised an irresistible attraction on military minds for centuries. Count Alfred von Schlieffen, author of the celebrated 'Schlieffen Plan', sought to achieve a strategic Cannae by encircling the French armies in a battle of annihilation. The plan failed to achieve the results for which its author hoped, but, on the Eastern front, a Russian advance into East Prussia was smashed at the Battle of Tannenberg; the southern prong of the Russian attack—General Samsonov's Second Army—was itself counterattacked, encircled and destroyed by Hindenburg and Ludendorff in a battle of envelopment from which the Tsarist army was never to recover fully. Even today Cannae is still taught in Russian military academies as the apogee of the general's art; certainly, the tactics of 'double envelopment', when employed successfully, as at Cannae or Sedan, can lead to dramatic results.

A successful double envelopment depends as much upon the inflexibility of its intended victims as it does upon the skill of its executors. The Russian winter offensive of 1942–43 brought about the encirclement and destruction of the German Sixth Army at Stalingrad. Similarly, the envelopment of the French at Sedan in 1870 was due largely to the cumbersome nature of the Army of Châlons and to the slowness with which it marched. Finally, though the battle of envelopment is undeniably a concept of great value, it cannot guarantee victory; Hannibal won Cannae, but Rome ultimately won the war.

By the end of the day, after frightful casualties on both sides, little ground had changed hands.

Further east, the 4th Army continued to be hard-pressed, although slightly less so than 9th Army on its left. The *XIX Corps*, supported by a division of the *XII Reserve Corps*, both of the *Third Army* thrust against the 4th Army's left at Sompius and nearly succeeded in breaking the French line. Although outnumbered in the center, the French 12th and Colonial Corps successfully resisted two corps of the *Fourth Army*, proving that firepower could be a fearsome defensive weapon when used by steady troops well-supported by field artillery. The French right performed notably less well than the center, and *XVIII Corps* and *XVIII Reserve Corps* succeeded in outflanking 2nd Corps of the French 4th Army and threatening the link between the 4th and 3rd Armies.

Oddly enough, there was no major action fought between the 3rd Army and its opponent the *Fifth Army*. Each side spent the day probing the other's defenses—which were exceptionally strong in both cases—and waiting for reinforcements which would permit a favorable resumption of the offensive. Toward evening General Sarrail received the 15th Corps from 2nd Army, but its arrival came too late in the day to support an attack of any importance. The German Crown Prince, commander of the *Fifth Army*, brought up elements of the *VI Reserve Corps*, but used them to strengthen his line rather than to launch an attack.

The second day of battle had ended less favorably for the Allies than the first. Kluck had largely succeeded extricating the *First Army*, and the 6th Army's advance against the German right flank was seriously compromised. On the other hand, the Allied line held everywhere and in some cases the Allies had gained ground. The French center, although hard-pressed, remained intact. The Germans, who had pursued a beaten foe for fourteen days, were unable to

comprehend the ability of the French to turn and attack. The seeds of doubt were already being sown at German Supreme Headquarters as to the final issue of the battle. Moltke was was losing his nerve.

On the extreme right of the German line the situation was far from ideal. The 6th Army occupied the position Betz-Etavigny-Puisieux-Marcilly-Chambry, and was faced by the four corps of the *First Army*. Opening the day with an attack by 45th Division against the German's center, Manoury hoped to use the 61st Reserve Division to ourflank the German left. Amidst fighting of the fiercest intensity, the Germans counterattacked in the afternoon using *IV Corps* to assault the French center between Puisieux and Etrepilly. On the 6th Army's right flank the French maintained a constant pressure in order to aid the decisive struggle on the left half of their line. The day ended with little gains on either side. Von Kluck's troops were now almost entirely north of the Marne astride the Ourcq. And although the *First Army* was no longer in danger of being overwhelmed by the French, the 6th Army was unlikely to be crushed by the weary Germans. It was a bloody stalemate, fought with an intensity that could not be long endured.

With von Kluck's troops engaged against Manoury's, the frontage along the Marne facing the BEF was only held by a rearguard of German cavalry. Advancing on the axis Nogent-Château-Thierry, the British encountered almost no

resistance until they reached the Petit Morin between La Ferté-sous-Jouarre and Sablonnières. After a stiff struggle in which the British made highly intelligent use of their field artillery they were able to crack the resistance of the German rearguard and cross the river. Making good progress through the day, they reached the line La Ferté-sous-Jouarre-Viels Maisons and were threatening Château Thierry.

General Franchet d'Esperey, commanding 5th Army, hoped to use this third day of battle to push the *Fourth Army* beyond Montmirail, thus relieving some of the pressure on the hard-pressed 9th Army. Advancing to the Petit Morin early in the morning almost as easily as the British on their left, the French met extremely heavy resistance in their attempts to cross that obstacle. The 18th Corps was able to force the river crossings but was soon held up in the region of Marchais-en-Brie. In the center, Montmirail fell to *III Corps* after an eight-hour battle which

Opposite: 'Papa' Joffre, commander of French forces at the Marne. Moltke lost his nerve; Joffre refused to have his eight hours of sleep disturbed. **Above:** The famous French '75', the formidable cannon used on the Western Front.

Below: German Q.F. gun, 1905 model, used at the Marne. Maximum range: 15,000 yards; Weight: two tons, three hundred-weight; Crew: five; Shell weight: 15 pounds.

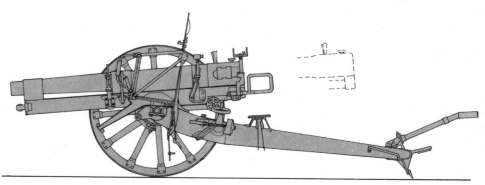

Above: Rations are issued to the 1st Cameronians on 8 September during the Battle of the Marne.
Above right: The 1st Cameronians move forward toward the Aisne the following day as the German flank is turned. **Below:** German soldiers man their machine gun positions as they defend a line north of the Marne on the Aisne after they were forced to withdraw from the Marne.

cost the Germans over 7000 casualties. On the right 1st Corps gained Vachamps and, more significantly, 10th Corps reached Charleville and then wheeled east to support 9th Army.

The center of the line held the key to the Allied success. With von Kluck engaged against the 6th Army, the British and 5th Army were able to make considerable progress against the thin German line in the sixty kilometer sector east and west of Château Thierry. Opposite 9th Army the situation was different. The Germans were making every possible effort to break the French line between Sézanne and Fère-Champenoise. The 9th Army's left was subjected to the severest punishment by the German *X* and *Guard Corps*, and by sheer weight of numbers the French were forced to give way, creating a serious bulge in the Allied line.

Immediately to the right of the 9th Army, the 4th Army was subjected to a pressure of almost equal intensity. His flanks threatened by the *Fourth Army*, de Langle de Cary was only able to hold his position with the aid of the 3rd Army on his right. It was here, in the French center, that the battle reached its climax. The 9th Army was able to hold its ground with the greatest difficulty. Its neighbor to the right had visibly reached the point of rupture. A combined attack by the *Third* and *Fourth Armies* succeeded in the afternoon in enveloping both flanks of the 4th Army. All through the day the situation remained critical and it was only toward nightfall that the French were able to send the 21st Corps into the line to sustain the 4th Army.

The opposing armies had now been engaged for three days in a battle of the most desperate intensity. The question was not whether one side would effect a brilliant Napoleonic maneuver and

sweep the other from the field. It was far more basic: which side would crack? The Battle of the Marne had become a question of will and nerve. It is perhaps indicative of the ultimate outcome of the battle that while Moltke was suffering a near nervous breakdown from the strain, Joffre was issuing his usual orders that under no circumstances was anyone to disturb his eight hours of unbroken sleep.

As the summer heat opened into severe rainstorm, the armies began the fourth day of of battle. The French 6th Army, while making some gains, was unable to cross the Ourcq and encircle the *First Army's* rear. Indeed, by the evening of the 8th, threatened with the whole weight of Kluck's force, the French were far from certain of being able to hold their positions. To strengthen the 6th Army, General Galliéni ordered reinforcements to Senlis and Creil.

Lacking transport, he created an instant legend by commandeering the 'taxicabs of the Marne'. Taxis packed with troops moved out to the field of battle from Paris as military transport proved insufficient. Whether or not the meters were running is anybody's guess. General Manoury ordered his retreating troops to turn and advance regardless of cost; he correctly appreciated that victory or defeat was now literally a matter of hours. It was the Germans who gave way first. Reacting to information that his exposed left flank—where a 'gap' of some thirty kilometers existed between the *First* and *Second Armies*—was being threatened by an advance of the BEF, Kluck ordered a withdrawal from the Ourcq, holding the line Nanteuil-Betz to delay the 6th Army should it attempt too rapid a pursuit.

Although the British were numerically small, their influence was conclusive. With little more

Above: Company D of the 1st Cameronians crosses a pontoon bridge over the Marne at La Ferté-sous-Jouarre on 10 September, 1914. **Top right:** the XI Hussars of the BEF pause at the Aisne. The crisis to defend Paris was behind them; the race to the Channel had begun. **Center right:** The long march back. German troops pass through a French village on their 'great retreat' after their failure to win on the Marne. **Right:** The French '75' in action.

than a cavalry division to oppose them they could, by a determined thrust, isolate the *First Army* from the rest of the German line. But three weeks of constant contact with the enemy had weakened Sir John French's resolution. Fearing to be caught alone and exposed in advance of the Allied line, French ordered an advance which minimized the risks. Pushing across the Marne at La Ferté-sous-Jouarre, Charly and Château-Thierry, the British were more significant for their presence rather than actual movements during this all-important day. Although the BEF had hesitantly nudged into the gap between the *First* and *Second Armies*, the Germans did not have the reserve to check the movement. By nightfall, the threat of a serious defeat hung over the German right.

Opposite the *Second Army*, the French 5th Army was ordered to push northeast to link up with the British on the Marne. Faced with little resistance, 5th Army was able to reach its objectives and increase the pressure on the Germans by threatening to push the *Second Army* northeast. The right of the 5th Army was, however, faced with a more difficult task: to aid the hard-pressed 9th Army by attacking the *Third Army*, which was slowly

pushing the 9th Army toward the marshes of St Gond. In this maneuver Franchet d'Esperey was equally successful and the Germans were forced to give way, all but eliminating the threat to the left flank of the 9th Army. Since the French center was holding its ground with increasing difficulty, the importance of the 5th Army's success cannot be overemphasized. If the 9th Army's front was not cracked by the evening of 9 September, the pressure on the German right would force von Kluck to continue his withdrawal, thus breaking the continuity of the whole German line.

The 9th Army's position was far from brilliant. On the 8th its left had barely held its own, whereas the right had lost substantial ground, perilously bending the French line. A further retreat could negate the success on the Allied left, and a German breakthrough would mean total disaster. Faced with this crisis, Foch responded in typical fashion, issuing an order of the day to attack which was brilliant in its ironic optimism.

Pivoting on his left, Foch used the 5th Army's support to strengthen his center and right. It was a maneuver which had the most important consequences. Three German corps, *Guard* of the *Second Army*, and *XII* and *XII Reserve* of the *Third*, pushed through the St Gond Marshes (near Fère-Champenoise) and forced the 9th Army's right to retire to Salon, forcing the center to fall back as well. But, pressed to breaking point, Foch managed to hold on for the extra day that was needed.

Foch's position was further aided by the 4th Army on his right which vigorously attacked the *Third Army* in order to lessen the pressure on the 9th Army. Pushing to within a mile of Sompius and moving laterally southwest of Humbauville, the 4th Army demonstrated a coordination with its neighbor which was notably lacking between the German army commanders.

But time had run out for the Germans. On 8 September Lieutenant-Colonel Hentsch was ordered by Moltke to visit each of the Army headquarters west of Verdun to assess the situation. In a move typical of the German Army, Hentsch, by virtue of his position as a General Staff Officer, was given full powers to 'coordinate the retreat, should rearward movements have to be initiated'. Moving from east to west, he became increasingly alarmed with each interview. Spending the night at *Second Army* headquarters, Henstsch found Bülow despairing of success. At 1100 on 9 September, Bülow issued orders for a a withdrawal. When Hentsch reached *First Army* headquarters at noon, orders had already been issued for a retreat. As Hentsch retraced his steps, he progressively ordered the *First, Second Third, Fourth* and *Fifth Armies* to the line of the Aisne. Having failed to break the French center, hard-pressed on their right, and lacking a firm hand to coordinate the army commanders in the the field, the Germans had no other choice. The Marne was a psychological rather than a physical victory for the Allies; it saved Paris, but ended with the Germans firmly ensconced on French soil. It was to take four more years of bloodletting through the stalemate of trench warfare to dislodge them.

1914 Coronel and Falkland

While the configuration of power in the Far East was being altered dramatically by the Russo-Japanese War of 1904–1905, the balance of power in Europe after 1900 was undergoing a fundamental re-alignment as well. The unification of the North German states in 1867 had produced a young and vigorous nation state which was challenging the status quo on the continent. Eventually the Triple Alliance of Germany, Austria-Hungary and Italy came to be one focus of power while Britain, France and Russia provided another. The conflict between the interests represented by these two centers resulted in the First World War which lasted from August 1914 to November 1918. World War I was a land war,

with only two encounters of note between the German and British navies. Early in the war, small squadrons of German and British ships clashed in what came to be known as the Battles of Coronel and the Falklands, and midway through the war the controversial Battle of Jutland took place. Described by First Sea Lord Winston Churchill as 'the saddest naval action of the war', Coronel and its sequel off the Falkland Islands were the first time that the British Navy had been challenged in open battle since Trafalgar.

After 1815 Britain had been undisputed master of the seas but during the latter part of the nineteenth century its fleet had slipped into a sad state due to neglect and parliamentary parsimony.

In 1889, however, the large task of reconstruction was begun with the Naval Defence Act. From 1900 Britain began to accelerate the expansion of her fleet in specific response to a perceived threat from her neighbor across the North Sea. Germany was undergoing rapid growth industrially, commercially and militarily and becoming a major power in Europe. The ambitious new state had also embarked on a program of naval expansion in the belief that a strong navy was necessary to protect German shipping, commerce and colonies throughout the world and that a strong battle fleet in particular was essential to German foreign policy. Not only would it increase Germany's alliance value and strengthen her diplomacy but combined with her formidable land power, the new fleet would give her a commanding influence in the world. It is clear that the Germans had taken the blue-water theories of Alfred Thayer Mahan to heart.

Anglo-German Naval Rivalry

Although Germany steadfastly maintained that her fleet was not intended for aggressive use, Britain came to view the German battle fleet as its main security problem. Between 1900 and 1905 Germany had launched fourteen battleships against sixteen for Britain, a fact which indicated to the British that Germany would be the second naval power in the world by 1906. The belief grew in the public domain and government circles that Germany aimed first at continental domination and then world hegemony. What other reason could there have been for her strong fleet and massive army? Thus Anglo-German relations deteroirated from 1900, not only due to naval rivalry but to political, commercial and colonial tensions as well. In Britain war came to be regarded as inevitable. In the words of First Lord of the Admiralty Sir John Fisher, '. . . that we have eventually to fight Germany is just about as sure as anything human can be, solely because she can't expand commercially without it'. In 1904 the German Ambassador to Britain reported 'Most of the papers regard every step in the progress of our Fleet as a menace to England'. The reaction was to end the long policy of British isolation, forming in 1902 the Anglo-Japanese alliance, in 1904 the *Entente Cordiale* with France and in 1907 affecting a rapprochement with Russia. Thus after 800 years of enmity and rivalry, Britain and France were brought together by the threat of Germany. The alliance with Japan and the destruction of Russian naval power in the Pacific during the Russo-Japanese War enabled Britain to bring most of her ships back from the east while a subsequent agreement with France left the French fleet with responsibility for the Mediterranean. As a result Britain was able to concentrate most of her battle fleet in home waters against the German threat.

The threat in fact was far more perceived than real. There was no basic conflict between German and British colonial and commercial interests. On the contrary, they were each other's best customers. Real German aspirations lay in Eastern Europe and it was as a result of events in Eastern Europe that war broke out. The basic problem was that due to her geographic position athwart Ger-many's sea approaches, any increase in German sea power posed a potential security problem for Britain, which is why she felt it necessary to concentrate her fleet in home waters after 1900. As the German naval attaché noted, 'The steadily increasing sea power of Germany constitutes the greatest obstacle to England's freedom of political action'. The war resulted from the various rivalries and aspirations of the continental powers, but when it did break out in August 1914, the Anglo-German naval rivalry had ensured on which side Britain would be. But the naval side of the First World War was almost entirely a non-contest between the British Grand Fleet and the German High Seas Fleet.

In 1906 Britain had 53 battleships to Germany's 20, a superiority which Germany would never have been able to overcome even with the most ambitious naval construction program. But in that year an event occurred which wiped out British superiority at the stroke of a bottle of champagne and rekindled the naval race on far more even terms. In December the HMS *Dreadnought* was launched, a launching which rendered every battleship then afloat or under construction obsolete. In the words of her creator, Admiral Fisher, the *Dreadnought* marked the 'beginning of a new naval epoch . . . today all nations start *de novo* . . .' Fisher had built the *Dreadnought* with such speed and secrecy that until she was launched it was not known what a radical design she embodied. The new ship caused a furor in Britain because she destroyed British superiority in battleships. The high cost of these new ships meant that fewer of them could be built compared to the old battleships. Fisher was severely criticized for this act, but he had had no choice. Not only was the technology available to build ships of this design, but it was known that the Americans, Russians and Japanese were all designing similar ships. By moving so rapidly and secretly, Fisher had given Britain almost a two-year lead in the dreadnought race.

The essential characteristics of the *Dreadnought* were gunpower and speed. The Spanish-American War of 1898 had convinced most navies that the big gun was the most important asset of the capital ship, a fact thought to have been confirmed in the Russo-Japanese War. At the same time, long-range firing was being developed. Until 1900 the effective battle range had been considered to be about 2000 yards with most captains expecting to come within a mile of the enemy and 'smother him with superior fire'. With the introduction of smokeless powder, new systems of fire control and more sophisticated range finders, accuracy at longer ranges advanced, until by 1914 16,000 to 18,000 yards was normal. Another reason for the increase in battle range was the increasing range and accuracy of the torpedo. Previously, battleships had only been vulnerable to other battleships, but now submarines and torpedo craft could launch torpedoes from distances up to 14,000 yards. The development of long range firing had an important effect on battleship design, as the varied armament of battleships had made fire control and accuracy at long range difficult due to different sizes of shell (and therefore splash), different rates of fire, and

mutual interference from blast and smoke. At long range lighter guns were useless while the heavy guns reached their peak accuracy. Speed was another essential in a battleship, since it was widely believed that in a fleet action both sides would use the line ahead, in which case the line 'with the superior speed must win . . . .'. Speed was 'the first desideratum in every type of battleship' wrote Fisher. Superior speed was the equivalent of having the weather gauge in Nelson's time, as it enabled a fleet to engage at the most advantageous moment.

The *Dreadnought* was a ship of 17,900 tons with 21 knots speed, two knots faster than any capital ship afloat or under construction. Ten twelve-inch guns were arranged so that six could fire ahead or astern, and eight on the broadside. Previous battleships could fire only two ahead or astern and four on the broadside; the *Dreadnought* was, therefore, equal to three battleships ahead or astern and two on the broadside. The only other armament was 27 twelve-pounders to repel torpedo boat attacks. Advances in gunnery had made the *Dreadnought* inevitable, for in the words of Admiral Jellicoe, 'The recent development of the prospect of hitting frequently at long ranges is the all important fact which has brought the value of the heaviest gun forward, and which culminates in the design of the *Dreadnought*'. The main armor belt of the new ship was eleven inches thick, while its hull had a large number of watertight compartments as a safeguard against torpedo and mine damage. Another innovation was the use of turbine as opposed to reciprocating engines. The former could operate at full speed for long periods whereas the latter tended to break down regularly. With its primary armament of eight to twelve large guns of the same caliber, the *Dreadnought* set the pattern for all subsequent capital ships of every navy. Awesome in its overwhelming power, the *Dreadnought* was the Edwardian ultimate deterrent.

Another of Fisher's brainchildren was the battle cruiser, the first of which was the *Invincible*. At 17,200 tons the *Invincible* was virtually identical to the *Dreadnought*, except that armor protection had been sacrificed for a 25-knot speed and there were only four turrets mounting eight twelve-inch guns plus anti-torpedo boat armament. 'Indeed, these Armored Cruisers are battleships in disguise' commented the Admiralty committee on ship design. The battle cruiser was to function as a super scout, forcing its way through the enemy screen of lighter ships to get information on the size and disposition of the opposing battle fleet, and then to act as a fast wing of the battle fleet in action. With the 23-knot German liners in mind, another use Fisher considered was the pursuit and destruction of armed merchant raiders.

With Germany now less than two years rather than decades behind Britain, the *Dreadnought* and *Invincible* ushered in the most intensive period of Anglo-German naval rivalry. Other countries were also in the race. The United States had let contracts for its first dreadnoughts – the *South Carolina* and the *Michigan* – in July 1906 while Japan had laid down the keel of an all-big-gun ship even before the Russo-Japanese War was over. The first German dreadnoughts and battle cruisers were laid down in 1907 and an ambitious naval program was launched in 1908, aiming at thirteen dreadnoughts to Britain's eighteen by 1912. As the race went on, size escalated as well as numbers. From the 17,900 tons and ten twelve-inch guns of the original *Dreadnought* in 1906, Britain had gone to the 28,000 tons and ten fourteen-inch guns of the *Canada* by 1915. The first German dreadnoughts were 18,800 tons with twelve eleven-inch guns, while the largest German ships at Jutland were 25,800 tons and ten twelve-inch guns. At the outbreak of war in 1914, Britain had twenty dreadnoughts and nine battle cruisers with twelve dreadnoughts and one battle cruiser under construction. To these must be added one Chilean and two Turkish dreadnoughts confiscated while under construction in Britain and 39 pre-dreadnought battleships. In addition to her 22 pre-dreadnoughts, Germany had thirteen dreadnoughts and five battle cruisers with seven of the former and three of the latter on the stocks. Thus Britain had maintained a decisive superiority in the new naval race, a superiority to which it could add one more advantage. The British Navy had confidence and the German Navy did not. With centuries of tradition behind it, the Royal Navy was better trained, more experienced and spent far more of its time at sea. Soldiers at sea rather than sailors, the Germans lacked a certain offensive spirit, even though they were hardworking and better educated. The German High Seas Fleet spent much of its time in harbor and usually trained in sheltered waters. While the opening naval encounter of the war at Coronel had little effect on British morale, it had a significant effect on that of the High Seas Fleet.

The German Navy's Passive Role

Well aware of British naval superiority, the German General Staff cast its navy in a passive role. The war was to be won by Christmas by Germany's incomparable army. The navy was to attack British commerce with submarines and surface raiders and prevent a landing on the German coast. But the war was not over by Christmas. In the first six months of the war, before the U-boat campaign began in earnest, the commerce war was carried on by detached cruisers and armed merchantmen. These ships were limited by coal and supply problems, and were a short-lived problem for the British, as the German bases from which they could operate soon fell. At the beginning of the war the Royal Navy immediately placed a distant blockade on the German ports to deny German naval forces and shipping access to the high seas. Since the German cruisers already on foreign stations had little chance of returning to Germany, they were ordered 'to carry on cruiser warfare against enemy merchant vessels and against contraband carried in neutral vessels, raid the enemy's coasts, bombard military establishments and destroy cable and wireless stations'. As the far-flung British empire was especially vulnerable to this sort of attack, these detached forces would assist the main fleet 'by holding many of the enemy's forces overseas'. The chief duty of these vessels was thus to damage the enemy as much as possible at the discretion of their captains since there was no way for orders to reach them from Germany. Nine cruisers were in foreign waters and were put to this use. The most successful was the light cruiser *Emden* which sank seventeen British ships in the North Pacific and Indian

Ocean in the first three months of the war before being sunk herself. In the Atlantic the *Karlsruhe* accounted for fifteen more ships. These losses were negligible when measured against total British shipping at this time, but public opinion demanded that action be taken.

The most dangerous threat, however, was the German China Squadron commanded by the aggressive Count Maximilian von Spee, a dangerous and resourceful adversary who had been in the Far East for almost two years. At the start of the war the 53-year-old von Spee had been on a training cruise at Ponapé in the Caroline Islands. Since Japan entered the war on the side of Britain on 23 August, it was obvious that his squadron could not long remain in the Pacific in the face of the Japanese Fleet. He therefore decided to operate off

the west coast of South America where there were important British trade routes protected by only a weak cruiser squadron and where he could use the friendly ports of Chile for coaling. Von Spee knew that the effectiveness of his force would be short, writing to his superiors, 'I must plough the seas of the world doing as much mischief as I can, until my ammunition is exhausted, or a foe of far superior strength succeeds in catching me'. But to the British, von Spee's existence presented a genuine threat. In the words of Churchill, 'He had no lack of objectives. He had only to hide and strike . . . So long as he lived, all the Allied enterprises lay under the shadow of a serious potential danger'. So Graf Spee made his way across the Pacific and arrived off the coast of Chile toward the end of October with two armored cruisers and three light cruisers. The armored cruisers were the *Scharnhorst* and the *Gneisenau*, 11,000-ton, 23.8-knot ships manned by the pick of the German Navy and renowned for their accuracy with the six 8.2-inch and six 5.9-inch guns of each ship. These were supported by the light cruisers *Nürnberg*, *Leipzig* and *Dresden*, each mounting ten 4.1-inch guns and capable of 23 to 24.5 knots.

At first the Admiralty was misled into believing that Graf Spee was heading west rather than east. But on 5 October, on the basis of an intercepted message from the *Scharnhorst*, they informed Rear Admiral Sir Christopher Cradock, commanding the South Atlantic station, that the German ships were definitely on their way to South America and instructed him to 'be prepared to meet them in company . . .'. On receiving this information Cradock proposed the formation of two forces, each strong enough to face von Spee independently, to operate on the east and west coasts of South America. This would counter the possibility of von Spee slipping past Cradock and raiding in the Atlantic. The Admiralty agreed and formed an east coast squadron under Rear Admiral A. P.

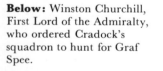

Below: Winston Churchill, First Lord of the Admiralty, who ordered Cradock's squadron to hunt for Graf Spee.

Stoddart consisting of the powerful armored cruiser *Defence*, three other cruisers and two armed merchantmen. But Cradock received no reinforcements other than the old battleship *Canopus*. His west coast squadron was thus composed of the 14,000-ton armored cruiser *Good Hope* mounting two 9.2-inch guns and sixteen 6-inch guns, the 9800-ton armored cruiser *Monmouth* with fourteen 6-inch guns, and the modern light cruiser *Glasgow* with two 6-inch and ten 4-inch guns. In addition, Cradock was lumbered with the *Otranto*, an armed merchant cruiser never intended for battle. Manned mainly by reservists, the *Good Hope* and *Monmouth* had been hurriedly commissioned at the start of the war and rushed off to the South American station without even having

had time to fire their guns. A further problem was that the armor piercing shells for the armored cruisers were obsolescent. So were the fuses of the lyddite common shells of all the ships.

The Admiralty knew that Cradock's ships were not fast enough to force an engagement with von Spee but assumed that at least the force was in no danger from the enemy as long as it had the *Canopus* to serve, in Churchill's words, as 'a citadel around which all our cruisers in those waters could find absolute security'. It was recognized that without the *Canopus* Cradock stood no chance against Graf Spee, but there was no alternative in the eyes of the Admiralty since all the dreadnoughts and battle cruisers were needed in home waters. Vice-Admiral Sir Doveton Sturdee, Director of Naval Operations, had proposed sending additional ships but this had been vetoed by Churchill and First Lord of the Admiralty Louis Battenberg. Cradock's order for the *Defence* to join him was also countermanded by the Admiralty on the grounds that the *Canopus* was sufficient reinforcement. Lightly armored even for a pre-dreadnought, the *Canopus* was in fact an old second-class battleship which had been scheduled for scrapping but was reprieved by the war. The maximum range of her four 12-inch guns was only 14,000 yards compared to the 13,500-yard range of the German 8.2-inch guns. Her crew consisted largely of untrained reservists whose gunnery efficiency was very low. As her chief engineer later said, 'Our fighting value was very small – our two turrets were in charge of Royal Naval Reserve Lieutenants who had never been in a turret before...'

The Admiralty's first mistake had been to use the British and Australian naval forces in the Far East to capture the harmless German colonies of Kaiserwilhelmsland in New Guinea, Yap, Nauru and Samoa instead of hunting Graf Spee down in the first days of the war. After belatedly recognizing the elimination of the German squadron as a high priority, their second mistake was the failure to concentrate enough force to deal with

Above: *Scharnhorst* and *Gneisenau* (left and right in background) leave Valparaiso with a light cruiser for their rendezvous in the Falklands. The ships in the foreground are Chilean cruisers.

the situation. The *Canopus* had arrived on 18 October with engines that needed overhauling, able only to make twelve knots. Cradock cabled this fact to London but then added, 'but shall trust circumstances will enable me to force an action'. Although Cradock apparently believed that he was expected to seek out a superior enemy force and bring it to action, Churchill placed his faith in the *Canopus* and made no effort to clarify what action Cradock was or was not expected to take. On 22 October another cable was received from Cradock stating that he was starting a sweep around the Horn and was leaving the slow *Canopus* to convoy his colliers. Again Churchill made no comment on the detachment of the *Canopus* or Cradock's course of action. Thus the Admiralty's third mistake was its failure to clarify its intentions to Cradock. In the last days of October Admiral Fisher replaced Battenberg as First Lord and immediately apprehended the situation. The *Defence* was dispatched to join Cradock posthaste while Cradock himself was ordered not to seek battle without concentrating all of his forces including the *Canopus*. But Cradock had already rounded the Horn and never received the cable.

Given the fact that his opponent was known to be superior in speed, gunpower, efficiency and numbers, Cradock's motivation for seeking an engagement is puzzling. Described by Fisher as 'one of our best officers', the 52-year-old admiral may have felt that he had to fight after being refused the *Defence* and told that he had sufficient force. The Nelson tradition of aggressively seeking out the enemy was still very strong in the Royal Navy, and a colleague of Cradock's was at that time up for court martial for not engaging a marginally superior enemy. One widely accepted explanation among his colleagues was that Cradock was 'constitutionally incapable of refusing or even postponing action, if there was the smallest chance of success'. Another common view was that Cradock, knowing his mission was impossible, wanted to damage Spee far from any German repair yards and force him to use up his irreplaceable ammunition. Whatever the reason, with good sea-room and plenty of time to escape on 31 October off Coronel, Cradock instead turned toward the enemy and engaged.

Cradock had sent the *Glasgow* to call at Montevideo for any messages from the Admiralty, but when the light cruiser touched at Coronel, von Spee learned of her presence and came south from Valparaiso to dispose of her. In response to the news from the *Glasgow* that she was intercepting wireless traffic from a German cruiser, Cradock in turn sailed north. Each thought that his quarry was a single ship, and neither admiral discovered the truth until the squadrons sighted each other at 1640 the following day fifty miles west of Coronel. With his dream come true – an inferior enemy cruiser force looking for a fight – von Spee immediately altered course so as not to be maneuvered into a lee position and to cut Cradock off from neutral waters.

The ensuing battle was hopeless for the British ships: 'the most rotten show imaginable' as one survivor described it. In single line ahead, Cradock tried to close the enemy to force the

The Battle of Coronel, 1 November 1914

Ships	Tonnage	Maximum Speed	Main Armament
British			
Glasgow	4800	25	2–6", 10–4"
Good Hope	14000	23	2–9.2", 16–6"
Monmouth	9800	18	14–6"
Otranto	12128	18	8–4.7"
German			
Dresden	3600	24.5	10–4.1"
Gneisenau	11000	23.8	6–8.2", 6–5.9"
Leipzig	3250	24.5	10–4.1"
Nürnberg	3450	24.5	10–4.1"
Scharnhorst	11000	23.8	6–8.2", 6–5.9"

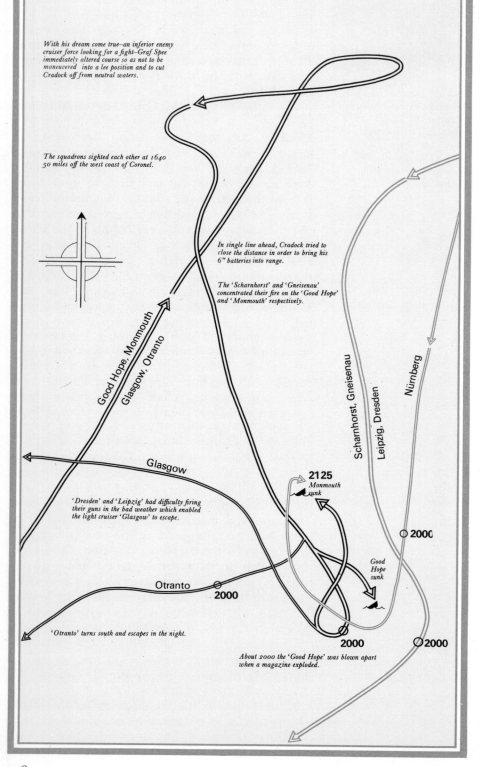

With his dream come true–an inferior enemy cruiser force looking for a fight–Graf Spee immediately altered course so as not to be maneuvered into a lee position and to cut Cradock off from neutral waters.

The squadrons sighted each other at 1640 50 miles off the west coast of Coronel.

In single line ahead, Cradock tried to close the distance in order to bring his 6" batteries into range.

The 'Scharnhorst' and 'Gneisenau' concentrated their fire on the 'Good Hope' and 'Monmouth' respectively.

Good Hope, Monmouth

Glasgow, Otranto

Glasgow

Scharnhorst, Gneisenau

Leipzig, Dresden

Nürnberg

2125 Monmouth sunk

'Dresden' and 'Leipzig' had difficulty firing their guns in the bad weather which enabled the light cruiser 'Glasgow' to escape.

Otranto

Good Hope sunk

○ 2000

'Otranto' turns south and escapes in the night.

○ 2000

○ 2000 ○ 2000

About 2000 the 'Good Hope' was blown apart when a magazine exploded.

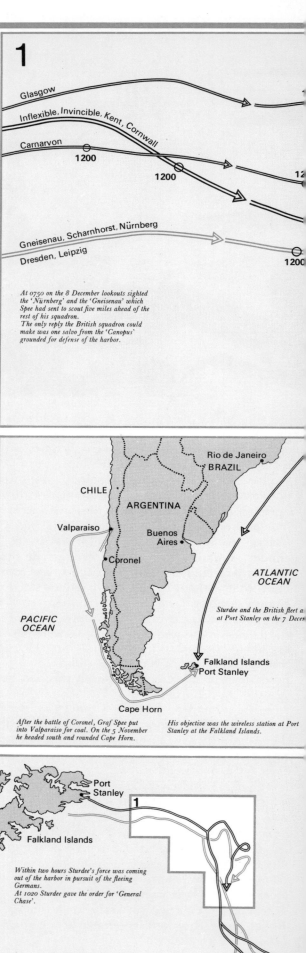

1

Glasgow

Inflexible, Invincible, Kent, Cornwall

Carnarvon ○ **1200**

1200

Gneisenau, Scharnhorst, Nürnberg

Dresden, Leipzig ○ 1200

At 0750 on the 8 December lookouts sighted the 'Nürnberg' and the 'Gneisenau' which Spee had sent to scout five miles ahead of the rest of his squadron.
The only reply the British squadron could make was one salvo from the 'Canopus' grounded for defense of the harbor.

Rio de Janeiro
BRAZIL

CHILE

ARGENTINA

Valparaiso

Buenos Aires •

• Coronel

ATLANTIC OCEAN

PACIFIC OCEAN

Sturdee and the British fleet a at Port Stanley on the 7 Decem

Falkland Islands
Port Stanley

Cape Horn

After the battle of Coronel, Graf Spee put into Valparaiso for coal. On the 5 November he headed south and rounded Cape Horn.

His objective was the wireless station at Port Stanley at the Falkland Islands.

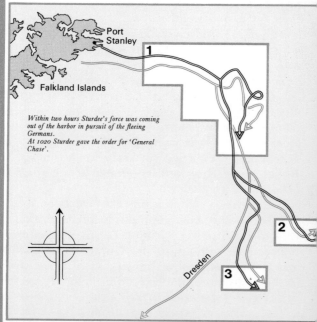

Port Stanley

1

Falkland Islands

Within two hours Sturdee's force was coming out of the harbor in pursuit of the fleeing Germans.
At 1020 Sturdee gave the order for 'General Chase'.

Dresden

2

3

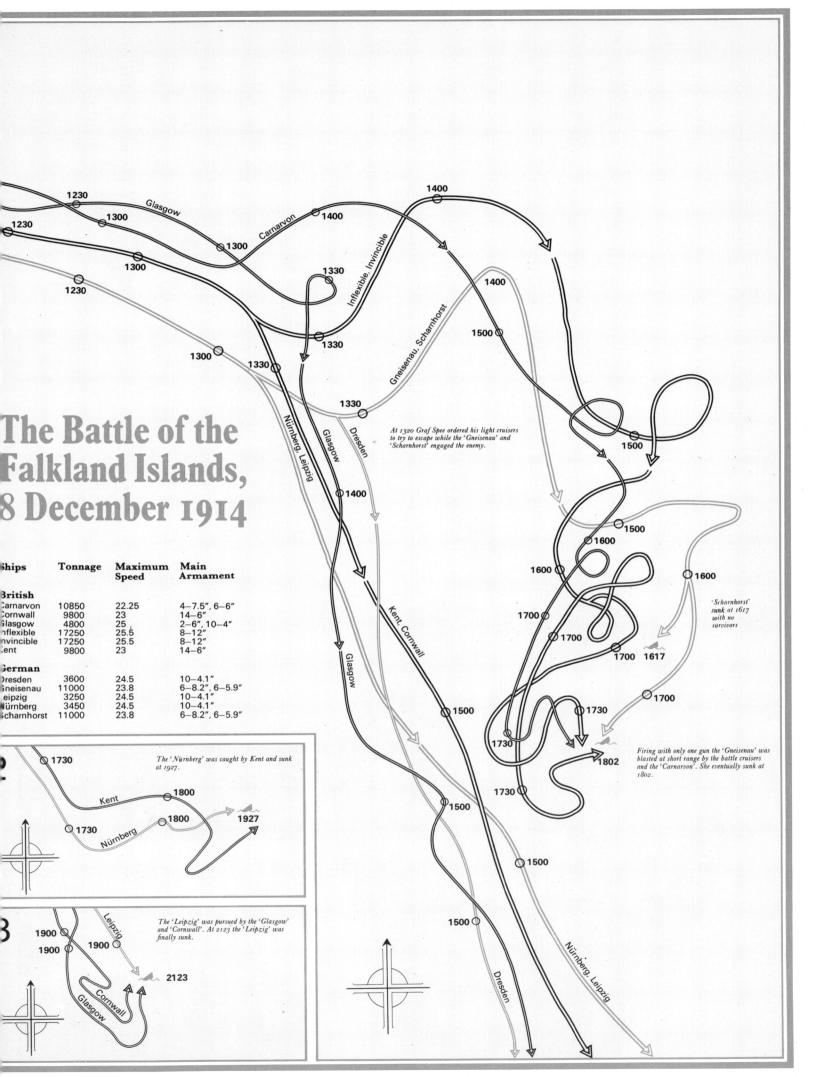

The Battle of the Falkland Islands, 8 December 1914

Ships	Tonnage	Maximum Speed	Main Armament
British			
Carnarvon	10850	22.25	4–7.5", 6–6"
Cornwall	9800	23	14–6"
Glasgow	4800	25	2–6", 10–4"
Inflexible	17250	25.5	8–12"
Invincible	17250	25.5	8–12"
Kent	9800	23	14–6"
German			
Dresden	3600	24.5	10–4.1"
Gneisenau	11000	23.8	6–8.2", 6–5.9"
Leipzig	3250	24.5	10–4.1"
Nürnberg	3450	24.5	10–4.1"
Scharnhorst	11000	23.8	6–8.2", 6–5.9"

At 1320 Graf Spee ordered his light cruisers to try to escape while the 'Gneisenau' and 'Scharnhorst' engaged the enemy.

'Scharnhorst' sunk at 1617 with no survivors

Firing with only one gun the 'Gneisenau' was blasted at short range by the battle cruisers and the 'Carnarvon'. She eventually sunk at 1802.

The 'Nürnberg' was caught by Kent and sunk at 1927.

The 'Leipzig' was pursued by the 'Glasgow' and 'Cornwall'. At 2123 the 'Leipzig' was finally sunk.

action before sunset. With the British between him and the sun, Spee was in a bad position and used his superior speed to keep the range at 18,000 yards until sunset. Then, with the enemy silhouetted against the horizon, von Spee quickly closed to 12,000 yards and opened fire. The two squadrons were on parallel courses but at this range only the two 9.2-inch guns of the *Good Hope* could answer the twelve 8.2-inch guns of the enemy so Cradock closed to 5500 yards to bring his six-inch batteries into range. A heavy sea was making it almost impossible to fight the main deck guns of the *Good Hope* and *Monmouth* which considerably reduced the gun power of the British line. The power of the British attack was further weakened by the poor quality of their shells, some striking and failing to explode.

The *Scharnhorst* concentrated her fire on the *Good Hope* while the *Gneisenau* blasted the *Monmouth*. Within five minutes decisive hits had been scored on each British cruiser. At 1930 the *Monmouth* veered out of line burning furiously and half an hour later the *Good Hope* was blown apart by an exploding magazine after taking more than 35 hits. Spee's crews had lived up to their reputation for excellent gunnery. By 2100 the *Nürnberg*

closed with the *Monmouth* which was then almost incapacitated and had only a few guns still in action. When the *Monmouth* refused to strike and made as if to ram, the *Nürnberg* dispatched her with shell fire at the point blank range of 600–1000 yards. Never intended to face warships, the *Otranto* had earlier turned south while the *Glasgow* also escaped because her adversaries – the small cruisers *Dresden* and *Leipzig* – had difficulty fighting their guns in the bad weather.

By superior force, skilful tactics and first class gunnery, von Spee had sunk two second-class enemy cruisers with the loss of all their crews and a rear-admiral while his own ships had suffered only six hits and two wounded. But the encounter had been costly in another way, for the German cruisers had used almost half of their 8.2-inch shells and these could only be obtained from Germany. After the battle Graf Spee put into Valparaiso to coal, and then received orders to try to break through to Germany with his ships. On 5 November he steered south with the intention of doing as much damage as possible on the way. His first objective was the wireless station at Port Stanley in the Falkland Islands where he also hoped to find a weak British cruiser squadron taking on coal.

The strategic gains reaped from Coronel by the Germans were practically nil – at best a temporary suspension of nitrate, copper and tin shipments from Chile and Peru. But the battle had been a blow to British prestige. Even though the losses at Coronel were negligible, they were still the first losses in battle in over a hundred years. Although the Admiralty blamed Cradock for disobeying orders by failing to concentrate his force, public reaction felt that the Admiralty had

Below: Rear-Admiral A. P. Stoddart commanded the cruiser squadron at the Battle of the Falklands.
Right, above and below: Two pictures of the German cruiser *Dresden*, sunk by the *Glasgow* five months after the Battle of the Falklands. The British ship violated Chilean neutrality to make certain of sinking the last survivor of Spee's squadron.

bungled by placing Cradock in a position where he had to face a superior enemy force. The setback also had its effect on the balance of neutral opinion. The news of the battle was received with great enthusiasm in Germany where Admiral Reinhard Scheer wrote that 'this news filled us in the fleet with great pride and confidence'.

The Search for Graf Spee

Within a day of learning of Coronel, Churchill and Fisher had developed plans to eliminate von Spee. The best course for the Germans would be to pass into the South Atlantic for operations there off the east coast of South America. Fisher therefore determined to create a powerful force to annihilate the raiders. He somewhat unjustly blamed the Director of Naval Operations, Vice-Admiral Sir Doveton Sturdee, for the faulty dispositions which had led to Coronel and fired him. The only post which was acceptable to Sturdee was command of the South Atlantic and South Pacific station. So ironically the man whom many held responsible for Coronel was charged with avenging it. The 55-year-old Sturdee was ordered to incorporate Stoddart's force and, using the Falklands as a base, to hunt and destroy the German squadron. The battle cruisers *Invincible* and *Inflexible*, identical 17,250-ton, 25.5-knot ships mounting eight 12-inch guns, were the core of his force; the remainder was Stoddart's armored cruisers *Defence*, *Cornwall*, *Kent*, *Carnarvon*, the light cruisers *Glasgow* and *Bristol*, and the armed merchant cruiser *Macedonia*. The two battle cruisers sailed on 11 November and arrived at Port Stanley on 7 December, having collected Stoddart's ships off Brazil on the way. Sturdee intended to leave the following day after coaling his

squadron, as the available intelligence still placed the Germans off the coast of Chile.

At 0750 the following morning, however, lookouts were surprised to sight two unidentified warships approaching from the south. Spee had sent the *Gneisenau* and *Nürnberg* to scout five miles ahead of the rest of his squadron. The British ships were still coaling and none had steam up, so if Graf Spee had come up with his entire force, he could have blasted each British ship as it emerged from the harbor. As it was, the only response the British could make was one salvo from the *Canopus*, now grounded for defense of the harbor. Aware neither of the unprepared state in which he had caught the British nor of the presence of two battle cruisers, von Spee decided not to risk an action and to use his superior speed to escape. The salvo from the *Canopus* had caused the two scouts to veer off while the British ships frantically got up steam. Within two hours Sturdee's force was coming out of the harbor in pursuit of the fleeing Germans. It was a calm, clear day with excellent visibility, ideal conditions for a shooting match. With plenty of sea-room and eight hours of daylight, Sturdee gave the order for 'General Chase' at 1020.

Von Spee fled southeast but at 1247, when the range had narrowed to 16,000 yards and his hindmost ship, the *Leipzig*, was coming under fire, the German admiral knew that the 12-inch guns and greater speed of the battle cruisers spelled the doom of his squadron. At 1320 he ordered his light cruisers to try to escape while the *Scharnhorst* and *Gneisenau* engaged the enemy. The three small cruisers scattered in the direction of the South American coast with three British cruisers hard on their heels. The *Nürnberg* was

Below: At about 1 p.m. the battlecruiser *Inflexible* opened fire on the German ships with her forward 12-inch guns.

Below: SMS *Scharnhorst*, which was launched in 1906. Displacement: 11,600 tons. Length: 474 feet. Beam: 71 feet. Draught: 24.5 feet. Speed: 22.5 knots. Armament: eight 8.2-inch, six 5.9-inch, eighteen .4-inch guns and four 18-inch torpedo tubes. Crew: 764 officers and men. **Opposite left:** A shell from the *Nürnberg* carried away the topmast of the *Kent*. The funnels are blistered from the intense heat generated during the chase. **Opposite right:** A six-inch casemate in HMS *Kent* after the Battle of the Falklands. The shell hole was caused by a hit from the *Nürnberg*. **Opposite center:** The armored cruiser *Kent* was hit several times by German shells during the battle. This is a hole in the engine room artificers' bathroom made by a 4.1-inch shell.

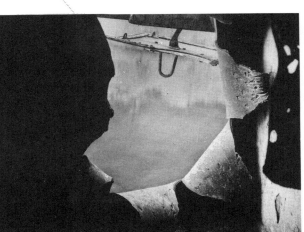

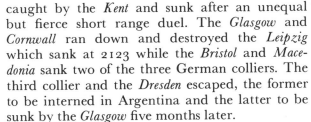

caught by the *Kent* and sunk after an unequal but fierce short range duel. The *Glasgow* and *Cornwall* ran down and destroyed the *Leipzig* which sank at 2123 while the *Bristol* and *Macedonia* sank two of the three German colliers. The third collier and the *Dresden* escaped, the former to be interned in Argentina and the latter to be sunk by the *Glasgow* five months later.

While the light cruisers were making their bids for survival, the armored cruisers were confronting the battle cruisers in another unequal struggle. Each admiral was maneuvering to get the range most suitable for his guns. Sturdee tried to keep a position where his 12-inch guns could outrange the 8.2-inch guns of the enemy, while von Spee tried to close the range to bring his 5.9-inch batteries into action and thus gain some advantage over the battle cruisers which had no intermediate armament. By 1500 von Spee had reduced the range to 11,000 yards and was hammering the battle cruisers with an accurate fire. Sturdee tried to counter by using his superior speed to open the range again and also to get clear of the battle smoke which was reducing his

gunnery efficiency. Even so, the 12-inch guns of the battle cruisers had already scored serious hits, for within half an hour the *Scharnhorst* was listing heavily and on fire. Disregarding signals to strike, she went down at 1617 with no survivors. Fighting with only one gun, the *Gneisenau* was blasted at short range by the battle cruisers and the *Carnarvon*, absorbing at least fifty 12-inch shells. She was listing, her upper deck a shambles and burning fiercely, but her captain refused to surrender, preferring instead to open his valves and blast out the sides of the ship with charges. The *Gneisenau* was finally abandoned at 1800 and 200 survivors were picked up.

Graf Spee had fought to the bitter end against hopeless odds, losing four of five ships and 2200 men as well as his own life. Sturdee's force had suffered little damage and few casualties, which only increased the jubilation in Britain over the victory. The Battle of the Falklands stilled public criticism of the Admiralty and reassured Britain's allies that the Royal Navy was still master of the seas. Even though he had achieved the Royal Navy's nearest approach to a smashing victory in the war, Sturdee still had his critics who pointed out that a weaker enemy had literally sailed into his backyard. Even Sturdee had to acknowledge this when he said of von Spee '. . . he gave our squadron a chance by calling on me the day after I arrived'. Fisher and Churchill were also cool toward him for allowing the

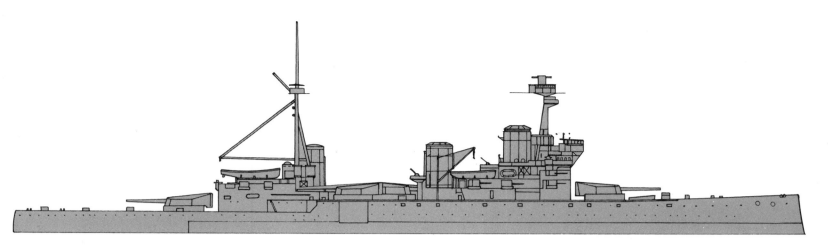

Dresden to escape. Being simply a stern chase, the action at the Falklands has no particular tactical interest, but it did have major strategic consequences. The stain of the defeat at Coronel was wiped out and morale in the service and the country received a substantial boost. A grave menace to British commerce and trade had been removed. Except for the *Dresden* and two armed merchant raiders, the Royal Navy was again in complete command of the seas. Within five months all of the surface raiders had been sunk or interned, but at that point the German submarine offensive began and was to bring Britain to the brink of starvation in a short time. After the Falklands, the Admiralty was able to strengthen the home fleet by recalling many ships from foreign stations, thus completing what Churchill termed the first phase of the naval war, the 'clearance of the seas and recall of foreign squadrons'. The consequent phases were the closing of the Elbe and the domination of the Baltic Sea.

The Battles of Coronel and the Falklands represented the first blow to British naval prestige and confidence in the war. The losses on each side were insignificant, but it was now clear the Germans could fight and fight well at sea. The British Navy could no longer afford to be overconfident. The two navies were to have only one more serious encounter during the war. Nineteen months after Coronel and the Falklands, Jutland was to be the second blow to British prestige.

Above: A battlecruiser of the *Invincible* class, armed with eight 12-inch guns and capable of 25½ knots. They were designed with a battle like the Falklands in mind, but were never used again with such striking success.

Opposite: The battlecruiser *Inflexible* stops to rescue German survivors of the *Gneisenau*. **Below:** The *Scharnhorst* (above left) has already sunk, but the *Gneisenau* is still firing all her guns at the *Invincible* (foreground).

Jutland

1916

The British Grand Fleet and the German High Seas Fleet met only once during the First World War. The result was the Battle of Jutland, a battle which has stirred controversy for over 50 years since its occurrence on 31 May, 1916. From Coronel and the Falklands to Jutland, there were only minor skirmishes between British and German surface units; the British blockade kept the High Seas Fleet in port while German U-boats kept the Royal Navy strained trying to cope with their highly successful attacks. Each side, however, kept a wary eye on the enemy battle fleet, hoping for the opportunity to strike a major blow. The British, who were already much superior materially at the outbreak of the war in 1914, had increased their margin of superiority by 1916. Jutland was the result of one German effort, not to defeat the Grand Fleet, but to reduce that margin of superiority.

In 1916 the Royal Navy had 33 dreadnoughts and ten battle cruisers, having added thirteen dreadnoughts since the war had begun. The German navy had added but five dreadnoughts, giving it a total of eighteen dreadnoughts and six battle cruisers. The two fleets which met at Jutland – the Grand Fleet and the High Seas Fleet – showed a similar disparity in strength.

The Grand Fleet put 28 dreadnoughts, nine battle cruisers, eight armored cruisers, 26 light cruisers, five destroyer leaders and 73 destroyers into the battle while the High Seas Fleet had 16 dreadnoughts, five battle cruisers, eleven light cruisers, six pre-dreadnought battleships and 61 destroyers. Thus during the battle the Grand Fleet had a 37:21 superiority in dreadnoughts and battle cruisers and a 102:78 edge in other ships. On paper the two fleets were roughly equal in speed at 24 to 25 knots, but in fact the British had an advantage of which they were unaware. The pre-dreadnought battleships limited the High Seas Fleet to eighteen knots but these ships had been included at the last minute thanks to the pleas of their officers. In the German fleet they were known as 'five minute ships', because that was how long they were expected to last in action against dreadnoughts.

The Grand Fleet also enjoyed a considerable superiority in gun power with 272 heavy guns in its battle fleet against 200 for Germany's and 72 against 44 in the battle cruiser squadrons. British capital ships almost always carried larger caliber guns than their opponents. Laid down in October 1912, the *Queen Elizabeth*, for example, mounted eight 15-inch guns with a broadside of 15,600

Right: Jellicoe on HMS *Iron Duke*, flagship of the Grand Fleet.

pounds while the *Kronprinz Wilhelm*, a comparable German dreadnought laid down in May 1912, mounted ten 12-inch guns with an 8600-pound broadside. Heavier shells are more accurate at long ranges than lighter shells and battle ranges were now 14,000 to 16,000 yards. The lighter German shells achieved the same penetrating power as the British shells, however, due to higher muzzle velocity. The Germans also had a better armor piercing shell. Although British armor piercing shells had a larger bursting charge, they were 'lamentably weak' for 12-inch guns and above when striking armor at oblique impact, but this was not recognized until after Jutland.

A new and far more effective system of fire control had been introduced in the Royal Navy in 1912. Termed 'Electrical Director Fire Control', it enabled all the guns of the broadside to be aimed and fired by one man using one sight in the conning tower. The result was a remarkable increase in accuracy. At Jutland all British dreadnoughts and battle cruisers had this system but only for their main armament. Fire control on German capital ships relied on an electrical 'follow the pointer' system which aimed and fired the broadside. The turret guns followed the lateral movement of the gunnery officer's periscope while elevation was determined by a 'range pointer'. Since they attached great importance to the initial estimation of range, the Germans had developed a stereoscopic range finder which was far more sophisticated and accurate than the British 'coincidence' range finder. The former was particularly superior in poor visibility and hence was a major factor at Jutland.

Because of the British preference for heavier guns, German ships were better armored than British, a fact which was made possible by their greater displacement. In the later classes of German dreadnoughts the armor belt was almost fourteen inches thick, while comparable British ships carried ten to twelve inches of armor. British battle cruisers had only nine inches of armor compared to twelve inches in German battle cruisers. German armored protection was also more comprehensive than that of British ships, whose turrets and magazines in particular were not properly protected; only the bows of German ships were inadequately armored. This British deficiency was the result of sacrificing some armor for heavier guns in dreadnoughts and a few knots extra speed in battle cruisers. Another significant difference was that German ships had a more complete watertight division below the waterline which gave better protection against mines and torpedoes.

Other weapons which were to influence the conduct of the fighting at Jutland were mines and especially torpedoes. After sinking eighteen ships in the Russo-Japanese war the mine had come into its own, especially in Germany. German mines were far in advance of British, since the Royal Navy had shown no interest in mines until after 1914. After registering its first successes in the American Civil War, the torpedo had had a checkered career. The Japanese had scored only four per cent hits in their war with the Russians, but further advances in technology had given the torpedo a 14,000-yard range and 45-knot speed, while the development of the gyroscope gave it far more accuracy. Delivery systems also improved with the advent of larger and faster sea-going destroyers and the submarine. Because of these developments, battleships now had to be screened by squadrons of destroyers to guard them against torpedo attacks by submarines and other destroyers. Thus the needs of the battleship increasingly shifted the role of the destroyer from offensive to defensive.

On the eve of Jutland, the German Navy was equal to the British in quality of ships, guns and gunnery, while in armor, shells, mines and torpedoes it was superior. At that time, however, British complacency was such that only the Admiral of the Fleet, Sir John Jellicoe, appreciated this fact, writing that 'it is highly dangerous to consider that our ships as a whole are superior or even equal fighting machines'. British naval superiority rested squarely and simply on the disparity in the size of the two fleets and on the confidence and experience of the British officers

Above: The German battlecruiser *Seydlitz* was very badly damaged at Jutland.

and ratings. A further British advantage was that at the beginning of the war, British naval intelligence had acquired captured German cipher and signal books and squared maps of the North Sea from the Russians. Thus through intercepted and decoded messages, the British often had advance knowledge of enemy movements. Eventually the Germans became suspicious and introduced variations in their codes, but this was offset by the development of directional wireless as a means of locating ships.

The tactical ideas underlying the dispositions for battle did not differ markedly from those of Nelson's time. The twin fetishes of the line ahead and centralized command had survived unchallenged down to 1916 because the nineteenth century had been devoid of occasions for testing them. Senior British officers, such as First Lord of the Admiralty Sir John Fisher, Admiral of the Fleet Sir John Jellicoe and others were firm believers in the line ahead while more junior officers such as Vice Admirals Sir Doveton Sturdee and Sir David Beatty argued for divided tactics, attack by divisions and using part of the battle fleet in an independent role so as to concentrate superior force on a part of the enemy. Tactics had not been much studied in the Royal Navy during the nineteenth century, while after 1900 most officers felt that technology had so changed naval warfare that the past had little to offer. For its part, the Admiralty preferred to leave strategy and tactics to those in command.

Below: British battleships *Royal Oak* and *Hercules* deploying into the line as the Grand Fleet comes into action at Jutland.

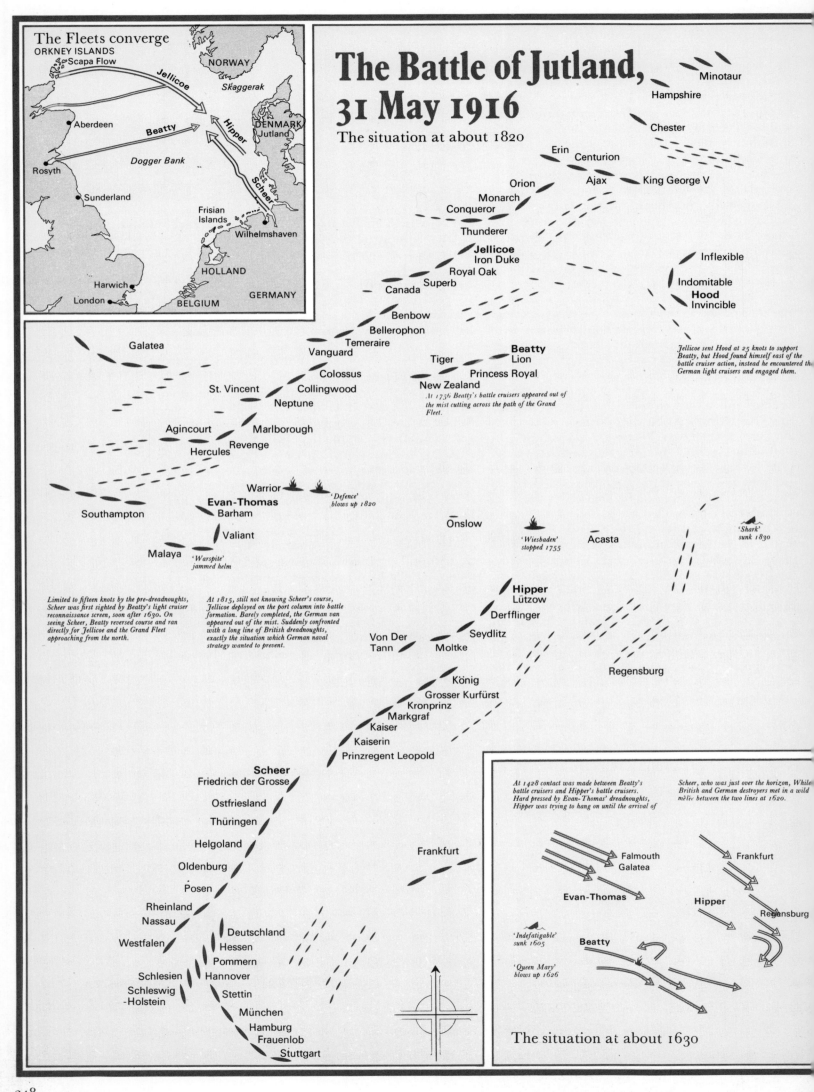

The Battle of Jutland, 31 May 1916

The situation at about 1820

The Fleets converge

ORKNEY ISLANDS
Scapa Flow
NORWAY
Skaggerak
Jellicoe
Aberdeen
Beatty
Hipper
DENMARK
Jutland
Rosyth
Dogger Bank
Scheer
Sunderland
Frisian Islands
Wilhelmshaven
HOLLAND
Harwich
London
BELGIUM
GERMANY

Minotaur
Hampshire
Chester

Erin Centurion
Orion Ajax King George V
Monarch
Conqueror
Thunderer

Jellicoe
Iron Duke
Royal Oak
Superb
Canada

Inflexible
Indomitable
Hood
Invincible

Benbow
Bellerophon
Temeraire
Vanguard

Beatty
Tiger Lion
Princess Royal
New Zealand

Jellicoe sent Hood at 25 knots to support Beatty, but Hood found himself east of the battle cruiser action, instead he encountered the German light cruisers and engaged them.

At 1756 Beatty's battle cruisers appeared out of the mist cutting across the path of the Grand Fleet.

Galatea

Colossus
St. Vincent Collingwood
Neptune

Agincourt Marlborough
Revenge
Hercules

Warrior
'Defence' blows up 1820

Evan-Thomas
Barham
Southampton
Valiant
Malaya
'Warspite' jammed helm

Onslow
'Wiesbaden' stopped 1755
Acasta
'Shark' sunk 1830

Limited to fifteen knots by the pre-dreadnoughts, Scheer was first sighted by Beatty's light cruiser reconnaissance screen, soon after 1630. On seeing Scheer, Beatty reversed course and ran directly for Jellicoe and the Grand Fleet approaching from the north.

At 1815, still not knowing Scheer's course, Jellicoe deployed on the port column into battle formation. Barely completed, the German van appeared out of the mist. Suddenly confronted with a long line of British dreadnoughts, exactly the situation which German naval strategy wanted to prevent.

Hipper
Lützow
Derfflinger
Seydlitz
Von Der Tann
Moltke

Regensburg

König
Grosser Kurfürst
Kronprinz
Markgraf
Kaiser
Kaiserin
Prinzregent Leopold

Scheer
Friedrich der Grosse
Ostfriesland
Thüringen
Helgoland
Oldenburg
Posen
Rheinland
Nassau
Westfalen
Deutschland
Hessen
Pommern
Schlesien
Schleswig-Holstein
Hannover
Stettin
München
Hamburg
Frauenlob
Stuttgart

Frankfurt

At 1428 contact was made between Beatty's battle cruisers and Hipper's battle cruisers. Hard pressed by Evan-Thomas' dreadnoughts, Hipper was trying to hang on until the arrival of Scheer, who was just over the horizon, While British and German destroyers met in a wild mêlée between the two lines at 1620.

Falmouth
Galatea
Frankfurt

Evan-Thomas
Hipper
Regensburg

'Indefatigable' sunk 1605
Beatty
'Queen Mary' blows up 1626

The situation at about 1630

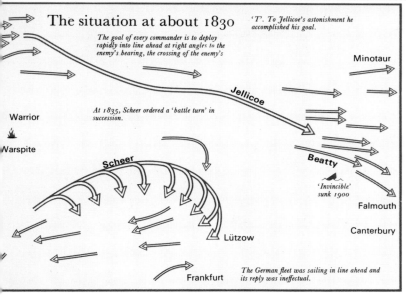

The situation at about 1830

The goal of every commander is to deploy rapidly into line ahead at right angles to the enemy's bearing, the crossing of the enemy's

'T'. To Jellicoe's astonishment he accomplished his goal.

At 1835, Scheer ordered a 'battle turn' in succession.

Minotaur

Jellicoe

Warrior

Warspite

Scheer

Beatty

'Invincible' sunk 1900

Falmouth

Canterbury

Lützow

Frankfurt

The German fleet was sailing in line ahead and its reply was ineffectual.

Ships	Tonnage	Maximum Speed	Main Armaments
British			
Barham	31000	24.5	8–15″, 12–6″
Chester	5200	25.5	10–5.5″
Defence	14600	23	4–9.2″, 10–7.5″
Galatea	3512	28.5	2–6″, 6–4″
Invincible	17250	25.5	8–12″, 16–4″
Iron Duke	26400	21	10–13.5″, 12–6″
Lion	26350	28	8–13.5″, 16–4″
Orion	22500	21	10–13.5″, 16–4″
Shark	935	30	3–4″
Tiger	28500	29	8–13.5″, 12–6″
Tipperary	1300	32	6–4″
Warrior	13550	23	6–9.2″, 4–7.5″
German			
Derfflinger	26180	27	8–12″, 12–5.9″
Kaiser	24380	23	10–12″, 14–5.9″, 8–3.4″
König	25390	23	10–12″, 14–5.9″, 8–3.4″
Moltke	22640	28	10–11″, 12–5.9″, 12–3.4″
Pommern	13200	18	4–11″, 14–6.7″, 20–3.4″
Rostock	4900	28	12–4.1″
Stettin	3550	25	10–4.1″
Von der Tann	19400	24.8	8–11″, 10–5.9″, 16–3.4″
V25	812	33	3–3.4″

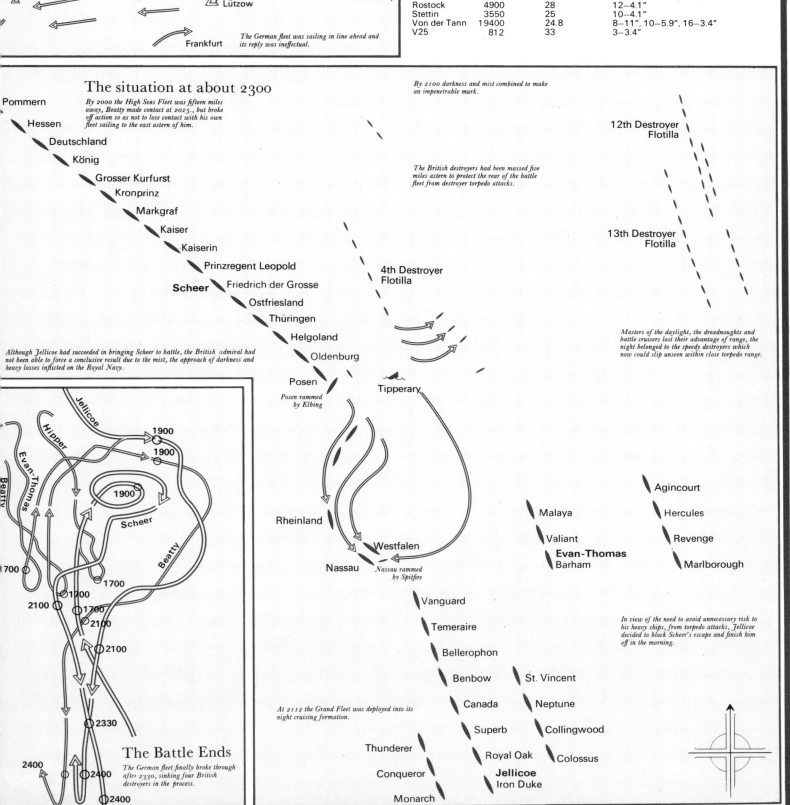

The situation at about 2300

By 2000 the High Seas Fleet was fifteen miles away, Beatty made contact at 2025., but broke off action so as not to lose contact with his own fleet sailing to the east astern of him.

By 2100 darkness and mist combined to make an impenetrable murk.

Pommern

Hessen

Deutschland

König

Grosser Kurfurst

Kronprinz

Markgraf

Kaiser

Kaiserin

Prinzregent Leopold

Scheer Friedrich der Grosse

Ostfriesland

Thüringen

Helgoland

Oldenburg

Posen

Posen rammed by Elbing

Rheinland

Westfalen

Nassau

Nassau rammed by Spitfire

4th Destroyer Flotilla

12th Destroyer Flotilla

13th Destroyer Flotilla

Tipperary

The British destroyers had been massed five miles astern to protect the rear of the battle fleet from destroyer torpedo attacks.

Masters of the daylight, the dreadnoughts and battle cruisers lost their advantage of range, the night belonged to the speedy destroyers which now could slip unseen within close torpedo range.

Although Jellicoe had succeeded in bringing Scheer to battle, the British admiral had not been able to force a conclusive result due to the mist, the approach of darkness and heavy losses inflicted on the Royal Navy.

Agincourt

Malaya

Hercules

Valiant

Revenge

Evan-Thomas Barham

Marlborough

Vanguard

Temeraire

Bellerophon

Benbow St. Vincent

Canada Neptune

Superb Collingwood

Thunderer Royal Oak Colossus

Conqueror **Jellicoe** Iron Duke

Monarch

At 2112 the Grand Fleet was deployed into its night cruising formation.

In view of the need to avoid unnecessary risk to his heavy ships, from torpedo attacks, Jellicoe decided to block Scheer's escape and finish him off in the morning.

Jellicoe

Hipper

Evan-Thomas

Beatty

1900

1900

1900

Scheer

Beatty

1700

1700

1700

1700

2100

2100

2100

2330

2400

2400

2400

The Battle Ends

The German fleet finally broke through after 2330, sinking four British destroyers in the process.

Some discussion had been generated by divided tactics but it was generally agreed that these offered too many problems. Coordination was one such problem. Wireless had not yet been developed for tactical use and even in the best visibility signaling was sometimes difficult, so that a commander-in-chief would be unable to keep control of a modern high speed fleet in a smoke-filled battle zone. Then there was the prospect that the enemy might turn the tables and achieve his own concentration of force against a division or independent squadron. And if the battle fleet minus its independent squadrons came up against the enemy, it would be too weak to achieve a decisive victory and might even be in danger. Tactical maneuvering by detached squadrons was also not feasible at ranges of 14,000 to 16,000 yards because the enemy could start a counter-maneuver before a maneuver of the attackers was completed. On the other hand, the line ahead still brought the greatest number of guns on the battleships in action, creating a blanket of fire, and was the best formation for maintaining the coherence of the fleet. What the advocates of divided tactics had failed to realize was that the development of long range gunnery made the concentration of ships of Nelson's tactics unnecessary, because all of a battle fleet's heavy guns could focus on any part of the enemy fleet without the ships themselves changing relative positions. Modern tactics relied not on tactical but on gunnery concentration.

Thus the general conception was that 'of an artillery duel in one long line on parallel courses', wrote a British officer. The goal was to 'deploy rapidly into line at right angles to the enemy's bearing' to achieve that dream of every commander, the crossing of the enemy 'T'. The Grand Fleet Battle Orders read: '. . . the ruling principle is that the "Dreadnought" fleet as a whole keeps together . . . the squadrons should form one line of battle'. The British strategy was to rely on superior numbers and a heavier broadside to defeat the enemy. No fundamental or comprehensive tactical doctrine united the commanders of the Royal Navy beyond general acceptance of crossing the enemy 'T'. This tactical conception only made sense if it was assumed that the enemy wanted to engage and would do so in line ahead. Although the Germans did normally use the line ahead, at Jutland the last thing they wanted was an action between the battle fleets.

The dominant tactical concept of the line ahead was related to a firm belief in the need for centralized command. Every movement of each squadron or division was initiated by the fleet admiral from his flagship. 'Devolution of authority was interpreted either as weakness or laziness' wrote an officer. Centralization was carried to such extremes that on occasion British ships had been known to collide with each other because orders to turn had not been received. Yet the system had its critics for, as Admiral Sturdee wrote, 'The system of signalling every movement from the fleet flagship tended to develop an acute

kind of tactical arthritis . . . valuable opportunities were frequently missed because no one would act without an order'. One of the main weaknesses of the British fleet at Jutland was the amount of centralization contained in the Grand Fleet Battle Orders. The Germans practised a much greater degree of centralization with a corresponding increase in the initiative of their officers.

The man responsible for containing the High Seas Fleet was 57-year-old Vice-Admiral Sir John Jellicoe, Commander-in-Chief of the Grand Fleet. With a long and distinguished career, Jellicoe was a genius in his own way and the officers of his fleet had absolute faith in him. In addition to his firm belief in the line ahead and the big gun, Jellicoe's strategy for the Grand Fleet emphasized defense. The main duty of the fleet was to stay 'in being' and in superior force; at all times, therefore, it was to be handled with caution. Sailing toward Jutland on 31 May, Jellicoe had virtually the entire British capital ship force under his command and was uncomfortably aware that, in the apt words of Churchill, he was 'the only man on either side who could lose the war in an afternoon'. Those who unfavorably compare Jellicoe's cautious tactics at Jutland with Nelson's bold stroke at Trafalgar should remember that Nelson commanded less than a third of the British battle fleet and thus could afford to take risks. To add to Jellicoe's concern, disaster could come to the Grand Fleet in ways other than from the guns of the enemy. To compensate for their inferiority in numbers, the Germans were making good use of mines, torpedoes, and submarine traps. One great fear of the British was that the balance of naval power would be suddenly and dramatically altered by these cheap means. The only way known in 1916 to neutralize mines, torpedoes and especially submarines was simply not to fight on the enemy's prepared ground. This forced Jellicoe to stifle his natural desire to bring the rival fleet to battle under any circumstances whatever.

A further reason for Jellicoe's caution lay not with the High Seas Fleet but on the other side of the Atlantic. In 1916 Britain was faced with the possibility of war with the United States over the blockade question and the taking of American ships into Allied harbors for contraband searches. 'One circumstance was in my mind throughout the action . . . This was the possibility of the United States coming into the war on the side of our opponents, a possibility which increased the desirability of not running unnecessary risks with the Grand Fleet', Jellicoe wrote in his own account of the battle.

Jellicoe's Strategic Concept
Jellicoe's strategic concept was that the Grand Fleet would be used to nullify any aggressive action by the High Seas Fleet, to cover its own vessels maintaining the blockade or protecting commerce, and to block invasion or landing raids. The elimination of the High Seas Fleet would be the ultimate fulfillment of these objectives but since they were also accomplished when the Germans lay at anchor in harbor, it made little sense to risk the Grand Fleet, especially in view of the danger of attrition from submarines and mines. As Jellicoe himself expressed it, 'There is no doubt that, provided there is a chance of destroying some of the enemy's heavy ships, it is right and proper to run risks with our own heavy ships, but unless the chances are reasonably great, I do not think that such risks should be run, seeing that any real disaster to our heavy ships lays the country open to invasion, and also gives the enemy the opportunity of passing commerce destroyers out of the North Sea'. Thus from the beginning British naval strategy recognized the fact that the maintenance of sea supremacy was far more vital than the defeat of the German Fleet. The entire British war effort – supply of home islands, communications with the Empire, support of the British Expeditionary Force in France, and the blockade of the German coast – hinged on this supremacy. However appealing the defeat of the High Seas Fleet may have appeared, it always remained secondary.

German naval strategy also was built on caution and defensive concepts but for entirely different reasons. The German General Staff had assigned the role of guarding the country from assault by sea to the navy. It was confidently expected that the German army would win the war on land in a short time, and the Kaiser himself had specifically ordered that the fleet was not to be risked. The German concept was that confrontation was unnecessary in any event since mines and submarines would take their toll of British ships. By 1916, however, the swift victory on land was yet to be attained. The balance of manpower was turning against Germany, and the pressure of the British blockade was becoming painful. In view of their deteriorating position, the Germans began to reassess their naval strategy in order to gain some relief from the blockade. The initial step in January 1916 was the appointment of Reinhard Scheer as commander-in-chief, the first genuinely able German fleet admiral of the war. Knowing full well that he lacked the ships to engage in the pitched battle envisaged by the British, Scheer's strategy was to try to reduce the

Below: Prince Henry of Prussia (with field glasses) and Admiral Scheer, Commander-in-Chief of the German High Seas Fleet.

Grand Fleet's margin of superiority. His basic approach was to create a situation in which the entire High Seas Fleet could overwhelm a part of the Grand Fleet, by enticing the Grand Fleet out with a sortie by the High Seas Fleet. Submarines and mines positioned off the British bases would account for some capital ships, while the High Seas Fleet itself would intercept and destroy any detached squadrons.

A specific operation was devised for mid-May. Submarines were to be stationed off the main British bases, especially the Grand Fleet base at Rosyth, to provide reconnaissance for Scheer and to cut down the British advantage with some well placed torpedoes. Admiral Franz von Hipper's First and Second Scouting Groups were to bombard Sunderland to bring Admiral David Beatty's battle cruisers out of the Firth of Forth. Hipper would then lead the battle cruisers to their destruction by the dreadnoughts of the High Seas Fleet, waiting 50 miles off Flamborough Head, before Jellicoe and the Grand Fleet could reach the scene. The key to this plan was extensive zeppelin reconnaissance to ensure that the Grand Fleet was not already in the North Sea. On 25 April the U-boats were recalled from their anti-commerce operations and dispatched to their battle stations on 17 May. With 30 May the last day that the submarines could remain on station – submarine endurance was barely two weeks in 1916 – Scheer experienced various delays until 29 May. Then bad weather ruled out the use of zeppelins, so an alternate plan was initiated. Hipper was to make a bold appearance in the Skaggerak as if searching for commerce and British patrol cruisers, in the hope of drawing part of the Grand Fleet to drive him off. The High Seas Fleet would then overwhelm this British force in waters close to home, with its retreat assured. The one exposed German flank could be guarded by cruisers and destroyers against surprise. With his flag on the battle cruiser *Lützow*,

Hipper sailed at 0100 on the 31st with the five battle cruisers of the First Scouting Group and the four light cruisers and three flotillas of destroyers of the Second Scouting Group. His orders were to show himself off the Norwegian coast before dark so that the British would discover part of the German fleet was at sea and sent out a force to chase it. An hour and a half later, Scheer and the sixteen dreadnoughts of the battle fleet followed, the admiral's flag in the *Friedrich der Grosse*.

After 17 May the suspicions of British naval intelligence had been roused when the U-boat fleet put to sea followed by no reports of sinkings. On 30 May it was known that the High Seas Fleet was assembling off Wilhelmshaven. At 1740 that day the Admiralty informed Jellicoe that 'Germans intend some operations commencing tomorrow' and ordered him to concentrate his ships 100 miles east of Aberdeen 'ready for eventualities'. With his flag in the *Iron Duke*, the Admiral sailed with 24 dreadnoughts, three battle cruisers, eight armored cruisers, twelve

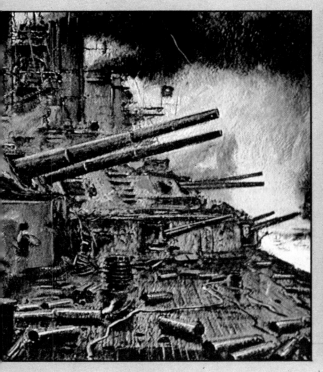

Far left: Despite heavy damage which put most of her guns out of action, the battlecruiser *Seydlitz* continued in action. Left: German battleships plow through shell bursts from the battleships of the Grand Fleet.

Left: The battleship *Warspite* was in action against seven battleships when her steering jammed at a crucial moment, but she survived with superficial damage. Below: The British battlecruiser *Lion* was the flagship of Sir David Beatty.

light cruisers, five destroyer leaders, 46 destroyers and a minelayer. One of the more colorful figures of the war, Vice Admiral Sir David Beatty, flying his flag in the *Lion*, led his battle cruiser force of six battle cruisers, four dreadnoughts, fourteen light cruisers, and 27 destroyers from the Firth of Forth with orders to join the battle fleet 90 miles west of the entrance of the Skaggerak. This flamboyant Irishman had a meteoric career in the service, becoming at 38 the youngest flag officer since Nelson. Married to a daughter of the Chicago millionaire Marshall Field, Beatty had a solid grasp of strategy and tactics and a passion for victory. As a result of the alertness of British intelligence in anticipating Scheer's sortie, the Grand Fleet was already at sea awaiting its rival. But due to a mix-up at the Admiralty between the intelligence branch and the Operations Division, Jellicoe was then informed that the German batttle fleet was still in harbor. The result was that Jellicoe later had little confidence in the subsequent information he received from the Admiralty and no immediate sense of urgency in making a junction with Beatty. Beatty's opinion of the mix-up was, 'What am I to think of [Operations Division] when I get that telegram

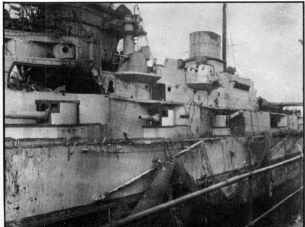

and in three hours time meet the whole German fleet well out to sea'.

Early on the afternoon of the 31st Beatty was sailing in two columns toward his rendezvous with Jellicoe with the four dreadnoughts of Rear-Admiral Evan-Thomas' Fifth Battle Squadron five miles to the rear. At 1415 the British ships swung around to the north, coming onto a converging course with Hipper's battle cruisers. A small Danish steamer was sighted simultaneously by the respective left wings of the cruiser screens of the two fleets. When each came to investigate, contact was made and firing began at 1428. Had it not been for this accidental contact, Jellicoe's Grand Fleet would have been in a position to intervene quickly, but at that time he was still 65 miles to the north and coming south while Scheer and the High Seas Fleet were 50 miles to the south coming north. At 1432 Beatty turned southeast to cut off the enemy's retreat, thinking that only German light cruisers were involved. Five miles to the rear, Evan-Thomas missed Beatty's signal and only turned at 1440, thus placing himself ten miles behind the battle cruisers. Still, the situation did not seem urgent. There was no reason to expect that the

Opposite above: The heavily damaged battle-cruiser *Seydlitz* lies half-submerged at the dock in Wilhelmshaven after the battle. **Top left:** The battlecruiser *Indefatigable* going into action minutes before she blew up. **Top right:** The British battleship *Valiant* at Rosyth. **Above left:** Shell damage to the German battlecruiser *Derfflinger*. **Above right:** The British battleship *Barham*, flagship of the 5th Battle Squadron, at Scapa Flow.

Bottom: The German battlecruiser *Moltke*.

German cruisers related to a larger force, since the Admiralty had placed the German fleet still at anchor.

A Misread Signal

After receiving a misread signal from his cruisers concerning 24 to 26 British dreadnoughts, Hipper had turned northwest to investigate. With the same intentions of joining the light cruiser action, Hipper and Beatty were now steaming toward each other at a combined speed of 45 knots. Sighting two columns of British battle cruisers coming over the horizon at 1520, Hipper reduced speed to eighteen knots and held his course, confident that he could hold his own without falling back on Scheer. After informing Scheer that the 'Enemy battle fleet is in sight' he then saw how the enemy was cutting between him and Scheer and turned 180 degrees southeast to catch Beatty between his battle cruisers and Scheer's dreadnoughts. With his destroyers and light cruisers in defensive position to beat off any destroyer torpedo attacks, Beatty now had his battle cruisers in single line ahead and ordered Evan-Thomas' squadron to come east at 25 knots from its position six miles to port. Although it was a windless day with excellent visibility, the smoke of the ships was already beginning to obscure the vision of the gunnery officers. As the range came down to 18,000 yards, Beatty turned east-southeast to clear the smoke and bring all of his guns to bear. With their superior range finders, Hipper's gunners found the range of the enemy some minutes before their own ships were sighted. As his guns were slightly outranged by those of the enemy, however, Hipper waited for the range to shorten to 16,500 yards. At 1548 both battle cruiser squadrons opened fire simultaneously.

The German gunners had the British ships neatly bracketed, scoring two hits each on the *Lion* and *Princess Royal* and four on the *Tiger* within the first three minutes. The fore turret of the *Princess Royal* and two turrets of the *Tiger* were knocked out of action temporarily. The range had narrowed to 12,900 yards before the British made their first hit with two shells from the *Queen Mary* which struck the *Seydlitz* at 1555. After over-estimating the range initially, British gunnery remained poor and somewhat confused in the coordination of targets. At 1600 both flagships were hit simultaneously, but the *Lützow* suffered no serious damage. The midship turret on the *Lion* was burst by a heavy shell, starting a cordite fire which would have blown up the ship had not a dying officer given the order to flood the adjacent magazine. The *Lion* took six more hits from the exceptionally accurate German fire and suffered more fires and flooding. The fight had become so hot by then that Beatty turned south and Hipper southeast. As the Germans continued to pound the British line with a deadly fire, Beatty was forced to shift a few degrees to starboard to alter the range. At the end of the two battle lines, now on more or less parallel courses, the *Indefatigable* and the *von der Tann* were matched in an unimpeded ship-to-ship duel. Within the space of fourteen minutes, the eleven-inch guns of the German ship sent

three shells crashing through the decks of its British adversary to explode a magazine, then hit her with another salvo which sank her. The *von der Tann* received not a single hit from the twelve-inch guns of the *Indefatigable*.

The British battle cruiser squadron was so badly mauled that it drew away to deal with its damage and put out the fires in the *Lion*. To keep Hipper occupied, Beatty ordered a flotilla of twelve destroyers to the attack, but before these could get into action Evan-Thomas' dreadnoughts appeared on the scene and turned onto a course parallel to Beatty's. Although the targets were obscured by smoke, the dreadnoughts smothered the rear of the enemy line with accurate salvoes of fifteen-inch shells, scoring serious hits on the *von der Tann* and the *Moltke* which were only saved because the inferior British shells were breaking up on impact instead of penetrating and bursting. Although the *Lion* still had fires, Beatty brought the battle cruisers back into the fray. At 1626 the *Queen Mary* was struck by five shells from the *Seydlitz* and the *Derfflinger* which either penetrated the armor of the British ship to explode in a magazine or ignited a magazine by the flash from their bursts. Whichever was the case, the ship was blown apart by her

was first sighted by Beatty's light cruiser reconnaissance screen which was two miles ahead of the battle cruisers. Just after 1630 Scheer sighted the two battle cruiser forces coming toward him, still hotly engaged. On seeing Scheer, Beatty reversed course and ran directly for the Grand Fleet approaching from the opposite direction. In order to become Scheer's advance force, Hipper also reversed course but in the process the *Seydlitz* was torpedoed in the side under her armor by a British destroyer. She was able to stay in line, however, due to her watertight compartments.

Beatty now steamed toward Evan-Thomas' squadron which was eight miles away and still blasting Hipper's rear to cover the retreat of the British battle cruisers. As the battle cruisers passed the dreadnoughts on an opposite course, Beatty signaled that the latter should turn in succession (one after the other rather than simultaneously) and follow him. Turning in succession requires considerably more time than turning simultaneously, and Scheer's approaching van was able to give the dreadnoughts a good dose of fire, the *Barham* and *Malaya* both taking hits. The dreadnoughts retaliated, however, with the

Left: Rear-Admiral Horace Hood, who was killed in the *Invincible*.

magazines and went down with all of her 1266 man crew. Just afterward, the *Princess Royal* was briefly obscured by smoke and spray, causing a signalman on the *Lion*'s bridge to report '*Princess Royal* blown up, sir'. Whereupon Beatty turned to his flag captain and said matter-of-factly, 'Chatfield, there seems to be something wrong with our damned ships today. Turn two points to port' – which was toward the enemy.

Hard pressed by Evan-Thomas' dreadnoughts, Hipper was trying to hang on until the arrival of Scheer who was just over the horizon. While Hipper considered easing his situation by ordering his destroyers to attack, the German flotilla leaders led their ships into action on their own initiative. The British destroyers had now got their attack underway and the two forces met in a wild *mêlée* between the two lines at 1620, a struggle in which two German ships were sunk and one British vessel disabled. The British dreadnoughts had turned away from the destroyer attack, and the longer range gave some relief to Hipper's outnumbered and outgunned battle cruisers. The British destroyers made several ineffectual attacks and then retired.

Limited to fifteen knots by the 'five minute ships' he had unwisely included in his fleet, Scheer

Right: One artist's misconception of the way the day battle of Jutland was fought. In reality ships never got so close to one another. The days of such close ship-to-ship conflict were long since past since the departure of the great sailing fleets. **Center:** A little closer to reality, this painting shows the battleship *Thüringen* sinking the British cruiser *Black Prince*. This only happened because the British ship had lost her way in the dark and blundered into the German Fleet. **Far right:** Another fanciful view of the night action. Although at times the ships drew close to one another, there was never a large-scale mêlée as depicted here. **Below:** A graphic representation of the British battle line firing. Clouds of coal and cordite-smoke rapidly obscured visibility.

Barham and the *Valiant* getting hits on the *Lützow* and *Derfflinger* while the *Warspite* and *Malaya* did the same to the leading German dreadnoughts, the *Grosser Kurfürst* and *Markgraf*. The faster British ships managed to retire out of range by 1730. The ships of Hipper's force had suffered greatly in the engagement thus far: the *von der Tann* had no guns operational, the *Lützow* and *Seydlitz* were heavily damaged and only the *Moltke* remained relatively unscathed. Still believing that Beatty's force was only an isolated squadron, Scheer signaled 'General chase'.

Despite the heavy damage to his four remaining battle cruisers, the speed of Beatty's force was unimpaired and he began to cut north-northeast across Hipper's path to get into position to cross the German 'T', signaling his ships 'Prepare to renew the action'. After this turn, however, Beatty lost touch with Scheer and even with Hipper who was steaming roughly parallel with him in the mist. Evan-Thomas was still in contact with Scheer but sent out no reports. At 1740 Hipper's ships appeared out of the mist 14,000 yards to the southeast. With the visibility advantage now on their side, the British battle cruisers and dreadnoughts laid down a heavy fire which the Germans could not return with any effect. Hit forward, the *Derfflinger* began to sink but was saved by her watertight compartments, while the hapless *Seydlitz* was struck many times by British shells and set afire. This fire forced Hipper to move to increase the range, a move which prevented him from seeing the approach of the Grand Fleet. His wireless was out in any event so that he could not have reported it nor was he able to report that Beatty and Evan-Thomas were still full of fight.

With its dreadnoughts in a six-column cruising formation screened by destroyers and light cruisers, the Grand Fleet had been steaming south toward its junction with the battle cruiser force. Eight miles ahead were the eight armored cruisers in line abreast as scouts in the increasingly poor visibility, while twenty miles ahead was the Third Battle Cruiser Squadron of Admiral Hood, composed of the *Invincible*, *Indomitable* and *Inflexible*. On receiving the first news of contact with the enemy, Jellicoe had sent Hood east to cut off the German light cruisers' escape through the Skaggerak in the belief that only a light enemy force was out. When news of the clash of the battle cruisers arrived Jellicoe sent Hood at 25 knots to support Beatty, but Hood found himself east of the battle cruiser action because Beatty had miscalculated his position by seven miles to the west. Instead, Hood's three ships encountered the German light cruisers and engaged them, an action which Hipper then came upon after he had swung east to escape from Beatty. Thinking that Hood was the van of the British battle fleet, Hipper fell back on Scheer and took his place at the head of the German battle line before 1900.

Visibility and Daylight Fade

Since only a few hours of daylight remained, it was now urgent that the Grand Fleet be deployed in battle formation. The already poor visibility was getting worse, raising the risk that the fleet might encounter the enemy in battle formation while it was still in cruising formation. To get his six columns into single line ahead, Jellicoe had to wheel them to the right or left, a maneuver which took at least four minutes. The position of the enemy determined which way

Below:
German torpedo boats come under fire from British ships during the opening stages of the battle.

and in what order the columns wheeled, and Jellicoe's main problem was his lack of information about the position of the enemy. Then a report from his cruisers, 'Large amount of smoke as though from a large fleet bearing east-south-east', caused Jellicoe to increase speed to eighteen knots. At 1630 his cruisers sighted Beatty's cruiser screen, but faulty signaling left the admiral no better informed about events to the south, although gunfire could now be heard in the distance. The wireless of the *Lion* had been shot away so any reports from Beatty to Jellicoe would have had to be sent through a third ship and no officer took initiative in this respect in the heat of battle. At 1750 Jellicoe's own cruisers sighted gun flashes and from that point he began to get regular reports. After receiving a signal from Jellicoe that a battle was imminent, the Admiralty realized its earlier mistake and from intercepted wireless traffic gave Jellicoe the enemy speed, course and position. With Beatty actually eleven miles northwest of his reported position, it now transpired that the Grand Fleet had miscalculated its own position as well; Jellicoe needed to know his position relative to Scheer before deploying the fleet. Hood was engaging the German light forces ahead and to port of the Grand Fleet when suddenly at 1756 Beatty's battle cruisers appeared out of the mist cutting across the path of the Grand Fleet and engaging an unseen enemy. When no response was received to his signal 'Where is the enemy's battle fleet?' Jellicoe repeated it and this time received answers from both Beatty and Evan-Thomas that Scheer was to the southwest. Still not knowing Scheer's course, which had always been northwest, Jellicoe deployed on the port column at 1815. His thought was to give his ships better visibility by firing toward the sunset, to cross the German 'T' if Scheer headed southeast, and to cut off the German retreat north to the Skaggerak or south to the Heligoland Bight. This deployment was barely completed as the German van appeared out of the mist. Suddenly confronted with a long line of British dreadnoughts, Scheer recoiled in amazement. Exactly the situation which German naval strategy was concerned to prevent was occurring – the High Seas Fleet was meeting the Grand Fleet in pitched battle.

The pall of heavy smoke over the battle area combined with the mist had masked the approach of the Grand Fleet and the Germans were taken completely by surprise. The dreadnought *Marlborough* opened fire at 1817, quickly followed by other British ships. The German fleet had been sailing in line ahead and, unable to turn to a more tactically advantageous course, Scheer could see that Jellicoe was crossing his 'T'. The *Lützow*, *Derfflinger*, *König*, *Grosser Kurfürst* and *Markgraf* all took hits while the Germans were unable to make an effective reply – a classic tactical situation. The seven battle cruisers of Hood and Beatty now combined to blast Hipper's five ships, hitting the *Lützow* nine times and the *Derfflinger* four. Although in a bad position for gunnery due to the light, the German ships found a target in the *Invincible* at 1831 and sank her with a salvo from the *Derfflinger* which exploded her magazines. Hipper's ships also sank an armored cruiser and

left another sinking. The *Lützow* was in such battered condition that she could only manage low speed and Hipper was taken off in a destroyer intending to transfer his flag, but the other battle cruisers were also too badly damaged with the exception of the *Moltke*, which Hipper finally succeeded in boarding around 2100.

In a desperate situation, at 1835, Scheer ordered a 'battle turn' in which each ship put its helm over hard and reversed course in succession beginning from the rear. Under cover of a smoke screen and a torpedo attack by German destroyers, this was the quickest way Scheer could get his line out of range. The German battle line followed by the battle cruisers and light cruisers, had disappeared into the mist heading west by 1845. Thinking that the German ships were momentarily hidden by the mist, it was over eleven minutes before Jellicoe realized that Scheer had withdrawn. The ships toward the rear of the British line saw the German maneuver but failed to report it, nor did the light cruiser squadrons inform the Admiral that the enemy had fled. For fear of destroyer torpedo attacks and possible mines laid by the retreating enemy and with only two hours of daylight remaining, Jellicoe declined pursuit and put his fleet into its six-column cruising formation. At first setting his course southeast, he then made two partial turns, edging close to Scheer while cutting off his retreat. Although Jellicoe had skilfully trapped Scheer into action, the poor visibility and the failure of his captains to keep him informed allowed the German admiral to escape.

After ordering his destroyers to the attack, Scheer did another battle turn to the east at 1855, probably thinking that he could cross the tail of the British fleet, hammer it in passing and regain his path home. But, mistaking Beatty's battle cruisers for the van of the Grand Fleet and thus misjudging its position, Scheer came directly against the center of the British fleet still heading south at 1910. This meant that the surprised Jellicoe was again crossing the equally surprised Scheer's 'T' at a range of only five miles. At 1912 the hapless *Lützow* was blasted by two dreadnoughts, bursting into flames and sheering off in a hopeless condition only to be sunk later by the merciful torpedoes of German destroyers. The entire British battle fleet then opened up on the lead ships of the German line, scoring many hits with an accurate fire. At 1920 Beatty's battle cruisers began scoring many hits on the German battle cruisers at 14,000 yards. The German reply was ineffectual: only the dreadnought *Colossus* was struck by a salvo of twelve-inch shells. Many of the German ships were heavily damaged, especially the *König* and *Grosser Kurfürst*. Facing annihilation for the second time that day, Scheer decided that the only way to extricate his battle fleet from this peril was to sacrifice his already battered battle cruisers. Receiving the signal 'Close the enemy and ram', the battle cruisers without Hipper to lead them charged the British fleet only to be met by a heavy curtain of fire. After suffering heavy damage, the battle cruisers were reprieved from their 'death ride' at 1917 when Scheer signaled 'Operate against the enemy's van'. This signal allowed the battle

Right: A German battleship fires a salvo.

cruisers to cover the retreat of the battle fleet as it performed yet another battle turn. At 1935 the German dreadnoughts were again heading west into the mist, followed by the battle cruisers, all of which survived the suicide attack, and the light cruisers.

At the same time the German destroyers had come in to make their attack but this was partly broken up by British destroyers and light cruisers so that only twenty destroyers were able to launch 31 torpedoes at a range of 8000 yards. The standard maneuver to counter such an attack was to turn away, so as Scheer was turning west, Jellicoe's ships turned east and continued in that direction for fifteen minutes until the attack was over. Again, due to the mist, Jellicoe failed to realize that Scheer had reversed course. 'No report of this German movement reached me' he later wrote, although some of his ships had witnessed it. As the Grand Fleet had once more lost contact with its adversary, it again turned on a southerly course, having missed its one chance of closing with the Germans after their second battle turn. By 2000 the High Seas Fleet was fifteen miles away. The still aggressive Beatty made contact at 2025, but after scoring some hits and driving the Germans farther west he broke off so as not to lose touch with his own fleet. Although Jellicoe had succeeded in bringing Scheer to battle, the British admiral had not been able to annihilate his adversary due to the mist, the approach of darkness, and Scheer's agility in refusing action.

As night fell, the strategic advantage lay with the Grand Fleet, for it barred the German escape to the east and had only to wait less than six hours before it could renew the encounter in daylight.

An Impenetrable Murk

By 2100 darkness and the mist had combined to make an impenetrable murk. Masters of the daylight, the dreadnoughts and battle cruisers lost their advantage of range; the night belonged to the speedy destroyers which now could slip unseen within close torpedo range. In line with orthodox British naval thought concerning night fighting, Jellicoe did not consider a night engagement which would expose his heavy ships to torpedo attacks by Scheer's destroyers. In view of the need to avoid unnecessary risks to the Grand Fleet, it made far more sense to block Scheer's escape and finish him off in the morning.

The Heligoland Bight was protected from intruders by minefields through which there were a number of swept channels. Scheer had three possible routes leading to these channels. One route was past the Horn Reefs and down the Frisian coast while a central route was past Heligoland. A southwest route would have taken the High Seas Fleet near the German coast and past the mouth of the River Ems, but at 180 miles this was the longest and the least probable since the British had a speed advantage. Jellicoe prudently elected to take a middle course south which covered all three possible escape routes, making Scheer's best chance to cut behind the Grand Fleet and run for the Horn Reefs passage. At 2112 the Grand Fleet was deployed into its night cruising formation. On a course due south at seventeen knots, the dreadnoughts were in three columns. The destroyers had been massed five miles astern to make the barrier larger and to protect the rear of the battle fleet from destroyer torpedo attacks. Separating the destroyers from the heavy ships also removed the possibility of confusion in the darkness. The battle cruisers had been stationed ahead and on the west flank of the battle fleet, which meant that the Germans could neither outrun nor get past the British to the south.

With the superior Grand Fleet blocking his escape and only waiting for daylight to annihilate him, the desperate Scheer decided that a night action offered his best chance. The losses from breaking through the British line would be preferable to certain destruction in the morning, so he opted for the shortest route home through the Horn Reefs passage. Covering its van with destroyers and light cruisers and placing the old battleships and limping battle cruisers in the rear, the High Seas Fleet made its bid for escape.

At 2200 British destroyers made contact with and fired on several light cruisers but were uncertain as to their identity. Between 2220 and 2230, the German fleet made various attempts to shove its way through the British destroyers and light cruisers in the rear bringing about repeated actions. Two German dreadnoughts were rammed by British destroyers, but after sheering off to the west the German fleet renewed its effort and finally broke through after 2330, sinking four British destroyers in the process. At 2215 a report of the beginning of these encounters was sent to Jellicoe, but it did not reach him until 2338. After that one message, the British rear sent no more reports to inform their commander that the quarry was

attempting to escape. The Fifth Battle Squadron of Admiral Evan-Thomas was stationed as an intermediate link between the rear and the battle fleet and was well aware of the action astern. Its two hindmost ships even saw the leading German dreadnoughts coming through, but neither of these ships reported the fact to Evan-Thomas, leading in the *Barham*, on the assumption that he also had sighted the Germans. Thus Jellicoe was left in ignorance as the enemy made good its escape.

Yet unmistakable clues that Scheer was making a break for the Horn Reefs were available to the British. From its directional wireless the Admiralty sent Jellicoe two messages on the German position. The first message contained an error and was obviously incorrect, but the second accurately gave the disposition, course and speed of the High Seas Fleet, adding that at 2114 it had been ordered home. What the message neglected to include was that Scheer had requested a dawn zeppelin reconnaissance over the Horn Reefs area. This message was received at 2330, the same time as a signal was received from the light cruiser *Bir-*

Above: The British light cruiser *Southampton* undergoes repairs after the battle. Note that the Zeppelin menace has already resulted in the fitting of an anti-aircraft gun (left).

Below: Torpedo boats and a battleship of the High Seas Fleet. Even moderately rough weather made the torpedo boats roll violently.

Above: The German battleship *Pommern* blew up after being hit by a single torpedo during the night action.

mingham that 'Battle cruisers probably hostile' were in sight and steering south. The British cruiser had seen the enemy as it was turning away from a British destroyer torpedo attack, and had got the course incorrectly but for Jellicoe, already distrustful of intelligence received from the Admiralty, this sighting confirmed his doubts and no action was taken. Inexplicably, Jellicoe made only one attempt at 2246 to inquire about the firing astern. Thus to the lack of initiative of his subordinates in transmitting vital information must be coupled the admiral's inertia.

The Last Contact

The last contact of the battle came just before dawn on 1 June. The Twelfth Destroyer Flotilla sighted the Germans, sent a contact report to Jellicoe at 0152 and then sank the dreadnought *Pommern*, thus accomplishing more than the entire battle fleet had so far managed. Probably due to wireless failure, the contact report never reached Jellicoe. When day broke around 0240, Jellicoe turned north with every expectation of meeting the High Seas Fleet. He then learned from the Admiralty that directional wireless placed the enemy near the Horn Reefs. On receipt of this disappointing news, a fruitless sweep for stragglers was made and then the Grand Fleet went home.

It was then that the second Battle of Jutland began, a battle which lasted until the British public was distracted by the advent of the Second World War some twenty years later. As one historian of the First World War has noted, no battle in all history has spilled so much ink as Jutland. Convinced of British superiority, both public opinion and the navy had been complacent and the navy even above criticism. Coronel had been explained away as due to the weakness of pre-

dreadnought ships, while the Falklands had demonstrated the superiority of the Royal Navy and proved the worth of the battle cruiser. Jutland thus came as an unpleasant surprise. The first British communiqué, issued before full details had been received from the returning fleet, was an honest attempt to give the known facts. And the facts were that Britain had lost three battle cruisers, three armored cruisers, eight destroyers and 6097 officers and ratings against German losses of one dreadnought, one battle cruiser, four light cruisers, five destroyers and 2545 casualties. The public reacted first with horror, then disbelief and finally outrage. Then a second communiqué was issued in which the estimates of German losses included all possibles and doubtfuls listed as probables so that on paper, British losses appeared to be slightly less than German ones. Public opinion was mollified still further when it became clear in the following weeks that Jutland was not a decisive German victory since the Royal Navy was still in command of the seas.

There also developed considerable discussion of the conduct of the battle, centering around Beatty's handling of the battle cruiser force and Jellicoe's failure to smash an inferior force which he had trapped. It is true that Beatty allowed his superior force of battle cruisers to be lured within range of the High Seas Fleet and lost a third of his ships in the encounter. He also committed two tactical errors which were then compounded by signaling mistakes. Initially Beatty had denied himself the support of Evan-Thomas's dreadnoughts by stationing them too far astern, and he then endangered these ships by waiting too long to signal his retreat so that they were exposed to the full force of the guns of the German van, only escaping serious damage by their excellent shooting. But to offset this, Beatty had then out-maneuvered Hipper so that Scheer was unaware of the approach of the Grand Fleet. Thus Beatty enabled Jellicoe to enter the battle at 1800 with the full strategic advantage on his side.

Given British naval strategy and the tactical assumptions of the day, Jellicoe handled the Grand Fleet cautiously but ably. He had his enemy at a severe tactical disadvantage twice and inflicted heavy damage. Where he can be faulted is in allowing Scheer to escape. The main reason lies in the execrable communications within the Grand Fleet, for if there was one factor which allowed the German fleet to survive, it was surely that Jellicoe's officers repeatedly failed to inform him of the movements of the enemy at vital moments. This factor characterized the action on the British side from beginning to end, from the initial difficulty which Jellicoe had in learning the position of the enemy to the end when the ships of the Fifth Battle Squadron watched the Germans make their escape without reporting it. This was surely the most damaging aspect of the lack of initiative – Sturdee's 'tactical arthritis' – which resulted from the preoccupation with centralized command. If one man was to control the fleet, however, then Jellicoe must also bear the blame for ignoring the signs and for his lack of suspicion that Scheer was making his escape.

On the German side, Jutland was quickly announced as a victory. Easily the best admiral on either side, Hipper had decisively beaten Beatty with superior gunfire, but then Scheer had been ambushed by Jellicoe in the confrontation of the battle fleets. Scheer in turn had out-maneuvered Jellicoe during the night to make his escape almost unscathed. Superior British strength forced Scheer to repeatedly break off the action. In tactical terms, therefore, an inferior force generally out-maneuvered a superior enemy and inflicted greater losses on it. Jutland can fairly be judged as a tactical victory for the Germans, a victory which demonstrated their skill and helped to dissipate their feeling of inferiority. Nor did Jutland discourage further initiative by the High Seas Fleet. Twelve weeks later, on 19 August, Scheer again tried to trap a part of the Grand Fleet by bombarding *Sunderland* as bait, but Jellicoe displayed his customary caution, Beatty lost another cruiser and no battle resulted. After this episode, it was fairly apparent that Scheer's strategy was not effective and the resources of the navy were increasingly thrown into the highly successful U-boat campaign. A last sortie by the High Seas Fleet was planned for 29 October, 1918 but by then morale in the German navy was poor and the crews mutinied and refused to sail. When the armistice came a few days later on 11 November, part of the terms were that all U-boats must surrender and the surface fleet be interned in an Allied harbor. On 21 November five battle cruisers, nine dreadnoughts, seven light cruisers and 49 destroyers were turned over to the Allies at Aberlady Bay inside May island. On that day Beatty said to his crew, 'I always told you they would have to come out'. Just before the Treaty of Versailles was signed the High Seas Fleet was scuttled by the Germans themselves.

Measured in terms of the goals of the two antag-

Left: All that was left of the battlecruiser *Queen Mary* after a cordite fire detonated her magazines.

onists, however, Jutland emerges as a strategic victory for Britain. Germany failed to weaken the Grand Fleet or shake its sea supremacy while it placed its own carefully husbanded battle fleet in mortal jeopardy. The Grand Fleet, on the other hand, 'nullified' the initiative of the High Seas Fleet and avoided any serious losses, precisely the defensively oriented strategy enunciated in Jellicoe's Grand Fleet Battle Orders. Thus neither the balance of naval power nor the strategies of the war were even slightly affected by Jutland. The battle could just as well have never taken place and indeed it might have been better for the Royal Navy had it not. The Navy lost great prestige in the eyes of the British public and the Allies and had their own complacency thoroughly shaken. The standard of German gunnery had been far higher than the British had expected and this by comparison reflected to some extent on British gunnery. Material deficiencies were also made manifest by the battle – the inferior armor piercing shell, the insufficient armor of British ships against plunging fire, and the lack of protection to prevent the flash of an explosion in a turret passing into the magazine. The latter was the most probable reason for the sudden demise of the *Queen Mary* and the *Indefatigable*. The utility of Fisher's beloved battle cruisers was questionable as well, since it appeared that skimping on armor for marginal extra speed was a dubious benefit. It must be remembered, however, that Jutland was only the second major naval battle of the steam age (Tsushima being the first), and therefore that the navies of the world had had little opportunity to experiment and to learn. After Jutland, no main fleet actions were to take place until the Second World War when battles would be fought under considerably different conditions as technology continued to revolutionize naval warfare.

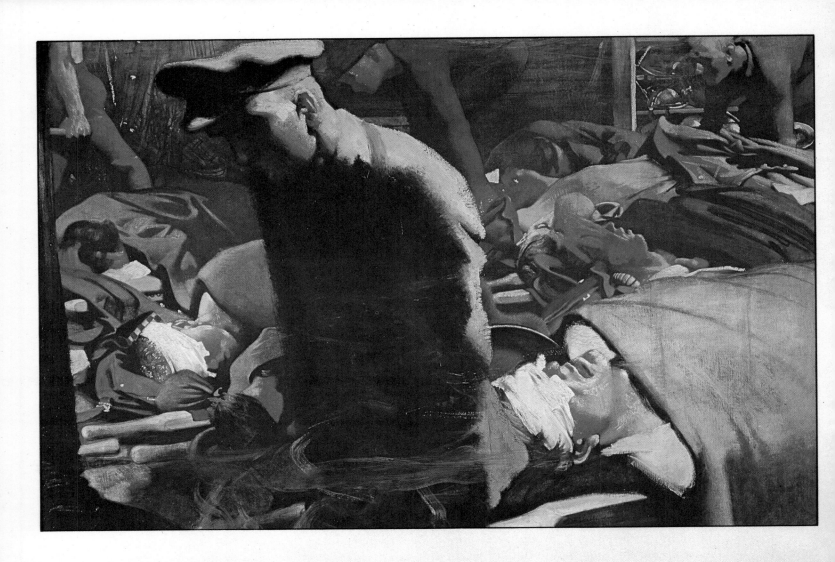

Somme

1916

The German army which retreated from the Marne on 10 September, 1914 was far from a defeated force. Too much had happened too fast, and the Allied follow-up was fatally hampered by the confusion of near defeat. By the end of September, the Germans turned to face the Allied armies astride the Chemin des Dames ridge, and, following the inconclusive 'race to the sea', and the mutual exhaustion of both sides, field fortifications were constructed sporadically until they formed an almost continuous system stretching from Switzerland to the North Sea.

Local fraternization in Christmas 1914 could not conceal a situation which, to the generals of both sides, was serious in the extreme. To a military generation believing in movement, flank marches and decisive thrusts, the deadlock was unacceptable. There were no flanks to turn, for the front ran from the North Sea to the Swiss border. There was only one possible solution: to break through the enemy's line and restore the war of movement.

A possible strategic alternative failed in 1915. Responding to Winston Churchill's suggestion, the British launched an attack against the Gallipoli Peninsula in late April, in an attempt to knock Turkey out of the war. But it was only in July that sufficient reinforcements were sent, and by then the Turks had heavily reinforced their own positions, significantly reducing the chances of British success. By the end of the year, the Dardanelles expedition had ended in dismal failure. Winston Churchill has convincingly argued that the Gallipoli campaign, if handled

Opposite: Human suffering on the Somme was horrendous. Mutilated men, some blinded by shellfire or gas attacks, were normal sights. The British lost 60,000 during the first hours of the months-long battle.

Below: Hopes were high in the British camp as the build-up for the Somme offensive continued. The Wiltshire Regiment marching to the trenches shared Haig's enthusiasm.

with sufficient determination and adequate force, could have succeeded. But his belief that it would have decisively changed the war is less credible. It was a long way from Istanbul to Berlin, even by way of Vienna, and there was no cheap way of beating Germany.

The British and French high command were largely unconvinced by Churchill's Eastern strategy. They believed that victory could only be won at the decisive point, where the German armies were concentrated—in northern France and Belgium. It was to this end that the Anglo-French armies in 1915 maintained a continuous initiative on the Western Front. On 10 March the British launched a limited attack at Neuve Chapelle. Supported by a brief but intense and effective artillery preparation, General Haig's First Army easily overwhelmed the German first line, but the narrowness of the frontage attacked, and the lethargic manner in which the initial success was exploited, gave the Germans enough time to close the gap. Yet the lesson of the battle glittered before the Allied eyes: given sufficient weight of fire, and adequate reserves, the German line could be broken.

The Allies, however, lacked both of these elements so essential to victory. Nor did they compensate by any particular astuteness in their tactics. In May the French were decisively checked between Lens and Arras at the same time as a British stroke at Aubers Ridge was repulsed. Too few reserves, too few heavy guns, too few men and unimaginative tactics. It was the formula for disaster. Between 15 and 27 May, the British continued their attacks on Festubert in conjunction with the equally fruitless French assaults around Lens. By the summer Allies' gains were negligible, at the cost of some 880,000 French and 183,000 British casualties in the period February-August. The Allies aimed at no less than a total breakthrough of the German lines. But, using a prolonged but relatively light preliminary bombardment which forfeited all surprise, they were successful nowhere. Often taking the first German positions relatively easily, the Allies were never able to successfully maintain the momentum of their initial assault. Furthermore, they were unable to find a tactical answer to the German use of machine guns in defense.

The 'New Armies'

The British 'New Armies' (volunteers) which appeared on the front in mid-1915, offered the British and French high commands a reserve which would enable them to break through the German lines and bring victory to, the Allies. The New Armies would provide the manpower necessary for an assault which would 'compel the Germans to retreat beyond the Meuse and possible end the war'. The 'big push' of 1915 was the idea of the French Commander-in-Chief, General Joffre. He envisaged a double stroke in Artois and Champagne to overwhelm the whole German line. General Sir Douglas Haig of the British First Army did not share Joffre's optimism, but was overruled by the C-in-C of the British armies in France, Sir John French. Despite his serious doubts, Haig agreed to an attack by six divisions of General Rawlinson's 4 Corps

and General Gough's 1 Corps. Following a four-day artillery bombardment which was badly hampered by lack of shells, the Allied attack was launched on 25 September. Impeded by a wind which prevented the effective use of gas, the British attack achieved only the most limited local gains, while the French in Champagne were equally unsuccessful. Although the assaults continued sporadically for two weeks, by 27 September the battle was an evident check for the Allies.

The twin Allied offensives of Autumn 1915 were a considerable improvement on those which took place in February and June. Planned with greater care, using more men and resources, they were a mechanical response to the problem posed by the deadlock. However, due to the military failures, Sir John French was replaced on 19 December 1915 by Haig. The problem which Haig faced in late 1915 was not really different from that which had existed twelve months previously. But he possessed more men and more *matériel* than Sir John French ever had at his disposal. With 36 British and Empire divisions in France by the end of the year, and the promise of significant increase in guns and shells, Haig had the two elements which he believed necessary to break the deadlock. Nothing could stop the assault of a half million men supported by a bombardment of a million shells. 1916 was to be the decisive year for the Allies, and for the British Army in particular.

Meeting at Chantilly on 5 December, 1915, the Allied commanders, under Joffre's influence, adopted the principle of a simultaneous offensive on the Eastern and Western fronts at a suitable date. Joffre claimed that, but for a lack of ammunition, the 'brilliant tactical results' of the September offensives would have produced a breakthrough. But the accumulation of sufficient stocks of ammunition was effected only slowly, and by February it was obvious that an offensive on the scale envisaged by Joffre could take place no earlier than the summer. Joffre pressed for an an attack over a 39-mile front, involving 40 French and 25 British divisions. It was an ambitious scheme which depended upon the Germans' remaining docile while the Allies methodically prepared for the assault. Unfortunately, the Germans were not to prove so helpful.

On 21 February, 1916, the French fortified zone at Verdun was subjected to a twelve-hour artillery bombardment of hitherto unparalleled intensity. That evening German troops moved forward into a battle of attrition which was designed to attract all the French army's reserves. The German attack seriously disrupted the Allied plans, reducing French participation from an original 40 divisions attacking over a 25-mile front to only five divisions over an eight-mile front.

The River Somme is a narrow stream, meandering through gently rolling hills. It is fine cavalry country, offering few natural obstacles to a horseman's progress. But what nature lacked, man had provided. Sir Douglas Haig said:

'During nearly two years preparation he (the enemy) had spared no pains to render these defenses impregnable. The first and second systems each consisted of

several lines of deep trenches, well-provided with bomb-proof shelters and with numerous communication trenches connecting them. The first of the trenches in each system was protected by wire entanglements, many of them in two belts 40 yards broad . . . . .

'The numerous woods and villages in and between these systems of defense had been turned into veritable fortresses. The deep cellars usually to be found in the villages, and the numerous pits and quarries common to a chalk country, were used to provide cover for machine guns and trench mortars . . . . . The salients in the enemy's line, from which he could bring enfilade fire across his front, were made into self-contained forts and often protected by mine-fields; while strong redoubts and concrete machine-gun emplacements had been conducted in positions from which he could sweep his own trenches should these be taken . . . . .

'These various systems of defense, with the fortified localities and other supporting points between them, . . . formed, in short, not merely a series of successive lines, but one composite system of enormous depth and strength.'

The plan of attack called for a five-phase advance. First, the attackers were to achieve a breakthrough of the German front on the line Maricourt-Sens, and then to gain the heights between Bapaume and Ginchy before pushing northwest to Arras, and completing the breakthrough. This was to be followed by an advance north, aided by a secondary attack from the area of Arras, and by strategic exploitation to 'roll up' the German line.

The British Fourth Army (General Rawlinson) was to bear the brunt of the initial assault. Eleven divisions were to attack, with five in immediate reserve and two in army reserve. The Third Army was to commit two divisions to a diversionary assault toward Gommecourt. No hopes were placed on the achievement of strategic surprise. The scope of the preparations was too vast to hide from the Germans, who enjoyed the great advantage of holding the higher ground. To compensate for the lack of surprise, the generals planned to crush the Germans in their trenches by a bombardment of unparalleled ferocity and duration. Approximately 1500 guns, one to every twenty yards of front, were to prepare the assault.

On the morning of 24 June, 1916 the British bombardment began. It was planned according to a program which exemplified the ultimate in contemporary military science. Scheduled to last five days (coded U, V, W, X and Y) prior to the infantry assault (Z Day) the preparation was divided into two periods: on U and V days the guns were to concentrate on wire-cutting and registration. Some 350,000 shells were fired in two days. The second period of bombardment, on days W, X and Y, was aimed at destroying the enemy defenses and further damaging the wire. Gas shells were occasionally to be used to confuse the Germans, but the large-scale use of gas was confined to midnight on Y/Z Day. A total of 1,627,824 shells were fired between 24 June and 1 July, the date upon which the attack actually took place. The most notable disadvantage of the bombardment was that it gave the Germans ample warning; the moment it ceased,

they knew the infantry assault was imminent.

On 8 May General Headquarters issued an instruction for 'Training of Divisions for Offensive Action'. The infantry was to attack 'in successive waves or lines, each line adding impetus to the preceding one where this is checked, and carrying the whole forward to the objective'. Although Haig himself favored an advance by small groups, his views were strongly opposed by his army commanders at their conference on 15 June, and the use of waves was confirmed. An added factor to the rigidity of the British battle order was the amount of equipment which the assaulting troops carried. It totaled about 66 pounds—a weight which the *British Official History* notes '. . . made it difficult to get out of a trench, impossible to move quicker than a slow walk, or to rise and lie down quickly'.

1 July 1916 was a day of blue skies and bright sun. The assault was set for 0730. It was expected to meet little initial resistance, coming as it did after 144 hours of continual bombardment. But the chalk of Artois proved ideal for deep dugouts:

'The garrisons of the first position remained below ground, close-packed, uncomfortable, short of food, depressed, but still alive and ready on their officers' orders when the barrage lifted, to issue forth with morale unbroken; . . .'

Nineteen Allied divisions, fourteen British and five French were ready to move into no-man's land. The Third Army, which held the line from Carency in the north to Hebuterne in the south sent two divisions, the 46th and 56th, to attack Gommecourt. The Fourth Army, which was the main assault force, was in position from Hebuterne to Maricourt, where it joined the French 8th Army. Rawlinson was ordered to send five corps forward on 1 July: 8, 10, 3, 15 and 13. With the 29th, 4th and 31st Divisions assaulting and 48th Division in reserve, 8 Corps was to attack in the area of Serre and Hamel, north of the Ancre. Further to the south, 10 Corps was to launch the 32nd, 36th and 49th Divisions south of the Ancre against Thiepval and Ovillers. In the center of the attacking line, 3 Corps was to take La Boisselle and press on to Contalmaison. Next in line, 15 Corps was to push two of its divisions

Opposite top: The Germans, prepared for the British attack, fire from their protected positions. **Opposite bottom:** A ration party of the Royal Irish Rifles pauses in a communications trench during the first day of the battle. **Below:** British soldiers assist two wounded German prisoners at La Boisselle during the third day of the offensive.

The Battle of the Somme, 1916

The Northwestern Front

Although the Germans had pushed the Russians well to the east, the battle lines which were drawn in the autumn of 1914 remained hard and fast along the trenches of the Western Front. The attempt to break through the wall of *trenches from Switzerland to the Channel was the dream of Allied and German generals alike. The Somme was Haig's dream which ended as a nightmare for the Tommies.*

The Battle of the Somme, 1 July, 1916

At 0730 along the whole front north of the Somme the Allied infantry went over the top. On the right the French XX Corps captured their objective. Immediately to their left, the British XIII Corps stormed into Montauban *and their other objectives. XV Corps was partially successful; capturing Mametz, however, Fricourt was not taken and from here northwards the British assault was unsuccessful, failing to achieve their objectives.*

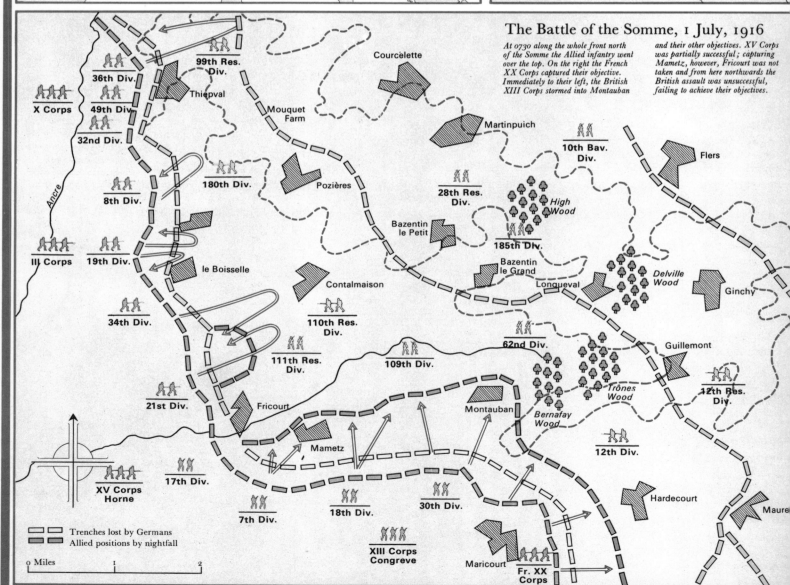

274

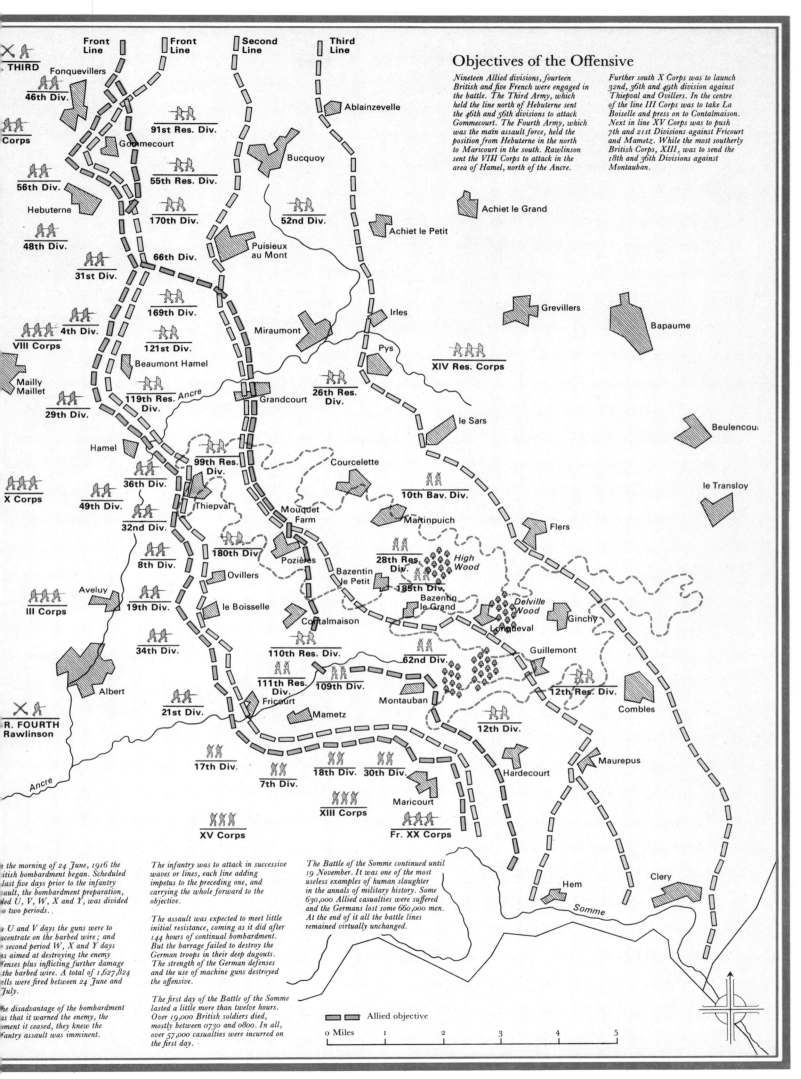

Objectives of the Offensive

Nineteen Allied divisions, fourteen British and five French were engaged in the battle. The Third Army, which held the line north of Hebuterne sent the 46th and 56th divisions to attack Gommecourt. The Fourth Army, which was the main assault force, held the position from Hebuterne in the north to Maricourt in the south. Rawlinson sent the VIII Corps to attack in the area of Hamel, north of the Ancre.

Further south X Corps was to launch 32nd, 36th and 49th division against Thiepval and Ovillers. In the centre of the line III Corps was to take La Boiselle and press on to Contalmaison. Next in line XV Corps was to push 7th and 21st Divisions against Fricourt and Mametz. While the most southerly British Corps, XIII, was to send the 18th and 36th Divisions against Montauban.

Front Line · **Front Line** · **Second Line** · **Third Line**

. THIRD

Fonquevillers
46th Div.
Corps
56th Div.
Hebuterne
48th Div.
31st Div.
VIII Corps
4th Div.
Mailly Maillet
29th Div.
Hamel
X Corps
36th Div.
49th Div.
32nd Div.
Aveluy
III Corps
8th Div.
19th Div.
34th Div.
Albert
R. FOURTH Rawlinson
21st Div.
17th Div.
7th Div.
XV Corps

Gommecourt
91st Res. Div.
55th Res. Div.
170th Div.
66th Div.
169th Div.
121st Div.
Beaumont Hamel
119th Res. Div.
Ancre
Grandcourt
99th Res. Div.
Thiepval
180th Div.
Pozières
Ovillers
le Boisselle
Contalmaison
110th Res. Div.
111th Res. Div.
Fricourt
Mametz
18th Div.
XIII Corps

Bucquoy
52nd Div.
Puisieux au Mont
Miraumont
Ablainzevelle
Achiet le Grand
Achiet le Petit
Irles
Pys
26th Res. Div.
Courcelette
Mouquet Farm
Bazentin le Petit
185th Div.
Bazentin le Grand
109th Div.
Montauban
30th Div.
Maricourt
Fr. XX Corps

Grevillers
Bapaume
XIV Res. Corps
le Sars
10th Bav. Div.
Martinpuich
28th Res. Div.
High Wood
Delville Wood
Longueval
62nd Div.
12th Div.
Hardecourt

Beulencou
le Transloy
Flers
Ginchy
Guillemont
12th Res. Div.
Combles
Maurepus
Hem
Clery
Somme
Ancre

At the morning of 24 June, 1916 the British bombardment began. Scheduled to last five days prior to the infantry assault, the bombardment preparation, coded U, V, W, X and Y, was divided into two periods.

On U and V days the guns were to concentrate on the barbed wire; and in the second period W, X and Y days was aimed at destroying the enemy defenses plus inflicting further damage to the barbed wire. A total of 1,627,824 shells were fired between 24 June and 1 July.

The disadvantage of the bombardment was that it warned the enemy, the moment it ceased, they knew the infantry assault was imminent.

The infantry was to attack in successive waves or lines, each line adding impetus to the preceding one, and carrying the whole forward to the objective.

The assault was expected to meet little initial resistance, coming as it did after 144 hours of continual bombardment. But the barrage failed to destroy the German troops in their deep dugouts. The strength of the German defenses and the use of machine guns destroyed the offensive.

The first day of the Battle of the Somme lasted a little more than twelve hours. Over 19,000 British soldiers died, mostly between 0730 and 0800. In all, over 57,000 casualties were incurred on the first day.

The Battle of the Somme continued until 19 November. It was one of the most useless examples of human slaughter in the annals of military history. Some 630,000 Allied casualties were suffered and the Germans lost some 660,000 men. At the end of it all the battle lines remained virtually unchanged.

Allied objective

0 Miles   1   2   3   4   5

against Fricourt and Mametz, leaving one in reserve. The most southerly British corps, 13, was to throw two divisions into the line southeast of Mametz and drive for Montauban.

The 13 Corps had three distinct objectives. During the initial assault, on 1 July, Montauban was to be taken and a line established east of the village to gain contact with the French 20th Corps. The attack was to be pressed forward into Montauban itself and was to finish the day on the Montauban-Mametz Ridge, a total advance of some 2500–2700 yards. The German second line was not to be breached during the first day's assault, and its capture was in any case contingent upon the success of 15 Corps' attack north of Fricourt. This would secure the left flank and rear of 13 Corps, permitting it to wheel to the right and advance east to the German second position, in accord with the French south of the Somme.

In front of 13 Corps were nine battalions of the *12th, 28th Reserve* and *10th Bavarian Divisions.* The first position was strongly held and consisted of parallel trenches with a reserve line 700–1000 yards to the rear. Three thousand yards further was the second line, while away to the rear lay a partially constructed third position. The defense system was scattered with isolated strongpoints, and Montauban had been turned into a fortress.

144 Hours of Shellfire

Preceded by 144 hours of continual shellfire and eight minutes of 'hurricane bombardment' by six trench mortar batteries, 89th Brigade had the honor of being first into the 800-yard-wide no-man's land. The artillery preparation had done its work well; little difficulty was experienced in seizing the German front trenches. By 0830 Dublin Trench had been reached; abandoned by the Germans, it was immediately occupied. To the left of the 89th, 21st Brigade was equally successful, traversing no-man's land with a minimum of casualties, although the 18th King's suffered from machine gun fire on its left due to the inability of 18th Division to make similar progress. Once this obstacle was cleared, the advance continued and the first objectives were secured by 0835.

The 18th Division had the task of seizing Pommiers, a penetration of some 1500 yards, preparatory to the assault on Montauban. Exploding two mines, one of 5000 pounds and the other a mere 500 pounds at 0727, the 6th Royal Berkshires dashed across the 200-yard no-man's land. Held up by some persistent machine-gunners, the British were not able to reach the reserve line before it was heavily manned. By 0837, the Germans were still offering stubborn resistance, although the 30th Division finally forced the German reserve to abandon its line.

By 0900 the First Objectives had been reached and the attack had begun on the Second Objective, Montauban village. Leapfrogging the 21st Brigade of 30th Division, 90th Brigade moved forward at 0930 and, despite heavy resistance, assaulted the village. An hour later, Montauban and 30th Division's share of the Montauban-Mametz Ridge had been secured. Although hampered by German artillery fire, the 30th Division established itself in Montauban, extending its line south and southeast into La Briqueterie, a useful vantage

point. Fifteen hundred yards of German trench had been seized to a depth of 2000 yards. By noon, the advance stopped because the commander of 30th Division was ordered to await the advance of flanking formations.

On the left, the 18th Division was experiencing equal success, although at a somewhat higher cost. Its progress lagged slightly behind that of 30th Division due to the tenacious resistance of the German reserve trench, which was only partially cleared by 0930. The last redoubt blocking the advance was not subdued until about 1400. The 30th Division's right was now freed, and reached the Montauban-Mametz road an hour later. Two hours of heavy fighting lay ahead of 54th Brigade, but by 1700 it had reached the northern flank of Montauban Ridge.

The 30th Division had lost a total of 3011 casualties, while the 18th Division lost 3115. It was, on the whole, a successful day for 13 Corps. It must be emphasized, however, that in no place had the corps 'broken through'. The enemy's first position had been penetrated, but the second line remained. Only if equal success was achieved along the whole of the attacking frontage could a real breakthrough be effected, now that the initial bombardment had ended.

Facing 15 Corps, which occupied the line directly to the left of 13 Corps, was the Fricourt salient, a position of awesome strength. The first 1200 yards of the German lines were composed of an intricate maze of trenches. Fricourt itself had been turned into a fortress, and was extremely well-protected by machine guns. The garrison was ensconced in particularly deep dugouts. Fifteen hundred yards from the foremost position of the German defense was a second line (Fritz Trench-Railway Alley-Crucifix Trench), which was supported by a third line (White Trench-Wood Trench-Quadrangle Trench), 2000 yards behind the German front. Some 2500 yards further back stood the second German position and 6400 yards beyond this (9000 yards from the front) was the third position.

The 15 Corps was to send two of its three divisions (17th division remaining as Corps Reserve) forward to seize the high ground between Mametz and Fricourt. The corps was to push on into the third line of the first German position, effecting a penetration of 3500 yards, while maintaining contact with 13 Corps to the right and 3 Corps to the left. If the preliminary stage of the battle met with success, subsequent days were to see the seizure of Bazentin le Grand and Longueval in the German third position.

The attack of 15 Corps was meticulously prepared by artillery fire. At 0625 an intensive bombardment commenced, followed by the hurricane bombardment and the explosion at 0728 of seven mines totaling 59,000 pounds of high explosive. Rising from their trenches and following a somewhat imperfect creeping barrage, the British troops benefited from the artillery's efforts.

On the right, the 91st Brigade (7th Division) was to drive on Mametz and seize the line of Fritz Trench. The 20th Brigade was to mask Fricourt, maintaining parity with the 91st Brigade on its right, and was later to assault Fricourt in conjunction with the 22nd Brigade. Crossing no-man's land relatively easily, the 91st Brigade met with sporadic resistance as it moved through the forward trench system, but had gained some 700 yards by 0745. By 0800, the first objective was almost secured and resistance remained relatively light. In front of Mametz, however, the assault bogged down in front of fierce machine gun fire. Aided by renewed artillery support and the progress of 13 Corps, the 91st attacked again at 1300, finally entering Mametz by about 1340. The 20th Brigade had even more trouble, for it was called to effect an intricate wheel in front of Fricourt. The task was further complicated by the cratered terrain, the result of the British mines. Here the British had difficulty crossing no-man's land. The 9th Devons in the center suffered cruelly from small arms and machine gun fire, but were able to take the German first trench, although they only

Above: More Germans are captured at La Boisselle, and one gets a free ride.

gained a somewhat precarious hold. On the right, the 2nd Gordon Highlanders were able to progress some 300 yards during the morning, but were eventually pinned down. Only 2nd Border Regiment, on the left, made relatively satisfactory progress. By mid-morning, though, the assault of 20th Brigade had ground to a halt.

The 21st Division was to push into the German trenches to the right and left of Fricourt, using the 63rd and 64th Brigades to take the first reserve line (Crucifix Trench) and eventually moving into Quadrangle Trench, while the 50th Brigade was reserved for the assault on Fricourt. It was this last objective which was the key to 15 Corps' attack. The preliminary bombardment had not succeeded in sufficiently reducing the defenses of Fricourt, so that 50th Brigade suffered heavy casualties and were unable to reach the village. Further

Below: Machine-gunners, with their gas helmets on, fire into a German communications trench near Ovillers in July 1916.

to the left, the 63rd and 64th Brigades were cut to pieces by the machine guns in the German front line which had survived the bombardment. Finally reaching the front line trenches, the 63rd and 64th were forced to remain where they were and await support. Although the 64th Brigade eventually penetrated Crucifix Trench, it was at the cost of such frightful casualties as to temporarily bring the assault to a halt.

General Horne, commander of 15 Corps, upon receiving reports of success to both his right and left, ordered the 22nd, 62nd and 50th Brigades to assault Fricourt at 1430. Although the 1st Royal Welsh Fusiliers of 22nd Brigade actually reached the outskirts of the village, 50th Brigade was decimated and made no progress; 7th Green Howards lost 15 officers and 336 men in three minutes.

The 15 Corps had progressed on its flanks to an average distance of some 2000–2500 yards. By afternoon 7th Division had consolidated its position, aided by the success of the 18th Division of 13 Corps against Mametz. To the far left, 21st Division, having fallen far short of its goal of Mametz Wood, was nevertheless in possession of the German front line. But the key to the German

Opposite left: British soldiers time their next attack; each seemed to be more futile than the next.
Left: Field Marshal Sir Douglas Haig, architect of the carnage of the Somme.
Above: General Sir H. S. Horne, Commander of 15 Corps at the Somme.
Below: British and German wounded on their way to the dressing station near Bernafay Wood.

position, in 15 Corps' sector was Fricourt, and there the check was complete. For this, 7th Division lost 3380 men, 17th Division 1155 and 21st Division 4256; a heavy price for such small gains.

The front from Becourt to Authville, facing the heavily fortified villages of La Boisselle and Ovillers, belonged to 3 Corps. The high ground of the Fricourt, La Boisselle and Ovillers spurs provided a serious impediment to a successful advance. The Germans anchored their defense on three strong redoubts (Sausage, Scots and Schwaben) and the two fortified villages. A second line ran from Fricourt Farm to Ovillers, and a third lay in front of Contalmaison and Pozières. The second position ran from Bazentin Le Petit to Mouquet Farm with a third positon about 4500 yards behind it.

Two divisions, the 8th and 34th, were to assault, with 1st division as Corps Reserve. On the right, 34th Division was to push across the Fricourt spur and take La Boisselle, and then move to the line Contalmaison-Pozières, stopping 800 yards before the German second position. At the same time, the 8th Division was to take the western slope of Ovillers spur as well as the village before advancing to the line Pozières-Mouquet Farm.

The 34th Division launched a four-pronged attack. The two columns on the left were to attack the flanks of La Boisselle, thus isolating it, rather than attempting to seize it by direct assault. It was assumed that the preliminary bombardment would deal with the garrison of the village. The columns, three battalions deep, were expected to advance some 2000 yards and reach the fourth German trench, the last in their first line system, by 0818. The German intermediate line, in front of Contalmaison-Pozières, was to be seized by 0858, whereupon the 101st and 102nd Brigades would halt, and the 103rd Brigade would pass through them to seize Contalmaison and part of Pozières. This was to be accomplished by 1010. The assaulting battalions left their trenches at 0730, and within ten minutes 80% of their troops had fallen. Although some troops of the right hand column were able to reach and take the first German trench, further progress remained impossible amidst a storm of machine gun and rifle fire. The other columns made no progress. The *British Official History* notes that the success of the 102nd Brigade 'depended on the bombardment having obliterated the defenses near the two villages (Ovillers and La Boisselle), and upon the chance that the defenders, demoralized...would surrender freely'. Unfortunately, this was not the case; the two leading battalions went forward with great determination but were all but annihilated before they reached the German front line. Two of the four columns never reached the German lines at all; one had made only small gains, and the extreme right-hand column seized part of the line but was pinned down there. No further progress was made during the day.

To the left of the 24th Division, the 8th assaulted Ovillers Spur with a three-column advance north and south of the ridge. Although part of the 25th Brigade, 2nd Lincolnshire, actually reached the German trench, vigorous counterattacks by riflemen and bombers drove them from the position by 0900. The three battalions of the

25th Brigade lost over 50% of their strength and the 1st Royal Irish Rifles succeeded in getting only ten men across no-man's land. On the left, the first two waves of the 70th Brigade got across with little difficulty and reached the second German trench, but were stopped dead by heavy fire.

By 0900 the advance had died away all over 4th Division's front. In some places, particularly on the left, the German lines had been reached, but nowhere had penetration totaled more than two or three hundred yards. When requested by divisional headquarters to prepare a second assault, the commanders of the 23rd and 25th Brigades replied that it was not 'advisable', given the condition of the German defenses, and their own heavy casualties. A similar reply was made later in the day by the commander of 70th Brigade. An assault was subsequently planned for 56th Brigade of 19th Division, but this was postponed. Some isolated infantry continued to hold out in small sections of captured trench and in no-man's land, but after 1430 no sign of British troops appeared from the German lines.

Out of approximately 17,000 troops of 3 Corps who went into action that morning, 11,500 were casualties, mostly by 0800, and the German line remained unbroken. The seven-day bombardment, while making the German defenses unrecognizable, had not made them untenable, and 3 Corps paid a heavy price to discover this.

The task facing 10 Corps was no easier than that of its neighbors. As in 3 Corps' sector, the German position was dominated by a fortified village, in this case Thiepval. Overlooking the British trenches, Thiepval was a formidable obstacle. The commander of 132nd Division was confident, however, that the preliminary bombardment would knock out this keystone of the German defenses in the sector, and this in turn would entail the collapse of the whole edifice. No contingency plan had been drawn up for use if the bombardment failed in its purpose. The southern half of the sector's defense hinged on the Leipzig Redoubt. Behind these formidable obstacles, independent strongpoints mutually supported each other with enfilade fire.

The 10 Corps was expected to seize the Thiepval Spur and the plateau beyond as its first objectives, a task which totally depended upon the effectiveness of the preliminary bombardment. The 32nd Division was to assault the German line between the Leipzig Redoubt and Thiepval, including both strongpoints. Meanwhile, 36th Division was to seize the plateau between Thiepval and St Pierre Divion, taking the latter. These two divisions were to go on to the German intermediate line, a penetration of 1500–2000 yards, and then press forward to Grandcourt.

The two brigades of 32nd Division which made up the first wave of the assault, 97th and 96th, met with various misfortunes during the day. Although the 17th Highland Light Infantry of 97th Brigade were able, under cover of the bombardment, to rush the front of Leipzig Redoubt, they were unable to get much further. Despite devastating fire from other sections of the line, the British managed to consolidate their hold. The left of the 97th was not able to reach the German trenches owing to the fire from Thiepval, which had not been

Opposite top: British infantry prepare to advance yet again at Guillemont, September 1916. **Opposite center:** The Indian troops of the Deccan Horse at Bazentin Ridge in July. **Left:** German dead in a captured trench between Ginchy and Guillemont, August 1916. **Left center:** The remains of a German soldier outside his dugout at Beaumont Hamel, November 1916. **Bottom:** Men of the 16th Irish Division return for a well-deserved rest after helping to take Guillemont, September 1916.

Meanwhile, through a lack of coordination, the 107th Brigade, not having received any counter-order, advanced past the halted 108th and 109th Brigades and attacked the Grandcourt line. Parts of the position were seized, although the garrison of Thiepval rendered it practically untenable by enfilade fire.

At 1445, 10 Corps Headquarters issued orders for an assault by the 146th Brigade of 49th Division, in reserve, against Thiepval, at 1600. Communications were difficult, and only a small fraction of the troops were able to move forward; the 1st/6th West Yorkshires lost half their strength in casualties in a gallant but vain assault. It was now the turn of the Germans, who opened a devastating trench-mortar barrage and began counter-attacking the isolated troops in Schwaben Redoubt; by 2230 the German 185th Regiment had retaken the position.

Before 8 Corps lay a series of spurs and valleys, which had been cleverly fortified to provide mutual support and enfilade fire. Beaumont Hamel, in the middle of the sector, was a fortress replete with machine guns and good protection for the soldiers who manned them. Four thousand yards behind the German front position a second line extended from Grandcourt to Puisieux, two fortified positions of great strength, while a third line lay another 4000 yards to the rear. The varied nature of the terrain was a serious disadvantage for the preliminary bombardment, as it was difficult for observers to check the fall of shot.

The 8 Corps hoped to precede its assault with a creeping barrage, which made no concessions to flexibility:

'At the commencement of each infantry attack the divisional artillery will lift 100 yards and continue lifting at the rate of 50 yards a minute...

'The rate of the infantry has been calculated at 50 yards a minute...

'The lines once settled cannot be altered. The infantry therefore must make their pace conform to the rate of the artillery lifts...'

The 29th Division pinned its hopes upon the devastating effect of a mine filled with 40,000 pounds of ammonal, fired at 0720 under a strongpoint in the German line. This brought about a serious error, for the divisional artillery switched to the second trenches when the mine went up, and the Germans were able to maintain a position on the far edge of the crater, under little artillery

subdued by the bombardment. The 96th Brigade suffered even more from machine gun fire and, although the Northumberland Fusiliers showed admirable courage by following 'a football drop-kicked by an eminent North Country player', they failed to cross no-man's land. At 0849, the 14th Brigade moved forward to assault the second German position. Not having been warned of the check to the 32nd, it was unprepared for the heavy fire it received, and could do little more than push some of its survivors into Leipzig Redoubt.

Perhaps surprisingly, 36th Division was able to seize a large part of its initial objectives. Leaving its trenches at 0715, and advancing to within one hundred yards of the German front line, 109th Brigade was able to reach the German trenches seconds before a firing line was established. They took the first trench and the advance was continued. By 0800 the German reserve trench was taken, as well as part of Schwaben Redoubt. Unfortunately 108th Brigade, to the left, was not able to seize St Pierre Divion, and its machine guns stood as a dyke preventing a rupture of the front. The failure of the 36th Division's left to break through north of the Ancre, which split the divisional frontage, necessarily limited the success further south. The failure of the 32nd Division to keep pace left the Ulstermen of the 36th in an exposed and uncomfortable position. At 0910 the 36th halted so as not to outpace its neighbors.

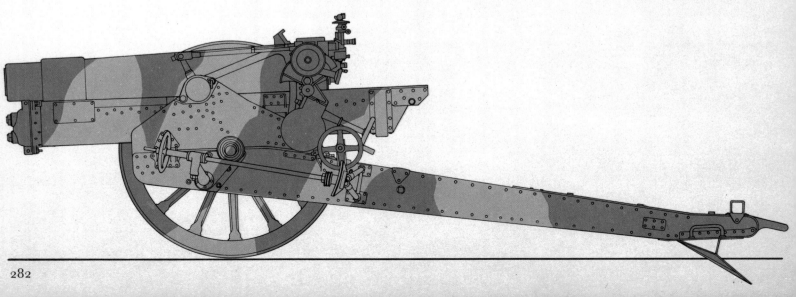

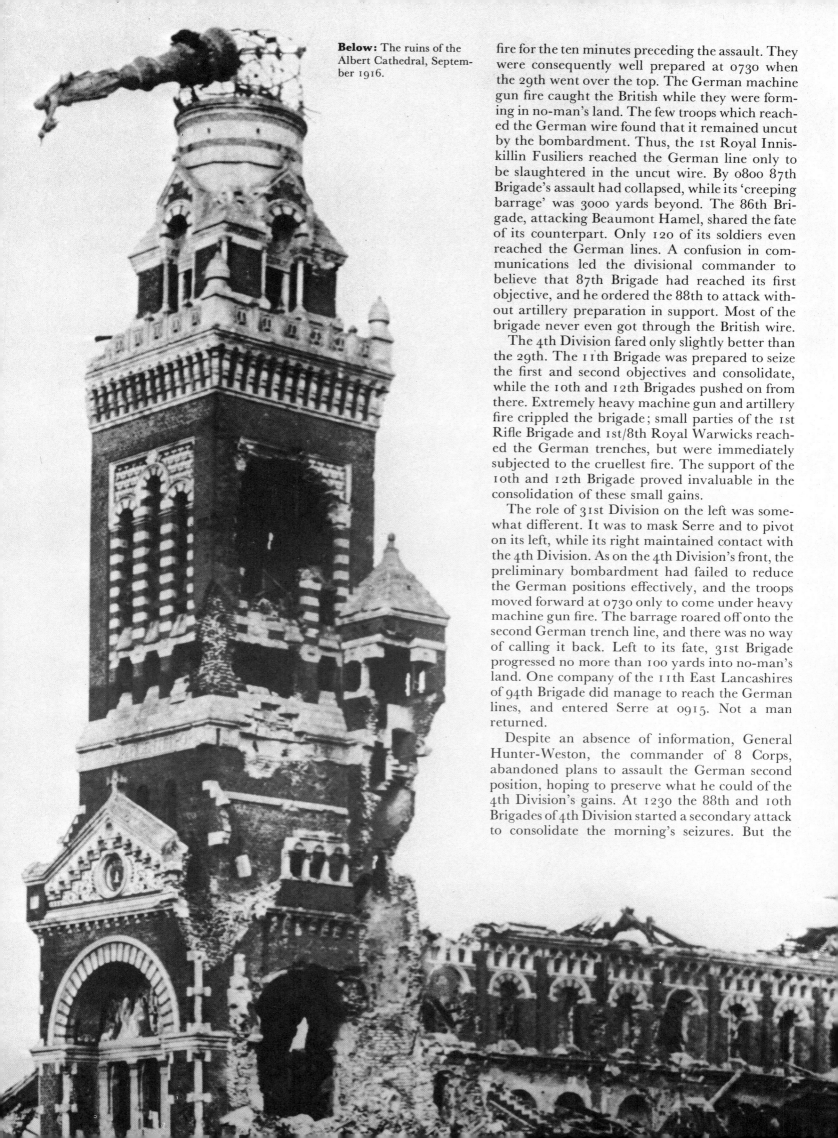

fire for the ten minutes preceding the assault. They were consequently well prepared at 0730 when the 29th went over the top. The German machine gun fire caught the British while they were forming in no-man's land. The few troops which reached the German wire found that it remained uncut by the bombardment. Thus, the 1st Royal Inniskillin Fusiliers reached the German line only to be slaughtered in the uncut wire. By 0800 87th Brigade's assault had collapsed, while its 'creeping barrage' was 3000 yards beyond. The 86th Brigade, attacking Beaumont Hamel, shared the fate of its counterpart. Only 120 of its soldiers even reached the German lines. A confusion in communications led the divisional commander to believe that 87th Brigade had reached its first objective, and he ordered the 88th to attack without artillery preparation in support. Most of the brigade never even got through the British wire.

The 4th Division fared only slightly better than the 29th. The 11th Brigade was prepared to seize the first and second objectives and consolidate, while the 10th and 12th Brigades pushed on from there. Extremely heavy machine gun and artillery fire crippled the brigade; small parties of the 1st Rifle Brigade and 1st/8th Royal Warwicks reached the German trenches, but were immediately subjected to the cruellest fire. The support of the 10th and 12th Brigade proved invaluable in the consolidation of these small gains.

The role of 31st Division on the left was somewhat different. It was to mask Serre and to pivot on its left, while its right maintained contact with the 4th Division. As on the 4th Division's front, the preliminary bombardment had failed to reduce the German positions effectively, and the troops moved forward at 0730 only to come under heavy machine gun fire. The barrage roared off onto the second German trench line, and there was no way of calling it back. Left to its fate, 31st Brigade progressed no more than 100 yards into no-man's land. One company of the 11th East Lancashires of 94th Brigade did manage to reach the German lines, and entered Serre at 0915. Not a man returned.

Despite an absence of information, General Hunter-Weston, the commander of 8 Corps, abandoned plans to assault the German second position, hoping to preserve what he could of the 4th Division's gains. At 1230 the 88th and 10th Brigades of 4th Division started a secondary attack to consolidate the morning's seizures. But the front-line troops were short of ammunition, especially bombs, and were slowly driven back into the German front trenches. The attack had to be postponed in order to prevent further congestion. The reorganized German defenses on each side of the salient effectively checked any reinforcements, although it took the Germans some time to clear the British from the captured trenches.

The attack on Gommecourt by 7 Corps was considered by Haig to be a diversionary assault designed to increase the frontage under attack. It was separated from the main sector of operations by a two-mile gap which was to be left unattacked. The objective of the assault, the village of Gommecourt, was a position of the greatest strength. It was, in effect, a single fortified position, the fruit of almost two years of German labor. The 7 Corps' orders clearly stated that the attack was 'to assist in the operations of the Fourth Army by diverting against itself the fire of artillery and infantry which might otherwise be directed against the left flank of the main attack near Serre'. No reserves were allocated in case of a breakthrough, although it would not have been impossible to shift troops to 7 Corps if the situation warranted such action.

Resting on high ground, Gommecourt was perhaps the strongest point in the German line. It was well-protected by deep dugouts, which provided sufficient protection from any but the most heavy guns. The unenviable task of assaulting this for-midable position went to 56th and 46th Divisions.

The 56th went over the top at 0730 with the 168th and 169th Brigades up and the 167th in reserve. The two forward brigades were expected to reach the German third trench, and the 169th was subsequently to move left to link up with the 46th Division behind Gommecourt. Just beating the Germans to their trenches after the bombardment lifted, the forward brigades seized two trenches relatively easily, and one other with more difficulty. Further progress was hampered by the German artillery barrage, which isolated the British troops in the German forward trenches.

The 46th Division, attacking at the same time as the 56th, did not fare nearly as well. The muddy ground and extreme width of no-man's land was disastrous for 137th Brigade on the right, which was caught in the open by German machine gun and artillery fire. The 139th was able to reach the German first trench, but again the German artillery fire quickly isolated those who were lodged in the German lines, and machine gun fire prevented an advance into the second and third German positions. Throughout the morning the 139th remained trapped, while repeated attempts to support them failed. Of the men of the 1st/5th and 1st/7th Sherwood Foresters who reached the German trenches none returned.

With 46th Division stuck fast either in no-man's land or in the first German trench, the Germans

Below: Horses, up to their knees in mud, carry an ammunition limber forward along what once was the Lesboeufs Road, November 1916.

turned their attention to the 56th, which had been considerably more successful. The Germans concentrated some thirteen reserve companies against the 56th and counterattacked behind the cover of a brief but severe artillery bombardment. Effectively isolated, the British began to run out of bombs by noon, and the Germans were able to push them back into the second line. Four hours later the second line was in German hands, and by 0930 the last British troops abandoned the German lines.

The first day of the battle of the Somme lasted a little more than twelve hours. The formula of more men, more guns and more munitions as the key to breakthrough and victory had proved to be false. Some 1,627,824 shells were hurled into the German trenches in a 144-hour bombardment. The rigidity of the plans, the lack of effective tactical and artillery support for the infantry, the strength of the German defenses, and their skillful tactical use of machine guns and artillery doomed the attack before it began. Over 19,000 British soldiers died, mostly between 0730 and 0800. In all, over 57,000 casualties. And yet:

'No braver or more determined men ever faced an enemy than those sons of the British Empire who "went over the top" on 1 July, 1916. Never before had the ranks of a British Army on the field of battle contained the pick of all classes of the nation in physique, brains and education. And they were volunteers, not conscripts. If a decisive victory was to be won, it was expected now.'

The failure of the British assault on 1 July did not end the battle. The offensive continued, with interruptions, until November, but British inability to achieve a clean breakthrough early on made it a long and bloody slogging-match. Newly arrived tanks were used in mid-September and achieved local success, but were too few in number to exercise a decisive influence upon the battle. The results of the battle remain a question of debate. Haig's expected breakthrough had failed to materialize, and the territorial gains of the Allies remained meager. The Germans had, however, sustained very heavy casualties—approximately 600,000 in all, roughly equal to the Allies' losses—and were in no position to replace them. One author has pointed out that Haig 'weakened the German Army in the west in much the same way as the Russian Army weakened Hitler's at Stalingrad'. He did so at the cost of frightful casualties, largely the result of tactical misappreciation and defective generalship. Yet it is, perhaps, too easy to make Haig the scapegoat for the bloodbath of the Somme. The Allies would not possess the means of breaking through the German lines in strength until the arrival of large numbers of tanks. Haig tried to apply the tactical lessons of 1914 and 1915, and his failure must be shared by the majority of British commanders at all levels.

Battle of Britain

1940

After the implementation of the armistice between France and the Axis forces of Germany and Italy on 25 June, 1940, the only opponent left in the field against Germany, the stronger by far of the two European Axis powers, was Great Britain and her empire. On paper the strength of the British position appeared relatively strong, despite the losses of the French campaign. But in reality Britain's position was a desperate one, redeemed only by the strength of the Royal Navy and Germany's almost total lack of expertise in amphibious operations. And it was to be on such operations, the Germans realized, that success in any proposed invasion of Great Britain would depend. The question of whether or not Germany ever really intended an invasion of Great Britain remains a thorny one: it seems that really in his heart of hearts Adolf Hitler was convinced that the fall of France would cause Britain to sue for terms, and that further prosecution of the war in the West would be unnecessary, leaving the German armed forces to devote their whole atten-

Far left: A member of the groundcrew carries a light bomb for loading onto the Junkers Ju 87 dive-bomber.
Left: Herman Goering, the commander-in-chief of the *Luftwaffe*, in earnest conversation with another German commander.
Below: A Junkers Ju 86 reconnaissance aircraft in flight.

Above: Winston Churchill became prime minister of Great Britain in the dark days of May 1940, and his 'bulldog' determination that the United Kingdom should not be defeated did much for morale during the Battle of Britain and the 'Blitz' of 1940 and 1941.
Below: Field-Marshal Albert Kesselring, commander of *Luftflotte* II points out with his baton something of interest to *Reichsmarshall* Goering.
Below right: German troops practise the assault landing techniques they would need if the invasion of Great Britain ever got under way.

tion to the problems of the invasion of Russia in 1941. The generals who would have to undertake the operation saw the whole venture as risky in the extreme, and wanted the landings to take place on a wide front; the admirals of Grand-Admiral Erich Raeder's navy, who would have to transport, protect and supply the invasion forces, fully realized the dangers posed by the Royal Navy, especially as their own forces had been sadly depleted in the Norwegian campaign, and wished the landings to take place on a narrow front, where their warships could offer a more concentrated defence against a Royal Navy intervention.

Realizing that such an invasion was a possibility at least, Raeder had in the winter of 1939 to 1940 ordered his staff to prepare a study of the problems of launching a large-scale amphibious operation against the southern shore of England. This study exposed large numbers of difficulties, and on 21 May, as the German *Panzer* forces were driving forward from Abbeville towards Boulogne and Calais after cutting the Allied armies into two portions, Raeder informed Hitler of the study. The *Führer* appeared uninterested, and instead ordered Raeder to consider how the Jews of Europe might be shipped out to Madagascar, where he had vague plans to settle them!

Operation Sealion

So convinced was Hitler that the British would 'come to their senses' and ask for terms that Hitler dallied on his special command train *Tannenberg* in the Black Forest from 25 June to 5 July before returning to Berlin. It was here, on 16 July, that he finally signed the celebrated *Führer* Directive No 16 for Operation '*Seelöwe*' or Sealion, as the invasion was to be designated. The aim of the operation was stated to be 'to eliminate the British

homeland as a base for the further prosecution of the war against Germany, and, if necessary, to occupy it completely'. On 19 July Hitler made his last appeal for the British to come to terms, but the ultimatum was sharply rejected by Prime Minister Winston Churchill.

The responsibility for the German Army's planning for Sealion fell to Field-Marshal Walther von Brauchitsch, the army commander-in-chief, together with a team of 12 other army and *Luftwaffe* generals. The preliminary plans were ready on 27 July: 41 divisions (six of them *Panzer* and three motorized), plus the *Luftwaffe's* 7th Parachute Division and the army's airlanding 22nd Infantry Division, were to descend on the southern shores of Great Britain soon after 25 August. Field-Marshal Gerd von Rundstedt's Army Group 'A' was to land two armies, the 16th between Ramsgate and Hastings, and the 9th between Brighton and Littlehampton, with another detachment landing on the Isle of Wight. Either simultaneously or shortly afterwards, Field-Marshal Fedor von Bock's Army Group 'B' would launch its 6th Army from the Cherbourg area against the Dorset coast between Lyme Regis and Weymouth. The initial stop-line for these forces ran between Maldon on the North Sea and Gloucester on the Severn river. Raeder was astounded by the plan, and pointed out emphatically that his naval forces could not support so extended a venture. To ensure adequate protection from the Royal Navy, the *Kriegsmarine* officers said, the landings should take place only between Ramsgate and Folkestone. The army in turn rejected so narrow a front, and eventually a compromise was worked out: the 6th Army attack was dropped, the 16th Army would land between Ramsgate and Folkestone, and the 9th Army's operation remained unchanged. This revised plan called for 27 divisions, nine of which would be landed on D-day, now put back to 21 September.

Both the army and the navy were still unhappy with the plan, which called for the collection of virtually all the motorized barges in northern Europe to the detriment of industry and civilian life alike, but nothing better could be worked out.

The *sine qua non* of the whole operation, though, was the suppression of the Royal Air Force and the Royal Navy, both of which could be expected to intervene with major attacks on the sealanes reaching to the landing beaches from Le Havre

to Rotterdam. The *Kriegsmarine* could achieve little, most of its heavy units having been sunk or damaged in the Norwegian campaign. Therefore the onus for the protection of the invasion forces fell on the *Luftwaffe*, the portly shoulders of whose commander, *Reichsmarschall* Hermann Göring, seemed well suited to the task. Ground support for the landings would have to be provided, the navy lacking the heavy-gun ships for the job, but first the *Luftwaffe* would have to eliminate the RAF, especially the fighter formations that might otherwise deny the German fighters access to the bomber forces.

That Hitler was well aware of this is indicated by his *Führer* Directive No 17, signed on 1 August. This called for an intensification of naval and air operations against Great Britain, and its first paragraph read: 'Using all possible means, the German air forces will smash the British air forces in as brief a period of time as possible. Their attacks will be directed in the first instance against formations in flight, their ground facilities, and their supply centres, then against the British aircraft industry, including factories producing anti-aircraft guns.' With this accomplished, the *Luftwaffe* was to turn its attentions to the country's ports, with the exception of those that would be needed for the invasion forces' supplies. Paragraph 5 of the directive, it should be noted, reserved exclusively to Hitler the right to order 'terror attacks' on British cities as measures of reprisal. At this stage Hitler was therefore thinking in terms of straight warfare only against military targets and their industrial bases, probably in the hope that the success of the *Luftwaffe* would yet persuade the British that further resistance was hopeless.

German and British air strength

So far as Germany was concerned, therefore, the future course of the war lay in the hands of the *Luftwaffe*. How well placed, then, was the German air force for the battle that lay ahead? Tactically its position was excellent: Germany's earlier successes had given her access to air bases in Norway, Denmark, Holland, Belgium and France, in effect a great arc running round Britain's east and south coasts. With the exception of the bases in Norway and Denmark, most of these bases were quite close to the air force's primary targets. As far as aircraft and aircrew were concerned, though, the picture was not quite so rosy: both had come through a hard time in the Western campaign, and the survivors were tired, aircrews in need of rest and rehabilitation, and the aircraft in need of thorough overhauls. German aircraft production, moreover, had been curtailed as it was expected that the war would soon be over, and so losses had not been made good. (Although it is often stated that the French air force was hardly a fighting arm to be reckoned with in 1940, it should be remembered that it had on its own inflicted losses of some 778 aircraft on the Germans.) Thus on 10 August, three days before *Adlertag* or Eagle Day, on which the German onslaught was to commence, the three German *Luftflotten* or air fleets deployed against Britain could muster only 2550 serviceable aircraft out of an actual strength of 3358 and an establishment strength of 3609. Three days later the *Luftwaffe's*

strength in the major combat types was as follows: Messerschmitt Bf 109 single-engined fighter 734, Messerschmitt Bf 110 twin-engined fighter 268, Junkers Ju 87 dive-bomber 336, and Dornier Do 17, Heinkel He 111 and Junkers Ju 88 twin-engined medium bombers 949. Total strength thus stood at 2287.

The German forces were deployed, as noted above, in three major formations: in Norway and Denmark was General Hans-Jürgen Stumpff's *Luftflotte* V; in Belgium and Holland was Field-Marshal Albert Kesselring's *Luftflotte* II; and in northern France was Field-Marshal Hugo Sperrle's *Luftflotte* III.

The British defence lay in the hands of Air Chief-Marshal Sir Hugh Dowding's Fighter Command, split up into four major sub-commands. Defending northern England and Scotland was Air Vice-Marshal R.E. Saul's No 13 Group, with headquarters in Newcastle; central England and northern Wales was the responsibility of Air Vice-Marshal Trafford Leigh-Mallory's No 12 Group; air operations over south-east England fell to Air Vice-Marshal Keith Park's No 11 Group; and finally the air defence of south-west England and southern Wales lay in the hands of Air Vice-Marshal Sir Quintin Brand. The chief burden of operations was to fall on Nos 11 and 12 Groups, whose commanders were unfortunately to disagree radically about the right tactics.

Fighter Command could deploy on 10 August

some 749 serviceable fighters out of an establishment strength of 1106. Although it thus seems that the fighter squadrons were considerably under strength, the position was tolerable as fighter production was increasing at a considerable rate (157 in January 1940, 325 in May, 446 in June and 496 in July). Far more important, though, was the lack of trained pilots, who numbered only 1341 on 13 July. Other commands had been combed for suitable pilots, but the number thus gained was relatively small. On 10 August Fighter Command had 1396 pilots, compared with an establishment of 1588, the deficiency thus being 192 pilots. This was always to be a critical factor in the battle to come, for a surplus of trained pilots would have enabled exhausted aircrew to be rotated more quickly. Only on 12 October was Fighter Command able to show a surplus: 38 pilots, the establishment being 1714 and the actual strength 1752.

Five main types of fighter featured in Fighter Command's inventory: the Gloster Gladiator biplane, the Boulton Paul Defiant single-engined turret fighter, the Bristol Blenheim twin-engined conversion, and the Hawker Hurricane and Supermarine Spitfire single-engined monoplanes. It was to be on the two last that the main burden of the battle fell.

What then were the principal merits of the British and German aircraft? On the British side,

the Hurricane and Spitfire were both excellent fighters, with an armament of eight .303-inch machine-guns. The Hurricane was slightly older in design than the Spitfire, but was available in larger numbers. Marginally slower than the Bf 109, the Hurricanes' prime virtues were good manoeuvrability and great strength, both great attributes in the attacks on the German bombers which were to be the Hurricanes' main opponents. The Spitfire was the better of the two British fighters in quality, and so was given the primary objective of taking on the German fighters, and thus facilitating the Hurricanes' attacks on the German bombers. There was little to chose in performance between the Spitfire and Bf 109, the Spitfire having a slightly smaller turning circle but the German fighter a higher rate of climb at average combat altitudes. Where the Bf 109 really scored, however, was in its ability to dive: its Daimler-Benz engine had a fuel injection system, whereas the Rolls-Royce powerplant of the two British fighters used a standard float carburettor; this meant that in a direct negative-g manoeuvre, such as when the nose of the aircraft was pushed down in a dive, the Rolls-Royce was starved of fuel and spluttered, unlike the Daimler-Benz which continued to run smoothly. In tactical terms, then, this meant that in order to break off combat the Bf 109 had merely to dive, whereas the British fighters had to half-roll and then dive

in a positive-g manoeuvre.

Of the other German aircraft, the most feared was the Ju 87 Stuka (*Sturzkampfflugzeug* or dive-bomber). Yet early combat operations were soon to dispel the aura of victory that the Stuka had won in Poland and in the west: the British fighters found that the type was a sitting duck, especially at the bottom of its dive, and that the Stuka was thus only effective where its own fighter forces enjoyed almost total air superiority, a situation which most certainly did not prevail in the Battle of Britain. After a severe mauling at the hands of Fighter Command in the battle the Stuka was revealed for what it was: a relatively effective ground-attack aircraft whose impact on land forces was as much psychological as physical.

The three medium bombers most widely used by the *Luftwaffe* were the Do 17, He 111 and Ju 88. All of them followed the standard German practice of grouping the crew members in an extensively glazed nose compartment. This had little or no bullet-proof glass, and thus proved an ideal target for the machine-guns of the British fighters. The performance of the He 111 and Do 17 was just about adequate, and that of the newer Ju 88 excellent, but the lack of crew protection, combined with a relatively weak defensive armament, gave the tactical edge to Fighter Command. Later in the battle, moreover, it was to be discovered that the range of these three

Above left: A formation of Heinkel He 111 medium bombers of *Kampfgeschwader* 55 in flight. The *Luftwaffe's* best medium bomber at the beginning of the war, by 1940 it had been joined by the superior Junkers Ju 88. In combat the He 111 had two main failings: lack of adequate defensive armament, and the grouping of all the crew in the vulnerable nose. **Below left:** A decisive factor in the Polish and Western campaigns, the Junkers Ju 87, most often known by the soubriquet *Stuka* (*Sturzkampfflugzeug* or dive-bomber), was revealed in the Battle of Britain to be a death-trap in the face of well handled defending fighters. **Above:** A Supermarine Spitfire IA fighter of No 19 Squadron taxies out for take-off, the two groundcrew helping the pilot navigate as the view from his cockpit was poor on the ground.

bombers, when carrying a full bomb-load, was quite short, especially when the *Luftwaffe* attempted to wage a strategic battle with three bomber types that had been designed for an essentially tactical role.

Of the major German combat aircraft this leaves only the much vaunted Bf 110 twin-engined twin-seat fighter. Designed as a heavy bomber destroyer (its German name was *Zerstörer* or destroyer), the Bf 110 had acquitted itself well in the Polish and Western campaigns as an escort fighter. Yet it had not been designed for this role, and the superior resistance offered by the RAF soon revealed that the Bf 110 was in fact a relatively clumsy aircraft that could not take on well-handled single-seaters. Although its speed was adequate, and its firepower heavy, the large dimensions imposed by the twin-engined layout meant that the Bf 110 just could not be as manoeuvrable as the Spitfire and the Hurricane. This meant that the Bf 110 received somewhat of a mauling in the battle, and thus a diminution in status in German eyes. It should be noted, though, that later in the war, the Bf 110 was to win great credit in the role for which it had been designed: fitted with radar, the Bf 110 proved an excellent bomber destroyer once the great Allied bomber fleets started to take the offensive air war into Germany.

Apart from aircraft, there were two other factors that militated against the Germans. First of these factors was the British use of radar in a relatively sophisticated fashion. Running round the eastern and southern coasts of Great Britain there were two types of radar, high and low altitude. This meant that German attacks coming in between the Shetlands and south Wales could be picked up by British radar; and although the sets in use were relatively primitive, skilled operators could interpret the information on their

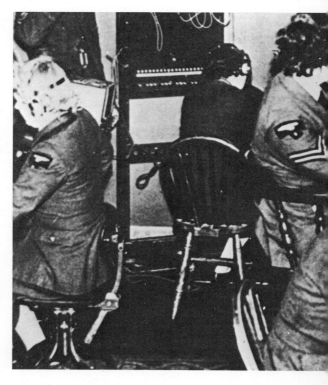

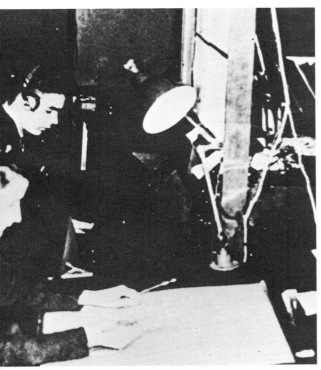

screens with some precision. The important thing about radar, though, was that the air defence of Britain had to a very great extent been modernized in concept to make full use of radar. The information from the stations round the coast was all fed to a series of filter rooms, where it was collated and assessed. Ground controllers could then direct the right number of squadrons to 'scramble' off the ground in time to meet the main threats. The whole system was seriously underestimated by the Germans, and this allowed Fighter Command to make the most effective use of its strictly limited resources. It should not be imagined, though, that this well run radar system was in any way a 'cure-all' for the excessive parsimony that had kept Fighter Command (and the other elements of the RAF and other armed services) starved of adequate men and *matériel* between the two world wars. In No 11 Group's area, for example, radar warnings preceded the arrival of a raid by only a short time, giving the defending fighters little chance to climb to the right altitude and assemble in useful numbers before combat was joined. The

Above left: Britain's victory was greatly aided by the existence of the network of Chain Home long-range radar stations round the east and south coasts of the country, together with the control system that turned the radar information into orders for the defending fighters. **Above:** The Group Operations Room of Air Vice-Marshal Park's 11 Group. It was here that the orders for the defence of South-East England were issued. **Left:** Plotters of the Women's Auxiliary Air Force in a 'filter room', where information from the radar stations was turned into visual form on the table map.

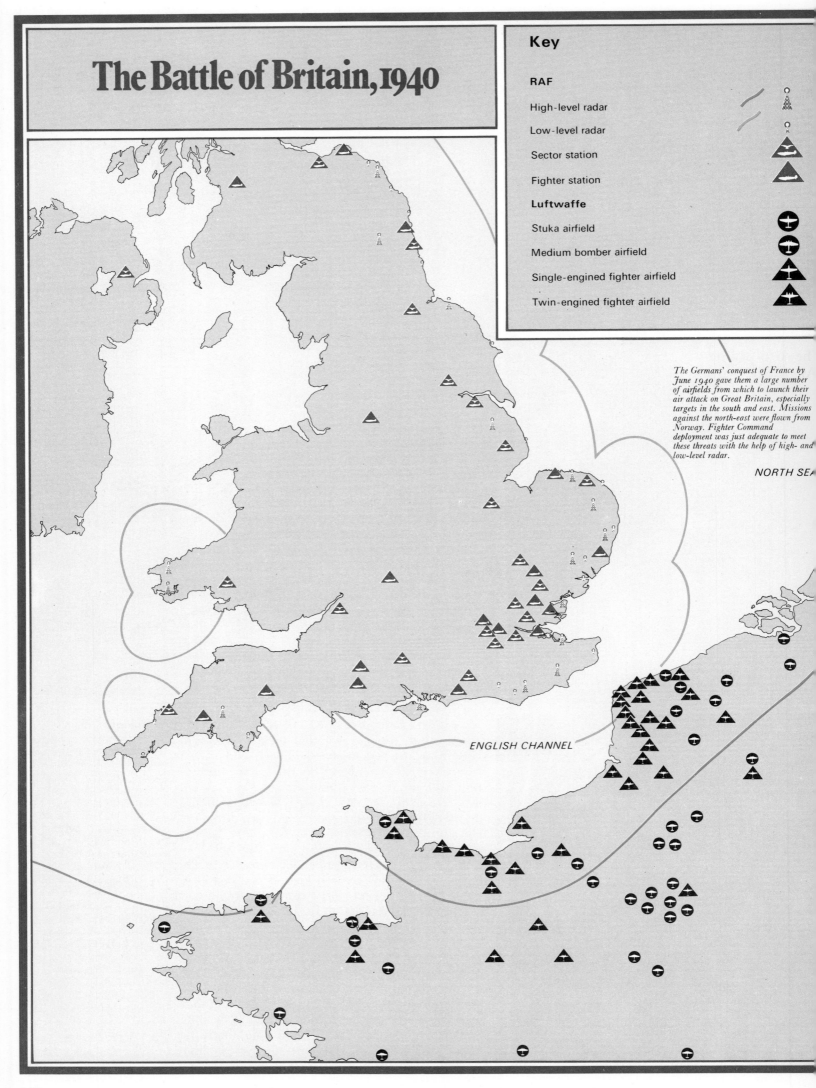

The Battle of Britain, 1940

Key

RAF

High-level radar

Low-level radar

Sector station

Fighter station

Luftwaffe

Stuka airfield

Medium bomber airfield

Single-engined fighter airfield

Twin-engined fighter airfield

The Germans' conquest of France by June 1940 gave them a large number of airfields from which to launch their air attack on Great Britain, especially targets in the south and east. Missions against the north-east were flown from Norway. Fighter Command deployment was just adequate to meet these threats with the help of high- and low-level radar.

NORTH SEA

ENGLISH CHANNEL

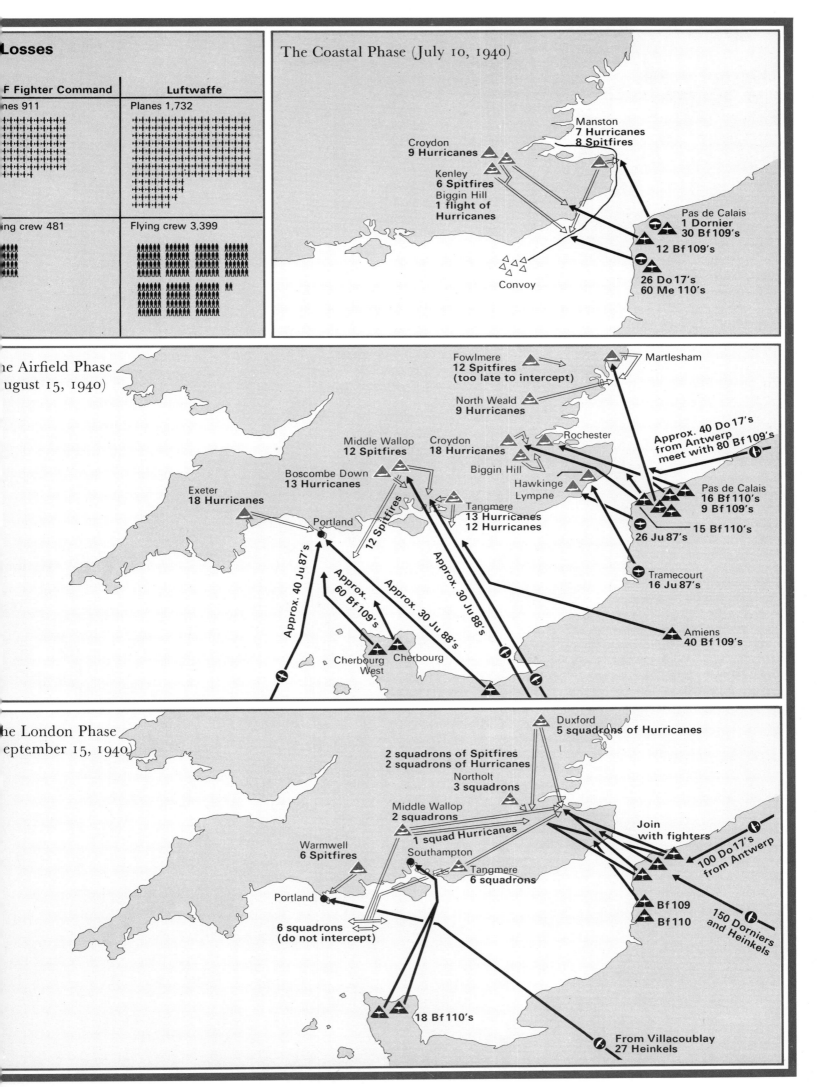

Losses

F Fighter Command	Luftwaffe
nes 911	Planes 1,732
╫╫╫╫╫╫╫╫╫╫╫╫	╫╫╫╫╫╫╫╫╫╫╫╫╫╫╫╫╫
╫╫╫╫╫╫╫╫╫╫╫╫	╫╫╫╫╫╫╫╫╫╫╫╫╫╫╫╫╫
╫╫╫╫╫╫╫╫╫╫╫╫	╫╫╫╫╫╫╫╫╫╫╫╫╫╫╫╫╫
╫╫╫╫╫	╫╫╫╫╫╫╫╫╫╫╫╫╫
	╫╫╫╫╫╫╫╫╫╫
	╫╫╫╫╫╫╫
ing crew 481	Flying crew 3,399

The Coastal Phase (July 10, 1940)

Croydon
9 Hurricanes

Kenley
6 Spitfires

Biggin Hill
1 flight of Hurricanes

Manston
7 Hurricanes
8 Spitfires

Convoy

Pas de Calais
1 Dornier
30 Bf 109's

12 Bf 109's

26 Do 17's
60 Me 110's

The Airfield Phase (August 15, 1940)

Fowlmere
12 Spitfires
(too late to intercept)

Martlesham

North Weald
9 Hurricanes

Middle Wallop
12 Spitfires

Croydon
18 Hurricanes

Rochester

Approx. 40 Do 17's
from Antwerp
meet with 80 Bf 109's

Boscombe Down
13 Hurricanes

Biggin Hill

Hawkinge
Lympne

Pas de Calais
16 Bf 110's
9 Bf 109's

Exeter
18 Hurricanes

12 Spitfires

Portland

Tangmere
13 Hurricanes
12 Hurricanes

15 Bf 110's

26 Ju 87's

Approx. 40 Ju 87's

Approx.
60 Bf 109's

Approx. 30 Ju 88's

Approx. 30 Ju 88's

Tramecourt
16 Ju 87's

Cherbourg
West

Cherbourg

Amiens
40 Bf 109's

The London Phase (September 15, 1940)

Duxford
5 squadrons of Hurricanes

2 squadrons of Spitfires
2 squadrons of Hurricanes

Northolt
3 squadrons

Middle Wallop
2 squadrons

1 squad Hurricanes

Join
with fighters

100 Do 17's
from Antwerp

Warmwell
6 Spitfires

Southampton

Tangmere
6 squadrons

Portland

Bf 109
Bf 110

6 squadrons
(do not intercept)

150 Dorniers
and Heinkels

18 Bf 110's

From Villacoublay
27 Heinkels

295

work of the radar stations, it should be added, was helped and confirmed by the Observer Corps, an organization of many thousand civilians who kept visual watch for the arrival of hostile aircraft over the coastline and then telephoned the information in to the main control centres.

The second other factor operating to the Germans' detriment was that as they were taking the war to Britain, the battle was fought over British soil. This had the effect of shortening Fighter Command's lines of communication: aircraft could take off, fight and then return to base for minor repairs, fuelling and arming with some ease. The Germans, on the other hand, had to fly from their bases, fight, and then get home again across the water. Quite apart from the extra strain this put on men and machines, it also meant that wounded crew had farther to go for medical attention, and damaged aircraft farther to fly without crashing. It also meant that RAF pilots who had to bale out landed on friendly territory or in the English Channel, where an efficient rescue service operated, whereas German aircrew often fell into the hands of their opponents. The importance of this factor was considerable. On 15 August, for example, the *Luftwaffe* lost some 70 aircraft to the RAF, with some 10 German aircrew being made prisoner; on the same day Fighter Command lost 28 Hurricanes and Spitfires in combat, but half their pilots rejoined their squadrons.

Such, then, were the main factors that played a part in the Battle of Britain, which started as a tactical opener for the German invasion plans, but which soon developed into the first decisive air battle in history, and the first major reverse for German arms in World War II. Unlike other decisive battles, though, it is hard to put definite dates on the battle. The Germans usually reckon the battle to have started on *Adlertag* (13 August); the British awarded a Battle of Britain Star (or Bar) to all aircrew of Fighter Command squadrons who had flown at least one operational mission between 10 July and 31 October, this making the British official dating for the beginning of the battle slightly more than a month earlier than the German one. Yet a more realistic date, despite the fact that it is 16 days before Hitler signed Directive No 16 for Operation '*Seelöwe*' and a month before the date on which he signed Directive No 17 for the intensification of air efforts against Great Britain, would be 1 July. On this day the hitherto light skirmishing that had taken place over the English Channel started to develop into far more serious fighting, with more than 12 raids, each made by more than 50 German aircraft, being met over the Channel and south coast.

Phase one

For practical purposes the Battle of Britain may be considered to have started on 1 July. This was to be the first of five quite distinct phases in the

battle, and lasted until 7 August. The objective of the German attacks in this phase was to cause the destruction of Fighter Command by a process of attrition: knowing that coastal shipping was of considerable importance to the British war economy, the Germans instituted a series of attacks on such shipping and the ports it used. Small numbers of bombers, escorted by large numbers of fighters, were sent out to attack coastal convoys. It was hoped that damage would be caused to the shipping, but the desired object of the exercise was to tempt Fighter Command into battle on terms advantageous to the German fighters and destroy large numbers of Spitfires and Hurricanes.

On the whole the Germans were successful in attaining their objects in this phase of the battle, principally because their fighter tactics proved superior to those of the British. In the 1930s the standard fighter tactics had evolved into somewhat cumbersome mass attacks, in which a whole squadron, of perhaps 12 fighters, would take on a single target. While theoretically sound, in that a continuous series of attacks would be kept up on one target until it was destroyed, the practice proved unsound in combat: it took too long for a squadron to form into battle formation of line ahead or line abreast from cruising formation, and was then unwieldy in combat. The Germans, with their experiences with the *Condor Legion* in the Spanish Civil War, had realized this as early as 1937 and thus evolved a far more flexible and practical type of tactics. While still loosely based on the squadron (*Staffel*) of 12 aircraft, the tactics were primarily based on the flight (*Kette*) of four aircraft, which in combat broke down into two sections (*Schwärme*) each of two aircraft. The rock-bottom tactical unit, therefore, was made up of two aircraft, a leader whose job it was to dispose of enemy aircraft, and his wingman, whose task it was to protect his leader. This German system soon proved its value in the Polish and Western campaigns, and soon impressed the Fighter Command pilots, many of them inexperienced, in the opening coastal phase of the Battle of Britain: while the Spitfires and Hurricanes were trying to form up into long lines, the more agile and flexible German formations were able to attack. The British cause was not helped, moreover, by the disastrous introduction of the Boulton Paul Defiant. Superficially similar to the Hurricane in appearance, the Defiant had no fixed forward-firing armament, relying instead on a four-gun turret mounted just aft of the pilot's cockpit. Although the type's first use, over the Dunkirk evacuation, had been impressive, for German pilots mistaking it for a Hurricane and closing in for a beam attack had been severely handled, the Germans now knew of the type's lack

of forward armament and overall performance, and despatched Defiants in large numbers, causing the type's immediate relegation to second-line and night-fighter duties.

Although British pilots who had served with the Advanced Air Striking Force in France during 1939 and up to the fall of France in 1940 had combat experience of the German fighter tactics, many of these had been lost in the closing stages of the Western campaign, and the survivors had not been able to disseminate their impressions very widely. The position was exacerbated by Dowding's courageous, and in the event entirely justified, refusal to allow any Spitfires to be sent to France in the closing stages of the disastrous campaign in that unfortunate country. Almost alone of senior British commanders he had realized that France was lost, and so British losses should be minimized to build up the defences of Britain, inevitably Germany's next target. For the most part, therefore, Fighter Command's pilots had little or no combat experience against the highly-trained Bf 109 pilots. This told considerably against them in the first phase of the Battle of Britain, but the survivors were quick to learn from their mistakes, and began soon to evolve their own version of the German tactics, the so-called 'finger four' formation, in which a section of four aircraft flew in positions relative to each other like the fingertips of the hand. The formation broke down simply into pairs for combat.

Statistically, the first phase of the battle may be summed up simply: between 1 July and 7 August Fighter Command lost 188 aircraft in combat; the Germans lost 248 aircraft in combat, with another 88 damaged to greater or lesser extent. (The Germans assessed damage in a complicated way, assuming 100% damage to represent the total loss of an aircraft, 60% or more a write-off with the possibility of cannibalization of parts, 45–59% severe damage requiring the replacement of major components, 40–44% the need to replace the engine, 25–39% local damage requiring repair and inspection, 10–24% local damage from gunfire requiring only local replacements, and less than 10% minor gunfire damage needing only local repair. For the purposes of 'lost' and 'damaged' figures, 60% damage and above has been assumed to represent a 'lost' aircraft and 10–59% a 'damaged' aircraft.)

Thus although the Germans lost the greater number of aircraft in this first phase, in proportion to their overall numbers they had come off slightly the better.

Sunday, 7 July, may be taken as a typical day in this phase of the battle. The air fighting centred round a British convoy heading east up the Channel. During the morning the Germans sent

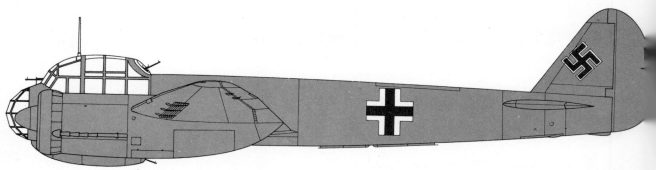

over three Do17P reconnaissance aircraft to shadow the convoy as it passed the Isle of Wight. Each of these three aircraft was shot down, one by each of Nos 145, 43 and 601 Squadrons, all of whom flew Hurricanes. The action farther along the coast in southern Kent during the morning consisted of 'free chases' by some 70 Bf 109s of *Luftflotte* II, none of which were intercepted by No 11 Group fighters. By 1930 the convoy was off southern Kent, and 45 Do 17Z bombers were despatched from Arras to bomb it, sinking one ship and damaging three others. British fighters had been scrambled, but a free chase by Bf 109s of *Jagdgeschwader* 27 caught many of them at a disadvantage and British losses in the ensuing *melee* totalled three. The German bomber attack by *Kampfgeschwader* 2 was finally beaten off, and the day's aerial activities finished with the onset of dusk, the RAF having suffered the loss of one Hurricane and six Spitfires and the *Luftwaffe* three Do 17Ps, one Do 17Z, two Ju 88As and three Bf 109Es destroyed and one Do 17Z damaged.

Aircrew casualties were four British dead and two wounded, and ten German dead and two wounded.

Phase two

The issuing of Directive No 17 by Hitler had the effect of hotting up the pace of operations, and the battle now moved into its second phase (8 to 23 August). Sporadic attacks on coastal convoys continued, but the main objectives of the German operations now became the radar stations along the coast and the forward bases of Fighter Command. (The weight of the attacks on this day meant that for some time it was taken by the British to be the official starting day of the Battle of Britain. But naturally there was no distinction at the time, the breaking-up of the battle into phases for subsequent analysis being somewhat arbitrary.) *Adlerangriff* or the eagle attack, as the opening of the offensive was called, had originally been scheduled for 10 August, but poor weather conditions had led the *Luftwaffe* high command into postponing the date into the 13th, and this phase reached its climax two days later on 15 August. The trouble, from the German point of view, with the battle on 15 August was that most of the senior field commanders were absent, called away to Göring's presence for a *post mortem* on the lack of total success on *Adlertag*. Although 13 August had been marked by some considerable successes, the effort had been marred by lack of liaison between the various subcommands of *Luftflotten* II and III, especially where the question of escort for the bombers was concerned. Often the fighters had turned up late or failed to arrive at all, and Göring was concerned

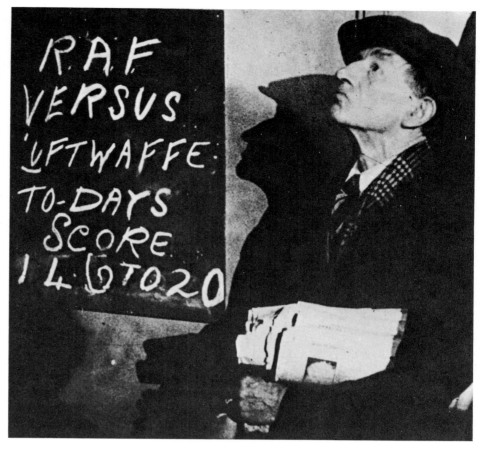

enough to summon the commanders involved to his home at Karinhall. The result, inevitably, was that the situation worsened—the commanders were all too aware of the failings of 13 August, and had prepared countermeasures. But without their presence at their own headquarters there was little way for the plans to be implemented. Statistically, the balance of losses on 15 August was as follows: Fighter Command lost, in combat, 28 aircraft and suffered damage to 13 others; the *Luftwaffe*, on the other hand, suffered losses of 76 aircraft with another three damaged. *Luftflotte* V's effort consisted of 63 He 111 bombers from Stavanger/Sola, escorted by 21 Bf 110s from Stavanger/Forus, which attacked Newcastle and Sunderland at about 1300, and 50 Ju 88s from Aalborg, which attacked Driffield at 1318. Feint attacks had been made by seaplanes, in the hope of confusing the radar picture, but the effect was spoiled by navigational errors, and No 13 Group's fighters were fully prepared. The Germans pressed home their attacks but suffered casualties in the order of 20%, far higher than could be sustained in a prolonged offensive. This was, therefore, the only major raid made by *Luftflotte* V from its bases in southern Norway and Denmark against the north-east coast of England, for Göring ordered the abandonment of any further efforts by this *Luftflotte*. At the same time Göring ordered that the Stuka should be

Above: A British 'scoreboard' for the day's air fighting shows a somewhat optimistic tally in favour of the Royal Air Force. At the time, however, the verification of pilots' claims was difficult, and throughout the war pilots and air gunners consistently claimed to have shot down more aircraft than in fact they had. Given the speed and general uncertainty of air combat, this was inevitable, and certainly does not mean that pilots wished to increase their 'scores' with fake claims.
Below, far left: The Junkers Ju 88 was Germany's best medium bomber of the battle, and was the war's most versatile aircraft. **Below left:** The Messerschmitt Bf 109 was Germany's fighter mainstay throughout the war, over 30,000 examples of the various models of this fighter being built.

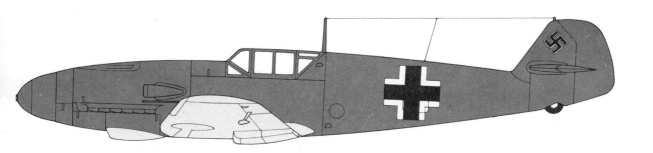

Right: An armourer reloads the magazine for one of the eight wing-mounted .303-inch Browning machine-guns of a No 19 Squadron Spitfire on Duxford airfield near Cambridge. The pilot waits in the cockpit. **Below:** Squadron-Leader D.R.S. Bader with other pilots of his No 242 Squadron, equipped with Hurricane fighters. Bader and his group · commander, Air Vice-Marshal Leigh Mallory, were proponents of the 'big wing' tactical doctrine— which worked well, but only if the big wing arrived in time to intercept the German raiding bombers. **Below right:** German bombs explode on the RAF station at Hemswell in Lincolnshire on 27 August.

withdrawn, so heavy had losses to the *Stukageschwader* been.

These losses had been incurred principally in attacks on coastal radar stations, which were for a time in danger of being destroyed. Several were in fact seriously damaged and in cases put temporarily out of action, and had the Germans continued to press this aspect of their offensive, the tide of the battle might very well have turned decisively against Fighter Command. As it was however, the Germans seemed satisfied with the initial *Blitz* against the radar stations, and after the withdrawal of the *Stukageschwader* failed to concentrate the efforts of their level bombers against the stations, especially those in south-east England. With hindsight it is possible to see that this was one of the Germans' worst blunders in the whole battle, for without the aid of radar the outnumbered British fighters would have had to operate 'blind', with little chance of making worth while interceptions of the increasing German bomber streams.

15 August was marked in the south of England by a number of major raids from bases all along the southern edge of the arc of German bases. From east to west, these raids attacked airfields

from Martlesham Heath to Portland. At 1135 Hawkinge was attacked by 16 Ju 87s of IV (Stuka) *Gruppe/Lehrgeschwader* 1 (IV (St)/LG1) from Tramecourt; at the same time Lympne was attacked by 26 Ju 87s of II/*Stukageschwader* 1, operating from airfields in the Pas de Calais area; Manston was attacked by fighters at 1205; Martlesham Heath came under attack from 16 Bf 110s and 9 Bf 109s of *Erprobungsgruppe* 210 at 1500; to the west, the Portland Bill was the target for some 40 Ju 87s from I/StG1 and II/StG2, operating from Lannion and supported by 60 Bf 109s from JG27 and JG53, operating from airfields in the Cherbourg area, and by 20 Bf 110s of V/LG2 from Caen; north-east of this, between 10 and 15 minutes later, Worthy Down came under bombardment from some 30 Ju 88s of II/LG1 from Orleans/Bricy at 1745, and Middle Wallop from some 30 Ju 88s of I/LG1, also from Orleans/Bricy, at 1750; support for these last two raids was provided by about 40 Bf 110s of *Zerstörergeschwader* 2 from airfields in the Amiens area; the main area of operations now moved to the east, with Eastchurch being attacked at 1845 and Rochester at 1850 by the 40 Do 17s of KG3 from Antwerp, escorted by some 80 Bf 109s of JG26 and JG54 from Pas de Calais airfields; the final major raid of the day was at 1900, when Croydon was the object of a raid by 15 Bf 110s and 8 Bf 109s of *Erprobungsgruppe* 210 from Pas de Calais airfields. It should also be noted that during the course of the afternoon, southern England, especially Kent and Sussex, had been harassed by a number of free chase operations flown by Bf 109s and Bf 110s.

Among the British fighter units involved were the Hurricanes of Nos 17, 1, 151, 32, 111, 43, 601, 249, 87 and 213 Squadrons, and the Spitfires of Nos 19, 54, 609 and 234 Squadrons. The picture is necessarily involved, perhaps even obscure, and appeared so at the time to the various controllers who had to try to handle each raid: as the radar and observer reports came in, these controllers had to assess their likely accuracy, the probable objectives of each German raid, the availability of defending fighter squadrons in the air, on the ground at readiness, on the ground refuelling and rearming, and the priority that should be given to each raid. The process was an extremely complex one, and it was to the great credit of the sector controllers that the day produced such decisive results for Fighter Command: 76 German aircraft destroyed and three damaged, for the loss of 28 fighters and damage to 13 others.

Although the phase was only two weeks long, the strain of almost continuous operations was beginning to tell on the pilots of Nos 10, 11 and 12 Groups early in the phase. The pilots of No 11 Group, in particular, were extremely fatigued as it was they who had to bear the brunt of operations. Although much has been made of the efforts of the pilots and the groundcrews who kept the fighters serviceable, it should also be remembered that Park and Dowding showed extreme skill in deciding the times at which exhausted squadrons should be pulled out of the line and replaced by rested and partially rested units. Without the efforts of these two men and their staffs, who made the hardest of decisions that would affect the lives and deaths of the men under their command, the battle might well have been lost during this second phase. By the time it ended on 23 August, losses to Fighter Command had been 303 aircraft, while those to the *Luftwaffe* had reached 403, with another 127 damaged.

Phase three

The third phase of the battle opened on 24 August and continued until 6 September. The objective of this phase was the elimination of aircraft production facilities and attacks on inland fighter bases. Yet again the *Luftwaffe* came close to victory, for within a few days of the beginning

of the phase the fighter airfields of the inland areas were as pockmarked with bomb craters, and littered with burned out aircraft wrecks as the fields farther south. Just as importantly, the control centres for the sectors were located on these airfields, and so suffered heavy damage as they had been provided with insufficient overhead protection. This inevitably meant that the co-ordination of the various fighter squadrons in the air suffered, facilitating the task of the Germans. The main effort against the airfields was naturally made by the bombers, but as the strength of the RAF fighter opposition had not diminished as quickly as had been expected, strong fighter elements were still used in an effort to tempt up Fighter Command aircraft under unfavourable circumstances. The main trouble with this concept was that the farther into England the fighters, especially the Bf 109s, had to penetrate, the more vulnerable they became, principally because their radius of action was so short. Over airfields to the south and east of London, for example, they had fuel for only some 15 minutes combat. Any longer period of high consumption activity at the extremes of the Bf 109s' range meant that a ditching in the Channel was very likely, especially if the engine or fuel system had been damaged.

Although in several respects not fully typical, the large-scale raids, or rather attempted raids, on the fighter bases at Debden and Hornchurch, the former near Bishop's Stortford and the latter north of the Thames river just to the east of London, serve to illustrate the type of raid that featured in this phase. Early in the afternoon of 26 August the radar screens of south-east England began to indicate that a major force was being assembled over Belgium. In fact it was some 80 Do 17s of KG2 and KG3, with escort provided by no less than 80 Bf 110s and 40 Bf 109s. As this considerable force approached the mouth of the Blackwater river in Essex, *en route* to Debden, 40 Do 17s and 40 Bf 110s peeled off towards Hornchurch, leaving 40 each of the Do 17s, Bf 110s and Bf 109s to press on towards Debden. It is worth noting at this stage that the presence of the Bf 109s was as escort to the Bf 110 escort-fighters, which had by now been proved all too vulnerable to the British fighters! Unfortunately for the Germans, though, the Bf 109s were operating at the very limits of their endurance, and half way between Debden and Colchester had to turn back for home or run out of fuel. The rest of the main force also turned for home, although some six to eight Dorniers pressed on alone and actually bombed Debden before heading for home unscathed. The rest of the main force fared worse, running into seven squadrons of Hurricanes and Spitfires. The Bf 109s, desperately short of fuel, avoided combat, leaving the Bf 110s and Do 17s to their fate. Losses were heavy, and seeing the fate of the main force, the group on its way towards Hornchurch also decided to abort and make for home in small groups.

The raid had been a failure, but had important repercussions on both sides. On the Germans' it was realized that free chase operations, such as that which had preceded the main raids to draw off the No 11 Group's fighters to Kent, were inefficient, and left the main force without adequate cover. On the British side it worsened the tactical quarrel between Park and Leigh-Mallory. Park, with most of his squadrons engaged over Kent, had had to call on Leigh-Mallory for aid. But Leigh-Mallory was an ardent advocate of the 'big-wing' theory, and it had taken too long for the squadrons he despatched to form up into a large body and arrive in time to engage the Germans. Park, who believed that the important thing was to engage the Germans before they had reached their targets, was prepared to send in single squadrons to break up large German formations, and was unhappy with Leigh-Mallory's tactics, which were theoretically sound—large numbers of aircraft grouped under single control would inflict correspondingly heavier casualties, but only if they got there in time. The trouble was that Leigh-Mallory's 'big wings' usually reached the German formations after they had bombed their targets. The problem remained largely unresolved during the Battle of Britain.

Below: German bomber crew receive their final briefing. **Below right:** Standing in front of a Bf 109 with 38 victory markings on its tail, Major Günther Lützow, the *Kommodore* of *Jagdgeschwader* 3 'Udet' from the middle of August 1940, talks to two of his pilots, *Hauptmann* Wilhelm Balthasar, holder of the Oak Leaves to the Knight's Cross of the Iron Cross and *Kommandeur* of JG3's III *Gruppe* (**centre**) and *Leutnant* Egon Troha, *Staffelkäpitan* of JG3's 9th *Staffel*. Lützow held the Oak Leaves with Swords to the Knight's Cross of the Iron Cross, and finally scored 108 victories, most of them on the Eastern Front.

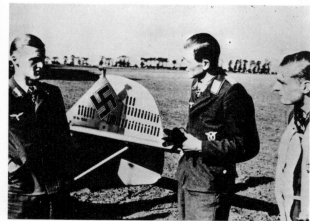

Nevertheless the third phase of the battle was a dire one for Fighter Command, which lost 262 aircraft to the *Luftwaffe's* 378, with another 115 damaged. The problem lay not in the supply of replacement aircraft, which was by now more than adequate, but the supply of pilots, either rested or from the operational training units. Pilot strength was down to under 1000, and these men were very close to the limits of exhaustion, despite Dowding's skills with rotation of squadrons. Yet again the Germans were on the brink of success when they again blundered, switching their attacks away from Fighter Command.

Phase four

On 24 August some German bombers had inadvertently bombed the outskirts of London, in direct contravention of Hitler's orders. In retaliation Churchill ordered that Berlin be bombed, which it was on the following night. Hitler was infuriated, and ordered that terror-bombing of London should start as soon as possible. The first raid broke on 7 September, ushering in the fourth phase of the battle, which may be regarded as having ended on 30 September, when large-scale day raids ended, although London was bombed daily for 57 days. The change of policy was disastrous for Germany: within an ace of tactical victory over Fighter Command, the *Luftwaffe* was ordered to turn its attentions towards a strategic goal for which it had never been designed or equipped. The raids on London were just what Fighter Command needed: the *Luftwaffe* could not attack London in strength without relaxing its pressure on Fighter Command. This allowed the British to build up the fighter arm quickly, and with the Germans' main target known in advance, the fighters were able to take the war to the Germans, inflicting terrible casualties on them as they made for London in mass formations by day. At last Leigh-Mallory's big wings had just the targets they needed, and decimated the German formations. The *Luftwaffe's* medium bombers, moreover, could not carry the bomb-load to destroy London, although enormous damage was caused, and the Bf 109s, now tied closely to the bomber units they were escorting, had to fly at an uneconomical speed and thus almost invariably ran short of fuel and had to turn for home before reaching London, thus leaving the bombers unescorted except for the Bf 110s, which could also have done with fighter escort! The greatest day in the battle came on 15 September, when the German bomber forces attacking London received a terrible mauling—the day has since been celebrated in Great Britain as Battle of Britain Day. By the end of the month, when this fourth phase, the daylight bombing of London, was called to an end because of the *Luftwaffe's* losses and near exhaustion, the RAF had suffered 380 aircraft losses to the Germans' 435, with 161 damaged.

Effectively the Battle of Britain was over, and Great Britain had come through one of the worst and most dangerous periods of her history. But Hitler was not satisfied, and it was decided that if daylight bombing was impractical, then London would be razed by a night *Blitz*, when the fighters defending the capital could not operate with any efficiency.

Phase five

There thus followed a fifth phase of the battle, with German fighter-bombers sweeping over southern England to keep the defences off balance while the night *Blitz* was prepared. The phase lasted from 1 to 31 October, and cost the Germans 325 aircraft, with another 163 damaged, to British losses of 265 aircraft. Yet the last phase was worse than useless: the whole object of the Battle of Britain, to pave the way for Operation 'Seelöwe', had disappeared with the indefinite postponement of this operation by Hitler on 17 September.

Top: Air Vice-Marshal Keith Park, who was a well-known figure in his white flying helmet, commanded 11 Group, which bore the brunt of the German attacks in the Battle of Britain. **Above:** Bomb damage in London after the *Luftwaffe* made the mistaken decision to bomb the British capital rather than persevere with attacks on Fighter Command and its bases.

Matapan

1941

The first big naval battle of World War II was fought off Cape Matapan in southern Greece on 28 March, 1941. Since the European war was composed mainly of land operations for geographical reasons, Matapan was the only large fleet action in the war which took place outside the Pacific theater. Matapan also marked a transition between the naval actions of World War I, fought with gun and ship-borne torpedo and the subsequent great carrier actions of the Pacific war. Indeed, the British fleet at Matapan contained two veterans of Jutland but at the same time assigned a crucial role to an aircraft carrier. The genesis of Matapan was a chain of complex and sometimes haphazard events which changed the Mediterranean from a backwater of the war to a major theater of operations for both sides.

As a result of Adolf Hitler's decision to invade Poland, Britain and France had declared war on Germany in 1939, but the German blitzkrieg had swept across Europe, bringing the capitulation of France in June 1940 and leaving Britain to stand alone against Hitler's European empire. At the same time, Benito Mussolini had brought Italy into the war against Britain, transforming the Mediterranean into an arena of war, for Britain had a Mediterranean fleet, large bases at Gibraltar, Malta and Alexandria, and vital interests to protect in that part of the world. After the capitulation of France, Hitler's main interest was the launching of Operation Barbarossa – the invasion of the Soviet Union – after which he planned to revert to the problem of Britain. The adventures of his erstwhile Italian ally, however, drew him into major commitments in the Balkans and North Africa on which he had not counted.

Although generally considering Europe south of the Alps to be Mussolini's domain, Hitler's relations with the Italian dictator were usually touchy. Neither Hitler nor Mussolini were by nature cooperators and it was also no secret that

the latter resented his subordinate role. By 1940 the relationship between Der Führer and Il Duce was already losing some of its strength. If Hitler was going to create an empire from the Atlantic to the Urals, Mussolini intended to build an Italian empire in the Mediterranean world. The German defeat of Britain and France gave him an opportunity to attempt to seize what he wanted: Corsica, Malta, Tunisia, part of Algeria, an Atlantic port in Morocco, French Somaliland and the British position in Egypt and the Sudan. First on his shopping list was the Adriatic coast of Greece. Knowing full well that Hitler would try to restrain him, Mussolini gave the German leader no advance notice of the invasion of Greece on 28 October, 1940, sending a letter antedated by five days at the last minute. Undertaken against the advice of all three Italian chiefs of staff, the attack struck through Italian-held Albania and was a complete failure. Within three weeks the counterattacking Greeks had driven the invaders off Greek soil. Mussolini had launched a war he could not finish, the first of a long series of disasters for Italy, and had seriously distorted Hitler's strategy, as the Germans were forced to intervene to retrieve the situation.

Mussolini had not planned to go to war to attain his objectives before 1942, but the fall of France forced him to advance his schedule. Except in naval terms, Italy was not a strong power. Her air force was obsolescent, her army poorly equipped and low in morale. But her navy ranked fifth in the world. In 1937 two modern battleships – the *Vittorio Veneto* and the *Littorio* – had been launched, while four others of World War I vintage had been rebuilt. There were nineteen modern cruisers, 120 destroyers and torpedo boats, and 100 submarines. There were, however, no aircraft carriers. During the great naval debate over aircraft carriers in the 1920's and 1930's, Mussolini had said that Italy itself was an unsinkable air-

Below: One of Italy's new battleships, the *Vittorio Veneto*. She was fast and well-armed with nine 15-inch guns.

Above: Admiral Sir James Somerville, commander of Force H, a striking unit based at Gibraltar. **Above right:** The Australian light cruiser *Perth*, which was on loan to Britain's Mediterranean fleet.

craft carrier and had not commissioned one for his navy. The Italian view was that a good air force could support their ships all over the Mediterranean, but unfortunately Italy did not have such an air force. With only the Mediterranean in which to operate, the Italian Navy was in fact a formidable force, so much so that in April 1940 France concentrated most of her naval strength in the Mediterranean. In May the French and British began combined naval operations and swept the Mediterranean while the Italian fleet prudently lay low. But in June France made armistices with both Germany and Italy, leaving Britain with but a small and overworked fleet in the Mediterranean. On 7 July Admiral Sir Andrew Cunningham, naval commander in the Eastern Mediterranean, completed negotiations with Vice Admiral R. E. Godfroy for the demilitarization of the French ships at Alexandria, thus sparing himself the need to fire on his former comrades-in-arms as had Admiral James Somerville at Oran.

Matched against the British Mediterranean fleet, the Italian Navy was superior in numbers while its ships were newer, faster and better armed. The Italians were, however, untrained in night operations, believing these to be impracticable for heavy ships, and were completely lacking in radar, which admittedly was a scarce and relatively untried instrument in 1940. Strengthening their Mediterranean fleet by the addition of a battleship and a carrier, the British shifted their main base from exposed Malta to Alexandria. The battle fleet consisted of three battleships, a carrier and a number of cruisers and destroyers. But even with the additions, the Italians would have been far superior materially had they wished to put to sea. The British ships were always in a poor state of repair due to constant use and no replacements. Destroyers and to a lesser extent cruisers suffered in terms of speed and operational efficiency as a result. On the other hand, the crews were experienced and morale high in the British ships, whereas the Italian sailors had logged little sea time and had no war experience.

As the British position in the Middle East was dependent on control of the eastern Mediterranean, the focus of British strength lay in Egypt where the Eastern Mediterranean Fleet under Admiral Cunningham and the Army of the Nile under General Sir Archibald Wavell were based at Alexandria. Facing Wavell across the Libyan desert was an Italian force of 215,000 men under Marshal Graziani, who was finally prodded into action by Mussolini in the fall of 1940. In December Wavell's mixed force of 30,000 British, Australian, New Zealand, French and Polish units counterattacked all the way to Benghazi in a brilliant campaign and in the process destroyed an Italian army six times its own size. Undertaken by the British largely to sustain morale on the home front, the campaign was the second major Italian disaster of the war. It forced Hitler to send General Erwin Rommel and his Panzer units to North Africa to support the Italians, and also caused him to take a closer look at British support of Greece, scene of the first Italian disaster, and at the need for German involvement in that campaign as well. Operation Barbarossa would have to wait until the Mediterranean had been tidied up.

Since the Italian entry into the war in June 1940 there had been skirmishes between the British and Italian fleets but no full scale action. Even with their superiority, the Italians were not challenging the British strongly since their operational aim was to maintain strong control in the central Mediterranean and to keep the sea route to Libya open. On 11 November, 1940 the British made a carrier based air strike on the Italian naval base at Taranto which put half of the Italian battle fleet out of action. For their part, the Italians made surprisingly successful torpedo boat attacks on British ships in various harbors. With German intervention in North Africa in February 1941, 400 German planes were based in Sicily and Rhodes to protect Rommel's supply lines between Sicily and Tripolitania. British shipping and bases came under heavy air attack. Malta was cut off and all but the eastern Mediter-

ranean became impassable to British convoys. The task of the British fleet had originally been to keep the lines of communication with Malta open and subsequently to attack Rommel's supply lines as well. At the same time the Royal Air Force had been giving modest assistance to the Greeks against the Italians. The Greek plight was raising strong Philhellene sentiment in Britain, but Churchill's proposal to increase aid to Greece in February 1941 had deeper political motivations. To maintain Britain's honor, he wished to uphold its 1939 guarantee of Greece. Successful British support of Greece would also encourage Turkish leaders to bring their country into the war against Germany. But perhaps most important, the Greek cause was very popular in the United States, and any aid, successful or otherwise, would add to British virtue in American eyes. Churchill's main goal was the creation of an alliance strong enough to defeat the Nazis, a goal to which American participation was essential. German intervention in Mussolini's Greek debacle was also expected imminently, and it was hoped that with British help the Greeks could clear out the Italians before Hitler struck. Thus on 4 March, 1941 Operation Lustre began the transport of British, Australian and New Zealand troops from Egypt to Greece, mostly in merchant ships. With the cruisers *Orion*, *Ajax*, *Perth* and *Gloucester*, Admiral H. D. Pridham-Wippell covered this traffic through operations in the Aegean Sea, thus adding yet another task to the burden of the Eastern Mediterranean Fleet. While British convoys ran north from Alexandria to Piraeus in support of the Greek campaign, German and Italian convoys went south from Sicily to Tripolitania in support of Rommel at the other end of the Mediterranean.

Believing two of the three British battleships to be out of action as a result of raids on Alexandria harbor, the German liaison staff suggested to the Italian Naval High Command on 9 March that the intensive traffic between Alexandria and the Greek ports carrying reinforcements and supplies

Above: The light cruiser *Orion*, Pridham-Wippell's flagship in the Aegean.
Left: Vice-Admiral Henry Pridham-Wippell, commander of the cruisers at Matapan.

Above: Admiral Andrew Cunningham, Commander-in-Chief of the Mediterranean Fleet, aboard his flagship *Warspite* in Alexandria.

twenty miles south of Gavdo Island, while Cattaneo's force made a sweep 50 miles to the north into the Aegean. Having destroyed all enemy convoys which could be found, they were then to rendezvous and return to base. Enemy warships were to be engaged only if conditions were entirely favorable to the Italian squadron. Air support, so crucial to modern naval operations, was problematical since it was not under the orders of Iachino who had to make requests for Italian planes to his own naval high command and for Luftwaffe support to the German liaison officers aboard his flagship. While at sea on 27 March, the *Vittorio Veneto* intercepted a message to Alexandria from a British reconnaissance plane reporting three Italian cruisers 80 miles east of Sicily and heading toward Crete. Both Iachino and Riccardi knew that the element of surprise was now gone and with it any chance of meeting a convoy, but Riccardi ordered the sweep to continue to avoid offending the Germans at whose instigation the operation had been mounted in the first place. Cattaneo was ordered not to penetrate the Aegean but merely to meet Iachino twenty miles off Gavdo Island at dawn on the 28th of March.

By 26 March the British Eastern Mediterranean Command had noted the increase in Italian air reconnaissance and concluded that a major Italian operation was imminent in view of the expected invasion of Greece by the Germans. A naval diversion to cover a landing in Cyrenaica or Greece or an attack on Crete might be in the offing but the most likely objective was the convoys of Operation Lustre. When the report of the Italian cruisers was received on the 27th, the Aegean was cleared of shipping and north and south bound convoys cancelled. If the enemy force could be located and if the British fleet could get to sea early enough, it might be able to bring the enemy to battle. The Italian cruisers were a source of much worry to the British command since these ships were faster and more heavily gunned than the old six-inch British cruisers. Known to his fleet as 'ABC', Admiral Andrew Brown Cunningham would have dearly loved to bring the Italian fleet to a decisive action and he thought it was just possible that there were battleships out in support of the Italian cruisers. He therefore hoisted his flag in the battleship *Warspite* and put out to sea with his fleet on the night of 27 March, having waited until after dark to deceive the ever present Italian reconnaissance planes. Admiral Pridham-Wippell with his force of cruisers was to meet Cunningham's squadron at 0630 on the 28th, 30 miles south of Gavdo Island.

The British Battle Squadron

The British battle squadron consisted of the *Warspite*, a modern ship mounting eight fifteen-inch guns and with 24-knot speed. The battleships *Valiant* and *Barham* had similar armament but both were veterans of Jutland and while the *Valiant* had been modernized, the *Barham* had not and could only manage 22 knots. The guns of these ships were inferior in range to those of the *Vittorio Veneto*. The *Formidable* was an armored aircraft carrier capable of $30\frac{1}{2}$ knots and carrying 27 planes – thirteen Fulmar fighters, four

was a particularly worthwhile target: 'The German naval staff considers that the appearance of Italian units in the area south of Crete will seriously interfere with British shipping, and may even lead to the complete interruption of the transport of troops, especially as these transports are at the moment inadequately protected'. The Italian Chief of Naval Staff, Admiral Riccardi, planned a reconnaissance in force to the island of Gavdo south of the western end of Crete, the first initiative of the Italian navy in the war thus far. With Admiral Angelo Iachino, Commander-in-Chief Afloat, in overall command, the force was divided into two groups. With his flag in the new 30-knot battleship *Vittorio Veneto*, mounting nine modern fifteen-inch guns, Iachino commanded the first group composed of the three cruisers *Trieste*, *Trento*, and *Bolzano* and seven destroyers. Within this group Admiral Sansonetti commanded the three cruisers and three destroyers while the remaining ships were under the direct orders of Iachino. Group two was Admiral Cattaneo's force of the cruisers *Zara*, *Fiume*, *Pola*, *Abruzzi* and *Garibaldi* and six attendant destroyers. Six of Iachino's eight cruisers were new 10,000-ton ships mounting eight eight-inch guns and capable of 32-35 knots.

Iachino was ordered to sail on 26 March to carry out an offensive reconnaissance to a point

Swordfish torpedo bombers and ten Albacore torpedo bombers, only five of which were fitted with long range tanks. The Fulmars were new and well-armed fighters, but the Swordfish and Albacores were old, slow biplanes. This fleet was screened by eight destroyers, each mounting from four to eight 4.7-inch guns and capable of 36 knots, whereas the Italian destroyers carried five or six 4.7-inch guns but could do 39 knots. Pridham-Wippell's Aegean cruiser force was composed of the *Orion*, *Ajax*, *Perth* and *Gloucester*, supported by four destroyers. The *Gloucester* was a 9600-ton vessel mounting a dozen six-inch guns, while the other three cruisers ranged between 6900 and 7200 tons and carried eight six-inch guns. All had 32-knot speeds compared to the 35 knots of their Italian counterparts. To add to the speed advantage already enjoyed by the Italians, the *Warspite* passed too near a mud bank as she left the harbor, fouling her condensers and reducing her speed to 20 knots. The battle fleet was thus limited to this relatively low speed. One advantage enjoyed by the British, however, was the fact that the *Formidable*, *Valiant* and *Ajax* were all equipped with the newest radar which had a range of 40–50 miles.

At dawn on the 28th, the British fleet was 150 miles south of the east end of Crete, at which time the *Formidable* turned into the wind and launched a dawn air search. At 0720 a report came in of four cruisers and four destroyers, followed a few minutes later by another report of four cruisers and six destroyers. The two forces were about 100 miles north of Cunningham's position and about twenty miles apart from each other. Hence it appeared that one force must be Pridham-Wippell but that the other must be the Italian cruisers. Then Pridham-Wippell reported Italian cruisers eighteen miles north of his position and heading east. Cunningham increased speed to 22 knots, the maximum then for the *Warspite* and the *Barham*, hoping to reach the scene and engage the enemy in two hours. In fact Pridham-Wippell had reached his assigned position, which was virtually identical with the scheduled rendezvous of Iachino and Cattaneo, and had then been sighted by an Italian reconnaissance plane.

All day on the 27th, Iachino had correctly believed the British battle fleet to be still at Alexandria. At dawn on the 28th, his own squadron was in three separate groups. Forty miles northwest of Pridham-Wippell was the *Vittorio Veneto* and four destroyers, ten miles to port was Sansonetti with three cruisers and three destroyers, while twenty miles to his port was Cattaneo with five cruisers and six destroyers. The *Vittorio Veneto* had catapulted a plane for a dawn air search and at 0643 this plane had reported the position of Pridham-Wippell's ships. Feeling that a convoy might be near, Iachino pressed on at 30 knots and ordered Sansonetti ahead to identify and then retire to the main force. At 0758 Sansonetti sighted Pridham-Wippell and reported him as thirteen miles away 'Evidently bound for Alexandria', but instead of retiring he pursued and shortly after 0800 opened fire with his eight-inch guns. With their superior speed, the Italian cruisers closed the British ships rapidly and concentrated their fire on the *Gloucester*. The British

ships were in line abreast, retiring at full speed since their six-inch guns were outranged, making smoke, and evading the enemy fire by 'snaking the line' or making alternate 30-degree turns. As the range shortened, the *Gloucester* opened fire but the Italians turned away out of range on a parallel course and continued their fire. Pridham-Wippell set his course straight for the main British force a hundred miles to the southeast, trying to draw the Italians with him, unaware that a second Italian force, that of Cattaneo, was also close by. At 0855 Sansonetti was recalled by Iachino who thought that he was already farther east than orders warranted. The Italian cruisers withdrew to the northwest, but Pridham-Wippell had drawn them 50 miles nearer to the British battle-ships and within range of an air strike from the *Formidable*. He then turned and began to shadow the Italians so as not to lose contact.

Cunningham had ordered the *Valiant* and two destroyers forward to support Pridham-Wippell, but when the action ceased they rejoined the main force without making contact with the British cruisers. An air strike had also been prepared by the *Formidable* but Cunningham did not want to launch it and reveal his strength until he was sure of the presence of the Italian battle fleet and close enough to overtake any enemy ship crippled by the strike. His general plan was to launch an air

Top: The Italian heavy cruiser *Zara*, which was sunk at Matapan. **Center:** The Italian heavy cruiser *Pola*, sister ship of the *Zara*. She suffered the same fate. **Above:** The Italian heavy cruiser *Fiume* firing her 8-inch guns. She ended up with her other two sisters at the bottom of the Aegean.

strike to slow or stop the Italians long enough for his battle squadron to get within range and make the kill. Although the engineers had now made the *Warspite* capable of 24 knots, the fleet was still limited to 22 by the old *Barham*. A variety of air reports were coming in but the picture was still confused for Cunningham, since there were three separate Italian forces. At 0905, for example, a report of three Italian battleships was received but Pridham-Wippell was only seven miles from their reported position at the time and would have made a visual sighting, so the report was discounted as 'manifestly incorrect'. This was actually Sansonetti whose three large cruisers had been mis-identified as Cavour class battleships to which they did bear some resemblance.

Italian air reconnaissance reports appeared confused to Iachino who also tended to discount them, assuming that the British fleet was still comfortably at rest in Alexandria harbor and that he was dealing only with a convoy escort. At 0900

he turned east to get north of Pridham-Wippell, after which he intended to order Sansonetti to reverse course and come back on his pursuers, catching them between his three cruisers and the *Vittorio Veneto*. Hard on the heels of Sansonetti, Pridham-Wippell sighted the *Vittorio Veneto* as the first fifteen inch salvo splashed around his ships from a range of twelve miles. Sansonetti had altered course according to plan and with his superior speed would shortly be in range. Once more in a desperate situation, Pridham-Wippell again headed toward Cunningham at full speed, making smoke furiously. Eighty miles away, Cunningham now knew the presence of at least one enemy battleship and launched the air strike from the *Formidable*, although he would have preferred to wait until his ships were closer. At the same time, he requested a strike from the naval air station at Maleme on the west end of Crete. The fire of the *Vittorio Veneto* was concentrated first on the *Orion* and then on the *Gloucester*. From a safe

Left: Fulmar fighters ranged on the flight deck of the carrier *Illustrious* with the battleship *Valiant* carrying out gunnery practice in the background.

Left: The battleship *Barham* was a sister ship of the *Warspite* and another veteran of Jutland which fought at Matapan. She had not undergone the same drastic modernization as her sister ship. **Below:** The aircraft carrier *Formidable* approaching Gibraltar.

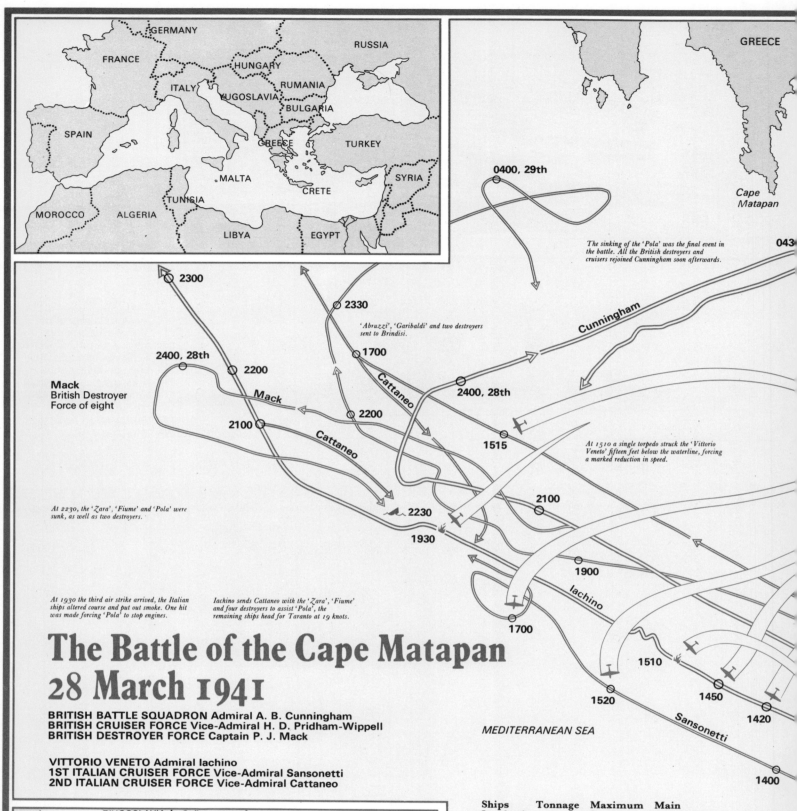

0400, 29th

The sinking of the 'Pola' was the final event in the battle. All the British destroyers and cruisers rejoined Cunningham soon afterwards.

Cunningham

2300

2330

'Abruzzi', 'Garibaldi' and two destroyers sent to Brindisi.

2400, 28th

1700

2200

Mack
British Destroyer
Force of eight

Cattaneo

2200

2100

Cattaneo

0430

Cape Matapan

GREECE

2400, 28th

1515

At 1510 a single torpedo struck the 'Vittorio Veneto' fifteen feet below the waterline, forcing a marked reduction in speed.

2100

At 2230, the 'Zara', 'Fiume' and 'Pola' were sunk, as well as two destroyers.

2230

1930

1900

Iachino

1700

At 1930 the third air strike arrived, the Italian ships altered course and put out smoke. One hit was made forcing 'Pola' to stop engines.

Iachino sends Cattaneo with the 'Zara', 'Fiume' and four destroyers to assist 'Pola', the remaining ships head for Taranto at 19 knots.

1510

1520

1450

1420

Sansonetti

1400

MEDITERRANEAN SEA

The Battle of the Cape Matapan
28 March 1941

BRITISH BATTLE SQUADRON Admiral A. B. Cunningham
BRITISH CRUISER FORCE Vice-Admiral H. D. Pridham-Wippell
BRITISH DESTROYER FORCE Captain P. J. Mack

VITTORIO VENETO Admiral Iachino
1ST ITALIAN CRUISER FORCE Vice-Admiral Sansonetti
2ND ITALIAN CRUISER FORCE Vice-Admiral Cattaneo

Iachino left Taranto on 26 March on an offensive reconnaissance to a point twenty miles south of Gavdhos Island, Crete.

Ships Involved	Tonnage	Maximum Speed	Main Armaments
British			
Ajax	6900	32	8–6", 8–4"
Barham	31000	22	8–15", 12–6", 8–4"
Formidable	23000	30.5	27 planes, 16–4.5"
Gloucester	9600	32	12–6", 8–4"
Orion	6900	32	8–6", 8–4"
Perth	6830	32.5	8–6", 4–4"
Valiant	31000	24	8–15", 20–4.5"
Warspite	31000	24	8–15", 8–6", 8–4"
Italian			
Abruzzi	7874	35	10–6", 8–3.9"
Bolzano	10000	32–35	8–8", 12–3.9"
Fiume	10000	32	8–8", 12–3.9"
Garibaldi	7874	35	10–6", 8–3.9"
Pola	10000	32–35	8–8", 12–3.9"
Trento	10000	32–35	8–8", 12–3.9"
Trieste	10000	32–35	8–8", 12–3.9"
Vittorio V.	35000	30	9–15", 12–6", 12–3.5"
Zara	10000	32	8–8", 12–3.9"

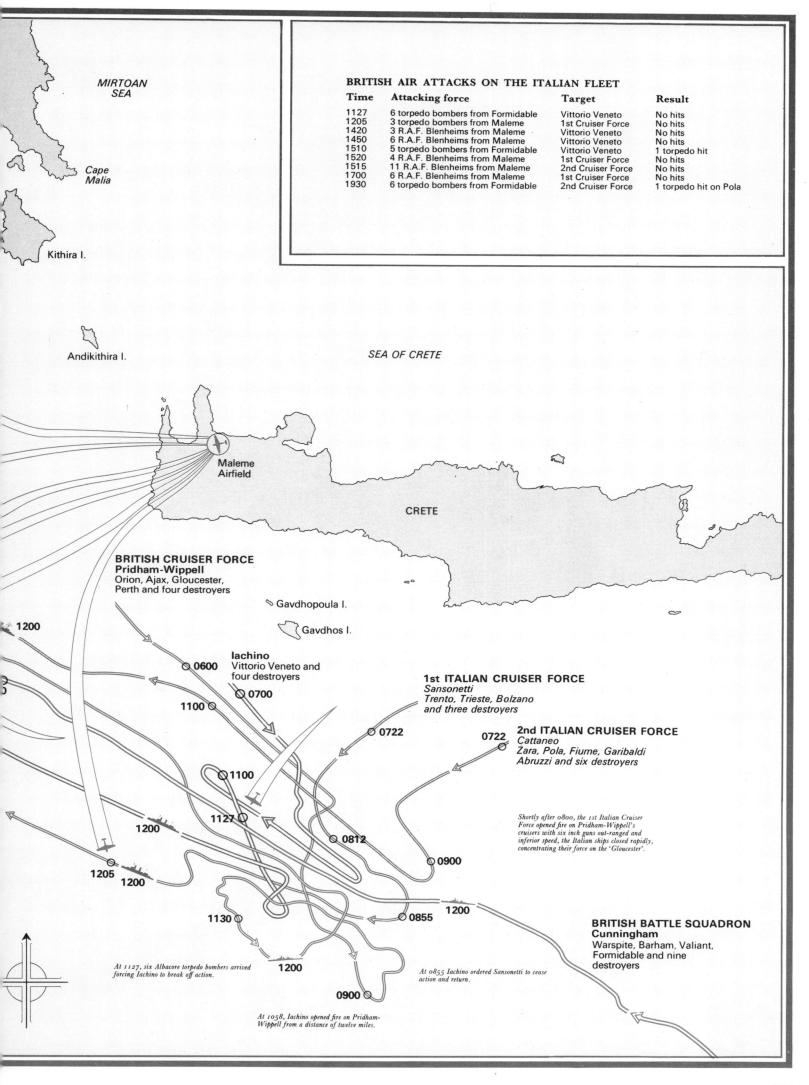

MIRTOAN
SEA

*Cape
Malia*

Kithira I.

Andikithira I.

SEA OF CRETE

Maleme
Airfield

CRETE

BRITISH AIR ATTACKS ON THE ITALIAN FLEET

Time	Attacking force	Target	Result
1127	6 torpedo bombers from Formidable	Vittorio Veneto	No hits
1205	3 torpedo bombers from Maleme	1st Cruiser Force	No hits
1420	3 R.A.F. Blenheims from Maleme	Vittorio Veneto	No hits
1450	6 R.A.F. Blenheims from Maleme	Vittorio Veneto	No hits
1510	5 torpedo bombers from Formidable	Vittorio Veneto	1 torpedo hit
1520	4 R.A.F. Blenheims from Maleme	1st Cruiser Force	No hits
1515	11 R.A.F. Blenheims from Maleme	2nd Cruiser Force	No hits
1700	6 R.A.F. Blenheims from Maleme	1st Cruiser Force	No hits
1930	6 torpedo bombers from Formidable	2nd Cruiser Force	1 torpedo hit on Pola

BRITISH CRUISER FORCE
Pridham-Wippell
Orion, Ajax, Gloucester,
Perth and four destroyers

Gavdhopoula I.

Gavdhos I.

Iachino
Vittorio Veneto and
four destroyers

1st ITALIAN CRUISER FORCE
Sansonetti
Trento, Trieste, Bolzano
and three destroyers

2nd ITALIAN CRUISER FORCE
Cattaneo
Zara, Pola, Fiume, Garibaldi
Abruzzi and six destroyers

*Shortly after 0800, the 1st Italian Cruiser
Force opened fire on Pridham-Wippell's
cruisers with six inch guns out-ranged and
inferior speed, the Italian ships closed rapidly,
concentrating their force on the 'Gloucester'.*

1200

0600

0700

1100

0722

0722

1100

1127

1200

0812

1205

1200

0900

1130

0855

1200

BRITISH BATTLE SQUADRON
Cunningham
Warspite, Barham, Valiant,
Formidable and nine
destroyers

*At 1127, six Albacore torpedo bombers arrived
forcing Iachino to break off action.*

1200

0900

*At 0855 Iachino ordered Sansonetti to cease
action and return.*

*At 1058, Iachino opened fire on Pridham-
Wippell from a distance of twelve miles.*

distance the battleship could have picked off the British cruisers one after the other, but at 1127 the strike force of six Albacores from the *Formidable* arrived. All aimed their torpedoes at the *Vittorio Veneto*, forcing her into evasive maneuvers, after which the entire Italian force broke off the action and headed northwest toward their home base. Although the British pilots thought that they had scored a hit, the *Vittorio Veneto* combed the tracks of the torpedoes successfully. Pridham-Wippell saw neither the air strike which saved him nor the retreat of the enemy. When the smoke cleared, there was only an empty horizon, and the cruiser force joined the main force at 1230. When signaled 'Where is the enemy?', Pridham-Wippell had to reply 'Sorry don't know; haven't seen them for some time'.

Cunningham's united force was now an estimated 45 miles east-southeast of Iachino, but unless the *Vittorio Veneto* had been slowed by a torpedo the lumbering British battleships would never catch the swift Italians. The air strike from Maleme had also missed their target; if the battleships were to get into action, a second strike from the *Formidable* would have to slow up the Italians. A force of three Albacores and two Swordfish with two Fulmars for cover was ready by noon. To launch and recover, however, the *Formidable* had always to turn into the wind, slowing the whole fleet. With two destroyers for a screen, the carrier was detached for independent operations while the remainder of the squadron steamed on at 22 knots. Launching its strike after noon, the *Formidable* rejoined the main force, which now had Pridham-Wippell's four cruisers sixteen miles in front as the van, at 1400.

After being attacked by carrier planes, Iachino had deduced that a carrier, four cruisers and attendant destroyers were at sea but he still believed the enemy battleships to be in port. Using air reconnaissance reports, he also calculated that the British were 170 miles behind him. With his superior speed and better gunned ships, he did not have to worry about a gun battle, but he was concerned about attacks from land-based planes. Several times that afternoon his ships had suffered high altitude bomb attacks by Blenheim bombers but were not hit. Unhappy about his vulnerability to air attack, Iachino later wrote in his account of the battle, 'I felt pretty well deceived by the lack of cooperation. We remained for the rest of the day without fighter cover'. Shortly after 1500 his fears were realized when the

second air strike arrived and scored a single torpedo hit on the key ship in the Italian squadron. Struck fifteen feet below the waterline near the port screw, the *Vittorio Veneto* immediately shipped a large amount of water and stopped engines. 'Enemy has made a large decrease in speed' was the jubilant report received at 1558 by Cunningham, who ordered Pridham-Wippell's cruisers to press on at full speed to make contact. A third air strike was launched at 1735. Six Albacores and two Swordfish were to take advantage of the cover of dusk to try to achieve a surprise attack. The 1830 air report placed the enemy 50 miles in front of Cunningham, making only twelve to fifteen knots. Even at that speed it would take the battleships four hours to get within gun range.

The Crippled *Vittorio Veneto*

Damage control and repair parties had worked hard on the *Vittorio Veneto*, however, and by 1700 she was able to make nineteen knots. Iachino still believed that the British surface forces were too far behind to catch him and that the main threat remained air attack. He therefore detached his two smaller cruisers, the 7800-ton *Abruzzi* and *Garibaldi*, and ordered them to Brindisi with two destroyers. Since his reduced speed had removed one of his biggest advantages and reduced his ability to maneuver, he arranged his fleet in five columns. The middle column was the *Vittorio Veneto* with two destroyers ahead and two astern. Three cruisers were ranged on each side and the flanks were covered by the remaining destroyers. Such a formation made any form of air or surface attack extremely difficult.

Spotted before its attack began at 1930, the third air strike met a furious curtain of anti-aircraft fire as the Italian ships altered course and put out smoke. Only one hit was made, but it forced the cruiser *Pola* to pull out of line with stopped engines. Iachino remained uninformed of this fact for another half-hour and then sent Cattaneo with the *Zara*, *Fiume* and four destroyers back to assist the stricken *Pola*, believing that the situation called for the presence of a flag officer to assess the damage and make decisions. 'It never occurred to me that we were within relatively short distance of the entire British force', he later wrote. 'I thought the British cruisers had decided to turn back leaving only two destroyers to deal with us'. The remainder of the fleet headed for Taranto at nineteen knots, then altered course at 2048 directly for Cape Colonne.

Opposite top: The Fairey Albacore torpedo bomber played a vital role in the preliminary phases of Matapan. **Opposite bottom:** The Fairey Swordfish torpedo bomber, although an antiquated design, had already been a deadly weapon against the Italian Fleet at Taranto. The Swordfish proved her worth again in the air strikes against the *Vittorio Veneto* before the main battle at Matapan.

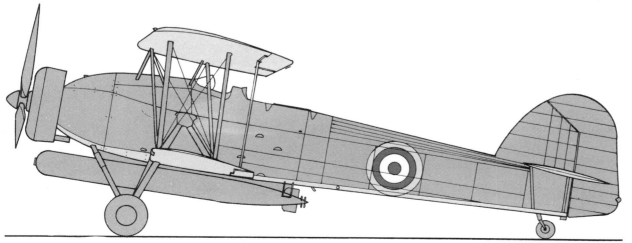

Left: The Fairey Swordfish had a maximum speed of 90 mph, but its virtues were its great maneuverability and its capacity to absorb punishment. Swordfish were frequently able to evade attacks from much faster fighters. Despite the fact that the first Swordfish were built in 1936, they were still being constructed at the end of World War Two.

Right: The Supermarine Walrus amphibian was carried on board British cruisers and battleships for spotting and reconnaissance duties.

Below: British battleships firing their 15-inch guns. The *Valiant*, followed by the *Barham* and *Warspite*, shown here on a gunnery exercise, were all later at Matapan. Their guns could fire a 1900-pound shell a distance of over twenty miles. **Below right:** The first intimation that the Italian cruisers had of the British presence at Matapan was a blaze of searchlights.

Pridham-Wippell's cruisers had pressed ahead and at 1918 they made visual contact with the enemy ten miles away. A few minutes later the force was witness to the third air strike. With the enemy crippled and in striking range, the hazards of a night attack were debated by Cunningham's staff, all of whom tended to be opposed. The essence of the dilemma was whether to risk the battle fleet in a night action with an enemy heavily screened by cruisers and destroyers, thus exposing the British heavy ships to night torpedo attacks, or to wait until morning and risk an attack by land-based German dive bombers. Although Cunningham wrote in his memoirs that he paid 'respectful attention' to the opinions expressed by his staff officers, one of these later said that in fact 'ABC' just looked at them and said 'You're a pack of yellow livered skunks. I'll go and have my supper now and see after supper if my morale isn't higher than yours'. The night orders were, predictably, 'If cruisers gain touch with damaged battleship, second and fourteenth destroyer flotillas will be sent to attack. If she is not then destroyed, battle fleet will follow in'. Four destroyers were left to screen the battleships and carrier while the remaining eight under Captain P. J. Mack went forward to attack the Italians who were now estimated to be but 33 miles ahead. Due to the increase in the speed of the *Vittorio Veneto* at 1700, however, the Italian squadron was actually 57 miles ahead. At the same time Pridham-Wippell's cruisers picked up a large ship dead in the water on their radar. Assuming it to be the *Vittorio Veneto*, Pridham-Wippell reported the position of the crippled *Pola* to Cunningham and gave her a wide berth as he continued his search for the rest of the enemy. Mack did not intercept this message and, unaware of the *Pola* and the easy target she would have made for his destroyers' torpedoes, swung to the north in an attempt to get ahead of the point where he had been told the Italian fleet was, in the hope of cutting it off.

Pridham-Wippell's report of a stopped ship caused Cunningham to think that the *Vittorio Veneto* had been left for the battlefleet to handle. In line ahead with the *Warspite* followed by the *Valiant*, *Formidable* and *Barham*, Cunningham headed straight for the target twenty miles distant. An hour later look-outs reported a large ship six miles ahead off the port bow. Ten minutes later the excited look-outs pointed out more ships crossing the bows of the British line only two miles away. In blissful unawareness Cattaneo's squadron was passing under the guns of three British battleships. 'Never in my life have I experienced a more thrilling moment . . . The enemy was at a range of no more than 3800 yards – point blank' wrote Cunningham, who was a great believer in the gun as a weapon. At 2227 the British destroyers turned their searchlights on the *Fiume* which then received broadsides of fifteen-inch shells from the *Warspite* and *Valiant* at 2900 yards. Five of the six shells in the *Warspite's* first salvo hit at intervals along the *Fiume's* length below her upper deck, while the sixth blew the aft turret completely over the side. 'One saw whole turrets and masses of other heavy debris whirling through the air and splashing into the sea . . . in a short time the ships themselves were nothing but glowing torches . . .' was the way Cunningham described the scene in his memoirs.

When suddenly fired on, Cattaneo's ships were paralyzed with surprise and unable to fight back. The Italians had no radar and could not use their main armament because they had no anti-flash ammunition and no means of gun laying and fire control at night. In any event, their main guns could not be brought into action on the spur of the moment. The attack was so overwhelming and unexpected that the Italian cruisers were completely shattered before resistance could begin. The *Fiume* was burning from stem to stern and listing heavily to starboard. While the *Warspite* continued to blast her with both her main and secondary armaments, the *Valiant* turned its guns on the *Zara* and poured in five broadsides in three minutes. The *Barham* then came up and gave her six more broadsides. Completely ablaze and with Cattaneo dead, the *Zara* was listed to port and heeled over in that direction. The *Fiume* sank at 2315 hours.

The *Formidable* had already hauled out of the battle line and steered north when three Italian destroyers counterattacked the battleships with torpedoes, forcing the latter to take evasive action and lift their fire from the hapless cruisers. Since his own destroyers had already been fired on mistakenly by his larger ships in the dark, Cunningham ordered his four destroyers to finish off the enemy ships with torpedoes, turned his battle line 90 degrees starboard on a northward course,

Left: The battleship *Warspite*, flagship of Admiral Cunningham at Matapan. This ship was a veteran of Jutland, but had been modernized twice and completely altered in appearance. She had eight 15-inch guns in four twin turrets and could steam at 24 knots. She saw the most arduous service of any battleship in World War Two. Built in 1914 *Warspite* served throughout World War Two.

and signaled the remainder of his forces that 'all forces not engaged should retire to the northeast'. At that moment Pridham-Wippell's cruisers were 35 miles east-southeast of Iachino's main force, unaware of the position of the elusive Italian admiral. Interpreting the message to include his force as well, Pridham-Wippell broke off his search and set course northeast as ordered. Mack's destroyers were 30 miles south-southeast of Iachino but continued their search, since for them the order had been qualified with 'after your attack'.

After their torpedo attack the three Italian destroyers were engaged by two British destroyers but with their superior speed, all three made good their escape by 2320, suffering only a few shell hits in the process. The remaining two British destroyers sank the other Italian destroyer. At midnight these two ships – the *Havock* and the *Greyhound* – discovered the abandoned *Zara* and the *Pola*. With no torpedoes left, they opened fire with their guns, then mistook the *Pola* for a battleship in the dark and hurriedly withdrew. A frantic signal concerning the sighting of a battleship 'undamaged and stopped' was received by Cunningham and also intercepted by Mack who was then, at 0030, sixty miles west-northwest of the battle area and 25 miles south of Iachino due to the latter's course change and increase in speed. Mack immediately raced toward the battle area at his full speed of 36 knots. Later the message was corrected from a battleship to a cruiser, but by then Mack had been steaming away from Iachino for almost an hour. Still not certain where the *Vittorio Veneto* really was, Mack decided to continue east and arrived at the battle zone after 0200 on the morning of the 29th. Drawn to the *Zara* by the light of her fires, Mack dispatched the abandoned ship with torpedoes. The *Pola* was then discovered and when illuminated by the searchlights of the British destroyers, was shown to have her guns trained fore and aft and her flag flying. On the upper deck was a thoroughly demoralized group of men which one British officer described as 'longing to surrender' and showing 'definite signs of inebriation'. These were apparently the non-swimmers of the *Pola's* crew, the others having gone over the side long before. After taking off this company, the *Pola* was sunk with torpedoes. The British officers who interrogated these prisoners wrote in their report 'Prisoners when asked why they failed to fire at us replied that they thought if they did we would fire back'. In fact, however, the electric power of the *Pola* was out and with it all her turrets.

The sinking of the *Pola* was the final event in the Battle of Matapan. All the British destroyers rejoined their main force soon afterwards, while Pridham-Wippell's cruisers arrived some hours later. At the time the British fleet was lying some thirty miles off Cape Matapan which gave its name to the battle. A dawn air search was sent out but found no sign of any Italian ships. The destroyers then returned to the battle area and picked up more than 900 survivors but were forced to break off this work as attacks by land-based German planes were expected. Cunningham sent a message to the Italian high command concerning the remainder of the survivors who were picked up two days later by the Italian hospital ship *Gradisca*. Later that day, as it returned to Alexandria, the British fleet was attacked by German Ju-88's, but no damage was sustained.

The Italian navy had lost the *Zara*, *Pola*, *Fiume* and two destroyers as well as Admiral Cattaneo and 2400 men. Unaware of these events when he reached Taranto with the remainder of his force, Iachino only learned of the disaster the next day in Rome when his superior, Admiral Riccardi showed him the British communiqué concerning the action. The stunned admiral blamed the disaster on the Italian and German air commands for not providing him with air cover and air reconnaissance reports, but he had in fact been operating most of the time at the extreme range of the Italian planes based at Rhodes and Scarpanto and to the east of the area normally covered by German planes. When Italy had entered the war, Iachino had felt that local air and sea superiority should have been immediately established by an all-out attack on Malta, which would have confined the British to the eastern Mediterranean. But as the Italian fleet stayed in port, its morale and ability to take the initiative fell drastically. The reinforcement of Cunningham's command and the air raid on Taranto caused the Italians virtually to relinquish any ideas of aggressive naval action until prodded by their German allies. Thus, the first fleet initiative of the Italian Navy was also its last. It did not engage the British again but stayed quietly in port until Italy made an armistice with the Allies in September 1943, after which it sailed to Malta and surrendered.

Although they were pleased to have further reduced the Italians' naval superiority by the elimination of three of the fast heavy cruisers which were such a threat to the older, slower British cruisers, there was considerable disappointment in the British fleet over the escape of the *Vittorio Veneto*. Iachino's ships had been saved by their increase in speed after the torpedoing of the *Vittorio Veneto* and their change of course. The British had simply been too slow to have had much chance of catching the Italians and what chance

there was had been nullified by British mistakes. Cunningham's order, which he himself later termed 'ill considered', for the fleet to withdraw to the northeast had caused Pridham-Wippell to break off his search while the mis-identification of the *Pola* had ended the search of the destroyer force. Yet in the darkness and confusion of Italian and British torpedo attacks, it was imperative for Cunningham to extricate his capital ships, for a hit on any of them would have reduced its speed and left it easy prey for German dive bombers the next day. It had been a cheap victory for Cunningham as it had cost only the Albacore which had torpedoed the *Vittorio Veneto*, shot down with its two-man crew.

Taranto followed by Matapan tipped the strategic situation in the Mediterranean in British favor, but this was all too brief. Preceded by a renewed and again unsuccessful Italian offensive in Albania, the anticipated German invasion of Greece began on 6 April. Operation Lustre, which the Italian Navy had tried to disrupt with such disastrous results for itself, had brought 50,000 British, Australian, and New Zealand troops to Greece. But British military cooperation with the Greeks was a series of muddles and misunderstandings. By the end of April resistance on the Greek mainland had ceased and the survivors of the Greek and Commonwealth forces had withdrawn to Crete which Britain had occupied six months previously. The defense of Crete was bungled as well, so the

Below: The battleship *Valiant* at anchor at Alexandria surrounded by nets to protect her against torpedo attack.

evacuation of that island began on 1 June. The British Navy suffered heavily in these operations: three cruisers and six destroyers were sunk, and two battleships, three cruisers and a carrier were damaged by German air attacks. In fact the navy had to suspend further operations around Crete with the evacuation only half-completed as further losses would have jeopardized its control of the eastern Mediterranean. More serious losses were suffered toward the end of the year when the old *Barham* was sunk by a German submarine and Italian midget submarines audaciously entered Alexandria harbor to put the battleships *Valiant* and *Queen Elizabeth* out of action for many months.

The strategic significance of Matapan is that it removed the potential threat of the superior Italian surface fleet to the British position in the eastern Mediterranean. While the Italians had no intention of using their fleet to dispute British control and did so only under German pressure, the British could not know this fact. For them the threat was real. Matapan secured Operation Lustre and made certain that the Italians would not try to interfere with the evacuation of Greece or Crete. Had the Italians made their sortie with the full support of the Luftwaffe during the evacuations of Greece and Crete, it might have been more than Cunningham's overextended force could have handled at that point. 'There is little doubt that the rough handling given to the enemy on this occasion served us in good stead during the subsequent evacuation of Greece and Crete. Much of these later operations may be said to have been conducted under cover of the Battle of Matapan' wrote Cunningham in his final dispatch. By midsummer Germany was in control of the Balkans. The North Africa campaign between Rommel's Afrika Corps and Wavell's Commonwealth forces then became the main focus of fighting in the Mediterranean until May 1943 when the Allies' Italian campaign began.

Matapan entailed a number of firsts in terms of naval warfare. It was the first time that carrier planes played a main role in a fleet action. For the first time, radar was used in a sea battle. It was also the first main fleet action of the British Navy since Jutland. It was, however, also a 'last' in the sense that it was the last fleet action in the European theater of war. Naval forces tended to play supporting roles in the European theaters, while the Pacific with its vast expanses of ocean and island fortresses was a naval war par excellence. Epic sea battles were to follow Matapan, but they took place in the Pacific. Thus Matapan was the last main fleet action of the Royal Navy.

Midway

1942

Opposite right: General Hideki Tojo, Premier of wartime Japan who made the ultimate decision to go to war against the United States.

Below: The raids of Jimmy Doolittle on Tokyo and other Japanese targets in 1942 came as a welcome tonic to Americans at home, who had heard nothing but bad news for months after Pearl Harbor. B-25s took off from the US carrier *Hornet* to get within range of Japanese cities. The showdown at Midway was yet to come.

The Midway campaign had been planned as the most important part of the second general offensive by the Japanese. On 5 May even before the Battle of the Coral Sea was fully underway, Imperial General Headquarters issued the order: 'Commander-in-Chief Combined Fleet will, in cooperation with the Army, invade and occupy strategic points in the Western Aleutians and Midway Island'. After the blunting of the Japanese southward thrust at the Coral Sea, Yamamoto pressed his view that any actions diverting the Japanese from their main problem – the American fleet – were dangerous. The Japanese admiral was under no illusions about Japan's position if the war was prolonged. The United States was mobilizing for war at full speed and if it was allowed to bring its might into play it would be irresistible. Japan had to strike again and at

once. Over the protests of many of his colleagues, Yamamoto gained acceptance of his view that the next move must be the conquest of Midway Island. The objectives of the Midway campaign were to gain bases in the Aleutians as the northernmost anchors of the proposed 'ribbon defense' and to gain Midway for a similar purpose but especially as a base for raids on the main American Pacific base at Pearl Harbor. The ribbon defense would thus have its anchors north to south at Kiska, Midway, Wake, the Marshalls, the Gilberts, Guadalcanal and Port Moresby. The main goal, however, was to draw out and destroy the remains of the American fleet, especially the carriers that had escaped at Pearl Harbor, before new construction replaced the initial losses. Yamamoto counted on Nimitz accepting that Midway was vital to American defense and send-

ing out his weakened fleet where Yamamoto could destroy it. Success in this battle was central to the entire Japanese strategic concept of the war. Victory would leave Japan master of the Pacific Ocean.

There were other reasons for seizing Midway. Lying only 2500 miles from Tokyo, the island could be used as a base for air raids on Japan. As a result of the raid by B-25 bombers led by Col. James Doolittle in April 1942, the Japanese were very sensitive about this prospect and had assigned hundreds of planes to defend Tokyo. The origin of the raid (actually the carriers *Hornet* and *Enterprise*) had never been discovered and Roosevelt's remark that it had come from Shangri-la had not illuminated the matter. Some Japanese officers suspected that Midway had been the base, and felt the capture of that island would protect the Emperor from the indignity of being bombed again. The island had also become an important base for the refueling of American submarines which were beginning to harass Japanese shipping. Thus Midway appeared to be the most appropriate target from several points of view.

Yamamoto was an undisputed genius, perhaps the only one Japan possessed in the war, with that rare combination of original ideas and the ability to translate them into action. He had, however, never been sanguine about Japan's ability as an island country, totally dependent on overseas supply, to wage war against an industrial giant like the United States. Before the war he had

frankly warned his Premier that 'If I am told to fight regardless of consequences, I shall run wild for the first six months or a year, but I have utterly no confidence for the second and third years'. After Pearl Harbor he wrote to his sister 'Well, war has begun at last. But in spite of all the clamor that is going, we could lose it. I can only do my best'. If he gained the annihilating victory he was seeking at Midway, Yamamoto planned to press on the Premier, General Hideki Tojo, the need for a negotiated peace with the United States, even to the point of proposing terms disadvantageous to Japan. In Yamamoto's eyes, victory at Midway was not only central strategically but essential for the survival of Japan.

However strongly Yamamoto felt about the Midway campaign, other Japanese had grave doubts concerning it for a number of reasons. Due to the speed Yamamoto was demanding, there was insufficient preparation and briefing of officers, and no time to digest the lessons of the action at the Coral Sea and the wisdom of the tactics used there. There was friction between Yamamoto's air wing and the rest of the navy which was beginning to suffer from general morale problems. More responsible officers particularly criticized Yamamoto for the speed which he was demanding as this required their two most powerful carriers to be excluded: the *Shokaku* and *Zuikaku* were still refitting and would have to be left behind. But the Japanese admiral felt that the political situation required immediate action and subordinated all else to this requirement. The Midway expedition sailed from Hashira on 21 May.

Yamamoto's Plan

Yamamoto had prepared a complicated plan for this battle. Division of force was always part of strategy for the Japanese, who liked diversionary tactics to confuse and pull the enemy off balance. The standard Japanese pattern for a decisive battle was to lure the enemy into an unfavorable tactical situation, cut off his retreat, drive in his flanks and then concentrate their own force for the kill. Hannibal at Cannae and Ludendorff at Tannenberg were the examples used in Japanese staff colleges for Yamamoto's strategy at Midway. Specifically, his plan called for a strike on Dutch Harbor in the Aleutians on 3 June to destroy the American base there and to cover an occupation of the Western Aleutians but especially to deceive Nimitz into thinking that the Aleutians were the main objective. In response Nimitz would rush north with his fleet while the Japanese bombed Midway on 4 June and occupied it on the following day. When the American fleet returned from its wild goose chase to the Aleutians not later than 7 June, it would be bombed intensively by Japanese carrier and Midway-based planes, after which any remaining ships would be sunk by the gunfire of Japanese cruisers and battleships. Yamamoto knew that the Americans had no fast battleships and probably only two carriers, as both the *Lexington* and *Yorktown* were believed to have been sunk at the Coral Sea. Fully counting on the element of surprise, Yamamoto expected no challenge from the enemy until after Midway had been secured.

If Nimitz did not fall for the Aleutian gambit, his forces still could not get to Midway before 7 June at the earliest. Even if he did not contest the occupation of Midway, the resulting pressure on Pearl Harbor would quickly force him to counterattack and Yamamoto would be waiting.

To carry out this plan, the Japanese force was divided into five sections. An Advance Force of sixteen submarines was to harass the American fleet as it came toward Midway either from the Aleutians or Pearl Harbor. The Main Striking Force under Admiral Nagumo, consisting of the big carriers *Akagi*, *Kaga*, *Hiryu* and *Soryu* and their screen, was to soften up Midway with air strikes so that the Midway Occupation Force under Admiral Kondo could make its assault. Kondo had 5000 men in twelve transports supported by two battleships, six heavy cruisers and numerous destroyers. Three hundred miles behind these forces was the Main Body under the immediate command of Yamamoto, composed of seven battleships and two light carriers screened by cruisers and destroyers. Yamamoto flew his flag in the awesome *Yamato* which, with its nine eighteen-inch guns, was the most powerful warship in the world. The Northern Area Force under Vice Admiral Hosogaya was built around the light carriers *Ryujo* and *Junyo* with two heavy cruisers, a destroyer screen and four transports carrying troops for the accupation of Adak, Attu and Kiska in the Aleutians. The Japanese Fleet totalled 162 warships and auxiliaries, including

323

Above: A Douglas SBD-3 Dauntless dive bomber warms up aboard the carrier *Yorktown*, which underwent speedy and extensive repairs after Coral Sea. Her appearance at Midway astounded Yamamoto. **Above right:** The airfield at Midway, which made up for the lack of aircraft carriers on the Americans' part. The Japanese had four, the US three; but the US had Midway.

Right: Wildcats aboard the *Enterprise* three weeks before Midway.

four heavy and four light carriers, eleven battleships, 22 cruisers, 65 destroyers and 21 submarines, almost the entire fighting force of the Japanese navy.

Yamamoto was indeed aiming a powerful and lethal blow at the United States. To parry this thrust, the United States had only the carriers *Enterprise*, *Hornet* and *Yorktown*, who had limped up to Pearl Harbor after the Battle of the Coral Sea in such poor condition that the enemy believed she had sunk. Working around the clock, the repair yard at Pearl Harbor made the *Yorktown* operational again in only three days, whereas in normal circumstances such repairs would have required not less than 90. There were no battleships, as the battle line of the Pacific Fleet now rested at the bottom of Pearl

Harbor. A force of old battleships on the American west coast was not included in any defense calculations because of its low speed. In addition to the three carriers there were eight cruisers and fifteen destroyers, more than Yamamoto thought the Americans could assemble at that specific moment.

The object of all this concern was a piece of coral only six miles in diameter lying 1136 miles west-northwest of Pearl Harbor. Since 1938 the United States had spent considerable sums fortifying Midway as an outpost of Pearl Harbor since, as Admiral Nagumo later wrote, 'Midway acts as a sentry for Hawaii'. The island served as base for 54 Marine Corps planes, 32 Navy Catalinas, 23 Air Force planes including seventeen B-17's, and six new Navy Avenger torpedo

324

bombers; an 'unsinkable aircraft carrier' as the Pacific Command thought of it. Midway also had two good search radars and in addition to its planes, the island was heavily defended by well dug in army and marine units.

The man responsible for countering the Japanese thrust was a 57-year-old Texan who was regular navy all the way. Chester W. Nimitz was a graduate of the US Naval Academy and had served in a variety of commands including submarine service in World War I. In 1938 he had been appointed to rear-admiral, followed by promotion to full admiral in 1941. Following the debacle at Pearl Harbor, he had been appointed Commander-in-Chief of the Pacific Fleet to salvage the situation. When he assumed command in the Pacific on 31 December, morale was at rock bottom, but Nimitz's calm demeanor and refusal to bring in new staff rebuilt confidence. Even though he was ordered to be on the 'strategic defensive' with his meager forces, he still was able to organize raids on Japanese bases in the Marshalls, New Guinea and New Britain in the spring of 1942. For over thirty years the American navy had been expecting war with Japan, thinking that when war came they would engage the Japanese Navy in the western Pacific in a series of epic Jutland-style battles. At Pearl Harbor, however, Yamamoto had destroyed the impressive facade of 'battleship row' and demonstrated that the bomb and air-borne torpedo rather than the big gun were the real striking power of the modern fleet while the fighter plane was its primary defense. By sinking its battleships, he had forced the American Navy completely into the age of carrier warfare. But Nimitz and his subordinates were already proving themselves apt students and developing a style of their own.

While Nimitz was the overall commander in the Pacific, the veteran of the Coral Sea, Rear-Admiral Frank Fletcher, was in tactical command of the forces mustered to defend Midway. In temporary command of Task Force 16 – the *Enterprise* and the *Hornet* – was Rear-Admiral Raymond Spruance; Rear-Admiral William Halsey (erroneously nicknamed 'Bull' by a confused journalist) had been hospitalized the month before. Since Fletcher had no air staff and Spruance had Halsey's, the latter exercised a virtually independent command. Neither did Fletcher control the Midway-based forces, the submarines operating in the area, or the force detached to defend the Aleutians.

With both the South and Central Pacific to defend, Nimitz would truly have been faced with a difficult decision as to how to dispose his modest forces had not American intelligence again come to his aid. By 10 May intelligence had confirmed what Nimitz already suspected, that the next objective was Midway. By decoding Japanese fleet messages, intelligence officers had also worked out the principal details of Yamamoto's plan with the approximate schedule and routes. While some of his officers thought that this was all an elaborate Japanese deception to cover a second raid on Pearl Harbor or even on the American West Coast, Nimitz predicted a full attack on Midway with the destruction of the American carriers as a primary goal and with enemy submarines penetrating to within 200 miles of Pearl Harbor. By 17 May Nimitz had decided not to abandon the Western Aleutians

Below: Douglas Dauntless dive bombers attack the Japanese Fleet at Midway. One ship is burning in the center.

to the enemy and formed the North Pacific Force under Rear-Admiral Robert 'Fuzzy' Theobald, comprised of two heavy cruisers, three light cruisers, a destroyer division, a nine destroyer strike group, six S-class submarines and many smaller craft. After concentrating his forces for the defense of Midway, Nimitz gave Fletcher and Spruance their orders: '. . . inflict maximum damage on the enemy by employing strong attrition attacks'. In the naval parlance of the time, that meant heavy air strikes. 'In carrying out the task assigned . . . you will be governed by the principle of calculated risk . . . the avoidance of exposure of your force to attack by superior enemy forces without good prospect of inflicting . . . greater damage on the enemy' added a further letter of instruction.

In the last few days of May, Japanese submarines were taking up stations east of Midway to intercept any American force that might be sent out to relieve the island but Nimitz had already stationed his carriers northeast of Midway beyond the range of the search planes of the approaching Japanese. From 30 May onwards, 22 Navy Catalinas from Midway were flying daily sweeps 700 miles out. A daily search-attack mission by the Midway B-17's to a point where the enemy was expected was also sent out. Nimitz was taking every precaution so that the Japanese could not sneak within plane launching range and achieve a Pearl Harbor type surprise at Midway. By 2 June Fletcher and Spruance were 375 miles northeast of Midway and conducting their own air searches.

Nagumo and the Japanese carrier force left Japanese home waters on 26 May, followed by Yamamoto's Main Body two days later. Nagumo's orders were to 'execute an aerial attack on Midway . . . destroying all enemy air forces stationed there' on 4 June to soften it up for the attack of the Occupation Force the following day. But the Japanese admiral was concerned, as his carriers had had hardly a month for maintenance and refresher training. 'We participated in the battle', he later wrote, 'with meager training and without knowledge of the enemy'. Even Yamamoto was in low spirits and suffering from stomach trouble from tension but morale in the fleet was high. Approaching Midway from the west, Nagumo's ships were covered by the many storms and fogs which occur there in May and June. Often the Japanese could hear American search planes above the clouds on their seemingly endless and fruitless missions.

The Aleutian Diversion
The Aleutian diversion began on 3 June according to schedule. Theobald had not actually reached Kodiak to take command until 27 May while the main body of his force did not finish assembling until after the first attacks on Dutch Harbor. On 28 May intelligence had informed Theobald of the enemy intentions but the admiral feared that this might be a maneuver to get behind him and seize Dutch Harbor in the Eastern Aleutians. He therefore deployed his force 400 miles south of Kodiak instead of trying to break up Hosogaya's force. On 3–4 June the Japanese light carriers easily got past the Ameri-

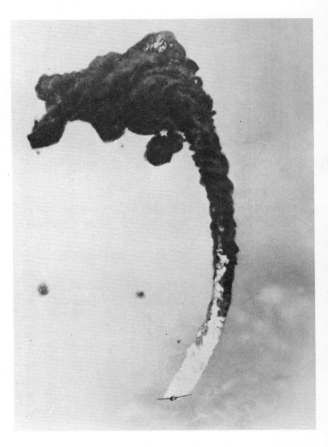

can force and heavily bombed Dutch Harbor unmolested. By the seventh, undefended Attu and Kiska had been occupied, but Army P-40's based on Unmak persuaded Hosogaya that occupying Adak would be too costly.

The third of June was also the day that a Midway-based Catalina first sighted a Japanese force precisely where intelligence had said it should be. This was probably Kondo's Midway Occupation Force. On the basis of the report, nine B-17's were sent out to attack from Midway but made no hits. The attack was subsequently renewed by four Catalinas which succeeded in torpedoing an oiler but without inflicting serious damage. At this time Fletcher's force was 300 miles east-northeast of Midway and 400 miles east of Nagumo. Based on the information then available, Fletcher decided that Nagumo would launch an air strike on Midway the following day, approaching from the northwest. Assuming that his presence was unknown to the enemy and would remain so until the Midway strike had been launched, Fletcher changed course in the evening to arrive at a point 200 miles north of Midway in the morning. From this position he could attack Nagumo the following day when the latter's position was certain. Thus on the night of 3–4 June, the two carrier forces were steaming toward each other on converging courses.

At 0430 on the morning of 4 June a hundred-mile search by ten planes was launched by the *Yorktown* as a routine precaution against the possibility of surprise by undetected enemy carriers. 215 miles to the west, Nagumo was launching his first strike on Midway. Although still sheltered by heavy cloud cover, the Japanese carriers were sighted by planes from Midway. At 0534 the report reached Fletcher, followed at 0545 by a further report of a heavy strike approaching Midway. A third sighting report at 0603 placed two Japanese carriers 200 miles west-southwest of

Fletcher. Although only two carriers had been reported, forty miles from their actual position, Fletcher now knew the approximate location of the enemy. Wishing to recover his search planes and wait for further information, he signaled Spruance to take the *Enterprise* and *Hornet* and 'Proceed southwest and attack enemy carriers when definitely located. I will follow as soon as planes recovered'. Even as this signal was being made, however, 108 Japanese planes were over Midway. At 0553 the radar on Midway had picked up the 36 Vals, 36 Kates and 36 Zekes 93 miles out. All planes capable of intercepting were immediately scrambled while the remainder were flown off to safer climes. The bulk of the interceptors were Marine Corps Buffaloes – old, slow and weak – which were easily swept aside by the efficient new Zekes. In twenty minutes of bombing a fair amount of damage was inflicted on the ground installations, but the runways were still usable. The anti-aircraft fire was good, and by way of compensation for the loss of 17 Buffaloes, about one third of the Japanese bomber force was shot down. Nimitz immediately ordered the Midway-based bombing planes to counterattack, so hard on the heels of the recent attackers were six navy Avengers and four army B-26's armed with torpedoes but with no fighter cover. One Avenger and two B-26's survived their attack which produced no hits.

Since according to Yamamoto's plan, no American forces and especially no carriers should have been in the vicinity of Midway for several more days, Nagumo's dawn air search had been routine and restricted. As a precaution, however, he had held back 93 planes and armed these with bombs and torpedoes in case any enemy surface forces were spotted. The returning planes of the Midway strike then radioed that the island was well defended and needed more softening up. The ten American planes from Midway arrived soon

Above left: Japanese aircraft goes down after being hit by anti-aircraft fire at Midway. **Above:** Heavy flak greets Japanese planes, which were shot down like clay pigeons over Midway. The smoke in the background comes from planes already shot down, as a cruiser moves into position on the left.

after, and emphasized this point with their attack. The Admiral then ordered the 93 planes to be rearmed with incendiary and fragmentation bombs for a second strike on Midway, a task which would take at least an hour, and the decks to be cleared for the recovery of the planes of the first strike. Only fifteen minutes after this order at 0728, Nagumo was amazed to receive a report from a reconnaissance plane catapulted from a Japanese cruiser: 'What appears to be ten enemy surface ships . . .' had been sighted to the northeast where no American ships were supposed to be. This was the first indication he had received of the presence of enemy ships but the report was vague and made no mention of carriers. After mulling the matter over for fifteen more minutes, he asked the reconnaissance plane for more information and ordered his planes to be rearmed once again for operations against ships. He did not wish to repeat Hara's great mistake at the Coral Sea by sending a major strike against a minor target but he was worried that the American actors might not be following Yamamoto's script for the drama. At 0809 the search plane reported five cruisers and five destroyers; at 0820 came the report 'The enemy is accompanied by what appears to be a carrier'. With his fears now realized, Nagumo felt he had been correct to order the second rearming of his planes but they could not take off once the rearming was completed because clear decks were needed for the recovery of the Midway strike planes.

While Nagumo was making these decisions, Yamamoto was becoming rattled as more attacks from shore-based planes were made on his ships. At 0755 sixteen Marine Corps dive bombers appeared, followed at 0810 by fifteen B-17's and at 0820 by eleven Marine Corps Vindicator bombers, but none of these strikes scored a hit of any kind. During this same period, the submarine *Nautilus* appeared, having intercepted the early reports of the Japanese position, and made her way to the scene posthaste. Under heavy depth charge attack from the Japanese destroyer screen, the *Nautilus* was only able to get off one inaccurate torpedo before she had to make her escape from the area. Once the various attacks had ended Nagumo could see that he was in a good situation. His own fleet was intact while over half the aircraft on Midway had been destroyed in the interception and in these ineffectual attacks. One more bombing would leave Midway ready for the assault of the Occupation Force and there was apparently only one American carrier to be dealt with. By this time, however, Spruance had determined his own strategy and American attack groups were already airborne.

Spruance had originally planned to launch a strike at 0900 at a distance of a hundred miles from the enemy, but on hearing of the attack on Midway his Chief of Staff, a brilliant if temperamental captain named Miles Browning, shrewdly deduced that Nagumo would order a second strike on the island and continue on his southeasterly course toward the target. The best opportunity for an American attack was while the Japanese planes were being refueled and rearmed for this second strike. Spraunce agreed with this strategy and began launching every operational plane he

had, except 32 Wildcats which were retained for Combat Air Patrol, in an all-out attack. More than an hour was required for the 67 dive bombers, 29 torpedo bombers and 20 Wildcats to be launched, but before this process was completed Spruance knew he had been sighted by a Japanese reconnaissance plane. Although he realized he had lost any element of surprise, he could not cancel the strike. Browning calculated that Nagumo could not completely recover his Midway strike planes before 0900 and must continue his course toward Midway until that time. Fletcher in the *Yorktown* had retrieved his search mission and was now on the same course as Spruance, but he held back his own attack force of twelve torpedo bombers, seventeen dive bombers and six Wildcats to see if any other carriers were in the vicinity. As no additional sighting reports came in, his planes were in the air at 0906. Like Nagumo, Fletcher had no wish to repeat the mistakes of the Coral Sea and held another deckload of planes in readiness.

The day was cool and clear with a 50-mile visibility at 19,000 feet. The four Japanese carriers were in a box formation in the center of a screen of two battleships, three cruisers and eleven destroyers. Recovery operations had begun at 0837 but Nagumo was understandably apprehensive as every few minutes reconnaissance planes reported the approach of a large force of carrier planes. Even before his recovery was complete, he turned east-northeast and signaled his ships 'We plan to contact and destroy the enemy task force'. Fueling and arming was hastily being done, exactly what Spruance and Browning had hoped for. Fortunately for Nagumo, his change of course caused 35 dive bombers from the *Hornet* to miss making a sighting. The strike had been launched at the limit of their fuel endurance and many of the planes had to continue on to Midway while a few ditched. Fifteen torpedo bombers from the *Hornet* located the Japanese ships by their smoke and attacked at 0925. They had lost their air cover and, pressing their attack in the face of heavy anti-aircraft fire and a flock of Zekes, were all shot down with only one pilot surviving the slaughter. At 0930 the torpedo bombers from the *Enterprise* came in, also without fighter cover. Ten of fourteen were shot down. At 1000 the torpedo bombers from the *Yorktown* arrived, shepherded by six Wildcats which were quickly overwhelmed by the Zeke's. Only five of the twelve torpedo bombers survived this attack, and three of the accompanying Wildcats went down as well. In all, only six of 47 planes returned after these attacks, which had registered no hits on the Japanese.

The massacre of the torpedo bombers had, however, prepared the way for the dive bombers of the *Yorktown* and *Enterprise* which arrived on the scene two minutes later. The violent evasive maneuvers forced on the Japanese carriers by the torpedo attacks had prevented them from launching more defensive fighters while those already airborne were at a low altitude after meeting the torpedo bomber attack and could not climb in time to meet the new threat. Thirty-seven dive bombers from the *Enterprise* had been searching for the Japanese ships and had only learned their position when the fighter group which had become

separated from the torpedo bombers informed Spruance that its planes were low on fuel, reporting the Japanese location as an afterthought. This was the first that Spruance and Browning had heard of their strike and the leader of the dive bombers could hear the latter screaming 'Attack! Attack!' over the radio, to which the leader replied 'Wilco, as soon as I find the bastards'. The dive bombers made their sighting and, diving from 14,000 feet swarmed over the *Akagi* and *Kaga* just as the carriers' evasive action from the last torpedo attack was ending. With 40 planes refueling on deck, the *Akagi* was hit three times within two minutes. One bomb exploded in the hangar detonating stored torpedoes. 'There was a terrific fire aboard ship which was just like hell' said a Japanese officer who survived. Another bomb exploded among the fueling planes on the flight deck. The carrier was burning fiercely and at 1047 an unwilling Nagumo was persuaded to transfer his flag to the light cruiser *Nagara*. By 1915 the situation aboard the burning ship was deemed hopeless and she was abandoned to drift northwards and be sunk by the torpedoes of a Japanese destroyer early the next morning.

The *Kaga* fared no better, taking four hits, one of which killed everyone on the bridge including the captain. The other bombs started fires in the gasoline and bomb storages. Soon the ship was a mass of flames from stem to stern and had to be abandoned. At 1925 the *Kaga* sank after severe internal explosions.

At the same time as the *Akagi* and *Kaga* were meeting their fates, seventeen dive bombers from the *Yorktown* were attacking the *Soryu*. Although they had started almost an hour and a half later than the other attack groups, by smart navigating they had managed to arrive simultaneously with the dive bombers of the *Hornet* and *Enterprise*. Attacking in three waves at one minute intervals,

they planted three 1000-pound bombs on the flight deck of the *Soryu* as she was turning into the wind to launch an attack group. The ship burst into flames and had to be abandoned within twenty minutes. Her captain was last seen standing on the bridge shouting 'Banzai!' By 1145, however, her fires had subsided and damage control parties were at work. By then the submarine *Nautilus* had caught up with the action and put three torpedoes into the *Soryu* which again set her blazing fiercely. At 1610 the gasoline storage exploded, breaking the ship in half and sending her down for good.

After the attacks most of the dive bombers barely made it back to their carriers and a few had to ditch because Spruance's staff had miscalculated Point 'Option', a point which moves in advance of the carrier and is calculated on the basis of course and speed as a guide for returning planes. Spruance was off schedule and his planes arrived at the Point 'Option' which they had been given only to discover that the carriers were 60 miles away. Some planes made it back literally on their last gallon of gasoline. The *Enterprise* had lost fourteen of 37 dive bombers, ten of fourteen torpedo bombers and one Wildcat. The *Yorktown* had lost seven of twelve torpedo bombers, two dive bombers and three Wildcats while the *Hornet* had lost all her torpedo bombers and twelve Wildcats, her dive bombers having failed to locate the enemy and landed on Midway. The returning fighter planes of the *Yorktown* gave Fletcher the first visual evidence that three Japanese carriers had been left burning. Aware now that there was a fourth enemy carrier, Fletcher launched a search mission to find the *Hiryu* which had been missed by the dive bombers.

Although three of his carriers were sinking, Nagumo still had the *Hiryu* untouched and with a full air group. He reasoned that the Americans had one or maybe two carriers which had probably already expended most of their planes. Deciding to continue the battle with the *Hiryu*, Nagumo radioed Yamamoto 'Sighted enemy composed of one carrier, five cruisers and six destroyers at position bearing ten degrees 240 miles from Midway. We are heading for it'. The first attack

group of eighteen Vals and six Zekes was launched at 1100, followed by a second attack group of ten Kates and six Zekes at 1331. The two reconnaissance planes which had located the American ships were ordered to guide the attack groups. Admiral Kondo had intercepted Nagumo's message to Yamamoto and signaled that he was coming north at 28 knots with the battle portion of the Midway Occupation Force to support the Main Striking Force. At the same time, Yamamoto ordered the light carriers *Ryujo* and *Junyo* south from the Aleutians to join the *Hiryu*.

At noon the *Yorktown* was refueling its fighters, with twelve Wildcats airborne as Combat Air Patrol and the last of its dive bombers on the circuit waiting to land, when radar showed between thirty and forty planes coming in only forty miles away. Evasive action began as the Combat Air Patrol went out to intercept. Both the Combat Air Patrol and the anti-aircraft fire of the cruiser and destroyer screen were highly effective. The interceptors knocked down ten Vals while anti-aircraft fire accounted for two more. But the remaining eight dive bombers hit the *Yorktown* three times. The first bomb damaged the boilers, bringing the carrier to a halt twenty minutes later. The second started a fire which was put out by flooding, while the third exploded on the flight deck causing many casualties and starting yet another fire. As the radar and communications had been knocked out, Fletcher transferred his flag to the cruiser *Astoria*. Damage control and repair parties worked quickly, however, and by 1340 the *Yorktown* could manage eighteen knots again. About 1630 the *Yorktown* was beginning to refuel its fighters when the radar of the attendant cruisers picked up the second attack group forty miles out. Low on fuel, the twelve Wildcats on Combat Air Patrol were no match for the fast Zekes and Kates. Coming in low from four different angles, four Kates were able to release their torpedoes at the short range of 500 yards, scoring two hits which ruptured most of the fuel tanks on the port side, jammed the rudder, cut all power and caused a seventeen degree list. Without power the list could not be corrected by counter-flooding. As her watertight integrity had been only half restored by the hasty repairs at Pearl Harbor, her captain was afraid that the *Yorktown* would capsize and gave the order to abandon ship at 1500.

The *Yorktown* continued to float for another 24 hours, having apparently reached equilibrium when her list became 25 degrees. The destroyer *Hughes* was detached to guard the carrier with orders to sink her if enemy surface ships appeared. At dawn the following day the commander of the *Hughes* informed Nimitz that the carrier could probably be saved. A small salvage party from the *Hughes* then boarded the vessel while other auxiliary ships including a fleet tug hurried to the scene. The salvage parties spent the day jettisoning anchors and other loose gear while the minesweeper *Vireo* tried to take the carrier in tow. On 6 June Fletcher sent a proper salvage party of 171 on the destroyer *Hammann* to attempt to get the *Yorktown* back to port. After transferring the salvage party, the *Hammann* lay along side the carrier to provide power for the work. But in the interim the *Yorktown* had been sighted by a Japanese reconnaissance plane which reported her position. Having been ordered by Yamamoto to finish the job, submarine I-68 penetrated the destroyer screen and put two torpedoes into the *Yorktown* and one into the *Hammann* which sank within four minutes. The *Yorktown* finally sank at dawn the following day.

Before the *Yorktown* was attacked Fletcher had sent out a search mission of ten planes to locate the *Hiryu*. After a fruitless three-hour search, one plane on its way home sighted the *Hiryu*, two battleships, three cruisers and four destroyers steering north about 110 miles west by north of the *Yorktown*. At 1530 the *Enterprise* turned into the wind to launch 24 dive bombers, including ten refugees from the *Yorktown*. The mission was without fighter cover since all operational Wildcats were now in a defensive role. At 1700 the attack group swept in on the *Hiryu* and scored four solid hits. One took out all facilities on the 'island' while the others caused uncontrollable fires. Three dive bombers were lost in this attack which was renewed an hour later by B-17's from Midway and Molokai. The land-based planes had their usual bad luck and scored no hits. At 1900 another strike of five Vindicators and six dive bombers – all the operational aircraft left – took off from Midway but failed to locate the target. The *Hiryu* continued to burn until at 0315 the next morning she was abandoned by all hands except the captain. She finally sank at 0900.

Yamamoto on the *Yamato*

During the carrier battle of the fourth of June, Yamamoto and the Main Body had been several hundred miles west of the Main Striking Force. With his flag aboard the *Yamato*, the admiral was receiving reports of the battle 'with the utmost consternation'. Three of his beloved carriers had been lost but the successful attack on the *Yorktown* meant that there was still a chance for victory since if, as Nagumo claimed, there had been only one American carrier, it was now non-operational at the least. With his overwhelming superiority in gun power, he could still annihilate his weaker enemy in a traditional naval engagement. Breaking radio silence at 0020, he ordered the Midway Occupation Force to retire to the northwest; its escort of battleships and cruisers under Kondo joined him the following day at noon along with the Aleutian force which had also been ordered south. It was not long, however, before the returning pilots of the *Hiryu* reported having seen three American carriers, information which was corroborated under duress by a captured American pilot. For the first time, Yamamoto was in possession of an accurate picture of American strength. A few hours later he learned that the *Hiryu* had been rendered non-operational by an American attack. 'The game is up, thought everybody on the *Yamato's* bridge', recalled one witness. Although personally shattered by the collapse of his plans, Yamamoto still hurried toward the remains of Nagumo's force, radioing Nagumo and Kondo that he intended to engage the enemy. Nagumo demurred and was peremptorily relieved in favor of Kondo, who was ordered to prepare for a night engagement. But as further reports revealed that all four Japanese carriers were either sunk or abandoned and that two American carriers were still operational, Yamamoto accepted the fact that he could more likely expect a dawn air attack than a night gun battle with the enemy. Around

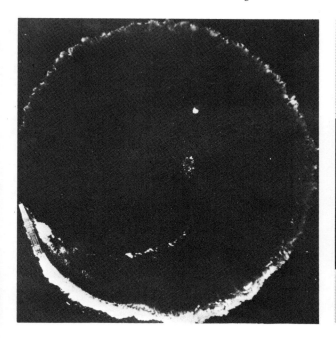

Far left: The Japanese carrier *Kaga* circles under the attack. *Kaga* as well as Yamamoto's other three carriers were all sunk at Midway. **Left:** Vice-Admiral Fletcher after Midway. His errors at the Coral Sea were not repeated at Midway, even though he finally lost *Yorktown*.

Below: Scene aboard the *Yorktown* after she was first hit. A bomb burst on the ship's funnel, which knocked out her boilers. **Right:** Japanese planes batter the *Yorktown*. **Center:** *Yorktown* listing badly just before she went under. **Bottom left:** Members of the crew and airmen of *Yorktown* examine the damage shortly before she sank. **Bottom right:** Survivors of *Yorktown* on a cruiser.

0300 on 5 June he accepted defeat and ordered all of his forces to turn west. Gloom lay like a pall over the retreating ships. 'We are retreating . . . It is utterly discouraging . . . The Marines, who were showing off, have not even courage to drink beer', wrote a Japanese officer in his diary.

At the end of the battle on 4 June, Spruance took stock of his situation. The *Yorktown* had been abandoned, the air groups of his two remaining carriers were decimated and there was no prospect of support from other American forces in sight. There were, however, other large units of the Japanese fleet which had not yet been located and these were known to include carriers. He also suspected that a fifth Japanese carrier might be in the vicinity. 'I did not feel justified in risking a night encounter with possibly superior enemy forces but on the other hand I did not want to be too far away from Midway the following morning. I wished to have a position from which either to follow up retreating enemy forces or to break up a landing attack on Midway', the admiral wrote in his report of the battle. He therefore headed east out of the battle area until midnight. Although Spruance was subsequently heavily criticized for withdrawing and allowing the defeated enemy to escape, he had made the correct decision. When Kondo heard of the first attacks on Nagumo's carriers, he headed north at high speed with two battleships, four heavy cruisers, a light carrier and his destroyer screen. Not far behind was Rear-Admiral Tanaka with ten more destroyers. By midnight this force was 125 miles from Nagumo. Had Spruance continued west he would have collided with this powerful fleet sometime close to 0100. The Japanese ships were well trained for night fighting while the American carriers had no night flying radar equipped planes. Even if Spruance had been able to hold his own against Kondo, Yamamoto and the Main Body were rapidly approaching from the northwest. Such a turn of events undoubtedly would have retrieved the victory for Yamamoto.

For all intents and purposes the Battle of Midway was over after the attack on the *Hiryu*. Before 0100 on 5 June, Yamamoto had cancelled a scheduled bombardment of Midway by four heavy cruisers under Rear-Admiral Kurita. These

Left: Rear-Admiral Raizo Tanaka, who followed Nagumo's carriers with a destroyer squadron. **Right** The last known photograp of the carrier *Hiryu*, taken from a Japanese aircraft.

Right: USS *Hornet*, one of three carriers at Midway. Displacement: 19,800 tons. Length: 809 feet. Beam: 83 feet. Draught: 22 feet. Speed: 32 knots. Aircraft: between 85 (if Devestators or Avengers) to 100 (if Wildcats). Crew: 306 officers and 2613 enlisted men (in wartime). Armament: eight 5-inch, sixteen 1.1-inch and 23 20-mm cannon.

cruisers and two destroyers were retiring 90 miles west of Midway when they were sighted by the submarine *Tambor* which was spotted by the ships at the same time. In making an emergency turn during evasive action, the cruiser *Mogami* collided with the *Mikuma*, smashing her own bow, catching fire and reducing speed to sixteen knots while the *Mikuma* began to leak oil. Kurita continued to withdraw at full speed with his other two cruisers, leaving the two destroyers as a screen for the cripples. Unable to get into a position to fire its torpedoes, the *Tambor* continued to track the enemy ships.

Interpreting the *Tambor*'s contact with Kurita's force as an indication that the enemy might still be considering a landing on Midway, Spruance quickly headed his carriers toward the island to give air support. He then received reports of the two damaged cruisers and later of Kondo's force 200 miles to the northwest. Confused air reports concerning the burning *Hiryu* led to speculation that two Japanese carriers might still be afloat. Spruance decided to ensure that no carriers escaped, and turned northwest about 1100 on 5 June. Two search-attack groups of dive bombers were sent out at 1500 but they found no major target and then failed to sink a nimble Japanese destroyer they chanced upon as they returned home. Later that evening Spruance gave up his efforts to find the carriers or Kondo and turned west to deal with the *Mogami* and *Mikuma*. Early the following morning reconnaissance planes located the cruisers which were soon subjected to attacks by 83 dive bombers and three torpedo bombers. The *Mogami* took five bomb hits,

The Battle of Midway, 4-5 June 1942

Attu

Agattu

Aleutian diversion began on 3 June according to schedule. Theobald had deployed his force 400 miles south of Kodiak. On 3-4 June the Japanese light carriers got past the American force and heavily bombed Dutch Harbor. By the 7th, undefended Attu and Kiska had been occupied.

Kiska

At 1331 on the fourth Yamamoto ordered the light carriers 'Ryujo' and 'Junyo' south from the Aleutians to join the 'Hiryu' since their presence was no longer necessary in the Aleutians.

Amchitka

Tanaga
Kanaga

ALEUTIAN ISLANDS

Unimal

Dutch Harbor

Unmak

NORTHERN AREA FORCE
Hosogaya
Light carriers Ryujo and Junyo, two heavy cruisers, a destroyer screen and four transporters

Adak
Atka
Amlia

Unalaska

MAIN STRIKING FORCE
Nagumo
Carriers Akagi, Kaga, Hiryu and Soryu, with cruiser and destroyer screen

When Kondo heard of the first attacks on Nagumo's carriers, he headed north at high speed with two battleships, four heavy cruisers, a light carrier and his destroyer screen. Not far behind was Tanaka with ten more destroyers.

Although personally shattered by the collapse of his plans, Yamamoto still hurried towards the remains of Nagumo's force, radioing Nagumo and Kondo that he intended to engage the enemy.

But as further reports revealed that all four Japanese carriers were either sunk or abandoned and that two American carriers were still operational, he accepted defeat and ordered all his forces to turn west.

MIDWAY OCCUPATION FORCE
Kondo
Two battleships, six heavy cruisers plus destroyers and twelve transports with 5000 men

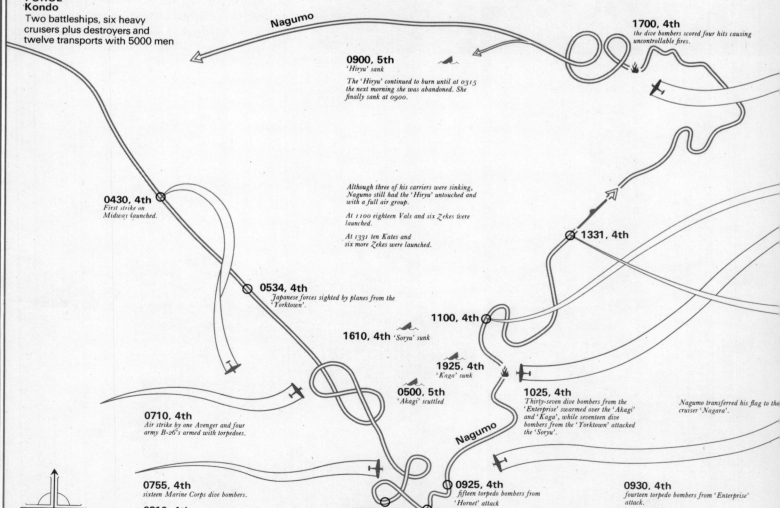

Nagumo

1700, 4th
the dive bombers scored four hits causing uncontrollable fires.

0900, 5th
'Hiryu' sank

The 'Hiryu' continued to burn until at 0315 the next morning she was abandoned. She finally sank at 0900.

Although three of his carriers were sinking, Nagumo still had the 'Hiryu' untouched and with a full air group.

At 1100 eighteen Vals and six Zekes were launched.

At 1331 ten Kates and six more Zekes were launched.

0430, 4th
First strike on Midway launched.

1331, 4th

0534, 4th
Japanese forces sighted by planes from the 'Yorktown'.

1100, 4th

1610, 4th *'Soryu' sunk*

1925, 4th
'Kaga' sunk

0500, 5th
'Akagi' scuttled

1025, 4th
Thirty-seven dive bombers from the 'Enterprise' swarmed over the 'Akagi' and 'Kaga', while seventeen dive bombers from the 'Yorktown' attacked the 'Soryu'.

Nagumo transferred his flag to the cruiser 'Nagara'.

0710, 4th
Air strike by one Avenger and four army B-26's armed with torpedoes.

Nagumo

0755, 4th
sixteen Marine Corps dive bombers.

0810, 4th
fifteen B-17's

0820, 4th
eleven Marine Corps bombers

0837, 4th
Recovering Midway strike Force.

0918, 4th
Nagumo turns east-north-east to intercept the American task force.

0925, 4th
fifteen torpedo bombers from 'Hornet' attack

0930, 4th
fourteen torpedo bombers from 'Enterprise' attack.

1000, 4th
twelve torpedo bombers and six Wildcats from the 'Yorktown' attack.

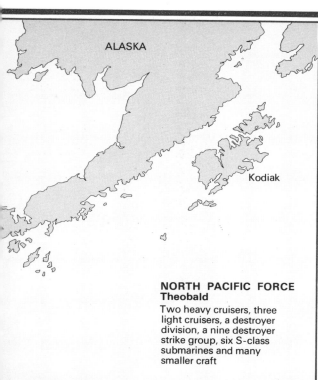

ALASKA

Kodiak

NORTH PACIFIC FORCE
Theobald

Two heavy cruisers, three light cruisers, a destroyer division, a nine destroyer strike group, six S-class submarines and many smaller craft

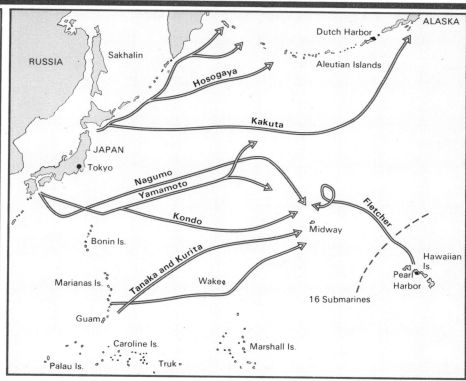

RUSSIA

Sakhalin

Dutch Harbor

ALASKA

Aleutian Islands

Hosogaya

Kakuta

JAPAN

Tokyo

Nagumo

Yamamoto

Kondo

Fletcher

Midway

Bonin Is.

Hawaiian Is.

Pearl Harbor

Marianas Is.

Tanaka and Kurita

Wake

16 Submarines

Guam

Caroline Is.

Marshall Is.

Palau Is.

Truk

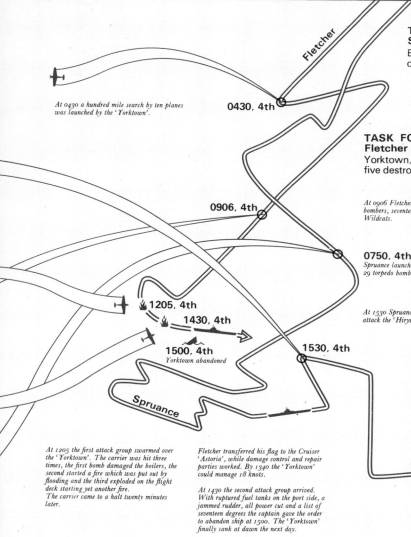

Fletcher

TASK FORCE 16
Spruance

Enterprise, Hornet, six cruisers and nine destroyers

At 0430 a hundred mile search by ten planes was launched by the 'Yorktown'.

0430, 4th

TASK FORCE 17
Fletcher

Yorktown, two cruisers and five destroyers

0906, 4th

At 0906 Fletcher launched twelve torpedo bombers, seventeen dive bombers and six Wildcats.

0750, 4th
Spruance launched 67 dive bombers, 29 torpedo bombers and 20 Wildcats.

After the attacks most of the dive bombers barely made it back to their carriers and a few had to ditch because of a miscalculated Point 'Option'.

The 'Enterprise' had lost fourteen of 37 dive bombers, ten of fourteen torpedo bombers and one Wildcat, while the 'Hornet' had lost all her torpedo bombers and twelve Wildcats, her dive bombers having failed to locate the enemy landed on Midway. The 'Yorktown' had lost seven of twelve torpedo bombers, two dive bombers and three Wildcats.

1205, 4th

1430, 4th

1500, 4th
Yorktown abandoned

At 1530 Spruance launched 24 dive bombers to attack the 'Hiryu'.

1530, 4th

Spruance

At 1205 the first attack group swarmed over the 'Yorktown'. The carrier was hit three times, the first bomb damaged the boilers, the second started a fire which was put out by flooding and the third exploded on the flight deck starting yet another fire.
The carrier came to a halt twenty minutes later.

Fletcher transferred his flag to the Cruiser 'Astoria', while damage control and repair parties worked. By 1340 the 'Yorktown' could manage 18 knots.

At 1430 the second attack group arrived. With ruptured fuel tanks on the port side, a jammed rudder, all power cut and a list of seventeen degrees the captain gave the order to abandon ship at 1500. The 'Yorktown' finally sank at dawn the next day.

Spruance

Spruance heads east out of the battle area until midnight.

For all intents and purposes the Battle of Midway ended after the attack on the 'Hiryu'.

Above: The *Mikuma* just before she sank. She was one of the last Japanese ships to go under, on the night of 6 June.

causing heavy casualties and fires, but survived to get to Truk. A bomb on the *Mikuma* detonated her torpedoes, forcing her crew to abandon ship after the second attack, and she sank during the night. The destroyer screen picked up survivors and then made its own escape. Reassessing his position after these attacks, Spruance decided to turn east as only four destroyers were left to screen his two carriers and six cruisers and all were low on fuel. Also, three days of hard action had exhausted his pilots. His ships were 400 miles west of Midway and could come within range of Japanese bombers on Wake or on a concentration of enemy submarines.

Yamamoto made one last try. Learning that the American carriers were east of the *Mogami* and *Mikuma*, he formed a task force of six heavy cruisers and ten destroyers, and at noon on 6 June ordered this force to attack Spruance and relieve the damaged cruisers. He also hoped that Spruance would get within the 600-mile range of the Wake based bombers and ordered air reinforcements to Wake from the Marshall Islands.

Later that day, he gathered the remainder of his force – the Main Body, Kondo's group, the Aleutian force and the remnants of Nagumo's force – to steam toward the *Mogami* and *Mikuma* and the Americans beyond. He continued in this direction until the morning of 7 June when he turned west to fuel. On the following day he continued a westerly course toward his home bases, having lost any hope of renewed engagement with the Americans. Even so, two heavy cruisers and a destroyer division were left east of Wake to send out heavy radio traffic in a vain attempt to lure the American carriers within bombing range.

The long run of Japanese victories in the war came to an abrupt end at Midway, the first defeat ever suffered by the Japanese navy. Before Midway the *Shoho* at the Coral Sea was the most serious loss suffered by the Japanese but at Midway they lost four heavy carriers, a heavy cruiser, 322 planes and 3500 men against one American carrier, 150 planes and 307 men. It was some time before the Americans even realized how

Yamamoto blamed the debacle on the failure of his advance screen of submarines to harass the Americans, but in fact responsibility rests with him. He had deployed his submarines to attack the Americans where his calculations said they should be rather than where they were. The battle was really lost when Yamamoto first divided his mammoth fleet and then devised a highly complicated plan of attack based on what he assumed the Americans would do. The plan was rigid and so was the Japanese response to a battle which did not follow their script. The Japanese commanders did not display the professionalism and knack of rapid adaptation necessary to cope with this kind of action. Even so, the crucial factor in the battle had to be the prompt and wise use of intelligence reports by the Americans. Without them Nimitz would not have known how to dispose his forces and the Japanese plan might well have succeeded. 'Had we lacked early information of the Japanese movements, and had we been caught with carrier forces dispersed . . . the Battle of Midway would have ended differently' wrote Nimitz. Another element was the leadership of Spruance, made Nimitz' Chief of Staff after the battle, who by destroying the Japanese carrier force left the rest of their fleet vulnerable to air attack and thereby forced it to withdraw. Even more than the Coral Sea, Midway demonstrated the central role of the carrier plane in naval warfare. Despite possession of infinitely superior gun power and a fleet which was largely intact, without air cover Yamamoto had to abandon the fight without firing a shot.

Midway was the debut of the Zeke, or Zero 3. The original Zero fighter was superior to its American adversaries, being more maneuverable and having a rate of climb three times more rapid than any American plane. The Zeke was an improvement on the Zero and by far the best plane on either side in the battle. But however superior the Zeke may have been, the Japanese pilots at Midway proved themselves to be definitely inferior, one more indication of the decline of the Japanese naval air force as the war progressed. The Americans were so disturbed by the non-performance of their torpedo bomber, the misnamed Devastator, that it was taken off the list of naval combat planes and replaced by the as yet untried Avenger. The Dauntless dive bomber, on the other hand, had more than proved its worth and was to become the most successful American carrier plane of the war.

The Battle of Midway had been a near miss but the meaning of their defeat was clear to the Japanese. They had lost the ability to strike when and where they chose and thus to govern the course of the war. The Japanese side of the war would now become a holding operation as the Allies seized the offensive. Forced into an unaccustomed defensive role, the conquest of Port Moresby, Fiji, New Caledonia and Samoa had to be abandoned by the Japanese. Imperial General Headquarters reverted to its original plan to consolidate its gains, leaving the initiative to the enemy. As Yamamoto had predicted, this meant Japan would be overwhelmed by the United States as soon as American economic mobilization was complete.

complete their victory had been, for they thought that two Japanese carriers had survived and returned to Japan. Defeated by a much inferior American force, the Japanese Navy emerged from Midway with great loss of prestige and with its air striking power badly crippled. News of the defeat was completely suppressed in Japan. 'Our forces suffered a reverse so decisive and so grave that details of it were kept as a secret from all but a limited circle, even within the Japanese Navy. Even after the war, few among high ranking officers were familiar with the details of the Midway operation' said a Japanese admiral after the war. Returning sailors were held incommunicado while the wounded were brought ashore at night. 'It was like being a prisoner of war among your own people' said one. At Japan's capitulation in 1945, all papers concerning the disaster, hitherto classified as top secret, were destroyed. The Japanese public only learned of the events that took place at Midway when survivors began to publish accounts in the 1950's.

El Alamein 1942

Opposite: General, later Field Marshal, Erwin Rommel, the Desert Fox of the *Afrika Korps* whose tactical skill made up for the inadequacy of men and matériel at his disposal.

The German blitzkrieg of 1939–40 which opened the Second World War was a complete success. Poland, Denmark, Norway, the Low Countries and France had quickly fallen to Hitler's Wehrmacht. Although total victory was not yet achieved thanks to 'the few' of the RAF who saved Britain from invasion, it looked all but over in Europe toward the end of 1940. Yet on the desert coast of North Africa the war of movement continued. Italy, already in possession of Libya, and backed by Nazi-influenced Vichy French North Africa, had only to plunge into British-held Egypt to take the Suez Canal and cut off Britain's lifeline of Empire and communication with India and the Far East. But the fortunes of war proved more than usually fickle in the Western Desert between 1940 and 1942. An Italian advance into Egypt in September 1940 was hurled back at Sidi Barrani in December, but German intervention in early 1941 brought about a rapid reversal of the situation. Lieutenant-General Erwin Rommel, an infantryman with a rare feel for the use of armor, struck back hard, driving the overextended British toward the Egyptian frontier. The ensuing lull saw both armies reinforced. The British Eighth Army was split into two corps, 8 and 30, with the latter containing most of the available armor. General Sir Claude Auchinleck was sent to take command of British forces in the Middle East, while General Sir Alan Cunningham took over the Eighth Army. Air Vice-Marshal Arthur Coningham commanded Air Headquarters Western Desert, soon to become the Desert Air Force, which provided Eighth Army with air support.

Rommel's command had also been expanded. It now contained three German divisions, *15th* and *21st Panzer*, and *90th Light*. The Italians fielded one good armored division, *Ariete*, a motorized division, *Trieste*, and four infantry divisions of less certain quality. Rommel had been promoted to general, and was in overall command

of the entire Axis force, now known as *Panzergruppe Afrika*. The German element, the *Deutsche Afrika Korps*, was commanded by General Crüwell.

Rommel feared that the continued British build-up would eventually crush *Panzergruppe Afrika* by sheer weight of numbers. He therefore sought permission to attack before British preparations were complete. Rommel's stroke was, however, pre-empted by a British offensive, 'Operation Crusader', which was launched on 18 November. After a bitter see-saw struggle, during which Auchinleck replaced the exhausted Cunningham with Lieutenant-General N.M. Ritchie, Rommel fell back westward, and mid-January 1942 saw him at Mersa Brega near El Agheila. Rommel, typically, refused to remain on the defensive, and on 21 January he jabbed forward once more. Benghazi fell on 29 January and Ritchie disengaged, falling back to a strong position just west of Tobruk, running from Gazala on the coast to Bir Hacheim in the desert.

Ritchie's withdrawal was followed by a four-month lull during which the Eighth Army was again reorganized, largely in an effort to produce better cooperation between infantry and armor. The new American Grant tank began to arrive; mounting a 75mm gun, it was a much more effective weapon than either the Stuart light tank or the Crusader medium tank, which it replaced.

The Panzer Mark III

The mainstay of Rommel's Panzer divisions was the Panzer Mark III mounting the short 50mm gun. The armor on many of these had been reinforced, and they were particularly resistant to the British two-pounder antitank round. The *Afrika Korps* was also receiving a trickle of Mark III specials with the long 50mm gun and a few Mark IVs with a 75mm gun. Italian tanks, mainly the Mark 13/30 and the improved Mark 14/41, were considerably inferior to the Germans'.

The adversaries were far from evenly matched in terms of antitank weapons. The British two-pounder was unable to cope with face-hardened armor, and its replacement, the six-pounder, though more effective, was soon to be outclassed by German tank development. Moreover, only 112 six-pounders were available to the Eighth Army in mid-1942. Although German antitank guns, properly speaking, were no more satisfactory than their British equivalents, the Germans possessed an important asset; the 88mm anti-aircraft gun used in the antitank role. Although the 88 had some tactical disadvantages,

Below: British 25-pounder gun, used during the Desert campaign. Weight: three tons, five cwt. Length: 19 feet 3 inches. Range: 13,400 yards. Crew: six.

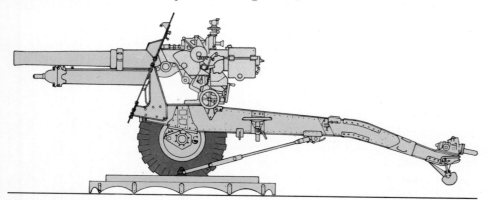

it had an extremely flat trajectory and a high degree of penetrating power. Properly deployed, a few 88s could hold off large numbers of tanks; Rommel habitually employed a screen of 88s to cover his own armor when threatened by attack.

Churchill's Visit

The Gazala battles in late May and early June exemplified the strengths and weaknesses of the contending armies. Rommel launched an attack which was bold to the point of rashness, but his adversaries, although fighting doggedly, reacted slowly. The eventual British counterattack met with a bloody repulse, and by 12 June Ritchie had decided to disengage. Tobruk, isolated and ill-prepared, fell on 22 June, and the Eighth Army continued its headlong retreat. Ritchie was relieved of his command by Auchinleck, who flew forward from Cairo to take over personally. His intervention failed to stem the tide; the Mersa Matruh position collapsed, and the British stumbled back to El Alamein, where work was in progress on a new defensive line.

El Alamein was a small station on the railway between Alexandria and Mersa Matruh. It was, in itself, a place of no importance. What gave El Alamein its great strategic significance was that forty miles to the south began the Qattara Depression, a huge salt marsh with a sharp escarpment running along its northern edge. The escarpment ended near Siwa, but south of Siwa stretched the Great Sand Sea, running south and east toward the Oasis of Kuffa. The potential of the Alamein position had been visible to British commanders for some time. One of Auchinleck's first acts had been to order the construction of defenses in the area, but these, planned on the now discredited 'box' concept, were far from perfect. They could only guarantee the security of the ground which they held physically or could cover with their fire, and several avenues of approach were left unguarded. In any event, the viability of the planned position was never put to the test, since two of the projected 'boxes' were overrun before they could be garrisoned.

On 2 July Rommel launched what he hoped

would be his final attack on the Eighth Army. Auchinleck fought the battle with commendable skill. *Ariete* was roughly handled by the New Zealanders on 3 July, and Auchinleck counterattacked two days later. Although Rommel was crucially short of armor, he managed to contain the counterstroke, but the battle ended with the British in firm possession of the vital ground of Ruweisat Ridge and Tel el Eisa.

Rommel had, for the time at least, been thwarted before Alamein, but Axis fortunes seemed in the ascendent in all other theaters of war. On 28 June Field Marshal von Bock opened his offensive in southern Russia. The initially modest strategic aim of this offensive had become inflated into a drive for the oilfields of the Caucasus. Bock's attack was to be exploited by a thrust through Rostov to the oilfield at Maikop and on to Baku on the Caspian Sea. Rommel, ironically, was only 550 miles from Haifa and its oil pipelines, while Bock was nearly a thousand from Baku. It is a measure of the low strategic priority given to the Western Desert by the German High Command that Rommel remained desperately ill-equipped. Men and *matériel* which would have brought about German victory in the desert could be squandered in a day's fighting in Russia.

Rommel Attacks

News of the defeat at Gazala and the fall of Tobruk was badly received in England. Churchill himself was particularly irritated by the latter, and decided to visit Cairo on his way out to meet Stalin at Tehran. Auchinleck, meanwhile, was planning to mount a powerful offensive in September, but suspected that Rommel would attack before then, probably against the Eighth Army's left rear. Rommel himself was ill and tired. He was pitifully short of tanks and fuel; his attack could not be launched until mid-August. Its direction was that anticipated by Auchinleck; it was to swing around the British southern flank, but in doing so would be met by the full force of Auchinleck's defensive preparations.

Churchill was preceded to Cairo by the Chief of

the Imperial General Staff, General Sir Alan Brooke. Brooke had hoped to do the groundwork for the inevitable command reshuffle before Churchill arrived, but, in the event, the two men landed in Cairo within a few hours of each other. Churchill came with certain preconceived ideas. Firstly, the forthcoming Anglo-American invasion of North Africa—'Operation Torch'—loomed large in his mind; he was eager that Rommel should be defeated in August or early September in order to have 'a decisive effect upon the attitude of the French in North Africa when ''Torch'' begins'. Secondly, he was opposed to any reinforcement of Persia and Iraq by troops from Egypt. The War Cabinet had been seriously worried by the possibility that the Germans would break through in the Caucasus and strike for the oil of the Middle East. By early August, however, it was apparent that the Russians would fight hard on the Caucasus front; the danger of a German thrust into Persia and Iraq was thus diminished.

The next few days saw a crucial sequence of decisions. Churchill and Brooke eventually agreed that Lieutenant-General W.H.E. Gott should take over the Eighth Army, while General Sir Harold Alexander was appointed to the newly-created Near East Command. This project, the result of much hard bargaining, rapidly became obsolete. Gott, flying back to Cairo from the desert on 7 August, was killed when his aircraft was attacked by German fighters. Brooke persuaded Churchill to replace him with Lieutenant-General B.L. Montgomery—Brooke's choice for the post in the first place. Auchinleck declined the proferred Middle East Command, which went instead to General Maitland Wilson. Auchinleck thus disappeared from the scene. He had, perhaps, been unfairly blamed for the Eighth Army's failures. Even his adversary Rommel pointed out that he was 'a very good leader', and paid tribute to his 'deliberation and noteworthy courage'.

Churchill left Cairo on 7 August. Before departing, he gave Alexander his overall directive for the campaign, stressing that 'your prime and main duty will be to take or destroy at the earliest opportunity the German-Italian Army commanded by Field-Marshal Rommel...' This, he added, 'must be considered paramount in His Majesty's interests'.

When Montgomery arrived in Egypt on 12 August, Auchinleck had not yet formally handed

Above left: Lt-Gen. (later Field Marshal) Bernard Montgomery addresses his troops after he took command of the Eighth Army.
Above: Italian prisoners taken at El Alamein eat rations of bully-beef after their arrival in POW camp.

Left: Soldiers of the *Afrika Korps* trudge forward during the first battle of El Alamein.

over to Alexander. However, when Montgomery drove forward to the Eighth Army's headquarters on the morning of 13 August, he was so unimpressed by the gloomy air of the place that he decided, despite orders to the contrary, to take command immediately. Having done this, he canceled all orders for withdrawal, and announced to the assembled staff his firm intention of staying put in the Alamein position. Retreat was out of the question. Although an immediate attack by Rommel might be difficult to repulse, he felt confident that this would not be the case in a week's time. Finally, he announced the appointment of Brigadier F.W. de Guingand as his Chief-of-Staff, and emphasized that de Guingand was to have full authority over his headquarters and staff.

It seemed probable to Montgomery that Rommel would launch an attack fairly soon. From Rommel's disposition, and particularly from strenuous mining activities in the north, it was likely that he would try to repeat his former success with a 'right hook' around the southern end of the British position. Full moon was on 26 August, and this seemed the most likely time for an attack. Plans were already in existence to meet such a threat; it is, indeed, a moot point as to how far Montgomery was able to profit by his predecessor's planning in this respect. What is certain is that Montgomery at once took steps to instill into commanders at all levels the belief that there would be no retreat. He disputed the

Far left: Australian artillerymen in action in the autumn of 1942. **Right:** 'Monty' with his famous hat covered with badges of the units which served under him in a photograph taken at the time of Alamein. **Below:** A German Mark III tank which was put out of action near Tel-el-Eissa Station in August 1942.

system of defensive 'boxes', and made forceful representations to General Headquarters, demanding that recently-arrived troops be sent forward sooner than the staff at Cairo had intended. These efforts produced the 44th (Home Counties) Division, most of which was sent to Alam Halfa Ridge. Further reinforcements also arrived, and with them came Lieutenant-General B.G. Horrocks to take command of 13 Corps.

By 26 August, the anticipated date of the attack, the Eighth Army was in a position to resist the expected onslaught. In the north, the 9th Australian and 1st South African Divisions held the El Alamein area. The 5th Indian division was strongly posted on Ruweisat Ridge with the 2nd New Zealand Division to its south, on Bare Ridge. To thwart a turning movement by Rommel, the 44th Division held Alam Halfa Ridge, with two armored brigades to its west and one to its south. Montgomery intended 'to stand firm in the Alamein position, hold the Ruweisat and Alam Halfa Ridges securely, and let him (Rommel) beat up against them'. The armor was not to rush forward to take on Rommel's tanks; it was to fight from hull-down positions at the western end of Alam Halfa Ridge. A substantial deception plan was also undertaken, with the hope of persuading Rommel that the southern flank was stronger than it in fact was.

Rommel was hampered by more than his worsening health. Although a grateful Führer had promoted him to the rank of Field-Marshal after the fall of Tobruk, he continued to be beset by contradictory orders emanating from a tangled chain of command; he was subordinate both to the Italian *Commando Supremo* and to Field-Marshal von Kesselring, German Commander of the Mediterranean theater. The problem of supply became more serious. British naval and air forces took a heavy toll of Axis convoys. General Bayerlein, the *Afrika Korps'* Chief-of-Staff, maintained that by mid-1942 only one-fifth of Rommel's supply requirements were arriving in North Africa. Even when *matériel* had been landed, it remained vulnerable. Most of the supplies came ashore at Benghazi and had to be moved eastward by truck under the watchful eyes of the Desert Air Force.

The whole question of supply was partially a consequence of a clash of operational priorities. The situation could have been improved by diverting all available air power to strike at Malta, the base from which many of the attacks on Axis shipping originated. This, however, would denude *Panzerarmee Afrika* of its air cover. In fact, both the *Commando Supremo* and Kesselring had favored calling a halt after the fall of Tobruk, in order to deal with Malta. Rommel, however, was backed by Hitler who authorized his drive to the Nile. It may, therefore, be argued that Rommel's advance from Tobruk was a strategic error, and that he himself was primarily to blame for the shortage of supplies which so imperiled his position in mid-1942.

Rommel launched his attack on the night of 30/31 August. The Desert Air Force hammered his troops as they advanced, and on 1 September the main armored attack broke against the Alam Halfa Ridge. Rommel called off the offensive on 3 September, though fighting went on for some days afterwards. The battle had cost Rommel 50 tanks; the British had lost slightly more, but, remaining in possession of the battlefield, were able to salvage some of these. The Battle of Alam Halfa—sometimes known as the first Battle of Alamein—was a sharp rebuff for Rommel, and it gave a useful fillip to the morale of the Eighth Army.

Montgomery began preparations for his offensive as soon as the Battle of Alam Halfa was over. Churchill continued to demand that it should be launched in September, but Montgomery and Alexander agreed that this was impossible, and 23 October was eventually selected as the target date. Montgomery emphasized three fundamental points during this pre-battle phase; leadership, equipment and training. Furthermore, steps had to be taken to ensure the continued security of the line. This was aided by extending the minefields to the south of the position. The other essentials were less easily tackled. The questions of training and leadership were closely interrelated. Montgomery's new mobile formation, 10 Corps, was commanded by Lieutenant-General Herbert Lumsden, formely of 1st Armored Division. He was not Montgomery's choice for the post, and was in open disagreement with his army commander over the plan for the forthcoming battle. Early in September, 10 Corps began to organize and train. It comprised three armored divisions; 1st, 8th and 10th, and was the Eighth Army's most powerful striking force.

Horrocks' 13 Corps

Lieutenant-General Horrocks' 13 Corps contained 7th Armored Division, newly reorganized and commanded by Major General John Harding, and two infantry divisions, 44th and 50th. Two Free French Brigade groups operated under command of the 7th. A major problem in both 10 and 13 Corps was the provision of adequate motorized infantry for the armored divisions. This eventually resulted in the 8th Armored Division being broken up; one of its brigades went to 10th Armored, the divisional troops formed the composite 'Hammerforce' in 10 Corps reserve, and the divisional headquarters were used for radio deception purposes. This complex reorganization required nearly a month, and 10 Corps was not fully concentrated until the end of September.

Lieutenant-General Sir Oliver Leese's 30 Corps, although a somewhat multinational force, found reorganization easier. It included the newly-arrived 51st Highland and 4th Indian Divisions; the latter relieved 5th Indian in early September. The corps was completed by Major-General

Freyberg's 2nd New Zealand Division which contained one armored and two infantry brigades, as well as the 1st South African and 9th Australian Divisions.

This extensive reorganization would in itself have proved difficult enough. It was complicated by the arrival of large quantities of new equipment, so that many units were forced to simultaneously reorganize, re-equip and retrain. The Eighth Army's tank strength rose, by the beginning of the battle, to 1029. Of these, 252 were new Shermans, mounting 75mm guns, more than a match for any of Rommel's tanks, even his few Mark IV specials. There were also 78 Crusader Mark IIIs, mounting six-pounder guns instead of models. Unfortunately, neither tank was immune from mechanical failure; the Crusaders proved the inadequate two-pounders carried by previous somewhat unreliable, and there were teething troubles with the Shermans.

Self-propelled artillery had also arrived, giving the armored divisions mobile fire support. Two types of guns were in use, the British 'Bishop', a 25-pounder mounted on the chassis of a Valentine tank, and the more reliable American 'Priest', with a 105-mm gun on a Grant chassis. Neither weapon had, however, arrived in sufficient quantity to replace the towed 25-pounder as the mainstay of British field artillery. Of the 1403 anti-tank

Above: Axis troops move forward in the desert sands.

Below: German soldiers laden with their field kits move up to the Alamein front.

guns available, 849 were six-pounders, a few of which, known as 'Deacons', were mounted on an armored chassis. Each infantry battalion now had eight two-pounders, while motor battalions each had sixteen six-pounders. Almost all the antitank regiments were equipped with the latter weapon.

The Desert Air Force, organized in two fighter groups and two light bomber wings, used the pre-battle period to rest and retrain, but kept up operations against Rommel's lines of communication. By 23 October Coningham had 750 aircraft available, of which 530 were serviceable.

Montgomery had considerable numerical superiority in all respects, though by no means the three-to-one ratio believed necessary for a set-piece attack. Rommel had only 104,000 infantry, just over half of them Italian, to Montgomery's 195,000. He was even more heavily outmatched in armor, with 489 tanks, of which 211 were German, mainly Mark IIIs. Only 30 Mark IV specials were available. In the air, too, Rommel was at a disadvantage; he had 675 aircraft in all, of which 350 were serviceable for the battle.

Rommel had decided, following his reverse at Alam Halfa, to dig in where he stood rather than to fall back to a position where the ground was better and supply easier. His engineers set to work creating a formidable series of defense works. The entire front of the Axis position was covered by minefields, or, as the Germans called them, 'Devil's Gardens'. These were not merely uniform expanses of mine-sown desert. They comprised several belts of mines running parallel to the front, with transverse sections to limit exploitation. Irregular strips on both sides of the main field strengthened weak points or shepherded attackers onto concealed positions. The mines were covered by fire from 'battle outposts' in the minefields themselves. Although in terms of sheer size the Axis position at Alamein was less impressive than the Russian defenses at Kursk, the planning of the minefields was certainly cunning in the extreme. Care was taken with concealment—although this was difficult in the desert, where the wind often blew away the sand that covered the mines—and with the use of booby-traps and similar devices.

Behind the minefields and 'battle outposts' ran a line of positions designed around dug-in tanks and anti-tank guns. These positions followed the minefields from Sidi Abd El Rahman on the coast to Qarat El Himeimat in the desert. Rommel himself had been ordered home to rest, but, before handing over command to General Stumme, he deployed *Panzerarmee Afrika* behind its increasingly strong defenses. The *15th Panzer Division* was in the north, south of Sidi Abd El Rahman, and *21st Panzer* was in the south northwest of Gebel Kalakh. As part of his policy of interleaving Italian and German formations, Rommel split up the Italian *XX Corps*, sending the *Littorio Division* to join *15th Panzer*, while the battered *Ariete* joined *21st Panzer*. *Trieste* and *90th Light Divisions* were in reserve in the north.

General Navarrini's *XXI Corps* held the forward positions in the northern sector, opposite the British 30 Corps. In the extreme north were two battalions of General Ramcke's parachute brigade, with some Bersaglieri. The Kidney Ridge area was the responsibility of *164th Division*. The *Trento Division* held Miteiriya Ridge, and the *Bologna Division* covered the western end of Ruweisat Ridge; both these formations were stiffened with German parachutists.

General Orsi's *X Corps* held the front south of Ruweisat Ridge. The *Brescia Division* was in the area of Bab El Qattara, with the *Folgore Parachute Division* to its southeast. The *Pavia Division* held the Axis right, toward Qarat El Himeimat, and curled round onto the Taqa Plateau. The flank was screened by German reconnaissance units.

The defensive concepts which underlay the planning of the Axis position had much in common with those prevailing on the Western Front in 1917–18. The essence of both was depth; Rommel anticipated that the minefields and 'battle outposts' would absorb much of the initial impetus of the attack, just as wire and machine guns had done 25 years previously. Should the

British armor attempt to move through its own infantry, it would collide with the antitank guns in the defensive positions, while its infantry and artillery support remained stuck in the minefield.

Rommel left Africa on 23 September, handing over to Stumme who had arrived less than a week previously. Stumme was handicapped not only by his inexperience of desert war, but also by the fact that several of his senior staff officers were sick. Furthermore, all but two of his German divisions had had changes of command over the previous weeks, and the *Africa Korps* itself was now in the hands of General Ritter von Thoma.

Montgomery briefed his divisional commanders and their chiefs of staff for 'Operation Lightfoot' on 15 September. His intention was to attack both flanks of the Axis position. The main weight would fall in the north, where 30 Corps was to force a gap to permit the armor of 10 Corps to move through and into the enemy rear. To the south, 13 Corps was to attack with the intention of distracting forces which might otherwise be employed against the northern attack. The assault was to go in under cover of darkness; the mine-fields would be breached and lanes cleared to enable the armor to move up at dawn. Once through the minefield, 10 Corps was to swing across the Axis supply routes and await the enemy reaction. Moonlight was essential for the first phase; this was largely responsible for the timing of the attack for 23 October, the night before the full moon.

Much thought was devoted to the important problem of mine-clearing. Some 'Scorpion' flail tanks were available, but these were distrusted and were not widely used. An electronic mine-detector had been recently developed, but only 500 were in the hands of the Eighth Army; many mines would have to be discovered by the more primitive method of prodding with a bayonet. A drill for minefield clearance was devised, and a school was set up at Burg El Arab to teach it. The expected rate of progress was 200 yards per hour using the mine detector, and considerably more if prodding was employed. The 24-foot gaps, once cleared, were to be marked by lights and wire to enable tanks and other vehicles to move safely through.

Above: German and Italian prisoners taken on the afternoon of 23 October.

Below: Italian infantry on the attack in October 1942.

Both 13 and 30 Corps were hampered in their training by the fact that they also had to hold the line. Although 10 Corps had no such responsibility, it was beset by problems of organization and re-equipment; some of its new tanks did not arrive until the day of the battle. Montgomery realized early in October that the army, and particularly 10 Corps, would not reach the required standard of training in time for the attack. He therefore decided to modify his plan. The breakthrough by 10 Corps was to be replaced by a 'crumbling' process by which the Axis infantry in the front line were to be destroyed while the British armor prevented any interference from Stumme's tanks. This was a sound concept; Field Marshal Model employed it at Kursk the following year, but lacking Montgomery's superiority in armor, he failed to achieve success.

The main blow was still to fall in the north, where 30 Corps, attacking on a front of four divisions, was to seize objective 'Oxalic', well inside the Axis position, and then open up two lanes in the minefield to permit 10 Corps to move through. Having passed through the infantry, 10 Corps was to hold the line 'Pierson', just west of 'Oxalic' to contain the enemy armor while 30 Corps 'crumbled' the infantry. Finally, once the 'crumbling' was complete, 10 Corps was to move forward against the Axis armor. Meanwhile, 13 Corps was to launch two attacks, one against Qarat El Himeimat and the Taqa Plateau, and the other towards Gebel Kalakh. It was hoped that these would draw some armor south, and would, furthermore, result in the mauling of *Folgore* and *Pavia*. The assault was to be prepared by a short but heavy artillery bombardment, concentrating first on the enemy guns before switching to the infantry.

Efforts at Tactical Surprise

Great efforts were taken to achieve tactical surprise. A complex deception plan was implemented, with emphasis being placed on the camouflage of real installations and concentrations, and the construction of dummy ones. Raids, both real and feint, were also employed in the weeks leading up to the offensive and on the night of 23 October itself, with the specific intention of tying down enemy reserves.

Although preparations for the offensive went well, all was far from serene among the British commanders. Lumsden disliked the role allocated to his corps; he would have preferred to give his armor more of a free rein. He also questioned the wisdom of the change of plan, arguing that it would be impossible for 10 Corps to break through unless 30 Corps had successfully cleared the minefields. Leese's three Dominion divisional commanders made the same point, claiming that they would require longer to carry out the 'break-in' phase. Montgomery, when approached by Leese, emphasized that there was to be no deviation from the plan; 10 Corps *would* move through 30 at dawn on the first day of the attack, come what may.

Battalion commanders were briefed by Montgomery on 19 and 20 October. He warned them that there would be no quick victory; they were to expect a long, hard slogging-match, lasting for

perhaps twelve days. Nevertheless, he declared, *Panzerarmee Afrika* was doomed; it would be unable to sustain a long battle and, providing the plan was adhered to, British victory was certain. Junior officers and men were briefed by their commanding officers on 21 October, and on the night of the 22nd the infantry of 30 Corps moved up to their forward positions. On the following morning Montgomery drove to his tactical headquarters on the coast, close to the advanced headquarters of 10 Corps, 30 Corps and the Desert Air Force. Telephone lines had been well-buried, and all vehicles were dug in. Montgomery's order of the day was read out to the waiting troops, concluding 'Let us all pray that "the Lord mighty in battle" will give us the victory'. The assaulting units continued their deployment undetected, and at 2140 the artillery of the Eighth army opened up on the Axis battery positions.

The flashes of over 1000 British guns lit the night sky as the infantry began their advance. To help them keep direction, Bofors anti-aircraft guns fired tracers on fixed lines, and searchlights crossed in the overhead. At 2200 the guns switched to the Axis forward positions, and the barrage buzzed and roared ahead of the advancing infantry. The Australians on the right of 30 Corps made good progress, but were finally brought to a halt about 1000 yards short of their objective. The Highland Division went forward to the sound of pipes, meeting with a brisk fire as it passed the minefield. The Highlanders spent a confusing and bloody night, and dawn broke to find them short of their final objective. Furthermore, the gaps through the minefield had not been fully opened, and the 1st Armored Division, trying to move forward, became involved in a scene of growing chaos. Freyberg's New Zealanders were more successful, seizing Miteiriya Ridge, though Brigadier Currie's 8th Armored Brigade, moving forward in the early hours of the morning, ran into minefields and was unable to get any further forward. The South Africans, the southernmost formation of 30 Corps, also made good progress, getting onto the southern end of Miteiriya Ridge by dawn.

While 30 Corps' attack had, despite some confusion and numerous casualties, generally reached its objectives, 10 Corps had had a less satisfactory night. Most of its units were delayed by difficulties in clearing lanes through the minefield, and soon much of the corps was spread out behind 30 Corps, with considerable congestion in some areas. Montgomery spoke to Lumsden and Leese at 0330 on 24 October, making it quite clear that, despite the slow progress, there would be no change of plan; the armor, he emphasized, had to get through. By dawn the situation had improved somewhat, though most of 10 Corps had been unable to get ahead of the forward elements of 30 Corps.

In the south, 13 Corps' plan of attack leaned heavily on Harding's 7th Armored Division, which, assisted by General Koenig's 1st Free French Brigade, attacked through Qarat El Himeimat towards the Taqa Plateau. The 44th Division put in a smaller attack further to the north, but lost heavily in the process. Harding's attack made little progress. His division experi-

Above: A German tank and its crew are taken in the desert.

Horrocks and Montgomery agreed that the plan should be changed; instead, 50th Division was to attack the western end of Munassib, supported by a brigade of the 7th Armored Division. This attack was also unsuccessful.

While Harding's tanks burned in the minefields, the Australians in the north began to 'crumble', and successfully attacked the *125th Panzer Grenadier Regiment* in the area of the coast road. The Highlanders on their left made more limited gains, and once again the armor spent a frustrating night, still unable to get clear of 30 Corps positions.

It was now clear to Montgomery that reappraisal was essential. Casualties in 30 Corps numbered over 4500, the Highlanders having suffered nearly half this total. Although 13 Corps had lost 1000 men it had failed to gain any ground at all, and while 10 Corps had suffered lightly, it had accomplished relatively little. The situation was, however, far from hopeful for the Germans. Rommel returned to his army on the evening of the 25th, and was not encouraged to hear that petrol stocks were dangerously low, precluding major movement. The infantry had suffered severely from British artillery fire and air attacks, and *15th Panzer*, used in a series of local counterattacks, now had only 31 tanks in action. Rommel concluded that the greatest threat to his position lay in the salient at Kidney Ridge, and ordered *15th Panzer* and *Littorio* to counterattack at dawn on the 26th. He went forward to watch the attack, and was depressed to observe the fierceness of British artillery fire and air strikes. He soon committed *90th Light* to the battle, but a day's furious fighting saw no conclusive result.

Montgomery had, meanwhile, finalized his new plan and issued orders accordingly. The Highlanders were to consolidate their position, and the Australians were to resume 'crumbling' on the night of the 28th, while 30 Corps was given time to recover; apart from this no other major moves were to be undertaken. Ten Corps was to nudge forward in the area of Kidney Ridge, at the same time preventing enemy armor from interfering with 30 Corps. Finally, Harding was to prepare to move north if required to do so.

Lumsden ordered Brigadier Bosvile's 7th Motor Brigade to attack points 'Snipe' and 'Woodcock' near Kidney Ridge at 2300 that night, and to form an anti-tank screen through which two armored brigades would advance the following morning. 'Woodcock' was taken but proved untenable. 'Snipe' was duly seized by 2nd Battalion, The Rifle Brigade, but the armor which should have moved through failed to do so. The Rifle Brigade was heavily attacked by German and Italian armor throughout the day, but in a brilliant defense, beat off these assaults, knocking out 37 tanks and self-propelled guns in the process. Thrusts toward 'Woodcock' gained little ground, and at about 1600 Rommel unleashed a major counterattack, using both his Panzer divisions, together with *Littorio* and elements of *Ariete*. The attack made no headway, and its failure profoundly disturbed Rommel. 'No one can conceive the burden that lies on me', he wrote to his wife, warning her that defeat was likely.

enced the same minefield problems as its counterparts in the north, and the French, after an initial success, were driven back, with the loss of the popular and gallant Colonel Amilakvari of the Foreign Legion. Horrocks decided to hold on to the ground that had been gained, and to résume the attack the following night.

The first that General Stumme knew of the offensive was the crash of the bombardment which heralded it. He did not immediately order his guns to reply, and the Axis counter-bombardment, by design or accident, took some time to get under way. Stumme was perplexed by the conflicting reports which arrived at his headquarters, and decided to go forward to investigate personally. While on this mission his car was shot at and Stumme himself, hanging onto the outside as his driver sped off, had a heart attack. His body was not found for 24 hours, and, though the capable Thoma took over, *Panzerarmee Afrika* was leaderless at a crucial stage in the action.

During the morning of 24 October 10 Corps tried to move forward through 30 Corps, in obedience to Montgomery's repeated urging, while the New Zealanders 'crumbled' to the south. By noon Montgomery had decided that the latter maneuver was likely to prove slow and costly, and he decided to switch the axis of the attack further north, where the Australians were to start 'crumbling'. The remainder of 30 Corps was to hold Miteiriya Ridge, while 10 Corps' main effort was to be directed toward Kidney Ridge. The Australians were to start their attack that night.

The same evening 13 Corps resumed their attack, while the 7th Armored Division and its supporting infantry spent another messy and fruitless night trying to force a way through the minefield. Early on the morning of 25 October

At 0800 on 28 October, Montgomery met Leese, Lumsden and their chief of staff. He informed them that 1st Armored Division, battered in four days hard fighting, was to be withdrawn to regroup, and the Kidney Ridge area was, for the time at least, to become a defensive front. The Australians were to attack, as planned, that night, and Lumsden was to be prepared to move westwards. Radio interceptions confirmed that *21st Panzer* had moved north, and orders were later issued for Harding to move up toward the coast, leaving one of his brigades in the south.

The New Zealanders had been pulled back into reserve on the 26th, and Montgomery informed Freyberg that he was to take over the Australian sector on the night of the 29th, with a view to launching an attack the following night, supported by infantry from 13 and 30 Corps. The Australian attack on the night of the 28th did not meet with the expected success, due largely to the problems of mines and night navigation.

There were by now growing doubts about Montgomery's wisdom. Churchill was increasingly dissatisfied with the conduct of the battle, forcing Brooke to defend Alexander and Montgomery against accusations of weakness and inactivity. On the 29th Montgomery was visited by Alexander, his Chief-of-Staff, Lieutenant-General McCreery and Minister of State Casey. Montgomery, radiating confidence as usual, stressed that all was well, and reminded his listeners that he had predicted a long fight. Nevertheless, neither McCreery nor Montgomery's own staff were altogether happy with the planned breakout, codenamed 'Operation Supercharge'. They felt that an attack along the coast by the New Zealanders would encounter Rommel's main strength, since this sector was vital for the safety of his supply dumps and lines of communication. De Guingand, backed by his senior intelligence

Above: Germans inspect a captured British tank.
Left: General von Arnim is taken into captivity after the collapse of the Axis effort in North Africa in 1943, when some 250,000 Axis forces remaining in Tunisia surrendered to the Allies. Alamein was the first step in the long road back from Egypt to Tunis.

officer, pointed this out to Montgomery, who wisely decided to change the axis of the attack. The Australians were to attack northward on the night of the 30th but the New Zealanders, instead of moving through them, would attack further south, just north of Kidney Ridge, on the night of the 31st. They would be reinforced with one armored and two infantry brigades, and liberally supported by artillery and air strikes.

The Australian attack in the Thompson's Post area on the night of the 30th made useful gains. Rommel declined to withdraw his threatened units in this sector, and instead ordered counter-attacks for the next day. This proved an error; Rommel's attention remained fixed on the coast while the real threat developed further south.

The last details of 'Supercharge' were arranged at a conference early on the morning of 1 November. The attack was to go in at 0105 on the 2nd, with two infantry brigades assaulting on a 4000 yard front. These brigades, one each from the 50th and 51st Divisions, were under the operational command of the New Zealand Division. They were to be followed by the armor, which, as in the original 'Lightfoot' plan, was to pass through the infantry once the latter's objectives were secure.

The infantry objective lay just east of the Rahman Track, while the objective of the 8th Armored Brigade was just beyond it, across the strongly-held Aqqaqir Ridge. Once 8th Armored were in possession of the ridge, 10 Corps was to take over the battle from 30 Corps, and the 1st

Opposite: A German Panzer halts to survey the action at Alamein. **Left:** Italian troops move forward in one of their last assaults of the action at Alamein. **Below:** Thousands of German prisoners are rounded up by the 1st Household Cavalry Regiment at the start of the Nazis' long retreat across the rim of North Africa.

Armored Division would move through the 8th Armored Brigade. The attack was to be supported by the guns of five divisions, strengthened by three extra artillery regiments.

The infantry attack went well. Its objectives were taken well before dawn, and just after 0600 Currie's 8th Armored Brigade moved up. The brigade had lost several of its tanks in the approach march, but swept forward with great *élan*, suffering heavily from the 88s and dug-in tanks on Aqqaqir Ridge. The Royal Wiltshire Yeomanry lost almost all its tanks; the brigade as a whole lost 87 in this attack. Nevertheless, the leading brigade of the 1st Armored Division moved forward as planned, only to be heavily engaged by German armor, and a fierce battle developed between the infantry line and the Rahman Track.

While this action was in progress some armored cars of the Royal Dragoons discovered that the southwestern edge of the salient was weakly held, and pushed forward into open country, doing considerable damage in the Axis rear. An attack by the 7th Motor Brigade on Tel El Aqqaqir failed that night, and the armor was unable to make any progress the following morning. Montgomery decided to press his attack through the southern portion of the salient, using the Highland Division and an Indian brigade, in an effort to break through the defensive crust and enable the armor to fan out.

Rommel had decided that the battle was hopeless on 2 November. The *Afrika Korps* ended the day with only 35 tanks, largely as a result of the fighting around Kidney Ridge; petrol and ammunition were both dangerously low. Rommel decided to pull back to Fuka, withdrawing his troops from the southern sector that night,

Above: German forces in full retreat toward Cyrenaica after Alamein.
Opposite left: A German half-track drags an artillery piece back into Cyrenaica as the retreat continues.

The Battle of El Alamein, 1942

Objectives of 'Operation Lightfoot'

The main blow was to fall in the north, where XXX Corps was to seize objective 'Oxalic', well inside the Axis positions, and then open up two lanes in the minefield to permit the armor of X Corps to move through. Having passed through the infantry, X Corps was to hold the line 'Pierson' to contain the enemy armor. Finally, on the Axis defenses were broken down, X Corps was to move against the Ax armor at 'skinflint'.

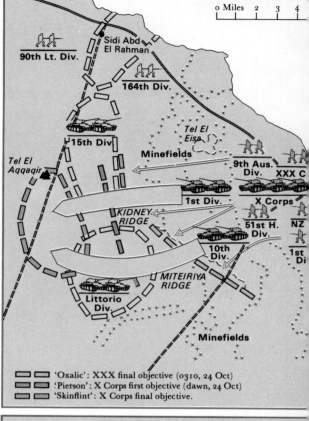

'Oxalic': XXX final objective (0310, 24 Oct)
'Pierson': X Corps first objective (dawn, 24 Oct)
'Skinflint': X Corps final objective.

The Balance of Forces at El Alamein

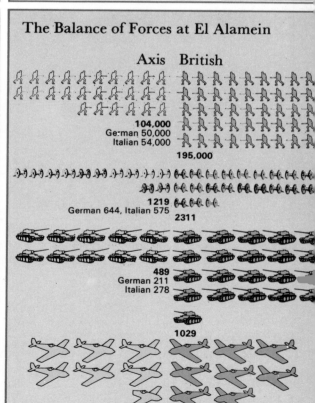

Axis   British

104,000
German 50,000
Italian 54,000

195,000

1219
German 644, Italian 575

2311

489
German 211
Italian 278

1029

675
German 275 (150 serviceable)
Italian 400 (200 serviceable)

750 (530 serviceable)

🚶 4000 men   🚚 50 tanks
⚙ 100 guns   ✈ 100 aircraft

Montgomery was only prepared to challenge the 'Afrika Korps' when he had established a clear superiority in tanks and men. His drive at Alamein was a frontal thrust based on sheer firepower and manpower which finally forced Rommel to retreat.

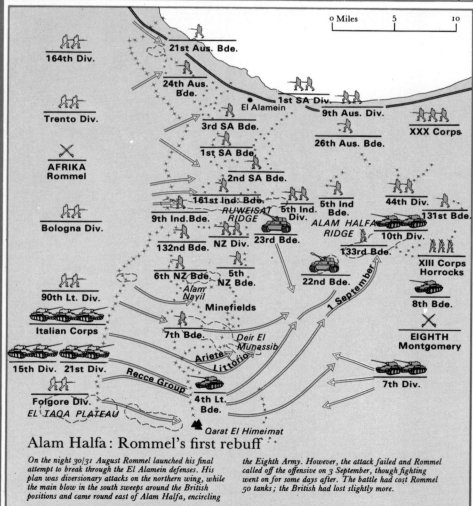

Alam Halfa: Rommel's first rebuff

On the night 30/31 August Rommel launched his final attempt to break through the El Alamein defenses. His plan was diversionary attacks on the northern wing, while the main blow in the south sweeps around the British positions and came round east of Alam Halfa, encircling the Eighth Army. However, the attack failed and Rommel called off the offensive on 3 September, though fighting went on for some days after. The battle had cost Rommel 50 tanks; the British had lost slightly more.

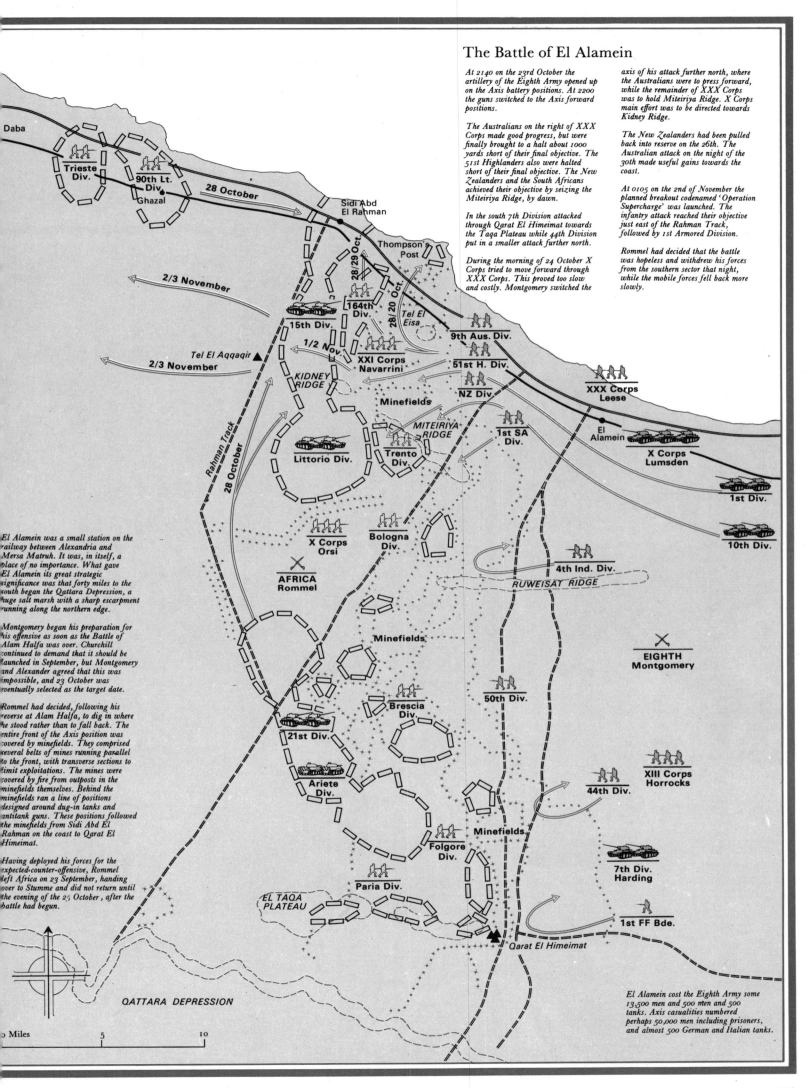

The Battle of El Alamein

At 2140 on the 23rd October the artillery of the Eighth Army opened up on the Axis battery positions. At 2200 the guns switched to the Axis forward positions.

The Australians on the right of XXX Corps made good progress, but were finally brought to a halt about 1000 yards short of their final objective. The 51st Highlanders also were halted short of their final objective. The New Zealanders and the South Africans achieved their objective by seizing the Miteiriya Ridge, by dawn.

In the south 7th Division attacked through Qarat El Himeimat towards the Taqa Plateau while 44th Division put in a smaller attack further north.

During the morning of 24 October X Corps tried to move forward through XXX Corps. This proved too slow and costly. Montgomery switched the axis of his attack further north, where the Australians were to press forward, while the remainder of XXX Corps was to hold Miteiriya Ridge. X Corps main effort was to be directed towards Kidney Ridge.

The New Zealanders had been pulled back into reserve on the 26th. The Australian attack on the night of the 30th made useful gains towards the coast.

At 0105 on the 2nd of November the planned breakout codenamed 'Operation Supercharge' was launched. The infantry attack reached their objective just east of the Rahman Track, followed by 1st Armored Division.

Rommel had decided that the battle was hopeless and withdrew his forces from the southern sector that night, while the mobile forces fell back more slowly.

El Alamein was a small station on the railway between Alexandria and Mersa Matruh. It was, in itself, a place of no importance. What gave El Alamein its great strategic significance was that forty miles to the south began the Qattara Depression, a huge salt marsh with a sharp escarpment running along the northern edge.

Montgomery began his preparation for his offensive as soon as the Battle of Alam Halfa was over. Churchill continued to demand that it should be launched in September, but Montgomery and Alexander agreed that this was impossible, and 23 October was eventually selected as the target date.

Rommel had decided, following his reverse at Alam Halfa, to dig in where he stood rather than to fall back. The entire front of the Axis position was covered by minefields. They comprised several belts of mines running parallel to the front, with transverse sections to limit exploitations. The mines were covered by fire from outposts in the minefields themselves. Behind the minefields ran a line of positions designed around dug-in tanks and antitank guns. These positions followed the minefields from Sidi Abd El Rahman on the coast to Qarat El Himeimat.

Having deployed his forces for the expected counter-offensive, Rommel left Africa on 23 September, handing over to Stumme and did not return until the evening of the 25 October, after the battle had begun.

El Alamein cost the Eighth Army some 13,500 men and 500 men and 500 tanks. Axis casualties numbered perhaps 50,000 men including prisoners, and almost 500 German and Italian tanks.

Above: A German soldier who fell at Alamein. **Left:** The race across the desert was on after Alamein. The battle decided the desert campaign, which ended only six months after the British breakthrough.

while the mobile forces in the north fell back more slowly. The fuel problem was so serious that many of the infantry would have no transport; their retirement would thus be a perilous affair. Rommel sent his ADC, Lieutenant Berndt, to explain the reasons for the withdrawal to Hitler, but before Berndt left the Führer sent an order countermanding the retreat. This proved difficult to execute, since units in the south had already began to fall back.

The night of 3 November saw confused fighting around Tel El Aqqaqir, which fell at first light on the 4th. Two armored divisions, 1st and 7th, pushed through the gap. *Ariete*, fighting hard, was surrounded and overwhelmed, but a clean break-through was delayed as much by the chaos behind the British front as by Axis resistance. By late afternoon Rommel realized that disengagement was essential if he was to avoid encirclement. The orderly withdrawal of his earlier plan was replaced by a general retreat. The coast road was crammed with vehicles, but the Desert Air Force, possibly due to a preference for bombing rather than strafing, failed to cause as much damage as Montgomery and his staff hoped.

Montgomery intended to cut off at least part of the retreating Axis Army by a series of left hooks through the desert. These achieved little, due partially to a number of particularly heavy storms which turned large areas of the desert into a quagmire and bogged down the pursuers. Montgomery has been criticized for the slowness of his follow-up, though it is likely that but for the rain Rommel would have been caught at Mersa Matruh on 6 November. As it was, the remnants of Rommel's mobile forces got away, but most of the helpless Italian infantry, isolated and without transport, were captured.

On 8 November the Allies landed in North Africa, and the Western Desert became a front of diminished importance. German reinforcements which, if delivered six months earlier, would have had a decisive effect, were rushed into Tripoli, but to no avail. Tripoli fell on 23 January, 1943; Montgomery forced the Mareth Line in late March, and on 13 May the last Axis forces in North Africa surrendered.

Alamein cost the Eighth Army some 13,500 men and 500 tanks. Most of the latter were, however, capable of repair. Axis casualties numbered perhaps 50,000, of whom 30,000 were prisoners. Rommel's tank losses were most significant; about 500 German and Italian tanks were either destroyed in the battle or captured subsequently.

Alamein's effect upon Allied morale was probably more important than its long-term influence upon the course of the war. While less significant in strategic terms than Stalingrad or Kursk, Alamein marked a watershed in Allied fortunes. Montgomery was criticized by some at the time, and has been criticized by many since, for his conduct of the battle. His plan has been condemned as pedestrian and his man-management as theatrical. Nevertheless, the fact remains that Alamein was the Eighth Army's first conclusive victory. It had had numerical superiority in the past, but had squandered it in indecision and discord. Montgomery brought a new drive and persistence to the Desert Army, and planned a set-piece battle in which its quantitative superiority could, for once, be fully employed. He achieved a victory when victories were few and far between. Churchill put it, with characteristic exaggeration, 'Before Alamein we never had a victory. After Alamein we never had a defeat'.

Kursk

It is deceptively easy for British and Americans to think of the Second World War largely in terms of theaters in which their own troops were engaged. This, however, tends to obscure the fact that, as Alan Clark has pointed out, to the Germans the war meant the war in the East. It was on the Eastern Front that the bulk of Germany's forces were deployed; North Africa, for instance, was little more than a sideshow. In the opinion of Field Marshal Erich von Manstein, probably the *Wehrmacht's* ablest strategist, the German defeat at Kursk in July 1943 marked a turning point in the war in the East, with the initiative passing into the hands of the Russians. The summer of 1943 can, indeed, be seen as a turning point in a wider sense.

Until that time the Germans, who had for the most part held the strategic initiative over the battlefields of Europe, had a reasonable hope of avoiding defeat in the war they had precipitated in 1939. True, their difficulties were increasing. Germany's mastery of Europe failed to conceal the restlessness and despair of the subjected populations who faced exploitation and often extermination. Germany, too, lacked the manpower, the industrial production, the oil and the transport facilities needed to capitalize on her gains and to totally defeat her enemies. The United States, moving into top gear on the production front, was flexing her muscles in Europe for the first time. But the European war was essentially decided in the East—on the Russian steppes where the German army was bled white in one of the most barbarous campaigns in history. Success in the East in 1943 might have enabled the Germans to deploy and successfully counter Anglo-American assaults in the West; it might still have been possible to fight to a standstill. After Kursk-Orel the war was lost for Germany, though there was no immediate end to it in sight. The battle banished any lingering doubts concerning the survival of the Soviet Union and opened the way for the Soviet drive that was to bring much of Eastern and Central Europe under Stalin's sway. In conjunction with the Allied victory in the Atlantic—the prerequisite for successful operations on the European mainland by the British and Americans—the battle ensured the victory of the Allies over Germany. It also heralded the emergence of the Soviet Union not simply as Europe's greatest power, but as a state that could only be compared in strength to the United States, with all the implications that contained for the future of Europe and the world.

Kursk-Orel was the last major offensive undertaken by the Germans on the Eastern Front. By that time they had been fought very largely to a standstill; thereafter their stance in the East was increasingly defensive. Driving deeply into the Soviet Union in 1941, the *Wehrmacht* had inflicted losses on the Soviet Army that by any normal standards should have been fatal, but the Russians had held at Leningrad and thrown back the last attacks on Moscow in December. Despite their local successes in the Moscow region during the winter, the Russians had been unable to substantially improve their strategic position and the German Army was able to launch a summer offensive in 1942 in southern Russia. Seeking to secure the granaries and mineral wealth of the Ukraine and the oilfields of the Caucasian approaches, the Germans crushed the weak Russian forces that opposed them but were drawn into battle at Stalingrad where, in vicious street fighting, their superiority in equipment and training were nullified. With the winter came a Soviet counter-attack that encircled German forces in the Stalingrad area and ultimately resulted in the destruction of the 230,000-strong German *Sixth Army*. But in trying to exploit their victory the Russians over-extended themselves; their armored thrusts were crushed around Kharkov in March, and the front stabilized on a line dictated by exhaustion and the spring thaw. The *Wehrmacht* had lost many of its best men and much of its equipment, but it had proved itself to be at least a tactical match for the Russians. German resilience was great, but was matched by that of the Russians, and as spring gave way to summer it became obvious that neither army could enforce its will upon its adversary.

For the Germans the spring of 1943 was a time of reappraisal and indecision. Despite two massive offensives they had failed to break the most formidable of their enemies, and they were faced with the prospect of Anglo-American action against southern Europe from North Africa where German and Italian forces stood on the edge of destruction at Tunis. In the Atlantic the U-boats had failed to starve Britain into submission and were suffering such losses that the outcome of the battle was no longer in any doubt. Politically, Italy was in deep trouble with Mussolini's credibility weakening with every defeat. Rumania, Hungary and Bulgaria had hardly been impressed by their German ally's defeat on the Volga, and there was a need to secure a victory that would put fresh heart into these countries and to forestall any Russian move that would bring the war closer to the Balkans.

Opposite: German tanks in action near the Kursk salient in the summer of 1943. Despite the introduction of the Panther and Tiger, two new German tanks, most of the tanks used by the *Wehrmacht* and *Waffen SS* were Pzkw IVs.

Only a victory in the East could stabilize the deteriorating situation, and it was becoming increasingly essential because of the Russians' increased industrial production. Throughout the war the Russians had enjoyed—and usually dissipated—an overall superiority of men, armor, artillery and aircraft but this had been offset by superior German tactics. By the spring of 1943, however, quality was being grafted onto an ever-increasing quantity that the Germans could not hope to match. It had therefore become essential for the Germans to bring the bulk of the Soviet Army to battle and to cripple it, in order to permit the redeployment of German forces in other theaters of war.

Preparations for the Offensive

Given that they were committed to make an attack in the East—a presumption that Colonel-General Heinz Guderian resisted—the Germans were faced with the twin problems of where, and with what forces, the attack should be made. Behind the enemy front there were no immediate objectives of strategic importance, in defense of which the Russians would be forced to commit their armies if attacked by the Germans. Leningrad, partially relieved in September 1942, offered a target, but room to maneuver was limited. Despite inflicting appalling losses on the Russians in November 1942 around Rzhev the Germans had been forced to abandon this salient and shorten their line the following March—with the result that thereafter Moscow was too far away for any successful attack to be considered. In the south, however, the front had stabilized in a manner that seemed more promising for a German attack. In the Bryansk-Orel-Kursk-Kharkov region the front had formed into a Russian-held salient sixty miles wide with the German Army Group Center holding the northern flank, and Army Group South the southern sector around Kharkov. From this salient the Russians threatened the entire German position in the Ukraine, since a breakout to the southwest might trap a major part of Army Group South against the Sea of Azov. The Russians had,

indeed, attempted this unsuccessfully, in February and March. Field Marshal Erich von Manstein, C-in-C Army Group South, anticipated such a Russian move and planned to lure any such attack toward the lower Dnieper and then strike it in the flank from Kharkov. This backhand battle of riposte was nevertheless rejected; there was no certainty as to where the Russians might attack and, much to Hitler's displeasure, such a technique would involve the temporary abandonment of ground. Instead, the Germans considered short but sharp thrusts on each side of the salient in May when the ground had dried. But here the Germans came up against an insoluble problem. In order to overwhelm the Russians in the salient—before they had time to shore up its defenses and possibly launch an attack of their own on the northern part of the Orel re-entrant—time was of the essence. The offensive had to be carried out as soon as possible after the ground had dried, but the Germans themselves were no better prepared in this sector than were the Russians. In January 1943 their eighteen Panzer divisions could muster between them only 495 battleworthy tanks and production was simply inadequate. Monthly production of the Pzkw IV—a tank not superior to the Russian T-34—only exceeded the hundred mark for the first time in October 1942, and the two new tanks, the Tiger and the Panther, were experiencing the teething problems inherent in any new equipment. Nevertheless, from April onwards German preparations for an offensive began, but by the beginning of May the first doubts began to grow in the minds of some of the field commanders.

Russia's Intelligence Network

The Russians, aided by an extremely efficient Intelligence network within the German Army High Command, had no illusions as to German intentions. They were thus able to choose between an offensive of their own to pre-empt the German blow, and a defensive battle in prepared positions, followed by a counterattack. Their experience of mobile operations convinced the Soviet High Command that the latter course of action was preferable. In open warfare, moving away from their supply dumps across a razed countryside, the Russians had been consistently outfought and outmaneuvered in the past; they lacked the experience and the means to maintain deep penetrations while the Germans still possessed mobile reserves. In defense, however, the ordinary Russian soldier had exhibited qualities of stoicism, bravery and self-sacrifice that made him a match for his German counterpart. Accordingly, the Soviet Command, playing to its strengths and not its weaknesses, prepared for a defensive battle, followed by heavy counterattacks once the main German assaults had been halted. Men, armor, artillery, aircraft and engineering equipment were moved to the area in profusion. By this time Soviet tank production was running at 2000 per month and the balance of manpower, equal in 1942, had swung in favor of the Russians.

Divided into three fronts—the Central, Voronezh and Steppe (Reserve)—the Kursk salient witnessed elaborate Russian preparations. Defenses were sited in depth, based on clusters of

Right: Field Marshal Erich von Manstein, C-in-C Army Group South, who helped plan the Kursk offensive. He was one of Germany's ablest strategists throughout the war.

anti-tank positions and minefields. Each of these small positions included three to five 76mm anti-tank guns, about five antitank rifles, and up to five mortars with infantry and engineer support. Because of the limited ability of the 76mm gun to destroy Tigers, strong points were mutually supporting and centrally controlled, and were covered by minefields in order to channel the German tanks into killing zones where they could be overwhelmed by sheer weight of numbers. By the time the battle opened the defensive systems were up to 110 miles deep, and consisted of six main belts within the salient alone. Behind it was a further defensive network that stretched back to the Don River. On the Central Front 3100 miles of trenches were dug.

Naturally, preparations on such a scale did not go unnoticed. The Germans soon became aware of the buildup, and many German generals believed that the Russians were simply too strong to be attacked at Kursk-Orel with any reasonable hope of success. On the other hand a battle would result in the commitment of the great majority of Russian reserves of manpower and armor, the very elements of the Soviet Army that the Germans sought to bring to battle. On balance, German planners believed that the task lay within their army's capabilities. The Russians had never withstood the opening of a blitzkrieg attack; difficulties in Russia had begun as the German tanks had fanned out on the limitless steppe. For this offensive, the attacking pincers had to travel only 60 miles—an apparently feasible task.

Nevertheless, the realization that the battle was assuming the nature of a head-on collision, a decisive trial of strength, did not recommend itself to the more perceptive German generals. Hitler himself was genuinely undecided whether or not to order the offensive, but with most of the Army High Command enthusiastic for the battle and no alternative offensive operation planned, the attack on the Kursk salient, 'Operation Citadel', was sanctioned scheduled for 4 July.

Despite the activities of the Russian partisans against the lines of communication (according to the Germans' own figures the partisans carried out 1092 attacks in June and 1460 in July behind the battle area) the Germans were able to concentrate a formidable striking force around the salient for the start of the battle. This force of 900,000 men, 10,000 artillery and 2700 tanks and assault guns enjoyed the support of 2500 aircraft. The main attacks were be handled in the north by *Ninth Army*, under the command of Field Marshal Walter Model, and in the south by *Fourth Panzer Army* and *Operational Group Kempf*, under the overall direction of von Manstein. Realization of the strength of the Russian defenses dictated a change of tactics. Instead of the usual opening attack in which the panzers streaked ahead of the infantry, Model proposed to use his infantry and artillery to drive a wedge through the Russian defenses into which the tanks would be fed. These had been the tactics used by Montgomery at Alamein in October 1942—but with one vital difference. Montgomery had enjoyed overwhelming superiority of numbers and equipment; and even then the attack had only just succeeded. Model, faced with greater in-depth defenses than

Above: Manstein scans Russian positions in June 1943. The planning of the Kursk offensive was meticulous, but the Russians were equally prepared. **Left:** German paratroops drop behind Russian lines in mid-June, prior to the great offensive.

The Battle of Kursk, 1943

The Balance of Forces involved at Kursk

	👤	🔫	🚗	✈
German	900,000	10,000	2700	2500
Russian	1,337,000	10,220	3306	2650

The German Offensive 4–12 July (southern front)

In the south where the two forces were more evenly matched than in the north, Manstein's forces made greater headway. After five days of conflict the Germans had succeeded in breaking through the first two Russian defense lines.

By the 7th the Germans had pried the Russians out of most of their positions on the Pena. On the 8th the German forces crossed the river.

On the morning of the 12th the German attack was met and repulsed. The losses

suffered prompted Hitler to abandon the offensive on the 13th, but Manstein was adamant in continuing the offensive. On 17th it was finally called off.

o Miles 10

'Operation Citadel' 4–12 July

The German attack was scheduled for 0330 on 5 July, but effectively the battle was under way by the afternoon of the 4th.

In the Bryanak-Orel-Kursk-Kharkov region the front line had formed into a Russian held salient 60 miles wide with the German Army Group Center holding the northern flank, and Army Group South the southern sector, around Kharkov. From this salient the Russians threatened the entire German position in the Ukraine. A Russian breakthrough would pierce the German front and open the road to Warsaw and eventual German defeat.

German High Command devised a plan to eliminate the salient. The plan, known as 'Operation Citadel', involved short but sharp thrusts on each side of the salient, intended to encircle the Russians within the bulge.

German preparations began in April. However, aided by an extremely efficient Intelligence network, the Russians were aware of the German intentions. Accordingly, the Soviet Command prepared for a defensive battle, followed by heavy counter attacks once the main German assaults had been halted. Men, armor, artillery, aircraft and engineering equipment were moved into the area. Defenses were sited in depth, based on clusters of antitank positions and mine fields. By the time the battle opened the defensive positions were up to 110 miles deep, and consisted of six main belts within the salient alone.

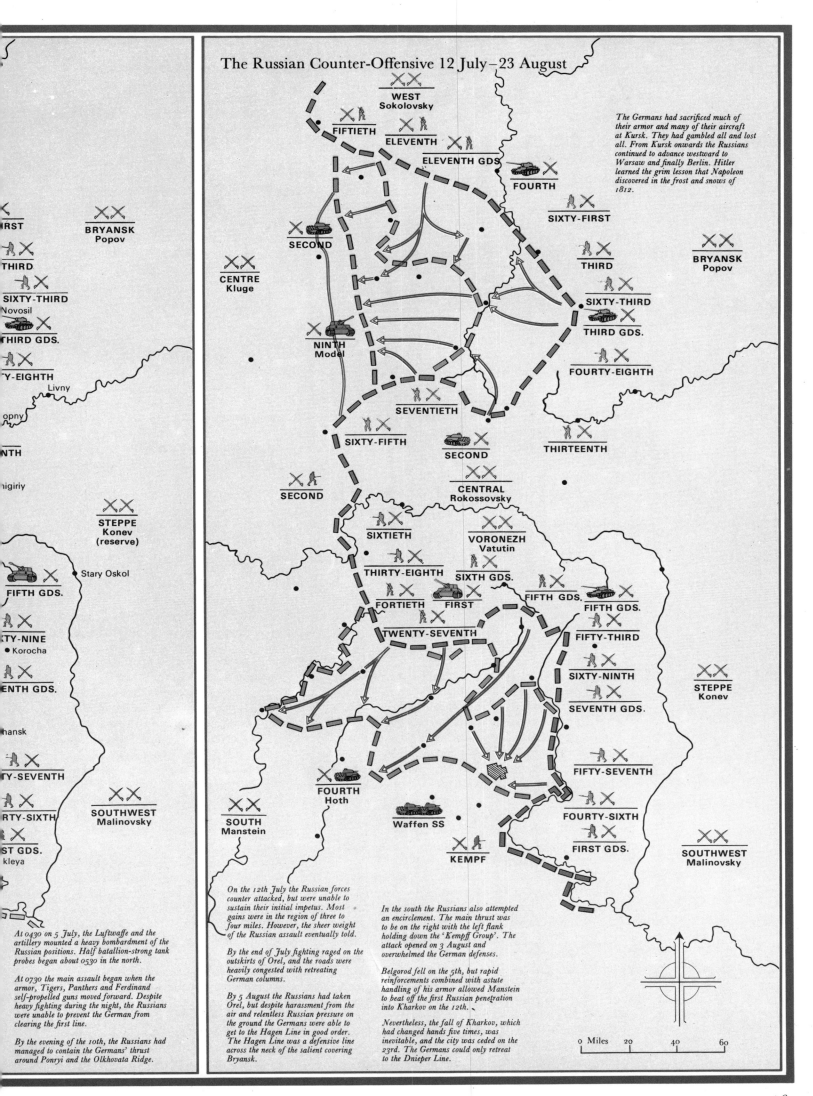

The Russian Counter-Offensive 12 July–23 August

WEST
Sokolovsky

FIFTIETH

ELEVENTH

ELEVENTH GDS.

FOURTH

SIXTY-FIRST

The Germans had sacrificed much of their armor and many of their aircraft at Kursk. They had gambled all and lost all. From Kursk onwards the Russians continued to advance westward to Warsaw and finally Berlin. Hitler learned the grim lesson that Napoleon discovered in the frost and snows of 1812.

FIRST

BRYANSK
Popov

THIRD

SIXTY-THIRD
Novosil

THIRD GDS.

SECOND

CENTRE
Kluge

THIRD

BRYANSK
Popov

SIXTY-THIRD

THIRD GDS.

-EIGHTH

Livny

NINTH
Model

FOURTY-EIGHTH

opny

NTH

SEVENTIETH

higiriy

STEPPE
Konev
(reserve)

SIXTY-FIFTH

SECOND

THIRTEENTH

SECOND

CENTRAL
Rokossovsky

Stary Oskol

SIXTIETH

VORONEZH
Vatutin

FIFTH GDS.

THIRTY-EIGHTH

SIXTH GDS.

FIFTH GDS.

FIFTH GDS.

-NINE
Korocha

FORTIETH

FIRST

FIFTY-THIRD

ENTH GDS.

TWENTY-SEVENTH

SIXTY-NINTH

SEVENTH GDS.

STEPPE
Konev

hansk

-SEVENTH

FIFTY-SEVENTH

-SIXTH

SOUTHWEST
Malinovsky

SOUTH
Manstein

FOURTH
Hoth

Waffen SS

FOURTY-SIXTH

T GDS.
kleya

KEMPF

FIRST GDS.

SOUTHWEST
Malinovsky

At 0430 on 5 July, the Luftwaffe and the artillery mounted a heavy bombardment of the Russian positions. Half batallion-strong tank probes began about 0530 in the north.

At 0730 the main assault began when the armor, Tigers, Panthers and Ferdinand self-propelled guns moved forward. Despite heavy fighting during the night, the Russians were unable to prevent the German from clearing the first line.

By the evening of the 10th, the Russians had managed to contain the Germans' thrust around Ponryi and the Olkhovata Ridge.

On the 12th July the Russian forces counter attacked, but were unable to sustain their initial impetus. Most gains were in the region of three to four miles. However, the sheer weight of the Russian assault eventually told.

By the end of July fighting raged on the outskirts of Orel, and the roads were heavily congested with retreating German columns.

By 5 August the Russians had taken Orel, but despite harassment from the air and relentless Russian pressure on the ground the Germans were able to get to the Hagen Line in good order. The Hagen Line was a defensive line across the neck of the salient covering Bryansk.

In the south the Russians also attempted an encirclement. The main thrust was to be on the right with the left flank holding down the 'Kempff Group'. The attack opened on 3 August and overwhelmed the German defenses.

Belgorod fell on the 5th, but rapid reinforcements combined with astute handling of his armor allowed Manstein to beat off the first Russian penetration into Kharkov on the 12th.

Nevertheless, the fall of Kharkov, which had changed hands five times, was inevitable, and the city was ceded on the 23rd. The Germans could only retreat to the Dnieper Line.

0   Miles   20   40   60

the British had encountered in the desert, had no marked numerical advantage. In the south Manstein concentrated eight of Germany's best armored divisions on a 30-mile front in order to implement the *panzerkeil* (armored wedge). By these tactics he intended to prise open the defenses by a series of thrusts in which the armor was concentrated along the cutting edge. The latest tanks, the Tigers, were concentrated at the tip, while in their wake were the lighter tanks, the Panthers and the Pzkw IVs, which would be backed up by the infantry. These would be followed by the artillery and mortar support. The Germans, in the south, intended to use the bludgeon rather than the rapier. In ordering the tanks not to stop to support disabled colleagues the German Command, anxious to maintain the momentum of the attack, effectively wrote off many of their tanks that were to be disabled. Damaged vehicles, often isolated from their own infantry, fell easy prey to untouched Soviet positions on the flanks of the thrusts.

The Soviets, on the other hand, were inferior in numbers along the axis of the German thrusts, but were superior in numbers and equipment in the salient area generally. Behind minefields with an average density of about 2200 antitank and 2500 anti-personnel mines per mile of front were some 1,337,000 soldiers, 20,220 artillery pieces and 3306 tanks—with one more Tank Army in reserve. Of the artillery 6000 pieces were 76mm antitank guns and 920 Katyusha multiple rocket-launchers. Only in the air did the Soviets lack any marked numerical advantage over the Germans, deploying about 2650 aircraft.

The Russians were confident in their ability to hold and defeat the German thrusts, despite the qualitative superiority of some of the latest German equipment. Months of preparation ensured that in the battle firepower and a tenacious defense would offset superior German technique, while in the critical opening stage mobility would be minimal. The Russians, bolstered by the knowledge that the Ural factories could more than easily replace their losses, were prepared to fight a gigantic battle of attrition, trading lives and equipment for the elimination of the German armor which had brought them close to defeat in 1941 and again in 1942.

Nevertheless, Helmuth von Moltke's adage that no plan ever survives the first contact of battle proved very accurate. Not only did the German plan go badly wrong, but Soviet deployment was also, in part at least, erroneous, and this was to lead to a critical situation which made the outcome of the battle an open question. The Russians were under the impression that the major German effort would be from the Orel salient against General Rokossovsky's Central Front with a smaller effort against General Vatutin's Veronezh Front in the south. The reverse proved to be the case, since Model deployed only three panzer divisions compared to Manstein's eight. The balance of Russian deployment essentially favored Rokossovsky, though this was redeemed by the deployment of reserves to help the southern sector. The German attack in the north was held relatively quickly. In the south, however, Russian losses were extremely heavy, German gains were more marked than in the north and the decision delayed. This was to mean the Russian plans for simultaneous counterattacks in the north and the south after the defensive battle lacked synchronization and failed to achieve either of the two super-encirclements planned.

The German attack was scheduled for 0330 on 5 July, but effectively the battle was under way by the afternoon of the 4th. In the south Manstein's forces undertook an artillery attack to make tactical gains in order to secure better start lines. On both fronts patrolling was undertaken and frequent clashes occurred, especially in the afternoon when the German engineers tried to clear their own wire and minefields ready for the attack. Prisoners and deserters gave the Russians the time of the attack and it was on this basis that the Russians began to bombard the German positions in the north at 0220. This disrupted German preparations and it was not until 0430 that the Luftwaffe and the German artillery mounted their reply. This provoked a second, far heavier, Russian counter-bombardment which was not particularly effective. Half-battalion strong tank probes began about 0530 in the north, but intense fire quickly drove them back. Two hours later the main assault opened with the armor, Tigers, Panthers and Ferdinand self-propelled guns moving forward. Because of their very thick front

armor the Tigers and Ferdinands were able to move through the first defense line, but it quickly became apparent that the one division used in this attack was not enough to overcome the resistance, which was far stronger than anticipated. By the afternoon all the armor had been committed, but with little return. On most of the front the Germans made no progress, though a 3½-mile penetration was achieved against the 15th and 81st Rifle Divisions of Thirteenth Army. A three mile break-in was made near Gnilets against the 132nd and 280th Divisions of Seventieth Army, but already there were signs that things were going wrong for the Germans. More than 100 tanks had been lost in the minefields where they had attracted the unwelcome attention of the antitank guns and the Soviet Air Force. Small-arms fire had forced the German infantry to go to ground with the result that the armor became isolated and ensnared in the Russian defense lines. Despite intense fighting during the night, however, the Russians were unable to prevent the Germans from clearing most of the first line. By placing fresh tanks in hull-down positions the Russians ensured that their next-day's firepower was not reduced very much despite their losses, but this did not prevent Model making the same depth of penetration on the 6th. Unfortunately for the Germans their assault had been most successful on the right flank where it had eventually been halted in front of a low line of hills north of Olkhovata. No major progress had been made in the center or on the left flank that could give aid and protection to the right. And it was against the German left flank that Rokossovsky had concentrated his armored reserves, though he sent three tank corps to the threatened sectors. Their rapid counterattacks on the morning of the 6th were relatively easily stopped, however, and the failure led the Russians to dig in their tanks. For the next four days positions in the north hardly shifted despite frenzied close quarter battles and ferocious armored clashes. Russian forces had turned the Olkhovata ridge into a formidable strongpoint, but wave after wave of German assaults finally cleared the village and the heights on the 8th. Nevertheless such were their losses that the Germans could not consolidate and the ridge was

to change hands six times in all. On the eastern sector the Russians managed to contain the German thrust around Ponyri, after bitter street fighting. This meant that by the 10th the front in the northern section of the salient had been stabilized, and the Germans, for the moment, were halted and exhausted.

In the South, where the two sides were more evenly matched than in the north, Manstein's

Above left: Kreim, Kluge and Model discuss tactics as the offensive begins.
Above: Artillery of the exhausted *SS Grossdeutschland Division* fire at the advancing Russians. This division was one of the strongest the Germans employed during the offensive.

forces made greater headway. Russian preparations had been hampered by lack of knowledge of
German intentions. With a concentration of five
panzer divisions north of Belgorod and three to
the east of the city, several options were open to
the Germans, all of which had to be anticipated
by the Russians. There was a risk that by attacking
on the right flank with the three armored divisions,
the *Kampf Group*, the Germans might be able to
roll up the defenses from the east. But the greatest
danger lay in the direct approach with the
Fourth Panzer Army making the main effort against
either Oboyan or Korocha. To meet these eventualities the Russians deployed Sixth Guard and
Seventh Guard Armies on the left and center of the
Voronezh front. Supporting Sixth Guard was the
reinforced First Tank Army with some 1304
armored vehicles. Ahead of these dispositions,
General Hoth, the commander of *Fourth Panzer
Army*, intended to try to sidestep the defenses and
engage the Russian reserves around Kursk and
further east. To prevent these reserves being
moved rapidly to the theater of operations, Hoth
chose to strike midway between Oboyan and
Korocha at Prokhorovka, a place where any
Russian reserves would have to detrain. Thus the
Russian defenses in the south were off-balance to
some extent before the battle began.

Russian Miscalculations
For the Russians in the south things began to go
badly as soon as the battle opened. They had
carefully planned a pre-emptive air attack designed to catch the German aircraft on the
ground, but this plan miscarried because the
Germans had installed radar in the area. This
gave the Germans enough time to get their
aircraft in the air and meet the incoming attack.
Soviet air losses were heavy—though the German
claim of 400 kills is certainly too high—and
this allowed the Germans to secure a local air
supremacy on 5 July. Some 2000 sorties were
flown in support of Manstein's attack which,
unlike Model's, committed most of its armor
from the outset. This plan proved quite successful
and *XLVIII Panzer Corps* was able to break
through 67th Guards Rifle Division and head for
the Psel River crossings and Oboyan. To the east

the *SS Panzer Korps* broke through the defenses of
52nd Guards Rifle Division and began to move
on Prokhorovka, but the *Kampf Group* faced
tougher opposition in Seventh Guard Army and
was only able to make slow progress towards
Rzhavets, a situation that bared the right flank
of the *SS Panzer Korps*.

For both sides the situation was critical.
Except on the front of the *XLVIII Panzer Corps*
the Germans had been unable to make continuous
gains, since the three SS Panzer divisions which
had punched separate holes through the Russian
lines had been unable to link up. Furthermore
Manstein's forces ran up against the same
problems that were to face Model when the
latter put in his attack—the tendency of the
Panthers to break down and catch fire rather
easily, and the danger of the armor and infantry
becoming separated. For the Russians, the loss

Left: Germans bring ammunition forward on a hastily-constructed railway built over partially flooded land near the Kursk salient. Appalling weather conditions at Kursk as elsewhere on the Russian front revealed the inadequacy of German preparations for a brutal war of this kind.

of their forward positions combined with their faulty initial dispositions meant that the decision in the south—and hence the salient generally—was in the melting pot; the familiar exhortations to fight to the last gave credit to the seriousness of the situation.

After the early successes on the 4th Hoth decided to cross the stream in the Sawidowka-Ssyrzew at dawn on the 5th, the areas to the south of the stream having been cleared during the night. Unfortunately, heavy rains swelled the stream to a torrent and inundated the surrounding fields. This gave the Russians a chance to reform, and a combination of human and natural obstacles prevented any German success in the area on the 5th. Nevertheless, on the following day *XLVIII Panzer Corps* was able to resume its offensive; they penetrated to Syrtzewo on the 7th, though some time was lost when *3rd Panzer Division* was forced to deal with a local Russian counterattack that regained part of Sawidowka. On the drying ground the Panzers were able to break almost to the main Russian artillery positions and attempts were made by *XLVIII Panzer Corps* to link-up with the SS Panzers who had managed to penetrate a further four miles on the right. By the 7th the Germans had pried the Russians out of most of their positions on the Pena. On the 8th German forces began to cross the river and successfully withstood a counterattack by T-34s from III Mechanized Corps in support of First Tank Army.

After five days of conflict the Germans had succeeded in breaking through the first two Russian defense lines, but only on the east flank of *XLVIII Panzer Corps* had the extremely strong *SS Grossdeutschland Division* managed to break into the third line. Russian resistance,

Left: Soviet anti-tank crew repulse a Panzer attack.

despite a slackening on the Pena on the 8th, was still fierce and the reserves—especially Fifth Guard Tank Army—were still uncommitted. Wheeling south from the Pena *6th Panzer Division* was able to crush the encircled 71st Guards Rifle Division by the 10th, securing the left flank, but Hoth's intention was to regroup for an attack toward Prokharovka to meet the Russian reserves. On the German right flank the *Kampf Group* was still struggling to make headway against Seventh Guard Army. Overall the result had been poor for the Germans; about 130 square miles of battered earth had changed hands and their maximum penetration had only been ten miles. Nevertheless the Russians had been forced to send some of their reserves to their right flank and this commitment was to weaken the forces they had nursed for the counterattack. The Fifth Guard Tank Army moved into the threatened

areas on the evening of the 9th after a 225-mile move, but it was held back for two more days to organize and prepare while the Germans exhausted themselves in clearing their flanks. For the Russians the crisis had passed. They had halted Model in the north and exhausted Manstein's forces in the south. With fresh troops and unworn equipment they were now ready to counterattack on two fronts against an enemy strained by a week of continuous heavy fighting.

In the south four armies, including the fresh Fifth Guard and Fifth Guard Tank Armies, were detailed to counter the anticipated German assault on Prokhorovka by the *XLVIII* and *SS Panzer Corps*. On the morning of the 12th about 700 German tanks moved out to attack, to be met by about 850 Russian tanks, mostly T-34s. In a head-on clash, as violent as it was unexpected, numbers told, for the Russians were able to

Above: Troops and tanks of the *SS Totenkopf Division* move forward. The soldier in the center is carrying a *Panzerfaust*, the German equivalent of a bazooka, a close-range anti-tank weapon. **Above right:** German machine-gun post during the night fighting at Kursk.

Below: Panthers and Tigers, introduced for the first time at Kursk, pause during a lull in the fighting.

get in close where their guns could penetrate the Tigers and their shorter barrels very often gave them the first critical shot. In a grueling eight-hour battle fought under a blazing sun and a cloud of dust that prevented close air support, the two armored formations played a deadly game of hide and seek. By evening the battlefield was in Russian hands, together with its booty of disabled tanks and wounded crews. About 600 tanks had been lost, roughly equally divided between the two sides. But whereas the Russians still had at least 500 intact, *Fourth Panzer Army* had less than two full strength divisions left and the tired *Grossdeutschland Division* had to go back into action to help extricate *3rd Panzer Division*. Even the belated gains of the *Kampf Group*, which finally managed to capture Rzhavets, could not restore the balance.

In the north too the Germans were in trouble as the Russians attacked in the northern part of the Orel salient in an attempt to cut off Model's armor. In all, some 490,000 combat troops and 1000 tanks and assault guns were in danger of encirclement, but fortunately for the Germans Rokossovsky's attack was weaker than it should have been and Model's forces were able to disengage.

These two counterattacks, combined with the losses suffered, prompted Hitler to abandon the

offensive on the 13th. Three days earlier Anglo-American forces had landed in Sicily and first reports were not encouraging for the Germans. Italian morale and fighting ability was low and it was obvious to Hitler that only by cutting his losses at Kursk and sending armor from Russia could the situation be stabilized. Field Marshal Gunther von Kluge, Model's superior, concurred with this assessment, especially since it would mean the extrication of his threatened forces, but Manstein was adamant in trying to continue the offensive. Either he failed to realize that 20% of his force had been lost in the previous day's eight-hour battle, or he believed that Soviet losses had been so great that victory was within his grasp. In fact he later claimed that Russian losses were four times as heavy as his own. He certainly believed that the Russians had exhausted their reserves and were in no state to meet any further German assault. In this he was quite wrong. Though the Reserve Front had committed its two Guard Armies, three more were unused, while in the north four armies, including two tank armies, remained intact. Manstein was confident that the battle should be continued until the Russian armor already deployed was defeated and he was convinced this could be achieved. Hitler conceded part of the argument and allowed Manstein to continue in the south. Some partial success was achieved when the *Kampf Group* virtually encircled the battered Sixty-Ninth Army near Rzhavets. To hold this thrust the Russians had to commit all the reserves not already allocated to the counteroffensive. Of the eight armies that made up the strategic reserve only one remained. But the Russian commitment of their reserves, and checking of *Kampf's* advance spelled the effective end of Citadel. On the 17th it was finally called off, though fighting continued in the south for another week.

The balance of forces and the initiative had swung heavily in favor of the Soviet Army, but its hope of twin encirclements, already thrown out of gear by Manstein's persistence, never materialized. Despite overwhelming numerical superiority in the northern salient—2:1 in men, 3:1 in artillery, 2.4:1 in tanks and 2:1 in aircraft—the Russians were unable to make the rapid progress necessary to catch Model's forces before

Left: German armor rolls forward across the Steppes. The two tanks closest to the camera have light plating protecting their tracks and turrets against bazooka fire. Below: A knocked-out Tiger is stopped, but the cost in Russian lives was dear.

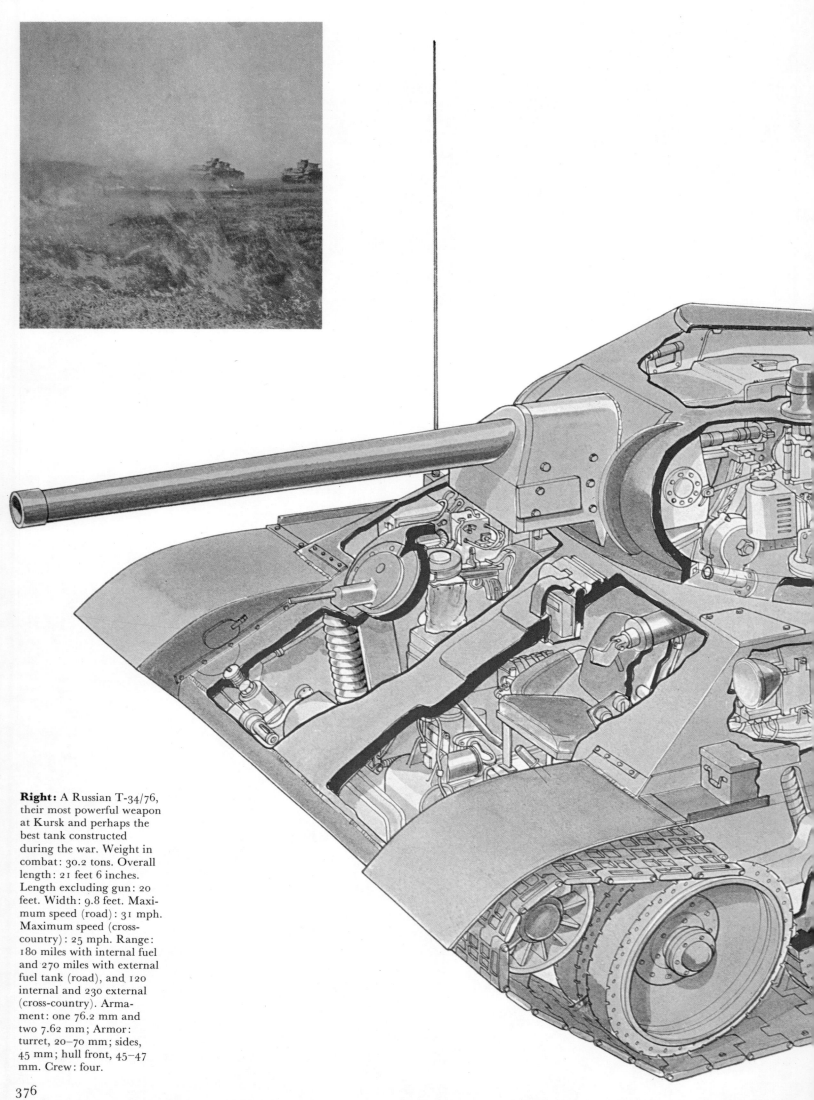

Right: A Russian T-34/76, their most powerful weapon at Kursk and perhaps the best tank constructed during the war. Weight in combat: 30.2 tons. Overall length: 21 feet 6 inches. Length excluding gun: 20 feet. Width: 9.8 feet. Maximum speed (road): 31 mph. Maximum speed (cross-country): 25 mph. Range: 180 miles with internal fuel and 270 miles with external fuel tank (road), and 120 internal and 230 external (cross-country). Armament: one 76.2 mm and two 7.62 mm; Armor: turret, 20–70 mm; sides, 45 mm; hull front, 45–47 mm. Crew: four.

Far left: German tanks found the opposition too much for them and the Kursk offensive slowed to a halt and then a retreat.
Right: A captured T-34 with German markings used by the *SS Leibstandarte Adolf Hitler* at Kursk.

they reached the safety of the Hagen Line, a defensive line across the neck of the salient covering Bryansk. During the two years the area had been in German hands elaborate field fortifications had been built, and these slowed down a Soviet Army unused to this type of operation. Despite the frightening scale of artillery support—attacking infantry regiments had five artillery regiments in support and Eleventh Guard Army massed one artillery piece every five yards for fifteen miles—the Russians were unable to sustain their initial impetus. On 12 July Eleventh Guards penetrated sixteen miles, but this was exceptional. Most gains were in the region of three to four miles, and attempts to feed in reserves failed to secure a lasting advantage. The sheer weight of the Russian assault eventually told, however. By the end of July fighting raged on the outskirts of Orel, and the roads in the area were heavily congested by retreating German columns. By 5 August what was left of Orel, and it was not very much, was in Russian hands but losses in the area were to continue for months to come. Before they left the Germans had strewn the region with mines and skillfully concealed booty traps. Despite harassment from the air and relentless Russian pressure on the ground the Germans were able to get to the Hagen Line in good order. Though no encirclement had been achieved during the pursuit, the Russians had good reason to be pleased; *Army Group Center* had lost 20% of its strength. Fourteen of its divisions, including all its armor, had changed beyond all recognition, and the two armies that had spearheaded the attack, the *Ninth* and *Second Panzer*, were never to recover.

In the south the Russians also attempted an encirclement, but to the southeast of the battle zone. On the Russian left flank the Southwest, South and North Caucasus Fronts had remained passive, while the Kursk battle raged. With the issue by and large resolved on the 12th, North Caucasus Front attacked in the Taman Peninsula, south of the Don, but was repulsed with appalling losses, while attacks by the South and Southwest Fronts met with only partial success and again incurred heavy losses. Russian lack of armor and heavy artillery on these fronts, combined with the fact that, as in the Orel salient, the Germans had had two years to prepare defensive positions, meant that progress was slow. But the German defenses along the River Mius were broken on 19 July and this prevented the despatch of forces to help Manstein's thrust on Rzhavets. The Russian breakthrough on the Mius threatened the whole of the German position in the south, but Hitler was unwilling to evacuate the Donetz basin and ordered counterattacks to be launched. After some heated exchanges between Hitler and Manstein, the latter counterattacked and eliminated the Russian bridgehead, capturing 18,000 prisoners. Yet nothing could stop the steady disintegration of the German position in the south; the Russians were now preparing encircling attacks on Kharkov.

The Russians intended to use a massive infantry attack to beat in the German front, and to feed in their armor to exploit their gains.

With over 650,000 combat troops, 12,000 guns, 2400 tanks and 1200 aircraft the Russians had nearly a 4:1 superiority on the ground and a 4:3 advantage in the air. Narrow frontage and massed artillery characterized the Russian plan. The main thrust was to be on the right with the left flank holding down the *Kampf Group*.

The Attack Opens

The attack opened on 3 August and quickly threatened to overwhelm the German defenses. Belgorod fell on the 5th—its capture and that of Orel prompted the first of the numerous victory salutes that continued to the end of the war—and in places the Russians achieved a 62-mile advance in five days. The *19th Panzer* and three infantry divisions were shattered in the Grayvoron region and even greater danger seemed to threaten the six divisions around Kharkov, which Hitler was determined to hold. Rapid reinforcement combined with astute handling of his armor allowed von Manstein to beat off the first Russian penetration into Kharkov by the 12th, and a heavy counter-attack halted an advance from the east of the city by First Tank Army. Nevertheless, the fall of Kharkov, which had already changed hands five times, could only be postponed and not prevented; its smouldering ruins were ceded on the 23rd. Von Manstein had decided to abandon the city contrary to orders. With Russian offensives being conducted along the whole length of the Russian front, with fresh drafts of men and equipment meeting about 25% of their losses, the Germans in the south could only retreat, hounded all the way to the Dnieper Line. By the new year the eastern Ukraine had been liberated and the Germans had to face Russian offensives throughout the year, not just in the winter—a sure sign of the changing picture in the East.

Losses in the battle are difficult to assess with accuracy. During the whole of the operations around the Kursk-Orel salients German records admit to 907,000 casualties, but the greatest loss had been among the cherished, once all-conquering Panzer divisions. At the height of the battle about 3000 tanks had been on the move at the same time, and it seems likely that about that number were destroyed, perhaps a few hundred more, with the balance of loss being about 40:60 against the Russians. Although Russian losses were no less than the German, the former could make up their casualties, while the latter could not. Kursk-Orel was the swan song of German armor, and the Russian headlines 'The Tigers Are Burning' signified not only the funeral pyre of the Panzer arm but the pall that overhung Germany's New Order and her hopes of victory.

Opposite above: SS Grenadiers await fresh orders during a pause in the withdrawal from the Kursk salient. **Left:** Russian SU-76 self-propelled guns enter Kharkov as the German front is rolled westward after Kursk: 23 August, 1943.

Allied Bomber Offensive

1943

In 1942 the only active land campaign that Britain and the United States could wage against Germany was that in North Africa, where the tactical genius of Field-Marshal Erwin Rommel enabled the German and Italian forces in North Africa to hold the British in a series of see-saw offensives despite the latter's general *matériel* superiority. The Allied position was strengthened later in the year when British and American forces landed in three separate places along the coasts of France's North African possessions, and so opened a two-front offensive against the Axis forces that were gradually being driven back into a smaller and smaller beach-head in Tunisia, which would finally capitulate in May 1943. Although the North African campaign was impor-

tant to the Allies, however, they realized that it was only a subsidiary: the war could only be won by direct action against Germany herself.

Bomber Command—equipment and tactics

During 1942 and 1943, the Allied leaders appreciated that this would be impossible on land, and therefore the bomber offensive, the only other means of taking the war to Germany, would have to be stepped up. Initially this would only be possible through the agency of RAF Bomber Command, under the energetic and forthright command of Air Chief-Marshal Sir Arthur Harris. Since the beginning of the war Bomber Command had been trying to take the war to Germany, at first with bombing attacks on military installations

and industrial targets, combined with leaflet drops on civilian areas, but the evolution of Bomber Command from a small pre-war force into a large and efficient sword-bearer had been a lengthy and at times apparently impossible task. Although some pre-war aircraft, notably the twin-engined Vickers Wellington and Handley Page Hampden, had proved themselves moderately successful, it had been foreseen before the war that four-engined heavy bombers would be necessary, and development of such types had been started in conjunction with that of better twin-engined machines. It was only in late 1940 that the first of the new bombers, the four-engined Short Stirling, entered service, and reasonable quantities of this, the Handley Page Halifax and Avro Lancaster, derived from the unsuccessful twin-engined Avro Manchester, began to enter service. With the Halifax and Lancaster, Bomber Command at last had the right aircraft, but now had to face the major problems of delivering with accuracy the greater bomb-loads of the new aircraft. Right up to the end of 1941, however, the bombing accuracy of most aircrews was abysmal, only a very small percentage of the bomb-load dropped falling within several miles of the intended target. The problem was really one of training, the majority of crews being so new to their tasks, as a result of Bomber Command's rapid expansion, that their ability to fly in close proximity to other aircraft for long distances, and to navigate with the degree of accuracy required, was strictly limited. The problem was further exacerbated by the gradual switch of Bomber Command's main efforts to night bombing as a result of the heavy casualties suffered in day raids in 1940 and 1941. With a few classic exceptions, Bomber Command under the leadership of Harris devoted itself almost exclusively to night raids, first against industrial targets and then against civilian residential areas. In such raids pinpoint accuracy was not essential, although with increased practice and training the navigational abilities of most crews were improving considerably.

The system eventually adopted, not without hesitation, by Bomber Command, was that the target would be marked just before the arrival of the main bomber force, by special 'pathfinders', formed into a separate group under the command of Air Vice-Marshal D.C.T. Bennett. These

Below: The Short Stirling I was Britain's first four-engined heavy bomber, but proved disappointing in combat, especially for its poor altitude performance.

pathfinders, skilled crews with the latest navigational and bombing aids, would mark the main target with red and green marker bombs, so that on arrival the main force could clearly see where they should drop their high explosive and incendiary bombs. The problems of the main force navigators were thus eased considerably, as on the outward leg of the sortie they had to arrive with only moderate accuracy over the target area. The return journey still posed problems, though, as the right airfield had to be found. Operationally, too, the approach to the target area was fraught with difficulties for the navigator and pilot. Early experience with the growing bomber numbers despatched against single targets had shown that the stream of bombers tended to straggle out in time and space, reducing the effectiveness of mass bombing, and giving the German defences, both night-fighters and AA guns, more opportunity.

The solution that gradually evolved was based on very careful timing and routing: squadrons took off from their airfields at specified times, rendezvoused in the right order over a predetermined spot and then struck off towards the target in a tightly concentrated stream, with a number of master navigators ensuring that the stream keep on the right course. Individual crews still had their work cut out, though, with keeping station in the bomber stream, avoiding collisions with other aircraft and then finding the right spot to bomb before turning for home.

Clearly the difficulty felt by most crews was that of navigating and bombing in the dark, when few landmarks might be visible, and the target would be blacked out. In 1943, however, three radio/radar aids to navigation and bombing entered widespread service, and at last Bomber Command had just about everything it needed to become a truly strategic air force. The threat that had been made with the first '1000-bomber' raid against Cologne on 30–31 May, 1942 was about to become a reality.

The first of these radio aids to enter service, in March 1942, was Gee, a navigation aid. In this, three ground stations in Britain broadcast a series of radio pulses; in the aircraft the navigator could determine his position by referring to a special map showing how the waves intersected and collating this information with the pulses coming in through his receiver.

The second aid, which entered service in March 1943, was Oboe, a bombing device: the aircraft flew along an arc of constant radius from a ground transmitter, the arc running over the target and the navigator keeping on the arc by means of a special receiver which told him if the aircraft were deviating to the left or the right; over the target the bombs were released when a signal from a second ground station, whose arc intersected the first's over the target, was received. Although relatively short in range, and usable by only one aircraft at a time, Oboe proved its worth in ensuring the accuracy of pathfinder aircraft on whose indicator markers the main force would bomb.

The best of the aids, which could be used both for navigating and for bombing, was H$_2$S, a radar device that 'looked' downwards and projected onto the navigator's screen a moving map of the

country over which the aircraft was flying. Skilled operators were able to work wonders with H_2S, which entered service in December 1942. The great advantage of H_2S over both Gee and Oboe was that the whole system was located in the aircraft, making ground stations, with their problems of range, unnecessary. The value of the new device was amply proved on the last day of 1942, when 13 aircraft fitted with H_2S marked Hamburg so well in very poor conditions that the main force inflicted heavy damage whereas previously it would have had to turn for home unable to find the target. These three devices, fitted to the Halifax, Lancaster and de Havilland Mosquito aircraft of the Pathfinder Force, in reality made possible Great Britain's contribution to the combined bomber offensive launched against Germany by the Allies in 1943.

German defences

In the face of the steadily growing threat of Bomber Command's raids, the Germans had

bomber visually and attack. Although a relatively clumsy system, in that the number of interceptions that could be made was limited, and in that British radio operators could sometimes interfere with the German controller's messages, the system worked well enough until the bomber streams sent over by the RAF became so large that even 100% successful interceptions would have been little more than pinpricks. The two main German night-fighters were the Messerschmitt Bf 110 and Junkers Ju 88. Both of these were adaptations, the first of a heavy 'bomber destroyer' and the latter of a medium bomber, but were very useful and successful night-fighters, especially when the Germans were able to fit them with more sophisticated radar enabling them to dispense with the limitations inherent in the Kammhuber Line's *Himmelbett* radar control in favour of the looser control of improved sets which could operate with more than one fighter at a time.

In time the war of radar versus radar was to become extremely complex and involved as both sides worked feverishly to devise systems that could not be jammed or distorted by the other side, while at the same time trying to do just this to the others! In the middle of 1943, however, the science of radar-derived night-fighting was still in its infancy and lacked the complexities of later operations. It was in the raid on Hamburg at the end of July 1943, however, that the British first used 'Window', millions of pieces of reflective tinfoil, dropped to produce an absolute mass of echoes that would totally confuse the picture on the German radar screens and make ground-controlled interceptions all but impossible. The failure of the *Himmelbett* system as a result of the first use of 'Window' brought home fully to the Germans the limitations of their present radar/night-fighter defences, and led to the replacement of Kammhuber by General Josef Schmid. The latter did much to raise the German night-fighter arm into a major and efficient force that during 1944 came close to stopping Bomber Command in its tracks. In the short term, however, there was little that Schmid could do, and the night-fighters had to recourse to '*Wilde Sau*' or Wild Boar tactics devised by Major Hajo Herrmann, in which single-engined

quickly improvized useful defences. Apart from the basic AA gun defences, based for the most part on 3.7-cm, 8.8-cm and 10.5-cm guns working in co-operation with searchlights, these defences were for the most part night-fighters operating in a system called the 'Kammhuber Line' after its developer, Major-General Josef Kammhuber, the head of the *Luftwaffe's* night-fighter arm. (It should be noted that the AA defences, unlike those of Great Britain, were part of the air force, both organizationally and tactically.) The Kammhuber Line, running along the northern parts of the territories controlled by Germany, consisted of a series of 'box' areas. A single night-fighter was allocated to each of these boxes, which in turn had two basic radar sets, one to detect the British bombers and the other to locate the German night-fighter. A controller in each box could then vector the fighter in close enough to a likely target for the fighter's own radar to pick up the victim and for the fighter's own radar operator then to direct his pilot in close enough to pick up the

Above: Air Chief-Marshal Sir Arthur Harris, Air Officer Commanding-in-Chief, Bomber Command, examines aerial photographs showing bomb damage to a German target after a raid. At the table in the foreground, WAAF interpreters with stereoscopic viewers examine further photographs to assess the extent of the damage.

fighters took off just before a raid and tried to attack bombers caught in the beams of search-lights or silhouetted against ground fires. The system was later improved upon by Major Viktor von Lossberg. The new tactics, in which the German fighters were ground-controlled into the bomber stream before it reached the target, being designated '*Zähme Sau*' or Tame Boar. These latter tactics proved highly successful in the winter of 1943, and to counter them Bomber Command had to call for night-fighters that would fly in with the bomber stream and tackle the German night-fighters. At the beginning of Operation 'Gomorrah', which was virtually to destroy Hamburg, these '*Wilde Sau*' and '*Zähme Sau*' tactics were in the future, although Herrmann was already trying to persuade Kammhuber to adopt the simple Tame Boar tactics. Kammhuber, however, was loathe to allow single-seater fighters to operate over areas designated as *Flak* responsibilities, and turned down the idea.

The raids on Hamburg

The origins of the four great raids in which Bomber Command razed Hamburg may be traced to the 'Pointblank' directive that emerged from the Casablanca conference between President Franklin D. Roosevelt, Prime Minister Churchill

and the Combined Chiefs-of-Staff Committee in the period between 14 and 23 January, 1943. The 'Pointblank' directive finalized some of the items in a general agreement on the bombing of Germany, in which the British were to tackle the German economy and civilian morale with night-time saturation bombing of cities, while the Americans, in the form of the 8th Army Air Force, were to try to reduce Germany's air strength with daylight precision raids against aircraft production facilities and against the *Luftwaffe* itself. These round-the-clock activities were then to be co-ordinated into devastating raids against German industry, with a view to destroying her capacity to wage a modern war. The order of priority for targets as laid down in the 'Pointblank' directive was: '(a) German submarine construction yards. (b) The German aircraft industry. (c) Transportation. (d) Oil plants. (e) Other targets in enemy war industry.' There was, however, a certain failure to co-ordinate the two forces' efforts, principally because the relevant commanders, Harris and Lieutenant-General Ira C. Eaker, chose to interpret the directive in different fashions. The order was in fact altered several times, with attacks on submarine construction gradually enjoying less priority as the U-boat threat diminished and the difficulty of inflicting decisive damage was realized.

Hamburg was clearly a target of importance: it was the second largest city in Germany, had an important communications role, and contained three large yards building U-boats. But by July 1943 it had been raided no less than 98 times, and the defences of the city were formidably strong. In the air there were 20 *Himmelbett* control boxes of the Kammhuber Line, with their aircraft operating from three large airbases; on the ground there were three smoke-generator groups charged with covering the area with impenetrable fog as soon as the approach of the bombers seemed imminent, plus 54 heavy *Flak* batteries and 22 searchlight batteries. These did indeed pose formidable problems for the British bombers, as earlier raids had discovered, and so on the afternoon of 24 July there was considerable gloom as crews discovered that the night's target was to be Hamburg. Even a carefully worded but slightly evasive note about 'Window', to be used for the first time, did nothing to improve matters. Yet 'Window' was to be the key to Operation 'Gomorrah', as the first raid was to prove.

As was their usual practice, the Germans had been listening in at their radio interception stations for signs of an impending British raid: testing of the bombers radio sets in the morning usually meant a raid that night, for faults discovered in the morning could be repaired in the afternoon; testing throughout the day meant that only routine maintenance was being carried out, and that no major attacks need be expected. During the morning of 24 July, therefore, the Germans had pretty clear indications that a major British raid was in the offing. But where would the bombs fall? the radio interception service could not provide this kind of information, so the controllers of the night-fighter and *Flak* services, together with the heads of the German civil defence organization, would have to wait until the first radar reports started to come in. In the evening of the 24th the German commanders waited anxiously: the forthcoming raid was clearly to be a major one, for since the raid on Aachen on the night of 13 to 14 July Bomber Command had been strangely quiescent. This was partially as a result of its exertions in the Battle of the Ruhr, which had started on 5 March with a raid on Essen and finished on 28 June with a raid on Cologne (after large portions of Essen, Duisberg, Düsseldorf, Wuppertal, Bochum and other cities had been destroyed), partially because replacements for men and machines had to be found and integrated into the system, and partially because Harris and his staff were preparing for a massive blow against a new target. For although the 'Pointblank' directive had laid down a specified list of objectives, the preamble of the directive stated: 'Your primary objective will be the progressive destruction and dislocation of the German military, industrial and economic system, and the undermining of the morale of the German people to a point where their capacity for armed resistance is fatally weakened.' As Harris himself pointed out: 'It gave me a very wide range of choice and allowed me to attack pretty well any German industrial city of 100,000 inhabitants and above.'

The first British bombers took off from Oakington at 2155 in the evening dusk of 24 July, and soon the skies over East Anglia, Lincolnshire and southern Yorkshire were loaded with the roar of engines as the bombers climbed slowly towards their cruising altitudes and headed out over the North Sea towards the rendezvous point. After two hours the force had linked up and taken up the right stations, and had set off for Germany nearly 800 aircraft strong: 73 Vickers Wellingtons, 125 Short Stirlings, 246 Handley Page Halifaxes and 347 Avro Lancasters, in all 791 bombers heading towards Germany at some 360 km/h (225 mph). *En route* to Hamburg the bomber stream was reduced by 45 aircraft turning back with some sort of mechanical or systems failure.

A radar station near Ostend was the first to detect the British force, and soon the headquarters of the *Reich's* fighter defence organization were fully manned by attentive personnel, waiting to detect and attack the intruders. These headquarters were located at strategic points in Germany and occupied Europe: the 1st Air Division at Deelen near Arnhem in Holland under the command of Lieutenant-General von Döring; the 2nd Air Division at Stade on the lower Elbe river under the command of Lieutenant-General Schwabedissen; the 3rd Air Division at Metz under the command of Major-General Junck; the 4th Air Division at Döberitz near Berlin under the command of Major-General Huth; and the newly-formed 5th Air Division at Schlessheim near Munich under the command of Colonel

Left: *Würzburg* was the most important German medium-range early warning radar until the British neutralised it with 'Window' in 1943. **Below:** A German U-boat sets off on a raiding mission from a concrete pen on France's Atlantic coast, guarded against sudden attack by a light *Flak* gun. U-boats and their pens were the Allies' prime heavy bomber target at the start of 1943.

Above: The de Havilland Mosquito was Britain's equivalent to the Ju 88, and was a sharp thorn in the Germans' side, especially as a nuisance bomber and pathfinder aircraft.

Harry von Bülow. At the headquarters of the 2nd Air Division, the first radar sightings had prompted the despatch of Bf 110 night-fighters of *Nachtjagdgeschwader* 3 from their bases at Stade, Vechta, Wittmundhaven, Wunstorf, Lüneburg and Kastrup to intercept.

Yet again, the Germans confidently expected that the Bf 110s, under *Himmelbett* control, would inflict severe losses on what were clearly the pathfinder aircraft for the main force. And then, from the German point of view, disaster struck: the radar 'blips' failed to move. The *Würzburg* sets, operating on a wavelength of 53 cm, were completely jammed, although the *Freya* sets, operating on the much longer wavelength of 240 cm, could just distinguish the bomber stream from the false echoes. But *Himmelbett* interception depended on the faultless operation of both the *Würzburg* and *Freya* of each ground-control box, and so the German night-fighters were now useless.

The bomber stream forged on entirely unattacked, leaving the impotent German defences to wait for the first visual sightings from coastal observers to indicate where the attack was to fall. 'Window' had proved totally effective, the multitude of tinfoil strips dropped by the bombers taking some 15 minutes to fall to the ground, all the time providing an echo like that which might be produced by 11,000 bombers. Even had the ground stations' radar sets been able to 'see' through the tinfoil cloud, the *Lichtenstein* sets carried by the Bf 110s could not, and so the chances of interception were minimal in the extreme, each strip of tinfoil producing the same radar picture as a large bomber. Stade, only a few miles from Hamburg, could not defend the city. A few fighters managed to find quarry, but the feelings of the majority may be summed up in the words of a night-fighter pilot:

'At 5000 metres my radio operator announced the first enemy on his *Lichtenstein*. I was delighted. I swung round on to the bearing, in the direction of the Rhur, for in this way I was bound to approach the stream. Facius proceeded to report three or four targets on his screens. I hoped that I should have enough ammunition to deal with them!

Then Facius shouted: "Tommy flying towards us at a great speed. Distance decreasing ... 2000 metres ...

1500 ... 1000 ... 500 ... he's gone."

I was speechless. Facius already had a new target. "Perhaps it was a German night-fighter on a westerly course," I said to myself and made for the next bomber. It was not long before Facius shouted again: "Bomber coming for us at a hell of a speed. 2000 ... 1000 ... 500 ... he's gone?"'

These fast-moving blips were, of course, tiny pieces of foil hanging almost stationary in the air, the speed indicated by the radar operator being that of the Bf 110 overtaking the foil. Some of the few real interceptions made by the nightfighters were the result of astute operators realizing that only blips that appeared to be stationary (i.e. were moving in the same direction as the fighter and at approximately the same speed) could be aircraft.

The attack plan was working perfectly, very few of the bombers having been engaged by the night-fighters. The most difficult moments so far had perhaps being to ensure that a bundle of 'Window' was dropped through the flare chute in each aircraft once every minute. The operational plan called for the pathfinders, 20 in number, to arrive over Hamburg at 0057 and mark the target area, dropping on the information provided by their H_2S radar sets, with yellow target indicators and illuminators. At 0058 another eight aircraft, this time bombing visually on the yellow markers already dropped, were to mark the target with red indicators. Then at 0102 the main force was to start bombing on the target indicators, the last aircraft passing over the target at 0105.

All went perfectly to plan. After forming up, the pathfinders and main force had headed out over the North Sea due east. At 0015 the pathfinders turned south-east into the Heligoland Bight, and at 0040 crossed the German coast. Ten minutes later, at 0050, the pathfinders turned south-south-east, onto the course on which they would attack, and arrived over the target right on schedule.

It had been clear for some 30 minutes by now that Hamburg was to be the bombers' target, and even if the fighters could not prevent the raid, the civil defence authorities could operate and get their charges into the air-raid bunkers. The full-scale raid alarm had been sounded at 0031, and

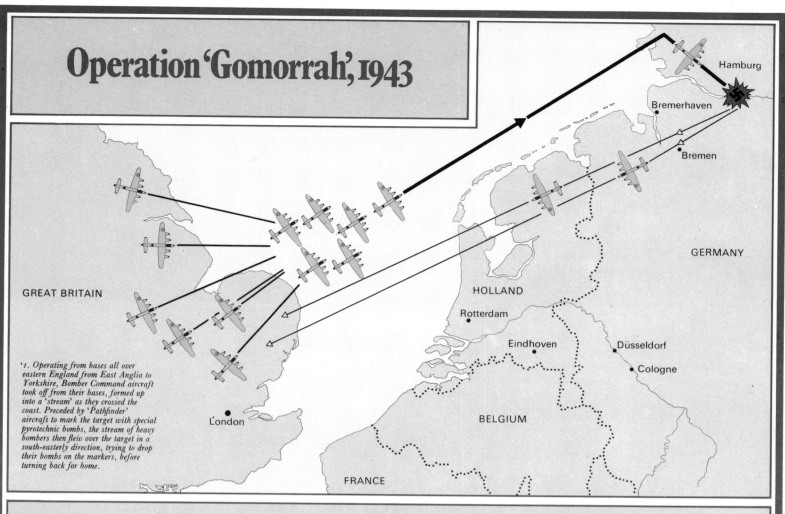

Operation 'Gomorrah', 1943

GREAT BRITAIN

GERMANY

HOLLAND

Rotterdam

Eindhoven

Düsseldorf

Cologne

BELGIUM

FRANCE

London

Hamburg

Bremerhaven

Bremen

'1. Operating from bases all over eastern England from East Anglia to Yorkshire, Bomber Command aircraft took off from their bases, formed up into a 'stream' as they crossed the coast. Preceded by 'Pathfinder' aircraft to mark the target with special pyrotechnic bombs, the stream of heavy bombers then flew over the target in a south-easterly direction, trying to drop their bombs on the markers, before turning back for home.

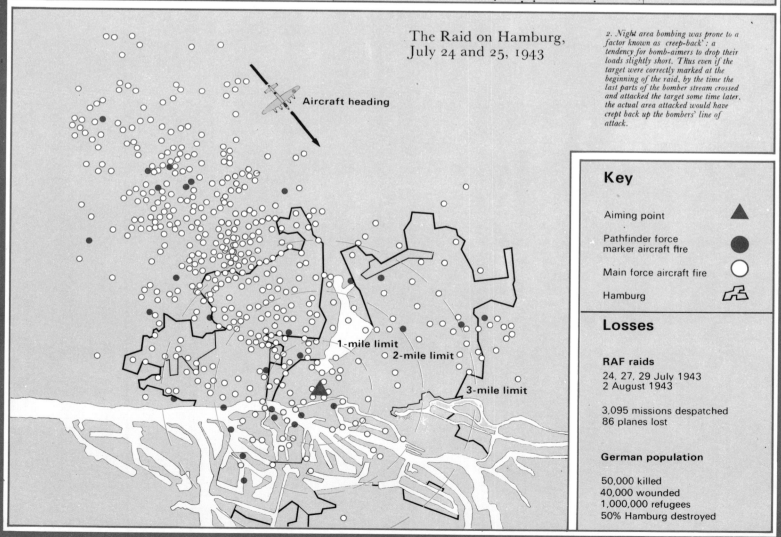

The Raid on Hamburg, July 24 and 25, 1943

Aircraft heading

2. Night area bombing was prone to a factor known as 'creep-back': a tendency for bomb-aimers to drop their loads slightly short. Thus even if the target were correctly marked at the beginning of the raid, by the time the last parts of the bomber stream crossed and attacked the target some time later, the actual area attacked would have crept back up the bombers' line of attack.

1-mile limit

2-mile limit

3-mile limit

Key

Aiming point

Pathfinder force marker aircraft fire

Main force aircraft fire

Hamburg

Losses

RAF raids
24, 27, 29 July 1943
2 August 1943

3,095 missions despatched
86 planes lost

German population

50,000 killed
40,000 wounded
1,000,000 refugees
50% Hamburg destroyed

as the civilians rushed to the bunkers, the defence of Hamburg now lay fairly in the lap of the *Flak* defences, aided by searchlights. Like the fighters, though, the *Flak* effort was dependent on radar to a great extent, and had also been blinded. The master searchlights, which most bomber crews feared considerably, were merely pointing up into the sky with no radar to direct them, and so it would be only by chance that the gunners would see a target they could engage. Predicted fire on individual aircraft was completely out of the question, so the local *Flak* commander, with 54 heavy and 26 light AA batteries under his command, ordered the guns to put up as heavy a fire as they could into a three-dimensional box in which he reckoned most of the bombers would have to fly to bomb accurately on the target markers.

Most of the bombers got through and dropped their loads with reasonable accuracy, and by 0150 the British were heading for home, relieved that at last there seemed to be a counter for the depradations of the German night-fighters and *Flak*. Only 12 aircraft (four Lancasters, four Halifaxes, three Stirlings and one Wellington) were lost—a loss rate of only 1.5%, well below the normal 6% loss rate for a raid on Hamburg, which would have cost about 50 aircraft. Some 92,000,000 strips of 'Window' were dropped, and it is interesting to note that No 103 Squadron, which bombed from above the main force, and therefore from above the 'Window', lost three Lancasters. The Stirlings, which would have lost proportionally the most aircraft, had a lower ceiling than the other types, and were thus well shaded by the 'Window' falling from above, thereby suffering smaller losses than might have been expected. This factor had been appreciated by Bomber Command, whose leaflet on 'Window' had advised the bomber crews to keep as close together as possible so that all might be protected by the bundles of 'Window' dropped by every aircraft.

The Americans took a hand on 25 and 26 July, with two raids on the port of Hamburg with 235 Boeing B-17 Flying Fortresses. The RAF returned to the attack on the 27th, when 722 bombers struck again at Hamburg, and the good weather that had helped this raid continued on into the 29th, when another 699 bombers attacked the city. The final blow against Hamburg, on 2 August, was hampered by heavy cloud, and only half of the 740 bombers claimed that they had attacked the target, the pathfinder indicators being all but invisible through the murk.

It was the second raid, on 27–28 July, for which the Battle of Hamburg has become best known. Little rain had fallen in the previous month, wood was tinder dry, and the previous day had been a scorcher. Into this tinder-box the RAF dropped an enormous weight of high explosive and incendiary bombs. The HE blew apart buildings and the incendiaries soon set fire to the wreckage. The bombing was well concentrated, and soon a 'firestorm' developed. In such a fire, the extreme heat of the concentrated fires produces a vast updraught, which causes more air, full of oxygen, to rush in at the bottom, fuelling the fire. The process is self-perpetuating until everything combustible in the area has been totally burned. Quite apart from this factor, moreover, intense heat is generated, winds of more than hurricane force are produced and the air is exhausted of oxygen.

Virtually nothing can survive such a firestorm, and its effects are appalling. As Major-General Kehrl, head of Hamburg's civil defence organization said: 'Children were torn away from their parents' hands by the force of the hurricane and whirled into the fire. People who thought they had escaped fell down, overcome by the devouring force of the heat, and died in an instant. Refugees had to make their way over the dead and dying. The sick and the infirm had to be left behind by the rescuers as they themselves were in danger of burning.' In the aftermath of the second raid *Gauleiter* Kaufmann appealed to all non-essential civilians to flee the city, which they did with alacrity, thereby reducing the number of victims of the next two raids.

Nevertheless the blow struck against Germany was an immense one. Some 9000 tons of bombs had fallen on the city, killing 30,482 people and destroying 277,330 buildings—more than half the city. The cost to the RAF had been small: 87 bombers lost and 174 damaged out of a total of more than 3000 sorties despatched. The value of 'Window' had been proved, and although the German night-fighters were able to come up with partial answers once they had got over their initial shock at the introduction of the new 'weapon', Bomber Command had secured a useful short-term advantage.

Below: A Handley Page Halifax I in flight. The Halifax bore the brunt of the British strategic night offensive against Germany together with the Lancaster. **Below left:** Bomb damage in the streets of Hamburg, devastated in July and August 1943.

Daylight raids by the USAAF

The saturation area bombing of RAF Bomber Command was, however, only half of the Allied strategic air effort, and while Harris was planning his next campaign, a huge onslaught against Berlin, it was the American daylight campaign that hit the headlines.

The instrument forged by the United States to take the bombing war to Germany was at first the 8th Army Air Force, commanded by Lieutenant-General Ira C. Eaker up to the end of 1943, and then by Major-General James H. Doolittle. This eventually became half of the Strategic Air Forces commanded by Lieutenant-General Carl A. Spaatz, the other half being the 15th Army Air Force in Italy. Loosely controlled from the other side of the Atlantic by General H.H. Arnold, the Strategic Air Forces (and in particular the 8th Air Force operating from Great Britain) were to partner RAF Bomber Command in devastating Germany in the manner envisaged in the 'Point-blank' directive.

The problem with any bi- or multi-national undertaking is the co-ordination of intent and effort. This applied with some force to the Anglo-American bombing effort in 1942 and 1943. For although the eventual decision that the USAAF should bomb by day, and that the RAF should bomb by night, appears simple and logical, it did not appear so at the time, and was the cause of considerable controversy. For many reasons, notably their possession of two good bombers (the B-17 and the Consolidated B-24 Liberator), the

Below: An American armourer at work in a camouflaged bomb dump. **Right, above:** The ground crew chief watches the pilot climb into the cockpit of his Republic P-47 Thunderbolt fighter. Note the droppable fuel tank under the fuselage, to give the 'Jug' extra range for escort missions. **Right, below:** The crew of a Boeing B-17 Flying Fortress bomber after a mission. The navigator has just thrown his flight pack into the back of the waiting truck.

availability of the excellent Norden bombsight, which made precision bombing from high altitude possible, and considerable pre-war experience and thought about strategic bombing, the Americans had decided that the only way in which Germany could be brought to her knees by the application of air power was the systematic elimination of key processes in her manufacturing industries, the throttling of her communications network and the destruction of her energy sources. All this was sound in theory. The British, however, who had combat experience against such targets in the face of improving German defences, pointed out that the cost in men and machines would be too high—it was for this very reason that they had turned from such pinpoint targets by day to area bombing by night.

The disagreement was academic during the first half of 1942, for it was only on 1 July, 1942 that the 8th Air Force received its first aircraft, a B-17E which had flown across the Atlantic to

land at Prestwick in Scotland. Marshal of the Royal Air Force Sir Charles Portal, the Chief of the Air Staff, supported by Harris, urged Spaatz, commanding the US air forces in Great Britain (the Strategic Air Forces were not formed until January 1944) to combine his forces with Bomber Command so that the size of the night offensive against Germany could be doubled or tripled. The Americans, however, were fully confident that their bombers could produce worthwhile results by day, no matter what the British experience had been. Their bombers, the American commanders claimed, could fight their way through to the targets in tight three-dimensional boxes, the guns of each Flying Fortress and Liberator covering the other aircraft in the box. In this way, the Americans thought, there was no way that the Germans could fight their way into the great boxes and cut them down.

Neither side would compromise, and so it was eventually decided that each would go for the type of bombing it thought best for its aircraft and tactics.

Key to the American approach was the US belief in the two basic bombers to be operated, the B-17 and B-24. Both were good machines, four-engined monoplanes with a heavy defensive armament of .5-inch machine guns. Combat experience, however, was soon to persuade the Americans that bomb-load was insufficient except at the expense of range, and that better armament and protection yet were needed. The faith of the Americans, though, is indicated in the rapid build-up of B-17 and B-24 groups in England during 1943: on 1 January there were five B-17

the B-17s and B-24s, despite Thunderbolt escort, were not invulnerable. Even if this was not a full lesson, the Americans were to be given a fuller one when 178 B-24s raided the oilfields at Ploiesti in Romania from Benghazi in North Africa on 1 August. Some damage was caused by the Liberators, but 48 of their number were shot down and another 55 badly damaged.

The Schweinfurt raids

These warnings and others were explained away by a number of factors, and Eaker finally decided that his forces were ready for a major deep-penetration mission against a strategic target in Germany. The target selected was Schweinfurt, one of the centres of the German ball-bearing industry. If the factories producing ball-bearings in this town could be destroyed, it was reasoned, a large proportion of Germany's war effort would be affected: the bearings needed for industry and the armed services would soon be unavailable, helping to bring Germany to her knees. At the same time the Messerschmitt factory at Regensburg, farther to the south, was also to be attacked. This had the advantage of keeping up the pressure against the German aircraft industry, and would also have the effect of drawing off and exhausting the German fighter defences, as the Regensburg force was to go in slightly before the Schweinfurt one.

The attack was scheduled for 17 August, with the 4th Bombardment Wing tackling Regensburg and then flying on to North Africa, and the 1st Bombardment Wing attacking Schweinfurt. Although the two missions were at first meant to be only ten minutes apart, various considerations meant that eventually something like four hours separated the two raids, with the result that the first raid warned the Germans that something was in the offing, and then gave them time to bring in as many fighters as possible to counter the first raid, and then have them nicely ready, rearmed

and two B-24; on 1 April five and five; on 1 July eleven and zero; on 1 October seventeen and four; and on 1 December nineteen and seven. Just as impressive are the number of sorties flown by these groups in the same months: 279, 379, 2334, 2159 and 5618.

Despite the eventual size of her war effort, though, the United States was relatively slow to bring the 8th Air Force to bear on Germany, preferring for this force to feel its way forward with raids against closer and less well protected targets in occupied Europe before committing them to deep-penetration raids into Germany proper. A number of raids in northern Germany were made, however, such as that of 11 June, 1943 against the U-boat yards at Wilhelmshaven, but the majority of raids made useful progress against targets such as marshalling yards in France. Eaker was keen to get to grips with his main adversary, the *Luftwaffe* and the factories that produced its aircraft, so as soon as he had received his first Republic P-47 Thunderbolt fighters fitted with underwing drop tanks to increase their range, he decided on a raid into Germany. On 28 July, just after the second British raid against Hamburg as part of Operation 'Gomorrah', the Fieseler factory at Kassel-Bettenhausen and the AGO facility at Aschersleben, both of which built Focke-Wülf Fw 190 fighters, were attacked, the Americans losing 22 bombers to the Germans' seven fighters. Clearly

Above: A Boeing B-17G in flight. This was the definitive model of this standard American bomber, and featured a chin turret as extra protection against German head-on attacks.
Far left: German fighter pilots discuss tactics against the Consolidated B-24 Liberator. The wires projecting from the model show the fields of fire of the aircraft's defensive machine-guns.

Above: Messerschmitt Bf 109G-1 fighters await delivery to the *Luftwaffe* outside the factory. Such factories were prime targets for the American bomber forces. **Above right:** The waist gunners of a B-17 watch for attackers, their .5-inch machine-guns ready. **Right:** The crew of a German *Flakvierling* 2cm quadruple AA gun ready for action. Note the man on the right, holding a small rangefinder.

and refuelled, when the Schweinfurt force arrived. Hopes that the Regensburg mission would maul the German interceptor fighters severely were, unfortunately, to be wildly optimistic.

As ordered, the Regensburg mission was flown by three Combat Wings, with 21 aircraft being supplied by each of the 4th Bombardment Wing's seven groups. The first Combat Wing was led by Colonel Archie J. Old's 96th Group, with Colonel Edgar M. Wittan's 390th Group as high group and Colonel William B. David's 388th Group as low group. The second Combat Wing had only two groups, Colonel Frederick W. Castle's 94th Group in the lead with Colonel Elliott Vandevanter's 385th Group as low group. The third Combat Wing also had only two groups, Colonel John K. Gerhart's 95th Group in the lead and Colonel Neil B. Harding's 100th Group as low group.

Poor weather meant a late start, and a diversionary raid on Arras had drawn off only 39 German fighters. The American escort was also understrength, and the third Combat Wing was left unprotected from the time it crossed the coast. Despite this, all at first seemed well. Then the German fighters began to attack in earnest, and

the B-17s started to fall: four by the time Eupen had been reached, another three by Kaiserslautern, and a further seven on the last leg to Regensburg, which was reached at 1156. The bombing run was made from a lower altitude than originally planned, and then the remaining B-17s turned south towards Africa. The Germans were dumbfounded, their fighters having broken off combat in order to refuel and rearm so that the bombers could once again be attacked as they returned to England. Nonetheless, another eight B-17s were lost *en route* to North Africa, where the first bomber landed at 1728. Of the 147 aircraft sent out by the 4th Bombardment Wing, 24 had been lost: it was an inauspicious start for the Schweinfurt mission.

This was to be flown by two task forces, each made up of two Combat Wings from the 1st Bombardment Wing. This meant a reshuffle of the squadrons involved, as the 1st BW had three Provisional Combat Bombardment Wings, each having four squadrons. One squadron was taken from each of the 101st, 102nd and 103rd PCBWs to make up the fourth Combat Wing. In all, 216 aircraft were put up by the 1st Bombardment Wing.

The first task force was based on the 101st and 102nd PCBWs, the former leading with Lieutenant-Colonel Clemens L. Wurzbach's 91st Group in the lead, with Colonel Joseph J. Nazarro's 381st Group as low group and Colonel William A. Hatcher Jnr's 351st Group as high group. In the 102nd PCBW, the lead, low and high groups respectively were Lieutenant-Colonel William M. Reid's 92nd Group, Lieutenant-Colonel Donald K. Fargo's 305th Group and Colonel George A. Robinson's 306th Group.

The second task force, the 103rd PCBW and the detached squadrons, had Colonel Maurice A. Preston's 379th Group in the lead, with Colonel Julius K. Lacey's 384th Group and Colonel Kermit D. Steven's 303rd Group, and then the nine detached squadrons forming the last Combat Wing. The force crossed the English coast at 1326, compared with the Regensburg's force's 0935.

The Germans were ready and waiting, and soon the American bombers were under attack from large numbers of fighters, single- and twin-engined, using all sorts of attack methods. Three B-17s had gone down by the time Eupen had been reached, another 12 by the time the force made its final turn towards Schweinfurt at Mainz,

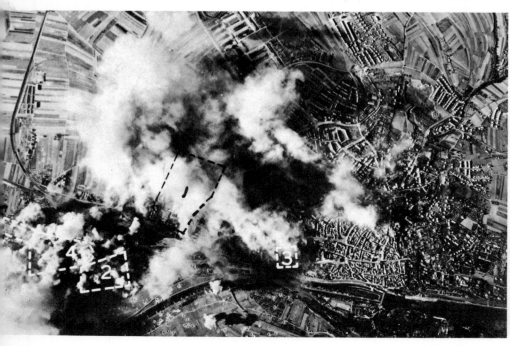

and a further six before Schweinfurt was reached at 1500. The bombing was good, and considerable damage was caused.

The Germans, waiting anxiously to see what the Americans would now do, were relieved to see them turn back for England. The attacks on the bomber force continued, and by Meiningen another three B-17s had succumbed, with another seven falling by Eupen and a further five before home was reached.

Total American losses were 60 aircraft, out of 363 despatched: 16% of the bombers despatched and 19% of those that reached their targets. As Major-General Adolf Galland, the German *General der Jagdflieger*, said: the day had been 'a disaster for the enemy'.

The whole question of daylight precision bombing was naturally enough called into question as a result of this joint raid. More importantly, perhaps, the losses were reported faithfully in the American press, and the US public was deeply shocked. Yet the 8th Air Force was still determined to press on with the type of bombing its commanders thought correct, despite the fact that the 17 August missions had shown that fighter

Far left, top: American commanders plan the course of future operations. Among those present are General Dwight Eisenhower, with Major-General Carl Spaatz on his left and Lieutenant-General Ira Eaker standing at the left. **Far left, centre:** A Consolidated B-24D Liberator of the 2nd Bombardment Division in flight. **Far left, bottom:** An 8th Air Force aerial photograph of the target area in Schweinfurt during the raid of 14 October 1943. The numbered sections are the target factories. **Above:** The Focke Wulf Fw 190 was the companion of the Bf 109 in the air defence of the Third Reich against American bomber forces. **Left:** B-17s of the 306th Bombardment Group in flight.

Right: An American air gunner poses in front of his B-17, loaded with .5-inch ammunition belts. **Far right:** Groundcrew empty spent cases from the fuselage of a B-17 after a mission.

escort right to the target and back was essential. For the next five weeks, therefore, the 8th Air Force contented itself with raids against *Luftwaffe* airfields in northern France, Belgium and Holland, where strong fighter escort could be provided. The planning staff, however, was preparing a blow which it hoped would avenge the humiliations of 17 August and vindicate the concept of deep-penetration raids against precision targets. The objective of the mission was again Schweinfurt, which was again to be attacked on 14 October.

The 8th Air Force had been reorganized on 13 September, the earlier Provisional Combat Bombardment Wings becoming Air Bombardment Divisions, and so the force of 291 B-17s despatched on the 14th was provided by the 1st and 3rd Air Bombardment Divisions, while the 2nd Air Bombardment Division broke off from the main force in the middle of the southern North Sea to make a feint attack on the Frisian Islands.

The two attacking divisions flew virtually straight to Aachen, where once again their escorting P-47s had to turn back for lack of fuel. Here the bombers started to fly evasive courses that would route them away from the main German *Flak* concentrations. But fully warned by radar of the impending raid, the Germans appreciated that it was the fighters, not the *Flak*, that the Americans should fear. And once the escort had turned back, once again the German fighters streamed in to the attack, using cannon, machine-guns, rockets and even bombs. Immediately the American losses started to pile up. As one American pilot put it: 'all hell was let loose . . . the scene was similar to a parachute invasion, there were so many crews baling out.' Yet the B-17s ploughed on, the 1st Division bombing Schweinfurt between 1439 and 1445, and the 3rd

Division between 1451 and 1457. The bombers then rallied to the south of the target area and set off home through the same sort of attacks they had had to face on their way to the target.

The B-17s started to cross the south coast of England at Beachy Head at 1700 and headed painfully for their bases in East Anglia. Their defeat had been crushing: of the 291 aircraft that had set out, no less than 60 had been shot down, with another 17 badly damaged and a further 121 less badly damaged. The loss rate was 20.6%, and the total casualty rate 68%.

Yet the second Schweinfurt raid was only one of four such deep-penetration raids during that week, Marienburg, Danzig and Münster having also been attacked. The cost had been prohibitive: 148 bombers and some 1500 aircrew. It was far too costly a type of bombing to be maintained, and the public outcry in the United States was only one of the reasons that such raids were temporarily abandoned. Yet the *Luftwaffe's* victory was not complete: the Americans had not abandoned the concept, but merely the way in which it had been implemented. They now realized how vulnerable their bombers were to determined fighter attack, and thus merely postponed the full implementation of the concept until the right escort fighter could be found. The right aircraft, the magnificent North American P-51 Mustang, was already in service with an Allison engine. It was at the time undergoing trials with a Rolls-Royce Merlin, and the pairing of the Mustang and Merlin was to produce just the aircraft the Americans needed, and produce what was arguably the war's finest all-round fighter. The P-51B Mustang appeared at the end of the year, and from that time onwards American daylight bombing deep into Germany became a force to be reckoned with.

The Schweinfurt Raids, 1943

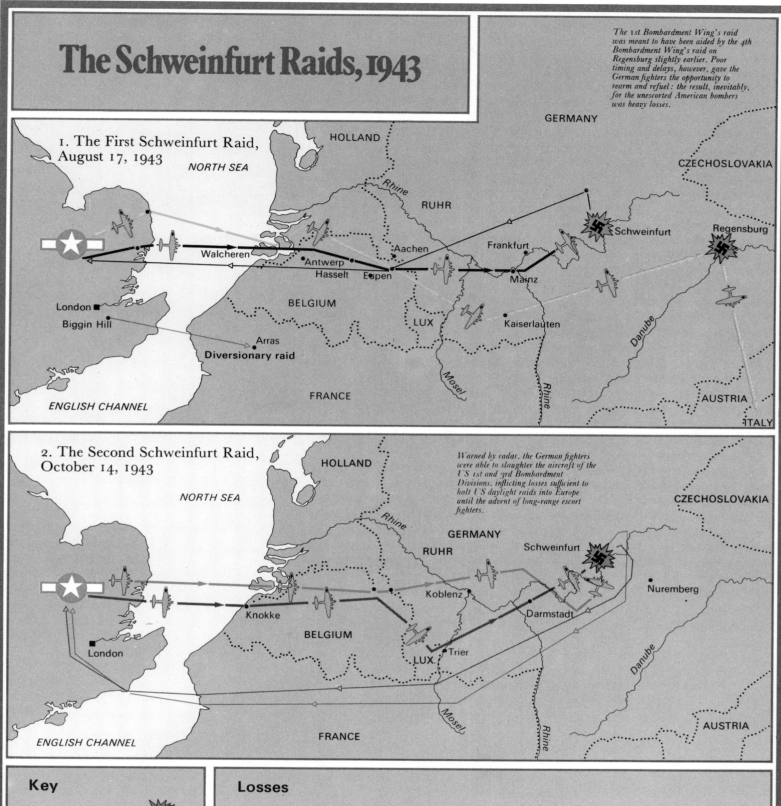

The 1st Bombardment Wing's raid was meant to have been aided by the 4th Bombardment Wing's raid on Regensburg slightly earlier. Poor timing and delays, however, gave the German fighters the opportunity to rearm and refuel; the result, inevitably, for the unescorted American bombers was heavy losses.

1. The First Schweinfurt Raid, August 17, 1943

NORTH SEA
HOLLAND
GERMANY
CZECHOSLOVAKIA
Rhine
RUHR
Schweinfurt
Regensburg
Walcheren
Aachen
Frankfurt
Antwerp
Hasselt
Eupen
Mainz
London
BELGIUM
LUX
Kaiserlauten
Danube
Biggin Hill
Arras
Diversionary raid
FRANCE
Mosel
Rhine
AUSTRIA
ITALY
ENGLISH CHANNEL

2. The Second Schweinfurt Raid, October 14, 1943

Warned by radar, the German fighters were able to slaughter the aircraft of the US 1st and 3rd Bombardment Divisions, inflicting losses sufficient to halt US daylight raids into Europe until the advent of long-range escort fighters.

HOLLAND
NORTH SEA
GERMANY
CZECHOSLOVAKIA
Rhine
RUHR
Schweinfurt
Nuremberg
Koblenz
Knokke
Darmstadt
London
BELGIUM
LUX.
Trier
Danube
AUSTRIA
FRANCE
Mosel
Rhine
ENGLISH CHANNEL

Key

Targets

1st Bombardment Wing

4th Bombardment Wing

1st Bombardment Division

3rd Bombardment Division

Losses

USAAF		LUFTWAFFE	
Losses first raid 17 August 1943		**First raid**	
Destroyed 148	++++++++++++++++	Aircraft lost	+++
Damaged 100	+++++++++		
Regensburg		**Aircraft claimed by USAAF**	
Total sent out 169	++++++++++++++++++	Destroyed 148	++++++++++++++++
Lost 24	++-	Damaged 100	+++++++++
Losses second raid 14 October 1943		**Second raid**	
Total sent out 260	++++++++++++++++++++++++++		++++
	+++++++++	**Aircraft claimed by USAAF**	
Lost 77	++++++++	Lost 104	+++++++++++
		Probably destroyed 26	+++
		Damaged 17	++

401

Leyte Gulf

The Coral Sea was the first check received by the Japanese navy while Midway was its first defeat. The Battle of Leyte Gulf was its last encounter as an independent fighting force. The biggest naval battle in history, Leyte Gulf saw every weapon except the mine employed on both sides. As a measure of their desperation, the Japanese introduced new and deadly air tactics for which the Americans had no effective counter. Leyte Gulf is significant because it was not only the last big naval clash of World War II but the last big fleet action in history. Since late October of 1944, there have been no major naval engagements. While the Korean, Vietnamese and the various Middle Eastern wars have seen some monumental land battles, navies have played a distinctly auxiliary role. Leyte Gulf was the last epic sea battle fought to date.

After Midway it was clear that the Allies were to have two major commanders in the Pacific. Admiral Nimitz and General MacArthur were the two personalities who dominated the direction of the Pacific theater. Early in the war Roosevelt and Churchill had agreed that the Pacific area including Australia should be under the direction of the American Joint Chiefs of Staff while the Middle East and India were under British control and the European-Atlantic area had joint Anglo-American command. The command in the Pacific was divided between MacArthur's Southwest Pacific Command comprising Australia, New Guinea, the Philippines and most of the Netherlands East Indies, and the Central Pacific Command under Nimitz. The navy had long anticipated a war with Japan in the Pacific and knew that such a conflict must be essentially naval in character; its chiefs did not want any competition from the army – Europe was the army's war – and in particular did not want navy forces under army command. Nimitz and Admiral Ernest King, Naval Chief of Staff, wanted to launch a purely naval campaign west from Hawaii via the Gilbert, Marshall, Caroline and Mariana Islands to Japan; MacArthur was expected to stay on the defensive in the Southwest Pacific. MacArthur refused to accept this role, however, and planned to launch his own campaign to Japan north from Australia via New Guinea and the Philippines. In fact, MacArthur wanted the entire Pacific fleet placed under his command to cover his advance along what he called the 'New Guinea-Mindanao Axis'. King and Nimitz were determined not to turn their war over to the army and were adamant concerning their amphibious cam-

paign across the central Pacific, cogently arguing that as long as the Micronesian 'spider webs' which the Japanese had spread across the Pacific remained, every point on the New Guinea-Mindanao Axis was vulnerable to air attack. A shorter route to Japan must be opened up by sweeping up the spider webs.

The navy had a sound strategic argument but MacArthur was taking other factors into consideration. He knew that the Western colonial powers had lost great prestige in Asian eyes by their poor showing against Japan. The only way in which this prestige could be recovered was to reconquer the colonies by force of arms. If the United States wished to re-establish its interests in the Philippines, the islands would have to be wrested from the enemy forcibly. Although an advocate of Filipino independence, MacArthur was concerned that the United States regain its economic position in its colony. Also, having promised the people of the Philippines that he would return, MacArthur intended to do so. Thus MacArthur and Nimitz were competing against each other to see who could defeat Japan first. Fond of this sort of confrontation, Roosevelt had approved the divided command in the hope of

Opposite top: The Japanese battleship *Yamato*, the biggest and most modern ship of its class in the world.
Opposite bottom: Vice-Admiral Gunichi Mikawa, who led Japanese forces at Rabaul during the great push back toward the Philippines.

Left: General of the Army Douglas MacArthur, wearing the British Order of the Knight Grand Cross of the Order of the Bath. He vowed to return to the Philippines after his forces were cornered at Bataan and Corregidor in 1942.

using the natural rivalry between the army and the navy to produce faster results. The navy openly hated MacArthur and welcomed the confrontation so much that Secretary of War Henry Stimson wrote 'the Navy's bitterness against MacArthur seemed childish'. 'Of all the faulty decisions of the war, perhaps the most inexpressible one was the failure to unify the command in the Pacific...' was MacArthur's subsequent view. The divided command was to have an important effect on the battle of Leyte Gulf.

Their smashing defeat at Midway again shifted Japanese attention to the Southwest Pacific. In an effort to retrieve some of their lost initiative, the Japanese high command formed a new Eighth Fleet under Admiral Mikawa to spearhead a fresh advance from Rabaul. New airfields were built at Rabaul and plans were laid for an infantry attack on Port Moresby over the Owen Stanley Mountains. Guadalcanal was to be occupied so that Japanese bombers would be able to menace the entire Allied position in the South Pacific. In July 1942, to counter this renewed threat and to get an Allied offensive underway, the Joint Chiefs of Staff finally formulated a strategy for the Southwest Pacific: to capture the New Guinea-New Britain-New Ireland area. In effect, this meant that MacArthur's American and Australian troops were to take the Solomon Islands and the northeast coast of New Guinea, along with Rabaul and adjacent positions in and around New Guinea and New Ireland. This was the origin of MacArthur's 'island hopping' program, the object of which was to break through the barrier of the Bismarck Archipelago and open the way to the Philippines.

The Allies opened their own offensive in the Southwest Pacific with MacArthur's troops fighting a long hard jungle campaign in New Guinea from July 1942 to January 1943 when the last Japanese were finally evicted. At the same time, navy and marine forces under Nimitz's command fought an equally difficult campaign for the recovery of Guadalcanal and Tulagi from August 1942 to February 1943, a campaign which involved seven major naval encounters and at least ten pitched land battles. With the victories in Papua and Guadalcanal, the initiative in the Southwest Pacific decisively passed to the Allies. MacArthur's campaign had been considerably strengthened in October 1942 by the appointment of Admiral William Halsey as commander of the naval forces in the Southwest Pacific. Like MacArthur, Halsey had a well deserved reputation for leadership, confidence and aggressiveness. Although 'island hopping' was proving successful, it was also proving too slow, and a new strategy called 'leap frogging' was devised. This meant by-passing the stronger Japanese positions sealing them off by sea and air and 'leaving them to die on the vine' or, as a baseball-minded member of MacArthur's staff put it, 'hitting 'em where they ain't'. This proved to be a wise course as it enabled the Southwest Pacific Command to by-pass the 100,000-man Japanese garrison at Rabaul and the 50,000-strong garrison at Wewak. By leap frogging MacArthur was able to gain control of New Guinea by 30 July, 1944 and could look across the Celebes Sea toward his next objective, Mindanao.

In the Central Pacific Nimitz was advancing atoll by atoll through the Marshalls and Gilberts, winning his victories by frontal assaults of overwhelming power. In June 1944 his forces began to attack Saipan, the key Japanese fortress in the Marianas. Saipan lay only 1350 miles from Tokyo and would be a valuable base for attacks on the Japanese home islands by long range B-24 bombers and the new B-29 super bomber. Loss of Saipan would also cut the lines of communications with Japanese forces to the south. Thus Imperial General Headquarters met the Allied attack on Saipan with the full force of the Japanese fleet. In the greatest air battle of the war, fifteen American carriers with 900 planes met five heavy and four light Japanese carriers with 370 planes. In what American pilots called the 'Great Marianas Turkey Shoot', the Japanese lost 315 planes in one day alone as well as a carrier, and several battleships and cruisers. The losses in planes and especially in pilots were irreplaceable at that stage of the war and Japan was never again able to launch an effective carrier force. The fall of Saipan was such an unmistakable sign of impending defeat that it brought down the war government of General Hideki Tojo.

With MacArthur now poised to cross the Celebes Sea to Mindanao and Nimitz occupying Saipan, Tinian and Guam on Japan's doorstep, the question of overall strategy was still unresolved despite fierce argument. Admirals King and Nimitz wanted to by-pass the Philippines, invade Formosa and then set up a base either on the Chinese mainland or in the Ryukyu Islands for the final assault on the home islands. MacArthur continued to insist on the liberation of the Philippines and on the use of Luzon as the base for the final assault on Japan. While Formosa had a hostile population, it was heavily defended and easily reinforceable from the Chinese mainland, Luzon was friendly and could easily be sealed off by Allied air and sea power. At a conference at Pearl Harbor in July 1944, MacArthur was finally able to convince Roosevelt and a dubious Nimitz of the merits of his 'Leyte then Luzon' concept. At the Octagon Conference at Quebec in September, the Allied Chiefs of Staff agreed that MacArthur and Nimitz should converge on Leyte and invade in concert in December. But within a week of this decision, Halsey's Third Fleet, spearheaded by the new Essex class fast carriers, found Japanese air opposition negligible while softening up Morotai, Yap and the Palau Islands. With no opposition from shore-based Japanese planes, MacArthur's forces could perform the ultimate in leap frogging, one long hop from New Guinea to Leyte, by-passing Mindanao and supported entirely by Nimitz's carrier-borne air power. In a remarkable example of strategic flexibility, the Octagon Conference advanced the date of the invasion of Leyte by two months to 20 October.

A Grim Struggle

For the Japanese, after their defeat in Guadalcanal and Papua, the war became a grim struggle to sell their short-lived conquests as dearly as possible. With control of 80% of the world's rubber, large quantities of tin, tungsten, man-

ganese, iron ore and the oil fields of the Netherlands East Indies, Japan should have been able to face a prolonged war. But Imperial General Headquarters was several generations out of date in its concept of war, concerning itself largely with battles, tactics and territory. The Japanese could and did design better warships and airplanes than the Americans but did not give top priority to producing large numbers of these weapons on which their defense rested. Although a pioneer of naval air power, Japan built only three aircraft carriers in 1943 (against 22 for the United States) and failed utterly to mobilize the manpower needed even for its restricted air forces. To exploit the resources she now controlled, Japan needed a large merchant fleet but made no effort to enlarge its merchant navy. By 1943 so much tonnage had been lost to bombing, mines and submarines that it was difficult to hold the overseas territories together. Yet the Japanese Navy made no adequate attempt to protect its merchant shipping through a convoy system, radar or asdic. For example, by 1943 Japan was already facing an oil shortage, a shortage which was severe enough to hamper production on the home front and curtail operations of the navy, because it no longer had the tanker capacity to move enough of this vital commodity from the Netherlands East Indies. This unimaginative planning and lack of coordination with the civilian sector of the economy meant that the essential weakness of the Japanese defense structure was economic. The Japanese were never able to exploit their huge resources to prolong the war.

The inability of the Japanese naval air force to seriously contest Nimitz' advance across the Central Pacific illustrates Japan's basic weakness by 1944. In two years of fighting 8000 navy planes had been lost and experienced pilots were in short supply. This huge loss of men and equipment had neither been foreseen nor prepared for and they could not be replaced. This was especially true of pilots, and the hasty training of replacements led to such a low level of fighting skill that

casualties mushroomed. One Japanese naval instructor wrote in his memoirs that 'The Navy was desperate for pilots, and the school was expanded almost every month, with correspondingly lower entrance requirements . . . We were told to rush the men through, to forget the finer points, just teach them how to fly and shoot . . . It was a hopeless task'. To make matters worse, the plane in which Yamamoto was making an inspection tour was ambushed by American fighters after American intelligence had decoded his route and schedule. No other Japanese admiral understood the use of air power so well. After his death the lessons taught by Yamamoto were forgotten and the navy fell back on its first love, the battleship.

By mid-1944 it was clear that Japan must fall back on an inner defense line extending from the Kuriles and the home islands through the Ryukyus, Formosa and the Philippines to the Netherlands East Indies. If this line could be maintained, Japan could still draw on the resources of her southern conquests and protect her lines of communication through the Formosa Straits and the South China Sea. Failure would mean that only the resources of China were left. As early as March 1944 Japanese strategists could see where the two prongs of the Allied offensive would meet, and the invasion of the Philippines was obvious to the Japanese long before the Allies had managed to agree on it among themselves. The main uncertainty was which island would be the first target. Although prepared to offer a 'general decisive battle' wherever the Allies struck, Japan's main interest was to hold Luzon, which would enable her to maintain communications with Malaya and Indonesia. Since she could not discover where the Allies would strike, four separate *Sho* (victory) plans were drawn up between 24 July and 1 August. *Sho* 1 covered the Philippines while the others concerned Formosa-Ryukyus, Honshu-Kyushu, and Hokkaido-Kuriles respectively. Although the other possibilities were covered, the

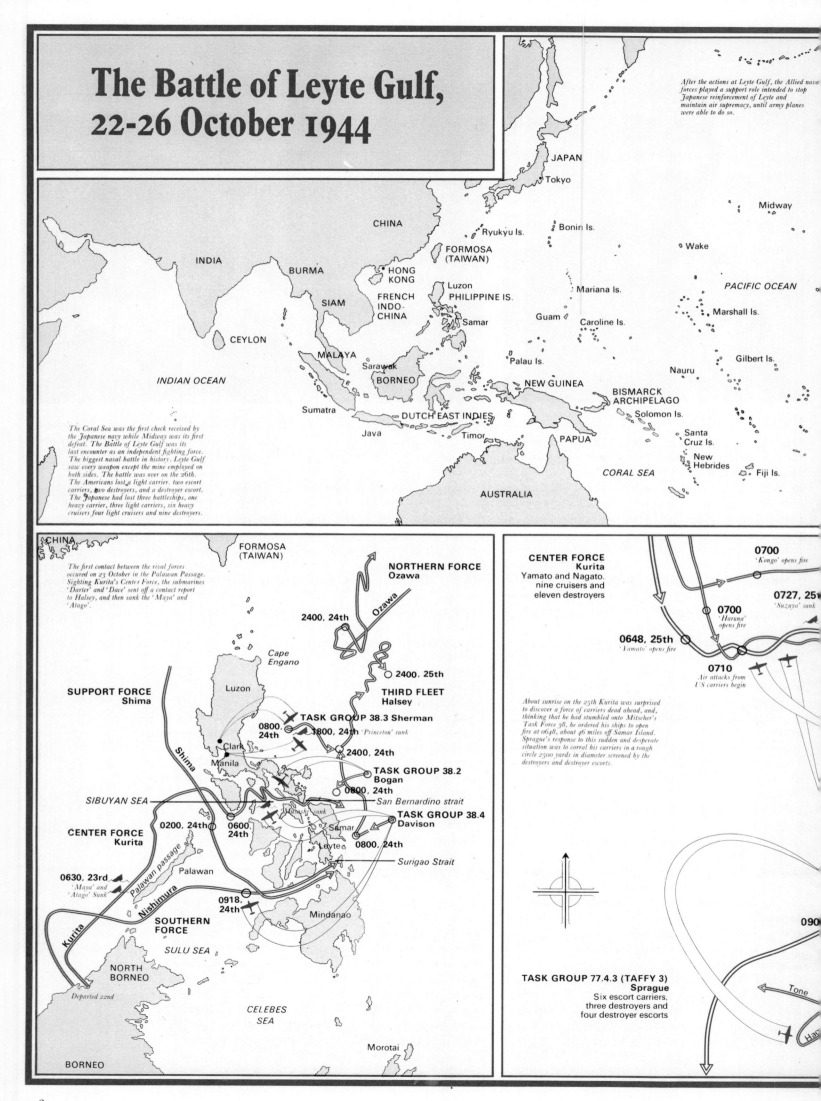

The Battle of Leyte Gulf, 22-26 October 1944

After the actions at Leyte Gulf, the Allied naval forces played a support role intended to stop Japanese reinforcement of Leyte and maintain air supremacy, until army planes were able to do so.

JAPAN

Tokyo

CHINA

Ryukyu Is.

Bonin Is.

Midway

FORMOSA (TAIWAN)

Wake

INDIA

BURMA

HONG KONG

Luzon

PHILIPPINE IS.

Mariana Is.

PACIFIC OCEAN

SIAM

FRENCH INDO-CHINA

Samar

Guam

Caroline Is.

Marshall Is.

CEYLON

MALAYA

Palau Is.

Nauru

Gilbert Is.

INDIAN OCEAN

Sarawak

BORNEO

NEW GUINEA

BISMARCK ARCHIPELAGO

Sumatra

DUTCH EAST INDIES

Solomon Is.

Santa Cruz Is.

Java

Timor

PAPUA

New Hebrides

Fiji Is.

CORAL SEA

AUSTRALIA

The Coral Sea was the first check received by the Japanese navy while Midway was its first defeat. The Battle of Leyte Gulf was its last encounter as an independent fighting force. The biggest naval battle in history. Leyte Gulf saw every weapon except the mine employed on both sides. The battle was over on the 26th. The Americans lost a light carrier, two escort carriers, two destroyers, and a destroyer escort. The Japanese had lost three battleships, one heavy carrier, three light carriers, six heavy cruisers four light cruisers and nine destroyers.

CHINA

FORMOSA (TAIWAN)

The first contact between the rival forces occured on 23 October in the Palawan Passage. Sighting Kurita's Center Force, the submarines 'Darter' and 'Dace' sent off a contact report to Halsey, and then sank the 'Maya' and 'Atago'.

NORTHERN FORCE
Ozawa

Ozawa

2400, 24th

2400, 25th

SUPPORT FORCE
Shima

Luzon

THIRD FLEET
Halsey

Cape Engano

Shima

Clark

Manila

TASK GROUP 38.3 Sherman

0800, 24th

1800, 24th 'Princeton' sunk

2400, 24th

SIBUYAN SEA

CENTER FORCE
Kurita

0200, 24th

0600, 24th

Musashi sunk

TASK GROUP 38.2
Bogan

0800, 24th

San Bernardino strait

Samar

TASK GROUP 38.4
Davison

0800, 24th

Leyte

Surigao Strait

0918, 24th

Mindanao

0630, 23rd
'Maya' and 'Atago' Sunk

Palawan

Nishimura

SOUTHERN FORCE

Kurita

Departed 22nd

NORTH BORNEO

SULU SEA

CELEBES SEA

Morotai

BORNEO

CENTER FORCE
Kurita
Yamato and Nagato, nine cruisers and eleven destroyers

0700
'Kongo' opens fire

0727, 25w
'Suzuya' sunk

0648, 25th
'Yamato' opens fire

0700
'Haruna' opens fire

0710
Air attacks from US carriers begin

About sunrise on the 25th Kurita was surprised to discover a force of carriers dead ahead, and, thinking that he had stumbled onto Mitscher's Task Force 38, he ordered his ships to open fire at 0648, about 46 miles off Samar Island. Sprague's response to this sudden and desperate situation was to corral his carriers in a rough circle 2500 yards in diameter screened by the destroyers and destroyer escorts.

090

Tone

TASK GROUP 77.4.3 (TAFFY 3)
Sprague
Six escort carriers, three destroyers and four destroyer escorts

Hag

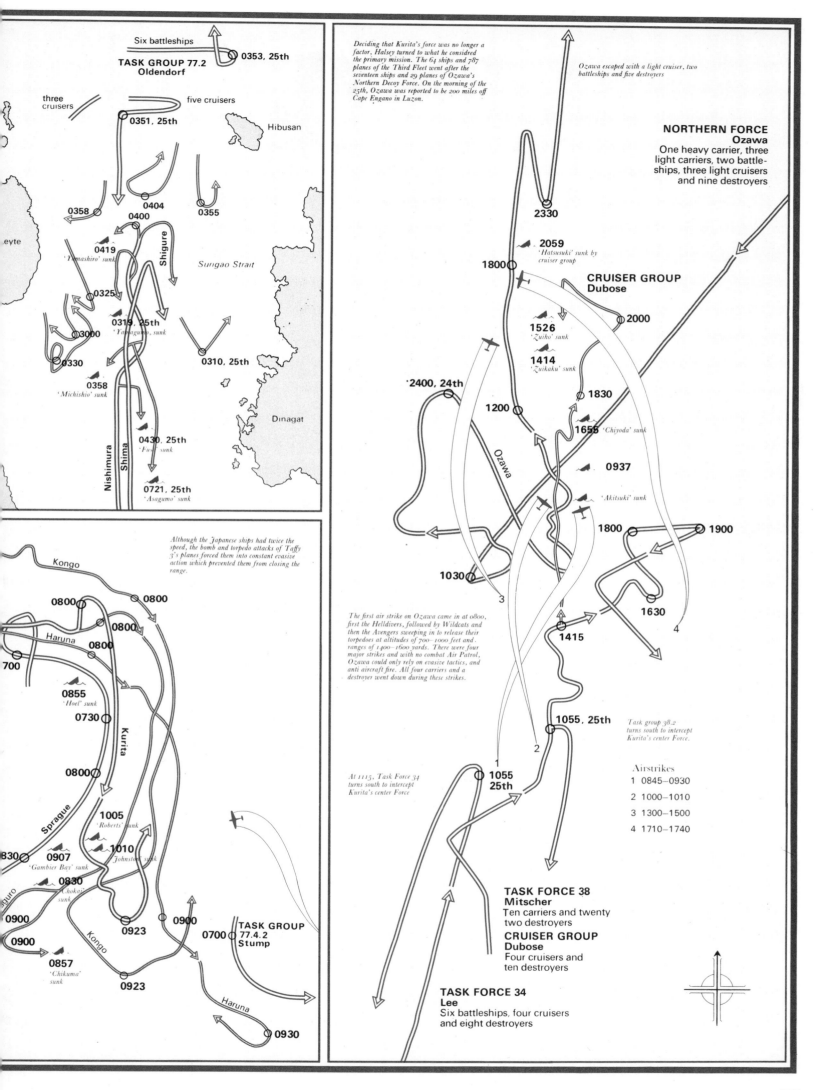

Six battleships

TASK GROUP 77.2
Oldendorf

0353, 25th

three cruisers

five cruisers

0351, 25th

Hibusan

0358

0404

0355

0400

0419

'Yamashiro' sunk

Shigure

Surigao Strait

Leyte

0325

0319, 25th

'Yamagumo, sunk'

0300

0310, 25th

0330

0358

'Michishio' sunk

Dinagat

Nishimura

Shima

0430, 25th

'Fuso' sunk

0721, 25th

'Asagumo' sunk

Although the Japanese ships had twice the speed, the bomb and torpedo attacks of Taffy 3's planes forced them into constant evasive action which prevented them from closing the range.

Kongo

0800

0800

0800

Haruna

0800

0800

700

Kurita

0855

'Hoel' sunk

0730

0800

Sprague

1005

'Roberts' sunk

0907

1010

'Johnston' sunk

0830

'Gambier Bay' sunk

0830

'Chokai' sunk

0900

0900

0923

0900

0900

Kongo

0857

'Chikuma' sunk

0923

0900

0700

TASK GROUP
77.4.2
Stump

Haruna

0930

Deciding that Kurita's force was no longer a factor, Halsey turned to what he considred the primary mission. The 64 ships and 787 planes of the Third Fleet went after the seventeen ships and 29 planes of Ozawa's Northern Decoy Force. On the morning of the 25th, Ozawa was reported to be 200 miles off Cape Engano in Luzon.

Ozawa escaped with a light cruiser, two battleships and five destroyers

NORTHERN FORCE
Ozawa
One heavy carrier, three light carriers, two battle-ships, three light cruisers and nine destroyers

2330

2059
'Hatsusuki' sunk by cruiser group

1800

CRUISER GROUP
Dubose

2000

1526
'Zuiho' sunk

1414
'Zuikaku' sunk

2400, 24th

1200

1830

1655
'Chiyoda' sunk

Ozawa

0937

'Akitsuki' sunk

1800

1900

1030

3

1630

4

The first air strike on Ozawa came in at 0800, first the Helldivers, followed by Wildcats and then the Avengers sweeping in to release their torpedoes at altitudes of 700–1000 feet and ranges of 1400–1600 yards. There were four major strikes and with no combat Air Patrol, Ozawa could only rely on evasive tactics, and anti aircraft fire. All four carriers and a destroyer went down during these strikes.

1415

1055, 25th

Task group 38.2 turns south to intercept Kurita's center Force.

2

At 1115, Task Force 34 turns south to intercept Kurita's center Force

1

1055
25th

Airstrikes
1 0845–0930
2 1000–1010
3 1300–1500
4 1710–1740

TASK FORCE 38
Mitscher
Ten carriers and twenty two destroyers

CRUISER GROUP
Dubose
Four cruisers and ten destroyers

TASK FORCE 34
Lee
Six battleships, four cruisers and eight destroyers

Japanese high command was certain that the Allies would attack the Philippines.

The basic elements of *Sho* 1 were that the Northern Force of Admiral Ozawa, built around the carriers *Zuikaku*, *Zuiho*, *Chitose* and *Chiyoda*, would decoy Halsey's Third Fleet to the north, thus removing the main American battle force from the vicinity of the real objective. Then Admiral Kurita's Center Force – the super battleships *Yamato* and *Musashi*, nine cruisers and supporting destroyers – would come through the San Bernardino Strait at the same time as the Southern Force of Admiral Nishimura came through the Surigao Strait to converge on Leyte Gulf. After destroying the gulf full of unprotected shipping and smashing the Allied beachhead, it is not clear what *Sho* 1 envisaged for Halsey's powerful Third Fleet when it returned from chasing Ozawa. Thus *Sho* 1 was a standard Japanese plan which employed division of force, diversions, unexpected attacks and a highly elaborate schedule.

Japan chose to regard the invasion of the Philippines as a crisis of the war. Although the naval air force had already been virtually eliminated, the fleet was still strong in surface ships. Ozawa's carriers had but 116 planes among them while land based air groups in the Ryukyus, Formosa and Manila could muster less than 200 planes. The carriers were therefore to be expended on the decoy mission while the battle would be decided by the gun power of the Japanese Navy.

If this plan succeeded, Japan would have achieved the equivalent of a second Pearl Harbor, destroying the American army as the navy had been smashed three years earlier. It would have been a year before the United States could replace the men and equipment lost at Leyte, and this was time which Japan desperately needed.

The Commander-in-Chief of the Combined Fleet was now Admiral Soyemu Toyoda, who directed operations from Tokyo. Toyoda was gambling on his forces making unimpeded contact with the enemy, free from air attack, and destroying them with overwhelming gun power. He accepted the probability that the Combined Fleet would be destroyed, but if the Philippines were lost, cutting Japan off from her only source of oil, the fleet would be immobilized from lack of fuel anyway. It was better, he thought, to go down fighting. *Sho* 1 was thus a huge *kamikaze* operation, a last desperate roll of the dice. Although Japanese intelligence had predicted that the invasion would come in the last ten days of October and that the target would be Leyte, it could be certain of neither time nor target. Due to the oil shortage, Toyoda could not activate *Sho* 1 until Allied ships were actually seen entering Leyte Gulf; if his forces were activated too soon, they would be short of fuel for the real engagement. Since the engagement off Saipan in June, now known as the Battle of the Philippine Sea, all the battleships and heavy cruisers had been stationed at Lingga Roads near Singapore in order to be near the sources of oil, while the carriers and their attendant ships had been in home waters waiting to embark new air groups as they emerged from the training schools. Thus the oil shortage meant that Toyoda could not activate *Sho* 1 early enough to catch the Leyte landings in their 'naked' stage as troops and equipment were being disembarked.

Allied preparations for the Leyte operation began immediately after the schedule was advanced by the Octagon Conference in September. Morotai was seized as a staging base against the Philippines for short range fighters and light and medium bombers. Peleliu was taken because an assault force had already been underway and Nimitz had not wanted to recall it. This was a

Top left: Kinkaid receives
the Distinguished Service
Medal from Admiral
Nimitz for his action in the
Coral Sea. Both were
responsible for the American
victory at Leyte Gulf two
years later. Above: Toyoda
sent his finest ships and all
that remained of his Navy
and Air Force against the
Americans at Leyte in a
desperate attempt to
prevent the collapse of
Japanese power in the
Pacific. Left: Kinkaid in
the Aleutians. He was transferred from that obscure
posting to a position of vital
importance at the head of
the Seventh Fleet in 1944.

Above: Vice-Admiral Mitscher, Commander of Task Force 38, part of Halsey's Third Fleet. He made the big raids on Formosa in October 1944. **Above center:** MacArthur 'returning' to the Philippines at Morotai. His forces fought for months against General Yamashita throughout the balance of the war in the jungles of the Philippines. **Above right:** MacArthur, walking through the water with his Chief of Staff, Sutherland, and President Osmeña (left) of the Philippines. Some critics said that MacArthur would have preferred to walk on the water.

mistake, as the defenders offered tough resistance for over two months. Early in October MacArthur's forces and Admiral Thomas Kinkaid's Seventh Fleet were gathering along the coast of New Guinea. When fully assembled, the invasion convoy totalled 738 ships, including 157 combat vessels, 420 amphibians, 84 patrol boats, minesweeping and hydrographic specialists, and 73 service ships. These were supported by Halsey's Third Fleet which comprised seventeen carriers, six battleships, seventeen cruisers and 64 destroyers. The invasion of the Philippines was being undertaken by the most powerful naval force ever assembled (though an even mightier force would gather for the invasion of Okinawa the following April). On 10 October the mammoth convoy began to move away from the shores of New Guinea with the minesweepers in the van.

The invasion of Leyte was being undertaken in one giant hop from New Guinea because it was believed that carrier planes could provide adequate air cover for the convoy and landings in view of the demonstrated air weakness of the Japanese. It was still necessary, however, to destroy Japan's remaining land-based air power before the landings took place. A major air assault was launched against Formosa to neutralize its air groups and deny it to the enemy as a staging base against the Philippines. Task Force 38 under Admiral Marc Mitscher was detached from the Third Fleet for this operation. In excellent flying weather between 12–14 October, planes from nine American carriers swarmed over the island, doing heavy damage to ground facilities. Under the command of Admiral Fukudome, 230 Japanese fighters rose to intercept but over a third were lost on 12 October alone. 'Our fighters were nothing but so many eggs thrown against the wall of the indomitable enemy formation' lamented the admiral. In the end Task Force 38 destroyed over 500 Japanese planes and 40 transports and smaller craft. These operations were supplemented by a series of B-29 raids from the American base at Chengtu in China.

In the week before the assault date of 20 October, army and navy planes attacked Japanese air bases in Luzon, Mindanao and the Netherlands East Indies while a naval sweep was sent against the Kurile Islands. They met little resistance as the Japanese were hoarding their planes in anticipation of the 'general decisive battle'. Allied knowledge of Japanese intentions and movements was both slight and wildly inaccurate. Halsey at least considered the possibility that the enemy would contest the landings but MacArthur's staff thought that a fleet action was not likely. 'The objective is relatively undefended – the Japanese will not offer strong resistance to the operation' was the estimate of General George Kenney, commander of the army air forces in the Southwest Pacific. On 20 October MacArthur's headquarters issued a statement that it would be impractical for the Japanese navy to use the San Bernardino or Surigao Straits due to navigational hazards and lack of space to maneuver. On 23 October Kinkaid and Halsey were still sceptical that the Japanese intended to use their fleet.

In fact, at 0750 on 17 October, Toyoda activated *Sho* 1 after receiving a message that American ships were approaching Leyte Gulf. The main battle force of Kurita sortied from Lingga Roads the following day. On the 20th, after topping up its fuel tanks at Brunei Bay in North Borneo, the force split. With most of the heavy cruisers, Kurita's five battleships set course for the Sibuyan Sea and the San Bernardino Strait. With its nucleus of two battleships, Nishimura's Southern Force headed for the Surigao Strait. Almost as an afterthought, two heavy cruisers, a light cruiser and seven destroyers under Admiral Shima were ordered from the Inland Sea to 'support and co-operate' with Nishimura. Undetected by the American submarines which had been sent to intercept any sortie, Ozawa's Northern Carrier Force slipped out of the Inland Sea on 20 October on its decoy mission.

Mine sweeping operations to clear the entrances of Leyte Gulf had begun on 17 October. By noon the following day rangers had secured the four islands at the mouth of the gulf. Rear-Admiral Jesse Oldendorf then moved his gunfire support ships from the Seventh Fleet into the gulf to bombard the beaches to cover the work of underwater demolition teams clearing obstructions from the landing areas. The assault day dawned with perfect weather and no surf. Only some light mortar fire opposed the landings. After the first wave was ashore, MacArthur and Sergio Osmena, who had become President of the Philippines after the death of Manuel Quezon, followed in a moment of high drama. Standing on the beach,

Above: Kurita's flagship at Leyte. Both ended up beneath the waters of Leyte Gulf.

MacArthur made the broadcast for which he had been waiting two and a half years: 'People of the Philippines, I have returned, By the grace of Almighty God, our forces stand again on Philip-ine soil – soil consecrated by the blood of our two peoples'. The speech had a tremendous impact on the Philippines and there on the beach MacArthur scribbled a note to Roosevelt urging him to grant the Philippines immediate independence. The following day, Dulag and Tacloban airfields and Tacloban town, which had the only docking facilities on Leyte, were in American hands. By midnight 132,000 men and 200,000 tons of supplies and equipment had been landed. General Walter Kreuger's Sixth Army then faced the difficult task of evicting 60,000 Japanese defenders from Leyte. By the 22nd, with the amphibious phase of the operation complete, most of the shipping in Leyte Gulf had departed. Only 28 Liberty ships and 25 Landing Ships Medium (LSM's) and Landing Ship Tanks (LST's) remained.

The first contact between the rival forces occurred on 23 October in the Palawan Passage between Palawan Island and the reefs bordering the South China Sea. Sighting Kurita's Center Force, the submarines *Darter* and *Dace* sent off a contact report to Halsey, the first news he had had of Center Force since the report of its departure from Lingga Roads, and then sank three enemy heavy cruisers, one of which was Kurita's flagship. By noon of the following day, Halsey had deployed three of the fast carrier groups of Task Force 38 on a broad front. Rear-Admiral Sherman's group lay to the north, Rear-Admiral Bogan's off the San Bernadino Strait, and Rear-Admiral Dawson's 60 miles off Samar. But before these groups could launch strikes against Kurita's ships, now in the Sibuyan Sea, Japanese planes from Luzon attacked Sherman's group which was in the position to do the most damage to Kurita. Three separate waves of 50 to 60 planes each swept in with bombs and torpedoes. Many were shot down by anti-aircraft fire and Combat Air Patrol planes but one dive bomber broke through to drop a 550-pound bomb which penetrated through the flight deck of the light carrier *Princeton*.

The torpedo storage of the vessel was detonated and she had to be abandoned to sink later that day. The other two carrier groups did launch attack groups which gave Center Force, who lacked a Combat Air Patrol since most available Japanese planes were attacking Sherman, a heavy working over. The super battleship *Musashi* took 19 torpedo and 17 bomb hits and sank with most of her crew. Other ships were hit as well but all except the cruiser *Myoko* were able to proceed. Although weakened, Center Force was still formidable with four battleships, six heavy cruisers, two light cruisers and ten destroyers. Kurita had made repeated requests to Admiral Fukudome, commanding the air forces in the Philippines and Formosa, for air cover but Fuku-dome had decided that attacking the carrier groups was the best way of relieving Kurita. By 1400 hours American reconnaissance planes reported that the Japanese ships were turning west as if withdrawing but in fact they were only re-grouping and assessing their damage. To avoid further air attack, Kurita asked permission to retire and run the San Bernadino Strait that night but Toyoda ordered him ahead. The air attacks in the Sibuyan Sea had lasted most of the day, putting Center Force seven hours behind schedule. There was now no way that it could keep its dawn ren-dezvous with Southern Force in Leyte Gulf.

While Center Force was being slowed down by the Battle of the Sibuyan Sea, Southern Force was approaching Leyte Gulf by its own route. Shima's supporting force was several hours behind Nishimura's squadron, the battleships *Fuso* and *Yamashiro*, the heavy cruiser *Mogami* and four destroyers. Before noon of the 24th, however, air reconnaissance had spotted Nishimura, leading Admiral Kinkaid of the Seventh Fleet to believe that the Japanese admiral intended to run the Surigao Strait that night. By 1830 of that same day Nishimura had been informed that Kurita could not keep to the time table, but when Toyoda signaled 'All forces will dash to the attack', Nishimura pushed on without even waiting for Shima to catch up. Since he had no air cover, the commander of the Southern Force believed that his only chance was to get to Leyte Gulf under cover of darkness. Kinkaid and Oldendorf in the meantime had laid a neat ambush for any enemy forces which tried to penetrate the gulf that night. A fifteen-mile battle line was formed between Leyte and Hibuson Island where the Surigao Strait enters Leyte Gulf. Six battleships, four heavy cruisers and four light cruisers were deployed to bar the way. Five of the battleships were now to

Left: The battleship *Musashi* blows up at Leyte Gulf. **Right:** Anti-aircraft fire from the USS *Sangamon* drives off Japanese dive bombers. **Below:** USS *Birmingham* hoses down the USS *Princeton*, which was sunk at Leyte on 23 October, 1944 during the the first phase of the battle.

have their revenge; they had already been sunk once at Pearl Harbor and had been refloated. Two destroyer divisions were deployed down the strait for torpedo attacks while a third was ordered to follow up the efforts of the first two and a fourth attended the battle line. As Kinkaid had no night-flying radar-equipped patrol planes, he had the strait patrolled by 39 torpedo boats with orders to report all enemy contact and then attack independently.

Contact was first reported at 2230, followed by more reports along the 50-mile length of the strait. Repeated PT boat attacks failed to score a hit, however, and by 0300 on the 25th the destroyer divisions were beginning their attacks. Nishimura was sailing in line ahead with the destroyers *Michishio*, *Asagumo*, *Shigure* and *Yamagumo* followed by the *Yamashiro*, *Fuso* and *Mogami*. Launching their torpedoes at ranges of 8200–9300 yards, the destroyers hit the *Fuso* which sheered out of line and began to burn and explode. The *Yamashiro* was also hit, and two of her magazines had to be flooded. The first Japanese destroyer was sunk while the second had her bow blown off and dropped out of line. When the follow up division of American destroyers made its attack ten minutes later, the *Yamashiro* received another hit and another destroyer was sunk, leaving only the *Shigure*. All of the American destroyers escaped without damage. During these attacks Nishimura ordered no evasive action nor took any notice of his damaged ships, even though the *Fuso* had gone down within 30 minutes of being torpedoed. Reduced to the *Yamashiro*, the *Mogami* and the *Shigure*, he maintained his course for his objective with single-minded concentration.

Oldendorf's formidable line had a left flank of three heavy and two light cruisers, a right flank of one heavy and two light cruisers, and a center of six battleships supported by a destroyer division.

Although the line was stationary, with Nishimura steaming toward it in single line ahead, the effect was the same as crossing the Japanese 'T'. At 0351 the American line opened fire, with the *West Virginia*, *Tennessee* and *California* doing most of the work as they were equipped with the new Mark 8 fire control radar. Fitted with the old Mark 3 radar, the other battleships had trouble finding targets, and the *Pennsylvania* never fired at all. Coming up at twelve knots, the *Yamashiro* could return the American fire only at visible targets since it had no fire control radar. It was supported feebly by the *Mogami* astern and the *Shigure* to starboard. By taking radical evasive action the *Shigure* escaped with only one hit but when the *Yamashiro* and *Mogami* began to retire at 0400 both had been heavily battered. A few minutes later the *Yamashiro* was burning brightly against the night; the *Mogami* stopped dead when its bridge was struck by shells, which killed most of the officers including the captain. Increasing their fire in rate and accuracy, the American battleships began to move up on the crippled enemy. The *Yamashiro* was retiring south at fifteen knots when she was struck by two torpedoes from the destroyer *Newcomb* lurking in the darkness. Immediately developing a 45-degree list, she quickly went down with Nishimura and most of her crew.

The *Shigure* was escorting the limping *Mogami* back down the strait as Shima was coming up past the burning hulks of some of Nishimura's ships. Having seen the flash of gunfire, Shima thought he was coming to the support of the van already engaged in wreaking havoc on a gulf full of unprotected shipping. The American PT boats were still patrolling the channel and knocked the light cruiser *Abakuma* out of formation with a torpedo. Two ships appeared on Shima's radar. He ordered his own destroyers to the attack, but when this failed he turned his ships to retire, joined by the *Mogami* and *Shigure*. As dawn appeared, Oldendorf began a general pursuit down the strait. The *Mogami*, which had fallen behind Shima's force, was discovered by three cruisers and received several more shell hits. Although 'burning like a city block', she was able to get up high speed and drive off some PT attacks, only to be sunk by planes some three hours later. The destroyer *Asagumo* with her smashed bow was sunk by two other cruisers. The *Abakuma* was dispatched the following day by New Guinea-based army bombers. The remaining two heavy cruisers and two destroyers of Shima made good their escape when Oldendorf decided to break off the pursuit and retire. With Kurita's Center Force still unaccounted for, the Seventh Fleet's main responsibility was the protection of the Leyte beachhead.

While his colleague Nishimura was being annihilated in the Battle of the Surigao Strait, Kurita was making his way 150 miles down the San Bernardino Strait unopposed. Halsey had accepted the inflated reports from his pilots of many sinkings in the Sibuyan Sea and had come to the conclusion that the Center Force 'could no longer be considered a serious menace to the Seventh Fleet'. Accepting air reconnaissance reports that Kurita was turning west in the afternoon to retire, and disregarding contradictory night sighting reports, he had not even alerted Kinkaid to the possibility that Center Force was a threat. He had then taken the entire Third Fleet north to chase Ozawa's decoy force, leaving not so much as a picket destroyer to watch the San Bernardino Strait. Due to an unclear message, both Kinkaid and Nimitz were under the impression that Halsey

had left a force of heavy ships to block any enemy penetration of the strait.

About sunrise on the 25th, Kurita was surprised to discover a force of carriers dead ahead and, thinking that he had stumbled onto Mitscher's powerful Task Force 38, he ordered his ships to open fire at 0648, about 40 miles off Paninihian Point of Samar Island. The crews of the ships, an escort carrier group with the code name 'Taffy 3', were equally surprised when shells began to splash around them as they were having breakfast on what was supposed to have been a day of routine operations. Often called jeep or Woolworth carriers, escort carriers were used to provide air support for landing operations until airfields ashore were usable. An escort carrier normally had a complement of 18 Wildcats and twelve Avengers. Taffy 3 consisted of six escort carriers, three destroyers and four destroyer escorts under the command of Rear-Admiral Clifton Sprague. Nearby were Taffys 1 and 2, similar escort carrier groups. The total complement of planes for the three groups was 235 Hellcats and Wildcats and 143 Avengers, but at 0648 that day few of these planes were available. A strike had been sent after Shima's ships as they escaped the massacre in the Suriago Strait while many others were engaged in patrol and other routine chores such as delivering fresh water to the troops on Leyte.

The 48-year-old Sprague, a former carrier commander at the Battle of the Philippine Sea, immediately turned his ships east into the wind and launched what planes he had. Ordering his group to the maximum escort carrier speed of $17\frac{1}{2}$ knots, he then began to broadcast urgent calls for assist-

Right: Two US carriers are pummeled by Japanese dive bombers. The plane which did the damage was shot down minutes later.

ance. The first response came from Taffys 1 and 2, over 130 miles away, who launched their planes in support. Before Sprague's unexpected SOS, Kinkaid had believed that a task force from the Third Fleet was covering the San Bernardino Strait and therefore had ordered only a modest night reconnaissance. When Sprague's cry for help came in, the ships of the Seventh Fleet were in Leyte Gulf refilling their ammunition lockers after their night battle with the Southern Force in the Surigao Strait and could not yet face another major engagement. The Third Fleet had let itself be taken out of the picture and could not send aid in time either. Halsey did order the air groups of Admiral McCain's task force to assist but McCain's ships were hundreds of miles to the east, and it would be hours before his planes could join the battle. Taffy 3 just had to fend for itself.

From the beginning Kurita bungled his golden opportunity. His staff officers reported the escort carriers as carriers, the destroyers as cruisers and the destroyer escorts as destroyers. When Taffy 3 was sighted the Japanese ships were sailing in anti-aircraft formation. On contact with the enemy a battle line of the heavy ships should have been formed and the destroyers sent in for torpedo attacks. But Kurita inexplicably ordered General Attack – every ship for itself – which threw his force into considerable confusion. Thus the Japanese squadron was not under proper tactical control as it came to the attack.

Sprague's response to this sudden and desperate situation was to corral his carriers in a rough circle 2500 yards in diameter screened by the destroyers and destroyer escorts. 'The enemy was closing with disconcerting rapidity and the volume and accuracy of fire was increasing', he later wrote. Faced with 'the ultimate in desperate circumstances', he ordered his destroyers and destroyer escorts to make a torpedo attack to divert the enemy, at the same time turning south-southwest to get nearer Leyte and his best hope of succor. This course offered the inside track to Kurita but the Japanese admiral preferred to keep the weather gauge and soon found himself due north of his quarry. Although the Japanese ships had twice the speed, the bomb and torpedo attacks of Taffy 3's planes forced them into constant evasive action which prevented them from closing in on the enemy.

The destroyers *Hoel*, *Heermann* and *Johnston* launched their torpedo counterattack. The *John-ston* got a hit on the cruiser *Kumano* which forced her, along with the bomb-damaged *Suzuya*, out of the battle. But on continuing her attack, the *Johnston* was hit at 0730 by three fourteen-inch and three six-inch shells. 'It was like a puppy dog being smacked by a truck', said one of her officers.

With all power gone and her engine room out, she still helped to break up an attack by Japanese destroyers by firing her guns manually. Then, said one survivor, 'We were in a position where all the gallantry and guts in the world could not save us' as three cruisers came up and blasted the hapless destroyer until she had to be abandoned. Trying to divert the enemy's major caliber fire from the carriers, the *Hoel* and the *Heermann* continued the unequal fight until the *Hoel*, hit 40 times, sank. The captain later noted that his crew 'performed their duties coolly and efficiently until their ship was shot out from under them'.

In spite of the efforts of the destroyers and the planes, which were making dry runs when out of ammunition to divert enemy fire from the carriers, the latter were taking a pounding. The *Kalinin Bay* had received thirteen eight-inch hits but managed to maintain her place in the formation. Center Force was somewhat scattered as four Japanese cruisers closed the range and sank the *Gambier Bay* at 0907. American planes then sank two of the cruisers, causing Kurita to break off the action. His communications were so poor that he apparently did not know what havoc his cruisers were beginning to work among the carriers. He intended to reassemble his scattered force and reorganize it for an attempt to get to Leyte Gulf. But when he was informed of the fate of the Southern Force, having already been attacked by submarines and planes in the Sibuyan Sea and with three more cruisers lost here, he decided to retire. At 1230 70 Wildcats and Avengers from Taffys 2 and 3 arrived to confirm him in this decision. As the Japanese ships turned away, a signalman on the bridge of Sprague's flagship yelled 'Goddammit, boys, they're getting away!'

Kurita's decision to retire was indeed prudent, for Oldendorf's battleships lay in wait at the mouth of Leyte Gulf and massive air attacks by land-based and Task Force 38 planes were being readied. Had it continued on, Center Force would undoubtedly have shared the same fate as Southern Force. As it was, Kurita's mistakes coupled with Sprague's determined resistance had enabled a weak and relatively defenseless

Above left: *Kamikaze* attack on the USS *Columbia*. These suicide missions, however frightening they were at first, only succeeded in destroying what was left of Japan's air power.
Above: A crew member of an escort carrier watches a Japanese bomb explode. The carrier set up a smoke screen to obscure the *kamikaze* pilots' vision.

Overleaf: Crew members of a rescue ship search for further *kamikaze* attacks as they help an LST already struck by a suicide pilot.

squadron to turn back the most powerful gunfire force Japan had put to sea since Midway. It was yet another demonstration of the helplessness of capital ships without air cover.

The travail of the Taffys did not end with Kurita's withdrawal for 25 October marked the first appearance of the *kamikaze*. Organized by Rear-Admiral Arima in 1944, the *kamikaze* were a special air corps designed to meet Japan's desperate need for air power. The Japanese naval air groups had been essentially eliminated, and land based planes were in short supply. American fighter pilots had become very competent at interception, while the invention of the proximity armed fuse for anti-aircraft shells made it nearly impossible for a bomber to get near enough to a ship to score a hit. Arima's *kamikaze* pilots were to crash their planes into the enemy ship, to detonate the bombs carried by the planes and start gasoline fires from the fuel. An added advantage was that obsolete planes and untrained pilots could be used. Such sacrifice for the Emperor appealed to the thousands of young Japanese who volunteered. Taffy 1 had the dubious distinction of being the first American force to endure a *kamikaze* attack; later that same day Taffy 3 underwent eight attacks, one of which sank the *St. Lo*. Between them, Kurita and the *kamikazes* had succeeded in sinking two escort carriers, two destroyers and one destroyer escort and badly damaging several ships on the 25th.

Kinkaid's Seventh Fleet was under Mac-Arthur's command for the Leyte landings with the specific mission of protecting the beachhead and providing fire support. Since MacArthur would have no cover from his own land-based planes, he had been guaranteed naval air support from Nimitz's command. Nimitz had assigned this task to the powerful Third Fleet under Halsey. Halsey's orders were to 'cover and support' the army in pursuit of the Allied objectives in the central Philippines and to 'destroy enemy naval and air forces in or threatening the Philippines'. But the orders went on to say 'In case opportunity for destruction of a major portion of the enemy fleet is offered or can be created, such destruction becomes the primary task'. Although the primary duty of a covering force in an amphibious operation is always the protection of the landing force, Halsey interpreted his orders to mean that his primary objective was to destroy the Japanese fleet if the opportunity appeared. Indeed, Halsey had a hand in drafting these orders with this very thought in mind. Not being under MacArthur's orders, he was not required to seek approval or even inform the army command of any action the Third Fleet might see fit to take. And *Sho* 1 was designed to offer the aggressive admiral the apparent opportunity to attain his primary objective.

All day on the 24th, Third Fleet search planes had been seeking a Japanese carrier force reported to have left the Inland Sea. Ozawa's Northern Force, equally anxious to be sighted, comprised one heavy carrier and three light carriers with a total of 116 planes between them. To make the force more attractive to Halsey two 'hermaphro-

Below: The wardroom of the USS *Sewanee* is used as a temporary sickbay during the Battle of Leyte Gulf.

dite' carriers – battleships with cut down super-structures to make room for a short flight deck but carrying no planes – were included, along with the screen of three light cruisers and nine destroyers. In the morning Japanese search planes discovered a part of Task Force 38 and Ozawa sent a 76-plane strike against it. Only 29 planes returned to Northern Force; the remainder were shot down, ditched, or landed on Luzon airfields. American search planes finally located Ozawa at 1540 but their report did not reach Halsey until 1700. The sighting of Japanese carriers was a red flag to 'Bull' Halsey, causing him to make a crucial error in judgement for which he received great criticism. Deciding that Kurita's force was no longer a factor, the admiral turned to what he considered his primary mission, the destruction of the Japanese carrier force, Around 2000 the 64 ships and 787 planes of the Third Fleet went after the 17 ships and 29 planes of the Northern Force. At 0220 on the morning of the 25th, the Northern Force was reported to be 200 miles off Cape Engano in Luzon. At 0430 the carriers prepared full deck-loads and launched at daylight. The first strike on Ozawa came in at 0800, first the Helldivers, followed by strafing Wildcats and then the Avengers sweeping in to release their torpedoes at altitudes of 700–1000 feet and ranges of 1400–1600 yards. There were five major strikes, and no Combat Air Patrol, Ozawa could only rely on evasive tactics and anti-aircraft fire. All four carriers and a destroyer went down during these strikes despite the fact that the Japanese anti-aircraft fire was

possibly the most deadly on either side during the war.

By 0820 Halsey was beginning to get urgent plain language appeals for help from Kinkaid but, anticipating a gun battle with Ozawa, he made no move to relieve Taffy 3 other than to direct McCain's distant task force to send air strikes when possible. As a result of a vague message from Halsey both Kinkaid and Nimitz assumed that he had left a force to watch the San Bernardino Strait. By 1000 even Nimitz was making inquiries as to where this force was and what Halsey was doing. In fact, Halsey had wanted to keep his battle force with him to clean up the enemy 'cripples' after the air strikes and to catch up with the two hermaphrodite carriers which had not succumbed to the air attacks. Largely because he now knew that Nimitz was concerned for the safety of the Seventh Fleet, he sent one carrier group and most of the battle line south at 1055. Even at top speed, however, this force could not have reached the strait before 0100 on the 26th. If this force had been detached immediately on Kinkaid's first appeal, it might have caught Kurita in the strait but as it was, the Japanese admiral escaped without further loss.

Halsey's remaining cruisers and destroyers were ordered in pursuit of Ozawa and finished off a crippled light cruiser and a large destroyer. Ozawa, who was considered the ablest Japanese admiral after Yamamoto, escaped with a light cruiser, the two hermaphrodite carriers and five destroyers. Although he later said 'We expected

Below: US sailors watch as the *Princeton* (background) is hit by Japanese dive bombers.

Above: USS *Darter*, one of the two submarines which saw the first action at Leyte Gulf, sinking Kurita's flagship. She was later hit badly and attempts to scuttle her were unsuccessful.

complete destruction in this mission', he had saved Center Force and his own from annihilation. Forced to use his carriers on what amounted to a suicide mission, the battle was a 'bitter experience' for him, coming as it did only five months after his defeat in the Battle of the Philippine Sea. Halsey, on the other side, had followed one error with another. The first was rising to the bait. The second was his failure to leave a strong part of his battle force behind to block the strait or even to inform Kinkaid that the strait was unguarded, while the third was his failure then to retain the battleships to complete the annihilation of Ozawa's force.

The End of the Battle

The battle was over on the 26th. The Allies had lost a light carrier, two escort carriers, two destroyers and a destroyer escort. The Japanese had lost three battleships, one heavy carrier, three light carriers, six heavy cruisers, four light cruisers and nine destroyers.

On the American side, it can be said that the air power of both the Third and Seventh Fleets was fully exploited but that the battle line of the former, with more gun power than the whole Japanese navy, never got into action through bad handling. The battle line of the Seventh Fleet engaged a Japanese force one-fifth of its strength and already decimated by destroyer attacks for a few minutes. With half of the surviving gun power of the Imperial Navy, the Center Force was allowed to sail undetected within gun range and take units of the Seventh Fleet by surprise. Only the fast reaction of air power prevented a major disaster. The Center Force then made its escape almost unmolested. The greatest weakness of the American side, however, was its divided command at the top. Had one commander, whether Mac-

Arthur or Nimitz, been in overall control at Leyte, Halsey could not have acted as he did. Before removing the Third Fleet from its station in the San Bernardino Strait for whatever reason, he would have had to ask permission of his superior.

For the Japanese side, it should have been obvious that *Sho* 1 was too complicated to succeed. There was bad coordination between the commanders, who showed an inability to avert disaster with new tactics and dispositions. Although brave and reasonably competent, the commanders were not up to maneuvering a modern fleet in battle and had no common doctrine of strategy or tactics to unite them. The best (or worst) example is Kurita who should have sunk all of Taffy 3 but failed because he lost tactical control of his force. The expenditure of Nishimura's Southern Force was pointless and again indicative of the Japanese inability to adapt a predetermined strategy to a new situation. In terms of command performance, the high points of the battle were Oldendorf's disposition and handling of the Seventh Fleet in the night battle of the Surigao Strait and Ozawa's execution of his decoy mission.

The great lesson of Leyte Gulf was the helplessness of a modern fleet without air cover. Taffy 3 was able to block a powerful force of battleships and cruisers for precisely this reason. Key events were, therefore, the Battle of the Philippine Sea in June and the October air strikes on Formosa. This earlier decimation of Japanese naval air power predetermined the Battle of Leyte Gulf. Had the invasion come in December as originally planned, new Japanese air groups would have been trained and the Imperial Navy could have put up a better fight.

After the actions at Leyte Gulf, the Allied naval forces played a support role intended to stop

Japanese reinforcement of Leyte and maintain air supremacy until army planes were able to do so. Although the initial landings had met with little resistance, Leyte ultimately proved a tough nut to crack, forcing MacArthur to commit a quarter of a million troops to the task. By the end of the year, however, only mopping up operations remained and preparations for the Luzon landings were well underway. After its desperate gamble at Leyte Gulf, the Japanese Navy ceased to be an independent fighting force and was relegated to an auxiliary role for the remainder of the war. Leyte Gulf was the death of the Japanese Navy, a death which meant that final defeat was imminent for Japan. As the Chief of Naval Staff, Admiral Yonai, said after the war, 'Our defeat at Leyte was tantamount to the loss of the Philippines. When you took the Philippines, that was the end of our resources'.

Conclusion

There have been no main fleet actions since Leyte Gulf nor are there likely to be any in the future, since the character of naval warfare has been completely revolutionized. From Trafalgar to Jutland the battleship constituted the striking power of a fleet, and as a result tactics were largely determined by the essential characteristic of the battleship – its reliance on gun power. During the nineteenth century the nature of naval warfare did not change radically because the development of the gun was more than matched by the corresponding development of armor. It was only after 1900 that the development of the mine, the torpedo and the submarine began to alter naval combat noticeably, but even though its position was now more vulnerable, the battleship still reigned supreme. Coronel and the Falklands were the last battles to be decided solely by gunfire

while it has already been seen how deeply the strategy, tactics and course of the action were affected by these factors at Jutland. In 1916 as in 1805, however, the essence of the sea battle was still two lines of battleships pounding each other with their guns.

While technical developments and innovations were influencing some facets of traditional naval warfare after 1900, in 1903 an event occurred which was a harbinger of a total revolution in naval warfare. In that year Wilbur and Orville Wright successfully flew the first airplane. The airplane developed rapidly as did its adoption for naval uses. In 1910 the first aircraft landing was made on the USS *Birmingham*, a light cruiser with a short flight deck. Throughout the First World War the Royal Navy experimented with airplanes and ships until by 1918, several modest aircraft carriers were in operational use in the North Sea. Japan acquired its first carrier in 1921, while the United States converted a collier into the USS *Langley* in 1922. During the time of the Washington Naval Limitation Treaty, a number of battle cruisers were converted to carriers, including the *Lexington* and *Saratoga* for the United States and the *Kaga* and *Akagi* for Japan. With the development of the 'Kate' torpedo bomber and the 'Zero' fighter, Japan achieved a definite superiority in carrier aircraft, a superiority which came as a rude awakening to Britain and the United States in 1941.

Between 1939 and 1945 the carrier came to dominate naval warfare. Already at Matapan in 1941, it was a carrier which struck the key blows and gave victory to the British. It was at Midway a year later, however, that the death knell of the battleship truly sounded. Although the Japanese had eleven battleships and the Americans none, the Japanese ships never got into action, the battle being wholly fought by carriers hundreds of miles away from each other. The role of the battleship was changing, a fact which Admiral Yamamoto for all his brilliance failed to grasp adequately. He committed the error of separating his carriers and battleships at a time when the carriers needed the anti-aircraft fire support of the battleships. It was a costly lesson, but one which the Americans learned well. For the remainder of the war, battleships were always assigned to provide support for American carriers. The role of the battleship thus came to be to provide anti-aircraft support and fire support for amphibious landings, while the carrier definitely became the predominant capital ship. This fact is reflected in the postwar period when the major navies ceased building battleships but continued the construction of carriers, culminating in the 75,000-ton nuclear-powered American carrier *Enterprise*.

At the present time, yet another technological revolution is threatening the supremacy of the carrier. The emergence of the atomic submarine and ultra-sophisticated missilry may well mean the relegation of the carrier to an auxiliary role alongside the battleship. Whatever the case, however, one fact stands out. Naval battles as Nelson, Jellicoe and even Nimitz knew them will never be repeated. The era of epic sea battles ended appropriately with the largest naval engagement in history at Leyte Gulf.

The Ardennes

1944

By the autumn of 1944 the once-powerful *Wehrmacht* had been forced onto the defensive on all fronts. North Africa was long since lost, most of France was in Allied hands, and the situation in the East deteriorated daily. After the mauling of the Panzers at Kursk, Germany's only hope on the Russian Front lay in fluid, mobile defense. Hitler's dismissal of Manstein, the leading practitioner of these tactics, only worsened the *Wehrmacht's* plight. June 1944 saw the crippling of *Army Group Center* which, despite substantial reinforcements which might more usefully have been employed in the West, was tumbled back to the Polish border.

The declining fortune of German arms was matched by growing discord within the Reich. The 20 July bomb plot was followed by a sharp increase in arrests and denunciations; suspicion and distrust between the army and the SS reached a new and dangerous level. However, in spite of the ferocity of Allied air attacks, German industrial production actually rose, and in August 1944 the record number of 869 tanks and 744 assault guns came off the assembly lines. But equipment was no use without soldiers to operate it; in a frenzied effort to get every available man

Opposite left: Field Marshal Gerd von Rundstedt, who was brought from retirement to direct the Ardennes offensive. He was forcibly retired by Hitler in 1944 after he advised him to surrender on the best terms possible when the Allies landed in Normandy.
Opposite right: Rundstedt inspects troops in his capacity as C-in-C West.
Below: An American 105-mm self-propelled howitzer crew takes on fresh ammunition as they prepare the counter-offensive in the Bulge.

Above: Walter Model, who was promoted to Field Marshal in 1944, commanded Army Group B in the Ardennes offensive.
Above right: General Hasso von Manteuffel, who commanded the Fifth Panzer Army in Hitler's last offensive.

into uniform the call-up age was lowered to 16½, and ruthless steps were taken to 'comb out' those in hitherto reserved occupations.

One of the consequences of the 20 July plot was the appointment of Heinrich Himmler, head of the SS, as commander of the 'Replacement Army'. Himmler added this office to his many others and, even without the Army-SS tension, it would have been difficult enough for any one man to cope. Himmler's new activities were indicative of the hostility between the agencies of the tottering Reich. The 'combing-out' process made thousands of men available; boys, businessmen, airmen without planes and sailors without ships. Instead of using them to reinforce weakened Army formations, Himmler posted them instead to new *Volksgrenadier* divisions, whose short training period was, in part at least, compensated for by very high *esprit de corps*. This was fostered by giving these divisions much of the new equipment. Most of the rest of it went to the SS, while for the battered Army divisions tanks, vehicles and guns were in short supply.

There was immediate employment at hand for the *Volksgrenadiers*. Hitler regarded the situation as far from hopeless. He was convinced that the Allies would soon be at each others' throats; the incongruous union between communist and capitalist could not survive for long. Germany could endure, she might yet triumph. The collapse of the alliance would, Hitler believed, be facilitated by striking a sudden and violent blow on one front. In August 1944 he had ordered that preparations should be made for an offensive on the Western Front in November. His generals maintained that troops would never be available in sufficient quantities, but the efforts of Himmler, Goebbels and the local *Gauleiters* proved them wrong.

But where were these new troops to be employed? An offensive against the Russians would be unlikely to achieve decisive results. In the West, however, things were different. The Allied

advance into Belgium had left the Ardennes—the hilly, wooded area where Belgium, Germany and Luxembourg meet—held by only six divisions. The events of 1940 had illustrated vividly that the area was passable to armor. To the undeniable tactical attraction of attacking a point where the enemy was weak, was added the historical appeal of staging a blitzkrieg on the very ground over which it had been so successful three and a half years before.

Desperate though the plight of the *Wehrmacht* was, there were certain factors favoring a limited offensive. The *Volksgrenadiers* would certainly enable the Germans to obtain local superiority. Of the 28 divisions available, eight were Panzer, and the Panther and Tiger tanks they contained were superior to the Shermans with which most British and American armored units were equipped. Surprise, an essential ingredient of blitzkrieg, was facilitated by the fact that the Allied commanders believed the Germans to be exhausted and quite incapable of a counter-offensive. On the other hand, there were two important factors militating against an attack. The first of these was Allied air superiority. The Luftwaffe, even by straining every nerve, could only hope to offset this on a local basis. Secondly, there was a critical shortage of fuel which was to severely limit movement on the ground.

The strategic aim of the Ardennes Offensive —often referred to as the Battle of the Bulge—was the capture of Antwerp and the encirclement of the four Allied armies north of the line Malmédy-Liège-Antwerp. This objective seemed unrealistic to the aged Field Marshal Gerd von Rundstedt, brought out of retirement to act as Commander-in-Chief West. 'Antwerp?' he inquired bitingly. 'If we reach the Meuse we should go down on our knees and thank God'. Von Rundstedt's command was little more than nominal; Hitler was to direct the battle personally. The three armies taking part in the offensive were to form *Army Group B* under Field Marshal Walter

Model, an excellent tactician who had shown his worth in the defensive battles in the East. Model's army commanders were an ill-assorted trio. SS General Joseph 'Sepp' Dietrich, a former regular NCO, led *Sixth SS Panzer Army*, which was to form the northern prong of the German trident. On his left was *Fifth Panzer Army* under General Hasso von Manteuffel who, at 47, had a brilliant record as a fighting general on the Russian Front. The less dramatic figure of General Erich Brandenburger commanded *Seventh Army* on the German left.

Planning the Operation

Rundstedt and Model discussed the operation with the three army commanders on 27 October. They reported in favor of a limited offensive with Liège as its target, but were overruled on 1 November by the arrival of an operations order which decreed that Antwerp should remain the objective. The attack was to be launched on an 85-mile front, between Monschau and Echternach. Dietrich was to cross the Meuse at Andenne and Huy, before thrusting straight for Antwerp. Manteuffel was to take Namur, Dinant and Brussels. Brandenburger was to cover Manteuffel's southern flank, an unspectacular but essential task. The advance was to be preceded by parachutists who were to seize major road junctions. SS Colonel Otto Skorzeny trained a special force which would wear American uniforms to sow confusion in the Allied rear.

Both Rundstedt and Model protested that the operation was too ambitious, and they were joined by Manteuffel, whose well-known tactical expertise persuaded Hitler to permit some small adjustments to the initial phase of the attack. The date for the launching of the offensive was initially to be 25 November. The concentration of the assaulting division took longer than expected, however, and the attack was steadily postponed, first to 7 December and finally to 16 December.

The Allied commanders, also were not without their problems. The rapid advance from the Normandy bridgeheads in August, and the subsequent liberation of Paris, could not conceal a serious difference of opinion between the Supreme Allied Commander, General Dwight D. Eisenhower, and his subordinate, Field Marshal Montgomery, commander of 21 Army Group. Montgomery wanted to push on north with his own army group and General Omar Bradley's 12 Army Group. This 'solid mass of 40 divisions' was to make for Brussels, and then for the Ruhr, thus crippling Germany's industry. Eisenhower envisaged a totally different approach. His plan was, in his own words, 'to push forward on a broad front with priority on the left'. Montgomery's plan might well have worked if implemented in August, but German resistance stiffened in September. 'Operation Market Garden', the seizure of the river crossings between Eindhoven and Arnhem, was only partially successful. This did not, however, curb Montgomery's enthusiasm. He continued to press for a drive into the Ruhr, but was eventually persuaded that the capture of Antwerp must be given first priority.

Antwerp fell on 4 September, although the port was not operational till 28 November. General George S. Patton's Third Army took Metz on 22 November, and the US Seventh Army entered Strasbourg the following day. Montgomery continued to argue, however, that the north was the crucial front, and stressed to Eisenhower that there should be a unified command of all forces north of the Ardennes. Eisenhower met Montgomery and Bradley at Maastricht in early December. It was decided to keep up pressure on the Germans in the north with a view to an attack on the Ruhr. For this purpose 21 Army Group would be reinforced with one American Army. The boundary between the two army groups was to be the Ruhr, not the Ardennes as Montgomery had wished.

The decision taken at Maastricht would un-

Center left: A Royal Tiger tank burns on a Belgian roadside as the German thrust to Antwerp is brought to a halt. **Near left:** General Dwight David Eisenhower, who was appointed as a Lieutenant General in 1942 to command American and Allied forces in Europe. After the success of 'Operation Torch', when this photograph was taken, he directed operations in Italy and France. His first major setback was suffered in the Ardennes. **Above:** Lieutenant General George S. Patton, commander of the American Third Army. 'Old Blood and Guts' was one of the most daring and controversial commanders in the US Army, who was tragically killed in a road accident soon after VE Day.

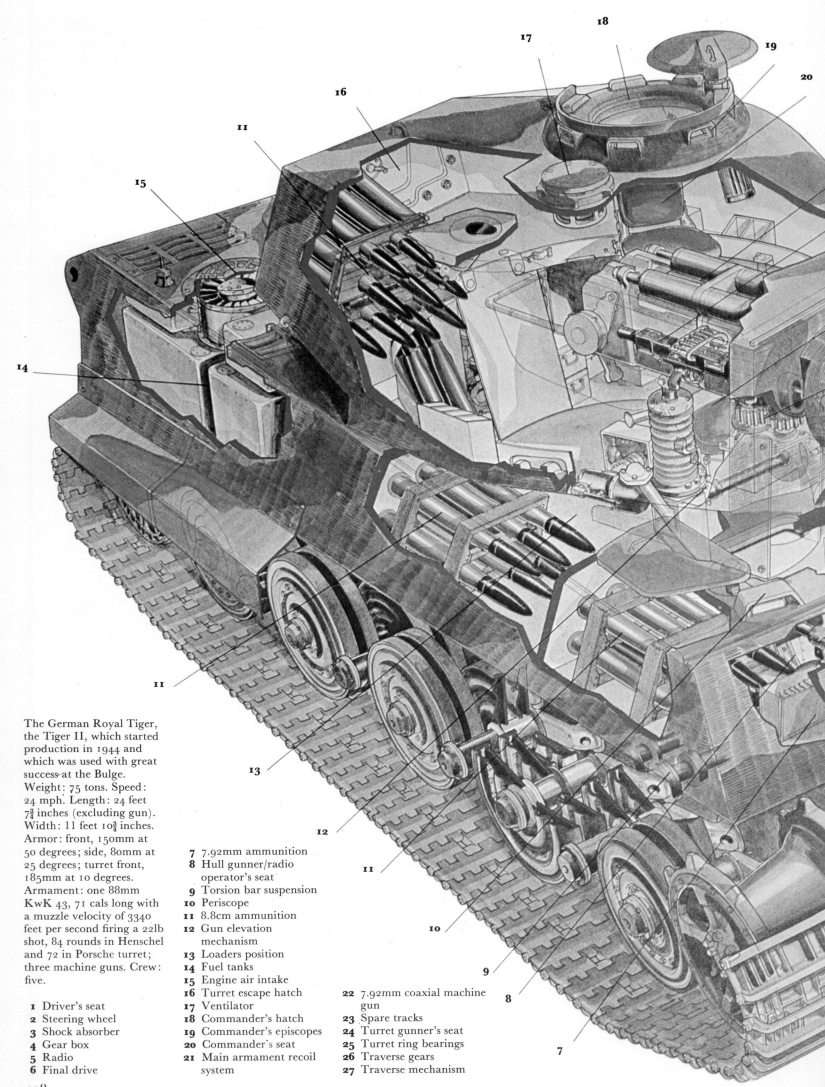

The German Royal Tiger, the Tiger II, which started production in 1944 and which was used with great success at the Bulge. Weight: 75 tons. Speed: 24 mph. Length: 24 feet 7¾ inches (excluding gun). Width: 11 feet 10¾ inches. Armor: front, 150mm at 50 degrees; side, 80mm at 25 degrees; turret front, 185mm at 10 degrees. Armament: one 88mm KwK 43, 71 cals long with a muzzle velocity of 3340 feet per second firing a 22lb shot, 84 rounds in Henschel and 72 in Porsche turret; three machine guns. Crew: five.

1 Driver's seat
2 Steering wheel
3 Shock absorber
4 Gear box
5 Radio
6 Final drive
7 7.92mm ammunition
8 Hull gunner/radio operator's seat
9 Torsion bar suspension
10 Periscope
11 8.8cm ammunition
12 Gun elevation mechanism
13 Loaders position
14 Fuel tanks
15 Engine air intake
16 Turret escape hatch
17 Ventilator
18 Commander's hatch
19 Commander's episcopes
20 Commander's seat
21 Main armament recoil system
22 7.92mm coaxial machine gun
23 Spare tracks
24 Turret gunner's seat
25 Turret ring bearings
26 Traverse gears
27 Traverse mechanism

doubtedly have been different had Allied intelligence fully appreciated the significance of *Sixth Panzer Army*. It had been detected early, but a SHAEF (Supreme Headquarters Allied Expeditionary Force) report of 12 November maintained that 'the Army's most obvious use is counterattack', pointing out that a lack of petrol precluded the launching of 'a true counteroffensive'. The move of *Sixth Panzer Army* to the area east of Aachen was seen as little more than an attempt by the Germans to buttress their crumbling front. Thus it was that, in mid-December, the Ardennes sector, irrelevant for the projected Allied thrust to the Ruhr, lay dangerously bare.

The threatened area was the responsibility of Lieutenant-General Courtney H. Hodges, US First Army. Most of the attack frontage was in the hands of Major General Troy H. Middleton's VIII Corps. On Middleton's left was the southernmost formation of V Corps, 99th Division, which had been in the line for only six weeks and was relatively inexperienced. This would have been serious enough. There was, however, an unguarded space of some two miles between the two corps. South of this lay the Losheim Gap, a classic avenue between Belgium and Germany, held only by 18th Cavalry Squadron, which had incomplete liaison with its right-hand neighbor, 106th Division. The 106th, holding the forward slopes of the Schnee Eifel Ridge, was totally inexperienced, and had arrived in its position only three days before the attack was launched. On its right stood the center formation of VIII Corps, 28th Division. This was, in contrast, a battle-tried division, but it had recently lost over 6000 men in the fierce fighting in the Hurtgen Forest, and was in the Ardennes to rest and reorganize. Hodges' only notable advantage was the presence of the excellent 2nd Division in the north. As part of Fifth Army's preparation for a thrust at the Koel Dams, this division had just launched a successful attack in the sector held by 99th Division. Its presence was to be of great value over the coming days.

At 0530 on 16 December 2000 German guns roared into life. While their shells pounded the American positions, the 200,000 men participating in Hitler's last offensive waited to move forward, their enthusiasm fired by the orders of the day issued by their commanders. 'Soldiers of of the Western Front, your great hour has struck', proclaimed von Rundstedt. 'At this moment the veil which has been hiding so many preparations has been lifted at last'. Model and his army commanders added their own bombast, and if any members of *Army Group B* lacked confidence that December morning, it was not the fault of their leaders.

The surge of fire came as a rude shock to the American front line units, many of whose members had previously been concerned with

nothing more important than the possibility of Christmas leave. As the fire died away, the German infantry and armor advanced, aided by searchlights bounced off low cloud.

German successes on the first day were dramatic but uneven. In the north, *LXXII Corps* of *Sixth Panzer Army* was checked before Monschau. The American attack toward the Roer Dams had reduced the forces available in this sector and, despite the furious assaults of *326th Volksgrenadier Division*, gains were limited. In particular, *LXXII Corps* failed to seize the Monschau-Eupen Ridge, whose capture was essential to the German plan. 'Hard Shoulders' were to be set up to bolster both flanks of the attack, and the Monschau-Eupen line was to form the northern shoulder. On the southern edge of the attack front, Brandenburger had the task of setting up a 'hard shoulder' across the Sauer at Echternach. This called for a complex river-crossing by his left-hand corps, *LXXX*. Brandenburger's *Volksgrenadiers*, aided by an effective preparatory bombardment, got across the river and successfully penetrated the American defenses. The US 4th Division, holding the sector, fought back with creditable tenacity, aided by a small number of tanks from the US 10th Armored Division. The *Volksgrenadiers* were poorly supplied with anti-tank weapons, and an American counterthrust into the village of Lauerborn achieved local success. The artillery of 4th Division, meanwhile, wreaked havoc amongst Brandenburger's horse-drawn artillery and transport, and impeded German pioneers in their efforts to bridge the Sauer. By nightfall, although the Germans were across the river in strength, the southern 'hard shoulder' had not been established.

Brandenburger's right-hand corps, *LXXXV*, had the dual task of cooperating with Manteuffel and assisting *LXXX Corps* in its seizure of the 'hard shoulder'. It was faced by 28th Division, whose 109th Infantry Regiment, dug in on high ground, assisted 60th Armored Infantry Battalion, to its south, to beat off *276th Volksgrenadier Division*. Thrusts by *352nd Volksgrenadier Division* against the 109th Infantry's left were also thwarted. The *5th Parachute Division*, Brandenburger's most northerly formation, made slightly better progress. The partial success of *Seventh Army's* right could not compensate for the failure of *LXXX Corps*. *Seventh Army* fell consistently short of its objectives in the subsequent days, and never provided *Fifth Panzer Army* with the necessary flank protection.

In the German center Manteuffel crashed through 18th Cavalry Squadron in the Losheim gap, and reached the St Vith road. On his left *XLVII Panzer Corps* crossed the Our, but was checked on the Clerf by the gallant 28th Division. To Manteuffel's right, Dietrich's men pressed forward rapidly. *Sixth Panzer Army's* main thrusts were delivered by *1st* and *12th SS Panzer Divisions*, both preceded by *Volksgrenadier* divisions who were to make the initial break, to permit the armor to funnel through the American position. The results of these tactics were not dissimilar to those of comparable plans at Kursk and Alamein. The *Volksgrenadiers* were very heavily shelled and were unable to get through the American line. The *12th SS Panzer Division* tried to move forward without infantry support, but was stopped dead; *1st SS Panzer* might have shared the same fate had its leading battlegroup not been commanded by a particularly ruthless and aggressive officer, SS Colonel Jochen Peiper.

Far left: A Nazi soldier directs the advance of German troops near a knocked-out US half-track on 16 December, at the start of the Ardennes offensive. **Above Left:** SS Colonel Jochen Peiper (with cigar) in a *Schwimmwagen* (amphibious Volkswagen) near Recht on 17 December, 1944. Peiper was responsible for the Malmédy Massacre which occurred on the same day. **Below left:** Two German infantrymen move forward past a burning vehicle as the attack continues. **Below:** Infantrymen of the US First Army move up to repel the German attack on 17 December, 1944 near Butgenbach on the German-Belgian frontier.

Above: Gliders brought reinforcements to the beleaguered 101st Airborne Division trapped in Bastogne.

Below: US infantrymen plunge forward through the wintry snows of the Ardennes.

Panzer Army, Peiper's failure to seize the Stavelot dump with its two million gallons of petrol was itself of prime significance.

While the German armor and infantry assaulted the American front, Otto Skorzery's special forces and Colonel von der Heydte's parachutists were employed against the American rear. Skorzery's men were quite successful; they destroyed several installations, spread disquieting rumors and caused a wave of saboteurmania behind the lines. Large numbers of roadblocks were set up, and troops whose presence was urgently required in the firing-line wasted hours in elaborate identity-checks. The parachutists, on the other hand, were dogged by bad luck. They were dropped 24 hours late; few of the aircraft found the dropping zone, and those parachutists that landed did so only with heavy casualties. Von der Heydte eventually collected 350 or so, and remained in the area of Baraque Michel for two days before ordering his men to return to their own lines in small groups. Few managed to make their way back; the majority, including von der Heydte, were captured.

On the second day of the offensive Manteuffel renewed his pressure on 106th Division, two of whose regiments became isolated on the Schnee Eifel Ridge. When reinforcements sent by VIII Corps failed to arrive in time, after being held up by retreating troops, over 8000 men surrendered in the most serious reverse incurred by American troops in Europe.

Eisenhower had immediately realized that the Ardennes thrust was a full blooded counter-offensive. He ordered 7th Armored Division to St Vith from its rest area near Aachen, and sent a combat command of 10th Armored Division to Bastogne. To Bastogne, too, he sent the US 101st Airborne Division, which set out from Reims on the evening of 17 December and arrived at its destination early on the 19th.

It was toward Bastogne that Manteuffel's main attack now developed. His advance was spearheaded by *XLVII Panzer Corps*, containing two good divisions, *26th Volksgrenadier* and *2nd Panzer*. The élite *Panzer Lehr* division was initially in reserve. Their high quality notwithstanding,

Peiper led his panzers past the chaos of the abortive *Volksgrenadier* attack, broke through the American lines, and took Honsfeld at dawn the following day. Unwilling to be burdened with prisoners, Peiper's men shot several captured Americans, setting a grim precedent for their subsequent behavior. After refueling with captured petrol at Bullingen, Peiper's force drove on to the Malmédy crossroads, where 86 American prisoners were machine-gunned in the infamous 'Malmédy Massacre', for which Peiper was later to be tried for his life. Peiper's objective was the Meuse bridge at Huy and, on the afternoon of 17 December, he seemed likely to reach it. However, his advance guard halted just short of Stavelot, deterred, it seems, by the large numbers of American vehicles in the area. This was the moment at which Peiper's leadership might again have tipped the scales, but, somewhat surprisingly, he failed to come forward to examine the situation personally. It was just as well for the Americans that Peiper did not cast his incisive glance over Stavelot, for it was held only by engineers, with no heavy weapons. Most of the vehicles there were moving petrol from a large fuel dump nearby. Since lack of fuel was one of the major causes of the limited advance of *Sixth*

the attackers' task proved difficult in the extreme. The *26th Volksgrenadier* had to cross two rivers, the Our and the Clerf, in the face of determined resistance. Although the isolated American strongpoints were eventually overcome with the aid of *2nd Panzer*, the advance went much slower than Manteuffel had hoped. The spirited defense of the Clerf line gave the Americans valuable time in which to reinforce Bastogne, and it was against Bastogne that Manteuffel's strength was ultimately to break.

Panzer Lehr was within five miles of Bastogne by dusk on 18 December. Although the commander of *XLVII Panzer Corps* was aware of the vital importance of Bastogne, he failed to infect Lieutenant-General Bayerlein of *Panzer Lehr* with the essential sense of urgency. Bayerlein halted at Magaret, and the route to Bastogne was lost; 101st Airborne Division arrived early the following morning.

Other Allied reinforcements were on their way. Hodges had bolstered up the Elsenborn Ridge south of Monschau with troops from the First Army's northern sector. Lieutenant-General W. H. Simpson of the US Ninth Army sent two divisions south to aid Hodges, and Eisenhower sent the US 82nd Airborne Division to Werboment, with the aim of blunting Peiper's thrust. On 19 December Eisenhower in a conference at Verdun laid down broad policy for preventing a breakout. Bradley and Montgomery were authorized to carry out limited withdrawals, but the west bank of the Meuse was to be the limit of such maneuvers. Lieutenant-General J.L. Devers was to extend his Sixth Army Group to the north to permit the US Third Army to intervene against the German left. Simpson was to carry out a similar extension to the South, to free more of Hodges' troops. Finally, Eisenhower took the decision, controversial but undeniably correct, to place all troops north of the breakthrough under Montgomery's command, while Bradley commanded those in the south. Pained though Bradley must have been by the temporary use of his First and Ninth Armies, there was logic in Eisenhower's decision. It was difficult for Bradley, whose headquarters were in Luxembourg, to control

armies with which his telephone links had been cut. Furthermore, by placing Montgomery in command of the northern sector, Eisenhower ensured that British reserves would be used to contain the breakthrough in this area.

Montgomery's immediate intention was, in his own words, 'to get the show tidied up and to ensure absolute security before passing over the offensive action..'. His efforts to 'tidy up' brought him into conflict with Hodges, whose headquarters he visited on 20 December. Montgomery suggested abandoning St Vith and the Elsenborn Ridge, but dropped the idea in the face of American protests. He even went on to authorize an advance by 82nd Airborne to the Salm, which *Sixth Panzer Army* had, as yet, been unable to cross in strength. Finally, Montgomery ordered Hodges to pull Major General J.L. 'Lightning Joe' Collins' VII Corps out of the line near Aachen to be strengthened for subsequent use as a counterattack force.

Although substantial steps had been taken to limit the German exploitation, the crisis was far from over. The *116th Panzer Division* of *XLVIII Panzer Corps* advanced into the void between Bastogne and St Vith, taking Houffalize on the evening of 19 December. The reconnaissance of

Above: Planes of the 9th Troop Carrier Command parachute supplies to the 'Battling Bastards of Bastogne', 23 December, 1944.

Below: US infantrymen outside St Vith in January 1945, during the counter-offensive which effectively destroyed the remnants of the German Army in the West.

The Battle of the Ardennes, 1944

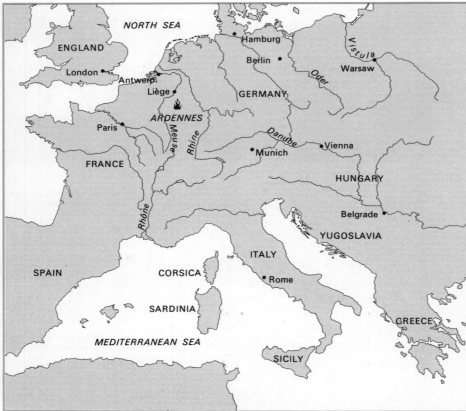

Objectives of the Offensive

The strategic aim of the Ardennes offensive was the capture of Antwerp and the encirclement of the four Allied armies north of the line Malmédy-Liège-Antwerp. Gerd von Rundstedt was to direct the battle. The three armies taking part in the offensive were to form 'Army Group B' under Model.

The German Offensive 16–24 December

At 0530 on 16 December 2000 German guns opened up on the American positions. As the fire died away, the German infantry and armor advanced.

German successes on the first day were dramatic but uneven. In the north 'LXXII Corps' was checked before Monschau. In the center Manteuffel advanced through the Losheim gap and reached the St Vith road. On his left 'XLVII Panzer Corps' crossed the Our, but was checked on the Clerf by the 28th Division. On the southern edge of the attack front, Brandenberger crossed the Sauer at Echternach in strength. Dietrich's men pressed forward rapidly, but only Peiper's battle-group of 1st SS Panzer Division broke through the American lines, took Honsfeld at dawn the following day. After refuelling at Bullingen, drove on to the Malmédy crossroads, and on the afternoon of the 17th halted just short of Stavelot.

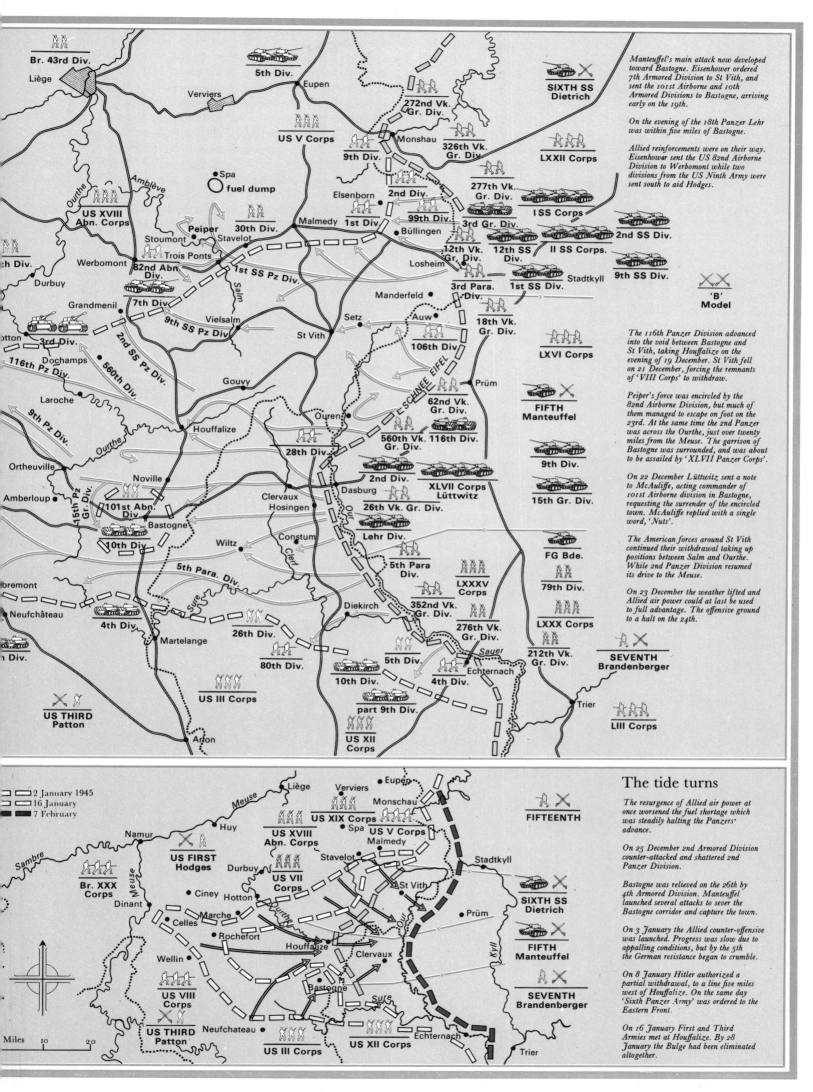

Br. 43rd Div.
Liège
5th Div.
Verviers
Eupen
SIXTH SS
Dietrich
272nd Vk. Gr. Div.
Monshau
US V Corps
9th Div.
326th Vk. Gr. Div.
LXXII Corps
● Spa
○ fuel dump
Elsenborn
2nd Div.
277th Vk. Gr. Div.
I SS Corps
2nd SS Div.
Amblève
Malmedy
1st Div.
99th Div.
Bullingen
3rd Gr. Div.
Ourthe
US XVIII Abn. Corps
Peiper
30th Div.
Stavelot
Losheim
12th Vk. Gr. Div.
12th SS Div.
II SS Corps
9th SS Div.
Stoumont
Werbomont
Trois Ponts
82nd Abn. Div.
1st SS Pz Div.
Salm
Stadtkyll
Durbuy
3rd Para. Div.
1st SS Div.
Grandmenil
7th Div.
Manderfeld
'B' Model
Vielsalm
9th SS Pz Div.
Setz
Auw
18th Vk. Gr. Div.
3rd Div.
2nd SS Pz Div.
St Vith
106th Div.
LXVI Corps
Dochamps
560th Div.
116th Pz Div.
Gouvy
Prüm
FIFTH Manteuffel
Laroche
9th Pz Div.
Ouren
62nd Vk. Gr. Div.
Ourthe
Houffalize
560th Vk. Gr. Div.
116th Div.
SCHNEE EIFEL
9th Div.
Ortheuville
28th Div.
Noville
Dasburg
2nd Div.
XLVII Corps Lüttwitz
15th Gr. Div.
Amberloup
101st Abn. Div.
Clervaux
Hosingen
26th Vk. Gr. Div.
15th Pz Gr. Div.
Bastogne
10th Div.
Wiltz
Constum
Lehr Div.
FG Bde.
5th Para. Div.
79th Div.
Neufchâteau
4th Div.
Diekirch
352nd Vk. Gr. Div.
LXXXV Corps
LXXX Corps
Martelange
Sure
Clerf
26th Div.
80th Div.
5th Div.
276th Vk. Gr. Div.
Sauer
212th Vk. Gr. Div.
Echternach
SEVENTH Brandenberger
10th Div.
4th Div.
US III Corps
part 9th Div.
Trier
US THIRD Patton
Arlon
US XII Corps
LIII Corps

Manteuffel's main attack now developed toward Bastogne. Eisenhower ordered 7th Armored Division to St Vith, and sent the 101st Airborne and 10th Armored Divisions to Bastogne, arriving early on the 19th.

On the evening of the 18th Panzer Lehr was within five miles of Bastogne.

Allied reinforcements were on their way. Eisenhower sent the US 82nd Airborne Division to Werbomont while two divisions from the US Ninth Army were sent south to aid Hodges.

The 116th Panzer Division advanced into the void between Bastogne and St Vith, taking Houffalize on the evening of 19 December. St Vith fell on 21 December, forcing the remnants of 'VIII Corps' to withdraw.

Peiper's force was encircled by the 82nd Airborne Division, but much of them managed to escape on foot on the 23rd. At the same time the 2nd Panzer was across the Ourthe, just over twenty miles from the Meuse. The garrison of Bastogne was surrounded, and was about to be assailed by 'XLVII Panzer Corps'.

On 22 December Lüttwitz sent a note to McAuliffe, acting commander of 101st Airborne division in Bastogne, requesting the surrender of the encircled town. McAuliffe replied with a single word, 'Nuts'.

The American forces around St Vith continued their withdrawal taking up positions between Salm and Ourthe. While 2nd Panzer Division resumed its drive to the Meuse.

On 23 December the weather lifted and Allied air power could at last be used to full advantage. The offensive ground to a halt on the 24th.

The tide turns

□■ 2 January 1945
□■ 16 January
■■ 7 February

Liège
Verviers
Eupen
Meuse
Monschau
FIFTEENTH
Namur
Huy
Spa
US XIX Corps
US XVIII Abn. Corps
Malmedy
Stavelot
Stadtkyll
US V Corps
Sambre
US FIRST Hodges
Br. XXX Corps
Durbuy
St Vith
US VII Corps
Meuse
Dinant
Ciney
Hotton
Ourthe
Prüm
SIXTH SS Dietrich
Celles
Marche
Our
Rochefort
Houffalize
Clervaux
Kyll
FIFTH Manteuffel
Wellin
Bastogne
US VIII Corps
Sure
SEVENTH Brandenberger
US THIRD Patton
Neufchâteau
Echternach
US III Corps
US XII Corps
Trier

Miles 10   20

The resurgence of Allied air power at once worsened the fuel shortage which was steadily halting the Panzers' advance.

On 25 December 2nd Armored Division counter-attacked and shattered 2nd Panzer Division.

Bastogne was relieved on the 26th by 4th Armored Division. Manteuffel launched several attacks to sever the Bastogne corridor and capture the town.

On 3 January the Allied counter-offensive was launched. Progress was slow due to appalling conditions, but by the 5th the German resistance began to crumble.

On 8 January Hitler authorized a partial withdrawal, to a line five miles west of Houffalize. On the same day 'Sixth Panzer Army' was ordered to the Eastern Front.

On 16 January First and Third Armies met at Houffalize. By 28 January the Bulge had been eliminated altogether.

the division pressed on toward the western branch of the Ourthe, hoping to find it with the bridges intact. South of *116th Panzer*, *2nd Panzer Division* of *XLVII Panzer Corps* was unable to help, since the Bastogne garrison blocked its path at Noville. By the time *116th Panzer* reached the river the bridges were blown and it thereupon fell back to Houffalize before resuming its advance northwest. Meanwhile, 2nd *Panzer* forced its way through Noville, and managed to cross the Ourthe west of Bastogne.

St Vith fell on 21 December. The town's fall was a blow to the Americans; St Vith was an important communications center, and its loss made the withdrawal of the remnants of VIII Corps in the St Vith horseshoe inevitable. By this time 82nd Airborne Division was in position along the Salm, and could probably prevent a new breakout in that sector. Peiper's force was encircled, and on 23 December much of it escaped on foot, abandoning over 100 armored

vehicles. But *116th Panzer Division* was likely to resume its advance from Houffalize, and, worse still, *2nd Panzer* was safely across the Ourthe, just over twenty miles from the Meuse. The garrison of Bastogne was surrounded, and was about to be assailed by *XLVII Panzer Corps*.

On the credit side, American retention of the Elsenborn Ridge seriously constricted *Sixth Panzer Army's* line of advance. Furthermore, artillery fire from 1st Division compelled Dietrich to edge south, bringing about a series of traffic jams as the left wing of *Sixth Panzer Army* became enmeshed with the right wing of *Fifth Panzer Army* north of St Vith. Both Rundstedt and Model had been disappointed by the slowness of the advance. The former had advocated calling a halt as early as 19 December, but Model argued that the operation could still succeed if Manteuffel were given command of some of Dietrich's panzers. Hitler opposed this, not wishing to put SS formations under army command. On 21 December the

increasingly congested state of the roads around St Vith at last brought about the transfer of two SS Panzer divisions to Manteuffel.

On 22 December Lieutenant-General von Lüttwitz of *XLVII Panzer Corps* sent a courteous note to Brigadier-General Anthony McAuliffe, acting commander of 101st Airborne Division in Bastogne. 'There is only one possibility', said the note, 'of saving the availed USA troops from total annihilation; that is the honorable surrender of the encircled town'. The message went on to warn McAuliffe that failure to capitulate would result in the destruction of his forces. McAuliffe, undeterred by this threat, replied with the one unequivocal word, 'NUTS!'

Away to the south, in a blinding snowstorm, Patton began his counterattack. In other sectors, the battle hung in the balance. The defenders of the St Vith horseshoe continued their withdrawal, taking up new positions between the Salm and the Ourthe. On the following day *116th* and *2nd SS Panzer Divisions* attacked in this area, dragging part of Montgomery's counterattack force into the battle. While Dietrich, having at last ceased his futile battering at the Elsenborn Ridge, swung two SS Panzer divisions into the central sector, *2nd Panzer Division* resumed its drive to the Meuse.

Yet the tide was turning. On 23 December the weather lifted, and Allied air power could at last be employed to full advantage. The fog and snow which had obscured the skies since the beginning of the offensive had been an added bonus for the Germans, preventing the Allies from striking their advancing columns. Once the skies were clear, the Luftwaffe had no hope of gaining even temporary air superiority. Its aircraft were driven from the sky by Allied fighters, while fighter-bombers raked the roads and bombers attacked concentrations, supply dumps and communications in the rear. The Luftwaffe, it is true, was not quite finished, and on New Year's Day mounted a 700-flare attack on Allied airfields. However, as General Adolf Galland later admitted, the Ardennes battle ruined the Luftwaffe in the West.

The resurgence of Allied air power at once worsened the fuel shortage which was steadily throttling Model's Panzers. Petrol had been in short supply even at the start of the offensive, and no sizable stocks of it had been captured. Lack of fuel imposed a constant strain upon German movement. It delayed the southward move of Dietrich's Panzer divisions, and brought Peiper to a halt. It is a measure of the *Wehrmacht*'s petrol crisis that when the leading tanks of *2nd Panzer Division* stopped at Celles, only four miles from the Meuse, it was lack of fuel, not Allied pressure, which brought them to a halt.

Shortage of petrol was not the only problem besetting *2nd Panzer Division* on Christmas Day 1944. Montgomery was, as we have seen, opposed to piecemeal counterattacks. He could afford to be, since he had deployed 30 Corps along the Meuse downstream of Namur, and felt confident of dealing with any German forces that might struggle as far as the river. Hodges was less calm, owing partly to a natural reluctance to give up ground for which his men had fought hard. When

Above: Brigadier-General Anthony McAuliffe confused the Germans by his one-word reply to the German offer to surrender: 'Nuts!' **Right:** Members of the 84th Division dig into snowy terrain after the German breakthrough; American lines held and the big push back began. **Center right:** Three German soldiers, sent behind the lines by Skorzeny disguised as Americans and trained to learn American English down to slang expressions and GI jargon, are caught, court-martialed and sentenced to death by firing squad. These soldiers, Cpl. Wilhelm Schmidt (being tied), Officer Cadet Günther Billings and Sgt. Manfred Pernass, were caught when they failed to give the proper password while armed with American weapons and driving an American jeep. Their mission was to sabotage communications across the Meuse. **Far right:** Pernass is taken down after his execution. **Right:** German prisoners are marched to the rear during the Allied advance.

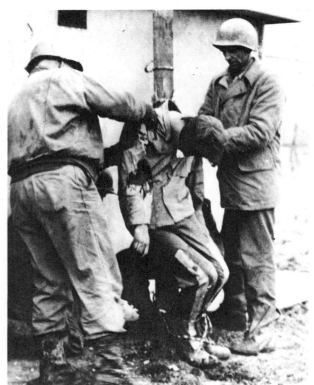

2nd Panzer reached Celles, the US 2nd Armored Division was within striking distance, and its commander, Major-General Ernest Harmon, asked his corps commander for permission to attack. The request was relayed to Hodges, who, on the evening of the 24th, tacitly authorized an attack. The next day 2nd Armored Division went forward, well supported by American aircraft, and shattered 2nd Panzer Division.

Nor was the defeat of 2nd Panzer an isolated occurrence. The 2nd SS Panzer Division, trying to force its way between the Salm and the Ourthe, was checked by the US 3rd Armored Division; 116th Panzer fared no better in the area of Marche, and Panzer Lehr was held up by VII Corps in the south. Bastogne, the ulcer on the German lines of communication, continued to hold out. Manteuffel launched a heavy attack on the town early on Christmas morning. His tanks were knocked out by well-sited American tank destroyers, and the infantry, denied armored support, were dealt with by McAuliffe's parachutists. At dusk on the following day the leading tanks of the US 4th Armored Division entered the town. Bastogne was relieved, and the southernmost prong of the German advance was in danger of being cut off.

There was a reappraisal on 28 December. The time seemed ripe for an Allied counterattack, but Montgomery and Bradley were unable to agree on this. Bradley favored immediate thrusts by the First Army in the north, and the Third Army in the south. Both armies were to be heavily reinforced—the former with four of Montgomery's divisions. Montgomery preferred to wait. He suspected that the Germans would make one more major effort, and he was not, like the Americans, in the fortunate position of expecting constant reinforcement. Eisenhower eventually authorized Montgomery to delay his attack till 3 January. This decision did not please Bradley or Patton; nor did Montgomery's demands for a continuance of the centralized command arrangement which, the Field Marshal insisted, was essential if the forthcoming Ruhr offensive was to be successful.

The Germans, too, took stock of the situation. Rundstedt again warned Hitler that the objective of Antwerp was clearly unattainable. The best that could be achieved was what Hitler had earlier termed the 'Small Solution'; a thrust toward Liège and the encirclement of Aachen. By 28 December Rundstedt felt that the time for even this was past. He recommended instead the withdrawal of the two Panzer armies to a line east of Bastogne, to prepare for the inevitable Allied counterattack. Hitler rejected both solutions. German setbacks had, he maintained, been incurred because his plan had not been followed to the letter. He was prepared to sanction a change of emphasis by two Panzer armies, but this jab to the northwest was to be purely temporary. Antwerp remained their goal. Hitler also believed that Patton had now become so overextended that a German offensive in Alsace would compel him to disengage from the Ardennes to meet it.

The Alsace offensive was launched on New Year's Day 1945. The Germans committed ten divisions in all, and the threat to Strasbourg gave rise to another inter-Allied crisis. American suggestions that the line should be rationalized to lessen the danger of a German breakthrough were opposed by General Jean de Lattre de Tassigny of the French 1st Army, who, naturally, was backed by General Charles de Gaulle. De Gaulle protested to both Roosevelt and Churchill, and eventually, partially due to Churchill's intervention, Eisenhower decided against withdrawal. Strasbourg was held, and though the offensive made slight progress, it did so at the price of 25,000 German casualties; if the Allied troops used to check it could not be employed in the Ardennes, neither could the German forces be engaged; the Alsace offensive simply whittled away at the already thin German reserves.

The battle in the Ardennes was not yet over. Manteuffel had launched several attacks on the corridor to Bastogne, but on 2 January, worried that his forward elements would be cut off by an American attack, he asked for permission to fall back to take up a defensive line running through Houffalize. Hitler refused, and on 3 and 4 January Manteuffel renewed his efforts to sever the corridor and take Bastogne. The capture of Bastogne remained as vital as ever, for even if, as Hitler now realized, a drive to Antwerp was impossible, retention of the Ardennes pocket could significantly delay the Allied Ruhr offensive. And, if the bulge was to be held, Bastogne had to be taken.

The failure of Manteuffel's last thrusts at Bastogne became obscured by the Allied counter-

Opposite: US motorized transport carries supplies and ammunition to the battle units as the Allied front widens. **Below:** Another German caught in GI uniform by MPs of the 30th Division in the vicinity of Malmédy. His sentence: death.

offensive. On 3 January, despite frightful weather conditions which totally prevented air cover and which turned roads into lethal skating-rinks, Collins began to advance from the Ourthe toward Houffalize. Progress was painfully slow, largely due to the appalling conditions which made it easy for a few desperate men behind a roadblock to hold up the advance for hours. Things were no easier on the Third Army front, but on 5 January the crust weakened. Model withdrew one SS Panzer division to aid Dietrich in the north, and Manteuffel took another out of the line to form an operational reserve. On 8 January Hitler at last authorized a partial withdrawal, to a line five miles west of Houffalize.

The policy of limited withdrawal could not survive for long. The Eastern Front had remained virtually stationary from August 1944 until the end of the year, but on 12 January the Red Army launched a massive offensive. Guderian had aptly compared the Eastern Front to a house of cards, and the ferocious Russian pressure compelled Hitler to take all available steps to shore up the crumbling structure. Dietrich's Panzer divisions were ordered back to St Vith on 8 January, and on the 22nd *Sixth Panzer Army* was transferred to the Eastern Front.

The US First and Third Armies met at Houffalize on 16 January. On the following day Bradley resumed command of the First Army, although the Ninth Army remained under Montgomery for the Ruhr offensive. The German retirement from the pocket never became a rout. Here the Germans were once more helped by the weather, which in early January again restricted Allied mastery of the air. Also, the Allied decision to not attack the shoulders of the bulge with the aim of cutting it off, made an orderly withdrawal possible. Manteuffel was pushed back by frontal pressure, rather than being compelled to fall back by threats to his flanks. His men, although demoralized by the failure of the offensive from which so much had been expected, retired with stubborn determination, aided by terrain and weather. On 22 January the skies cleared once more, and Allied aircraft hammered German columns on the Our crossings. By 28 January the bulge had been eliminated altogether.

The fighting had cost the Americans 81,000 men and considerable quantities of equipment. Yet while American losses could be quickly replaced, the 100,000 German casualties imposed a further strain upon dwindling German manpower. The same was true of equipment; German tank and aircraft losses could never be repaired. It is too easy to see the Ardennes offensive as simply another of Hitler's strategic blunders.

There was some logic behind it. An offensive would permit the *Wehrmacht* to seize the initiative and to employ its armor in what many German generals regarded as its prime role, the attack. It would also spoil the Allied offensive into the Ruhr, and might substantially weaken Allied unity. The fact that Hitler undertook the operation in defiance of the opinion of his professional military advisers is, in itself, no guarantee that Hitler was wrong. He had, after all, been right, in the face of serious military opposition and over the same ground, in 1940.

This logic, such as it was, rested upon false premises. Firstly, the Allies were by no means in such disarray as Hitler imagined. Although the Ardennes offensive did put stresses, both political and military, upon the Allies, it totally failed to induce defeatism in London or Washington. Far from weakening Allied resolve, the offensive strengthened it. Secondly, Hitler's desire to mount a new blitzkrieg was at variance with bald facts. The 1940 attack had succeeded because the Germans possessed air superiority over the Ardennes; their columns could use the narrow roads and bridges without danger of attack. To attempt the same task with the roads worsened by winter was dangerous enough; to attempt it in the face of Allied air power was fatal. The American retention of Bastogne, and the long defense of St Vith further reduced the roads available, compressing the German lines of supply into a dangerously narrow bottleneck. Shortage of petrol, too, placed growing stresses upon movement in and behind the battle area.

Finally, none of the senior German commanders believed that the offensive could succeed. As Dietrich put it, 'All I had to do was to cross the river, capture Brussels, and then go on to take the port of Antwerp. The snow was waist deep and there wasn't room to deploy four tanks abreast, let alone six armored divisions. It didn't get light till eight and was dark again at four, and my tanks can't fight at night. And all this at Christmas time'. Manteuffel, the most sanguine as well as the most capable of the German army commanders, said after the war that while the offensive was justifiable in strategic terms, the tactical and logistical problems it entailed were bound to bring about its failure.

Although the offensive had caused the Allied commanders considerable loss of sleep, it had never produced a climate similar to that of, for

Below: An example of how even the heaviest German tank could be wiped out by a direct hit. This Panther was knocked out near Bastogne on 3 January, 1945.

instance, March 1918, when the Germans threatened to break through on the Western Front. But the rifts in the Allied command were not easy to heal. Montgomery's cool, even clinical handling of the northern sector was praiseworthy, but his subsequent interviews with the press made implications which Bradley, in particular, found objectionable. Churchill took a less partisan view. Speaking in the House of Commons, he pointed out that there had been 30 or 40 times more Americans than British engaged, and 60 to 70 times more American casualties. It was, in his opinion, the greatest American battle of the war and an ever-famous American victory.

Yalu River

At dawn on 25 June, 1950, the armed forces of the Democratic People's Republic of Korea (North Korea) swept south over the 38th parallel and invaded the Republic of Korea (South Korea) in an effort to overrun the country and annex it to the North before the South could receive aid from the Western world. The invasion was on a wide front, and at first seemed to have an excellent chance of success.

Origins of the Korean War

The origins of the Korean War (1950 to 1953), as the conflict came to be called, were both complex and yet basically simple. After her success in the Russo-Japanese War (1904 to 1905), Japan had annexed the Korean peninsula. During World War II, however, the Allies had promised Korea freedom once Japan had been defeated. First made at the Cairo Conference (December 1943), the promise was reaffirmed at the Potsdam Conference (July 1945). But Korea was not liberated by force of arms during World War II, and when Japan surrendered in August, a hurried Allied agreement allowed for the temporary

Above left: The reconnaissance camera of a Republic RF-80 records a strafing run against a Korean village used as a laager for North Korean armoured vehicles. Visible on the road is a T-34 tank.
Left: An American ground-crew man refuels the wing-tip fuel tank of a Lockheed F-94B Starfire fighter in August 1953.

'partition' of Korea: the 38th parallel was chosen as an arbitrary dividing line, and the Japanese forces to the north of this line would surrender to the Russians, those south of it to the Americans. The idea was then that democratic elections should be held, and that the country should be unified under an elected government. After two years of fruitless negotiation on the subject with the Soviet Union, the United States took the problem to the United Nations Organization, which adopted the American point of view and called for free elections. The USSR refused this and on 15 August, 1947, the second anniversary of the Russian and American partition agreement, the Republic of Korea was declared in Seoul. Shortly afterwards the Democratic People's Republic of North Korea, a Russian puppet, was declared in Pyongyang. The Russians set about developing North Korea's army and air force on Russian lines with Russian equipment, but purportedly left

North Korea in December 1948; a similar role was played by the Americans, albeit on a far smaller scale, for South Korea. They had pulled out their forces (with the exception of an advisory group) by June 1949. As soon as the Americans had gone, the North Koreans started a low-key campaign of sabotage, terrorism and guerilla raids against South Korea.

Seeing that there was no chance of the southern half of the Korean peninsula being joined with the northern one under a communist victory in free elections, the Russians with the agreement of the Communist Chinese (who had gained final victory over the Nationalist forces of Chiang Kai-shek in 1949) set about masterminding a military campaign that would give the North Koreans victory in one fell swoop. The Russians themselves provided thousands of technical personnel for both combat and logistical purposes.

The course of the war

North Korea's armed forces consisted of some 130,000 men in 10 divisions and a brigade of Russian T-34 medium tanks. Air power consisted of some 150 Russian aircraft, mostly Yakovlev

China had threatened to enter the war on overt terms should the UN forces cross the 38th parallel, and on 25 November 18 Chinese divisions, some 180,000 men strong, tore into the UN forces and sent them reeling back towards the 38th parallel. The North Korean and Chinese offensive was resumed on 1 January, 1951, but after a series of offensives and counter-offensives, the front gradually stabilized along the 38th parallel by 22 April. Thereafter fighting continued almost unabated in the same general area, both sides suffering very heavy casualties.

Russian and American air involvement

The success of the United Nations offensive in the autumn of 1950 had the effect not only of bringing Chinese ground forces into the war, but also of persuading the Russians that if they were not to see the crushing of their client, considerable *matériel* would have to be supplied. Among other items, this aid took the form of powerful air reinforcements, together with the necessary ground-crew and aircrew. As a major part of the UN offensive scheme was based on the interdiction of the communist supply routes, by the destruction of all means of communication and convoys using them, the Russians decided that the best application of their air power would be in a defensive role. Thus there began to appear in North Korea the first examples of the new generation of Russian fighters, the Mikoyan-Gurevich MiG-15. With the arrival of the new fighter the air war over Korea intensified considerably, and from November 1950 to April 1952 the MiGs flew a monthly average of over 2000 daytime sorties. The highest average for a month came in December 1951, when over 4000 sorties were flown. During 1953 the MiGs also flew night sorties against raiding B-29 and B-26 bombers, but their lack of onboard equipment of a sophisticated nature limited them to co-operation with ground-control radar and searchlights, which severely hampered their effectiveness.

The Americans had already deployed one jet fighter, the Lockheed F-80 Shooting Star in Korea, but this was a design of strictly limited performance, dating from the closing stages of World War II. Nevertheless, the Americans were confident of their overall air superiority in the closing months of 1950.

The first jet combats

Then, late on the afternoon of 1 November, six North American P-51 Mustangs patrolling along the southern shore of the Yalu river, the crossing of which was denied to the Americans for political reasons, were attacked by six swept-wing jet fighters that emerged from Manchuria across the river, attacked and then returned without shooting down any of the Mustangs. It was clear that the Americans, for the first time in Korea, had to face a superior combat aircraft.

A second generation turbojet-powered interceptor, based on Russian and captured German research into the amelioration of compression problems at high subsonic speeds by the sweeping back of the flying surfaces, the MiG-15 had entered design in March 1946, and had first been seen by westerners at the 1948 Soviet Aviation

Yak-7s, Yak-9s and Yak-11s, with a fair number of Ilyushin Il-10s. The South Koreans, on the other hand, were barely trained for para-military operations, with their 100,000 men in eight divisions with negligible artillery, armour and air support.

It is not surprising, therefore, that the North Koreans made rapid progress in their drive south after 25 June. Although the Americans decided swiftly to aid the South Koreans, there were few troops and equipment available in the Far East, so little of material use to the South could be achieved. The United Nations, meanwhile, decided to take a united stand against the North Koreans and authorized its member states to send troops and support elements to Korea. General of the Army Douglas MacArthur was appointed to lead the United Nations' forces, predominantly American in composition. The effect of these political moves would in the long run produce results, but in the short term the South Koreans, with minimal US support, were forced back towards the south-east tip of Korea, where a final defensive perimeter was established around the port of Pusan at the beginning of August. With the stabilization of this perimeter the North Koreans' only realistic chance of finishing the war in one bold stroke was gone, and the allies of each side could now be expected to take a major part in the war.

By the end of July the North Korean air force had been reduced to about 18 aircraft, and there was little that the North Koreans could do when the United Nations launched a joint offensive on 15 September, the US 8th Army breaking out from the Pusan perimeter and the US X Corps pulling off one of the great military coups of all time by landing in hazardous conditions at Inchon, half way down the North Koreans' lines of communication and harassing their rear. The North Koreans fell back in disarray, hotly pursued by the United Nations forces, and by the end of November the UN forces were lodged deep in North Korea, in places almost along the Yalu river forming the boundary between China and North Korea.

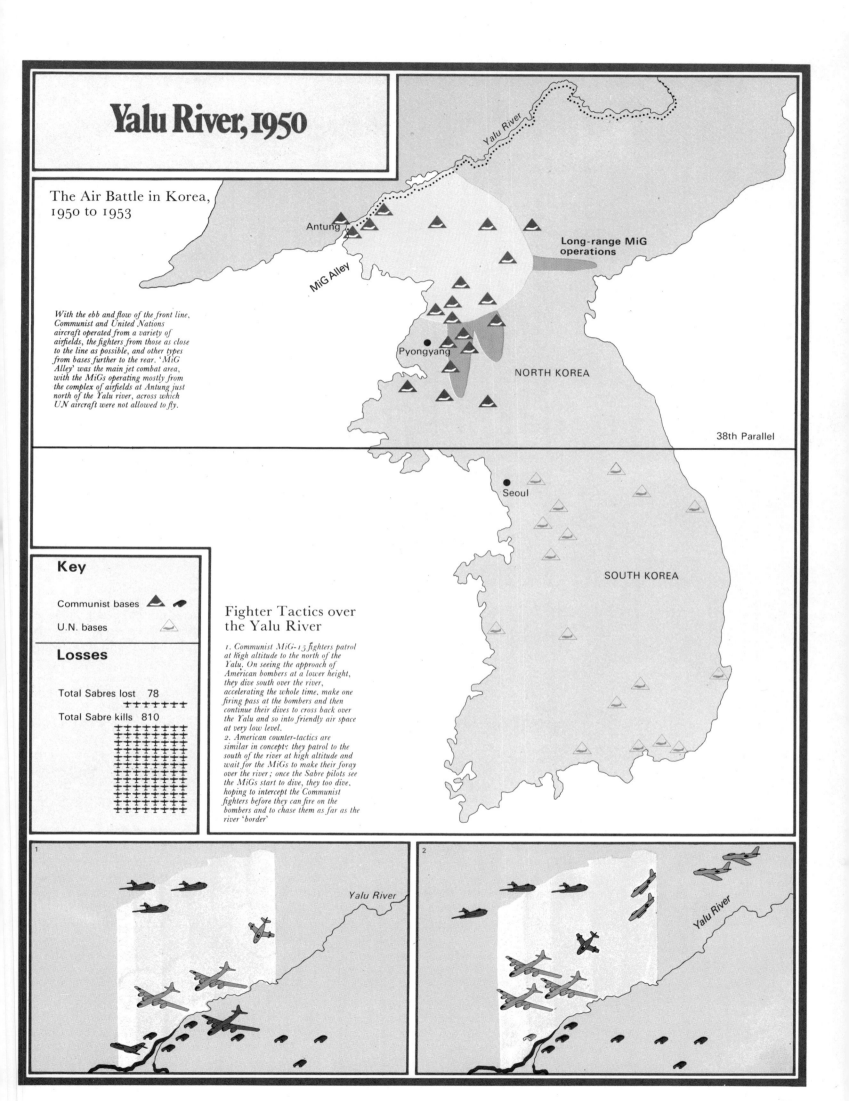

Yalu River, 1950

The Air Battle in Korea, 1950 to 1953

With the ebb and flow of the front line, Communist and United Nations aircraft operated from a variety of airfields, the fighters from those as close to the line as possible, and other types from bases further to the rear. 'MiG Alley' was the main jet combat area, with the MiGs operating mostly from the complex of airfields at Antung just north of the Yalu river, across which UN aircraft were not allowed to fly.

Yalu River

Antung

MiG Alley

Long-range MiG operations

Pyongyang

NORTH KOREA

38th Parallel

Seoul

SOUTH KOREA

Key

Communist bases

U.N. bases

Losses

Total Sabres lost   78

╈╈╈╈╈╈╈

Total Sabre kills   810

Fighter Tactics over the Yalu River

1. Communist MiG-15 fighters patrol at high altitude to the north of the Yalu. On seeing the approach of American bombers at a lower height, they dive south over the river, accelerating the whole time, make one firing pass at the bombers and then continue their dives to cross back over the Yalu and so into friendly air space at very low level.

2. American counter-tactics are similar in concept: they patrol to the south of the river at high altitude and wait for the MiGs to make their foray over the river; once the Sabre pilots see the MiGs start to dive, they too dive, hoping to intercept the Communist fighters before they can fire on the bombers and to chase them as far as the river 'border'.

Yalu River

Yalu River

Day display just outside Moscow. It was realized only in Korea, however, how impressive the type's performance was: this was due in part to the advanced and carefully thought-out design, and in part to the use of licence-built examples of a British engine, the Rolls-Royce Nene, virtually handed to the Russians in 1946 by the Labour government by an Anglo-Soviet Trade Agreement.

The MiGs increased in numbers rapidly in Korea, and on 8 November there occurred the world's first combat between jet fighters, when MiG-15s attacked the F-80 escort of a group of B-29s on a bombing mission. In every respect the MiGs were technically superior, but the Americans escaped without loss, one of the F-80s, flown by Lieutenant Russell J. Brown of the 51st Fighter Interceptor Wing, actually managing to shoot down a MiG. Here at least there was some consolation for the Americans, for it was clear even from these early encounters with the MiGs that the American pilots were in every respect

superior to their communist counterparts. There thus quickly developed the odd situation in which one side possessed considerably superior *matériel*, but could not take real tactical advantage of this because the other side possessed far superior pilots, enabling the American aircraft to keep out of harm's way.

For the most part, American pilots enjoyed the legacy of aerial expertize and success in World War II. There were many veterans of the air war against Germany and Japan, and newer pilots had benefited from training under combat-experienced pilots and instructors, and from close association with World War II pilots in their squadrons. Unlike the communist pilots, moreover, the Americans were well suited and trained to the full use of sophisticated electronic equipment such as radar gunsights, this latter in particular giving them a decided combat 'edge'. It is possible to see, therefore, that although they enjoyed a tactical advantage because of the restrictions on UN pilots, and possessed slightly better aircraft, this was more than balanced, when combat was joined, by the overall superiority and experience of the American pilots. It is in this, therefore, that lies the key to the communists' failure to win overall air superiority and the Americans' excellent kill:loss ratio.

The tactics used by the communists were simple and should have proved effective: having deduced that the Americans were not allowed to cross the Yalu, the communists climbed to altitude on their own side of the river, and then drove across the river in a dive at maximum speed to make a single firing pass before turning to recross the river, still in a dive. The fighter could then climb in safety again, and repeat the attack. The tactics were used by both piston- and turbojet-powered fighters, but the losses suffered by the Yakovlev and Lavochkin fighters soon meant that only the MiGs posed a real threat to the Americans.

By December 1950, the strength of the MiG-15 deployed by the Communist Chinese air force had risen to about 150, evidence of the large-scale production of the type in the Soviet Union, and of the importance the Russians placed on both the need to stave off US bombing and reconnaissance attacks, and the desire to acquire combat experience with this new venture in fighter design. To a great extent the Chinese air force was an

extension of the Red Air Force, with its aircraft almost exclusively of Russian origins. At the same time the instructors, senior tactical leaders and many technicians were Russians. Thus the aircraft could be tested in combat under 'Russian' conditions, but without the expenditure of too many Russian lives. Early in 1951, in addition, the Russians started setting up a comprehensive radar network on the north side of the Yalu. This enabled the MiGs to operate more efficiently, and also allowed the Russians to develop the equipment and techniques of radar-controlled interception without fear of US reprisal.

It was clear, though, right from the first encounters with the MiGs over North Korea, that the F-80 could not meet the new Russian jet on anything like equal terms, and so the latest American fighter, the elegant North American F-86A Sabre, would have to be deployed in the theatre. Like the MiG-15 the Sabre was a second-generation jet fighter, and featured swept flying surfaces. Thus in December 1950 the 4th Interceptor Wing was rushed over to Korea via Japan.

The Sabres made their first operational flight, a sweep along the Yalu, on 17 December. The events of the day were to prove typical of the air fighting along the Yalu in the months to come. Led by the commander of the 336th Squadron, Lieutenant-Colonel B.H. Hinton, a detachment of P-86A-5s from Kimpo airfield set off on an armed reconnaissance of the Yalu. Flying at 9750 metres (32,000 feet) at a speed of 760 km/h (472 mph), the patrol spotted four MiG-15s patrolling some 2135 metres (7000 feet) under them. Hinton led his aircraft down, and in a brief combat one of the MiGs was sent down, its rear fuselage swathed in flames; the remaining three escaped in high-speed dives towards the Manchurian border. The one untypical factor in this brief clash was that it was the Sabres that 'bounced' the MiGs.

More typical, perhaps, was another sortie by four aircraft under Hinton just two days later. The Americans clashed with six MiGs which, however, raced through the American formation in head-on passes. Not a shot was fired, though, and by the time the slightly less agile American fighters had turned in pursuit of the MiGs, the latter had escaped across the Yalu.

The communists did at times stay to fight, as the Americans found out three days later. This time eight Sabres met a larger formation of MiGs at 12,190 metres (40,000 feet). The MiGs swept in with determination, the muzzle flashes of their cannon in striking contrast with the rather subdued flashes at the mouths of the Americans' machine-guns. Before the MiGs dived away one of the Sabres had been knocked down in flames. Later in the day, though, the Sabres returned to the scene, where this time they met some 15 MiGs. A short but savage battle followed, and in this encounter the Americans more than evened the balance, disposing of six MiGs without loss to themselves.

Escalation of the air war

Combat in the following weeks, though, showed that the Sabres would not have things entirely their own way, for a variety of tactical considerations gave a certain advantage to the communist pilots. For a start, it soon became apparent that in many respects the MiG-15 was a better combat aircraft: it possessed a higher rate of climb, speed, ceiling, acceleration and turning radius than the Sabre. To balance this slightly, the F-86 had greater stability (this making it a considerably superior gun platform), a better weapons system (in its radar gunsight), longer range, higher rate of fire(although its armament was only six .5-inch machine-guns, compared with the MiG-15's two 23-mm cannon), superior medium altitude performance and better diving characteristics.

Technically, therefore, the MiG-15 had slightly superior attributes in its fighter characteristics. Tactically, however, the Sabre pilots were far superior to their communist counterparts, and it was this factor that proved decisive in the battles that were to come.

The fact that they were operating over North Korean territory gave the communists great 'battlefield' advantages: the MiGs were operating from airfields just over the Yalu, whereas the Sabres had to fly up from Taengu or Kimpo, which reduced their patrol time to a maximum of only a few minutes. To conserve fuel the Sabres cruised at lower speeds than was advisable tactically, and this added to the MiG's advantage, for the latter could now make their diving firing pass and break away before the Sabres had accelerated to a reasonable combat speed. The Sabre pilots quickly worked out a counter, however: 'combat loiter' speed on patrol was reduced yet further, but four flights of Sabres were sent into the same area at five minute intervals at high speed to engage any MiGs that might have been tempted down onto the first flight. The tactics worked excellently, as was shown on 22 December, when six out of 15 MiGs were shot down in a brief battle with eight Sabres. By the end of the year the Sabre pilots had flown 234 missions, resulting in 76 combats during which eight MiGs had been destroyed, two probably destroyed and seven damaged.

The Russians and Chinese were not overly dismayed, though, and pressed on with the build-up of their forces in Manchuria. The objective of this was eventually to secure air superiority over north-western Korea. The communists' chance came in January 1951, when the 4th Interceptor Wing was pulled back to Japan, the necessary maintenance facilities for its Sabres not being

available in Korea. While the Sabres were absent the communists struck, and the 75 MiGs of a complete air division at Antung gained air superiority over north-west Korea. Even the reappearance of the Sabres, now operating from Suwon, did not entirely remove the communists' superiority. March was occasioned by several large-scale combats, but the Sabres scored no kills. Indeed, the MiGs fared better, at times being able to dive through the Sabre top cover to engage the bombers below, the close escort of Republic F-84 Thunderjets being unable to deal with the MiGs.

The scale of the communist effort is indicated by the battle of 12 April, when some 50 MiGs took on 39 B-29s escorted by Sabres and Thunderjets. Three B-29s were shot down and another six damaged, the Sabres claiming four MiGs destroyed and six damaged, and the Thunderjets three probables. The last seems an unduly optimistic claim. Quite apart from the MiGs' material successes, though, what amazed and concerned the American pilots was the determination of the MiGs' pilots. Only later was the reason revealed by a defector: in March large numbers of Russian, Polish and Czech pilots began to arrive for three-month tours of operational flying. As General O.P. Weyland, commanding the Far East Air Force, pointed out, the main reason for this short stay in the front line (US pilots did eight months per year in the combat zone) was probably the Russian desire to give as many of their own and their satellites' pilots as possible experience of jet warfare. At the same time whole squadrons of Russian MiGs were attached to the Chinese air force, their aircraft having the Russian markings replaced by Chinese ones.

It was clear towards the end of April 1951 that the communists were preparing airfields in North Korea (i.e. south of the Yalu) in expectation of a major air offensive. Accordingly the US heavy bombers virtually destroyed these fields in a series of major raids at the end of the month, the Sabre escorts also scoring convincingly over the MiGs. The failure of the planned air offensive made the communists revert to the earlier diving attacks from across the Yalu. During May there was only one major clash, in which 36 Sabres knocked down three of 50 MiGs and damaged another five.

During the next month the squadrons (regiments) of the Red Air Force joined combat on the communist side. Although the reason for it was not known by the American pilots, the entry into combat of regular Soviet units was indicated by the general rise in flying standards on the communist side. Although the Sabres were still enjoying a highly favourable kill:loss ratio (only one Sabre having been lost in combat so far), they now started losing more of their number as the MiG pilots probed far south of the Yalu. On 18 and 19 July a Sabre was lost on each day, and others were lost thereafter. Yet these communist incursions into the south were of little practical value, for the pilots kept their aircraft at high altitude, where they enjoyed a performance

Below: Air-launched torpedoes from Douglas A-1 Skyraider aircraft of the United States Navy hit the wall of the Hwachon Dam. The breach of the wall, in May 1951, caused severe flooding, which in turn greatly hampered a planned North Korean attack.
Above right: A Douglas B-26 Invader of the 452nd Bomber Wing (Light) drops its bombs during an interdiction mission. **Below right:** Another B-26 of the 452nd BW attacks a communist train and railway junction.

advantage over the Sabres. This meant that for the most part the UN fighter-bombers could operate below the MiGs unmolested. On the few occasions when the MiGs did attack lower down, the F-80 and F-84 pilots were usually able to look after themselves, and also managed to down a few MiGs.

The communists' build-up of aircraft was continuing all the while, and by the middle of the year the three main MiG bases at Antung, Ta-ku-shan and Ta-tung-kou contained 300 MiGs or more, with another 150 in reserve in China. Despite the fact that the Americans had only 44 Sabres in Korea, with a further 45 in reserve in Japan, the MiGs were pushed back onto the defensive. This occurred despite Russian experimentation with a number of different tactical schemes designed to test out the Americans' combat efficiency. One of these, the 'Yoyo', consisted of a circle of MiGs at their service ceiling, from which sections would break off to make firing passes before climbing up to rejoin the safety of the parent circle. The very same tactic had been used by the Germans from 1944 onwards for attacks on the American bomber streams.

The pace of operations increased again in September, when formations of up to 75 MiGs

Below: Republic F-84 fighter-bombers played a great part in the United Nations' ground support effort.

were met. This gave the Russians and their allies a numerical advantage in combat of up to four-to-one on many occasions, yet for the loss of three Sabres, one Mustang, one Shooting Star and one Thunderjet, the Americans could claim the destruction of 14 MiGs. The pace increased yet again in October, when the communists flew some 2500 missions, losing 32 MiGs to an American loss of 15 aircraft. The reason for this increase in the air fighting of October was that once again the communists were attempting to build up new airfield complexes south of the Yalu, and the Americans were determined to prevent them being brought into service, no matter what the cost. Despite this feeling, however, the vigour with which the communists launched their fighter attacks on the big American bombers had the effect of putting them off their balance, with the result that they could not neutralize fully all the new airfields. Consequently, for the first time in the war some MiGs, about 25 in number, were able to start operating from a base south of the Yalu, in this case Uiju.

This last fact, combined with the tactical draws of the air fighting of the month, finally convinced the planners of the US Air Defense Command that a greater effort was needed in Korea. Within a fortnight, exemplary speed for a large organization, a further 75 Sabres were on their way to Korea via Japan. These aircraft were to be operated by the 51st Fighter Wing, and were an improved version of the Sabre, the F-86E. This featured an all-flying tail and powered controls, making the aircraft far more responsive. Taking

over from the tired 4th Fighter Interceptor Wing in January, the 51st Fighter Wing made its presence felt immediately, its improved aircraft and fresh pilots downing 25 MiGs for no loss in January 1952.

That the communists appreciated this change in equipment and manpower became quickly apparent as large formations of MiGs virtually disappeared from the North Korean skies, their place being taken by small groups rarely numbering more than a dozen or so. Nevertheless serious air fighting continued. Then in May the Russians sprang a surprise on the Americans, when suddenly MiGs began to appear by night. At last the Russians had finished their GCI (Ground-Controlled Interception) system, and the MiGs, despite their lack of radar gunsights and other sophisticated electronic equipment, began to take a toll of the American bombers, which had been forced to operate by night to avoid the attentions of the Russian day fighters.

The night-fighting MiGs drew their first blood on 10 June, when they shot down the alarming total of three B-29s out of a formation of four over North Korea. It seemed that the Americans had suppressed one threat only to raise another in its stead.

But despite such successes, the communist air forces failed to gain any real measure of air superiority. Yet they were at the same time continuing to build up considerable air power north of the Yalu. During December 1952, for example, estimates put the number of aircraft available to the units on the northern bank of the Yalu at some 2100 aircraft, of which some 1300 to 1500 were jets. Of these jets, it was reckoned that about 950 were MiG-15s. More dangerously, perhaps, photographic reconnaissance revealed that the Russians had also deployed in the theatre some 100 jet bombers, the latest aircraft produced by Russia, Ilyushin Il-28 twin-jet medium bombers. Although they could not hope to operate by day, the Il-28s could have operated with relative safety in the night, for the Americans possessed no high performance night-fighter or even the GCI equipment to allow day fighters to be used at night with any chance of success. Alert to the possibilities that the Americans might react with atomic weapons to such a provocation, however, these bombers were never used.

Sporadic air fighting continued during the closing months of the year, and on 18 November there occurred the only overt Russian effort to tackle American tactical support operations. While attacking Hoeryong, aircraft of the US Navy's Task Force 77 saw MiGs climbing from the Russian base at Vladivostok. Although they carried no national markings, the aircraft could only be Russian. On joining combat, however, they lost one of their number to a Grumman Panther and the rest then made off.

Although they felt that they had the measure of the MiGs by the end of 1952, the American pilots were surprised at the beginning of 1953 when the MiG pilots seemed to improve yet again. This was due, no doubt, to the introduction of the new model of the MiG, the MiG-15*bis* with uprated engine and improved electronics. Confident of the abilities of their new machines, the Russian pilots, many of them flying in aircraft marked with the Russian star, at last stayed to fight. Unfortunately, for them, their new aircraft were not enough to turn the scales, and in January 1953 the Americans destroyed 37 MiGs for the loss of only one Sabre.

The war in Korea was gradually winding down at this time as the armistice negotiators went through the wearying round of talks that finally ended the war with the armistice of 27 July, 1953. The war in general had been a costly one, but the performance of the Sabres had been one of the factors that had allowed the United States to prevail generally in the air war. For the loss in combat of only 68 of their own number, the North American F-86 Sabres of the United States

Air Force had claimed the destruction of 810 aircraft: one Ilyushin Il-12, six Lavochkin La-9s, no less than 792 Mikoyan-Gurevich MiG-15s, nine Tupolev Tu-2s and two others. The grand total of communist aircraft destroyed by all the United Nations air units was only 1050, so the importance of the Sabre may easily be gauged.

It should always be remembered, though, that to a great extent the USSR had achieved its aims in the air—it had tested its aircraft, personnel and other equipment to the full against the likely enemy, had acquired much American equipment, especially radar and other electronics, and was then able to digest this information at leisure and implement the conclusions to produce a far more formidable air force for the future.

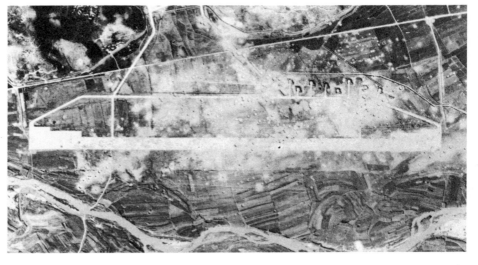

Six Day War
1967

Right: A Russian-made SA-2 surface-to-air guided missile captured from the Egyptians is towed back to Israel. In general, Israeli tactics were more than adequate to cope with these missiles.

Since her establishment in 1947, the state of Israel has been in a state of hostility with her Arab neighbours. The rights and wrongs of the whole Arab-Israeli situation form a complex pattern too involved to be treated satisfactorily here, so all that need be said is that although, at the present the animosity between Israel and the 'Arabs' seems to be continuing unabated, there seems in general to be a lessening of the tension between Israel and individual Arab states, notably Jordan and Egypt. Nonetheless, it should be noted that in the 30 years since her formation, Israel has fought four major wars against her Arab neighbours, and in the intervals between these large-scale conflicts has survived a fairly continuous war of attrition in conventional terms and continuous harassment from Palestinian guerrilla movements.

The Israeli Defence Force/Air Force

This semi-permanent state of war has turned the Israeli Defence Force into one of the most efficient and sophisticated armed forces in the world. The economic situation of the country will not permit large standing forces to be maintained, however, and the main strength of the Israeli forces thus rests on well-trained reservists, who can in general join the full-time cadres of their formations within 72 hours of the mobilization signal. One primary exception to this rule, though, is the Israeli Defence Force/Air Force, for the nature and sophistication of modern air war precludes in general the use of reservists as combat pilots. The IDF/AF is therefore based on a large cadre of permanent aircrew, with reservists joining in secondary capacities. Fairly continuous combat experience has helped the IDF/AF develop into a first-class force, well suited to the operational requirements it is designed to undertake. All in all, therefore, the IDF/AF may in most respects be considered the elite formation of the whole IDF.

At the time of the Six-Day War in 1967, most of the IDF/AF's equipment was of French origin, a legacy of the support and encouragement the new state had enjoyed from France since its formation. (This aid was to be cut off peremptorily, shortly after the Six-Day War, when Israeli commandos raided Beirut airport in the Lebanon, destroying several Arab airliners in retaliation for a Palestinian attack. Thereafter the United States became the Israelis' prime supplier of weapons as well as of finance.) Geared to fight only relatively short wars, the Israeli economy

being unable to sustain any prolonged large-scale conflict, the IDF/AF is relatively 'tooth' heavy (i.e. it has a relatively large combat element and a relatively small administrative and logistic 'tail'). Thus for a total mobilized strength of some 20,000 men, the IDF/AF could put into the air a strength of some 450 aircraft, of which about 350 could be classified as combat aircraft suitable for first line duties. These combat aircraft were, as noted above, mostly of French origin, and were in some cases of relatively venerable vintage: the best aircraft fielded by the IDF/AF were some 73 Dassault Mirage III Mach 2+ delta-winged interceptor and ground-attack machines; the principal fighter-bombers were 20 Dassault Super Mystères and about 50 of the older Dassault Mystère IVA; for less arduous combat situations the IDF/AF could also call on 48 obsolescent Dassault Ouragan fighter-bombers, 60 Fouga Magister training aircraft modified as light ground-attack aircraft, and about 25 obsolescent Société Nationale de Constructions Aéronautiques du Sud-Ouest (SNCASO) Vautour II ground-attack bombers. To support this offensive force the Israelis had about 20 Nord Noratlas and Boeing Stratocruiser transports and some 25 helicopters of various types. In world terms, the only two really first-line aircraft deployed by the Israelis were the Mirage and Super Mystère, both

supersonic, and armed with inbuilt 30-mm cannon and provision for air-to-air missiles. With the exception of the Vautours, the combat radius of the Israeli aircraft was in the order of some 650 km (400 miles), which would apparently limit the IDF/AF's ability to strike deep into Arab territory.

The organization of the IDF/AF was into 13 squadrons: four of interceptors, five of fighter-bombers and ground-attack aircraft, two of transports and two of helicopters. In organization and equipment, therefore, there was little remarkable in the IDF/AF. What was remarkable, however, was the efficiency and ability of the pilots and other aircrew, the sophistication of the tactics, and the general superiority of the groundcrew, who managed to make a very high proportion of the IDF/AF's overall strength serviceable before the beginning of the war, and thereafter kept a very high percentage serviceable despite combat damage and other adverse factors.

The Arab Air Forces

The main opponent for the IDF/AF in this war, as in the other Arab-Israeli conflicts, would be the Egyptian Air Force. After World War II it had used British equipment and methods for the most part, but the disaster of the 1956 war, in which the Israelis had won total superiority and plunged through the Sinai to the Suez Canal, led to a reordering of the whole of the Egyptian armed forces along Russian lines with Russian support and equipment. With the aid of generous Russian terms, the Egyptians had thus been able to turn their armed forces between 1957 and 1967 into the apparently most formidable forces in the Middle East. Although their air force was only about the same in size as the IDF/AF, the Egyptians' was possessed of some of the very latest Russian aircraft and missiles, supplied in some cases even before the Warsaw Pact forces had received such equipment. Front-line equipment thus consisted of about 130 Mikoyan-Gurevich MiG-21 fighters, 80 MiG-19 fighter-bombers, 180 MiG-17 and MiG-15 fighter-bombers, 20 Sukhoi Su-7 fighter-bombers, 30

לפני הפגיעה

2 בפגיעה
הפלת מיג 21-70.7

3 אחרי הפגיעה

combatant but provider of considerable economic aid to the combatants; and to the south-west of Egypt. The strategic implications of this encirclement are obvious. Slightly less obvious are the tactical problems of Israel's position: she was a long, thin country running along a north-south axis, and Arab forces stood a strong chance of cutting the country in two across this axis. The Arab air forces, moreover, could attack any part of Israel with their tactical aircraft, let alone their larger bomber formations, whereas the converse most certainly did not apply to Israel, which could attack only the areas of the Arab opponents close to her own frontiers.

Although not individually comparable with the Egyptian or the Israeli air forces in numbers, equipment or training, the air forces that could be deployed by the Lebanon, Syria, Iraq, Jordan and possibly Saudi Arabia posed a great threat to Israel. The Lebanon could put some 35 aircraft into the air, mostly Hawker Hunters of limited combat use. Syria was better off, with an air force numbering about 9000 men and 120 aircraft, all of them Russian. Organization and equipment were on Russian lines, with one MiG-21 and one MiG-19 squadron, and two MiG-17 squadrons. The problem with the Syrian air force, though, was lack of trained aircrew and groundcrew, and although the Russian advisers in Syria were making good progress, the war caught the Syrian air force in a difficult position. Iraq was also able to field an air force on Russian lines, in this case of about 220 aircraft: 1 Tu-16, 1 Il-28, 3 MiG-15 and MiG-17, and two MiG-21 squadrons. There were also transport and helicopter squadrons, but as with the Syrian air force, trained personnel were in scanty supply and this was seriously to hamper the Iraqi air force's war effort. Jordan was poorly placed with her air force, having only 22 Hawker Hunter ground-attack fighters in two squadrons, plus a few elderly transport aircraft and only three helicopters. As with Syria and Iraq, trained personnel were wholly inadequate—there were only 16 pilots for the 22 Hunters, for example. Saudi Arabia, finally, had only about 40 aircraft, and these in the event remained non-combatant. In all, however, the Arab states who could become involved in a war with Israel possessed some 895 aircraft, whereas Israel could muster only some 350 first-line machines against them. In the war to come, though, this material imbalance was to be more than offset by the Israelis' superior training and tactical expertise.

The Israeli plan

The exact cause and responsibility for the Six-Day War, which began in the early hours of 5 June, 1967, will in all probability never be known. Clearly the Arab nations, especially Egypt and Syria, were threatening Israel militarily. But whether their preparations were in earnest, or merely 'sabre-rattling', remains an enigma. Considering the overwhelming strength deployed against them (2790 tanks against 800; 540,000 men against 264,000; and the aircraft figures already quoted), the Israelis had decided that a pre-emptive strike against the Arabs was essential as soon as war appeared imminent. And it was this pre-emptive strike, launched originally by the

Tupolev Tu-16 reconnaissance bombers and 40 Ilyushin Il-28 bombers. In support the Egyptians had some 90 transport aircraft (Ilyushin Il-14s and Antonov An-12s) and 60 Russian helicopters. Training had been conducted by Russian advisers and some combat experience, albeit against minimal opposition, had been gained in the Yemen. All in all, though, the Egyptian Air Force seemed formidable, especially as the combination of its bombers and MiG fighter cover gave it the ability to deliver strategic strokes against Israel's main cities. Unfortunately for them, the Israelis possessed no similar capability, and the threat to their civilians weighed heavily on the politico-military leadership. Like the Israeli fighters, moreover, the Russian MiGs had inbuilt 30-mm cannon as well as an air-to-air missile capability, and this gave them a material equality with the Israelis. Under Russian tutelage, though, the Egyptian pilots had developed extreme confidence in their overall superiority to their Israeli counterparts. The confidence was based on propaganda rather than fact, however, as the war that was about to break out would prove.

One of the main tactical and strategic problems faced by Israel in any confrontation with the Arab powers lies in the fact that she is surrounded on three sides by her opponents: to the north lies the largely neutral Lebanon, which did, however, harbour large Palestinian guerrilla elements; to the north-east is Syria, with Iraq behind her but not contiguous with Israel; to the east is Jordan; to the south-east is Saudi Arabia, a non-

The Six Day War, 1967

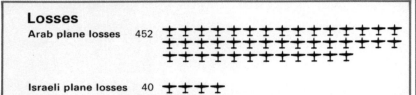
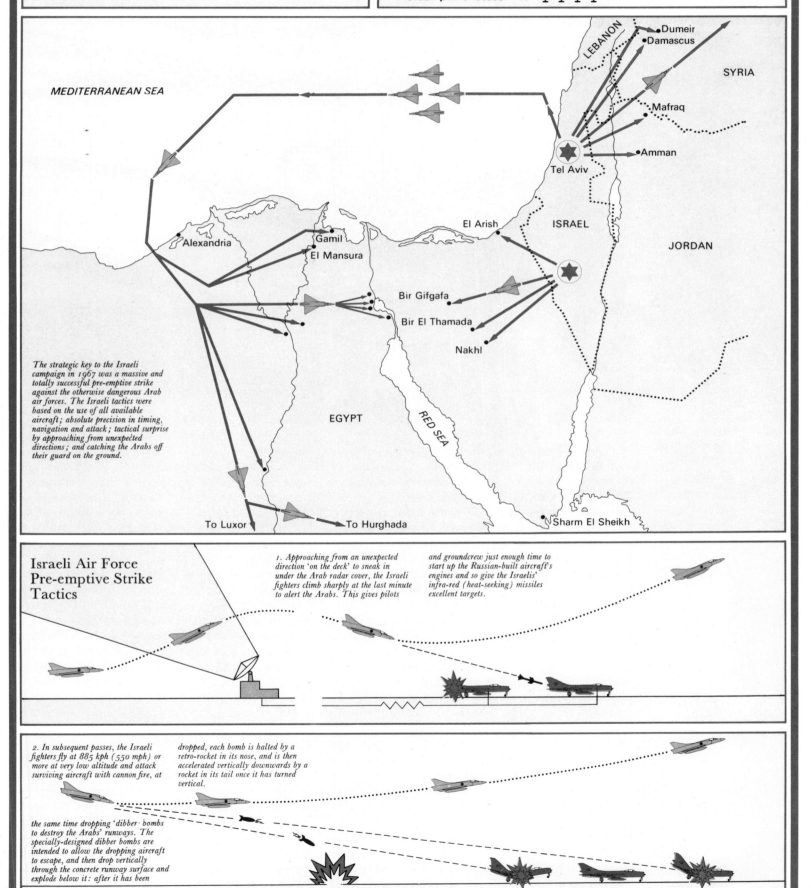

MEDITERRANEAN SEA

LEBANON

SYRIA

Dumeir

Damascus

Mafraq

Amman

Tel Aviv

ISRAEL

JORDAN

El Arish

Alexandria

Gamil

El Mansura

Bir Gifgafa

Bir El Thamada

Nakhl

EGYPT

RED SEA

Sharm El Sheikh

To Luxor

To Hurghada

The strategic key to the Israeli campaign in 1967 was a massive and totally successful pre-emptive strike against the otherwise dangerous Arab air forces. The Israeli tactics were based on the use of all available aircraft; absolute precision in timing, navigation and attack; tactical surprise by approaching from unexpected directions; and catching the Arabs off their guard on the ground.

Israeli Air Force Pre-emptive Strike Tactics

1. Approaching from an unexpected direction 'on the deck' to sneak in under the Arab radar cover, the Israeli fighters climb sharply at the last minute to alert the Arabs. This gives pilots and groundcrew just enough time to start up the Russian-built aircraft's engines and so give the Israelis' infra-red (heat-seeking) missiles excellent targets.

2. In subsequent passes, the Israeli fighters fly at 885 kph (550 mph) or more at very low altitude and attack surviving aircraft with cannon fire, at the same time dropping 'dibber' bombs to destroy the Arabs' runways. The specially-designed dibber bombs are intended to allow the dropping aircraft to escape, and then drop vertically through the concrete runway surface and explode below it: after it has been dropped, each bomb is halted by a retro-rocket in its nose, and is then accelerated vertically downwards by a rocket in its tail once it has turned vertical.

IDF/AF, which was to decide the course of the war. On this both Major-General Moshe Dayan, the Defence Minister, and Major-General Yitzhak Rabin, the Chief-of-Staff, were agreed. In the short term the threat posed by the Arab air forces, especially the strategic bombers, was paramount, and considerable thought had been exercized into means of defeating this menace before it could be used. At the same time it was realized that even the elimination of the bomber menace would leave the Arab air forces with a considerable tactical superiority, and so means of reducing this imbalance were sought.

The plan finally decided upon was bold, and had the advantages of tactical simplicity allied with superior training, surprise, determination and excellent planning taking full advantage of the Israelis' abilities and weapons. That the threat posed by the bombers was a real one can be seen readily enough from the fact that the Egyptian air force alone could deliver some 300 tons of bombs in a single strike, and the other Arab air forces another 200. And whereas Cairo was nearly 30 minutes flying time from the nearest Israeli air base, Tel Aviv was only 4½ minutes from the Egyptian forward base at El Arish just to the west of the Gaza Strip. Further to increase this imbalance, the Arabs deployed fairly considerable numbers of the Russian SA-2 'Guideline' surface-to-air missiles (SAMs). The Israelis, on the other hand, had to a certain extent

discounted the effectiveness of SAMs, and thus had only a few American Hawk missiles, enough to provide a scanty defence of Tel Aviv and more substantial protection for the Israeli nuclear research establishment in the Negev desert.

The Israeli air forces, therefore, had long prepared for an all-out aerial pre-emptive strike against the Arab airfields at the first sign of hostilities, the object being to 'take out' a large proportion of the Arab aircraft in 'sitting duck' positions on the ground. The plan was simple enough in essence, but was complex to execute. Split-second timing was needed to catch the Arab aircraft in just the right positions, and the runways would also have to be destroyed to prevent, or at least to hamper, their use by surviving Arab aircraft. The problem in such an operation was how to secure surprise, always a difficult matter in modern war, when radar can warn the defence when the attackers are still many miles distant. The plan worked out by the IDF/AF's staff was shrewd and took full advantage of known Arab routines, especially those of Egypt: knowing that the Israeli aircraft were short-ranged for the most part, the Arabs would expect any attack to come straight in; the Israeli staff, therefore, planned a raid to come in from the Arabs' rear, where less comprehensive radar watch was kept. Flying a circuitous approach to the target, the Israeli fighters would come in fast and low, underneath the primary radar cover.

They would thus be close to their objectives before they were spotted.

While the planners worked out the schedules, offensive loads to be carried and the other logistical aspects of the operation, in a remote area of the Negev desert the Israeli pilots were undergoing intensive training in low-level operations and navigation, while groundcrew practised the rearming and refuelling of their aircraft so that returning fighters and fighter-bombers could be 'turned round' for another mission with minimum delay—in the event, many aircraft were turned round in well under five minutes, an extraordinarily short time for a sophisticated modern combat aircraft.

The first Israeli strikes against Egypt

At 0745 on 5 June, Israeli aircraft struck at nine Egyptian airfields in simultaneous raids. Their timing was impeccable—approaching the Egyptian airfields from their rear, the Israeli fighter-bombers arrived over their targets at just the right moment. Dawn, about three hours earlier, had seen considerable Egyptian activity, for this was the time that an Israeli raid might be expected, and standing patrols of MiG fighters had been up in the air; at 0745, though, visibility was excellent, and the standing patrols had been brought down, the conditions being seemingly against an Israeli attack. Duty controllers had relaxed, but senior commanders

had yet to arrive for the day's work, when all of a sudden radar operators picked up the 'blips' of fast aircraft approaching from the rear. These were the Israeli fighter-bombers, which had approached 'on the deck' and then climbed sharply through the Egyptian radar cover at a nicely determined range from their target airfields. The height gained in the climb put the attackers at just the right altitude for their strikes, and also 'warned' the Egyptians of the impending raid. Pilots rushed from their ready stations to man their aircraft while mechanics started up the engines. Just at this moment the Israeli aircraft appeared and released their French Nord AS-30 air-to-surface missiles. These infra-red (heat-seeking) missiles then had perfect targets in the exhaust gases of the MiG fighters; just as importantly, the aircraft were caught in the open preparing for take-off, so their destruction blocked the runway and usually killed the pilots.

In the first strike, eight of the nine airfields (El Arish, Jebel Libni, Bir Gifgafa and Bir Thamada in the Sinai; Kabrit on the Suez Canal; Abu Sueir and Cairo West in the Nile delta; and Beni Sueif south of Cairo) designated were eliminated within 15 minutes. Only Fayid on the Suez Canal was taken out late—because the Israeli pilots had difficulty finding it.

The planning had been masterly, and was in fact aided by the fact that Field-Marshal Ali Amer, Egypt's commander-in-chief, and General Mahmoud Sidky, Egyptian air force commander, were flying across the area in an Ilyushin to visit bases in the Sinai. The Egyptian AA gunners had thus been instructed not to fire, which in itself aided the Israelis, and at the same time the fact meant that the two most relevant Egyptian commanders were unavailable for 90 minutes while they flew back to Cairo to take command.

These first strikes had been launched by the Israeli Mystères, with a top cover of some 40 Mirages. The only Egyptian aircraft in the air at the time of the first strike were four trainers, which quickly fell to the Israeli fighters. Each wave of Israeli aircraft spent about ten minutes over the target, in this time making about four attacking passes before ammunition, rockets and bombs were exhausted. In the first three passes

Above left: Neatly lined up aircraft, such as these MiG-17 fighter-bombers on an airfield near Cairo, provided the Israeli strike aircraft with perfect targets.
Below: Local defence for Arab airfields lay in the hands of AA gunners such as this one, seen with his 14.5-mm heavy machine-gun.

the runways and dispersal areas were engaged with cannon and missile fire, and during the last pass the Mirage fighter-bombers sprang a last surprise on the Egyptians—the newly developed 'concrete dibber' bomb designed to destroy runways. Dropped from low altitude, these bombs were retarded after dropping to allow the parent aircraft to get away from the area, then turned vertical and accelerated into the concrete runways by a rocket motor in the tail. Their speed driving them through the concrete, the bombs then detonated, ripping large craters in the runways and thus rendering them useless. After ten minutes the first wave broke off to return home, refuel and rearm, its place over the target being taken by the second wave, which had taken off ten minutes later than the first wave. A third wave took over from the second, and a fourth from the third. Meanwhile the first wave had returned to base, where the groundcrew got quickly to work, and flew back to take over from the fourth wave. Mission after mission was flown until 1200, by which time Egypt's air force had virtually ceased to exist. Only eight MiGs had managed to get off the ground, and these were shot down for the loss of two Mirages.

The pattern was repeated over other Egyptian airfields, and by 1200 17 major airfields, including Cairo international airport, had been attacked. The cost to Egypt was devastating—in the order of 300 aircraft, including 30 Tu-16 and 27 Il-28 bombers, 70 MiG-19 and 90 MiG-21 fighters and fighter-bombers, 12 Su-7 fighter-bombers, and 32 transports and helicopters.

Egyptian repair work was hampered in the morning by the fact that Israeli aircraft were overhead the whole time, and by the fact that the dibber bombs (which were not used in the Sinai so that the advancing Israeli forces would take intact airfields) had delayed action fuzes. Israeli losses had been minimal, despite the spirited defence put up by the Egyptian AA gunners later in the morning. But without fighters the Egyptians were at a severe disadvantage, and the SAM-2 then proved useless at low altitude, its take-off and acceleration being far too slow to enable it to deal with the low-flying, fast Israeli aircraft. For virtually no losses, therefore, the IDF/AF had during the morning of 5 June wiped out about six-sevenths of the Egyptian Air Force's serviceable strength. During the afternoon Israeli aircraft resumed their attacks, revisiting the scenes of their morning triumph to deal with any 'stragglers', and destroying some 23 Egyptian radar sites.

The victory was complete, and ranks as the single most crushing blow ever inflicted by one air force on another of comparable size and equipment.

Attacks against Jordan and Syria

Yet this victory was only one part of the Israelis' effort for the day. Convinced by the Egyptians and Iraqis that they were striking into Israel, King Hussein of Jordan decided to throw in his lot with the other Arab nations during the morning of 5 June, and ordered his Hunters to attack Israeli airfields, where four aircraft were claimed destroyed. On their return home, however, the Jordanian aircraft were caught on the ground by

an Israeli strike of eight Mirages shortly after noon. Eighteen Hunters were destroyed, and the Jordanian air force's runways destroyed. None of the pilots was killed, and Hussein sent them off to fly Iraqi Hunters for the rest of the war. Yet Jordan had lost her air force, and on the ground her army, fighting desperately and often brilliantly, was being forced slowly backwards out of the Jordanian part of Jerusalem. At the same time the Israeli armoured and mechanized forces were thrusting deep into the Egyptian positions in the Sinai, unhindered by Egyptian airpower.

It was then the turn of Syria. At 1215 some 16 Mystères arrived over the complex of four airfields south of the Syrian capital, Damascus; only 20 minutes later the Syrian air force had virtually ceased to exist, its aircraft being nothing more than twisted piles of burning metal on cratered runways. Some 45 of the 120 available Syrian aircraft had been destroyed, many of the remnants were unserviceable, and many pilots had been killed.

There was only one brief, and·in the event inconclusive, clash between Israel and Lebanon before the latter opted for a hostile neutrality. The other main enemy to be faced by Israel was Iraq, but the latter's only real air effort was restricted to one minor attack by a single Tu-16. During the early afternoon, though, Israeli aircraft struck at an Iraqi airfield, as a warning as much as a raid, destroying some seven aircraft. Thereafter the Israelis were content to leave the Syrian, Iraqi and Jordanian air forces alone, and concentrated their efforts on eliminating the last vestiges of Egyptian airpower and on supporting the fast moving spearheads of their ground forces, now deep in the Sinai *en route* to the Suez Canal, which was reached in the north during the 7th. On the same day, in the centre of the Sinai front, Israeli aircraft blocked the western exit of the Mitla pass, thereby denying any escape route to the Egyptians trapped to the east of it.

During 8 June the remnants of the Egyptian air force struck three times at the Israeli forces in the Sinai, but could make no real impression, and were severely handled by the exuberant Israeli fighter pilots. As the main Israeli forces had by now reached the Suez Canal, the IDF/AF was able to turn its attentions to the Syrians, whose heavy artillery had proved particularly troublesome to the Israeli positions on the Golan heights. These artillery positions were quickly subdued, but the air force then had to turn its attention to the Syrian positions and bunkers on the top of the heights. Egypt had agreed to a ceasefire during the evening of 8 June, but the stubborn Syrians finally ceased fighting only at 1930 on 10 June, during which time the IDF/AF had inflicted severe losses on them on the Golan heights and on the retreat back towards Damascus.

The Israeli victory was a great one in overall terms, but an absolutely crushing one in the air. More than 1000 sorties were flown by the Israelis on each of the first two days of the Six-Day War, with some pilots making as many as eight sorties. Some 26 out of 240 aircraft used were lost in this two-day period, the Arabs in turn losing about 415 aircraft.

Index

476

Acknowledgments

The publishers would like to thank the following individuals and organizations for their kind permission to reproduce the photographs in this book:

Associated Press 370 above, 443 centre, 452, 458-459, 461 above right, 464-465 above, 465 below, 468-469; **Australian War Memorial** 410 right; **Balzer/Trans Ocean** 426 left; **Bapty & Co.** 290; **Bell Helicopter Co.** 448-449; **Boeing Company** 394-395 above, 396-397, 461 centre right; **Bundesarchiv** 4-5, 288 below left, 343 below, 372-373; **Camera Press Ltd.** 290-291, 292 above, 292-293 above and below, 296-297, 299, 300-301 above and below, 301, 302 left and right, 303 above, 462-463, (Israel Press & Photo Agency) 470, 471 above, (Marvin E. Newman) 464-465 below, 465 above, 471 below, (I.W.M.) 386; **Dorke** 223; **Mary Evans Picture Library** 146 above right; **Flight International** 390-391; **Fox Photos** 380-381, 385 right; **Giraudon** 62-63, 63 above, 64 above, 65 above left and right, 67, 70, 71, 73 above and below, 74, 76 inset, 76-77, 78-79, 80, 84, 85, 166, 170, 180-181, 182 above left; **Robert Hunt Library** endpapers, 36-37, 42, 66-67, 70, 88, 128 above left, 130, 142-143, 154-155, 167, 169 below, 171 left and right, 176 below left and right, 177 below left, 178 above and below, 180 above, 181 above left and right, 182 above right, 184 centre and below, 185 above, 188 above and below, 189 above and below, 190 above, 190-191, 191 above, 192 insets, 193 inset, 194 above left and below, 194-195, 196 inset, 197 inset, 198, 200-205, 206 left, 207, 208 below, 208-209, 210-213, 216 above left, 216-217, 217 above left, 218, 219 left and

right, 220-221, 222, 224-225, 225 above, 226-227, 229 above left and right, 231 above right, 231 below, 234 below, 241 above left, 250 above, 252-253 above, 253 above right, 256-257 below, 257 right, 258-259, 262 above and below, 263 below, 264, 279 above right, 288 below right, 303 below, 304, 306 above left, 309 above, centre and below, 321 above, 326, 331 right, 334 left, 341, 343 above left, 346 above and below, 347 below, 348-349, 351 above and below, 353 above, 354 above, 354-355, 355 above, 356-357, 356 below, 362, 365 above and below, 368 left and right, 369 above left and right, 370 below, 371 above, 373 above, 374 above left and right and below, 375 above, 376, 377, 378 above, 378-379, 409 above right, 410 centre, 415, 424 above left and right, 426 centre, 432 above and below, 438 above left, 441, 442 above left, 443 below, (H. Roger Viollet) 38; **Illustrated London News** 149 above and below; **Imperial War Museum** 8-9, 216 above right, 217 above right, 224 above left and right, 226 above, 227 above and centre, 228-229, 231 left, 232, 233 above and below, 234-235, 238 left and below right, 239, 241 below left, 241 right, 242 above, 244 above left and right, 244-245, 246, 247 above and below, 250 below, 251, 252-253 below, 253 centre, 254 above, 254-255, 255 insets, 256-257 above, 263 above, 265, 266 above, 266-267, 268 above and below, 270-271, 272 above and below, 273, 276, 277 above and below, 278 above, 278-279, 279 above left, 280 above and centre, 280-281, 281 above and centre, 282, 283, 284-285, 288 above, 289, 296 above right, 305, 306 above right, 307 above and below, 308, 310 above, 310-311, 311 above and

centre, 314 above and below, 316 left and right, 318-319, 322 below, 327, 328, 333 below left inset, 334-335, 342, 343 above right, 344 above, 344-345, 345 above, 349 above, 351 centre, 352, 360-361, 360 below, 396 below, 371 below, 383 above right, 398 below, 398-399 below, 402 above, 403, 405 right, 410 left, 416, 417 right, 424-425 below, 426-427, 427 right, 430 insets, 439 above left and right, 440; **Keystone Press Agency** 382-383 above; **Library of Congress** 106, 107, 108 above, 109 above and below, 111, 112 above right, 124-125, 125 above, 126, 127 above, 129, 132-133, 135 below right, 138-139, 139 above, 146 above left, 146-147, 148, 150, 152 above right and below, 153 above and below, 156-157, 157 insets, 160 above and below left, above and below right, 161, 162-163, 163 above left, 165; **Mansell Collection** 152 above left, 164; **Sidney L. Meyer** 122 right; **J.G. Moore Collection** 286-287, 384-385 above, 384 below; **Musee de la Marine** 23 below, 25, 28-29, 32, 52-53, 53 above; **National Army Museum** 82-83, 86 insets, 86-87, 87 inset, 89 above and below, 90-91, 91 insets, 92 inset, 92-93, 96, 98, 99, 100, 101, 102 inset, 102-103, 103 inset; **National Maritime Museum** 2-3, 10-22, 23 above, 30-31, 33 above and below, 34-35, 39 above and below, 40 above, 40-41, 42-43, 44 above, 45 above, 46, 47, 48 above and below, 50 above, 50-51, 51 above, 56-57, 58 above, 58-59, 59 above, 60-61, 104-105, 104 below left, 117 inset, 120-121, 121 inset, 228 inset, 238 above right, 242-243, 258-259 insets, (J. Webb) 6; **Novosti Press Agency** 75 below, 375 below; **Popperfoto** 231 centre right, 400 left and right, 466, 469; **F.D. Roose-**

velt Library 116-117; **Suddeutscher Verlag** 1, 382-383 below, 387 above and below, 390 inset, 394 below, 396 left, 397 below, 398-399 above; **J.W.R. Taylor** 388 above; **Victoria and Albert Museum** 186 above, 186-187; **H. Roger Viollet** 65 below, 75, 104 below right, 168 left and right, 169 above, 172 inset, 172-173, 174, 176 above, 177 above, 177 below right, 179 above and below, 182-183, 183 above left and right, 184 above, 184-185, 221 above; **U.S. Air Force** 320-321, 392 left, 392-393 above and below, 398 above and centre, 433 above, 446 above, 446-447, 450, 452-453, 453 right, 454, 454-455 above and below, 456-457 above and below, 460 left, 460-461 above, 461 left, 461 below right; **US Army** 353 below, 427 centre, 430-431, 433 below, 436-437, 437 above left and right, 438 above right, 438-439, 442 above right and below, 443 above, 444-445; **US Marine Corp.** 324 above right; **US National Archives** 108, 112-113, 122 left, 123, 322, 324 above left and below, 325, 330, 331 left, 332-333, 333 above, centre and below right insets, 338-339, 364, 408, 411, 412-413, 413 inset, 414 above and below, 417 left, 418-419, 420, 421; **US Navy Photo** 112 above left, 113 above, 114 above and below left, 114-115, 116-117 above inset, 116 below inset, 119, 127 below, 128 below, 128-129, 129 above right, 133 above, 134 above and below, 135 above and below left, 136-137, 137 below, 140-141, 144, 192-193, 196-197, 206 above and below right, 323, 329, 402 below, 405 left, 409 above left and below, 412 above, 422-423, (US National Archives) 456 left; **West Point Museum Collection, US Military Academy** 163 above right; **Zennaro** 347 above.